Creo Parametric 3.0: Introduction to Solid Modeling Part 1

Student Guide

2nd Edition

ASCENT - Center for Technical Knowledge®

Creo Parametric 3.0: Introduction to Solid Modeling Part 1

2nd Edition

Prepared and produced by:

ASCENT Center for Technical Knowledge
630 Peter Jefferson Parkway, Suite 175
Charlottesville, VA 22911

866-527-2368
www.ASCENTed.com

Lead Contributor: Scott Hendren

ASCENT - Center for Technical Knowledge is a division of Rand Worldwide, Inc., providing custom developed knowledge products and services for leading engineering software applications. ASCENT is focused on specializing in the creation of education programs that incorporate the best of classroom learning and technology-based training offerings.

We welcome any comments you may have regarding this student guide, or any of our products. To contact us please email: feedback@ASCENTed.com.

AS-CRP3-ISM2-SG1 // RS-CRP3-ISM2-SG1

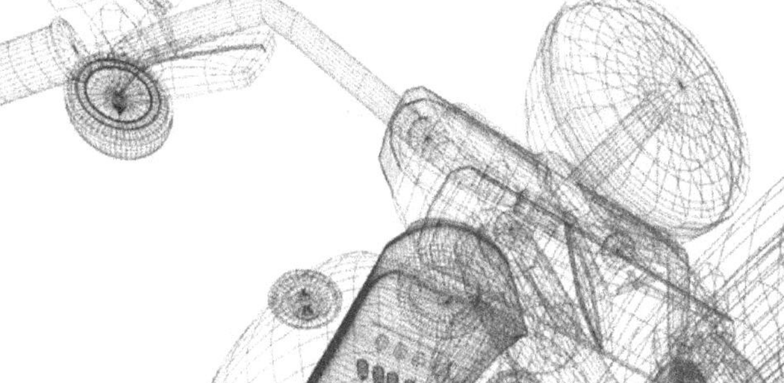

Contents Part 1

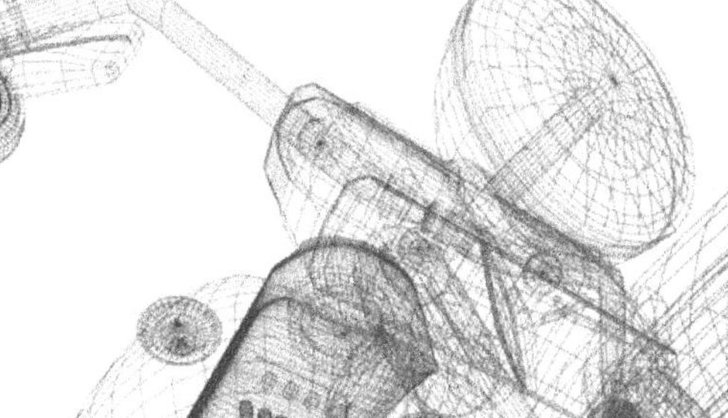

Contents Part 2

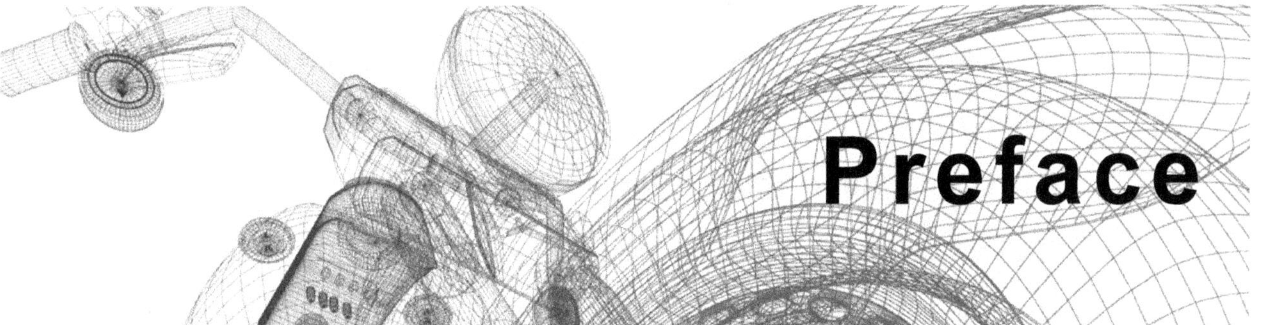

Preface

The *Creo Parametric 3.0: Introduction to Solid Modeling* student guide provides you with an understanding of the process of designing models with Creo Parametric 3.0 through a hands-on, practice-intensive curriculum. You will learn the key skills and knowledge required to design models using Creo Parametric 3.0, starting with 2D sketching, through to solid part modeling, assembly creation, and drawing production.

Topics Covered:

- Creo Parametric fundamentals and interface
- Principles behind design intent
- Manipulating a model
- Creo Parametric file management
- Part creation and modification
- Sketching and creating geometry
- Sketcher mode functionality (sketching and dimensioning)
- Datum features
- Duplication techniques (patterns, mirroring)
- Creating relations to capture design intent
- Creo Parametric customization
- Design documentation and detailing
- Feature management
- Sweeps and blends
- Assembly creation and manipulation
- Parent/Child relationships in Creo Parametric models
- Model Analysis
- Feature failure resolution
- Effective modeling techniques

Note on Software Setup

This student guide assumes a standard installation of the software using the default preferences during installation. Lectures and practices use the standard software templates and default options for the Content Libraries.

Lead Contributor: Scott Hendren

Scott has been a trainer and curriculum developer in the PLM industry for almost 20 years, with experience on multiple CAD systems, including Creo Parametric, Creo Parametric, and CATIA. Trained in Instructional Design, Scott uses his skills to develop instructor-led and web-based training products.

Scott has held training and development positions with several high profile PLM companies, and has been with the Ascent team since 2013.

Scott holds a Bachelor of Mechanical Engineering Degree as well as a Bachelor of Science in Mathematics from Dalhousie University, Nova Scotia, Canada.

Scott Hendren has been the Lead Contributor for *Creo Parametric 3.0: Behavioral Modeling* since 2017.

In this Guide

The following images highlight some of the features that can be found in this Student Guide.

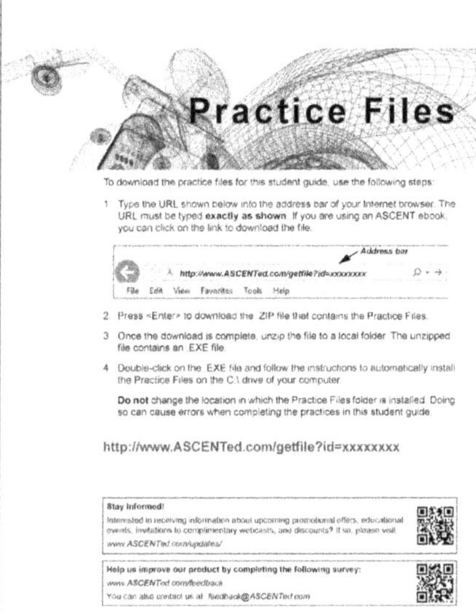

Practice Files

To download the practice files for this student guide, use the following steps:

1. Type the URL shown below into the address bar of your Internet browser. The URL must be typed **exactly as shown**. If you are using an ASCENT ebook, you can click on the link to download the file.

   Address bar

   http://www.ASCENTed.com/getfile?id=xxxxxxxx

   File Edit View Favorites Tools Help

2. Press <Enter> to download the .ZIP file that contains the Practice Files.
3. Once the download is complete, unzip the file to a local folder. The unzipped file contains an .EXE file.
4. Double-click on the .EXE file and follow the instructions to automatically install the Practice Files on the C:\ drive of your computer.

   Do not change the location in which the Practice Files folder is installed. Doing so can cause errors when completing the practices in this student guide.

http://www.ASCENTed.com/getfile?id=xxxxxxxx

Stay Informed!

Interested in receiving information about upcoming promotional offers, educational events, invitations to complimentary webcasts, and discounts? If so, please visit: *www.ASCENTed.com/updates/*

Help us improve our product by completing the following survey:

www.ASCENTed.com/feedback

You can also contact us at: *feedback@ASCENTed.com*

FTP link for practice files

Practice Files

The Practice Files page tells you how to download and install the practice files that are provided with this student guide.

Chapter 1

Getting Started

In this chapter you learn how to start the AutoCAD® software, become familiar with the basic layout of the AutoCAD screen, how to access commands, use your pointing device, and understand the AutoCAD Cartesian workspace. You also learn how to open an existing drawing, view a drawing by zooming and panning, and save your work in the AutoCAD software.

Learning Objectives in this Chapter

- Launch the AutoCAD software and complete a basic initial setup of the drawing environment.
- Identify the basic layout and features of AutoCAD interface including the Ribbon, Drawing Window, and Application Menu.
- Locate commands and launch them using the Ribbon, shortcut menus, Application Menu, and Quick Access Toolbar.
- Locate points in the AutoCAD Cartesian workspace.
- Open and close existing drawings and navigate to file locations.
- Move around a drawing using the mouse, the **Zoom** and **Pan** commands, and the Navigation Bar.
- Save drawings in various formats and set the automatic save options using the **Save** commands.

Learning Objectives for the chapter

Chapters

Each chapter begins with a brief introduction and a list of the chapter's Learning Objectives.

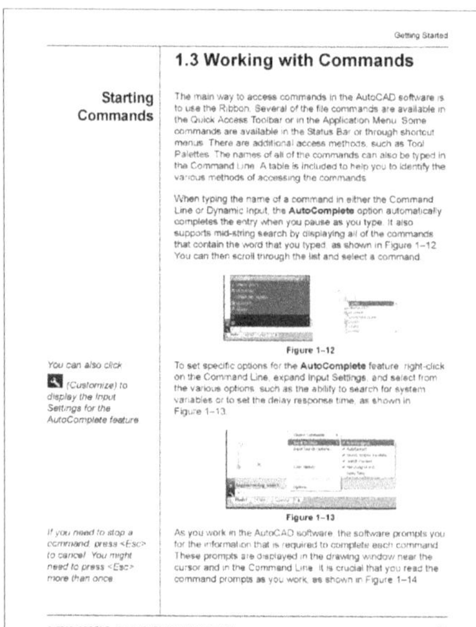

Getting Started

1.3 Working with Commands

Starting Commands

The main way to access commands in the AutoCAD software is to use the Ribbon. Several of the file commands are available in the Quick Access Toolbar or in the Application Menu. Some commands are available in the Status Bar or through shortcut menus. There are additional access methods, such as Tool Palettes. The names of all of the commands can also be typed in the Command Line. A table is included to help you to identify the various methods of accessing the commands.

When typing the name of a command in either the Command Line or Dynamic Input, the **AutoComplete** option automatically completes the entry when you pause as you type. It also supports mid-string search by displaying all of the commands that contain the word that you typed, as shown in Figure 1–12. You can then scroll through the list and select a command.

Figure 1–12

You can also click (Customize) to display the Input Settings for the AutoComplete feature.

To set specific options for the **AutoComplete** feature, right-click on the Command Line, expand Input Settings, and select from the various options, such as the ability to search for system variables or to set the delay response time, as shown in Figure 1–13.

Figure 1–13

If you need to stop a command, press <Esc> to cancel. You might need to press <Esc> more than once.

As you work in the AutoCAD software, the software prompts you for the information that is required to complete each command. These prompts are displayed in the drawing window near the cursor and in the Command Line. It is crucial that you read the command prompts as you work, as shown in Figure 1–14.

© 2015, ASCENT - Center for Technical Knowledge® 1–9

Side notes

Side notes are hints or additional information for the current topic.

Instructional Content

Each chapter is split into a series of sections of instructional content on specific topics. These lectures include the descriptions, step-by-step procedures, figures, hints, and information you need to achieve the chapter's Learning Objectives.

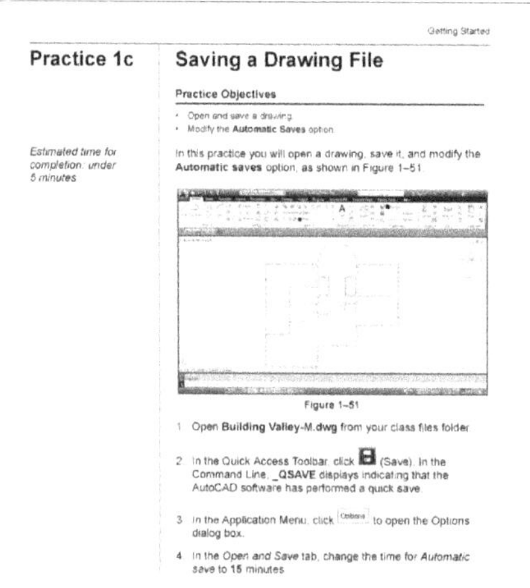

Getting Started

Practice 1c Saving a Drawing File

Practice Objectives

- Open and save a drawing.
- Modify the **Automatic Saves** option.

Estimated time for completion: under 5 minutes

In this practice you will open a drawing, save it, and modify the **Automatic saves** option, as shown in Figure 1–51.

Figure 1–51

1. Open **Building Valley-M.dwg** from your class files folder.
2. In the Quick Access Toolbar, click (Save). In the Command Line, **_QSAVE** displays indicating that the AutoCAD software has performed a quick save.
3. In the Application Menu, click Options to open the Options dialog box.
4. In the *Open and Save* tab, change the time for *Automatic save* to **15** minutes.

Practice Objectives

Practices

Practices enable you to use the software to perform a hands-on review of a topic.

Some practices require you to use prepared practice files, which can be downloaded from the link found on the Practice Files page.

Getting Started

Chapter Review Questions

1. How do you switch from the drawing window to the text window?
   a. Use the icons in the Status Bar.
   b. Press <Tab>.
   c. Press <F2>.
   d. Press the <Spacebar>.
2. How can you cancel a command using the keyboard?
   a. Press <F2>.
   b. Press <Esc>.
   c. Press <Ctrl>.
   d. Press <Delete>.
3. What is the quickest way to repeat a command?
   a. Press <Esc>.
   b. Press <F2>.
   c. Press <Enter>.
   d. Press <Ctrl>.
4. To display a specific Ribbon panel, you can right-click on the Ribbon and select the required panel in the shortcut menu.
   a. True
   b. False
5. How are points specified in the AutoCAD Cartesian workspace?
   a. X value x Y value

Chapter Review Questions

Chapter review questions, located at the end of each chapter, enable you to review the key concepts and learning objectives of the chapter.

Command Summary

The following is a list of the commands that are used in this chapter, including details on how to access the command using the software's Ribbon, toolbars, or keyboard commands.

Button	Command	Location
	Close	• **Drawing Window** • **Application Menu** • **Command Prompt:** close
	Close Current Drawing	• **Application Menu**
	Close All Drawings	• **Application Menu**
NA	Dynamic Input	• **Status Bar:** expand Customization
Exit Autodesk AutoCAD	Exit AutoCAD	• **Application Menu**
	Open	• **Quick Access Toolbar** • **Application Menu** • **Command Prompt:** open, <Ctrl>+<O>
	Open Documents	• **Application Menu**
Options	Options	• **Application Menu** • **Shortcut Menu:** Options
	Pan	• **Navigation Bar** • **Shortcut Menu:** Pan • **Command Prompt:** pan or P
	Recent Documents	• **Application Menu**
	Save	• **Quick Access Toolbar** • **Application Menu** • **Command Prompt:** qsave, <Ctrl>+<S>
	Save As	• **Quick Access Toolbar** • **Application Menu** • **Command Prompt:** save
	Zoom Realtime	• **Navigation Bar:** Zoom Realtime • **Shortcut Menu:** Zoom

Command Summary

The Command Summary is located at the end of each chapter. It contains a list of the software commands that are used throughout the chapter, and provides information on where the command is found in the software.

Practice Files

To download the practice files for this student guide, use the following steps:

1. Type the URL shown below into the address bar of your Internet browser. The URL must be typed **exactly as shown**. If you are using an ASCENT ebook, you can click on the link to download the file.

2. Press <Enter> to download the .ZIP file that contains the Practice Files.
3. Once the download is complete, unzip the file to a local folder. The unzipped file contains an .EXE file.
4. Double-click on the .EXE file and follow the instructions to automatically install the Practice Files on the C:\ drive of your computer.

   Do not change the location in which the Practice Files folder is installed. Doing so can cause errors when completing the practices in this student guide.

http://www.ASCENTed.com/getfile?id=talentum

Stay Informed!

Interested in receiving information about upcoming promotional offers, educational events, invitations to complimentary webcasts, and discounts? If so, please visit:

www.ASCENTed.com/updates/

Help us improve our product by completing the following survey:

www.ASCENTed.com/feedback

You can also contact us at: *feedback@ASCENTed.com*

Introduction to Creo Parametric

Understanding how Creo Parametric models are built and how they react to change is fundamental to designing robust and intelligent models. In addition, learning the Creo Parametric working environment is important as the environment contains many different components (e.g., toolbars, tabs, menus, etc.). Learning to interact with all of the components increases your modeling efficiency.

Learning Objectives in this Chapter

- Understand how Creo Parametric models are constructed using a feature based approach.
- Describe the five key attributes of Creo Parametric and how they contribute to creating robust parts and assemblies.
- Understand design intent and how dimensioning contributes to building a robust model.
- Navigate the ribbon, toolbars, menus, and selection methods to locate and execute commands.
- Open existing files and create new files.
- Pan, zoom, rotate, and look at specific objects in a model using the various model orientation commands.
- Assign display styles to your models to accurately visualize them in your working environment.
- Learn object selection techniques to efficiently select objects in your models.

1.1 Solid Modeling

Solid modeling is the creation and manipulation of solid, 3D representations of a model. Creo Parametric is used to design solid 3D part models and create drawings of parts, as shown in Figure 1–1. The part models and drawings can then be used for manufacturing.

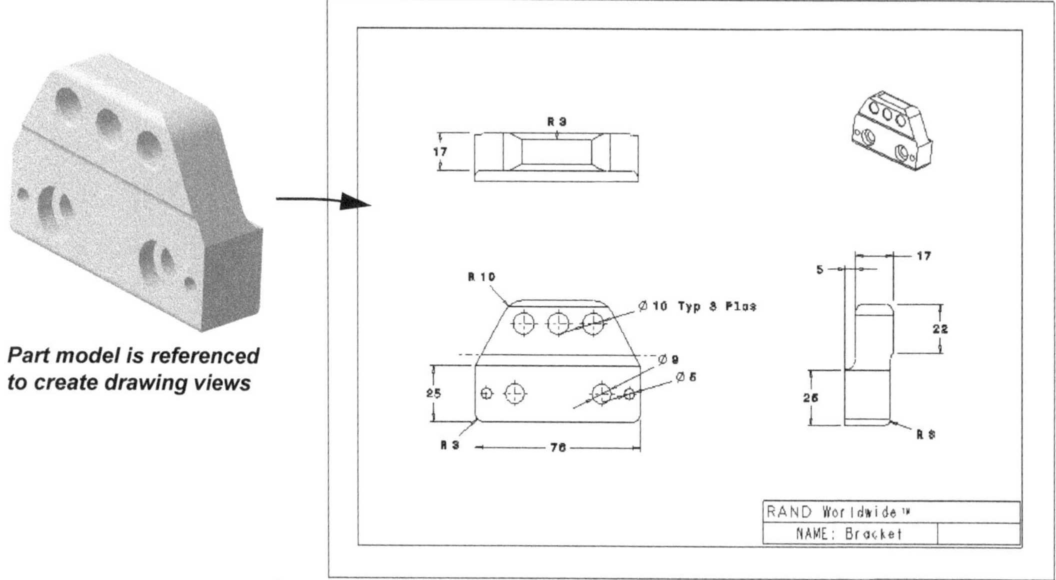

Figure 1–1

Creo Parametric can produce two kinds of 3D models: Solid and Surface (surface models are covered in the *Creo Parametric: Surface Design* training guide).

Additionally, you can place existing models relative to one another in an assembly. The assemblies can then be referenced by a drawing, as shown in Figure 1–2.

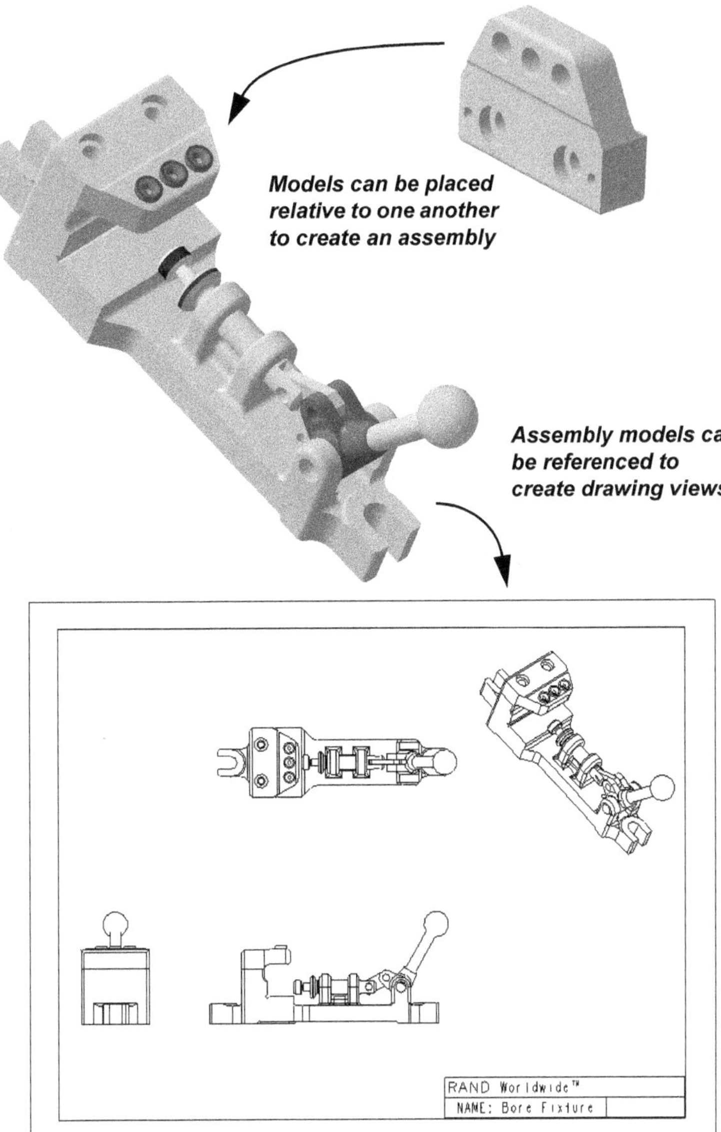
Models can be placed relative to one another to create an assembly
Assembly models can be referenced to create drawing views
RAND Worldwide™
NAME: Bore Fixture

Figure 1–2

1.2 Creo Parametric Fundamentals

Creo Parametric has the following four key attributes:

- Feature-based
- Parametric
- Associative
- Relations

Feature-Based

Creo Parametric is a feature-based modeling program, which means that a part evolves by creating features one by one until it is complete. Each feature is individually recognized by the system. Figure 1–3 shows a part model consisting of several individual features.

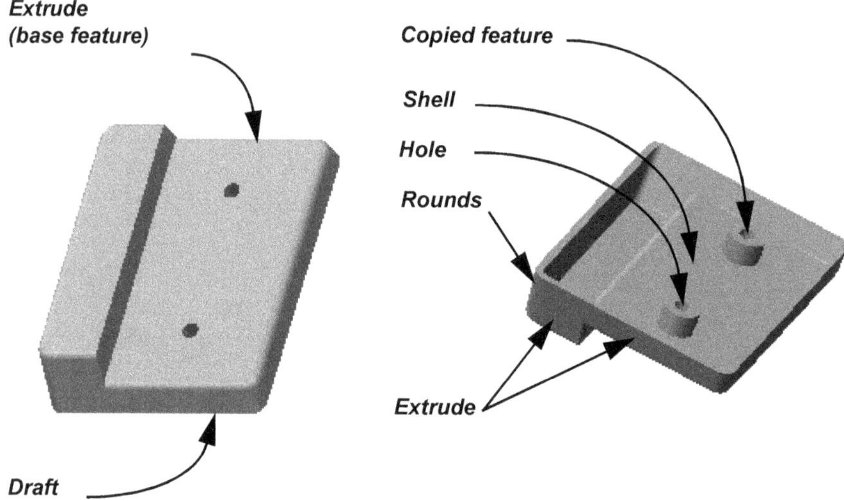

Figure 1–3

Extruded features can either add or remove material from the model. Extrusions that remove material are casually referred to as cuts.

To start a design, create a simple extruded base feature that approximates the shape of the part and continue to add additional features until the part is complete, as shown in Figure 1–4.

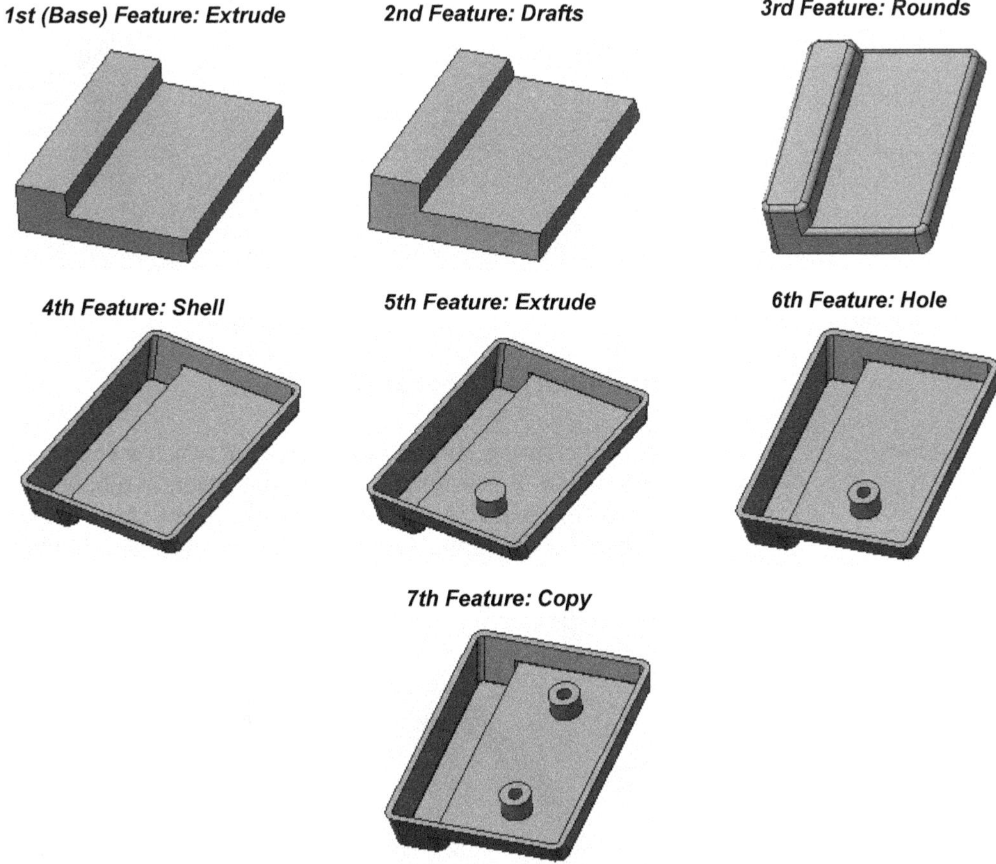

Figure 1–4

The following primary feature types are discussed in this training guide:

- Sketched
- Engineering

Sketched Features

A sketched feature is created by sketching its shape or profile and it can be any shape and size. To create a sketched feature, you must sketch a 2D cross-section on the placement surface and then add dimensions to define and locate the sketched geometry with respect to the model, as shown in Figure 1–5.

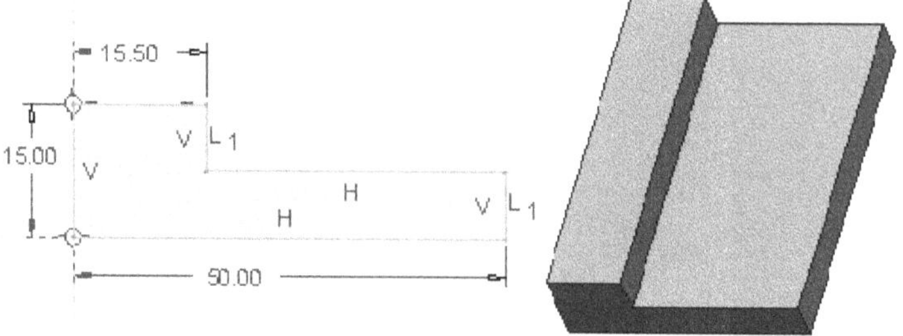

Figure 1–5

Engineering Features

An Engineering feature is a feature for which a shape is predefined. For example, the cross-section of a hole feature is a circle. To create an Engineering feature, you must define the location of the feature and the references required to locate the feature with respect to the existing geometry. Figure 1–6 shows an example of a hole feature.

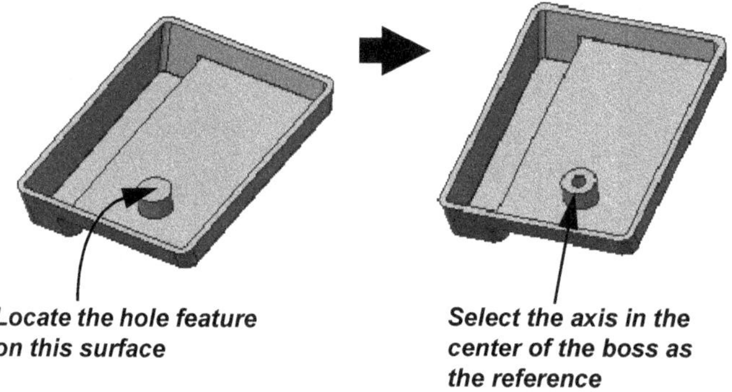

Figure 1–6

Parent/Child Relationships

Parent/child relationships are formed between features as a model is created.

Feature-based modeling requires that features be added one by one. As a result, *parent/child relationships* are created as new features reference existing features. For example, the hole shown in Figure 1–6 cannot exist without the cylindrical extruded feature because the hole's placement references exist in the extrusion. Parent/child relationships are created with all features.

Parametric

Creo Parametric is a parametric modeling tool. When creating geometry, precise dimensions are not required; only a conceptual idea of the shape of the object is required.

Geometry is said to be dimension-driven because dimensions are automatically applied to a part in the Creo Parametric software. However, you can change the applied dimensions and redimension as required. Dimension values can be modified to incorporate changes in a model, as shown in Figure 1–7.

*Creo Parametric automatically assigns names (e.g., d1, d2) to dimensions. You can display either the name or value of the dimension. To switch between these two display modes, select **Model Intent > Switch Symbols** in the Model tab.*

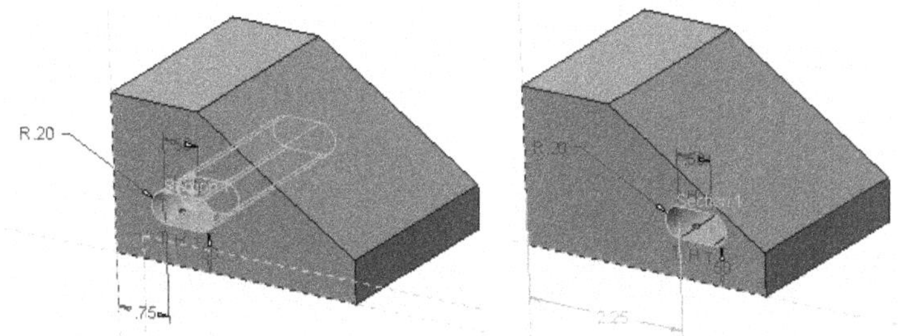

Figure 1–7

Dimensioning is an important step in the modeling process. In addition to the dimensions that are created automatically, you can create your own dimensions.

- When creating them, consider those that are going to be shown in drawings and be aware of any resulting parent/child relationships. Consider changes that might be made to the model in the future and how easily the dimensions facilitate these changes.
- Periodically modify the dimensions to test *what if* scenarios. This is called *flexing the model* and helps to eliminate future problems by verifying that the model behaves as expected when changes are incorporated.

Associative

Creo Parametric is fully associative, which enables you to work with the same model in different modes (e.g., Part mode, Assembly mode, or Drawing mode) and changes made to a model in any of the modes propagate to all other modes, as shown in Figure 1–8.

A change made anywhere is reflected in all modes.

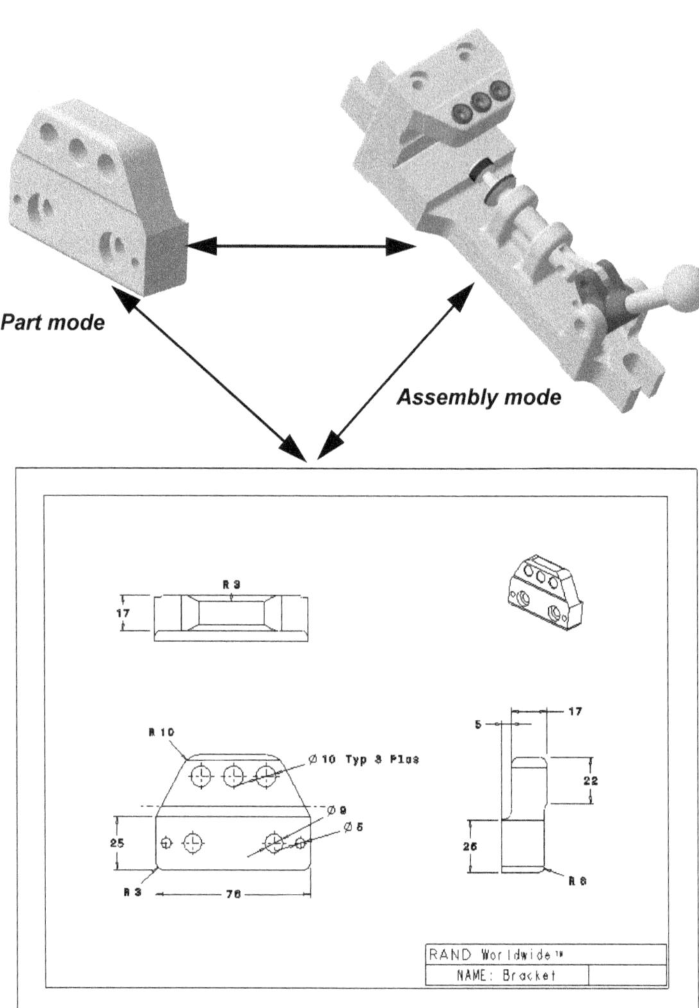

Figure 1–8

Assembly Relationships

Models built in Creo Parametric Part mode can be used as components in assemblies. Assemblies are created by constraining components with respect to one another, rather than constraining them relative to one global position. The addition of these constraints incorporates parent/child relationships between components and builds intelligent assemblies.

Relations

Creo Parametric relations are user-defined mathematical equations used to capture and control design intent. Relations are created by writing equations using dimensions or parameters from the model, and help establish robust models.

For example, the following relation can be used to keep a hole centered on a block, as shown in Figure 1–9:

```
/* Relations to center hole
d5=d1/2
d6=d2/2
```

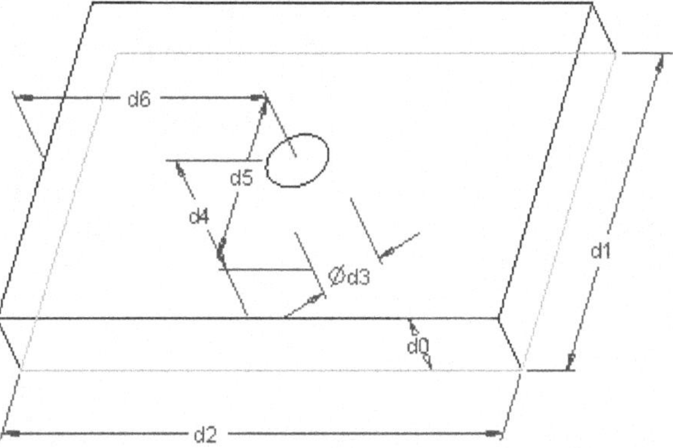

Figure 1–9

1.3 Design Intent

The key to building robust, parametric, feature-based, solid models is to construct them so that their behavior is flexible and predictable. The result of constructing them this way is known as the *design intent*.

Creo Parametric also provides tools that enable you to change your design intent.

- Design intent can be captured in a variety of ways. When creating models in the Creo Parametric software, pay special attention to the features used, how they are created (pick and place or sketched), and the dimensioning scheme.
- The parent/child relationships established during feature creation and the explicit relations set up after feature creation are also important for incorporating design intent.
- There are various ways to incorporate the design intent into a models.

Dimensioning Scheme

One method of capturing design intent is to determine the feature's dimensioning scheme. Figure 1–10 shows an example of a part with a hole. When the base feature increases in length, the design intent of the hole determines how it behaves. If the hole is dimensioned to the end of the base feature, the hole moves, but remains 3.00 from that end. If the hole is dimensioned to the face, it remains 6.00 from that face.

Figure 1–10

Symmetrical Geometry

A second method is to create symmetrical geometry. The design intent for the part shown in Figure 1–11 is to have the extruded cut remain at the center of the part. Constraining the cut from either end of the base feature does not capture the design intent. It is recommended to construct the base feature and cut relative to a center datum reference, or to use relations to capture this design intent.

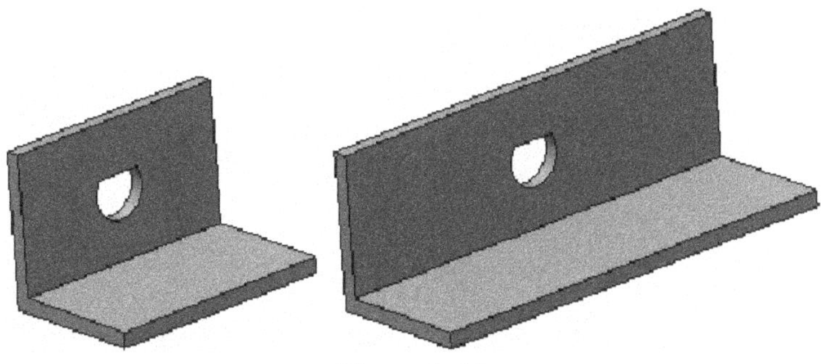

Figure 1–11

Depth Options

A third method is to determine the type of depth required for your feature. Figure 1–12 shows a part a part with a hole, whose design intent is for the hole to pass through the entire model. When the base feature changes from *5.00* to **6.00**, the resulting geometry displays differently depending on the depth option set for the hole. If the hole is given a blind depth value of **5.00**, it no longer passes through the entire part. Therefore, the hole depth must also be changed to maintain the design intent. A better solution is to set the depth option for the hole to **Through All**. In this scenario, the hole always passes through the part, regardless of the height of the base feature.

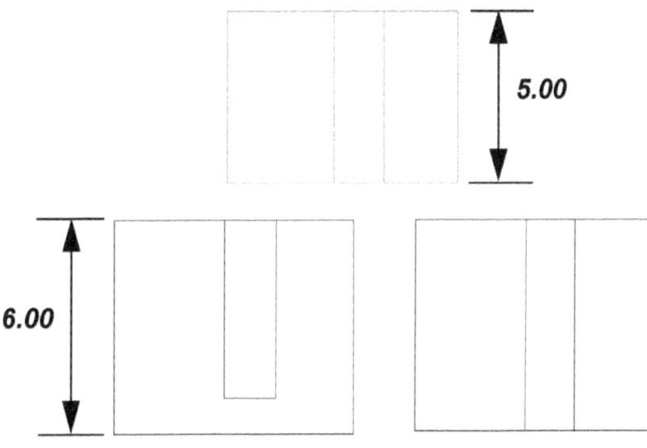

Figure 1–12

1.4 Creo Parametric Interface

The Creo Parametric user interface enables you to work with your models in a variety of ways using a ribbon style interface with tabs. Its development addresses ease of use, accessibility, and efficiency. Figure 1–13, Figure 1–14, and Figure 1–15 show the current layout of the Creo Parametric software interface.

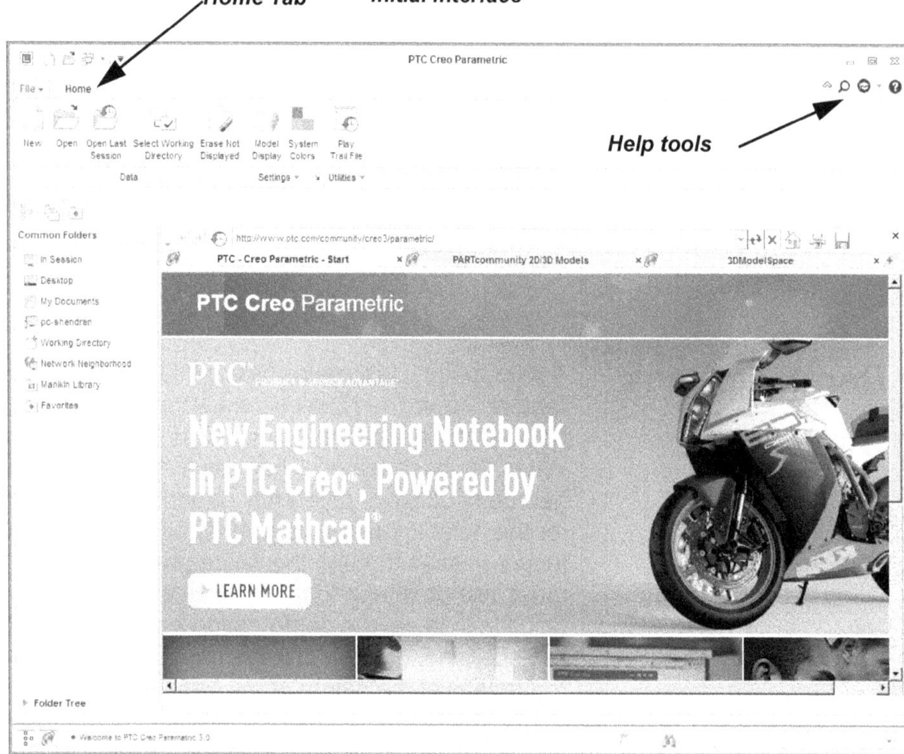

Figure 1–13

1. Navigator	Contains multiple tabs for the Model Tree, Folder Browser, and Favorites.
2. Quick Access Toolbar	Used for quick access to frequently used icons.
3. Ribbon	Contains collections of functions grouped together in tabs.
4. Tabs	Contain collections of related icons.
5. Groups	Used to further organize related ions in the tabs.

6. Creo Parametric Browser	Displays the contents of the embedded web browser and other pages such as feature information.
7. Status Bar	Displays the regeneration status. Also has icons for controlling the display of the navigator and browser.
8. Selection Filter	The options in this drop-down list enable you to refine what you can select in the model.

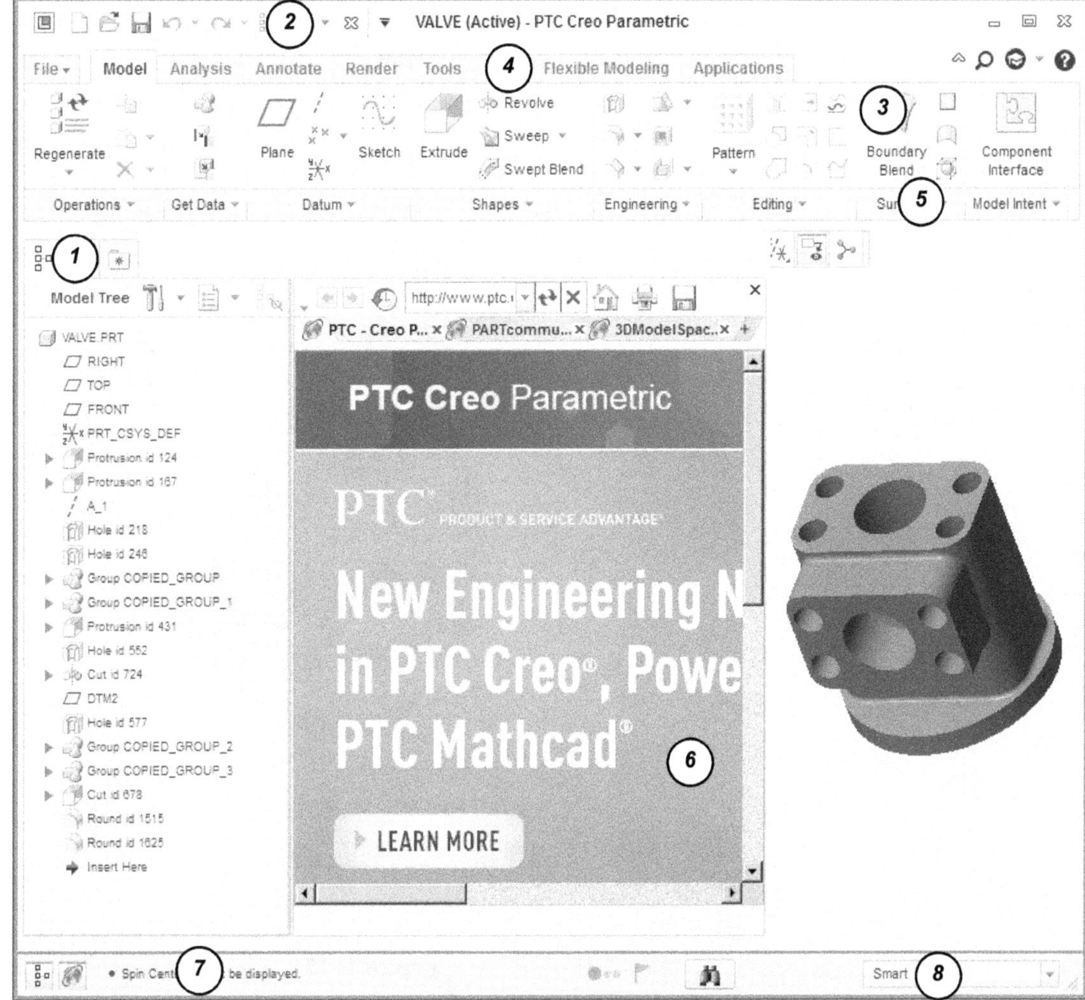

Figure 1–14

1. Dashboard	Contains options used when creating features.
2. In-graphics Toolbar	Contains icons to control the display of the model
3. Graphics (Main) Window	Displays the model.
4. Contextual Menu	Can be displayed by right-clicking.
5. Message Window	System messages and prompts display in the multi-line message window.

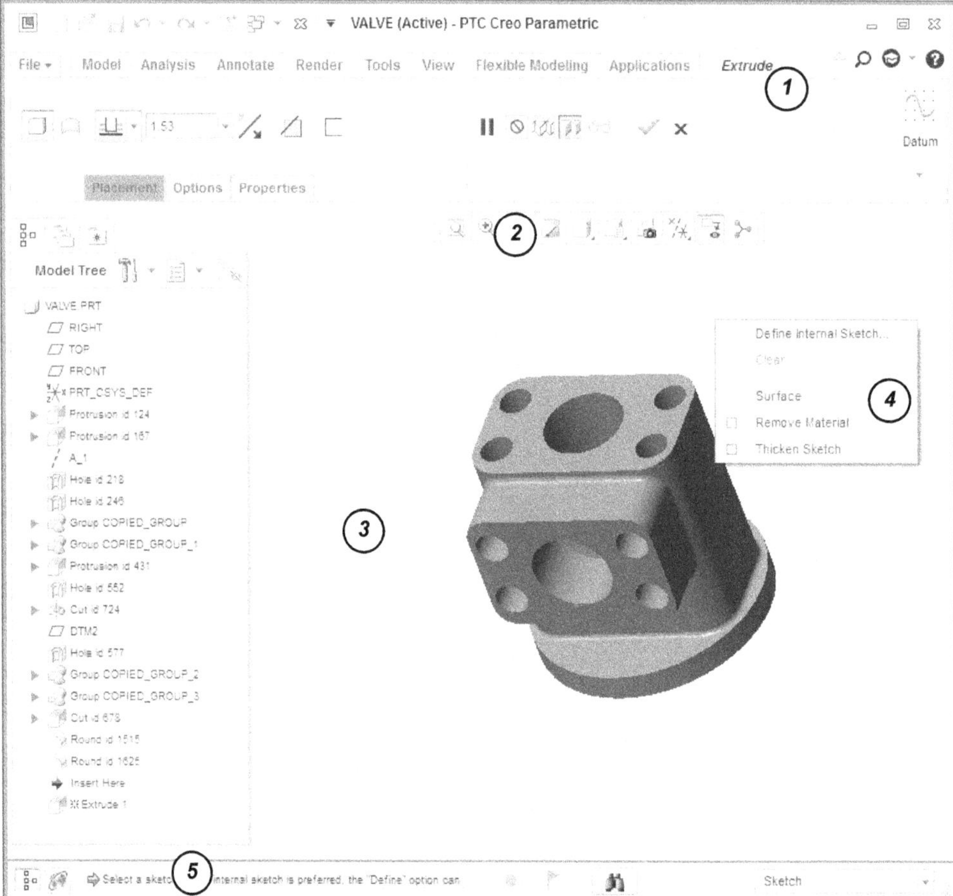

Figure 1–15

Menus

In the Creo Parametric software, menus are used to create and manipulate a model. Examples of the different menu types are described as follows:

- Group Overflow Buttons: Display additional options in the Ribbon, as shown in Figure 1–16.

- Menu Manager: In limited cases, the menu manager is used to run specific operations and displays at the right side of the main window as shown in Figure 1–17.

Figure 1–16 Figure 1–17

- Contextual Menus: Right-click on features in the model or model tree to display contextual menus, as shown in Figure 1–18.

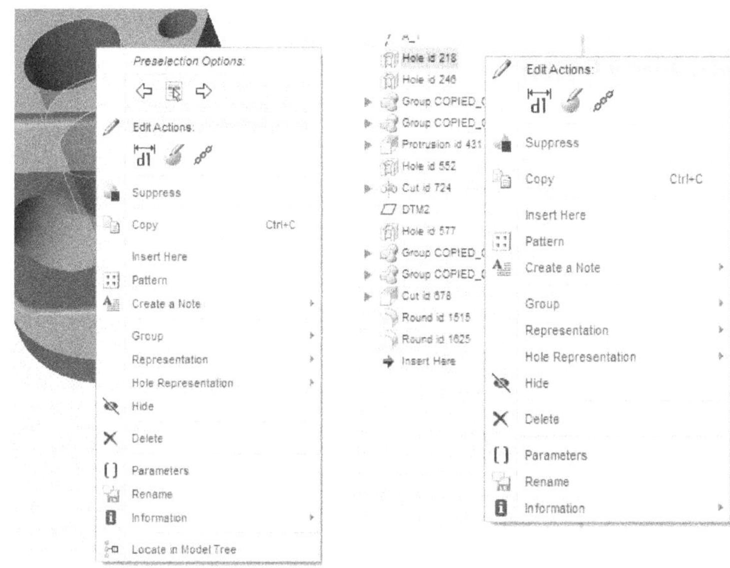

Figure 1–18

- When the option is selected, it highlights in blue, indicating that it is the active option. Options that are dimmed or grayed are not available for selection if they are not applicable to the action being performed. Some selections in the menus display additional options. Figure 1–19 shows the additional menus associated with the Info selection.

Figure 1–19

Toolbars

The shortcut icons, available in the toolbars, enable you to select commonly used options with one click of the mouse. Additional toolbar icons can be added to the toolbar or the ribbon by selecting **File>Options**. The default icons found in the In-graphics toolbar are listed as follows:

Icon	Description	Icon	Description
	Refit		Saved Orientations
	Zoom In		View Manager
	Zoom Out		Datum Display Filters
	Repaint		Annotation Display
	Display Style		Spin Center

Tabs and Ribbons

The Creo Parametric software uses a ribbon style interface with tabs. Tasks are grouped under tabs and common icons related to the task are grouped under the tab. For example, all icons related to the display, orientation, and model setup are located in the *View* tab as shown in Figure 1–20.

- The ribbon can be collapsed for more viewing space by clicking ⌃ or by double-clicking on a tab. Click once on the tab to temporarily retrieve the ribbon. To return the ribbon to the default display, click ⌄ or double-click on the tab.

Minimize ribbon

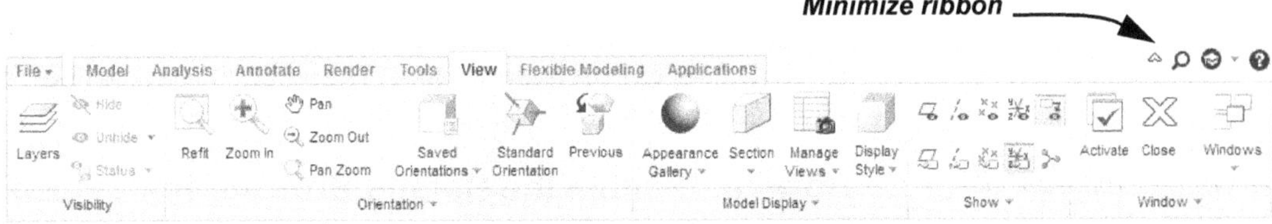

Figure 1–20

File Tab

The *File* tab contains menu choices that enable you to perform some basic tasks, as shown in Figure 1–21. Previously opened files are also listed in the *File* tab, enabling you to quickly access the files.

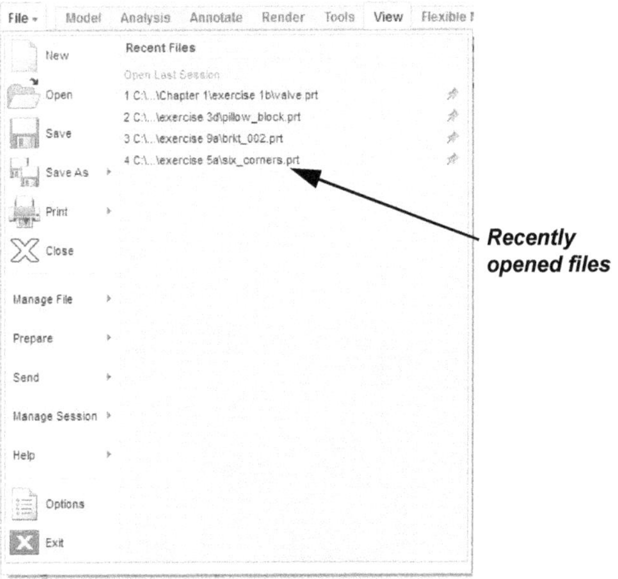

Figure 1–21

Creo Parametric Browser

By default, the software launches with a browser window that covers the main graphics window. The browser provides you with the standard capabilities of any internet browser. The default address opens PTC's Creo Parametric 3.0 Home page (**http://www.ptc.com/community/creo3/parametric/**). The page contains links to tools to help you learn and become productive.

- **PARTcommunity 2D/3D Models** is a webpage that enables you to search for free 3D CAD models and 2D drawings. You can download the files to your system.
- **3DModelSpace** is a webpage located in one of the default tabs of the software. It is a web search engine for 3D and 2D CAD files of purchased items. These DAC files can be used by engineers in their product designs.

To change the default browser address, set the config.pro option ***web_browser_ homepage*** *to the required URL.*

How To: Disable the Default Browser from Opening Each Time Creo Parametric is Launched

1. Expand the *File* tab and select **Options**. The Creo Parametric Options dialog box opens.
2. Select **Window Settings**.
3. In the Browser settings, clear the **Expand the browser during startup** option.
4. Click **OK** to close the dialog box.

The browser's size can be set as a percentage (%) of the window's width by selecting ***Window Settings*** *in the Creo Parametric Options dialog box.*

Figure 1–22 shows the browser icons and how to deactivate the browser.

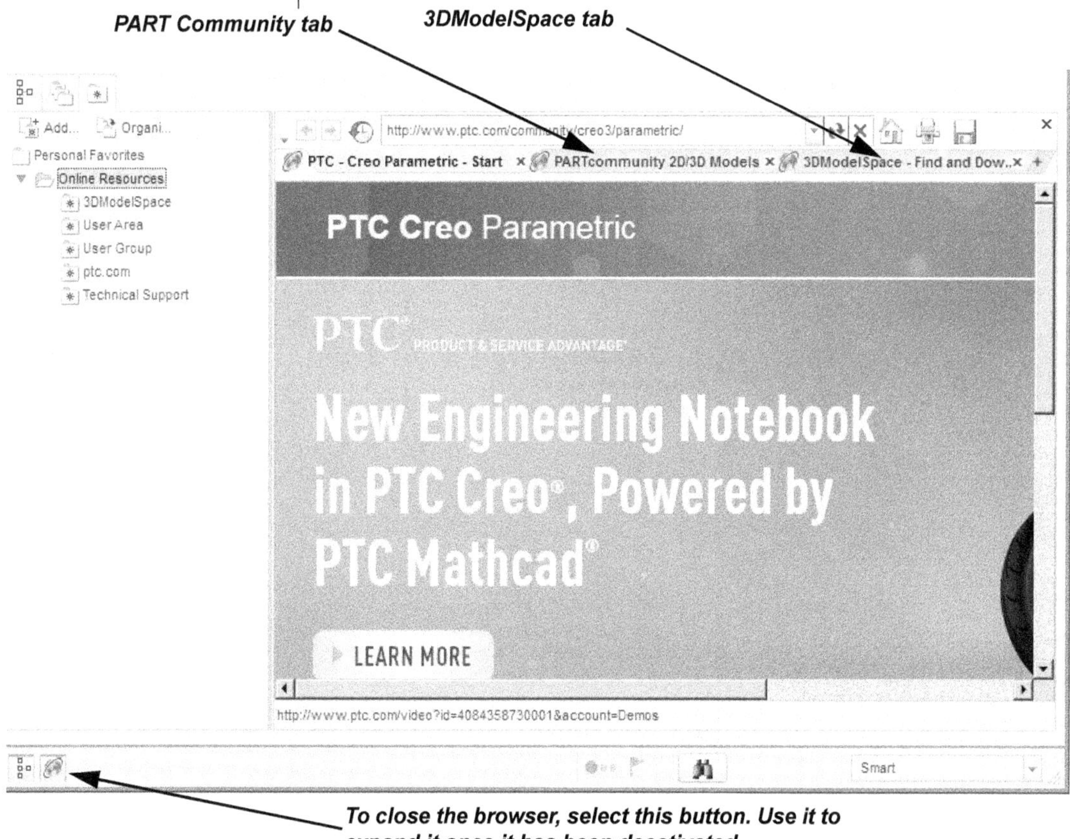

Figure 1–22

Some of the icons in the *Tools* tab provide feedback in the browser (e.g., (Feature Information) or (Model Information)). Certain information is provided with a hyperlink (blue font and underlined) to the model, as shown in Figure 1–23. This enables you to highlight the information directly in the model for easier identification. Click (Show Browser) in the lower left of the window to hide the browser.

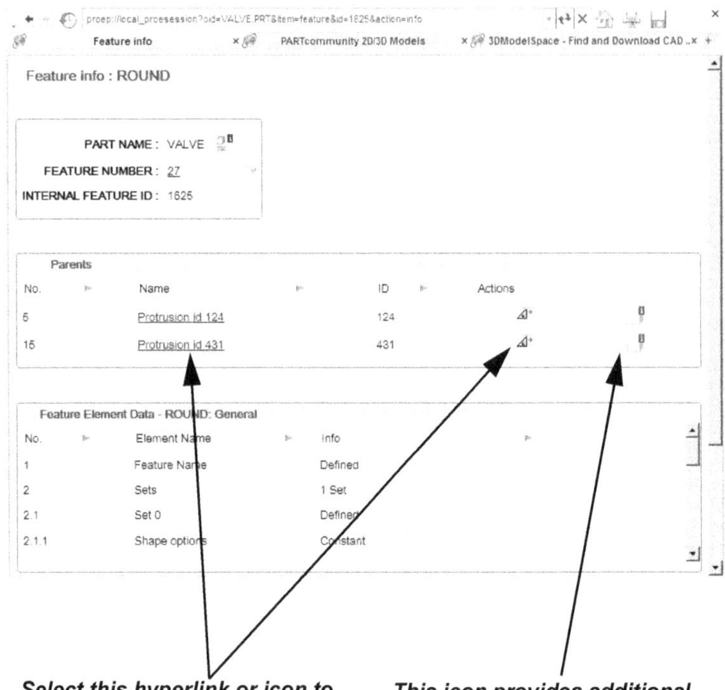

Figure 1–23

Navigator

The Navigator, found on the left section of the interface, includes the following components:

- Folder Browser
- Model Tree
- Favorites
- History

Folder Browser 

The *Folder Browser* is the default tab that displays when you launch Creo Parametric. It enables you to browse the local file system and local network. When you select one of the directories listed in the Folder Navigator, the browser is replaced with detailed information about the directory and its files, as shown in Figure 1–24. You can set the Working Directory by right-clicking on the directory and selecting **Set Working Directory** or by clicking (Select Working Directory) in the *Home* tab.

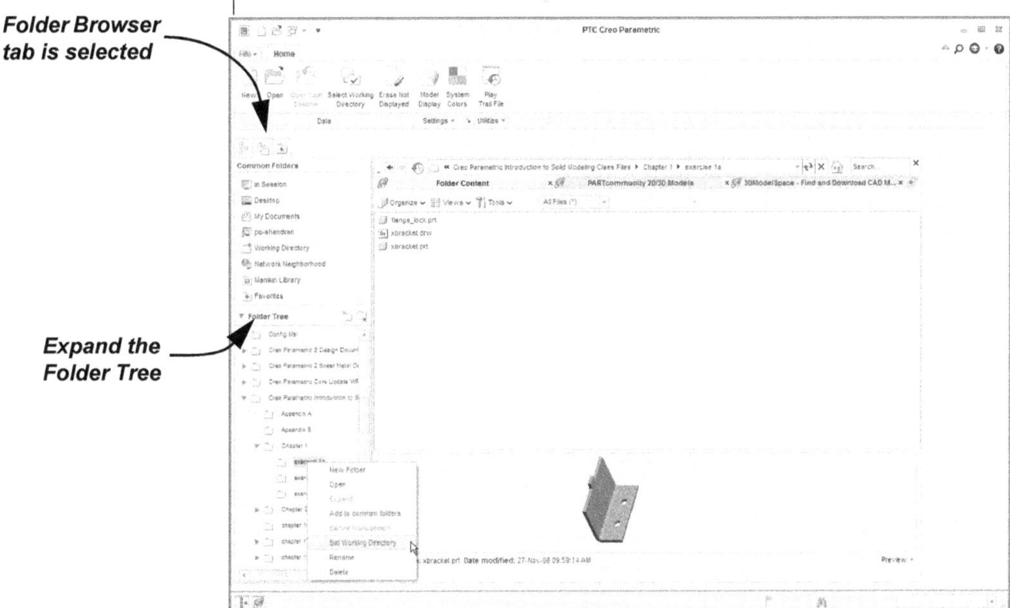

Figure 1–24

Additional locations such as Windchill servers, ftp locations, etc. can be added to the Folder Navigator by selecting ***File>Manage Session>Server management****.*

Select the filename in the directory and then select the **Preview** option at the bottom right to preview models using ProductView Express (installed by default with the Creo Parametric software). The model displays at the bottom of the browser, as shown in Figure 1–25. Select the **Preview** option again when you have finished viewing the model.

Figure 1–25

- You can open files directly from the directory listing by double-clicking on them.

Model Tree

The model tree is activated in the Navigator when a file is opened, as shown in Figure 1–26.

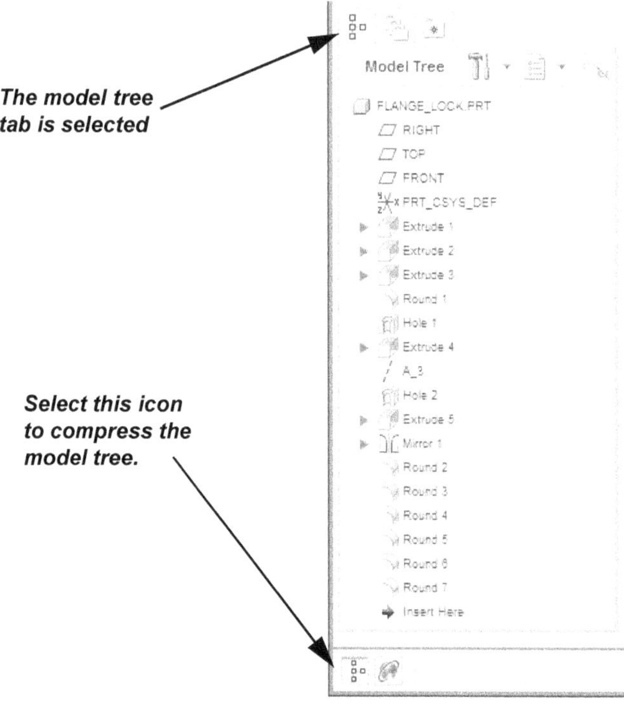

Figure 1–26

Customizing the model tree is discussed later in this training guide.

The model tree displays all of the features contained in your models. All features or components are listed in the order of creation. It is a powerful tool that can be used for any of the following actions:

- Selecting features.
- Renaming features.
- Accessing commonly used options (e.g., **Delete** or **Edit Definition**).
- Searching.

- Creating and editing parameters.
- Editing features.
- Viewing information on features.
- Changing the order of features (click and drag).
- Inserting features or components.
- Opening components in an assembly.

- (Show): Enables you to switch between the model tree and layer tree, collapse or expand the items in the model tree, or enable highlighting on the model. It can be found at the top of the Navigator.

- (Settings): Enables you to customize the filter settings and column display and open/save the model tree settings.

To customize the model tree to show or remove specific information (e.g., remove all suppressed features), select the (Settings)>**Tree Filters**. Select the required options in the Model Tree Items dialog box, as shown in Figure 1–27.

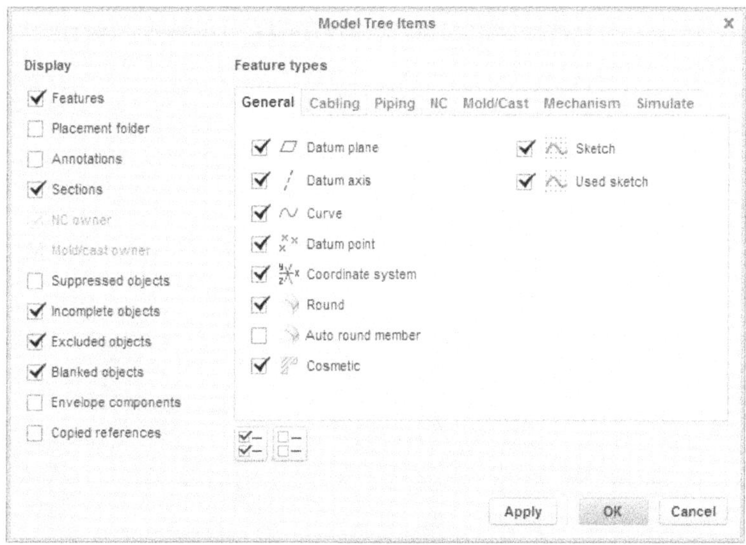

Figure 1–27

The display of the columns of the model tree can also be customized to include additional information on your model. To add or remove columns to the model tree, select the (Settings)>**Tree Columns**. The Model Tree Columns dialog box displays as shown in Figure 1–28. Select an option in the **Type** menu to add column information. Common Type options are described as follows:

Options	Description
Info	Enables you to add columns of information regarding your model (Status, Feat #, Feat ID, Feat Type, Feat Name).
Model Params	Enables you to add a column in the model tree that displays the model's parameters and their values.
Feat Params	Enables you to add a column in the model tree that displays the feature parameters and their values.
Simplified Reps	Enables you to add a column in the model tree indicating the simplified representation name and the features/components that were selected to create it.
Layer	Enables you to add a column to the model tree that indicates layer names and their status.
Note	Enables you to add a column to the model tree that displays information on a note (Note ID, First Line, Note Display, URL, Note Type).
Reference Control	Enables you to add a column to the model tree that displays information on reference control for components in an assembly.

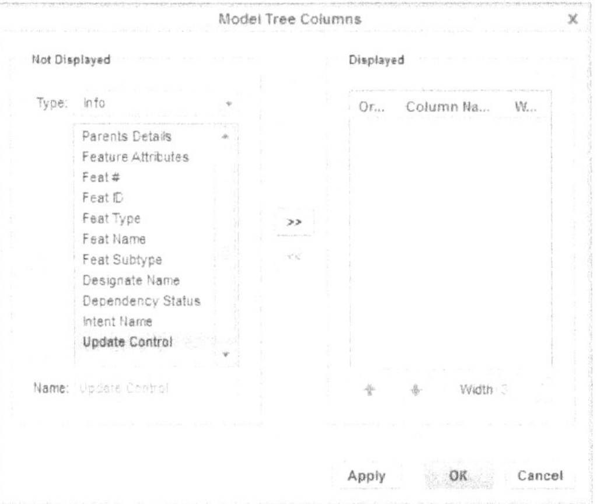

Figure 1–28

Favorites

The *Favorites* area in the Navigator can be accessed by clicking (Favorites). This area enables you to bookmark your favorite websites, as shown in Figure 1–29.

Favorites are saved each time the Creo Parametric software is closed.

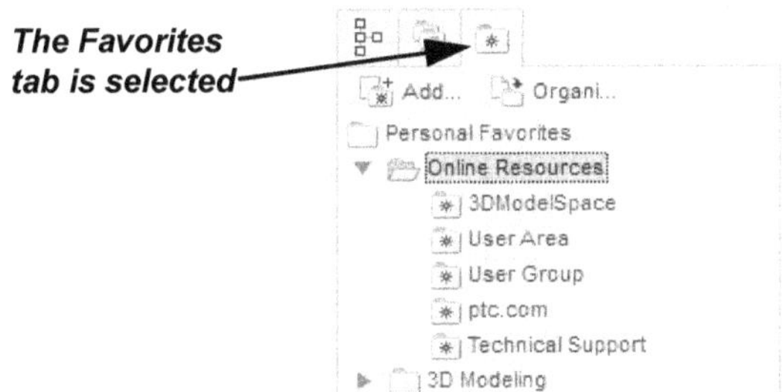

Figure 1–29

- To add bookmarks to your list, access the webpage and click (Add Favorite). By default, all bookmarks are included at one level.
- Click (Organize Favorites) and use the Organize Favorites dialog box to create, rename, and delete folders.

History

By default, the *History* area in the Navigator is disabled. To enable it, access the browser and click (History tool). Once enabled, this area provides you with a list of all of the websites that have been previously visited, as shown in Figure 1–30.

The History Browser is not the same as the history list created in your standard browser.

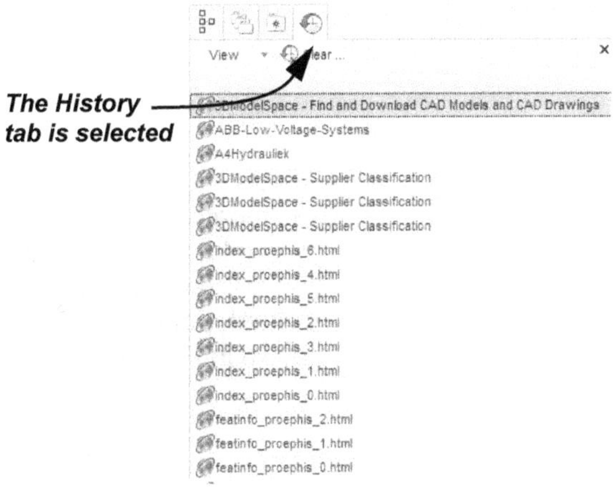

Figure 1–30

*The **config.pro** option, web_browser_history_ days, enables you to specify the number of days to store the history record.*

Click **View** in the History Browser to display the history according to the following criteria:

- By Date
- By Site
- By Most Visited
- By Order Visited Today

To clear all of the history recorded from your browser, click (Clear History). To disable the History Browser, click ✕ in the top right corner of the Navigator.

Feature Creation Controls

When you create a feature, you can define a variety of elements or properties, such as sketch, direction, and depth. To define these elements, you use either the ribbon interface or a feature dialog box.

Dashboard

Features such as extrusions and rounds are created using the dashboard interface.

When creating most features, a tab that corresponds to the feature being created displays in the ribbon at the top of the Creo Parametric window. This tab is referred to as the feature dashboard. All elements can be defined using the available icons and panels. Figure 1–31 shows the dashboard that is used to create an **Extrude** feature. The options in the tab vary depending on the feature being created.

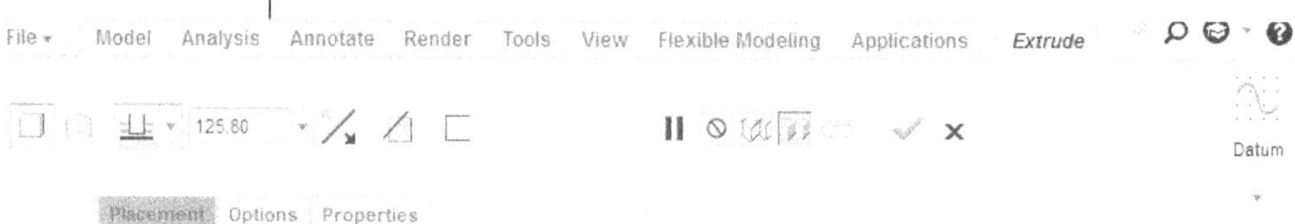

Figure 1–31

Panels display when you click the icons in the bottom row of the dashboard and enable you to select references, define additional elements, and modify the properties of the feature. The icons that display in the top row vary according to the feature being defined. For example, the Options panel for an extrude feature is shown in Figure 1–32.

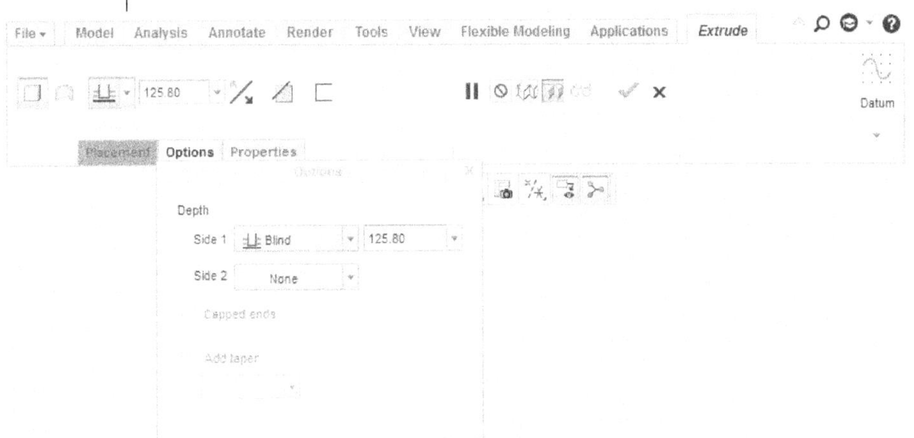

Figure 1–32

The icons that display on the right side of the dashboard are accessible for all features and are described as follows:

Icon	Description
	Pauses feature creation and enables you to access other features.
	Resumes feature creation.
	Removes the preview from the view window.
	Displays an outline of the new geometry before the feature is finalized.
	Displays a preview of the geometry and enables you to continue to make changes to the geometry.
	Displays a preview of new geometry before the feature is finalized. Enables you to verify that the geometry will regenerate given the current parameters.
	Completes the feature. Results display in the main window.
	Exits or cancels out of a dashboard.

Message Window

The message window at the bottom of the main window displays information and prompts. It can provide information and require you to enter information, as shown in Figure 1–33.

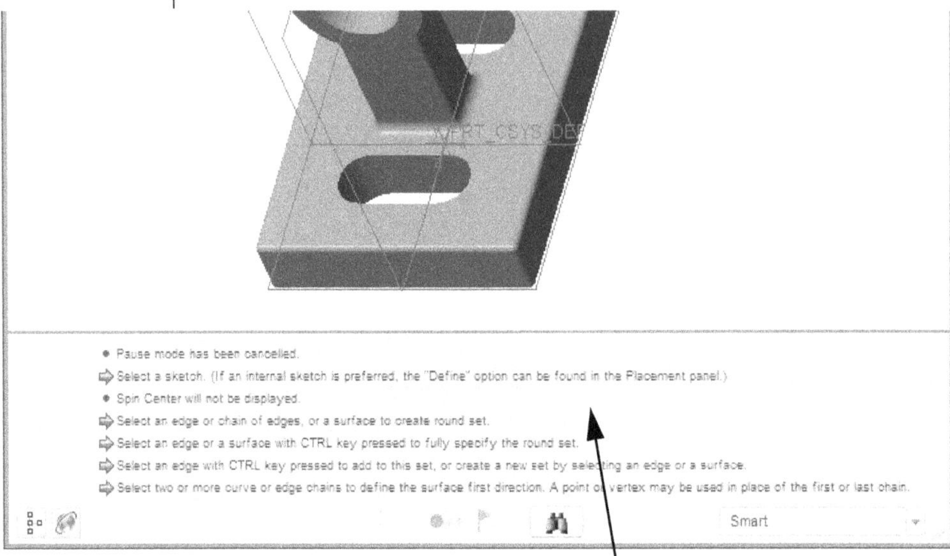

Figure 1–33

By default, the number of visible message lines is set to two. To change this, select the top border of the message window and once ≑ displays, drag up or down as required.

The current system prompt is located at the bottom of the message line and the old prompts can be found by scrolling upward. You can use the scroll bars on the right side of the message window to display the old prompts. You can also click (Message Log) in the *Tools* tab to display older message lines.

Help Options

Several help tools are available at the top right corner of the main window as shown in Figure 1–34. These options can help provide direction when you are using a new tool or trying to locate the tool.

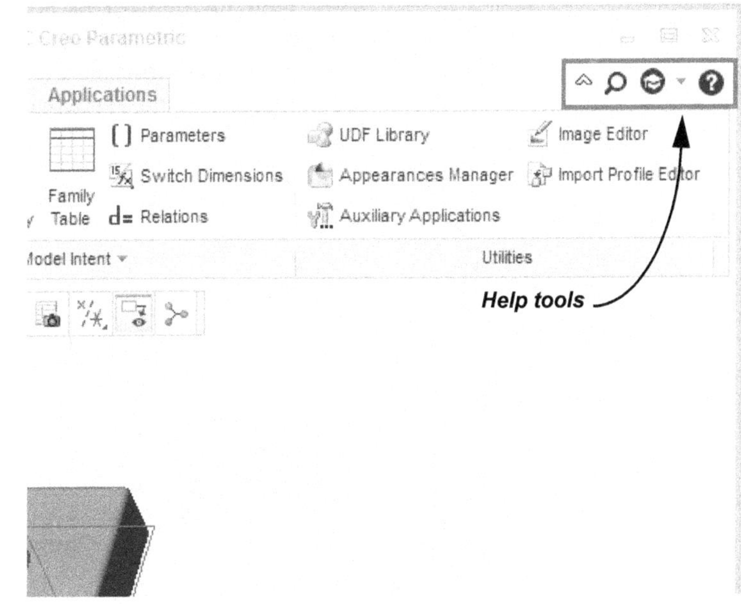

Figure 1–34

The icons available are described as follows:

Icon	Description
≈	Minimizes the ribbon to only display the names of the tabs.
⚲	Command search helps you to find an existing command in Creo Parametric.
⊖	The **Learning Connector** option requires you to set up an account and enables you to search for topics.
?	Creo Help tool enables you to search for topics.

- (Command Search): Launches the command search, as shown in Figure 1–35.

Figure 1–35

If you type the name of the command that you are looking for, the tool lists one or more commands that match your search. If you hover over the listed command, the location for that tool highlights in the associated tab and location, as shown in Figure 1–36.

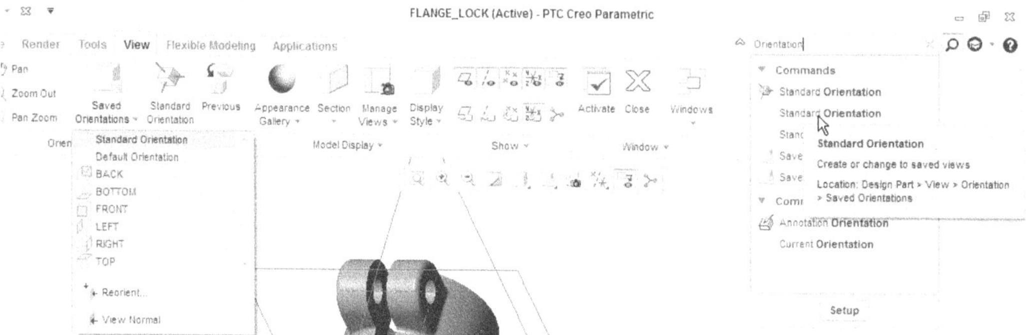

Figure 1–36

- (PTC Creo Parametric Help): Opens the Creo Help dialog box, as shown in Figure 1–37. You can select a topic or search for a topic by typing key words and clicking **Search**.

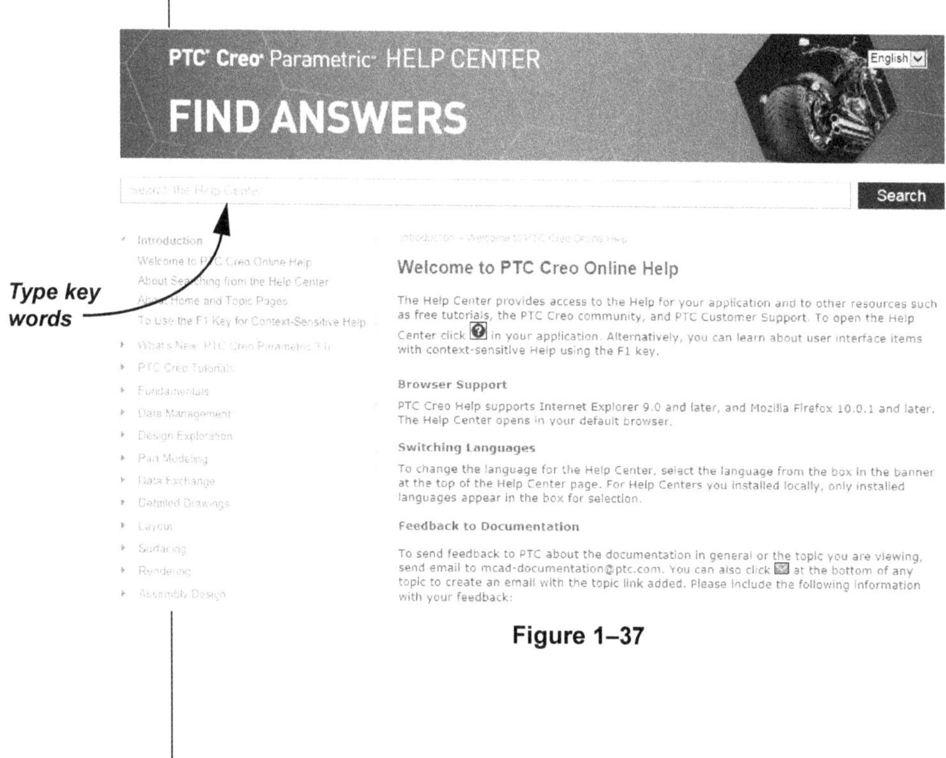

Figure 1–37

Commands

Icons can be of different sizes, depending on the size of the main window. When the window becomes smaller, the icons might lose their labels and the large icons become smaller, as shown in Figure 1–38. This enables the entire ribbon to be displayed. Icons called *split icons* contain an arrow indicating that other commands are available in the flyout, as shown in Figure 1–39. Clicking an icon that contains an arrow launches the command. Clicking the arrow next to the icon opens the corresponding flyout menu, as shown in Figure 1–40.

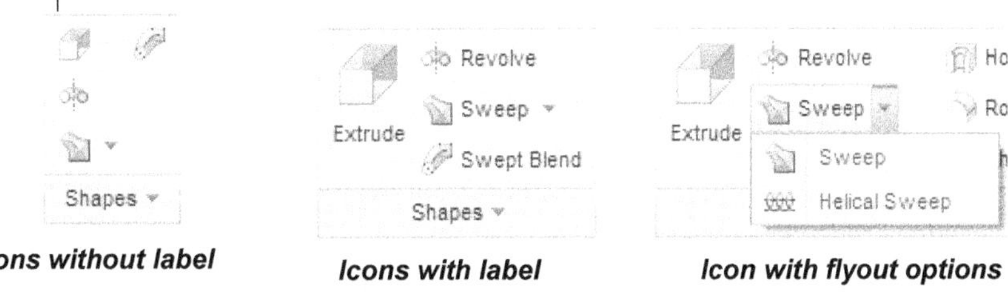

Icons without label ***Icons with label*** ***Icon with flyout options***

Figure 1–38 **Figure 1–39** **Figure 1–40**

- Hovering the cursor over an icon opens a tool-tip containing a brief description of any item, such as a menu option, icon, or model geometry.

Traditional hotkeys also work. For example, you can press <Ctrl>+<Z> to undo a previous task.

- Hotkeys are another method that you can use to select tabs or commands. You can display the hotkeys for the tabs and other commands by pressing <Alt>. The hotkeys display below the command or tab, as shown in Figure 1–41. To remove the display of hotkeys, select anywhere on the screen or press <Alt> again.

Press <Alt>+<1> to activate the new file command.

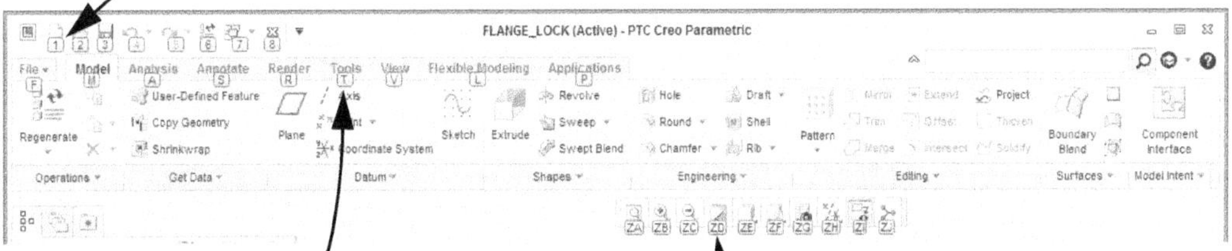

Click <T> to activate the Tools tab.

Note that the hotkey for repaint is <Alt>+<ZD>.

Figure 1–41

1.5 Manipulating a Model

Modes

This training guide covers the following four basic modes of operation in Creo Parametric:

- Sketcher mode
- Part mode
- Assembly mode
- Drawing mode

*The **New** and **Open** options are also available using <Ctrl>+<N> and <Ctrl>+<O> respectively.*

To work in these modes, click (New) to create a new file. Alternatively, you can click (Open) to open an existing file. When you create a new file, you must select a type of file to create in the New dialog box. This determines the Creo Parametric mode. All existing files are stored with mode-specific extensions. The New and File Open dialog boxes are shown in Figure 1–42.

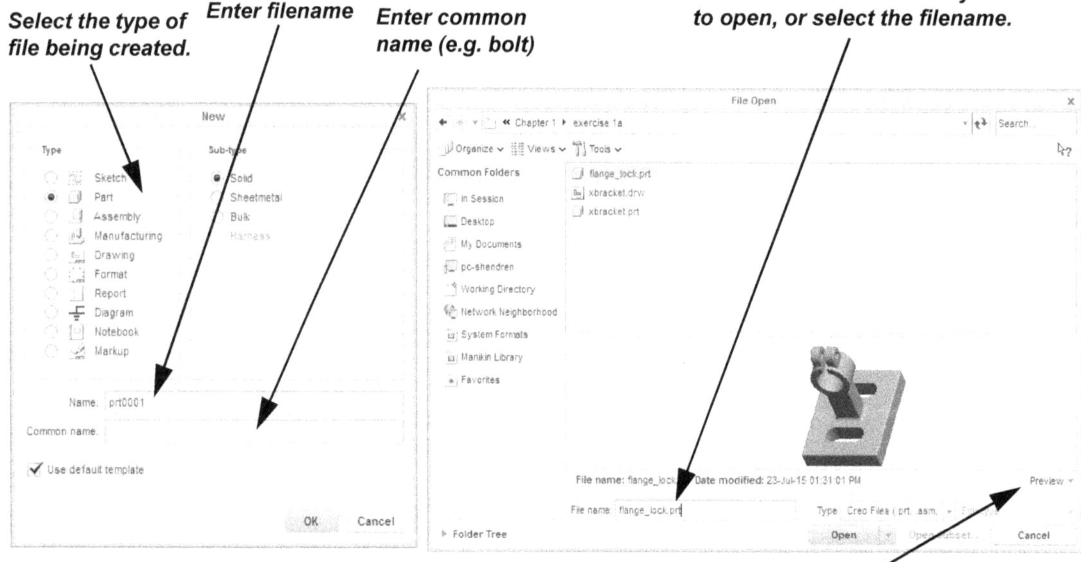

Figure 1–42

The File menu displays the most recently opened files. They can be quickly retrieved by selecting the name of the file.

Multiple Windows

Multiple files can be opened in a Creo Parametric session. The first file that is opened displays in the main graphics window. If this file is not closed before another file is opened, the next file displays in a separate window. Both windows contain the same menu options.

Alternatively, you can activate an open window by selecting it.

- When a file is opened, it becomes the active window. To activate a previously active window, expand (Windows) in the Quick Access Toolbar and select the name of the file, as shown in Figure 1–43.
- ✓ in front of the filename indicates the active file.

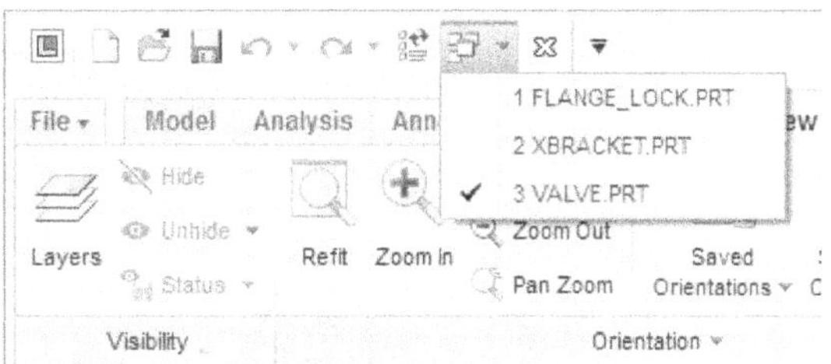

Figure 1–43

- If you no longer need to have a file open, you can remove it from the display. To remove a file from the graphic display, select **File>Close Window**. The model is no longer displayed but is still in memory.

File Naming

Files created in the various modes are given different filename extensions. When you create a new file or open an existing file into any mode, Creo Parametric automatically knows the correct extension. You do not need to enter the extension with the filename.

Creo Parametric permits a maximum of 31 characters in a filename. Periods and spaces are not permitted. Certain operating systems might not permit other characters in filenames. All files are stored in lowercase regardless of whether they are entered with uppercase letters.

The extensions used for the four modes discussed in this training guide are listed as follows:

Mode	Extension	Example
Sketcher	.SEC	groove.sec
Part	.PRT	key.prt
Assembly	.ASM	padlock.asm
Drawing	.DRW	padlock.drw

Model Orientation Using Two Planar Surfaces

The model does not have an explicit top, bottom, right, left, front, or back. The orientation options are all relative to your monitor, as shown in Figure 1–44. To fully orient a model in 3D, two perpendicular planar surfaces must be selected as references.

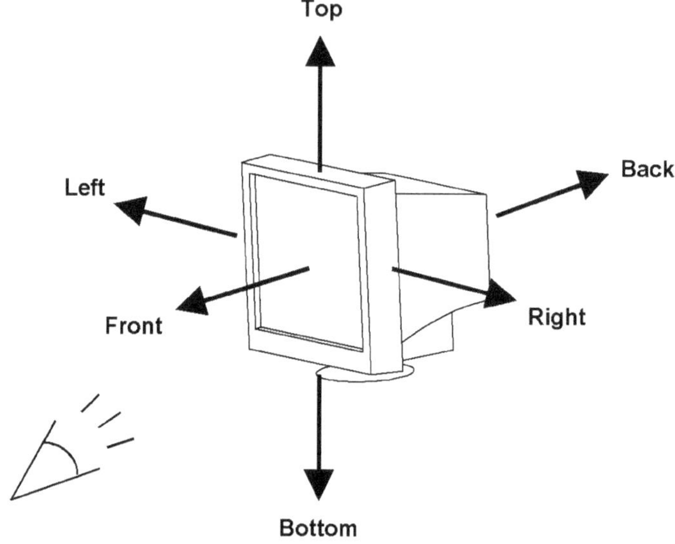

Figure 1–44

You can orient the model using the surfaces shown in Figure 1–45.

Press <Ctrl>+<D> or click (Saved Orientations) and select ***Standard Orientation*** *to return to the default orientation.*

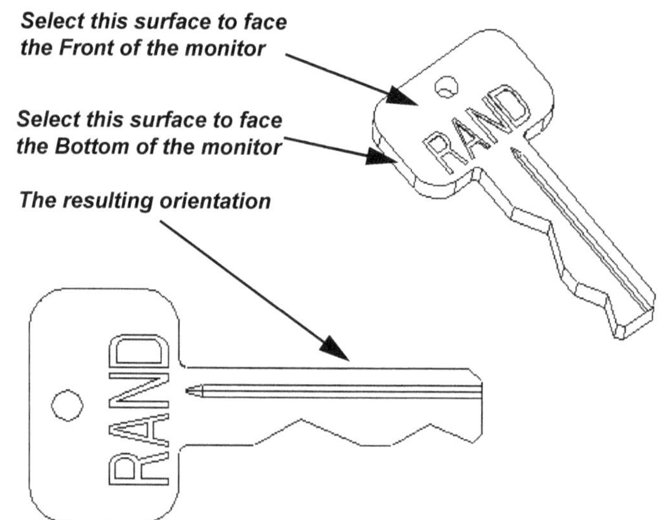

Figure 1–45

View Normal

You can quickly orient the model into a planar orientation by clicking (Saved Orientations) from the In-graphics toolbar, and then clicking (View Normal). Select a planar surface, and the system will automatically define a second reference so that the selected surface is oriented parallel to the screen.

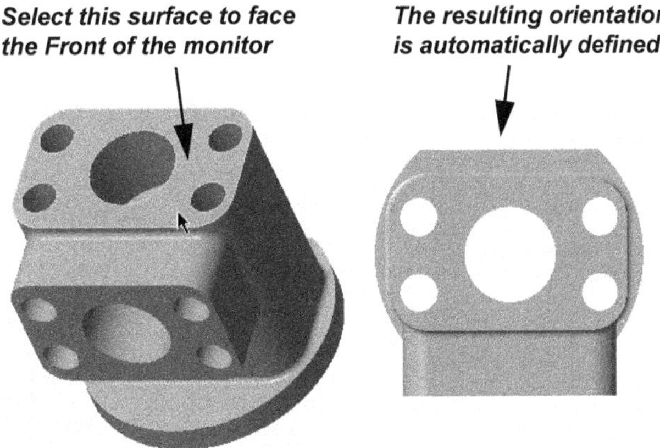

Figure 1–46

Spin, Pan, Zoom

The three standard controls for spinning, panning, and zooming work as follows:

- To spin the model, press and hold the middle mouse button and move the mouse as required to spin the model. When the (Spin Center) displays, the system spins the model about this location. Otherwise, the model is spun about a selected location. The selected location can be anywhere in the main graphics window, including selected geometry (entities, edges, or vertices). To select geometry, you can use the Geometry selection filter.
- To pan the model, press and hold <Shift> and the middle mouse button and move the mouse as required.
- To zoom the model, press and hold <Ctrl> and the middle mouse button and move the mouse up or down as required. You can also use the mouse scroll wheel to zoom the model.
- To zoom in on a specific area of the model, press and hold <Ctrl>, press and release the middle mouse button, and drag the bounding box to define the zoom area.
- To turn the model, press and hold <Ctrl> and the middle mouse button and move the mouse right or left as required.

Practice 1a Opening and Manipulating a Part

Practice Objectives

- Open part and drawing files and navigate between them using the **Windows** command in the Quick Access Toolbar.
- Change the visual style and orientation views of the model for improved visualization.
- Delete features and modify dimension values associated with a model to verify associativity between a part and its drawing file.

In this practice, you will practice using the Creo Parametric interface before you begin creating new models. You will then use the **Zoom**, **Pan**, and **Rotate** commands to orient the model shown in Figure 1–47.

Figure 1–47

Task 1 - Open the flange_lock.prt model.

You can also set the working directory by clicking (Select Working Directory) in the Home tab.

1. Set the current working directory by selecting **File>Manage Session>Select Working Directory** and select the *C:\Creo Parametric Introduction to Solid Modeling\Chapter 01\ practice 1a* folder.

*To open files you can also select **File>Open**.*

2. In the Quick Access Toolbar at the top of the main window, click (Open).

3. In the File Open dialog box, select **flange_lock.prt** and click **Open**. The model displays in the main window and the model tree displays all of the features in the model, as shown in Figure 1–48.

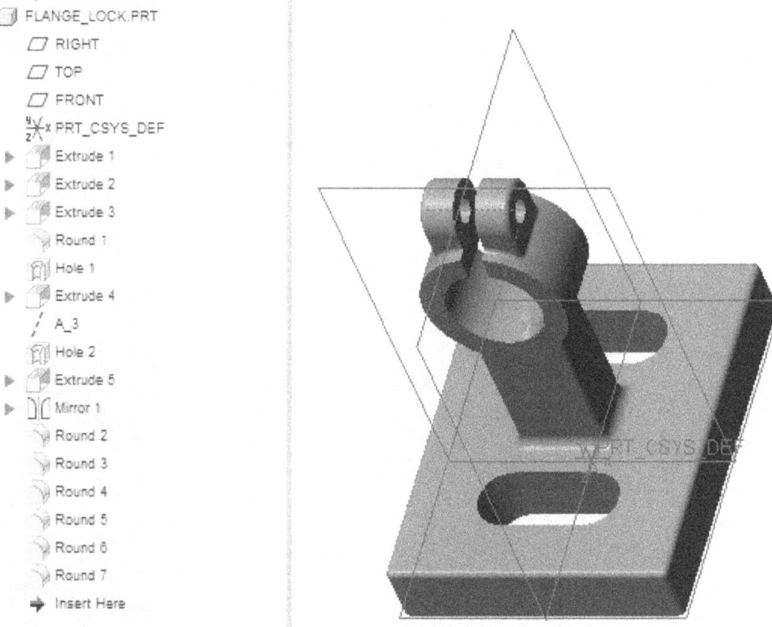

Figure 1–48

Note that the model name displays in the header of the Creo Parametric window and at the top of the model tree listing. The name in the model tree identifies the model as a part (.PRT) file. The model consists of solid geometry and datum features that were used as references when creating the solid geometry.

Task 2 - Zoom in and out on the model.

1. Press and hold <Ctrl>.
2. Hold the middle mouse button.

3. Move the mouse back to zoom in forward to zoom out on the model. If your mouse has a scroll wheel, use it to zoom in and out on the model.

To refit the model to the screen you can also click (Refit) in the Orientation group in the View tab.

4. In the In-graphics toolbar at the top of the view window, click (Refit) to refit the model in the center of the screen, as shown in Figure 1–49.

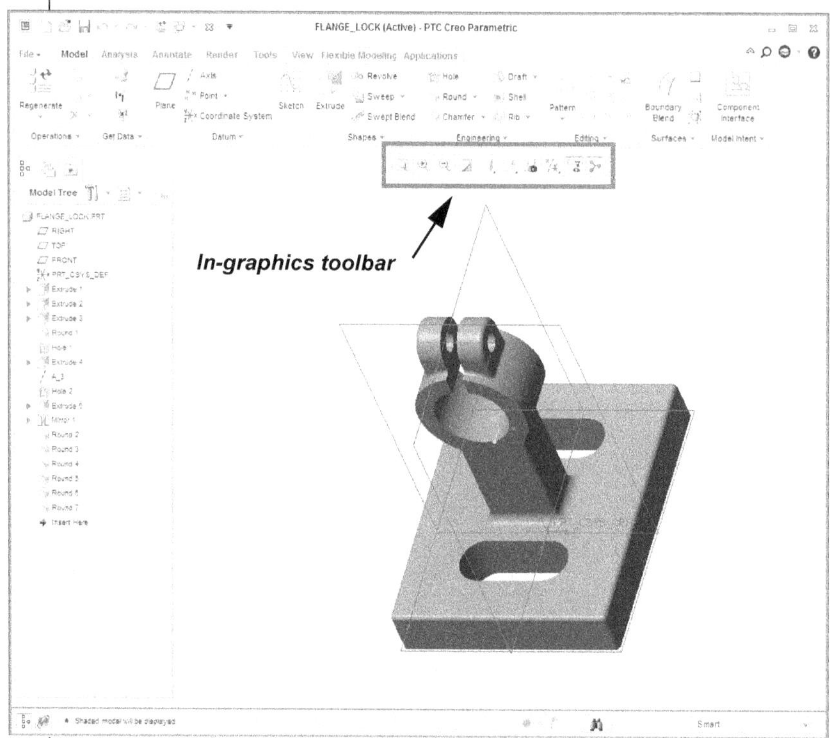

Figure 1–49

5. Press and hold <Ctrl>.
6. Hold the middle mouse button.
7. Move the mouse right or left to turn the model.

You can also click (Refit) in the View tab of the ribbon.

8. In the In-graphics toolbar, click (Refit) to refit the model in the center of the screen.

Task 3 - Zoom into an area of the model and zoom out on the model.

1. In the In-graphics toolbar, click (Zoom In).
2. Select a location on the model using the mouse button to define a corner of the bounding box zoom area.
3. Drag the mouse to draw a box over the area to zoom.
4. Press and release the mouse button again when the box is the required size.
5. In the In-graphics toolbar, click (Zoom Out). The Creo Parametric software automatically zooms out on the model. Continue to click this icon to zoom out further on the model.
6. In the In-graphics toolbar, click (Refit).
7. If your mouse has a scroll wheel, move the cursor over the model, then scroll up to zoom out and scroll down to zoom in.
8. Move the cursor to the right of the model and scroll up and down. Note that the system zooms in and out on the location under the cursor, as shown in Figure 1–50.

Figure 1–50

9. Click (Refit).

Task 4 - Pan the model on the screen.

1. Press and hold <Shift>.

2. Hold middle mouse button.
3. Move the mouse to drag the model.
4. Click (Refit).

Task 5 - Spin the model around the tri-colored spin center.

1. Hold the middle mouse button on any location in the main window.

To orient the model to its default orientation you can also press <Ctrl>+<D> or click (Standard Orientation) in the Orientation group in the View tab.

2. Move the mouse to spin the model. The Spin Center can be used as an orientation reference.
3. Click (Saved Orientations) and select **Standard Orientation** to return to the standard isometric orientation.

Task 6 - Manipulate the view display of the model.

The ability of a system to spin a shaded model depends on the quality of the graphics hardware. By default, the model display is set as shaded ((Shading) is selected in the In-graphics toolbar at the top of the view window).

You can also select different model display options by clicking (Display Style) in the Model Display group in the View tab.

1. In the In-graphics toolbar, expand (Display Style) and click (No Hidden) from the flyout menu to set the *View Display* to **No Hidden**.
2. Repeat the previous step to set the *View Display* to (Hidden Line), (No Hidden), (Wireframe), and (Shading With Edges).

Datum planes, axes, points, and coordinate systems are features that can exist in the model. They are discussed later in the training guide.

3. In the In-graphics toolbar, click (Datum Display Filters), then click **(Select All)** to toggle off the display of all datum entities.
4. Expand (Display Style) and click (Shading) to return the *View Display* to **Shaded**.

Task 7 - Orient the model by selecting two orientation constraints.

When orienting models, two perpendicular surfaces must be selected. ***Front*** *and* ***Top*** *are the default reference options.*

1. In the In-graphics toolbar, expand (Saved Orientations) and click (Reorient). The Orientation dialog box opens, as shown in Figure 1–51.

2. For the **Front** surface, select the surface shown in Figure 1–52.

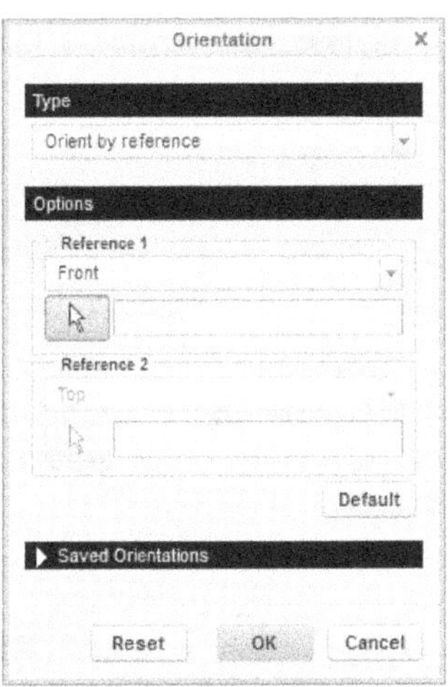

Figure 1–51

Figure 1–52

3. In the *Reference 2* area, select **Bottom** from the drop-down menu, and then select the surface shown in Figure 1–53.

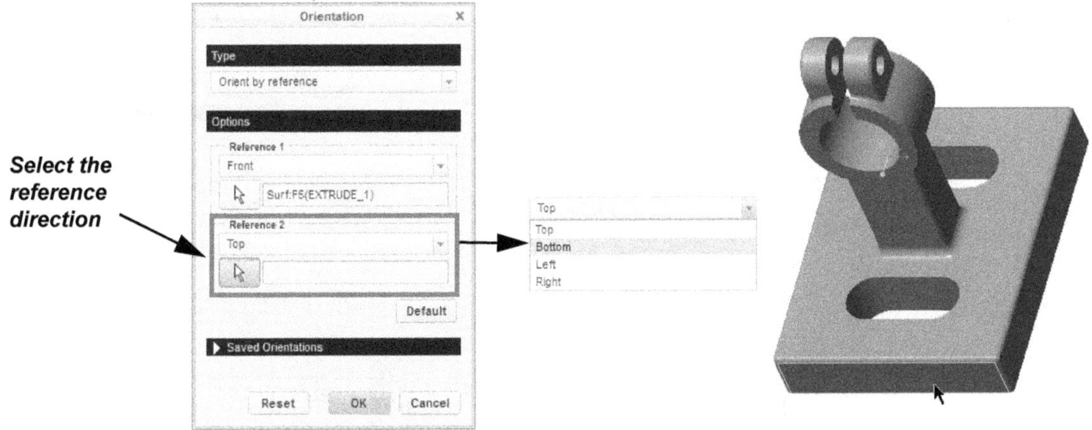

Figure 1–53

The model automatically reorients, as shown in Figure 1–54.

Figure 1–54

To retrieve a saved orientation, expand (Saved Orientations) and select the name of the saved view.

4. In the Orientation dialog box, select the **Saved Orientations** heading. In the expanded *Saved Orientations* area, in the *Name* of the new view, enter **view1**, as shown in Figure 1–55.

Figure 1–55

5. Click **Save** to save the view.

6. Click **Reset** to return to the default orientation.

Task 8 - Practice orienting the model.

Remember:

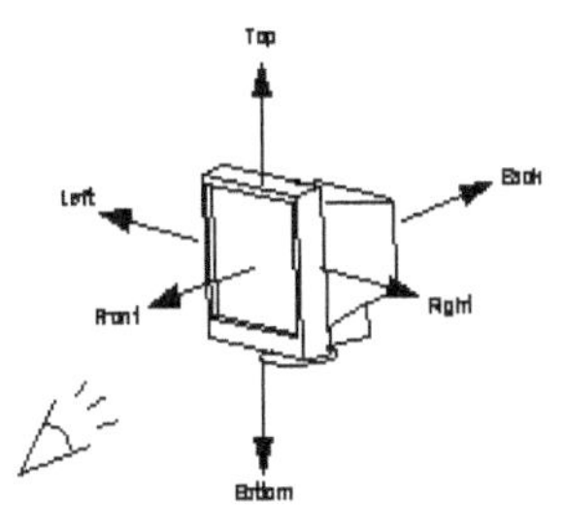

1. Select any two orientation constraints to define the views shown in Figure 1–56.

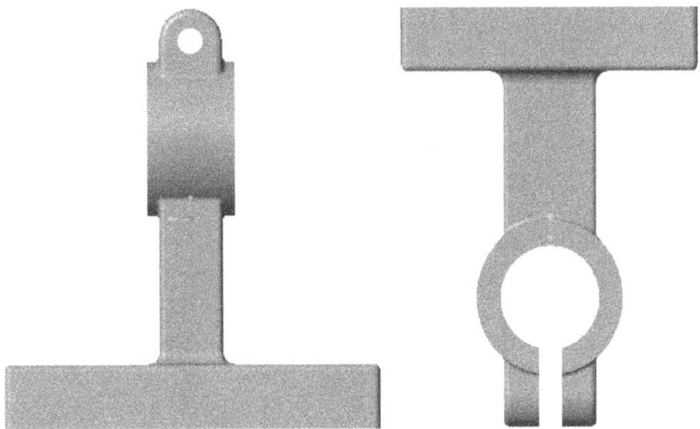

Figure 1–56

2. In the dialog box, click **Reset** to return the model to the default view.
3. Click **OK** to close the Orientation dialog box.
4. In the In-graphics toolbar, expand (Saved Orientations) and click (View Normal).
5. Select the surface shown in Figure 1–57. The model automatically reorients, as shown in Figure 1–58.

Figure 1–57

Figure 1–58

6. Press <Ctrl>+<D>.

7. In the In-graphics toolbar, expand (Saved Orientations) and click (View Normal).

8. Select the surface shown in Figure 1–59 to reorient the model.

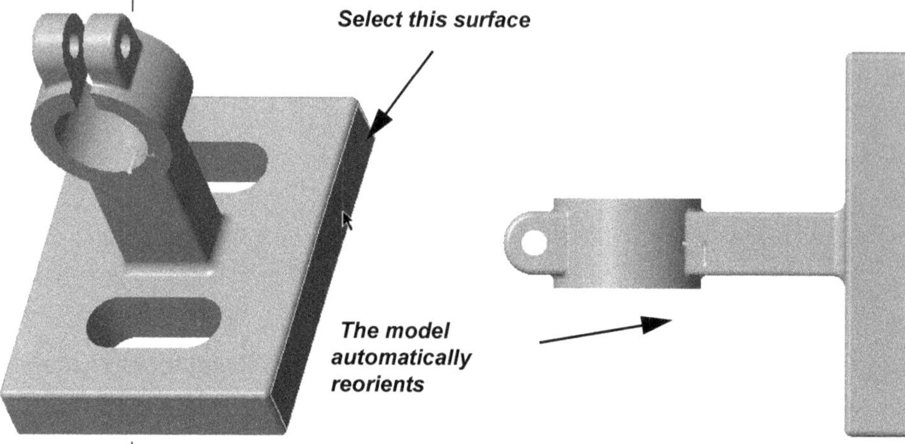

Figure 1–59

9. Press <Ctrl>+<D>.

Task 9 - Edit feature dimensions on the model.

1. In the model tree, select **Hole 1**.

2. Right-click and select (Edit).

3. In the main window, double-click on the **80.00** diameter dimension.

When the model regenerates, the system recalculates the model geometry. The length of regeneration time depends on the complexity of the model.

4. Set the new value to **50.00**, as shown in Figure 1–60. Press <Enter>.

5. Click on the screen twice and the size of the hole updates as the model regenerates. Note that you click once to clear the feature selection, move the mouse slightly, and a second time to trigger the regeneration.

6. In the model, select **Round 3**, hold the right mouse button and select (Edit) as shown in Figure 1–61.

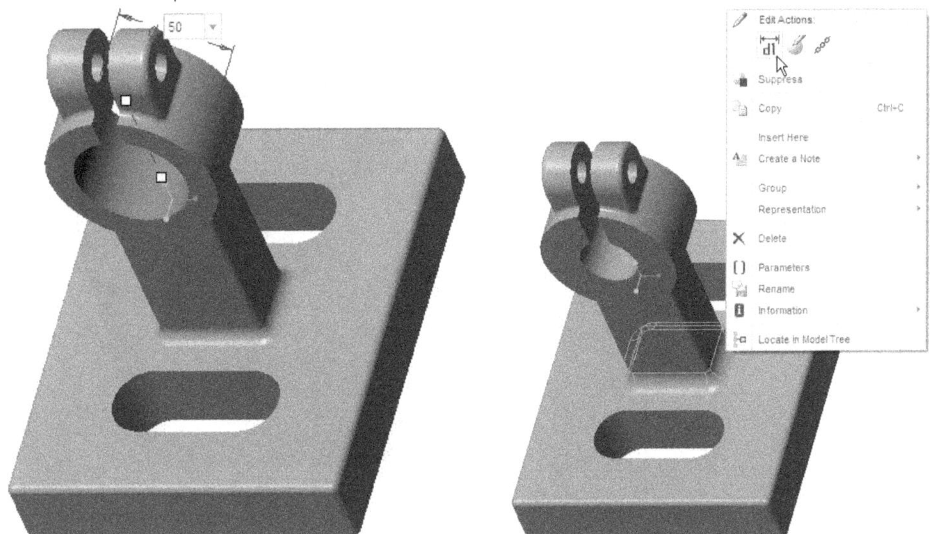

Figure 1–60

Figure 1–61

7. Set the radius round to **15 units.**

8. As an alternative to entering the dimensional value, you can dynamically drag the open arrows of the dimension. Double-click the oblong cut (**Extrude 5**). Note that the dimension locating the oblong cut is **77.50**, as shown in Figure 1–62.

9. Select the bottom arrow shown in Figure 1–63 and drag the position of the oblong cut to approximately **89.75**, as

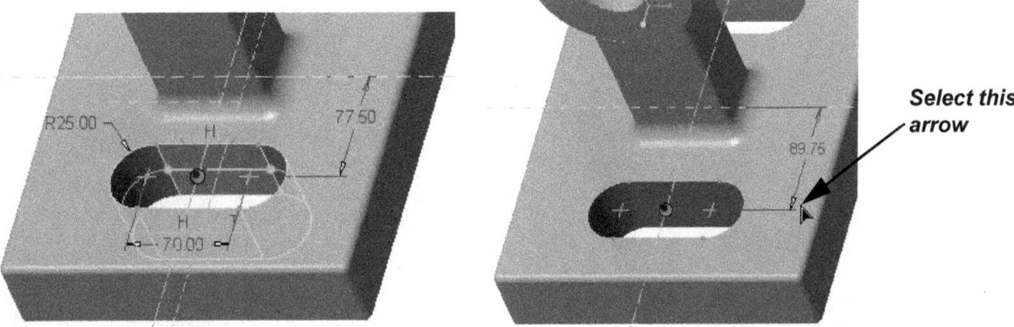

Figure 1–62

Figure 1–63

10. Change the post height (**Extrude 2**) from *275* to **350 units** using either method.

11. Click twice on the screen or click (Regenerate) in the Quick Access Toolbar to regenerate the model. The model displays, as shown in Figure 1–64.

Figure 1–64

*To save files you can also select **File > Save** or press <Ctrl>+<S>.*

12. In the Quick Access Toolbar, click (Save)

Task 10 - Delete features from the model.

You can use <Ctrl> to select multiple features at the same time in your model.

1. Select **Hole1** directly on the model, hold the right mouse button, and select **Delete**, as shown in Figure 1–65.
2. In the Delete dialog box, click **OK**. The hole and cut are deleted. The model displays as shown in Figure 1–66.

The cut feature is a child feature of the hole. You are prompted to select an action for the child feature.

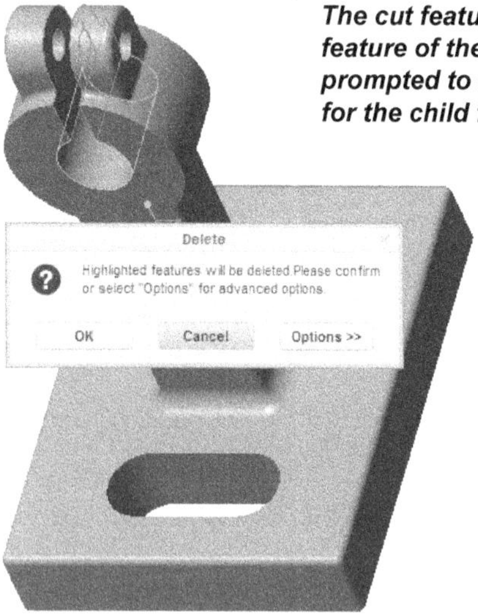

Figure 1–65

Figure 1–66

Alternatively, you can click (Close) in the Quick Access Toolbar.

3. To close the active working window, select **File>Close**. The model is no longer displayed but is still in memory.

Task 11 - Open files.

1. In the *Home* tab, click (Open).

The previous files that were opened are listed in the File tab on the right under Recent Files. This enables you to quickly access these files without using the Open dialog box.

2. If required, click (Working Directory) in the Common Folders area of the Open dialog box.
3. Double-click **flange_lock.prt**. The model was not saved with the deleted features. However, the **flange_lock** file (with the deleted features) still remains in the active working memory until it is erased. This active working memory is termed *in session*.
4. Select **File>Manage Session>Erase Current** to erase the file from memory. This does not affect the file saved on the system disk.
5. In the Erase Confirm dialog box, click **Yes**.
6. Open **flange_lock.prt** again. The model displays with all of its features because it was not saved after the features were deleted.
7. In the Quick Access Toolbar, click (Close).

Task 12 - Open multiple Creo Parametric windows.

The Creo Parametric environment enables you to work with multiple open windows.

1. Open **xbracket.drw**. The header of the main window displays the name of the drawing. The word **Active** after the name indicates that this is the active window.

*You can also open the drawing model by selecting the model in the model tree, right-clicking and selecting **Open**.*

2. Open **xbracket.prt**. A second window opens containing the drawing model.
3. The window containing **xbracket.drw** is still open. In the Quick Access Toolbar, click (Windows).

   xbracket.drw and **xbracket.prt** are listed but **xbacket.prt** is the active file. These can be selected to activate the appropriate window.

Task 13 - Delete the rectangular tab protrusion on the model.

1. In the menu bar, expand [icon] and verify that **xbracket.prt** is the active file.

2. In the model tree or main window, select the rectangular tab protrusion as shown in Figure 1–67, right-click and select **Delete**. Click **OK** to confirm deletion of the tab.

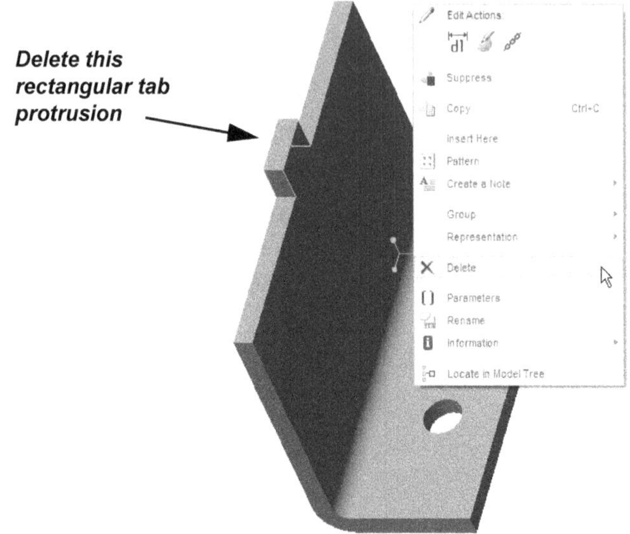

Figure 1–67

Task 14 - Edit the length of the bracket in the drawing.

1. In the Quick Access Toolbar, expand [icon] and select **XBRACKET.DRW** to activate the drawing, as shown in Figure 1–68.

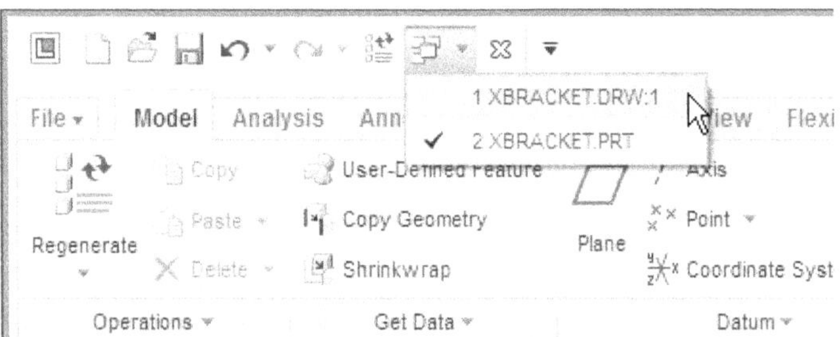

Figure 1–68

2. The drawing updates now that the tab protrusion has been deleted. If it does not update, click (Update Sheets) in the *Review* tab.

3. Select the **10.00** length dimension, hold the right mouse button and select **Modify Nominal Value**.

4. Set the new *Dimension* to **8** and press <Enter>.

5. In the Quick Access Toolbar, click (Regenerate Active Model) to regenerate the model.

6. Activate the window containing the part to verify that the model has changed.

To repaint the model you can click (Repaint). This option refreshes the work area by eliminating residual graphics or returning graphics that might have disappeared.

7. Click (Save) to save the model.

8. Click (Close) close the part file.

Task 15 - Edit the diameter dimension of the hole in the drawing.

1. Ensure that the window containing the drawing is active.

2. Set the hole *Diameter* to **.5** and regenerate the model. Note that the diameter of both holes has updated simultaneously. This is because the holes were created using the **Pattern** option.

Task 16 - Save the drawing and close the window.

1. Save the drawing and close the window.

2. In the *Home* tab, click (Erase Not Displayed) to erase all of the files from memory.

Practice 1b Model Tree Manipulation

Practice Objectives

- Manipulate the model tree display.
- Select and operate on features from the model tree.

Task 1 - Toggle the display of the model tree on and off.

1. In the *Home* tab, in the ribbon, click (Select Working Directory) and navigate to the *Chapter 01\practice 1b* folder. Click **OK**.

2. In the Quick Access Toolbar at the top of the main window, click (Open).

1. In the File Open dialog box, select **valve2.prt** and click **Open**.

Removing the model tree from the display gives you more room to work with your model.

2. To remove the model tree from the display, click (Model Tree) in the lower left corner of the Creo Parametric window.

3. To return the model tree to the display, click (Model Tree) again.

4. To resize the model tree, click and hold the cursor on the right-hand border of the model tree. The cursor changes as shown in Figure 1–69.

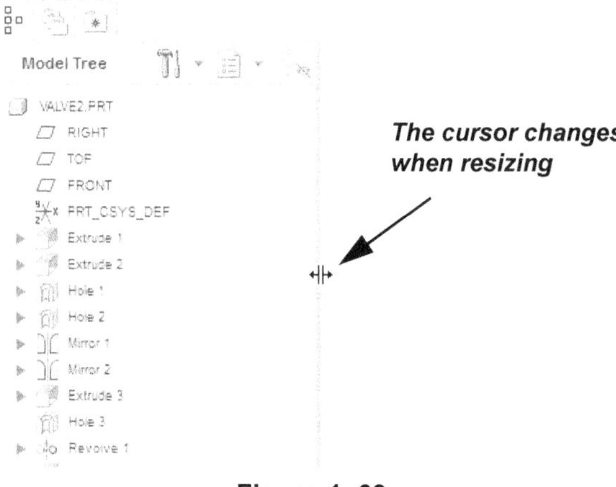

Figure 1–69

5. Drag the border right to increase the model tree width, and left to decrease it.

Task 2 - Conduct a feature operation directly in the model tree.

1. Press and hold <Ctrl> and select **Round 1** and **Round 2** from the model tree.
2. Right-click and select **Suppress**.
3. Select **OK** to confirm suppression of the features. The model and model tree update to temporarily remove the features, as shown in Figure 1–70.

Feature suppression is covered later in this guide.

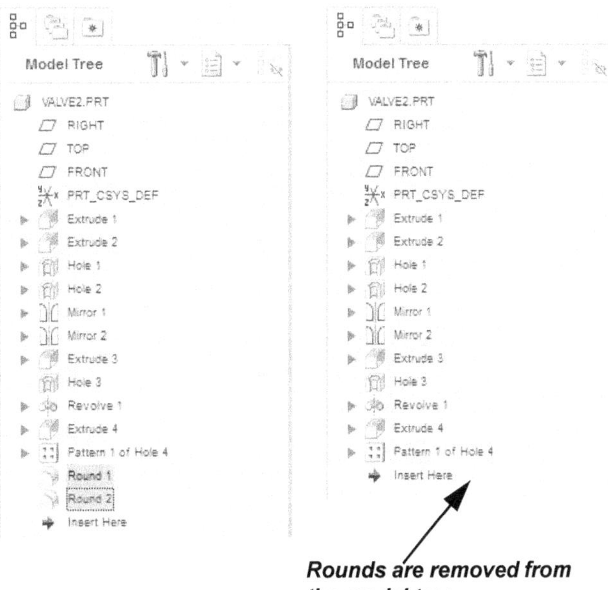

Figure 1–70

Task 3 - Manipulate the display of the items in the model tree.

1. In the model tree, select (Settings) and click **Tree Filters**. The Model Tree Items dialog box displays.
2. Select **Suppressed objects** to display any suppressed features in the model tree.
3. In the *General* tab, in the Feature Types section of the dialog box, select **Datum plane** and **Coordinate system**.

4. Select **OK** and close the Model Tree Items dialog box. The model tree displays, as shown in Figure 1–71.

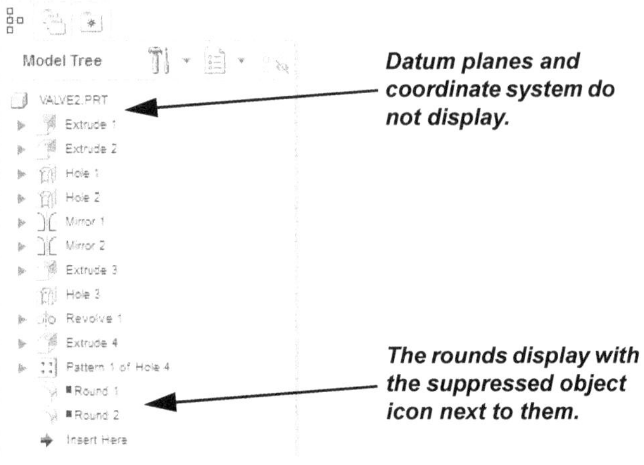

Figure 1–71

Task 4 - Manipulate the column display of the model tree.

1. In the model tree, select (Settings) and click **Tree Columns**. The Model Tree Columns dialog box displays.
2. Press and hold <Ctrl> and select **Feat #** from the Not Displayed list.
3. Select to » (Add Column) to add the feature number to the Displayed column.
4. Repeat the previous two steps for **Feature Status**, and **Feat Type**.
5. In the **Type** menu, select **Layer**. Each item in this list enables you to add additional columns to the model tree.

Layers are discussed later in this guide.

6. Add **Layer Names** to the column display.
7. Select **OK** to close the Model Tree Columns dialog box and update the model tree.

The model tree, model tree filters and model tree columns can be used to select objects and entities efficiently.

8. Resize the model tree window and drag the column dividers to display the columns and model tree as shown in Figure 1–72.

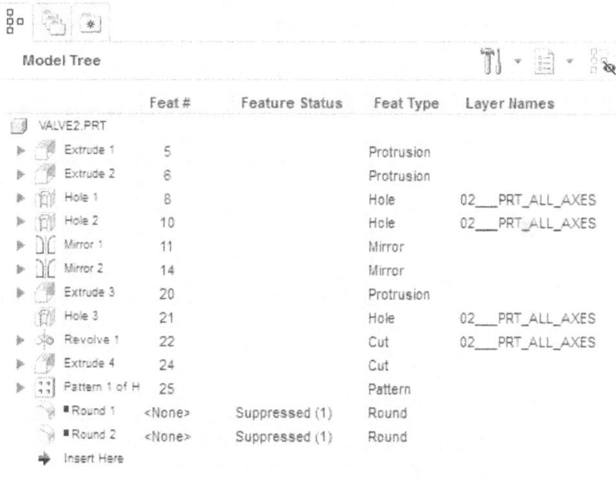

Figure 1–72

9. In the Quick Access Toolbar, click (Close).

10. In the *Home* tab, in the ribbon, click (Erase Not Displayed).

Chapter Review Questions

1. Which of the following are the key attributes of the Creo Parametric software? (Select all that apply.)
   a. Feature-based
   b. Parametric
   c. Associative
   d. Relations
2. Which of the following represent features for which a shape is predefined? (Select all that apply.)
   a. Sketched
   b. Engineering
   c. Extrude
   d. Revolve
3. After editing the dimensions of a part model, you must open all of the drawings referencing that part to make the same dimension changes.
   a. True
   b. False
4. Which of the following actions can be initiated in the model tree? (Select all that apply.)
   a. Select features
   b. Search
   c. Insert features
   d. View feature information
5. Creo Parametric part files have the _______ filename extension.
   a. .asm
   b. .prt
   c. .drw
   d. .sec
6. Selecting the **TOP** orientation option enables you to view the top of the model.
   a. True
   b. False

7. To spin the model, which mouse button do you need to click and hold?
    a. Left
    b. Middle
    c. Right
8. Which of the following answers describes the purpose of the (Regenerate) option?
    a. It refreshes the screen after spinning the model.
    b. It changes the display mode of the model from hidden line to shaded.
    c. It re-calculates the geometry after dimension changes.
    d. It opens a new model.
9. Which of the following orientation option combinations can be used to orient a model? (Select all that apply.)
    a. **Right** and **Top**
    b. **Front** and **Back**
    c. **Back** and **Left**
    d. **Top** and **Back**
10. **File>Manage Session>Erase Current** option erases the current file from your system's hard disk.
    a. True
    b. False

Command Summary

Button	Command	Location
	Open	• **Ribbon:** *Home* tab • Quick Access Toolbar • File>New • **Hot Key:** <Ctrl>+O or <Alt>+2
	Select Working Directory	• **Ribbon:** *Home* tab • File > Manage Session > Select Working Directory
	Save	• Quick Access Toolbar • File>Save • **Hot Key:** <Ctrl>+S or <Alt>+3
	New	• Ribbon: Home tab • Quick Access Toolbar • File>New • **Hot Key:** <Ctrl>+N or <Alt>+1
	Pan	• **Ribbon:** *View* tab in the Navigate panel • Navigation Bar • <Shift>+MMB
	Zoom In	• **Ribbon:** *View* tab in the Orientation group • In-graphics toolbar • Scroll Wheel • **Hot Key:** <Alt>+Z+B
	Refit	• **Ribbon:** *View* tab in the Orientation group • In-graphics toolbar • **Hot Key:** <Alt> +Z+A
	Zoom Out	• **Ribbon:** *View* tab in the Orientation group • In-graphics toolbar • **Hot Key:** <Alt>+Z+C • Scroll Wheel
	Repaint	• In-graphics toolbar • **Hot Key:** <Crl>+R or <Alt>+Z+D
	Regenerate	• **Ribbon:** *Model* tab in the Operations group • Quick Access Toolbar • **Hot Key:** <Ctrl>+G or <Alt>+6
	Undo	• Quick Access Toolbar • **Hot Key:** <Ctrl>+Z or <Alt>+4
	Redo	• Quick Access Toolbar • **Hot Key:** <Ctrl>+Y or <Alt>+5

	Display Style	• **Ribbon:** *View* tab in the Model Display group • In-graphics toolbar • **Hot Key:** <Alt>+ZE
	Saved Orientations	• **Ribbon:** *View* tab in the Orientation group • In-graphics toolbar • **Hot Key:** <Alt>+Z+F
	Help	• Help toolbar • (*press < F1>*)

Managing Your Creo Parametric Session and Files

File management options in Creo Parametric enable you to organize your files. Managing your files is important for effectively controlling your design data. In addition to PDM (Product Data Management), these file management options offer methods for saving, duplicating, and deleting files.

Learning Objectives in this Chapter

- Understand how files are stored and retrieved.
- Understand the different options in the File tab.
- Understand the versions of the part and how to show the part versions in the File dialog box.
- Understand the differences between the erase commands.

2.1 Managing Creo Parametric Files

Most companies have some form of PDM (Product Data Management) system setup in their organizations. Most of the capabilities discussed in this chapter are handled via the PDM system.

It is important to understand how Creo handles files when not using a PDM system, in the event you are ever working offline. This chapter covers how Creo Parametric handles files when working with them locally.

RAM is considered temporary storage (or In Session working memory) and the system hard drive is considered permanent storage.

All work done in the Creo Parametric software uses the system's memory (RAM). Files are only stored to the system's hard drive when the file is saved, as shown in Figure 2–1.

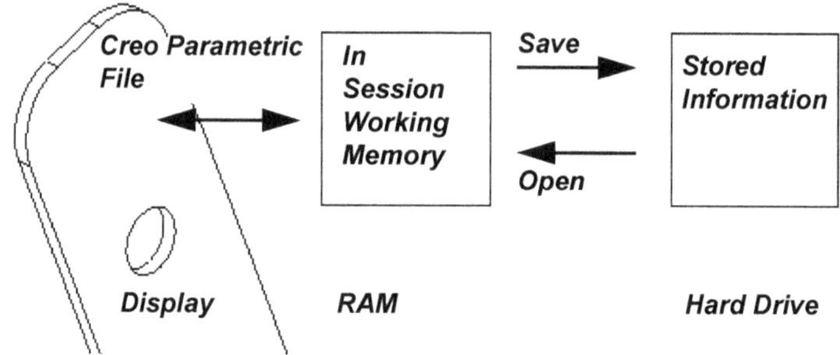

Figure 2–1

Files remain in RAM until one of the following occurs:

- Files are erased using one of the **Erase** options.
- The Creo Parametric session is closed.

General Steps

Use the following general steps for file management when working on a model:

1. Save the initial model design and any subsequent changes made to it.
2. Delete any unwanted versions of the model.
3. Close the window.
4. Erase the file from memory.

Step 1 - Save the initial model design and any subsequent changes made to it.

Once a design has been created or changes have been made to the model, it is recommended to store the files in a permanent location on your hard drive. Files can be saved using any of the following options:

- Save
- Rename
- Save a Copy
- Save a Backup

Save

To save a model, click (Save) in the Quick Access Toolbar or select the **File>Save**. The Save Object dialog box opens, as shown in Figure 2–2.

You can also press <Ctrl>+<S>.

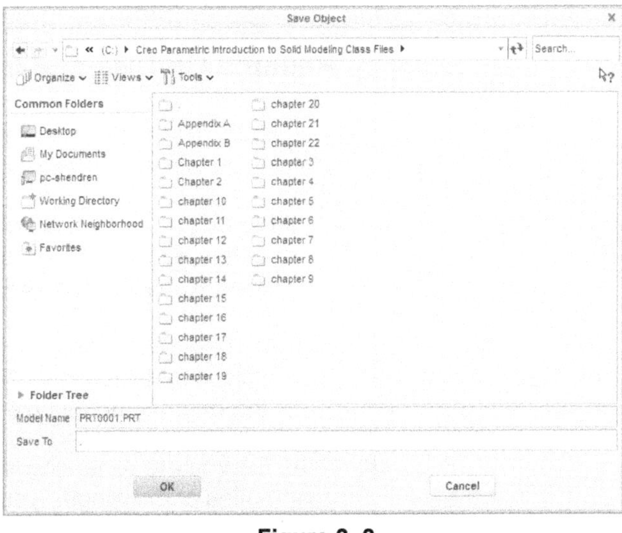

Figure 2–2

You can also click the middle mouse button at this point, to store the file on the hard drive.

- Press <Enter> or click **OK** in the Save Object dialog box to store the file on the hard drive.
- When you save a file using **File>Save**, the model is automatically saved to the current working directory (for a new file) or the directory from which it was retrieved (for an existing file).

Rename

To rename the existing file, select **File>Manage File>Rename**. The Rename dialog box opens, as shown in Figure 2–3. Enter a new name for the model and select whether to rename the file in session and on disk or only in session.

Figure 2–3

Rename In Session

If you rename the file in session, the file is only renamed in RAM. Subsequently, selecting **File>Save** creates a new file in the directory in which the original model is stored. The original model remains unchanged.

Rename On Disk and In Session

This option depends on whether the original model is stored in the current working directory:

- If the original model is not stored in the current working directory, the **Rename on disk and in session** option acts like the **Rename in session** option.
- If the original model is stored in the current working directory, the file is renamed in RAM and on the hard drive. All versions of the original model take the new name.

If the file you are renaming is associated with other files (i.e., assemblies or drawings), you must bring all of them into session by opening them. This ensures that all of the associated files are updated with the correct model name, once the file is renamed. For example, if an assembly is comprised of several part models and you rename one of those parts without the assembly in session, the part will be considered missing when you later open the assembly. Once the associated file is renamed, all of the reference files must be re-saved to ensure that the change is applied.

Save a Copy

You can copy an existing file to a new name while retaining the existing file using the **Save a Copy** tool. This enables you to explore different design options. To save a copy of an existing file, select **File>Save As>Save a Copy**. The Save a Copy dialog box opens, as shown in Figure 2–4.

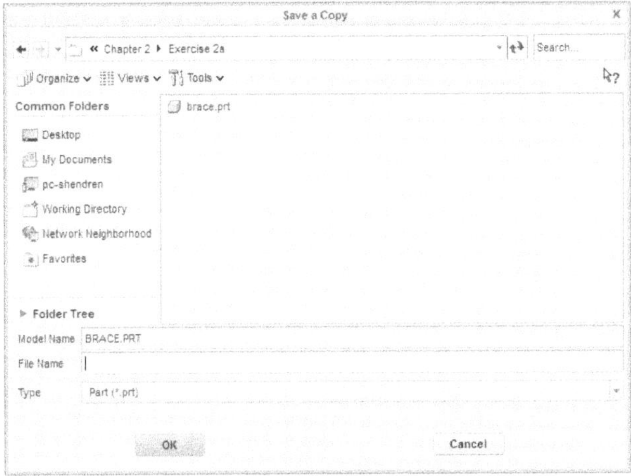

Figure 2–4

By default, the copied file is stored in the current working directory. You can select a different directory in which to save the file, by navigating to the appropriate folder.

- Enter a new name for the file and click **OK** to save it to the hard drive. Note that the original file remains in the active window, so you must open the new file to work with it. If you do not want to save changes in the original file, erase it from the session without saving. (See Step 4 - Erase the file from memory.)
- In the example shown in Figure 2–5, the part **bracket_2.prt** originally contained two holes. A design change requires the model to have four holes. Once the holes are created, the file is saved as **bracket_4.prt** using the **Save a Copy** option. As a result, the current file in RAM is still **bracket_2.prt** and **bracket_4.prt** is saved to the hard drive. To ensure that the additional holes do not display in the original file, it is erased without saving.

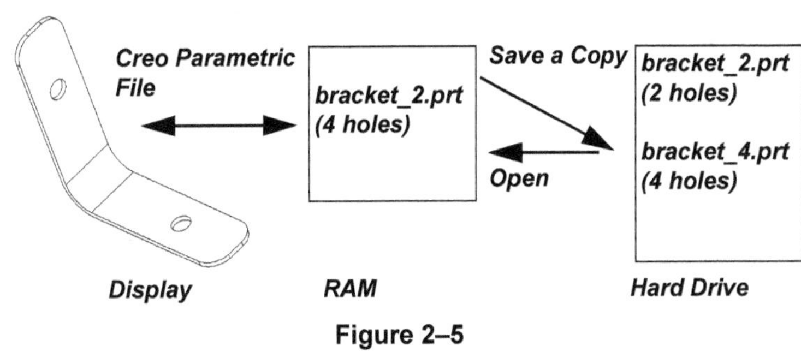

Figure 2–5

Backup

To avoid losing your work, you can create a backup copy of your file by selecting **File>Save As>Save A Backup**. The Backup dialog box opens, as shown in Figure 2–6.

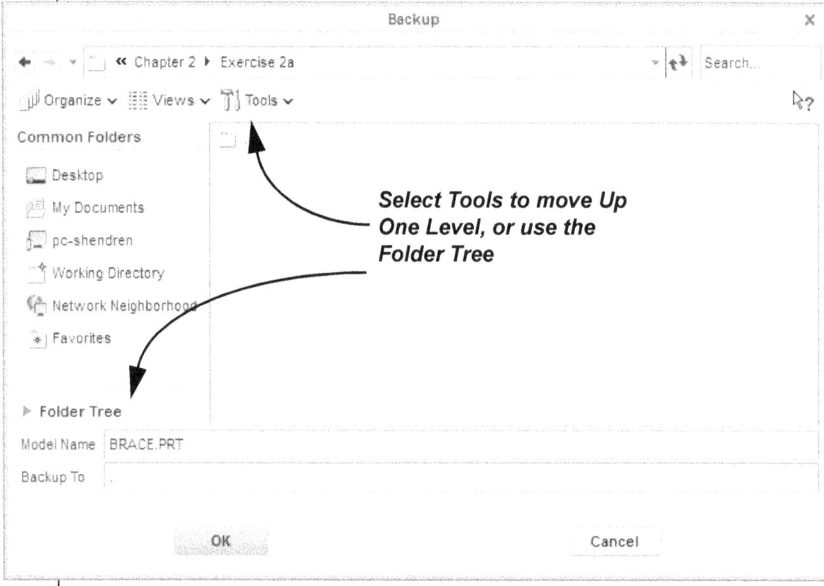

Figure 2–6

- Browse to the target directory. The original filename is maintained and the backup copy is stored in the new directory. The original model remains in the active window. The changes saved to the backup file remain independent to the original file.

Backup also saves the backups of any associated files to the backup directory.

- It is recommended to save your changes often and/or create a backup file. The software does not have an automatic save function and does not prompt you to save your files when exiting the program.

Step 2 - Delete any unwanted versions of the model.

Each time a file is saved, an updated version of that file is stored on the hard drive. For example, if **brace.prt** is saved three times, it is stored as three different files in the directory. Each version of the saved file has a numbered extension appended to the end of the filename. The highest numerical extension represents the most recently saved model, as shown in Figure 2–7.

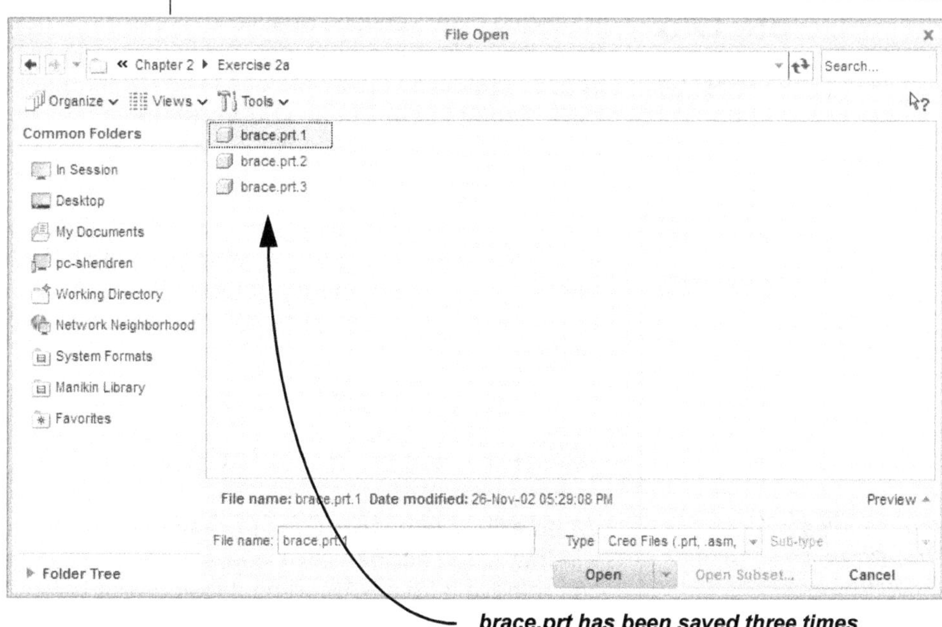

Figure 2–7

To display a list of versioned files, select **Tools > All Versions** as shown in Figure 2–8.

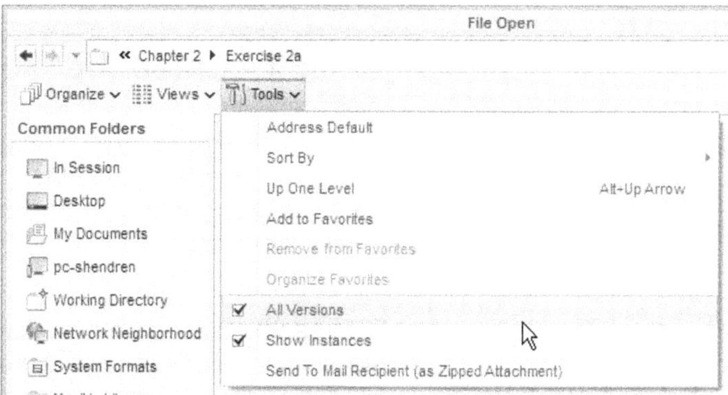

Figure 2–8

To help manage the number of files that you have stored on the hard drive, it is recommended that you delete any unwanted versions of your models.

Delete Old Versions

Retaining older versions of a file is useful if you need to retrieve them later. However, each new file takes up additional disk space. If retaining older versions is no longer required, select **File>Manage File>Delete Old Versions** to remove all but the most recent version of the file.

Delete All Versions

If a file is no longer required, remove it and all of its versions from your hard drive by selecting **File>Manage File>Delete All Versions**. This permanently deletes the files from the hard drive and RAM. It is recommended to use this option with extreme caution.

Step 3 - Close the window.

*You can also select **File>Close** to close an active window.*

When a file is opened in Creo Parametric, it displays in the active window. If you accidentally close a window without saving, you can retrieve it from RAM without losing your work. The information on the hard disk is not accessed.

- (In Session): Enables you to review the files in RAM. It can be found in the Common Folders list. You can also open the files in the dialog box.

Step 4 - Erase the file from memory.

Once the files have been saved, it is recommended that you erase them to clear your RAM. Files can be erased from the current display or erased from memory if their window has already been closed.

Erasing Current Files

Files can be erased from the current display in the active window by selecting **File>Manage Session>Erase Current**. Ensure that all of the changes are saved before erasing the file as erasing it completely removes it from RAM. Only the last saved version of the model can be accessed.

Erasing Not Displayed Files

Files that were previously closed still exist in RAM. To erase these files, select **File>Manage Session>Erase Not Displayed**. Erasing files ensures that only the required ones are in session. Try to erase files when you have finished working with them to minimize the amount of information stored in RAM. Too much information in RAM slows down the system. If you are not sure which files are currently in session, click (In Session) in the Common Folders list.

- For example, three parts (**bracket_2.prt**, **bracket_4.prt**, and **bracket_6.prt**) are in session, as shown in Figure 2–9. Suppose **bracket_2.prt** and **bracket_4.prt** have previously been saved and **bracket_6.prt** has not yet been saved. If you close all three windows and select **File>Erase>Not Displayed**, **bracket_6.prt** would no longer exist, while **bracket_2.prt** and **bracket_4.prt** would remain because they were previously saved.

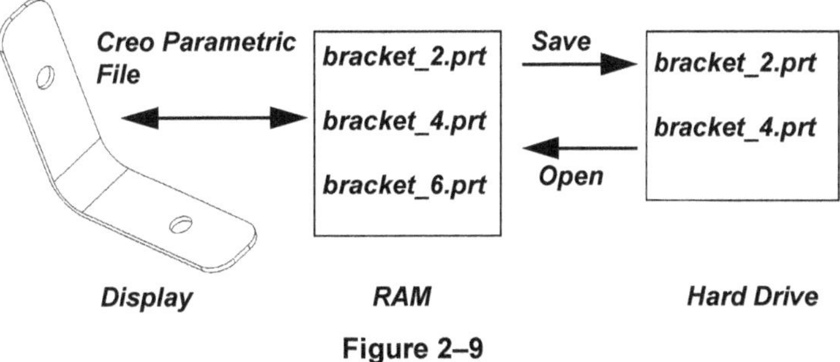

Figure 2–9

Practice 2a Managing Files

Practice Objectives

- Display the different versions of a part.
- Rename a part, save a copy, or erase files from memory using the *File* tab.

In this practice, you will open a model with which multiple saved versions are associated and practice using the file management options covered in this chapter.

Task 1 - Open a part file.

1. Set the working directory to the *Chapter 02\practice 2a* folder.
2. In the Creo Parametric Navigator, click (Folder Browser), if required. In the Common Folders list, select **Working Directory**. The Browser displays as shown in Figure 2–10.

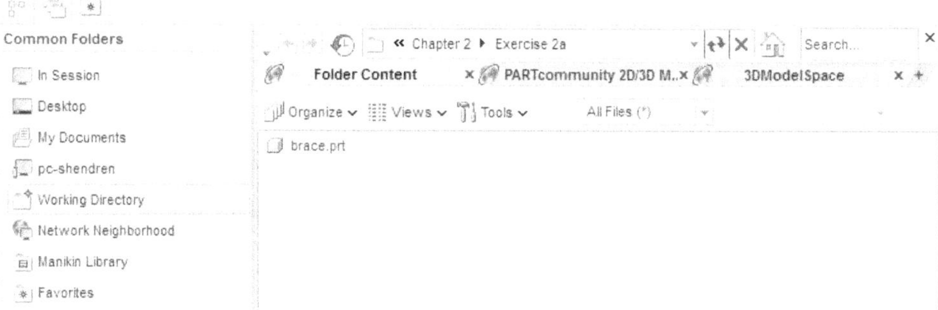

Figure 2–10

This is an alternative way to browse the contents of directories.

3. Select **brace.prt** and select **Preview**, as shown in Figure 2–11.

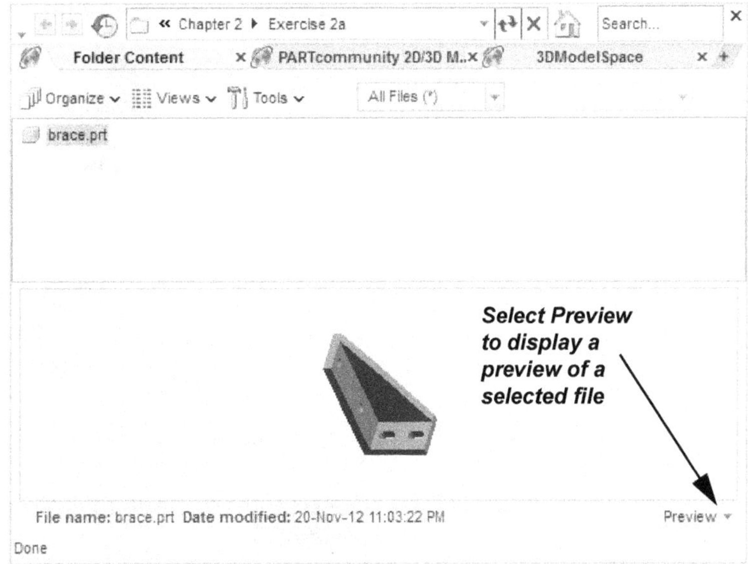

Figure 2–11

4. In the Browser, select **Tools>All Versions**, as shown in Figure 2–12. The file structure displays all of the saved versions of the models. There are several different versions of **brace.prt**.

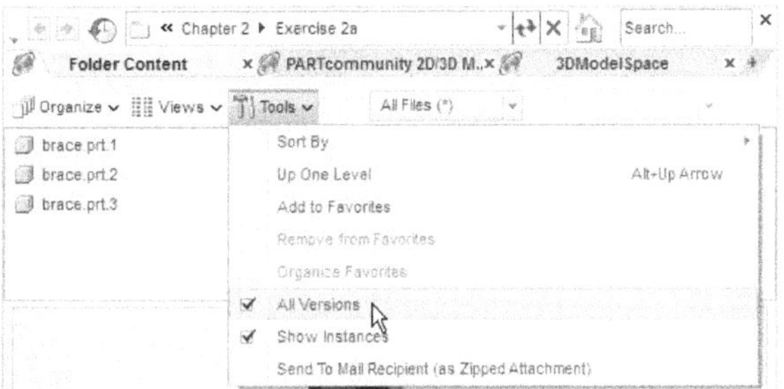

Figure 2–12

5. Select **brace.prt.1**. Note that the original version of the model displays in the *Preview* area.

If a previous version is opened, modified, and saved, it becomes the latest version of the part.

6. Double-click on **brace.prt.3** to open the latest version of the model.

7. Set the model display as follows:

   - *(Datum Display Filters)*: All Off
   - *(Spin Center)*: Off
   - *(Display Style)*: (Shading)

The model displays as shown in Figure 2–13.

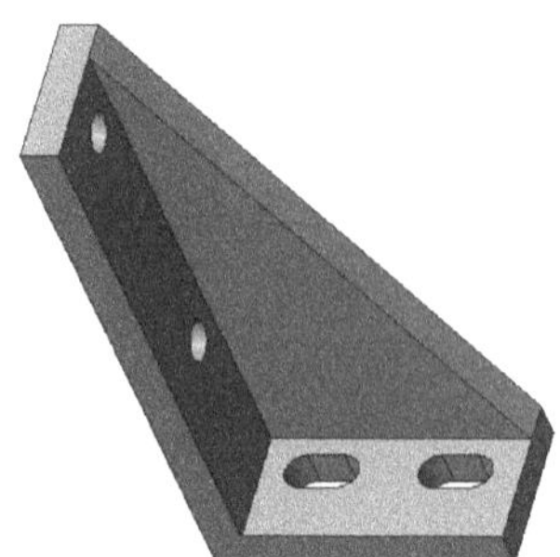

Figure 2–13

Task 2 - Rename the part.

1. Select **File>Manage File>Rename**. Rename *brace.prt* to **holder**.

This renames the part in the current session and permanently renames it on the hard drive

2. Select the **Rename on disk and in session** option.
3. Click **OK**.
4. Use the Browser to display the working directory and confirm that all versions of the part have been renamed as **holder.prt**, as shown in Figure 2–14.

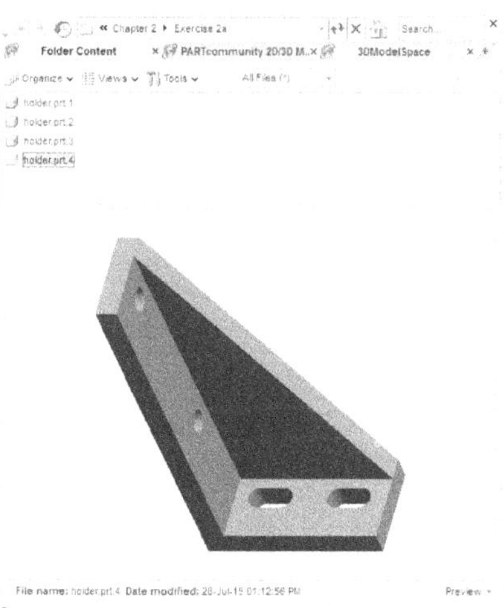

Figure 2–14

5. To close the browser window, click ✕ in the top right corner.

Task 3 - Modify and save the part with a new name.

1. Click (Model Tree) in the Navigator, if required.
2. Delete **Extrude3**. The part displays as shown in Figure 2–15.

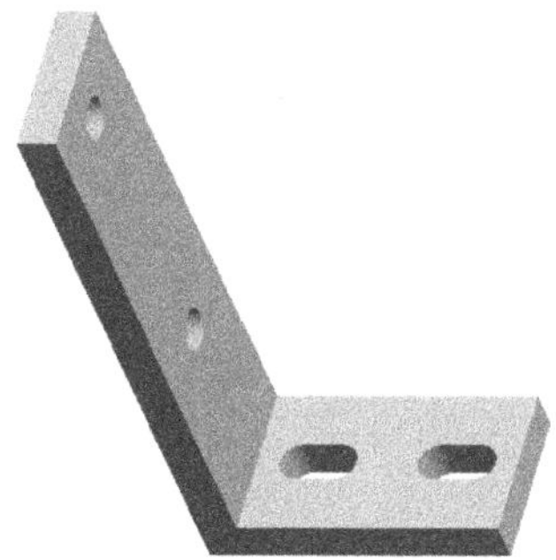

Figure 2–15

3. Select **File>Save As>Save a Copy** to save the changes made in the model.
4. In the Save a Copy dialog box, click (Working Directory).
5. Save the model with the name **stabilizer.prt**, as shown in Figure 2–16.

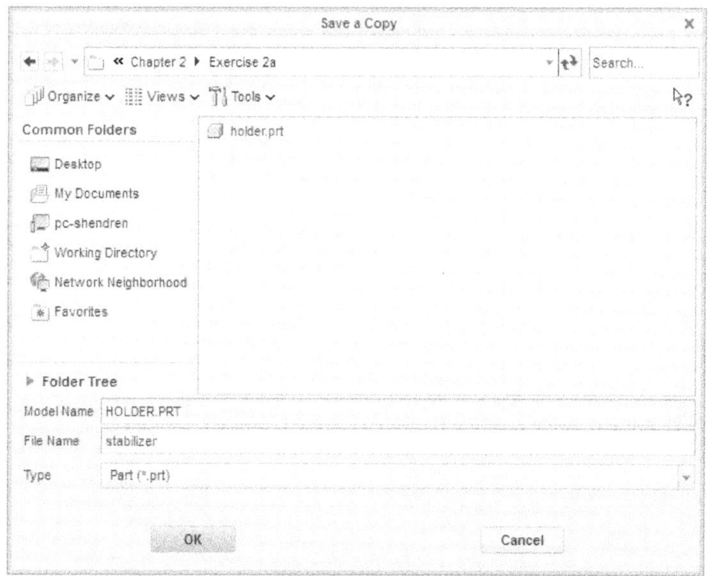

Figure 2–16

6. Click **OK**.

Task 4 - Erase a single file from RAM.

1. Select **File>Manage Session>Erase Current** to erase **holder.prt** from RAM. Click **Yes** to confirm.

2. Open **holder.prt**. The model contains the original geometry. The changes were only saved in **stabilizer.prt**.

3. Open **stabilizer.prt**. Observe the geometry.

4. Close all files.

5. In the *Home* tab, click (Erase Not Displayed) to remove all files from memory.

Chapter Review Questions

1. What are the locations in which files exist while you are working on them in Creo Parametric? (Select all that apply.)
    a. Hard drive
    b. RAM
    c. Display
2. Which of the following statements is true regarding saving a file? (Select all that apply.)
    a. Click (Save) to save a file.
    b. When you save a file, it automatically prompts you for the directory in which you want to save it.
    c. When saving a file using (Save), the current name can be changed by entering the new name at the message window prompt.
    d. Each time a file is saved, an updated version of the file is stored on the hard disk.
3. If you open a file and decide that you do not want to save the changes, and that you want to start over and continue to work on the model, select **File>Close** and reopen the part.
    a. True
    b. False
4. Which of the following statements is true regarding the **Save a Copy** option?
    a. Any files that reference the file being copied must be in session.
    b. The copied file becomes the active model once saved.
    c. The copied file is stored in the current working directory.
    d. The **Save a Copy** option is the same as renaming the file.
5. Which of the following options enables you to create a duplicate of a model by copying it to a new name?
    a. Save
    b. Rename
    c. Save a Copy
    d. Backup

6. Which of the following options enables you to create a copy of a model in another directory while maintaining the original name?
    a. Save
    b. Rename
    c. Save a Copy
    d. Backup
7. Erasing files from the display removes them from RAM.
    a. True
    b. False
8. Select **File>Manage File>Delete Old Versions** to remove all of the versions of a model from the system disk.
    a. True
    b. False
9. Which of the following series of menu selections must be made to save the current file to a new name and erase the original file without saving it?
    a. Select **File>Save As>Save a Copy**, enter a new filename, and click **OK**. Select **File>Manage Session>Erase Current**.
    b. Select **File>Save As>Save a Copy**, enter a new filename, and click **OK**. Select **File>Manage Session>Erase Not Displayed**.

Command Summary

Button	Command	Location
	Save	• Quick Access Toolbar • File>Save • **Hot Key:** <Ctrl>+S or <Alt>+3

Selection

Working with 3D models requires the selection of entities when creating, editing, or redefining geometry. Due to the potential complexity of the models, you may have to select hidden geometry, multiple features or multiple entities. This chapter covers the various scenarios and tools you will encounter while modeling in Creo Parametric.

Learning Objectives in this Chapter

- Understand various selection methods for selecting geometry.
- Understand how to select hidden geometry.
- Use Selection Filters to narrow your selection options and make selection easier.
- Understand how to select Chains of edges.

3.1 Selecting Features

To interact with the model, you must select entities such as surfaces, edges, and datums. Multiple methods are available to help you select the entities you want to work with.

Preselection Highlighting

As you move the cursor over the model, selectable features will highlight, as shown in Figure 3–1. You can select any feature after it highlights.

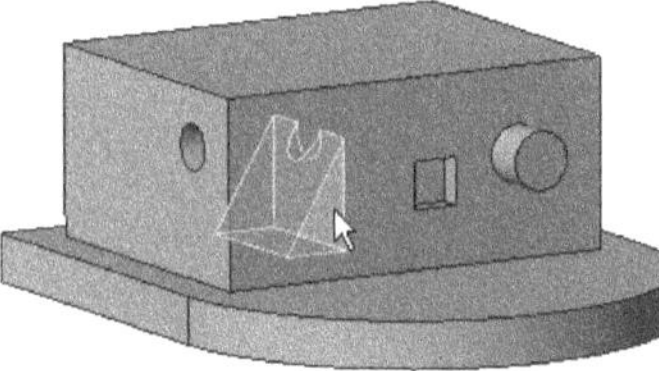
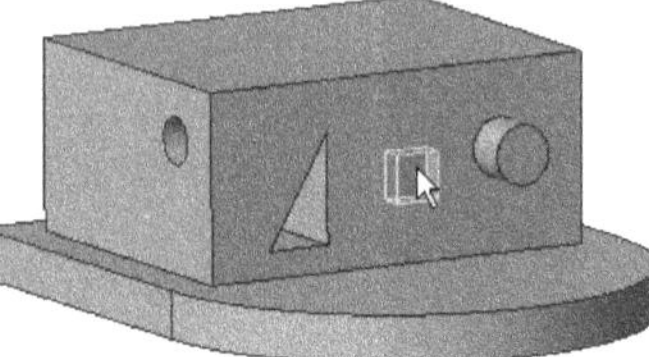

Figure 3–1

- To select the edges that are created by a feature, select the feature and then applicable edge, as shown in Figure 3–2.
- Multiple entities can be selected at once by holding <Ctrl> while selecting. The system creates a selection set, and indicates the number of selected entities in the **Selected Items** area in the lower right corner of the Creo Parametric window as shown in Figure 3–3.

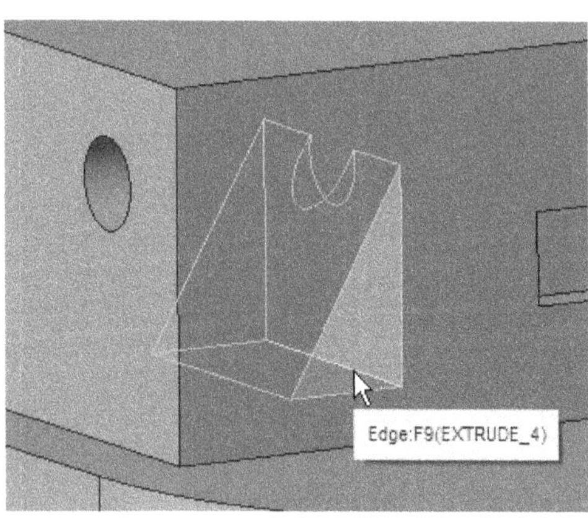

Figure 3–2

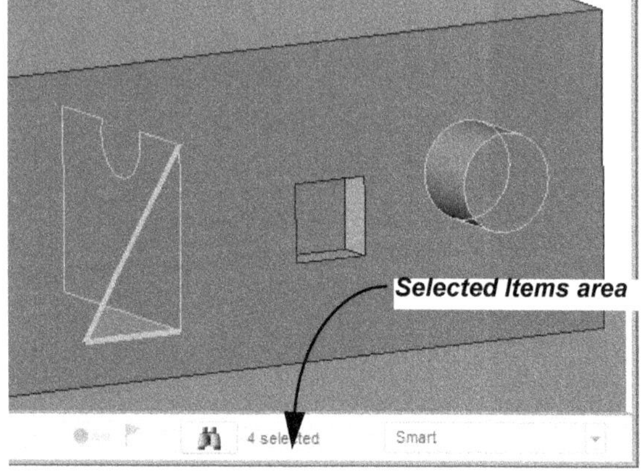

Figure 3–3

If you double click the **Selected Items** area, the Selected Items dialog box displays as shown in Figure 3–4.

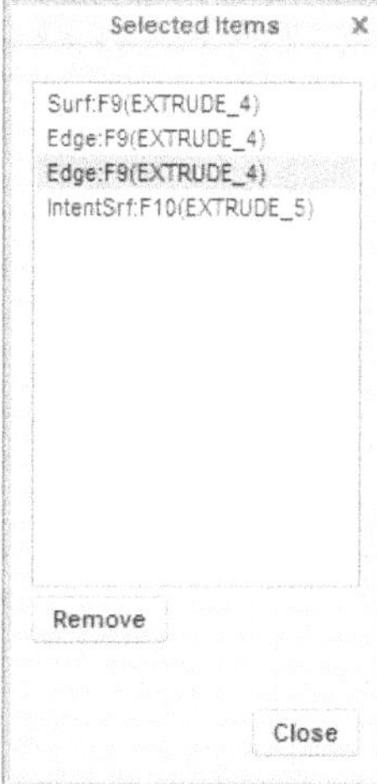

Figure 3–4

Select any entities in the list and click **Remove** to remove them from the selected items set.

Model Tree

You can directly select features in the model tree by clicking the feature name. To ensure highlighting, click (Show) in the model tree and enable **Highlight Geometry**. Any feature selected in the model tree will then highlight in the model, as shown in Figure 3–5.

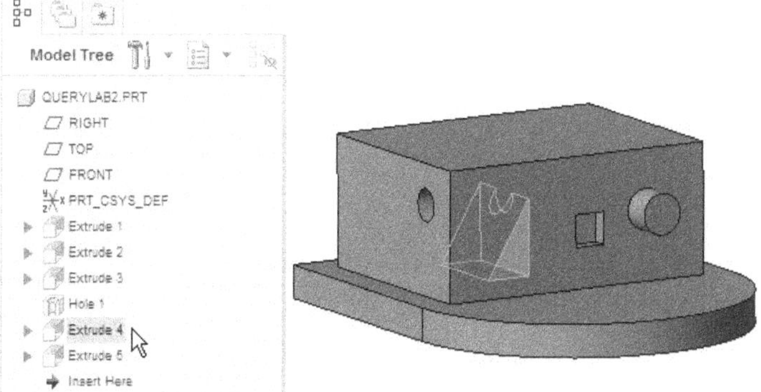

Figure 3–5

- You can also have the system highlight features in the model as you move the cursor over them in the model tree by clicking click (Show) and enabling **Preselection Highlighting**.

- In the model tree, you can use <Ctrl> and <Shift> in the same fashion you would with a Microsoft Office application. Press and hold <Ctrl> to select multiple, individual features.
- Select a feature, press and hold <Shift> and select another feature, and the system will select the two features, plus all features in between, as shown in Figure 3–6.

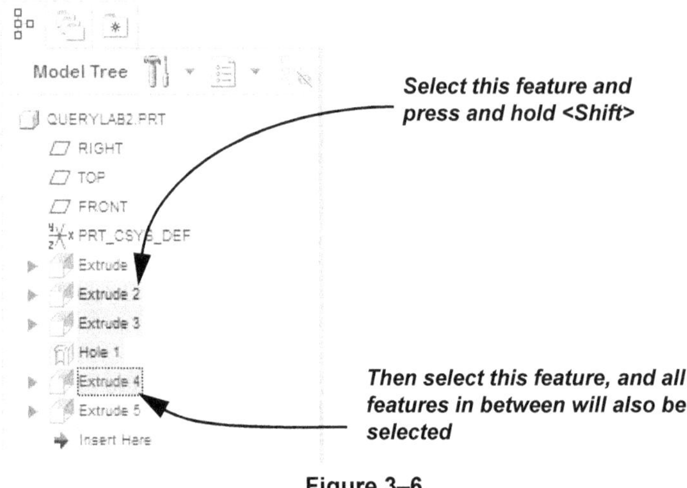

Figure 3–6

Note on Model Tree Features

In legacy versions of the Creo Parametric (Pro/ENGINEER) software, features were labeled in the model tree differently than they are currently. Figure 3–7 shows a model created with a legacy version, while Figure 3–8 shows a model recreated in the Creo Parametric software.

Legacy Model Tree Listing

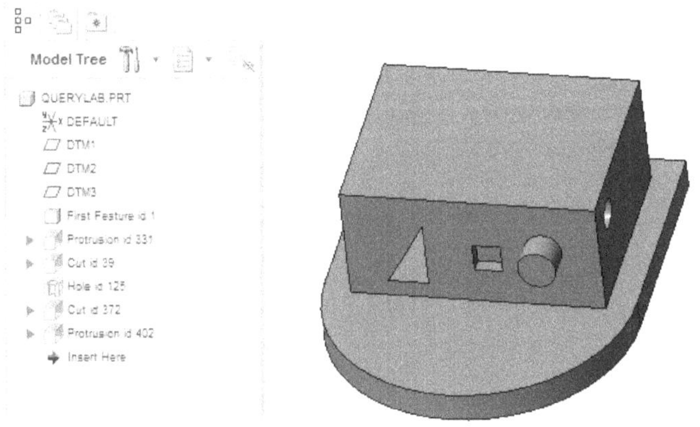

Figure 3–7

Modern Creo Parametric Model Tree Listing

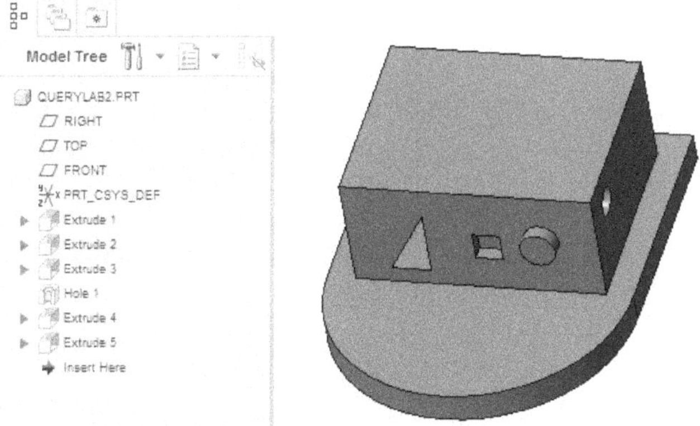

Figure 3–8

Although this course will focus on the modern listing, it is important to be aware of the difference, as you will likely have to work on a legacy model at some point. For that reason you will see both listings used in this course. Whether legacy or modern, features are selected and edited in the same manner.

3.2 Selecting Hidden Features

In some model orientations, features are hidden. To select these features, you can reorient the model so that the features are no longer hidden. However, this technique is not efficient. To select hidden features, you should query through the model using your mouse or the Pick From List dialog box. For example, the model shown in Figure 3–9 contains a number of features that are hidden when the model is in the default orientation.

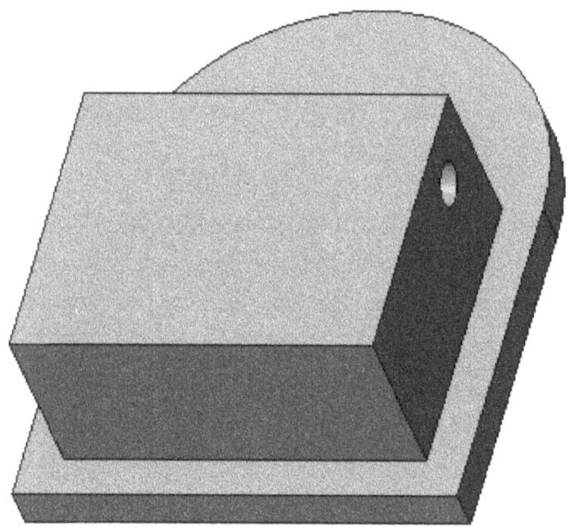

Features hidden when shaded

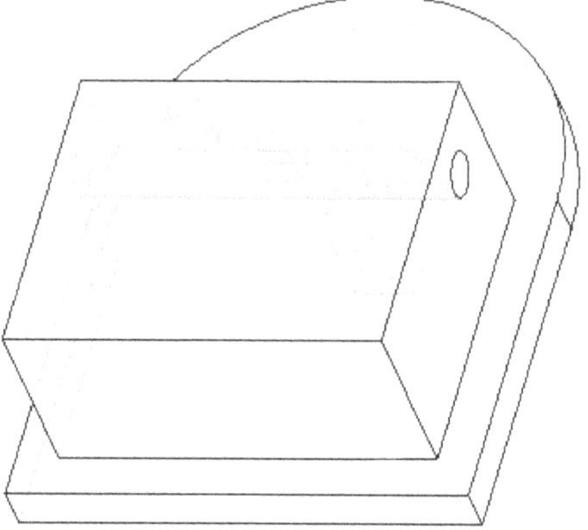

Features display in Hidden Line mode, but still cannot be selected directly

Figure 3–9

Query Selection

You can set the model display to hidden line to help identify the location of the feature.

How To: Select Hidden Features Using the Mouse

1. Hover the cursor directly over the feature, even if it is hidden. The feature directly below the cursor highlights.
2. Right-click to toggle through to the next feature in the mode. Repeat the click action to step through all features that lie directly below the cursor.
3. Once the feature you want is highlighted, click to select it.

Pick From List

It is recommended to review a list of all of the features that can be queried based on where the cursor is located.

How To: Review All of the Features

1. Position the cursor directly over the feature, even if it is hidden. The feature number and type display in a pop-up box, indicating the current feature.
2. Hold the right mouse button and select (Pick From List). The Pick From List dialog box opens, as shown in Figure 3–10.

The features that display in the Selection dialog box depend on the location of the mouse when you select (Pick From List).

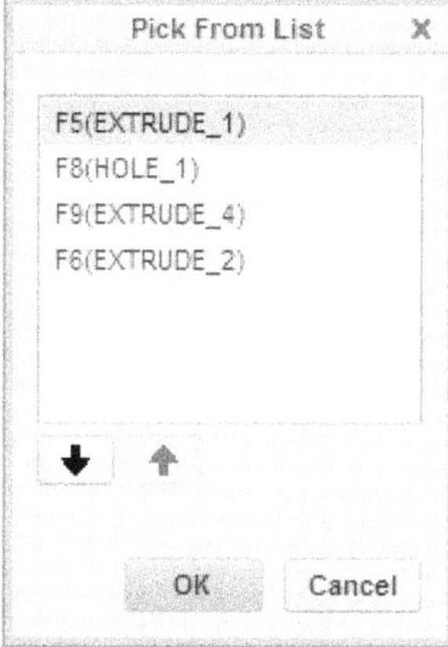

Figure 3–10

3. Select the feature in the selection list or use the up and down arrows to navigate to the required feature.
4. Click **OK** to accept the selected feature.

3.3 Selection Filter

When modeling, you often need to select specific types of entities, such as features, edges or curves, or datums. The selection filter in the bottom right corner of the main window enables you to filter entities, features, or components so that you can only select the type of object required. The system only selects the entities applicable to the selected option.

- For example, if you select **Datums**, you can only select datums on the model. To only select surfaces and edges, use the **Geometry** option. The options in the drop-down list vary depending on the mode in which you are working. For example, the options for Part mode display are shown in Figure 3–11.

Figure 3–11

- The selection filter can also be deactivated by holding <Alt> and selecting the item. This can be useful for quickly selecting edges or surfaces.

3.4 Selecting Chains

Chains

Chains consist of a collection of edges or curves that are related either by tangency or by a common vertex. When you establish a chain you are collecting edges or curves into a group to more efficiently perform modeling actions.

- To create curve chains, you select an entity, press and hold <Shift>, and then select the additional entity or entities.
- There are two types of chains: Non-rule based and Rule-based.

Non-rule Based

The two types of Non-rule based chains are described as follows:

- **One-by-One Chain:** A chain of individual curves and edges that you select. Typically, you would create a One-by-One chain if the entities you select are from different features or exist across multiple features. If you hover over the entities, a box displays indicating the chain type, as shown in Figure 3–12.

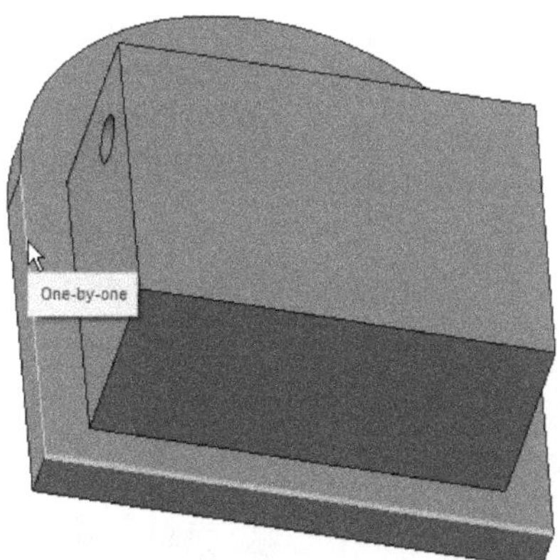

Figure 3–12

- **Intent Chain:** When features are created in Creo Parametric, they result in new edges and surfaces. These edges and surfaces can then be used as references for additional features, and so on. Changes to the original features can result in lost references and feature failures.

An Intent Chain is established and preserved by the feature that created it, not by the entities of that feature. Consider the example shown in Figure 3–13.

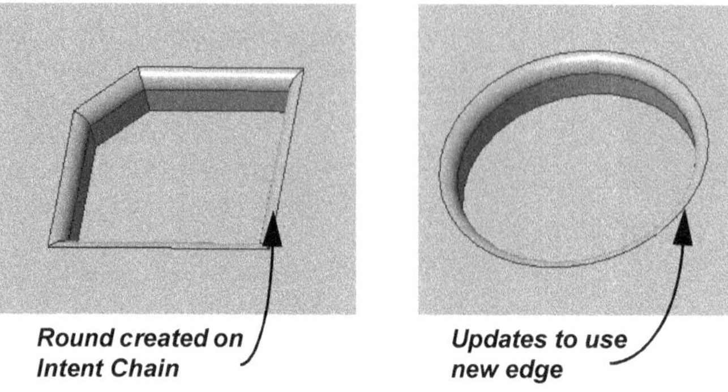

Figure 3–13

The round is created on the Intent Chain of edges formed by the cut. When the section is redefined to have a circular section, the round simply updates to use it. Without intent edges, the round would have failed after the edit.

Rule Based

The three types of Rule based chains are described as follows:

- **Partial Loop Chain:** A chain that begins at a start-point, follows an edge, and ends at the end-point of a selected edge or curve. This is also known as a From-To chain. If there is a possibility of multiple chains, you can right-click to step through the possibilities, as shown in Figure 3–14.

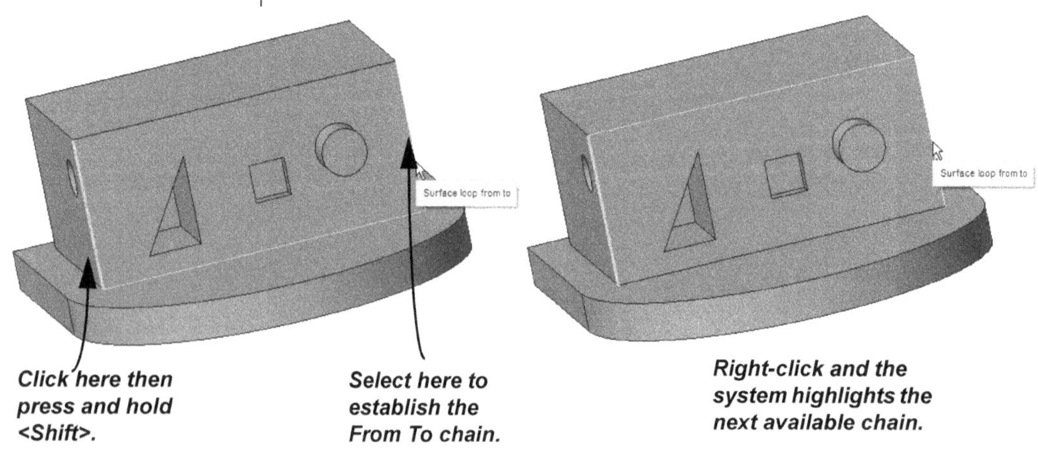

Figure 3–14

- **Complete Loop Chain:** A chain that contains a loop of curves or edges that encompasses the curve, quilt, or solid surface it belongs to.

  By right-clicking a third time, they system highlights the surface loop, as shown in Figure 3–15.

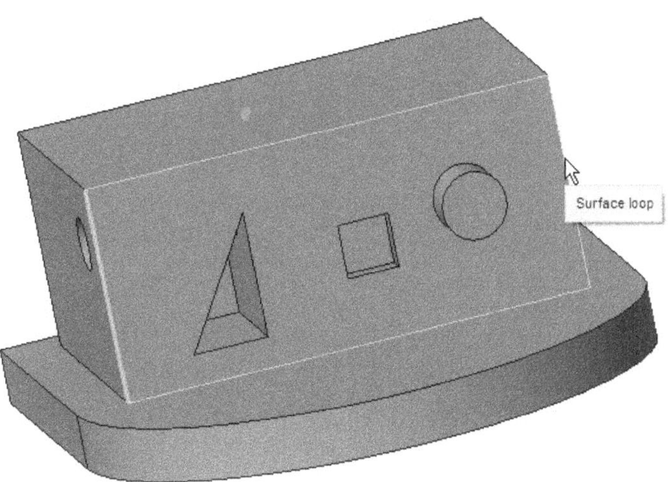

Figure 3–15

- **Tangent Chain:** A chain defined by the selected entity and the end of the adjacent tangent entities, as shown in Figure 3–16.

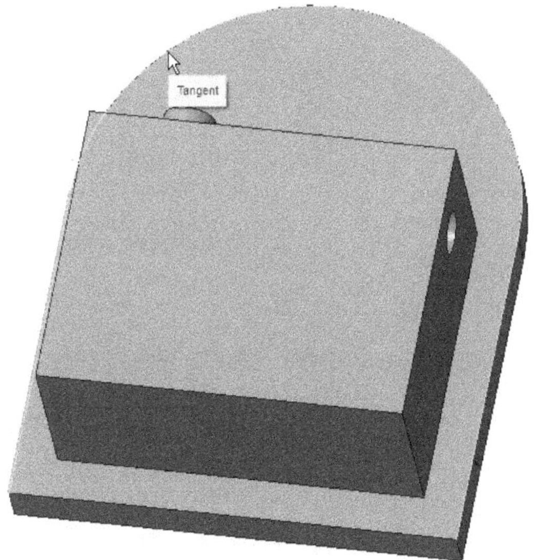

Figure 3–16

Practice 3a Selecting Geometry

Practice Objective

- Select hidden features in a model using the Pick from List option and the mouse buttons.

In this practice, you will edit the dimensions associated with the two hidden features, as shown in Figure 3–17. To edit these features you will use selection techniques for quickly selecting hidden features without having to reorient the model.

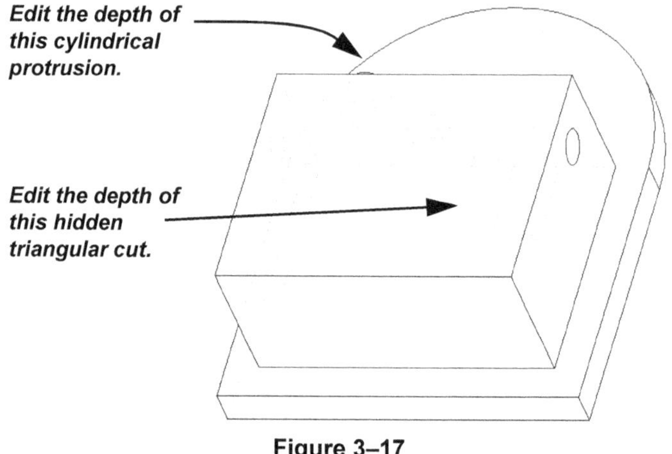

Figure 3–17

Task 1 - Open the querylab2.prt model and set the initial display.

1. In the Home tab, click (Select Working Directory) and select the *Chapter 03/practice 3a* folder.
2. Open **querylab2.prt.**
3. Set the model display as follows:
    - *(Datum Display Filters)*: All Off
    - *(Spin Center)*: Off
    - *(Display Style)*: (Hidden Line)

Task 2 - Use the Selection Filters.

1. With the selection filter set to **Smart**, move the cursor to the location shown in Figure 3–18 and note that the entire feature highlights.
2. Move the cursor to the location shown in Figure 3–19 and note again that the entire feature highlights.

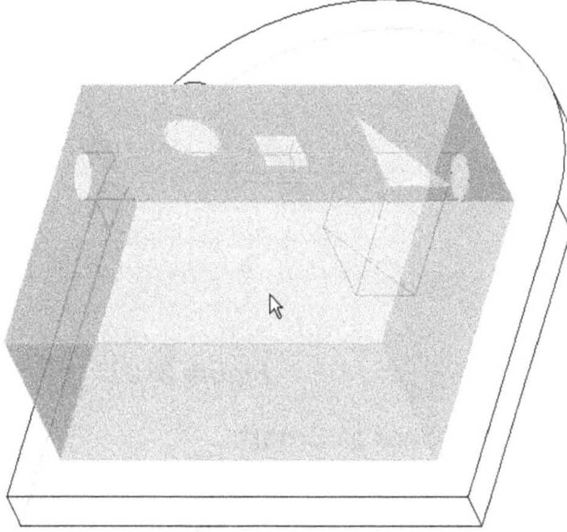

Figure 3–18

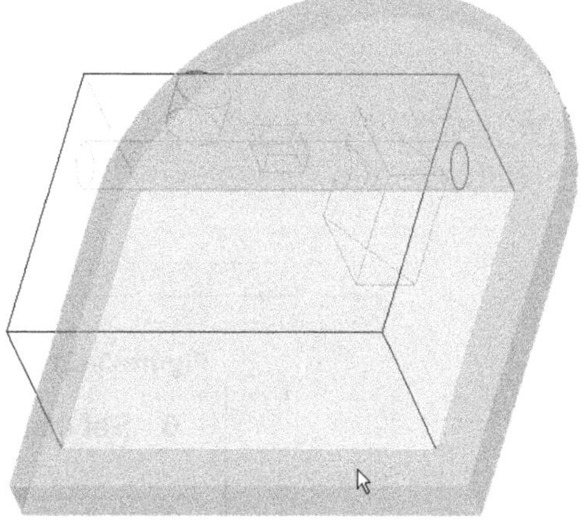

Figure 3–19

3. Select **Geometry** from the Selection Filter, as shown in Figure 3–20.

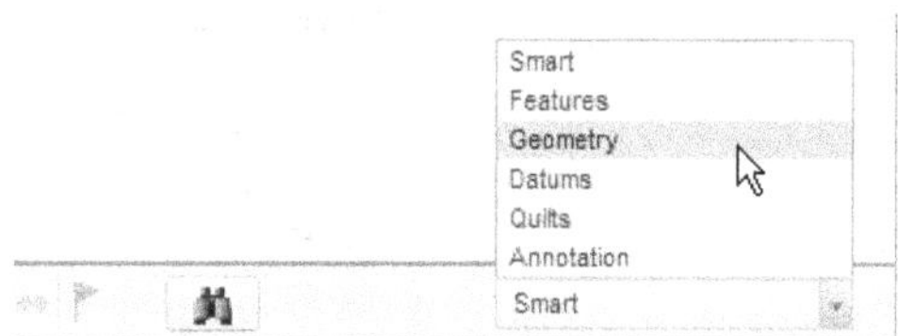

Figure 3–20

The selection filters can be used to narrow down your selection options.

4. Move the cursor to the location shown in Figure 3–21. Note that now only the surface itself highlights.
5. Move the cursor to the location shown in Figure 3–22. Note again that only the surface itself highlights.

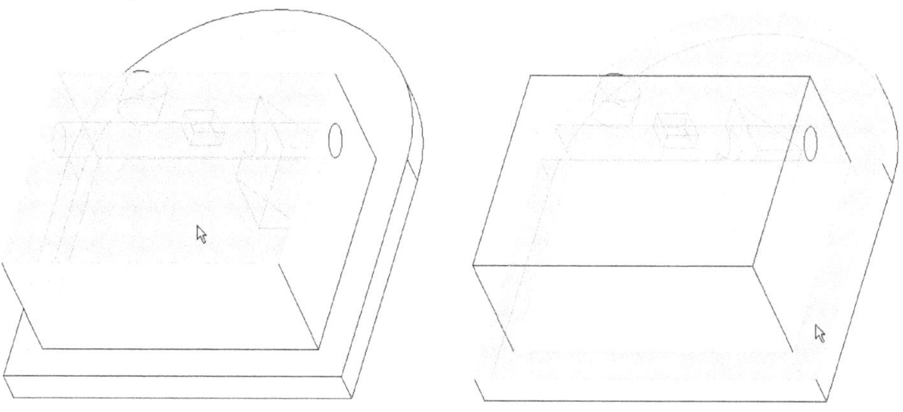

Figure 3–21 **Figure 3–22**

6. Set the Selection Filter back to **Smart**.

Task 3 - Edit the depth of the hidden triangular cut.

Keep the model in its default orientation at all times.

1. Hover the cursor over the model. Once a feature is recognized, it highlights and a help line displays indicating the feature. Hover the cursor over the feature, as shown in Figure 3–23.
2. Right-click and the cut feature located directly below the original mouse location is highlighted, as shown in Figure 3–24.

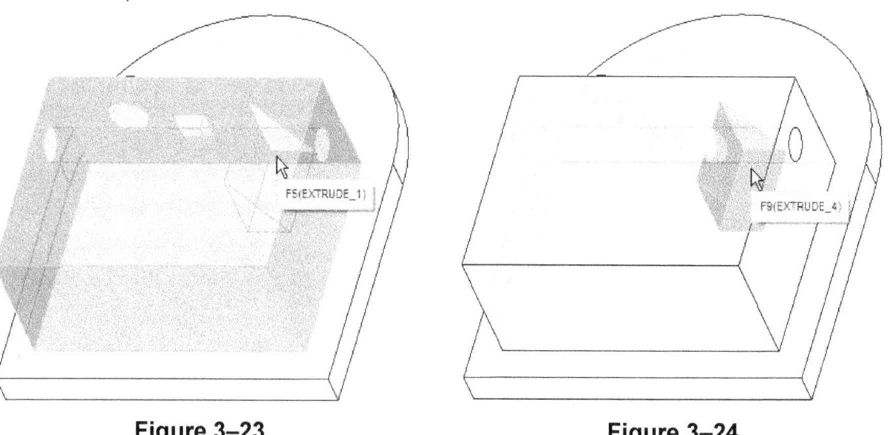

Figure 3–23 **Figure 3–24**

3. Keeping the cursor in the same location, select the model again using the mouse button. **Extrude 4** highlights in green and becomes the active feature.

4. Hold the right mouse button and select (Edit). All of the dimensions associated with this feature display.

5. Double-click on the 30 depth dimension and enter **50**.

6. Click twice on the screen to regenerate the model.

Task 4 - Edit the diameter of the circular extrusion.

As an alternative to right-clicking to toggle through the selection list, you can review the list by selecting (Pick From List) to open the Pick From List dialog box.

1. Hover the cursor over the location shown in Figure 3–25. Hold the right mouse button, and select (Pick From List).

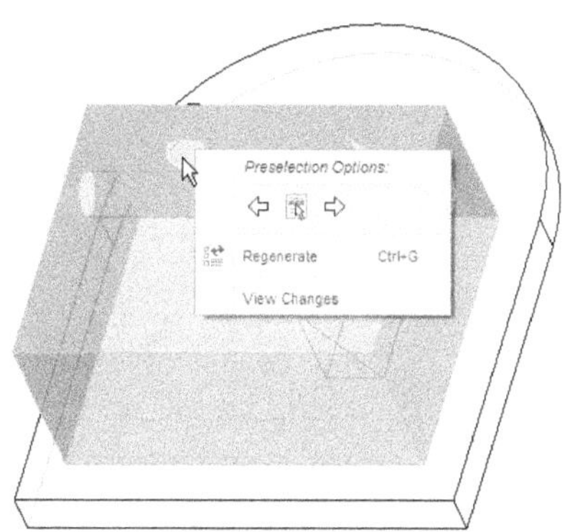

Figure 3–25

The Pick From List dialog box opens, as shown in Figure 3–26.

The features that display in the Pick From List dialog box might vary depending on where the cursor is located when you select (Pick From List). The Pick From List dialog box lists all of the features that lie beneath the selected location.

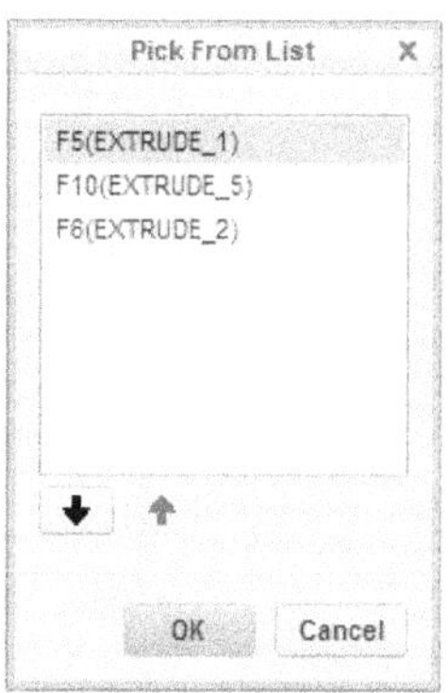

Figure 3–26

2. In the selection list, select **F10(EXTRUDE_5)** and click **OK**. The cylindrical protrusion highlights in green.

3. Hold the right mouse button and select dl (Edit). All of the dimensions associated with the feature display on the model.

4. Double-click on the **12.5** diameter dimension, and enter **20**.

5. Click twice on the screen to regenerate the model.

Task 5 - Select edges to create rounds.

Rounds are covered in detail in later chapters.

1. Select the edge highlighted in Figure 3–27. Then, press and hold <Shift>.

2. Move the cursor to the position shown in Figure 3–28 and note the **One by One** curve highlights.

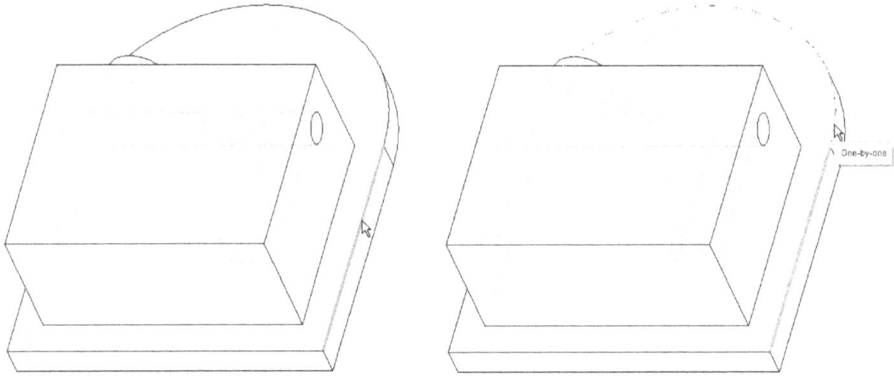

Figure 3–27 **Figure 3–28**

3. Right-click once and the Tangent chain highlights, as shown in Figure 3–29.

4. Right-click again and the From To chain highlights as shown in Figure 3–30.

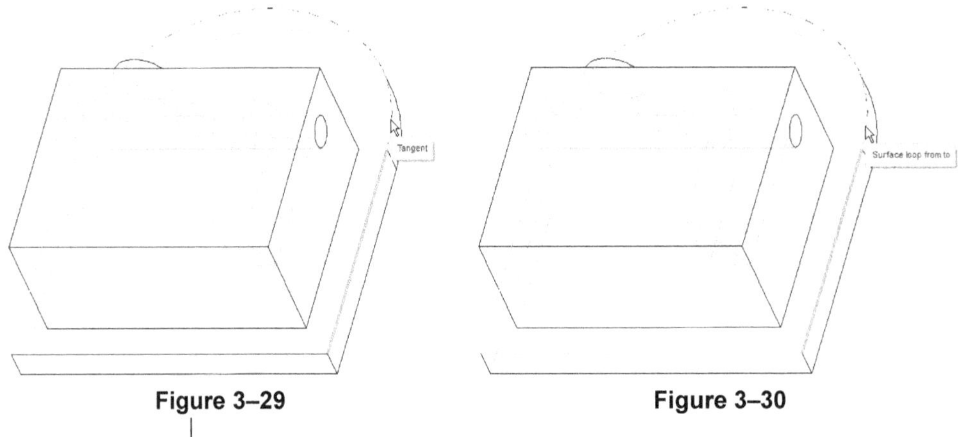

Figure 3–29 **Figure 3–30**

5. Right-click again and the next From To chain highlights as shown in Figure 3–31.

6. Right-click again and the Surface Loop chain highlights as shown in Figure 3–32.

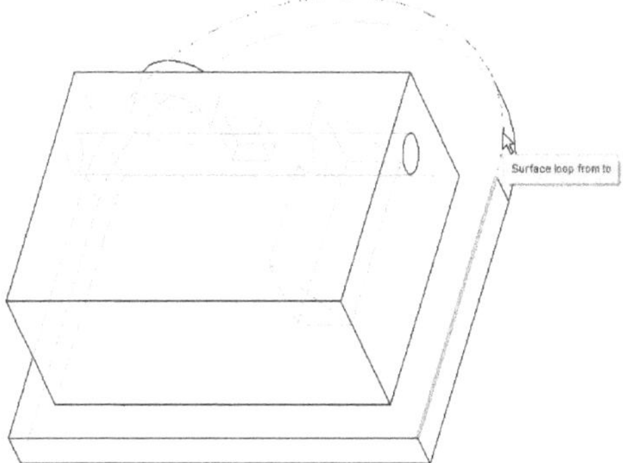

Figure 3–31

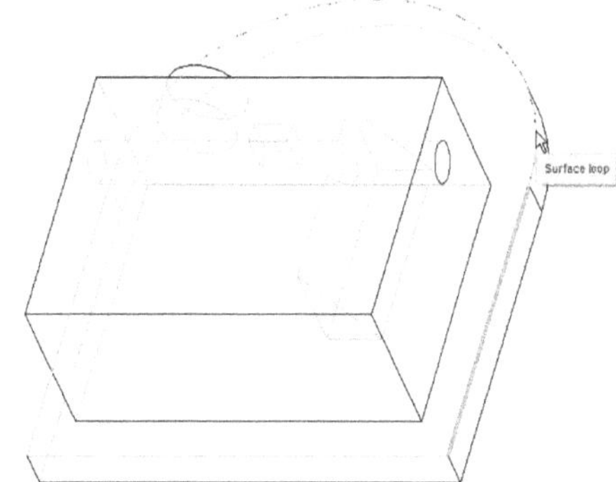

Figure 3–32

The Pick From List tool is an efficient way to step through multiple selection option.

7. Press and hold the right mouse button, and select (Pick From List).

8. Click through the list and note that the same chains highlight as the previous few steps.

9. Select the **Surface loop** chain, as shown in Figure 3–33.

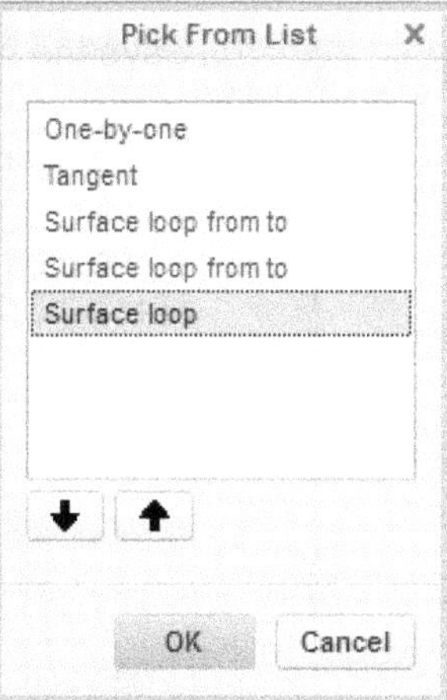

Figure 3–33

10. Click **OK** in the Pick From List dialog box.

11. Right-click and select **Round**, as shown in Figure 3–34.

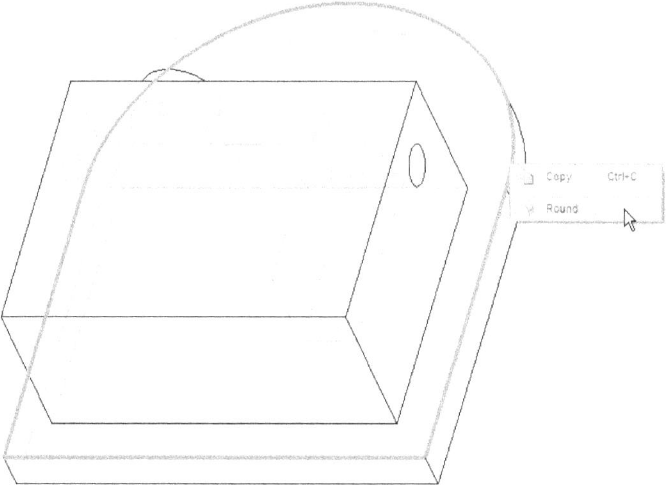

Figure 3–34

12. Set the *Radius* to **2.00**.

13. Click (Complete Feature).

14. Set the display to (Shading With Edges).

15. Save the model.

16. In the Quick Access Toolbar, click (Close).

17. In the *Home* tab, click (Erase Not Displayed) to erase all of the models from memory.

Chapter Review Questions

1. Features can be selected on the model or in the model tree.
   a. True
   b. False
2. The system will highlight features as you mouse-over the model. This is referred to as:
   a. Selection
   b. Query Select
   c. Preselection Highlighting
   d. Selection Filter
3. When you prehighlight a feature, you can right-click to step through all features in the model.
   a. True
   b. False
4. If you want to limit selection to only Surfaces and edges, you can set the selection filter to:
   a. Datums
   b. Geometry
   c. Features
   d. Quilts

5. The most efficient Chain option for selecting the edges shown in Figure 3–35 is:

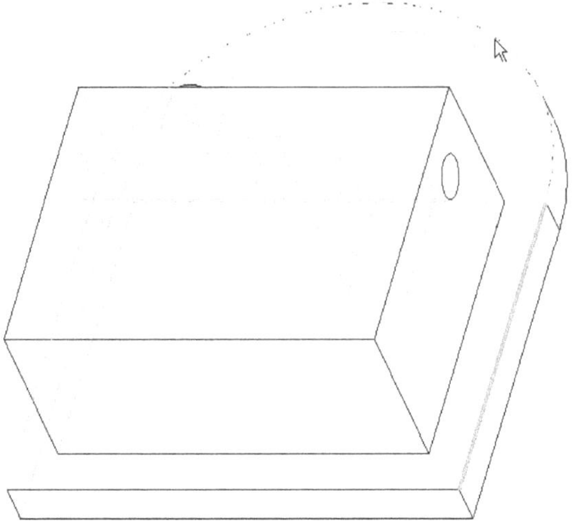

Figure 3–35

   a. **Surface loop from to**
   b. **Surface loop**
   c. **One-by-one**
   d. **Tangent**

Command Summary

Button	Command	Location
	Save	• Quick Access Toolbar • File>Save • **Hot Key:** <Ctrl>+S or <Alt>+3

Sketching Geometry

Sketching is the foundation for creating many different feature types. Sketches can be created in a solid feature, or you can create them independently as 2D geometry. When a sketch feature is created on its own, it can later be selected to generate 3D geometry.

Learning Objectives in this Chapter

- Sketch geometry using the basic sketch tools.
- Sketch the geometry using additional tools in the Sketch tab.
- Dimension and constrain 2D entities, and use construction geometry in a sketch to capture the design intent for the feature.

4.1 Sketching Tools

Many features require a sketched section to define the profile of the geometry. These are referred to as Sketched Features, and include Extrude, Revolve and Sweep features, among others.

You can create a stand alone sketch, then select that as your profile, or you can create the sketch while defining the feature. This chapter discusses the basic tools available in the *Sketch* tab of the ribbon. In later chapters, you will learn how to use sketches to create solid geometry.

Sketches are non-solid 2D geometry features. The sketching tools used to create a sketch are the same as those used to create any sketched feature. This section focuses on creating sketches.

General Steps

Use the following general steps to create a sketched datum feature:

1. Start the creation of the sketch.
2. Create the geometry for the sketch.
3. Complete the sketch.
4. Add and delete constraints, as required.
5. Add and delete dimensions, as required.
6. Modify dimensions, as required.
7. Complete the sketch.

Step 1 - Start the creation of the sketch.

To create a sketch, click (Sketch) in the Datum group in the *Model* tab.

Step 2 - Create the geometry for the sketch.

The selection of a sketch orientation reference is optional.

Once you have started the creation of the sketch, you must define the sketch plane and sketch orientation in the Sketch dialog box shown in Figure 4–1.

Figure 4–1

Sketch Plane

Select the sketch plane first. You can select a datum plane or planar surface as the sketch plane. The 2D sketch is sketched on this reference.

Sketch Orientation

Once a sketch plane has been defined, Creo Parametric automatically selects a default sketch orientation plane. The sketch orientation reference is used to orient the model into 2D for sketching. It is similar to selecting the sketch orientation reference for a base feature. If the default selection is not the required orientation, you can use any of the following methods in the Sketch dialog box to change or override the reference:

- Change the Sketch view direction by clicking **Flip**.
- Change the Reference in the Sketch dialog box, by selecting the default Reference and selecting the required reference plane or surface in the model.
- Change the **Orientation** option in the Sketch dialog box, using the drop-down list.
- Select **Setup>Section Orientation>Flip Sketching Plane** in the *Sketch* tab.
- Select **Setup>Section Orientation>Flip Section Orientation** in the *Sketch* tab.
- Change the Reference by selecting **Setup>Section Orientation>Set horizontal reference**.
- Change the Reference by selecting **Setup>Section Orientation>Set vertical reference**.

The selection of the sketch orientation reference is optional.

If you to start sketching without an orientation reference, Creo Parametric uses a projection of the X-axis of the default coordinate system for the horizontal orientation of the sketch.

- Once the sketch orientation has been defined, click **Sketch** to enter Sketcher mode.
- If enough default sketching references are available to fully place the sketch, you can begin sketching immediately. If required, you can access the References dialog box by clicking (References) in the Setup group, in the *Sketch* tab of the ribbon. The References dialog box opens as shown in Figure 4–2.

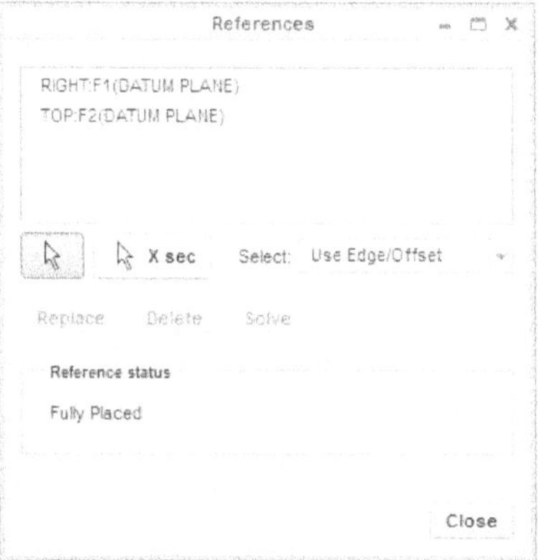

Figure 4–2

Sketch references can be defined using the References dialog box, as with any other sketch. Once defined, click **Close**. References can also be added while sketching. For example, if you are sketching a line, a reference can be added by holding <Alt> and selecting an object to reference. The reference is added to the References dialog box.

- Build the sketch shape using geometry tools. You only need to sketch the general shape, then add dimensions and constraints to define your design intent.

With the references selected, you are now ready to sketch the geometry using the geometry creation tools in the Sketching group of the Sketch tab shown in Figure 4–3. The options available for sketching are described in detail as follows.

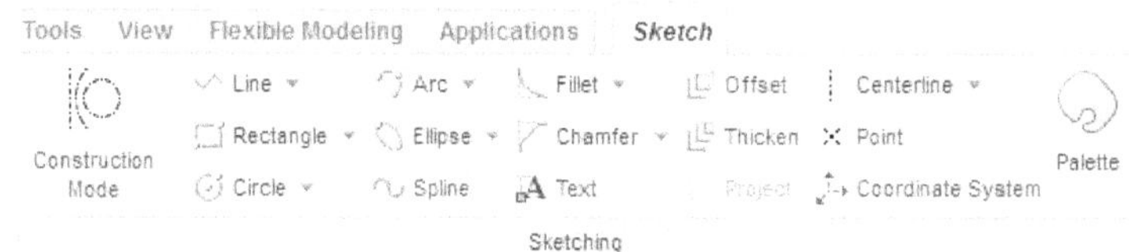

Figure 4–3

Icon	Procedure
(Line Chain)	Select the location required as the start of the line. A rubber band line displays, attached to the cursor. You can then select the location for the end of the line. Continue selecting locations to create additional attached lines. Click the middle mouse button to complete the line creation.
(Line Tangent)	Select the location required for a line to be tangent to an entity. A rubber band line displays, attached to the cursor. Select a second location required for a line to be tangent to an entity. Click the middle mouse button to complete the line.
(Corner Rectangle)	Select the location of the first vertex and drag the rectangle to the required size. Click to place the other vertex and complete the rectangle creation.
(Slanted Rectangle)	Creates a rectangle at any angle.
(Center Rectangle)	Select a center point and a corner to create the center rectangle.
(Parallelogram)	Creates a parallelogram.
(Center and Point)	Select the location of the centerpoint and drag the circle to the required size. Click to complete the circle creation.
(Concentric)	Select a reference circle or arc to define the centerpoint (the selected reference circle can be a sketched entity or model edge). A rubber band circle displays, attached to the cursor. Drag the mouse until the circle is the required diameter. Click the left mouse button to create the circle.
(3 Point)	Creates a circle by selecting three points along the circle.
(3 Tangent)	Creates a circle by selecting three entities that you want the circle to be tangent to.
(3-Point / Tangent End)	**3-Point Arc:** Select the locations for the endpoints of the arc. Select an additional point for the radius. **Tangent End Arc:** Select an endpoint of an existing entity to define tangency. Select a location for the endpoint of the arc.

(Center and Ends)	Select the location of the centerpoint of the arc. Select the endpoints of the arc.
(3 Tangent)	Select a start location on an existing arc or circle. Select a second and third location on two other arcs or circles.
(Concentric)	Select a reference circle or arc to define the centerpoint (the selected reference circle can be a sketched entity or model edge). A rubber band circle displays, attached to the cursor. Drag to the required diameter. Click to start the arc, drag the mouse around the diameter, and click again to complete the arc.
(Center and Ends)	Select the location of the centerpoint of the arc. Select the endpoints of the arc.
(Conic)	Select the location of each endpoint, then click to locate the peak of the conic arc.
(Centerline)	Creates a construction centerline used to help define geometry. No solid geometry will be created. Select the location where you want to intersect the centerline. A centerline displays, attached to the cursor. Select a second location through which the centerline passes.
(Centerline Tangent)	Creates a construction centerline that is tangent to two sketched arcs or circles.

Construction Geometry

As with centerlines, construction entities are used as a reference and do not create solid geometry. To create construction geometry, click (Construction Mode) in the Sketching group in the *Sketch* tab. Once it has been toggled on, any geometry that is created becomes construction geometry and is not shown when exiting sketch mode.

- Any entity can be converted to a construction entity by selecting the entity, right-clicking, and then selecting **Construction**. Figure 4–4 shows an example of a construction geometry that has been used to sketch a hexagon with only one dimension.

To toggle a construction entity back to solid geometry, select the geometry, right-click and select ***Solid****.*

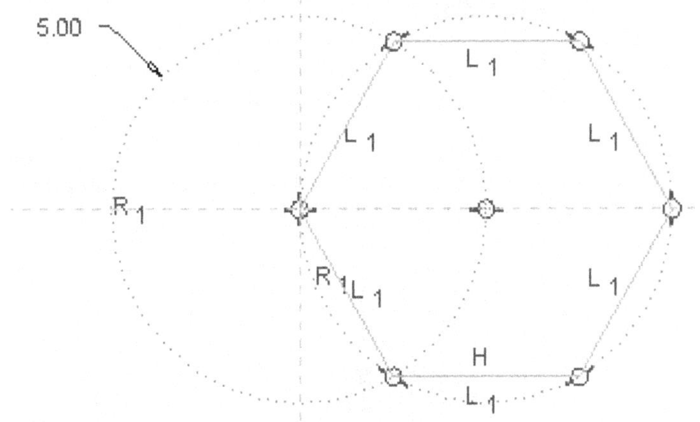

Figure 4–4

Step 3 - Complete the Sketch.

Creo Parametric provides easy-to-use sketcher editing and modification tools, so you are not required to sketch precisely. You can easily make changes using some of the following editing tools.

Tools for editing sketch geometry are accessible in the Editing group in the *Sketch* tab as shown in Figure 4–5.

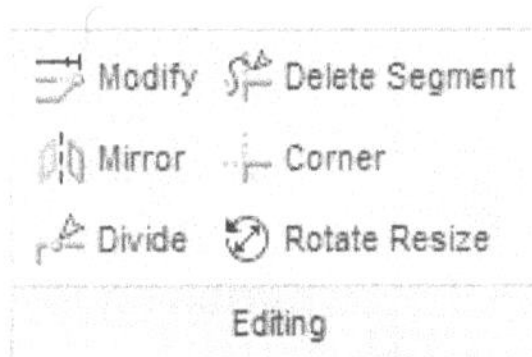

Figure 4–5

Divide

To divide an entity into two, click (Divide). You can also select at the intersection of two entities and divide both of them. The sketch shown in Figure 4–6 is created by sketching a line and dividing it along its length.

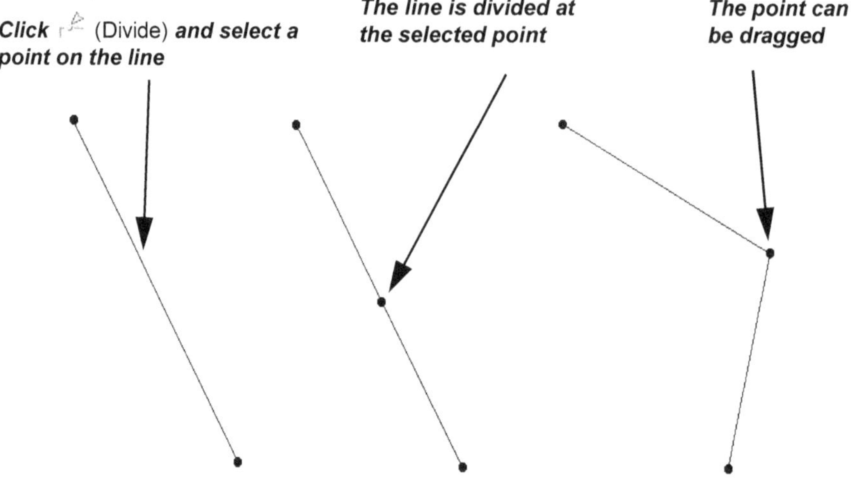

Figure 4–6

Corner

To trim two entities with respect to each other to form a corner, click (Corner). The **Corner** sketching tool trims or extends the entities, as required. Select an entity on the segment that you want to remain unchanged.

The sketches shown in Figure 4–7 are created by sketching a rectangle using the **Line** geometry tool and using the **Corner** sketching tool to create the final geometry.

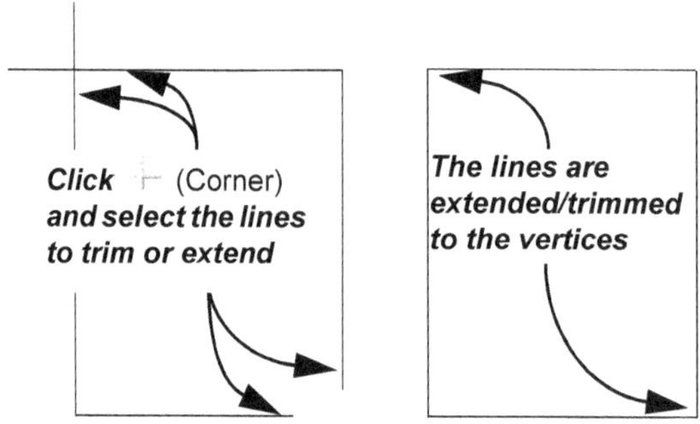

Figure 4–7

Delete Segment

To dynamically trim segments on your sketch, click (Delete Segment). This tool temporarily divides all of the entities at their intersection points with other entities. You can select individual segments to delete. Alternatively, you can press and hold the left mouse button and drag a spline through those segments to delete multiple segments at the same time.

- For example, the sketch shown on the right in Figure 4–8 is created by sketching the geometry on the left and trimming the inside section of the circle, as shown in the middle sketch.

Dynamically trim the circles by sketching a spline through the sections that are to be removed

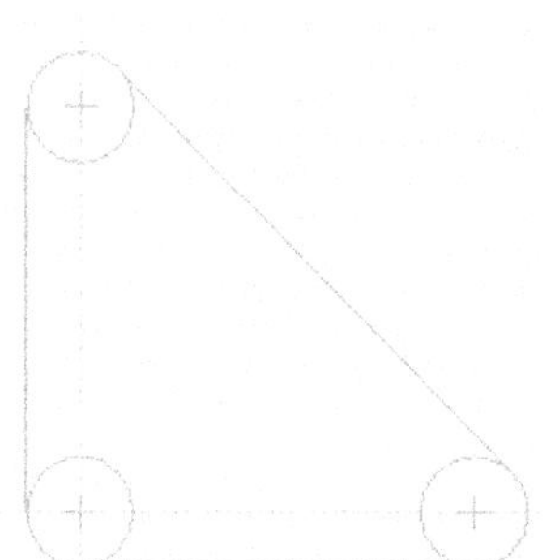

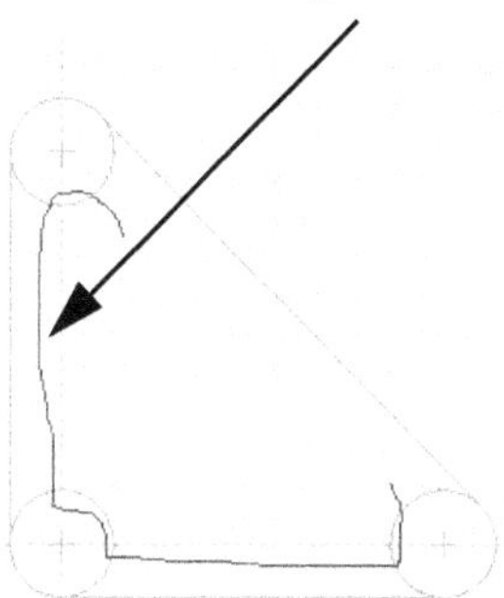

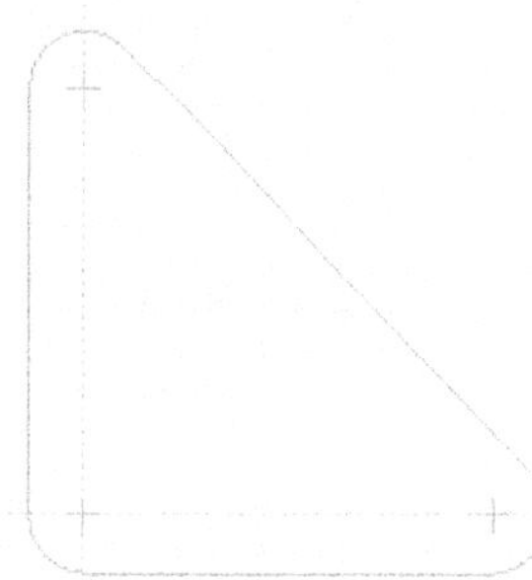

Figure 4–8

Mirror

To mirror selected entities about a centerline, select the entity(ies) to be mirrored, select the centerline, and click (Mirror). The sketch is created using the **Mirror** sketching tool, as shown in Figure 4–9.

Select the entities, click (Mirror), ***and select the centerline***

The entities are mirrored about the centerline

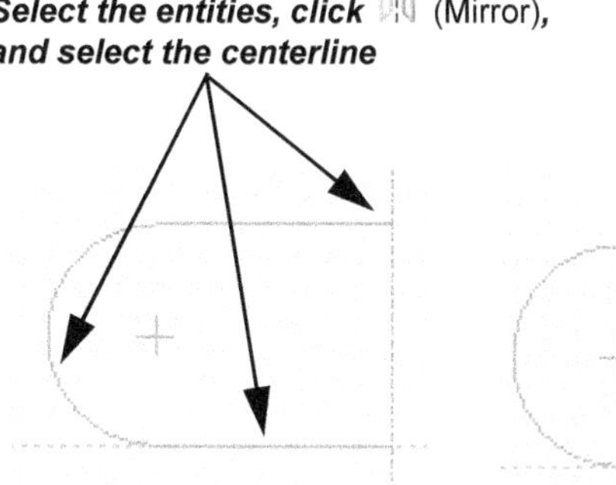

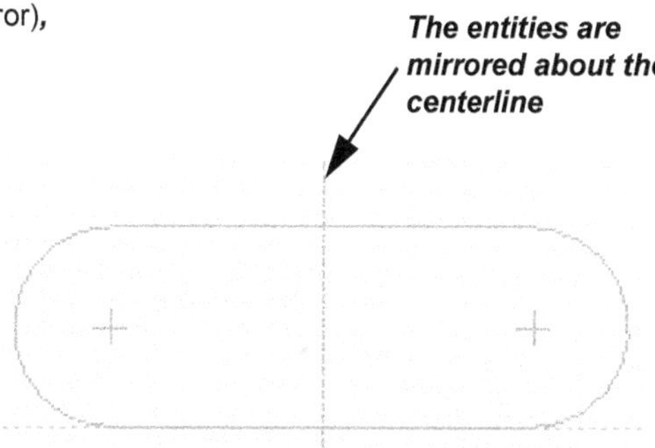

Figure 4–9

Step 4 - Add and delete constraints, as required.

Constraints control how sketched entities behave. For example, if two lines are constrained to be equal in length, they remain equal even when the geometry of the sketch changes. If the new geometry does not accommodate the constraints, the Resolve Sketch dialog box opens, indicating where you must resolve the constraints or the changes.

As you sketch geometry, Creo Parametric automatically defines constraints as the cursor drags, in a certain tolerance. You can add or delete constraints, as required.

The following describes some basic constraints.

Horizontal and Vertical

The lines are constrained to be horizontal (H) and vertical (V), as shown in Figure 4–10.

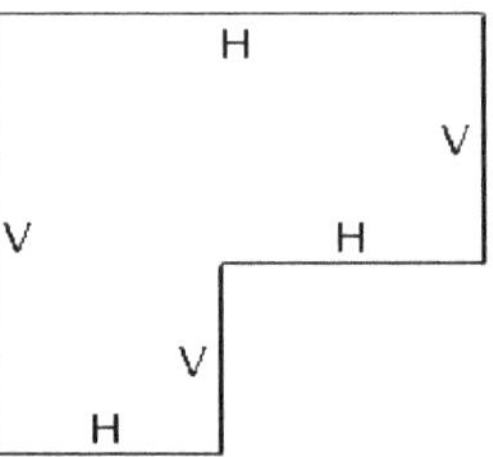

Figure 4–10

Tangent

The arc is constrained to be tangent (T) to the geometry line at its endpoint and tangent to the horizontal centerline, as shown in Figure 4–11.

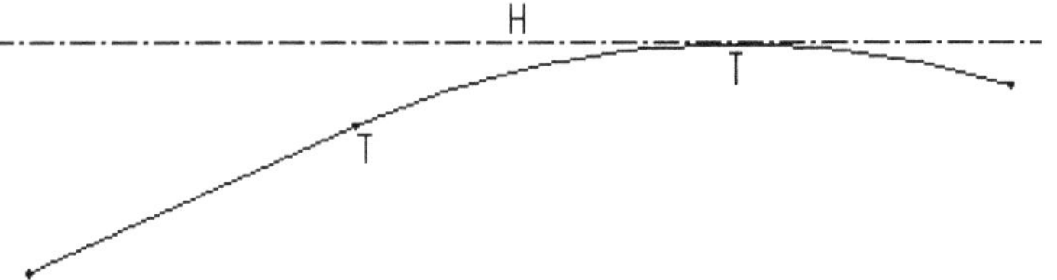

Figure 4–11

Equal Length

The lines are constrained to be equal in length, as shown in Figure 4–12. Lines with the equal length constraint display the same $L_{\#}$ symbol.

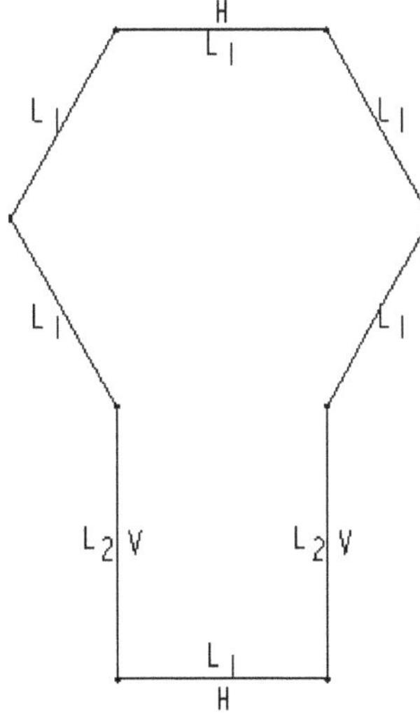

Figure 4–12

Equal Dimensions

The horizontal dimension is constrained to be equal to the vertical dimension, as shown in Figure 4–13. Dimensions with the equal dimension constraint display the same E1 symbol.

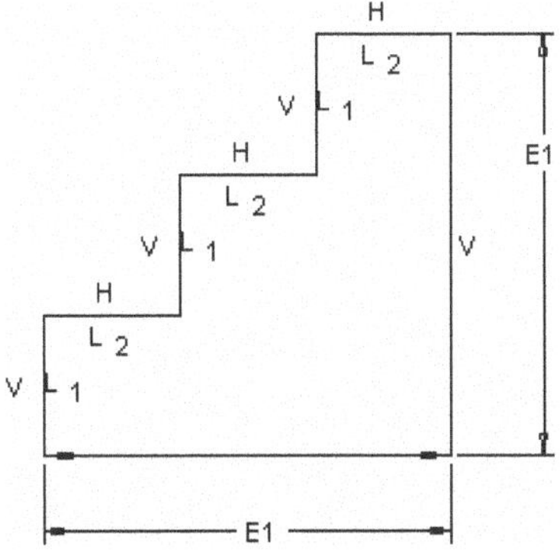

Figure 4–13

Point on Entity

The centerpoint of the large arc is constrained to lie on the horizontal line (⦿), as shown in Figure 4–14.

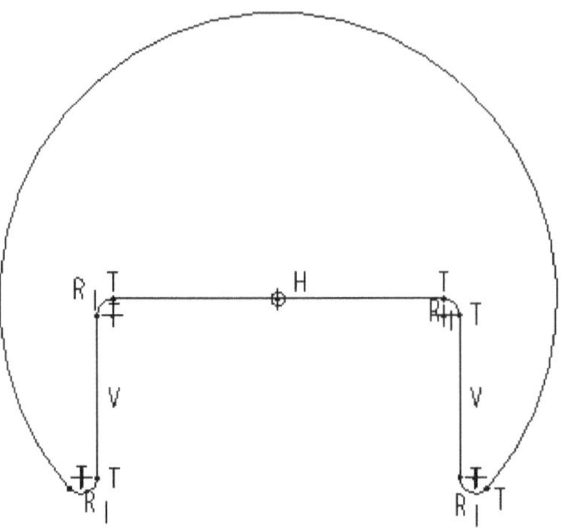

Figure 4–14

Equal Radius/ Diameter

The two fillet arcs are constrained to have equal radii (R_1), while the radius of the larger arc (R_2) is constrained to be equal to the diameter of the construction circle, as shown in Figure 4–15.

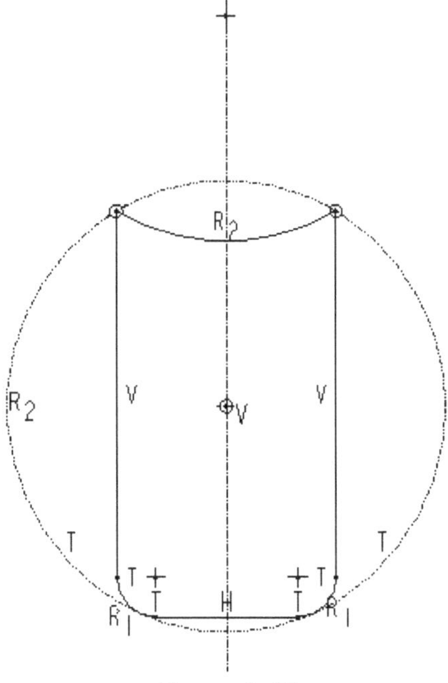

Figure 4–15

Horizontal and Vertical Alignment

The two vertices are constrained to line up horizontally (▬), while the circle centerpoints are constrained to line up vertically (▮), as shown in Figure 4–16.

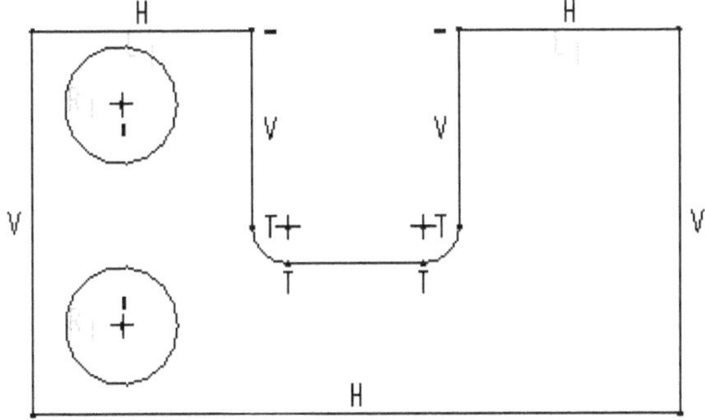

Figure 4–16

Mid-point

The end of the arc is constrained to lie on the mid-point of the adjacent line, as shown in Figure 4–17.

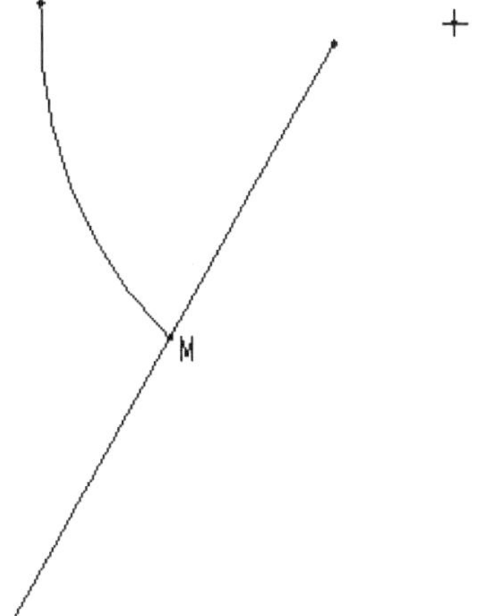

Figure 4–17

Coincident

The endpoints of the line and the arc are constrained to be coincident with the centerpoint of the construction circle, as shown in Figure 4–18.

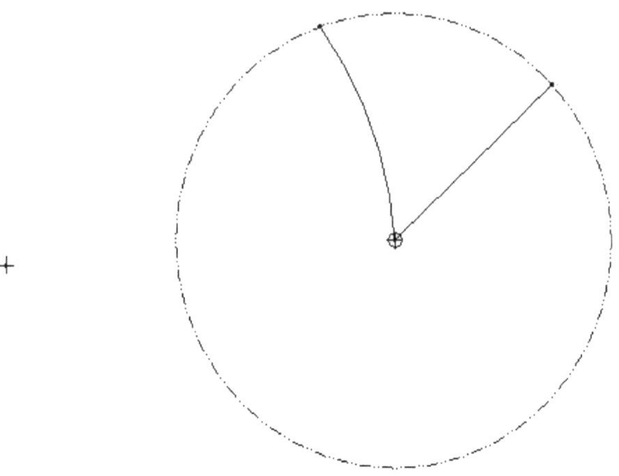

Figure 4–18

Symmetry

Vertices with the adjacent arrow (→) symbols are constrained to be symmetric about the centerline, as shown in Figure 4–19.

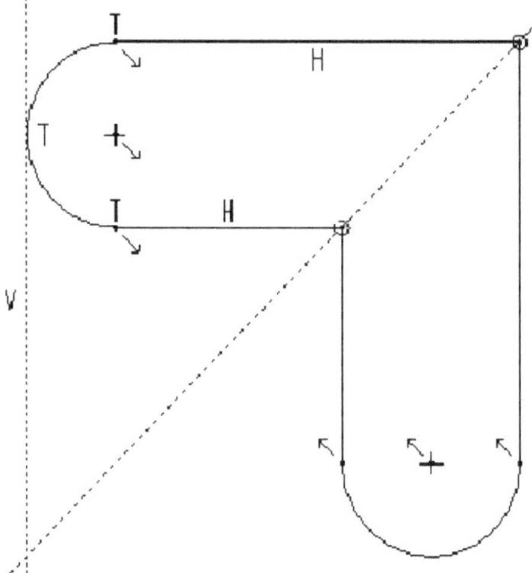

Figure 4–19

Collinear Constraint

The line is constrained to be collinear with the centerline, as shown in Figure 4–20.

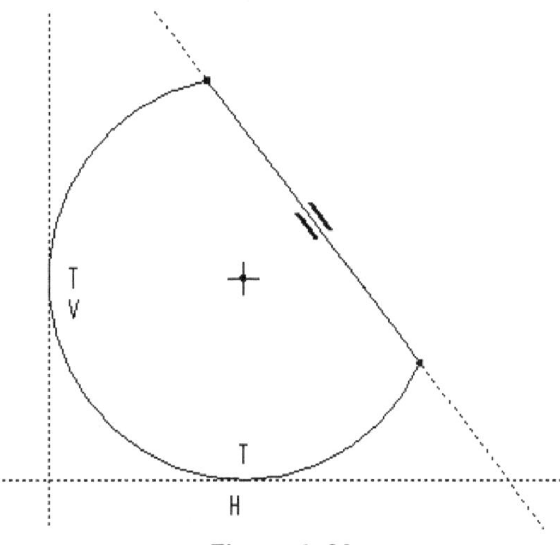

Figure 4–20

Parallel and Perpendicular

Parallel and perpendicular lines are indicated by the // and ⊥ symbols, as shown in Figure 4–21.

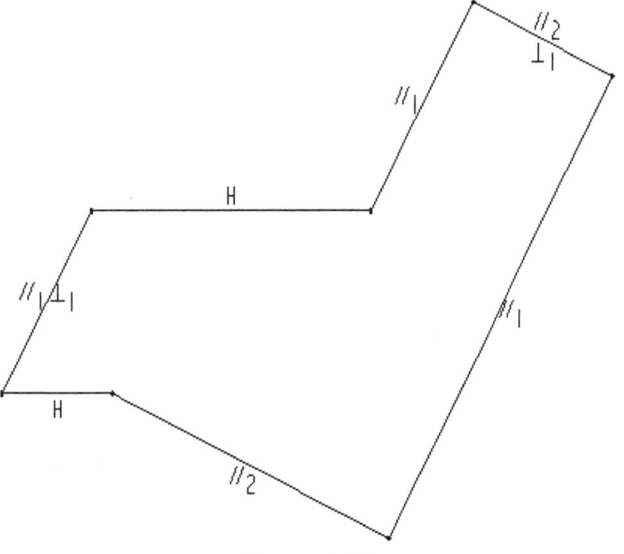

Figure 4–21

Constraint Control

You can control the constraints as you sketch the geometry. Before you select the final location for the entity, you can control a constraint in the following ways:

- Right-clicking consecutively toggles the status of the highlighted constraint between locking, disabling, and enabling.
- When a constraint is disabled, Creo Parametric does not automatically define that constraint while sketching. To enable a constraint, right-click again. For example, the graphic on the left side of Figure 4–22 shows the equal length constraint as disabled. You can continue to drag the entity, but the lengths no longer remain equal.
- <Shift> can also be used while you drag a sketched entity to automatically disable constraints.
- When the sketch is complete, the disabled and locked constraint symbols no longer display in the sketch.

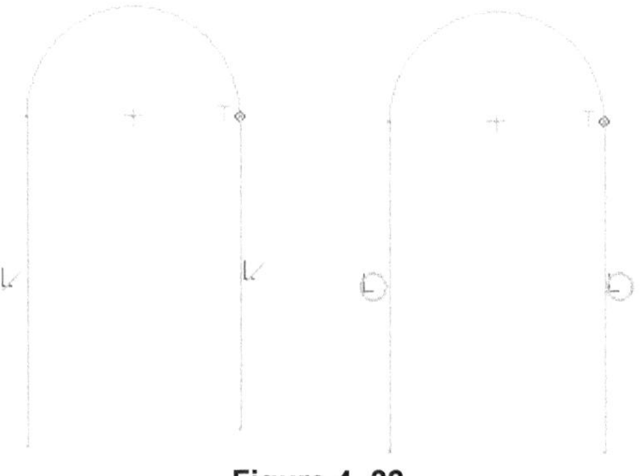

Figure 4–22

Assigning Constraints

When entities have been sketched, you can manually add constraints to the geometry. These constraints are located in the Constrain group in the *Sketch* tab. Additionally, tools for defining sketch constraints are accessible in the Constraints group in the *Sketch* tab, as shown in Figure 4–23.

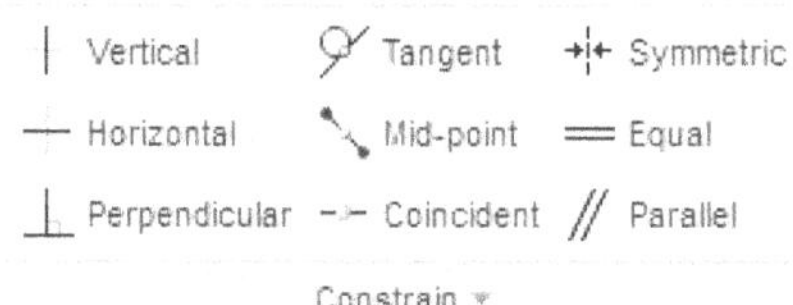

Figure 4–23

You can also access the constraints using the contextual menu. Select the sketch entities and right-click to display the relevant constraints in the contextual menu.

The constraint options are described as follows:

Icon	Description
(Vertical)	Makes a line vertical.
(Horizontal)	Makes a line horizontal.
(Perpendicular)	Makes two entities perpendicular.
(Tangent)	Makes two entities tangent.
(Mid-point)	Places a point in the middle of a line.
(Coincident)	Creates the same points, points on entity, or collinear constraints.
(Symmetric)	Makes two points or vertices symmetric about a centerline.
= (Equal)	Creates equal lengths, equal radii, equal dimensions or same curvature constraints.
// (Parallel)	Makes two lines parallel.

Depending on the type of constraint you want to assign, you are prompted to select the entities to which the constraint is going to apply.

Figure 4–24 shows an example of two arcs that were sketched and automatically dimensioned so that they have two independent radius dimensions. Figure 4–25 shows an example where the equal radii constraint is applied to the section by clicking = (Equal) and selecting the arcs. Both arcs are of equal radius as indicated by the R_1 symbol.

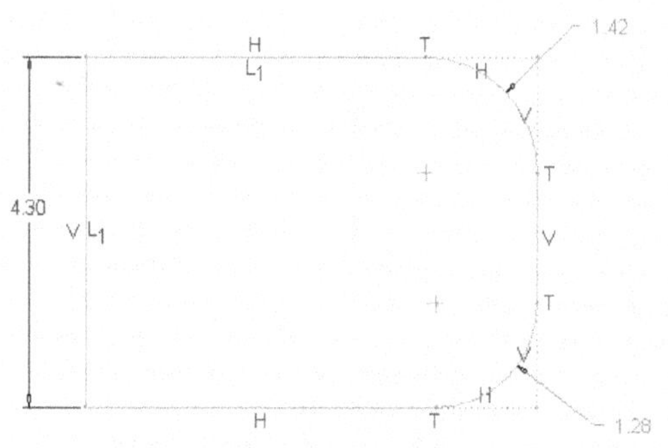

Figure 4–24

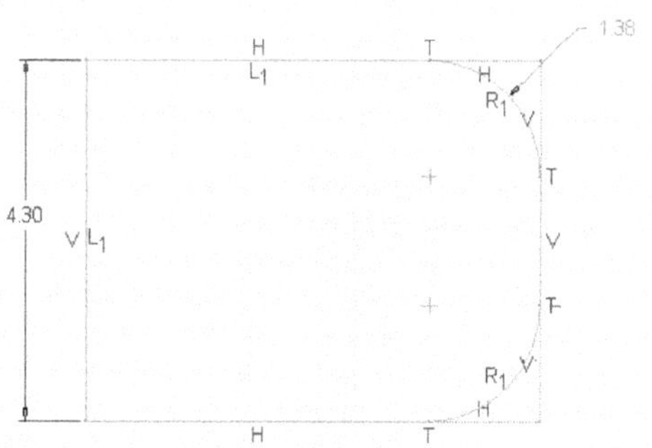

Figure 4–25

Figure 4–26 shows the sketch before being constrained and Figure 4–27 shows the sketch after being constrained. The center of the arc is aligned with the horizontal entity. The constraint is assigned by clicking (Coincident) in the Constraints dialog box and selecting the center-point and horizontal line.

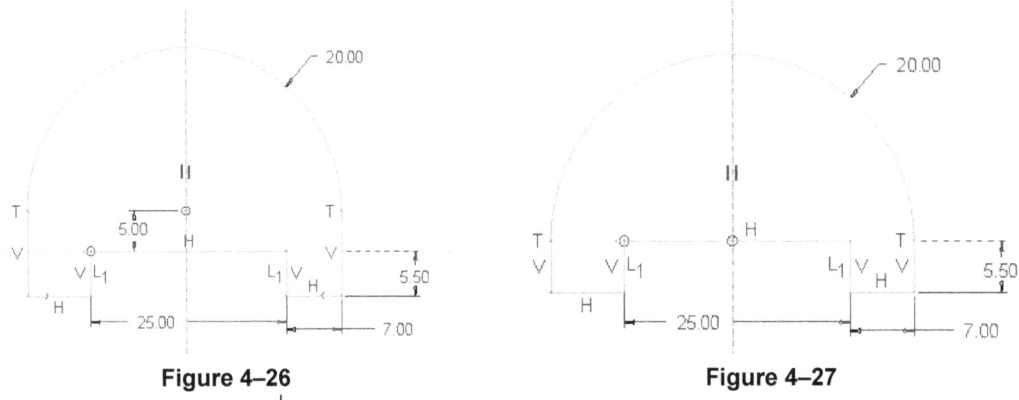

Figure 4–26

Figure 4–27

Step 5 - Add and delete dimensions, as required.

As you sketch, dimensions are added and removed automatically so the geometry is always located with respect to the references but is not over-dimensioned. Dimensions created by Creo Parametric are referred to as *weak* dimensions. As you sketch additional geometry, the system automatically removes them to avoid over-dimensioning.

The dimension icons can be found in the Dimension group in the *Sketch* tab as shown in Figure 4–28.

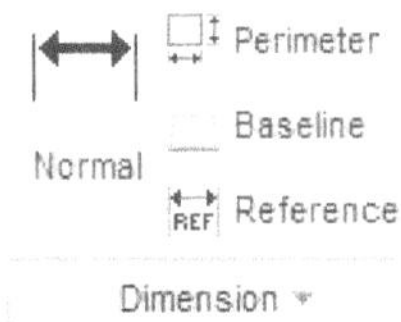

Figure 4–28

*You can also create dimensions by selecting the entity, right-clicking and selecting **Create Dimension**.*

To create additional dimensions, click ⟷ (Normal), select the entities to dimension, and click the middle mouse button to place the dimension. Once the dimensions have been created, they can be immediately changed to the required values. Dimensions that you create are referred to as *strong* dimensions and cannot be automatically removed from the sketch. Strong and weak dimensions display as shown in Figure 4–29.

Weak dimensions display in light blue. Strong dimensions display in blue.

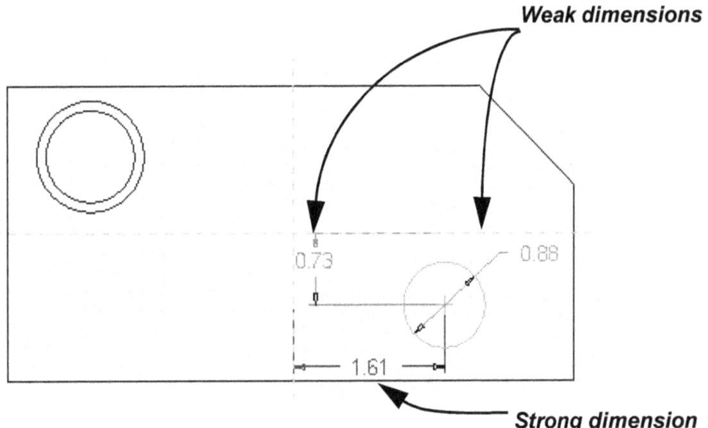

Figure 4–29

Strong dimensions are considered required dimensions. Weak dimensions that are important to your design intent should be made strong to ensure that the dimension value is not removed by the system as you continue to sketch geometry.

- To make a weak dimension strong, select the dimension value, right-click and select **Strong**. A weak dimension also becomes strong when you modify its dimension value. To modify the dimension value, double-click on the value and enter a new one in the field that displays.
- There are several common types of dimensions that can be created in Sketcher mode. They are described in continuation.

Linear Dimensions

The placement of the dimension determines whether it is a horizontal or vertical dimension. Keep the design intent in mind when considering the dimensioning scheme.

To create a linear dimension, click (Normal) and select the entity(ies) to dimension using the left mouse button. Move the cursor to the required location and place the dimension using the middle mouse button. The different methods for dimensioning the linear entities are shown in Figure 4–30.

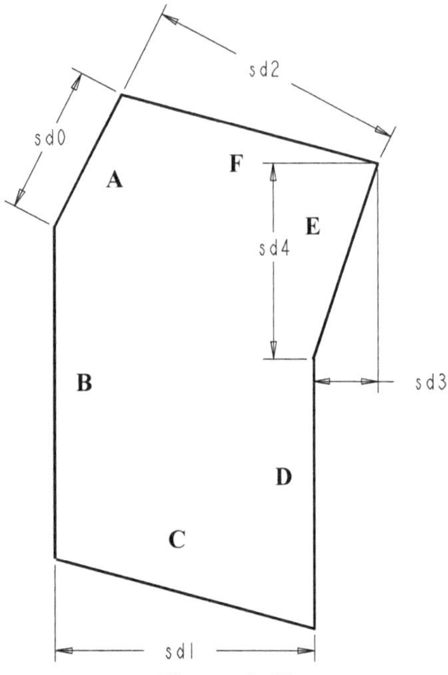

Figure 4–30

Dimension	Procedure
To place dimension sd0	Select line **A**. Position the cursor where you want to place the dimension and click the middle mouse button.
To place dimension sd1	Select lines **B** and **D**. Position the cursor where you want to place the dimension and click the middle mouse button.
To place dimension sd2	Select line **A** and the vertex between lines **E** and **F**. Position the cursor where you want to place the dimension and click the middle mouse button.
To place dimensions sd3 and sd4	Select the two vertices at the ends of line **E**. Position the cursor where you want to place the dimension and click the middle mouse button.

Center/ Tangential Dimensions

To dimension the distance between circles and arcs, click (Normal) and select the two entities. Move the cursor to the required location and place the dimension using the middle mouse button. To place a slanted dimension, place the dimension at a point along a line that joins the two entities that are being dimensioned. A sketch with center/tangential dimensions is shown in Figure 4–31.

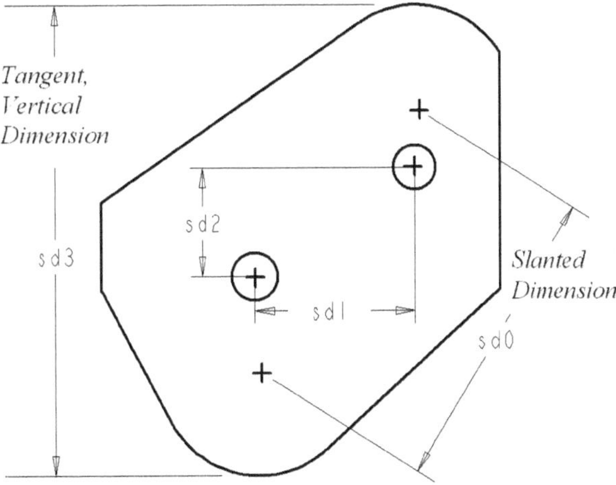

Figure 4–31

Radius/ Diameter Dimensions

To create a radius dimension, click (Normal) and select an arc or a circle. Move the cursor to the required location and place the dimension using the middle mouse button. To create diameter dimensions, select an arc or circle twice and place the dimension using the middle mouse button. A sketch with radius/diameter dimensions is shown in Figure 4–32.

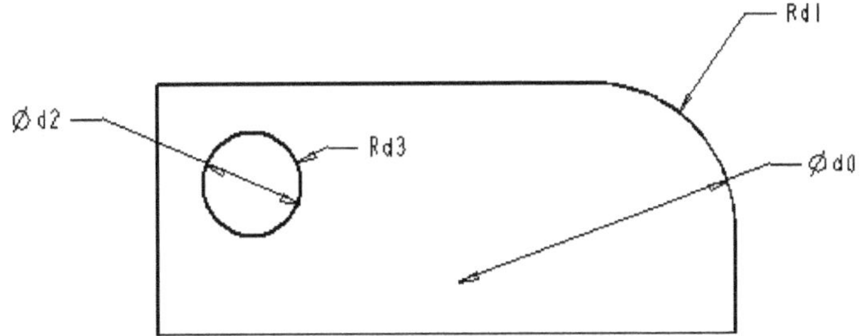

Figure 4–32

You can also change a Radial dimension to a Diameter dimension by right-clicking and selecting **Convert to Diameter**, as shown in Figure 4–33. The same process can change a Diameter dimension to a Radial dimension.

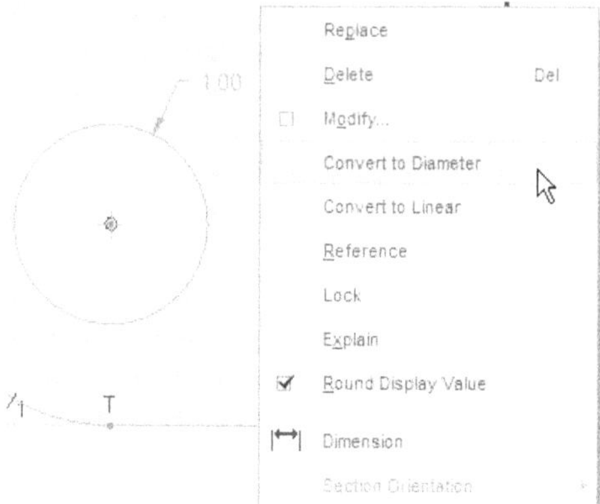

Figure 4–33

Angular Dimensions

For an angular dimension, select lines **A** and **B** and place the dimension using the middle mouse button. The resulting angle is dependent on the placement location of the dimension, as shown in Figure 4–34.

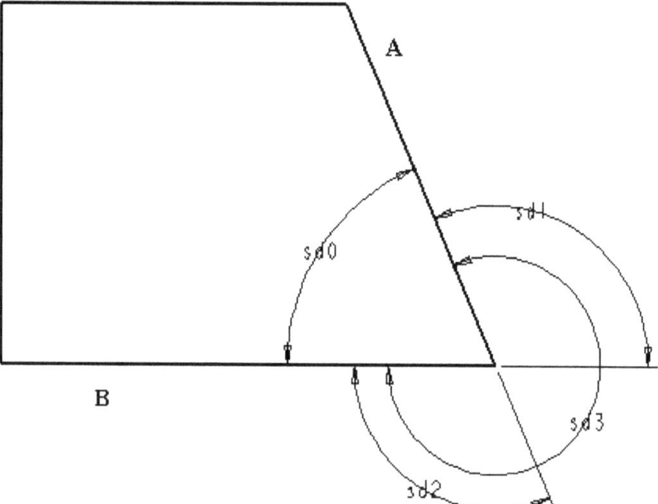

Figure 4–34

To dimension an arc angle, select the arc (the selected arc turns red) and the two end points and place the dimension using the middle mouse button, as shown in Figure 4–35.

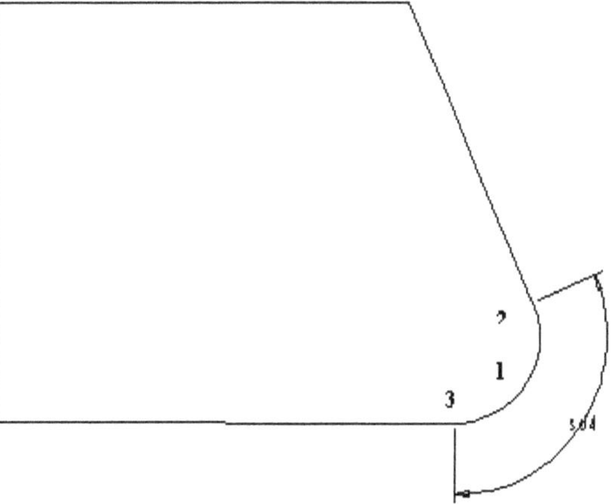

Figure 4–35

Revolved Section Dimensions

Only half of the cross-section of a revolved feature needs to be sketched. It is then revolved about the centerline at a specified angle. You can use any combination of the following selections to create a diameter dimension on the section of a revolved feature. In the example shown in Figure 4–36, the sd0 dimension is created by selecting the geometry, selecting the centerline, and then selecting the geometry again. The **sd1** dimension is created by selecting the centerline, point, and centerline again. In both cases, click the middle mouse button to place the dimension. Using either of these selection techniques results in a diameter dimension.

This type of dimensioning scheme can also be used to dimension symmetrical entities.

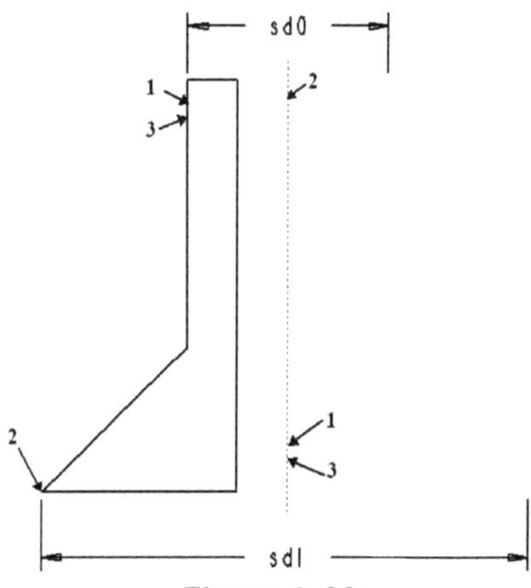

Figure 4–36

Step 6 - Modify dimensions, as required.

You can also modify multiple dimensions on a sketch using the Modify Dimensions dialog box.

Once dimensions have been placed, modify them to suit your design intent. You can modify a dimension in the sketch by double-clicking on the dimension value and entering a new one in the field that displays.

Step 7 - Complete the sketch.

*If you have accessed Sketcher independently (through **File>New> Sketch**), select **File> Save** to save the file with the .SEC extension.*

*Sketches display in light blue. You can modify the color by selecting **File> Options>System Colors>Graphics**.*

Once you are satisfied with the geometry, dimensions, and constraints, exit the Sketcher mode and complete the sketch by clicking ✓ (OK). The completed sketch is shown in Figure 4–37.

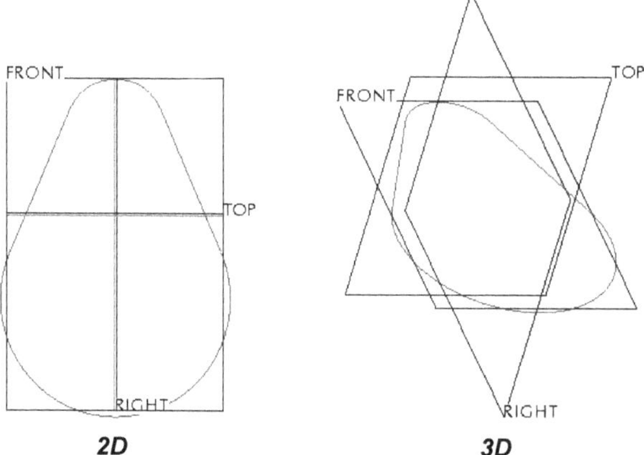

Figure 4–37

4.2 Trimming Tools

When you create a sketched feature, such as an extruded cut or protrusion, you can sketch a new section or select existing sections. Existing sections can be created as sketches.

Fillet Option	Procedure
(Circular)	Select two entities. A fillet arc with a circular profile is created between the two entities, with construction lines that extend to the intersection point.
(Circular Trim)	Select two entities. A fillet arc with a circular profile is created between the two entities. The center of the arc is located by dimensions.
(Elliptical)	Select two entities. A fillet arc with an elliptical profile is created between the two entities, with two construction lines that extend to the intersection point and two that extend to the center of the elliptical arc.
(Elliptical Trim)	Select two entities. A fillet arc with an elliptical profile is created between the two entities. the center of the ellipse is located by dimensions.

4.3 Interactive Practice

The sketch shown in Figure 4–38 is successfully regenerated using only four dimensions. This is possible because of sketcher constraints. Consider which constraints are used for each un-dimensioned entity. Discuss these constraints with the class. A possible solution is shown in Figure 4–39.

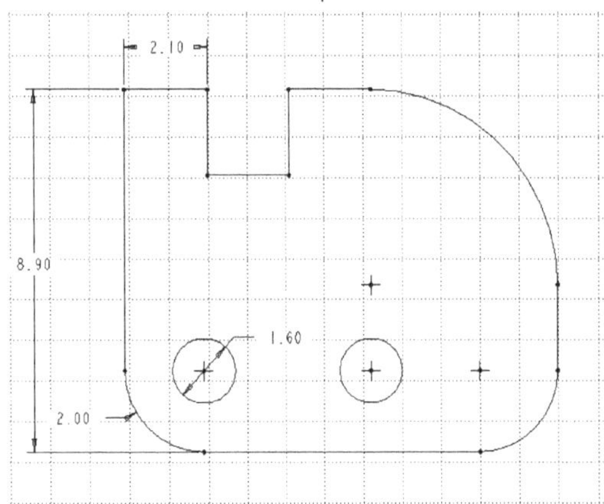

Figure 4–38

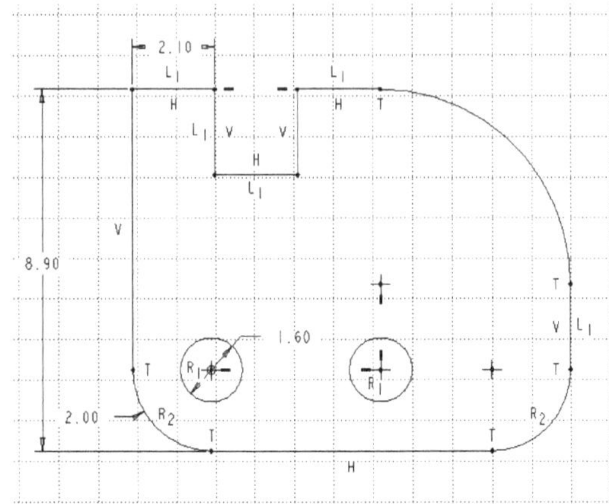

Figure 4–39

Practice 4a

Create a Sketch

Practice Objectives

- Create a 2D sketch object.
- Use multiple sketch tools in the *Sketch* tab.
- Add additional constraints and dimensions to the sketch to ensure that it captures the required design intent.

In this practice, you will create a stand alone sketch to learn how to create geometry, add dimensions, and add constraints. You will create the sketch shown in Figure 4–40.

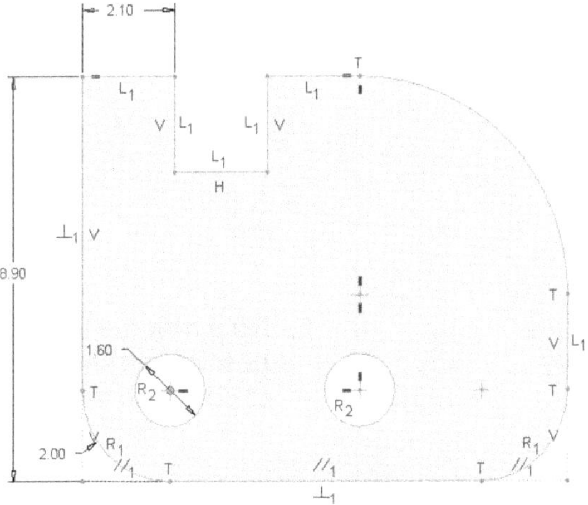

Figure 4–40

Task 1 - Create a new sketch.

1. Set your working directory to the *Chapter 04\practice 4a* folder.
2. Click (New).
3. Select **Sketch**. Set the *Name* to **sketch**.
4. Click **OK**.

Task 2 - Toggle on the grid and start sketching.

1. In the In-graphics toolbar, select (Sketcher Display Filters).

We will use the grid as a visual aid for the creation of this sketch. In general, you will not need it toggled on.

2. Select (Disp Grid) to toggle on the grid display.
3. In the Sketching group of the ribbon, click (Line Chain).
4. Select approximately in the location shown in Figure 4–41.

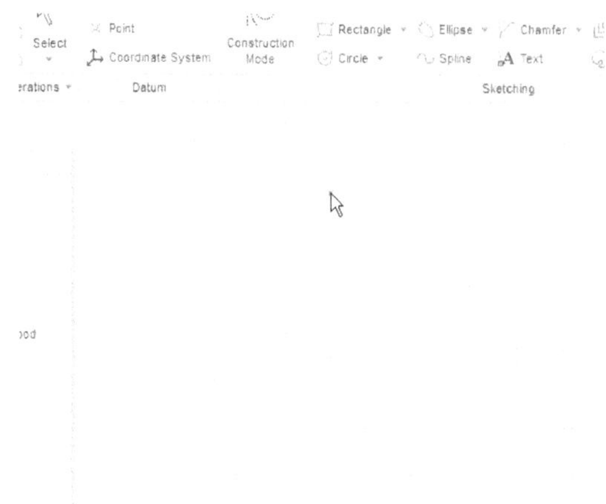

Figure 4–41

5. Note how the line rubber bands but will snap to the Vertical position, as shown in Figure 4–42. Click the location shown to complete the first line.

Figure 4–42

6. Move the cursor to the right until the **H** symbol displays and click the location shown in Figure 4–43 to complete the second line.

Figure 4–43

7. Click the location shown in Figure 4–44 to complete the third line.

Figure 4–44

8. Right-click and select (3-Point / Tangent End), as shown in Figure 4–45.

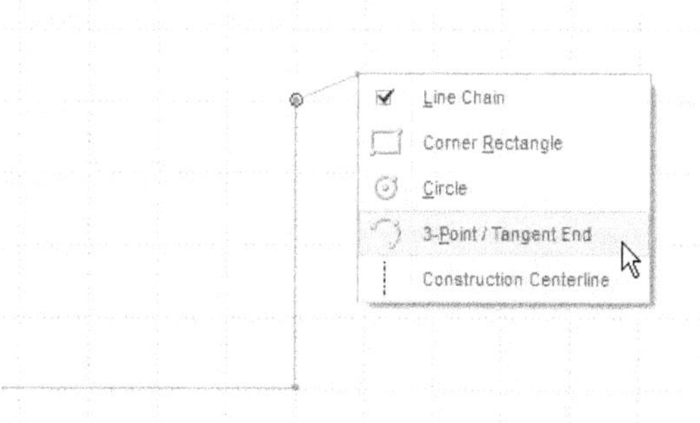

Figure 4–45

Note the Tangent constraint at the beginning and the two colinear constraints at the end.

9. Click the end location as shown in Figure 4–46.

Figure 4–46

10. Right-click and select (Line Chain).

Note the equal length constraints that are automatically established if you sketch the lines roughly equal.

11. Click the open end of the arc, and create the two lines shown in Figure 4–47.

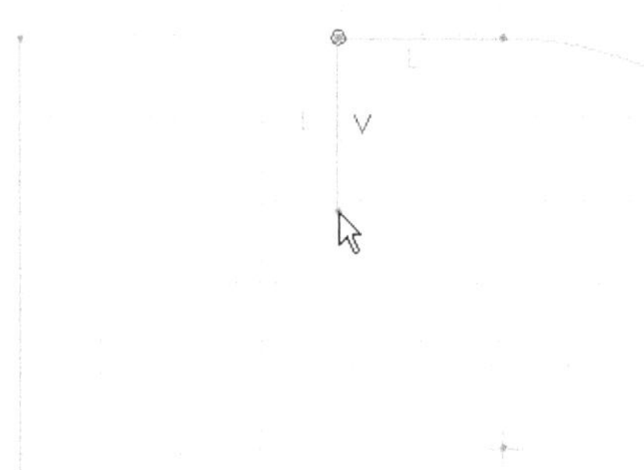

Figure 4–47

12. Sketch the remaining three lines as shown in Figure 4–48. Ensure the final point snaps to the endpoint of the first line.

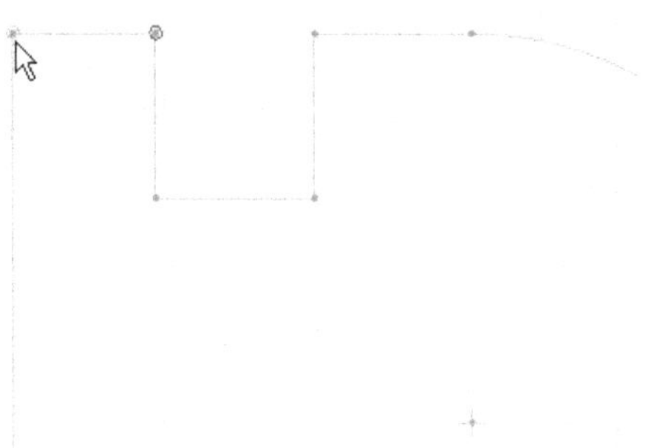

Figure 4–48

13. Click the middle mouse button to complete the sketch. The sketch displays approximately as shown in Figure 4–49.

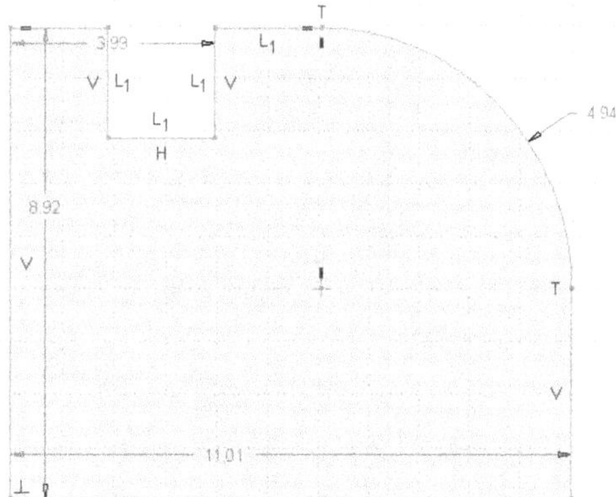

Figure 4–49

Task 3 - Add the filleted corners.

1. Right click and select (Fillet).
2. Select the location shown in Figure 4–50.

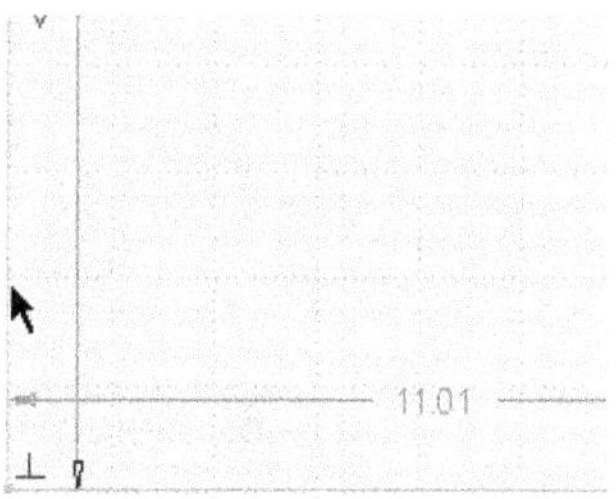

Figure 4–50

3. Select the location shown in Figure 4–51.

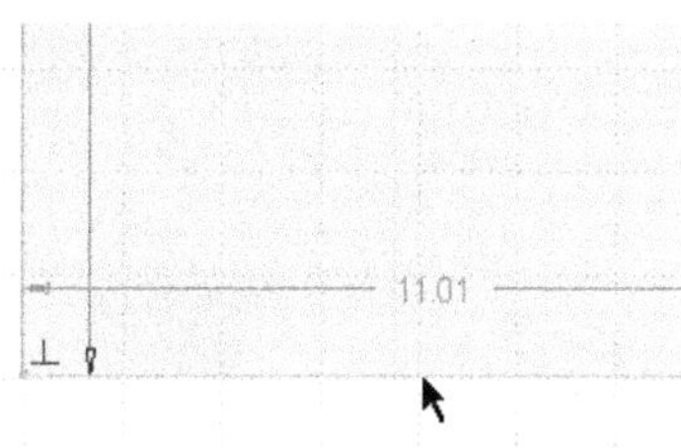

Figure 4–51

Note that the radius is defined by the point selected in Figure 4–53, which is closest to the corner.

4. The system creates a radius as shown in Figure 4–52.

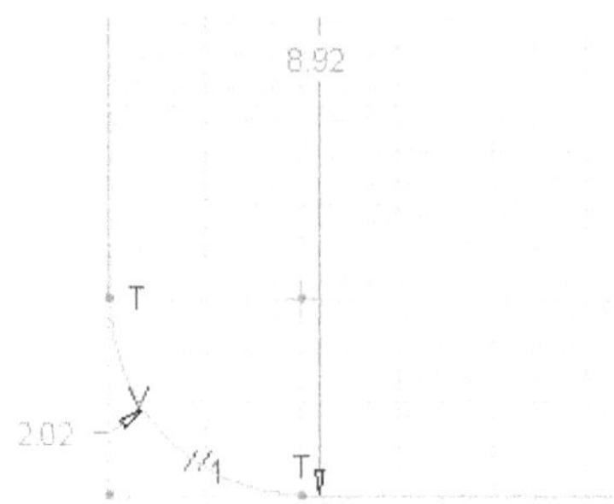

Figure 4–52

5. With (Fillet) still enabled, select the location shown in Figure 4–53.

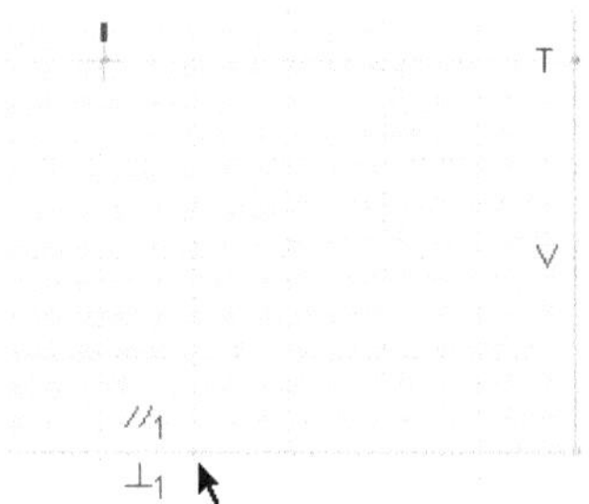

Figure 4–53

6. Select the location shown in Figure 4–54.

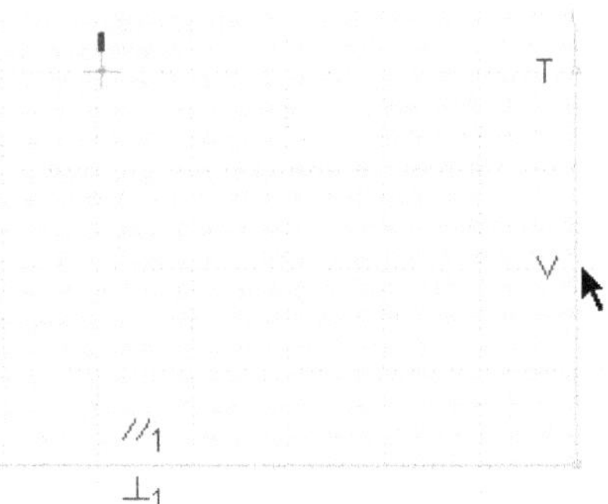

Figure 4–54

7. The system creates a radius as shown in Figure 4–55.

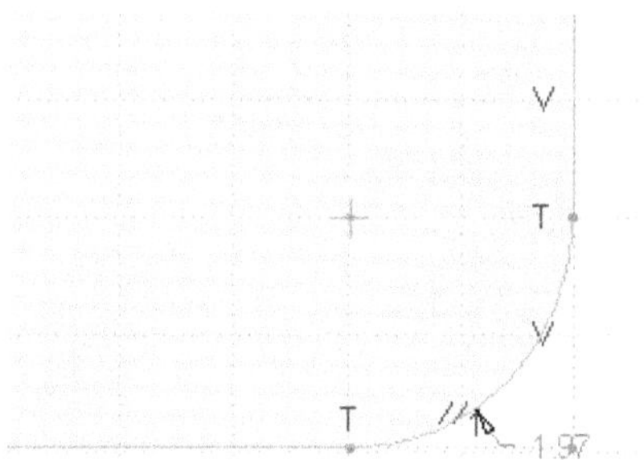

Figure 4–55

Task 4 - Add the Two Circles.

1. In the In-graphics toolbar, select (Sketcher Display Filters).
2. Select (Disp Grid) to toggle off the grid display.
3. In the Sketching group in the ribbon, select (Circle).
4. Move the cursor until it *snaps* to the center of the arc shown in Figure 4–56 and left click to start placing the circle.

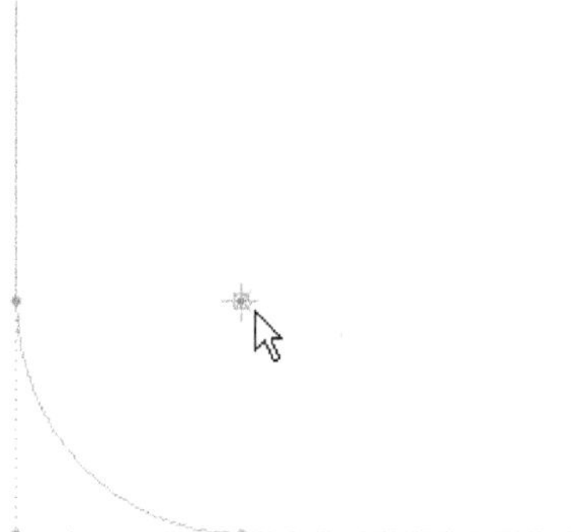

Figure 4–56

5. Move the cursor to the approximate position shown in Figure 4–57 and left-click to complete the circle.

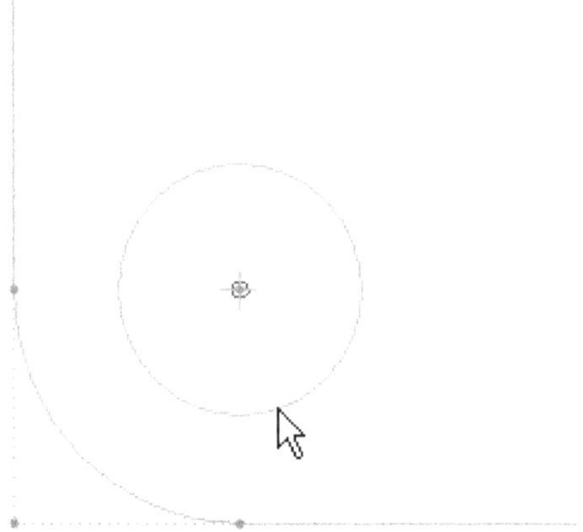

Figure 4–57

6. Create another circle in the approximate position shown in Figure 4–58. Ensure no automatic constraints are applied.

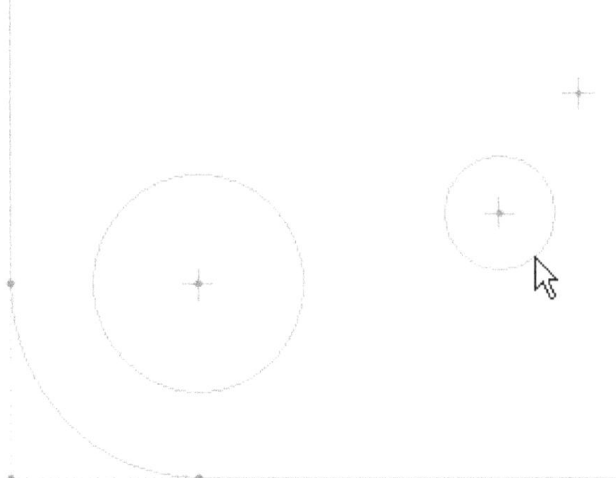

Figure 4–58

7. Click the middle mouse button to stop sketching.The model should display approximately as shown in Figure 4–59. Do not be concerned if your dimensions and constraints are different.

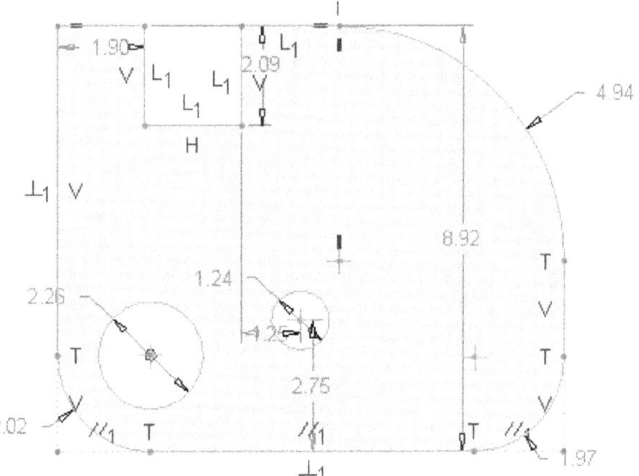

Figure 4–59

Task 5 - Add constraints to remove dimensions.

1. In the Constrain group in the ribbon, click (Horizontal) and select the center of each circle. The circles align horizontally as shown in Figure 4–60.

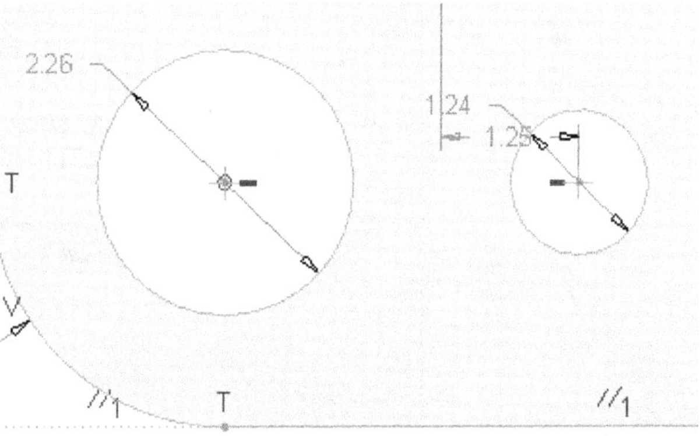

Figure 4–60

2. Click ⊦ (Vertical) and select the center of the large arc and the right circle, and the model updates as shown in Figure 4–61.

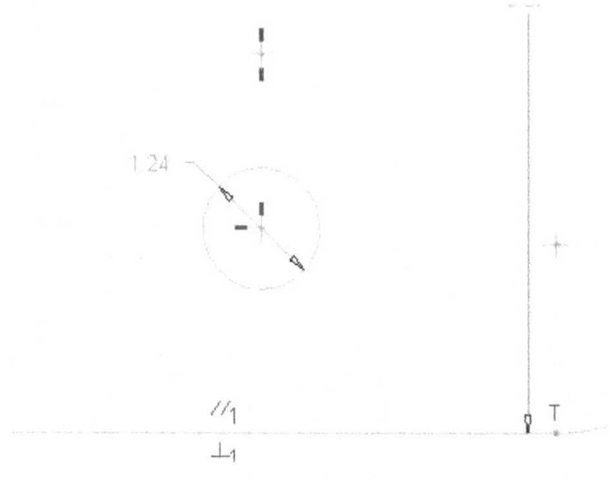

Figure 4–61

3. Click = (Equal) and select the two smaller arcs. The model updates as shown in Figure 4–62.

Note that the two arc are made equal in radius, denoted by the ***R1*** *symbol. The sketch uses the dimension of the first arc selected.*

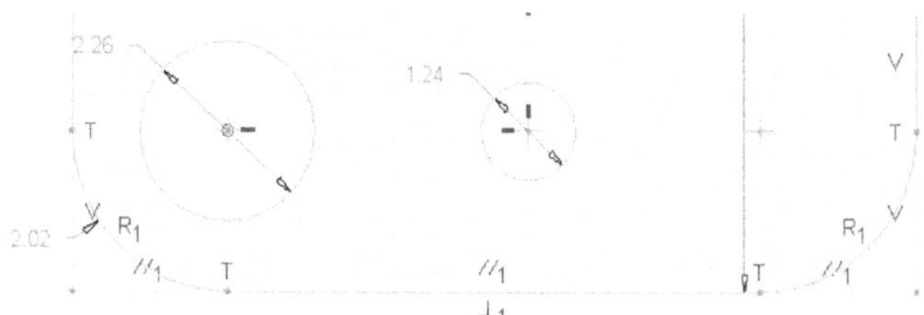

Figure 4–62

4. Click = (Equal) to select two new entities (otherwise you will continue making entities equal to the first arc).

5. Select the two circles and the system makes them equal as shown in Figure 4–63.

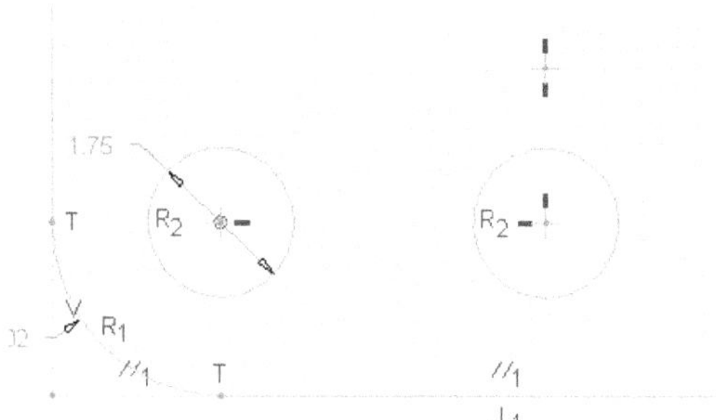

Figure 4–63

6. Click ═ (Equal) to select new entities.
7. Select one of the lines already marked as **L1** and select the top left horizontal line, as shown in Figure 4–64.

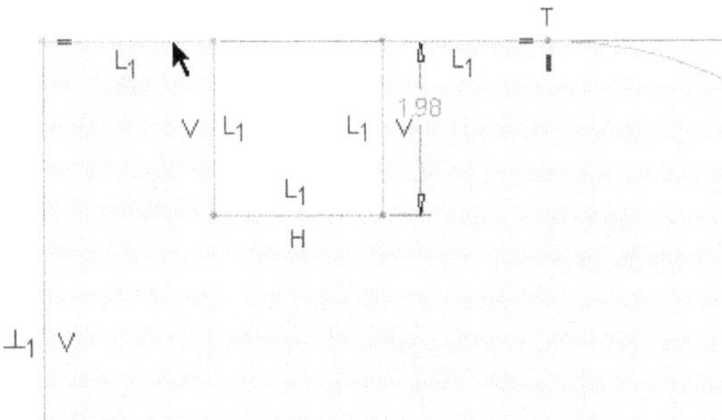

Figure 4–64

8. Select the vertical line between the two arcs on the right, making it also equal, as shown Figure 4–65.

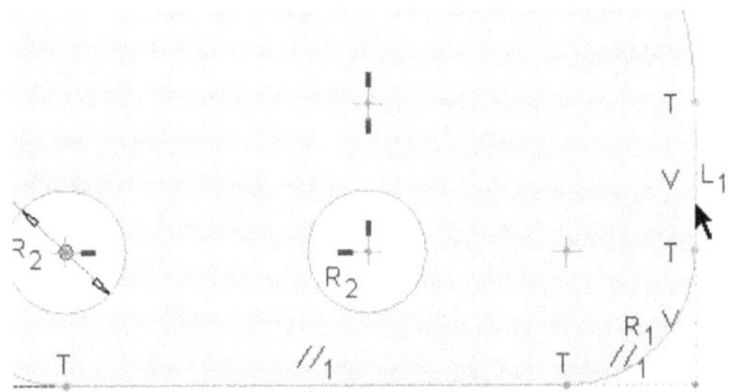

Figure 4–65

Task 6 - Edit the dimensions to complete the sketch.

1. In the Dimension group in the ribbon, click ⟷ (Normal).
2. Select the line shown in Figure 4–66.

Note that the weak dimension is replaced with the strong dimension.

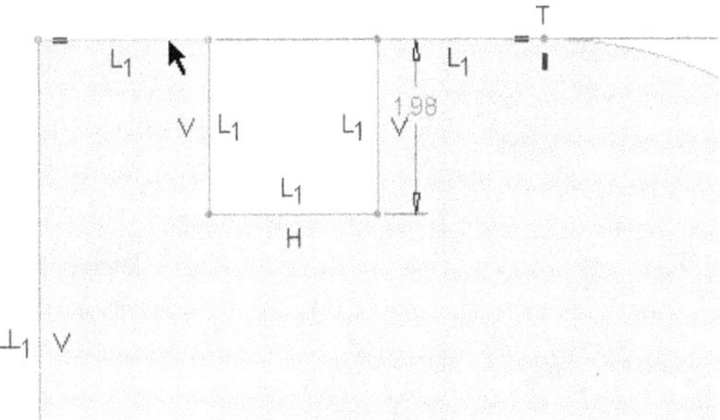

Figure 4–66

3. Move the cursor to the location shown in Figure 4–67, click the middle mouse button to place it, set the value to **2.1**, and press <Enter>.

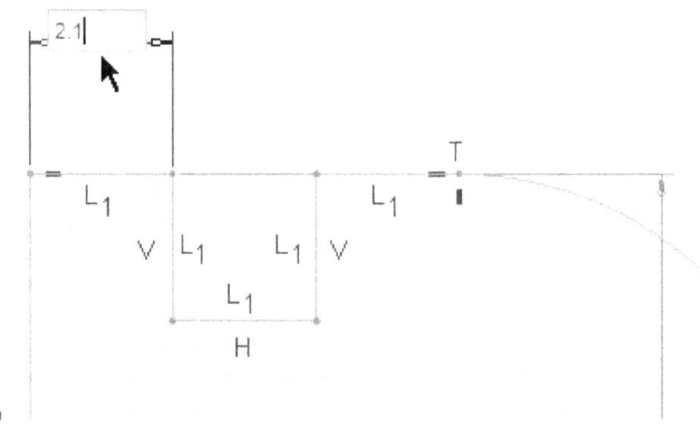

Figure 4–67

The weak dimension is again replaced with a strong dimension.

4. Select the two lines shown in Figure 4–68.

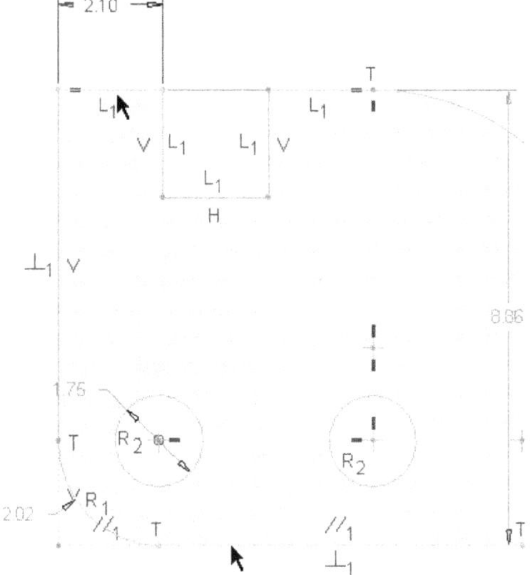

Figure 4–68

5. Move the cursor to the location indicated in Figure 4–69, click the middle mouse button, set the value to **8.9**, and press <Enter>.

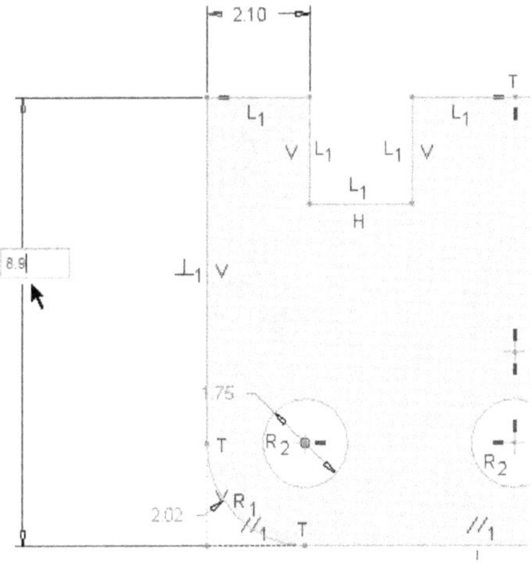

Figure 4–69

6. In the Operations group in the ribbon, click (Select).

7. Double-click the *Radius* dimension for the lower left arc and set it to **2**. Press <Enter>.

Directly editing a weak dimension will convert is to strong.

8. Double-click the *Diameter* dimension and set the value to **1.6**. Press <Enter>. The completed sketch displays as shown in Figure 4–70.

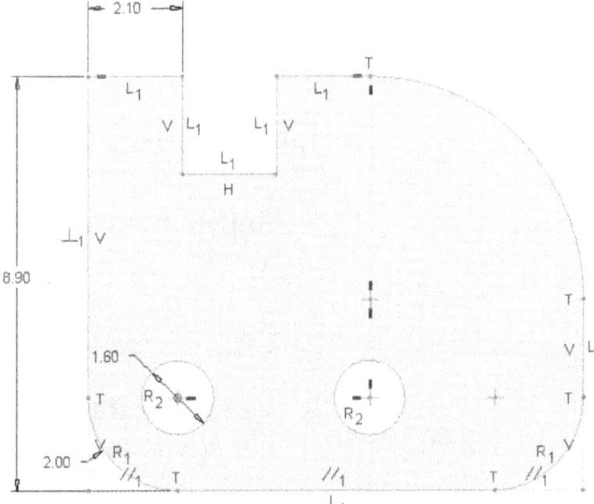

Figure 4–70

Practice 4b Create a Sketch in a New Part

Practice Objectives

- Create a 2D sketch in a new part using references.
- Create a 2D geometry using the line, arc, tangent line, and trim tools in the Sketch tab.
- Add additional constraints and dimensions to the sketch to ensure that it captures the required design intent.

In this practice, you will create the sketches shown on the left in Figure 4–71. These curves can be used later to create the solid geometry shown on the right.

Figure 4–71

Task 1 - Create a new part.

1. Set your working directory to the *Chapter 04\practice 4b* folder.
2. Click (New) to create a new part.
3. Verify that **Part** and **Use default template** are selected. Set the *Name* to **gauge**.
4. Click **OK**.

5. Set the model display as follows:

    - (Datum Display Filters): Only (Plane Display)
    - (Spin Center): Off
    - (Display Style): (Shading)

6. Select datum plane **FRONT** from the model tree as the sketch plane for the first sketch.

Always review the default selections made by Creo Parametric. They might not meet your design requirements.

7. In the Datum group in the *Model* tab, click (Sketch) to begin creating the sketch. The *Sketch* tab becomes active.

8. In the Setup group in the ribbon, click (Sketch Setup) to investigate how the sketch plane has been established. The Sketch dialog box opens as shown in Figure 4–72.

Figure 4–72

9. Note that the Sketch Plane you selected is listed, and datum plane **RIGHT** has been selected as the sketch orientation reference plane for this feature. You could select different references here if required. Click **Cancel** to return to the sketch.

Task 2 - Sketch a rectangular section.

You can sketch in 3D as well, but we will do so in 2D until you are more familiar with the tools.

1. In the Setup group in the ribbon, click (Sketch View) to orient the model to the sketch view.

2. Click (Rectangle) to sketch a corner rectangle.

3. Start the rectangle at the intersection of datum planes **RIGHT** and **TOP** and drag it to the top-right quadrant, as shown in Figure 4–73. If the horizontal and vertical edges become close to the same length and the L_1 symbol displays next to them, indicating that the automatic equal length constraint has been added. When this symbol displays, click the left mouse button to complete the rectangle.

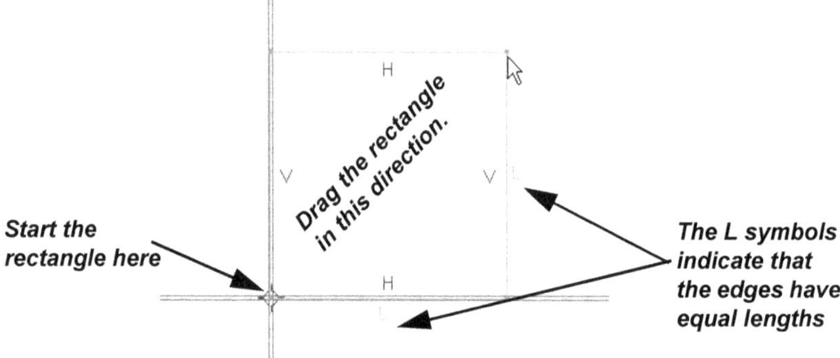

Figure 4–73

4. Modify the dimension of the rectangle. Click (Select), double-click the dimension, and enter **1.5**.

5. Press <Enter> to complete the modification. The sketch displays as shown in Figure 4–74.

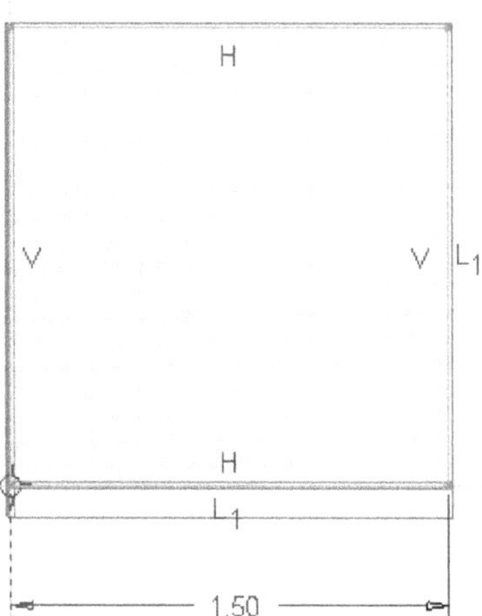

Figure 4–74

Task 3 - Sketch a center-and-ends arc.

1. Expand the (Arc) flyout.
2. Click (Center and Ends) to create a center-and-ends arc.
3. Select the vertex in the upper right corner of the rectangle. This vertex is the center of the arc.
4. Sketch the arc from the top horizontal edge to the right edge of the rectangle, as shown in Figure 4–75.

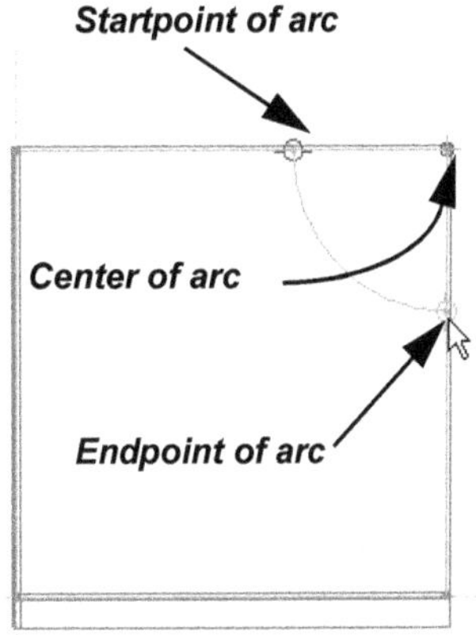

Figure 4–75

5. The arc displays as shown in Figure 4–76.

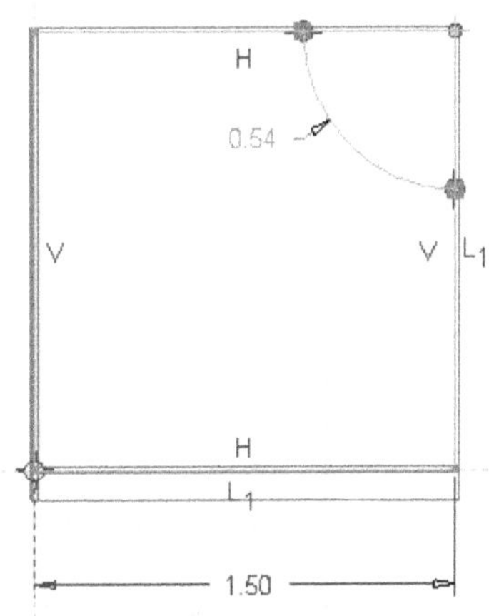

Figure 4–76

Note the highlighted vertices and that the sketch is no longer filled in due to the multiple loops. In the next task these entities will be trimmed.

6. Modify the value of the *Radius* dimension to **0.60**.

Task 4 - Corner trim the arc and edges of the rectangle.

When trimming to a corner, select each entity on the portion you want to keep.

1. In the Editing group, click (Corner) to corner trim the arc and edges of the rectangle.
2. Select the top horizontal edge of the rectangle in the location shown in Figure 4–77.

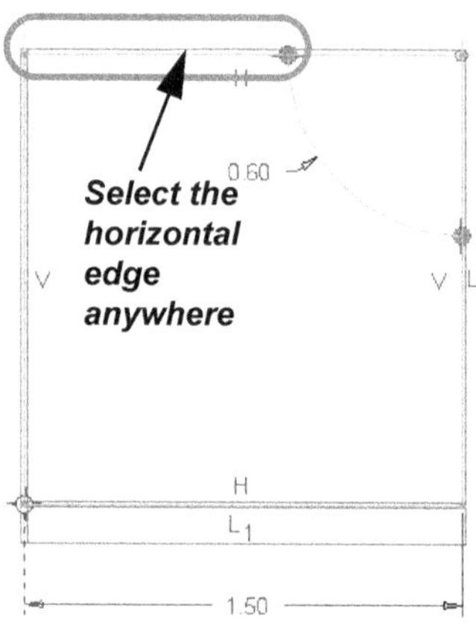

Figure 4–77

3. Select the arc. The entities are trimmed to a corner, as shown in Figure 4–78.

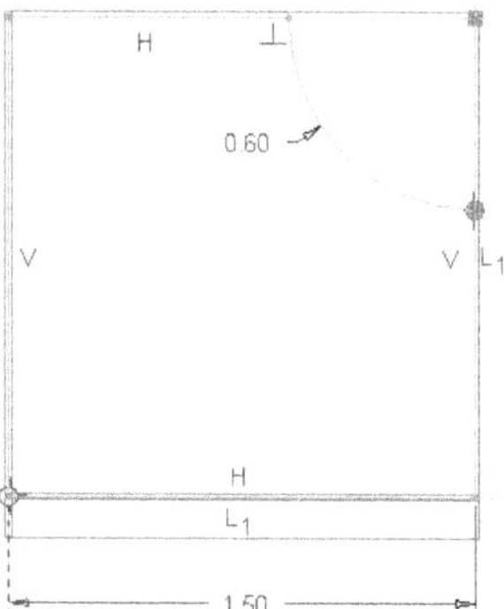

Figure 4–78

4. Corner trim the arc and the right vertical edge of the rectangle in the same way. Remember to select the edges on the portions you want to keep. The sketch displays as shown in Figure 4–79.

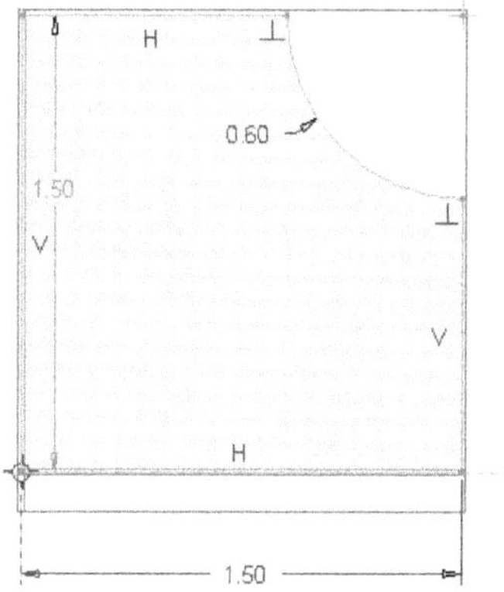

Figure 4–79

5. The sketch is now filled in because it is a closed loop. In the Inspect group of the *Sketch* tab, click (Shade Closed Loops) to toggle the shading off.
6. Click (Shade Closed Loops) again to toggle it back on.

Task 5 - Apply the equal length constraint.

The equal length constraint was removed when the top and right side of the rectangle were trimmed. The constraint can be re-applied to the bottom and left sides so that a single dimension controls these lengths.

1. Note that two dimensions control the height and width of the remains of the rectangle. To apply the equal length constraint, click = (Equal) in the Constrain group,
2. Select the bottom edge and the left edge. The sketch displays as shown in Figure 4–80. The extra weak dimension has been removed, and the L_1 symbols display next to the edges.

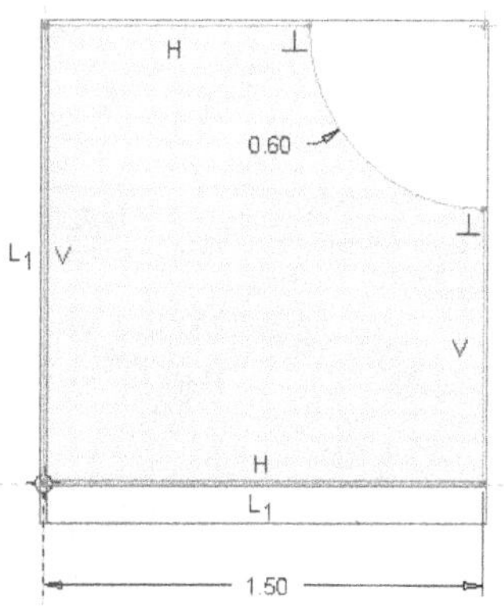

Figure 4–80

Task 6 - Complete the feature and rename it.

1. Click ✓ (OK) to complete the sketch.
2. Return the model to its default orientation by clicking <Ctrl>+<D>. The sketch displays as shown in Figure 4–81.

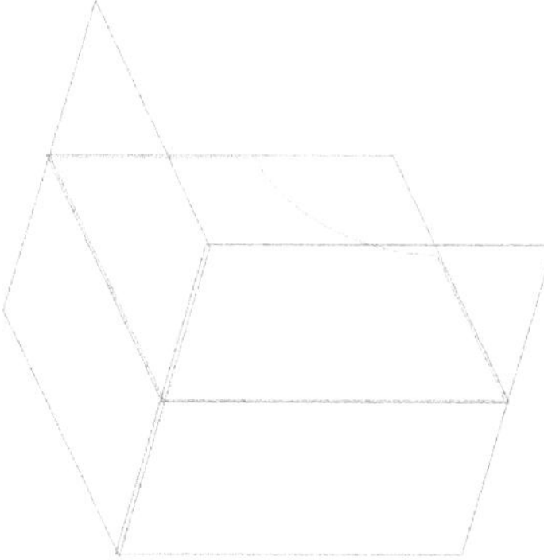

Figure 4–81

3. In the model tree, select **Sketch 1**, right-click, and select **Rename**. You can also select the feature twice in the model tree.
4. Set the new *Name* of the sketch to **front_profile**. The model tree displays as shown in Figure 4–82.

Figure 4–82

Task 7 - Create the second sketch.

1. Select datum plane **TOP** from the model tree as the sketch plane for the second sketch.
2. Click (Sketch) to begin creating the sketch. The *Sketch* tab becomes active and the system automatically selects a sketch orientation reference plane.
3. Click (Sketch View) to orient the model.

The first sketch feature that was created cannot be seen because it is perpendicular to the current sketching plane.

You can temporarily toggle off the display of Sketcher dimensions clicking (Sketcher Display Filters) and clearing the (Disp Dims) option. The display can also be controlled for constraints, vertices, and the Sketcher grid.

Task 8 - Sketch an obround section.

1. Click (Circle) to sketch two circles as shown in Figure 4–83. Sketch the circles so that they have equal radii and their centers are aligned vertically, as indicated by the constraint symbols. The circles are sketched in the lower right quadrant of the intersection of datum planes.

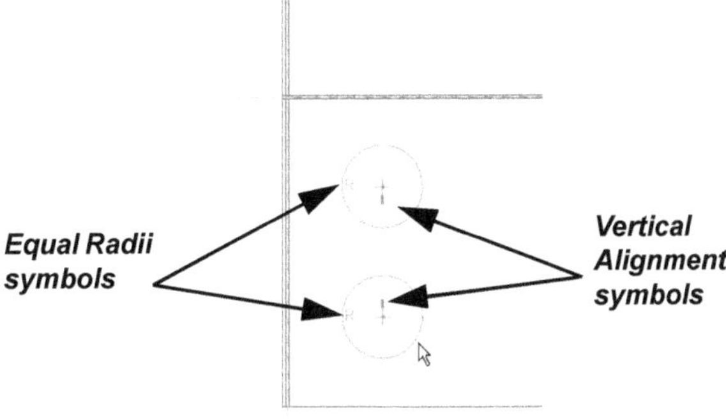

Figure 4–83

2. In the Sketching group, expand the (Line) flyout.
3. Click (Line Tangent) to sketch a line that is tangent to two entities.
4. Select the left side of the two circles. A line tangent to both circles is sketched, as shown in Figure 4–84.

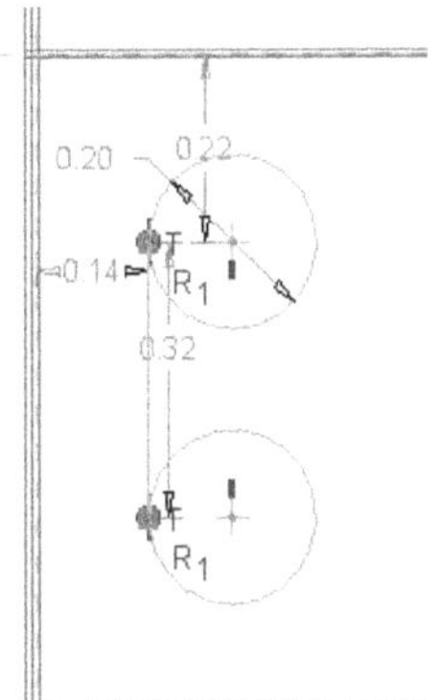

Figure 4–84

5. Sketch a second line tangent to the right sides of the circles, as shown in Figure 4–85.

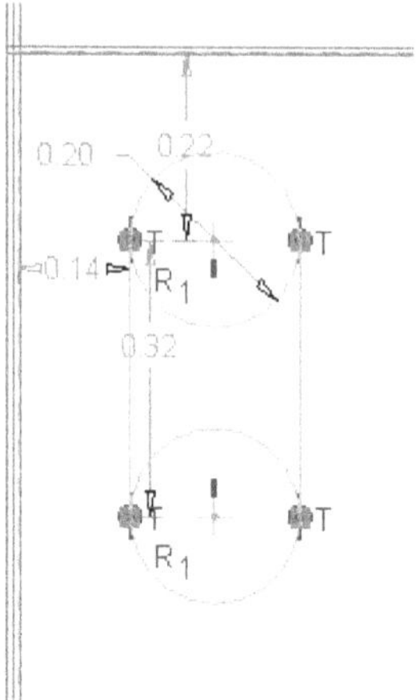

Figure 4–85

6. In the Editing group, click (Delete Segment). When you select this option, all of the entities are temporarily divided where they intersect other entities.

7. Select the inner segments for trimming. Press and hold the left mouse button and drag a selection spline through the inner segments of the two circles, as shown in Figure 4–86.

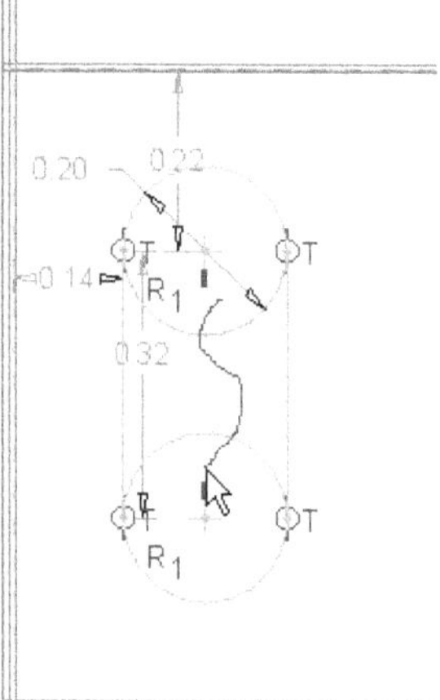

Figure 4–86

8. Release the left mouse button to delete the selected segments. The sketch displays as shown in Figure 4–87.

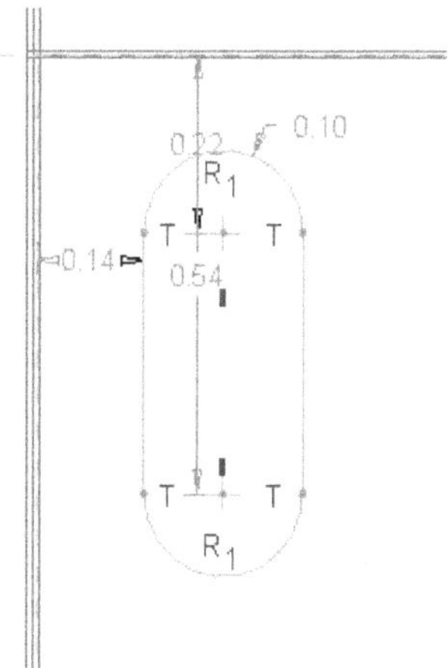

Figure 4–87

9. Click (Normal) to create dimensions. The current dimensions are the weak dimensions automatically created by the Creo Parametric software.

10. Create the dimension **0.23** shown in Figure 4–88. Select the two vertical lines and place the dimension with the middle mouse button. Do not worry about the value of the dimension because you will modify it once you have completed creating all of the required dimensions.

You can move a dimension to a new position. Click (Select), select the dimension by holding the left mouse button, and drag the dimension to the required position.

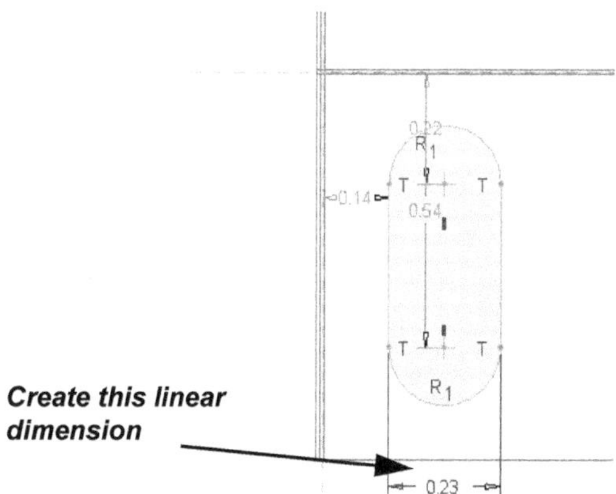

Figure 4–88

11. Create the dimension **0.18** shown in Figure 4–89 by selecting the center of the lower arc and the vertical cyan reference entity. Place the dimension with the middle mouse button.

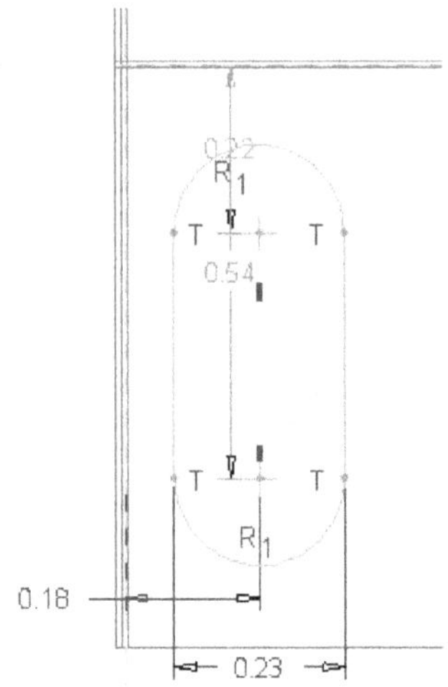

Figure 4–89

12. Create the dimension **0.60** shown in Figure 4–90 by selecting the two arcs. Select the arc entities, not their centers. Place the dimension with the middle mouse button.

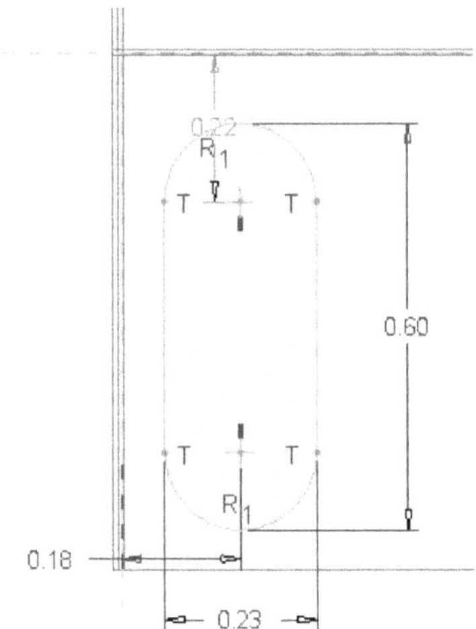

Figure 4–90

13. Finally, create the dimension **0.06** shown in Figure 4–91, by selecting the edge of the upper arc and the horizontal reference entity. Place the dimension with the middle mouse button.

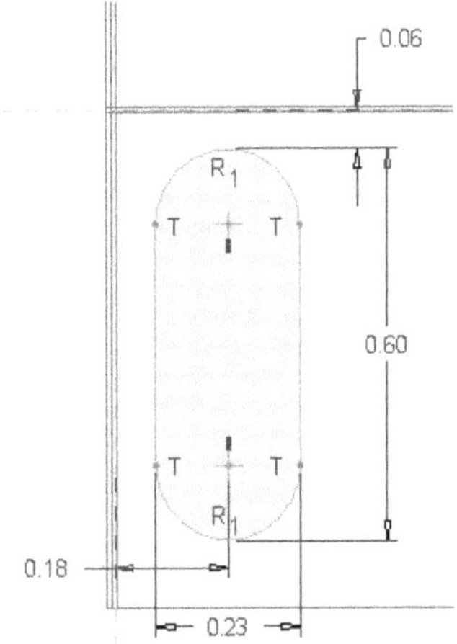

Figure 4–91

14. Double-click on each dimension to enter the new values shown in Figure 4–92.

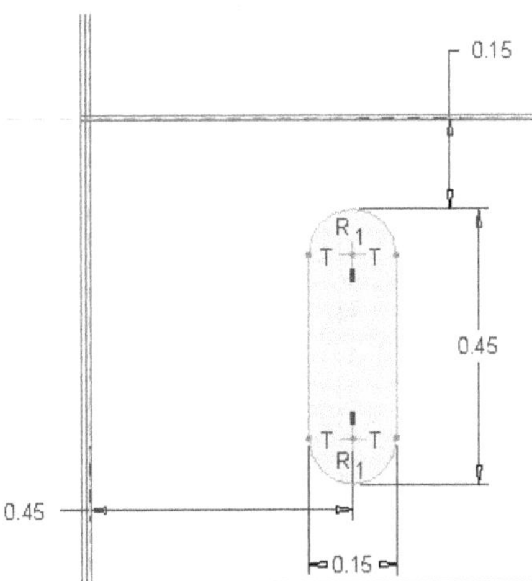

Figure 4–92

15. The sketch is now complete. Click ✓ (OK) to finish the sketch feature.

16. Press <Ctrl>+<D> to return to default orientation.

17. Click (Datum Display Filters) and select (Plane Display) to toggle off the display of the datum planes.

18. The model displays in the default orientation, as shown in Figure 4–93.

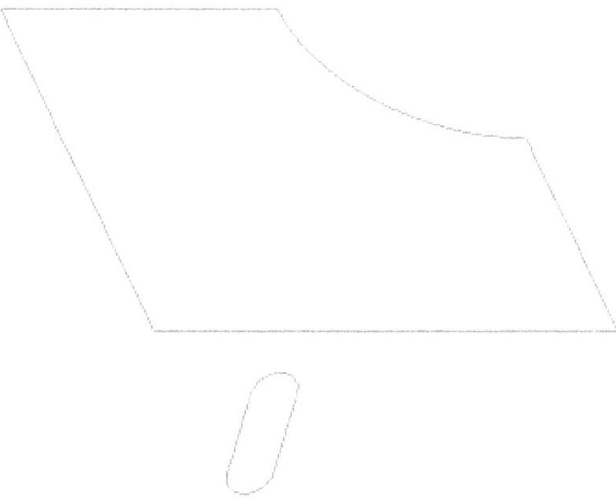

Figure 4–93

19. Save and erase the model.

Practice 4c Sketch on Existing Geometry

Practice Objectives

- Open an existing part model and add a 2D sketch on an existing surface in the model.
- Create the 2D sketch using the Centered Rectangle command.
- Modify the existing entities into a alternate sketch using the **Delete Segment** command.
- Modify and dimension sketched entities.
- Create an extrude feature using the 2D sketch.

In this practice, you will create a sketch in a part that already contains solid geometry. Instead of selecting a datum plane as the sketching plane, you will select a surface on the solid geometry. The sketch displays as shown in Figure 4–94.

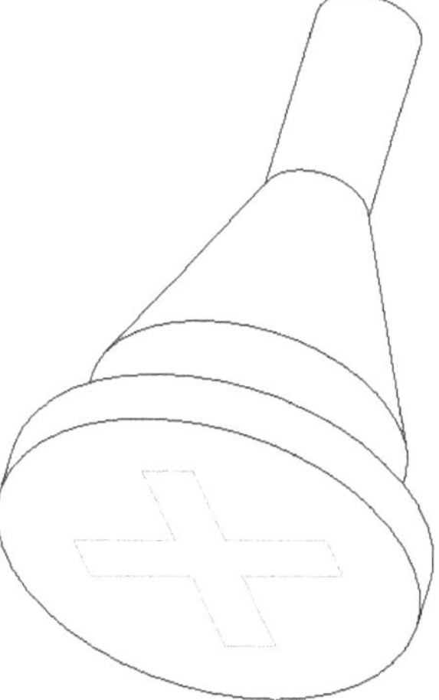

Figure 4–94

Task 1 - Open a part file.

1. Set the working directory to the *Chapter 04\practice 4c* folder.
2. Open **control_shaft.prt**.
3. Set the model display as follows:
    - *(Datum Display Filters):* All Off
    - *(Spin Center):* Off
    - *(Display Style):* (No Hidden)

You can also hold <Alt> to disable the Smart selection and select the surface.

The Selection Filter is in the lower right corner of the Creo Parametric window.

Task 2 - Start the creation of the sketch on the protrusion.

1. To help select a solid surface, change the *Selection Filter* to **Geometry**, as shown in Figure 4–95.

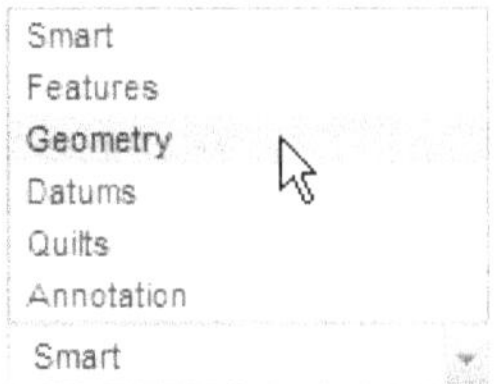

Figure 4–95

2. For the sketching plane, select the surface of the solid, as shown in Figure 4–96.

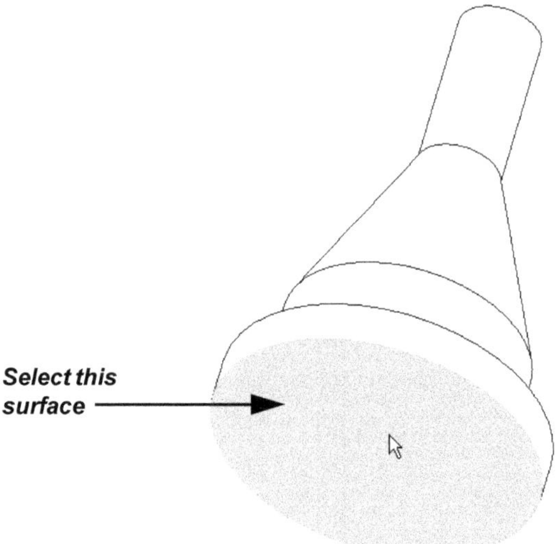

Figure 4–96

3. Click (Sketch) to create a sketch.

4. Click (Sketch View) to orient the model.

You can sketch in 3D orientation, but will sometimes find it easier to sketch in 2D.

5. Click (References) to open the Reference dialog box. Note that the Coordinate system and the **TOP** datum plane were automatically selected as references as shown in Figure 4–97.

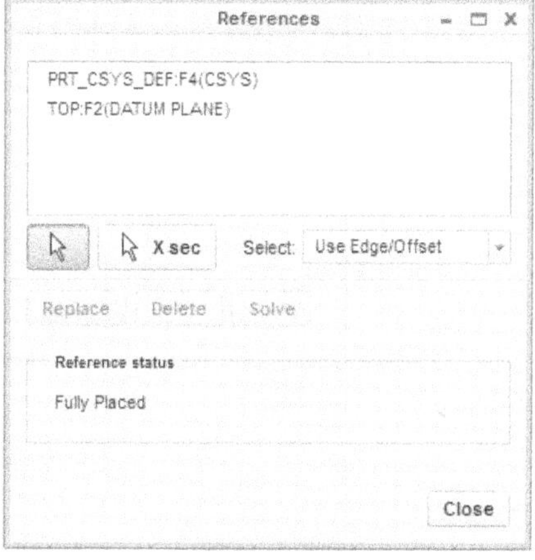

Figure 4–97

6. Select the **RIGHT** datum plane from the model tree as an additional sketcher reference, and close the References dialog box. The model displays as shown in Figure 4–98.

*You can also right-click and select **References**.*

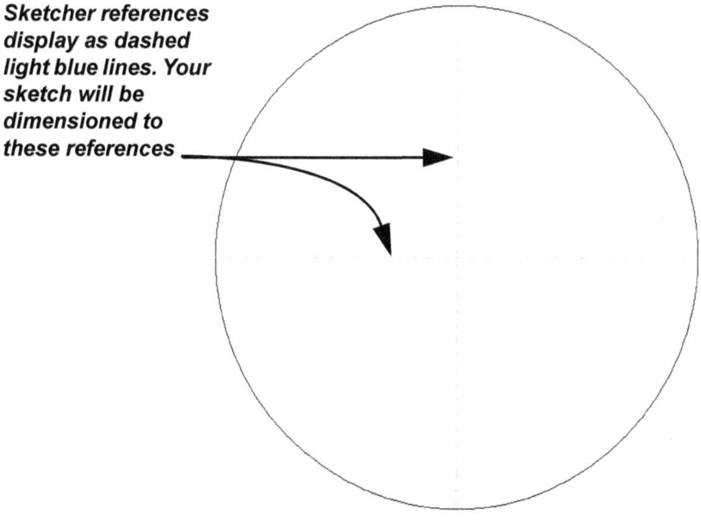

Figure 4–98

7. Expand (Rectangle) and click (Center Rectangle). Begin the sketch by clicking on the intersection of the two sketcher references for the centerpoint of the rectangle, as shown in Figure 4–99.

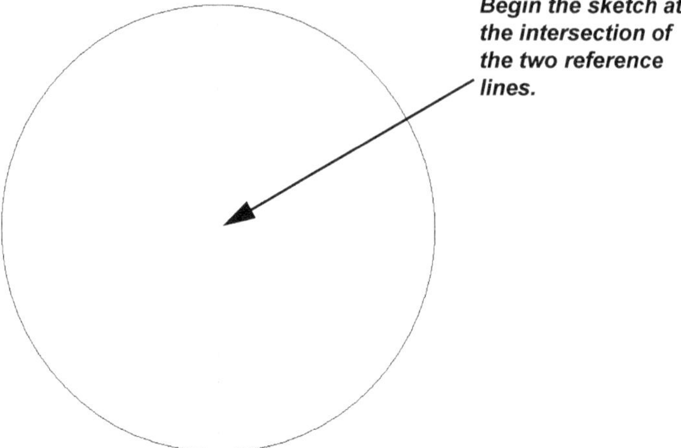

Figure 4–99

8. Click the endpoint location of the rectangle, as shown in Figure 4–100. This creates a rectangle in the center of the geometry.

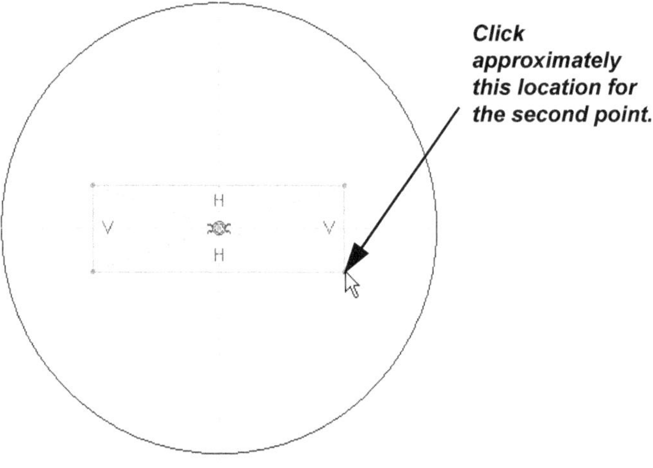

Figure 4–100

To dimension a line, click the line, then click the middle mouse button where you want to place the dimension.

9. Click (Normal) and dimension the rectangular sketch, as shown in Figure 4–101.

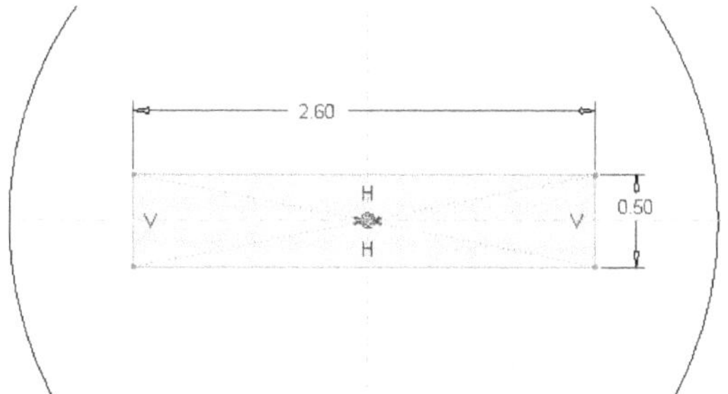

Figure 4–101

10. Sketch another centered rectangle vertically, as shown in Figure 4–102.

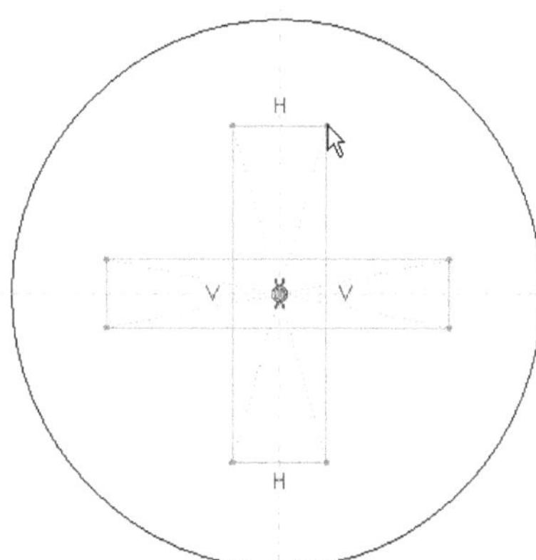

Figure 4–102

11. Click (Delete Segment) to trim away the segments shown in Figure 4–103.

You can drag a continuous line or select the individual segments, There are 16 individual segments.

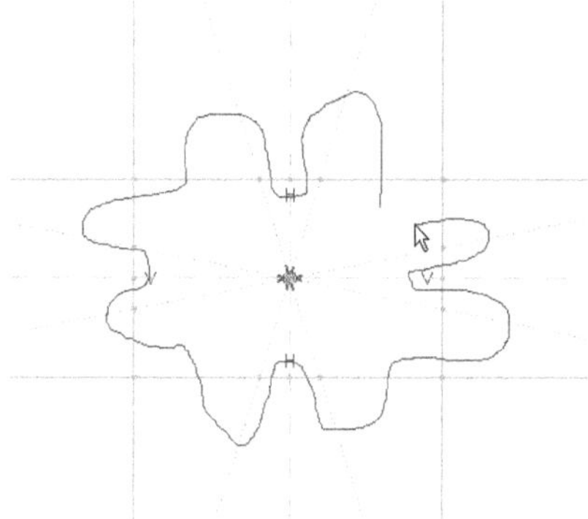

Figure 4–103

12. Dimension the sketch shown in Figure 4–104. Apply constraints as required to create a fully constrained sketch that is only controlled by the two dimensions shown in Figure 4–104. Note that the dimensions can be on any appropriate line, not necessarily on the lines shown.

Use the constraint icons or select the entities and use the contextual menu to apply the constraints.

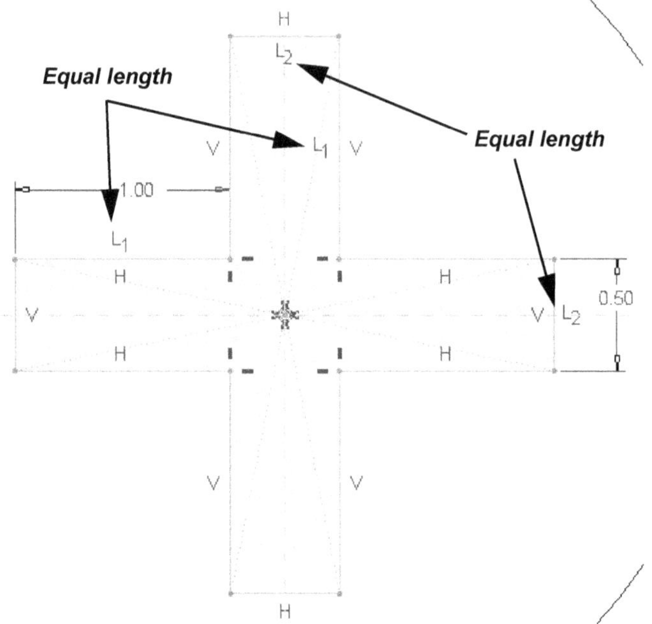

Figure 4–104

13. Exit Sketcher. The completed sketch displays as shown in Figure 4–105.

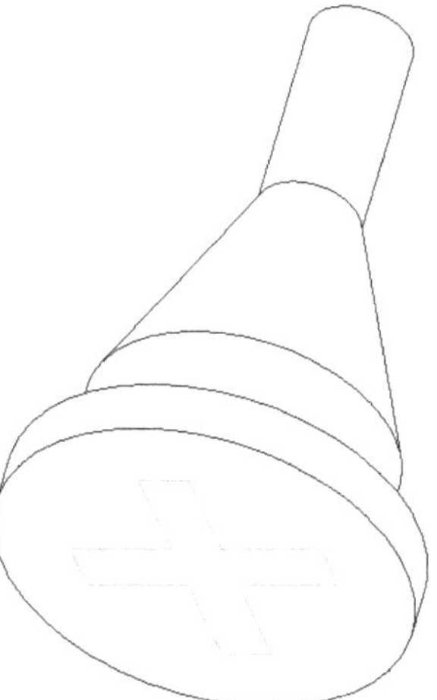
Figure 4–105

14. Press <Ctrl>+<D> to return to Standard Orientation.

15. Select the **Sketch 1** feature in the model tree, if required.

16. In the Shapes group in the *Model* tab, click (Extrude).

17. Set the *Depth* to **1.0**, as shown in Figure 4–106.

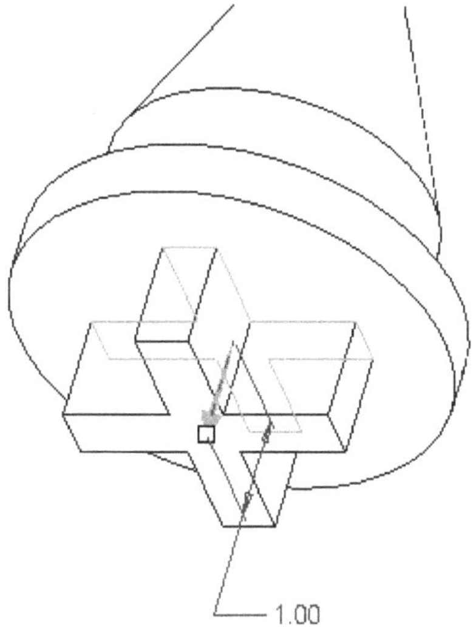

Figure 4–106

18. Click (Complete Feature).

19. Save the part and erase it from memory.

Practice 4d Create a Sketch

Practice Objectives

- Create a new sketch using the sketch and orientation planes.
- Create geometry using the mirror, trim, and fillet tools.
- Apply dimensions and constraints so that the sketch captures the design intent and is fully constrained.

In this practice, you will create a sketch in a new part. You will use many of the techniques used in previous practices. The sketch is shown in Figure 4–107.

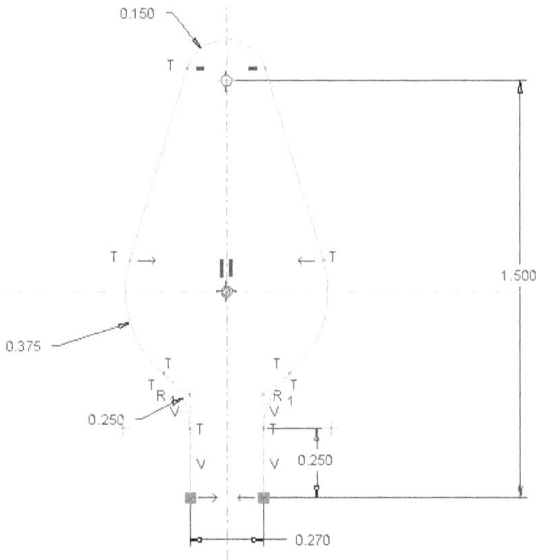

Figure 4–107

Task 3 - Create a new part.

1. Set the working directory to the *Chapter 04\practice 4d* folder.
2. Click (New) to create a new part, and set the *Name* to **clip**.
3. Click **OK**.
4. Set the model display as follows:
   - *(Datum Display Filters):* All off
   - *(Spin Center):* Off
   - *(Display Style):* (Shading)

Task 4 - Create the sketch.

1. Click (Sketch) to create the sketch feature. Use datum plane **FRONT** from the model tree as the sketching plane and click **Sketch**.

2. Click (Sketch View) to orient the model.

3. Sketch a circle at the intersection of the sketcher references as shown in Figure 4–108.

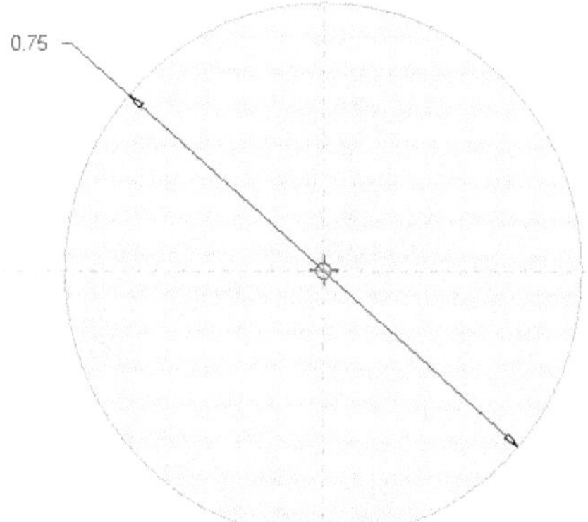

Figure 4–108

4. Select the *Diameter* dimension, right-click and select **Convert to Radius**, as shown in Figure 4–109.

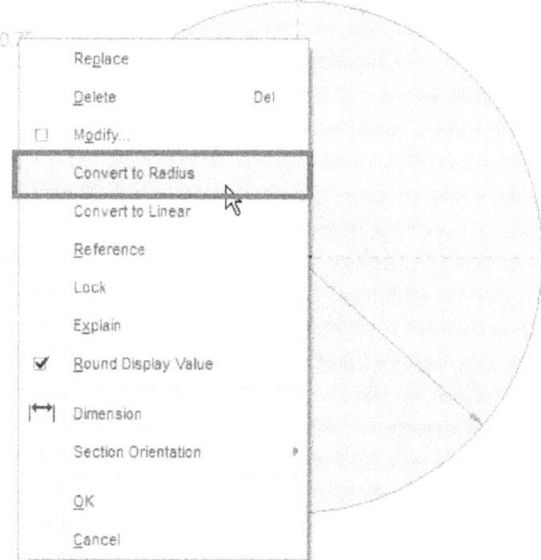

Figure 4–109

Depending on your system setup, the dimension may only display two decimals. You will learn how to change that in a later chapter.

5. Set the *Radius* to **0.375**, as shown in Figure 4–110.

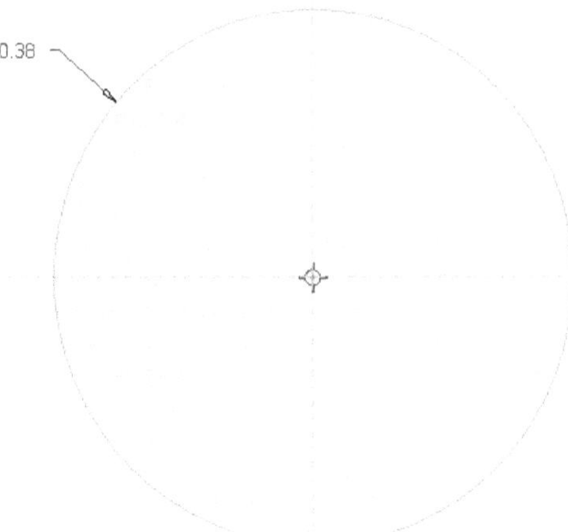

Figure 4–110

6. Sketch a second circle and dimension it with a *Radius* of **0.15**, as shown in Figure 4–111.

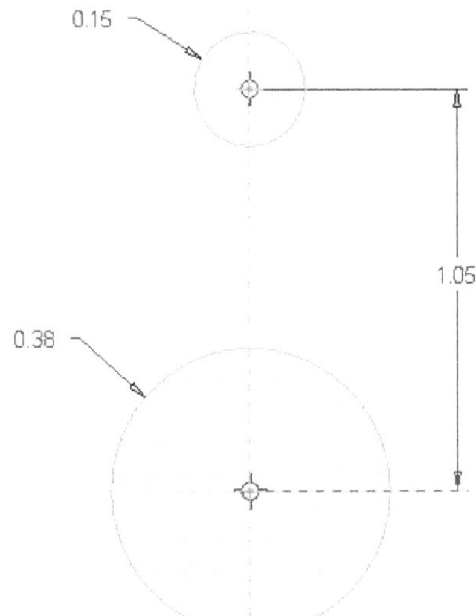

Figure 4–111

7. Expand the (Line) flyout and click (Line Tangent), then sketch two lines that are tangent to the circles, as shown in Figure 4–112.

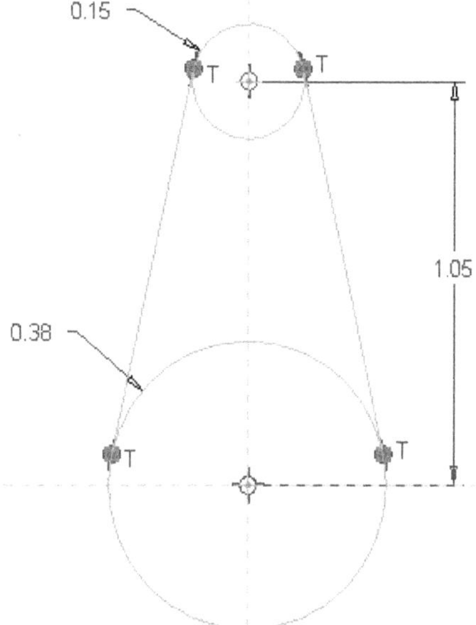

Figure 4–112

8. Sketch the vertical line shown in Figure 4–113. Remember to click the two points, then click the middle mouse button to complete the line chain. Do not worry about the exact length.

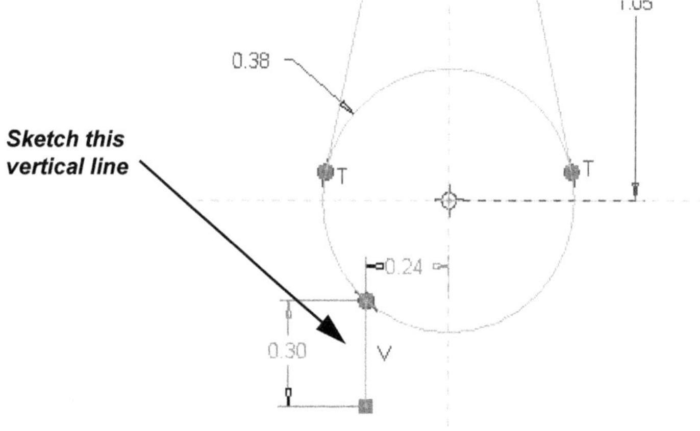

Figure 4–113

You can also sketch a centerline by clicking (Centerline) in the Sketching group.

9. Right-click and select **Construction Centerline**. Click anywhere on the vertical sketcher reference and select the vertical sketcher reference again. The vertical centerline displays as shown in Figure 4–114.

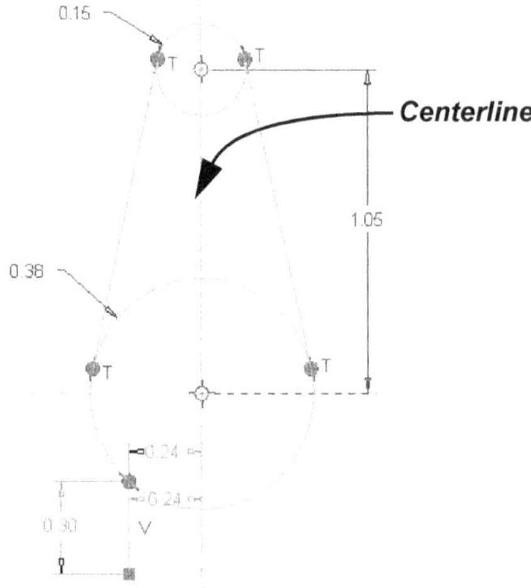

Figure 4–114

Task 5 - Mirror a sketched entity.

1. Select the vertical line sketched at the bottom of the lower circle, as shown in Figure 4–115.

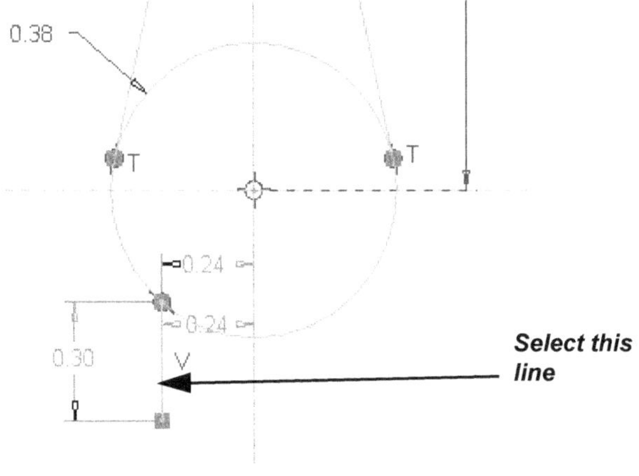

Figure 4–115

2. In the Editing group, click (Mirror) to create a mirror copy of this line.

3. Select the vertical centerline about which to mirror. The new line displays symmetric about the centerline with the original line, as shown in Figure 4–116.

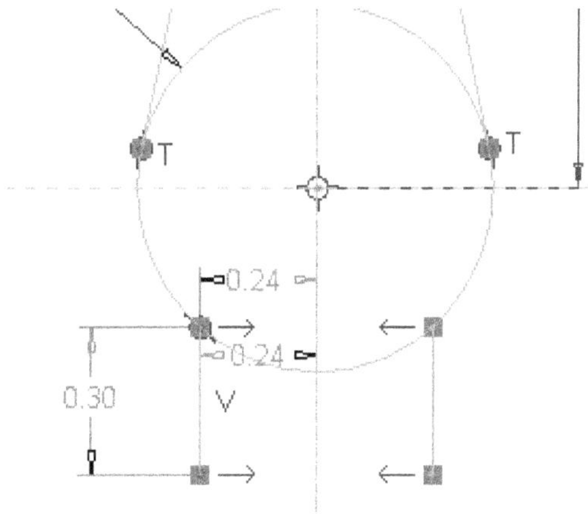

Figure 4–116

4. Click (Delete Segment) to trim the unnecessary segments of the circles. The sketch displays as shown in Figure 4–117.

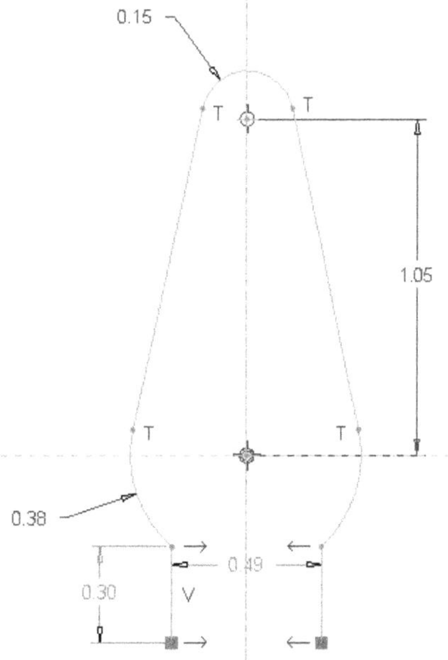

Figure 4–117

5. Click (Fillet) to sketch a circular fillet between the arc segment and vertical line. Select a location on the arc (as shown in Figure 4–118), for the first point. Select a location on the line for the second point as shown in Figure 4–118.

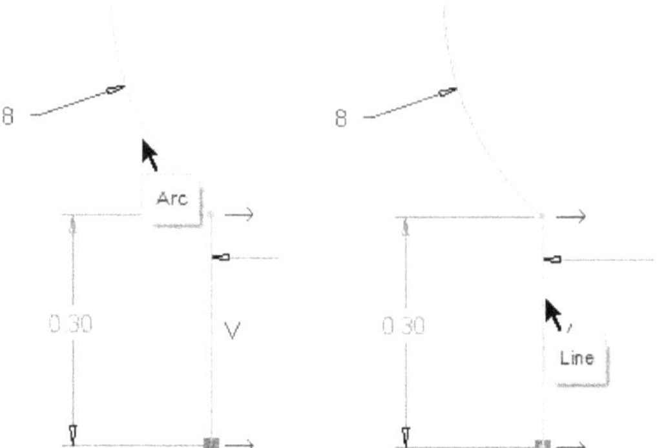

Figure 4–118

6. Sketch another circular fillet on the opposite side between the vertical line and arc segment. The sketch displays, as shown in Figure 4–119.

Sketch this circular fillet ***Sketch this circular fillet***

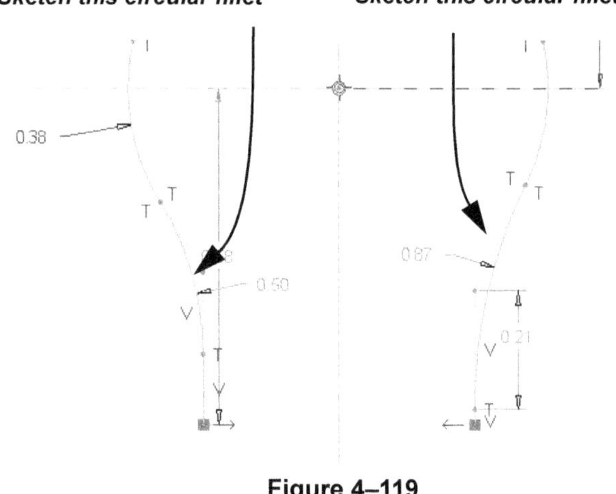

Figure 4–119

7. Note that the original entities have been trimmed.

8. Constrain the radii of the two fillet arcs to be equal, as shown in Figure 4–120.

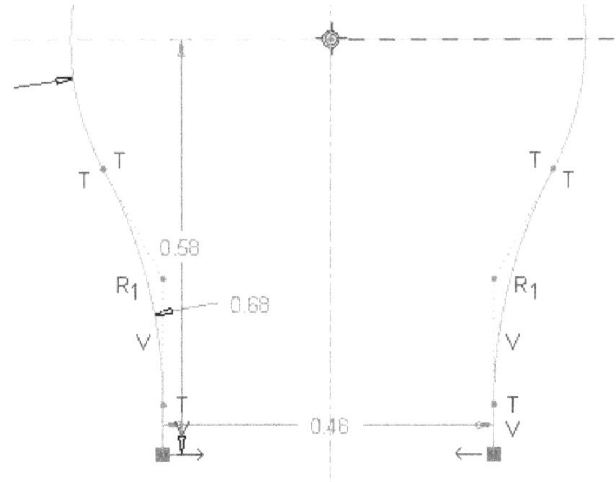

Figure 4–120

9. Create the constraints and dimensions in Figure 4–121 and modify the values.

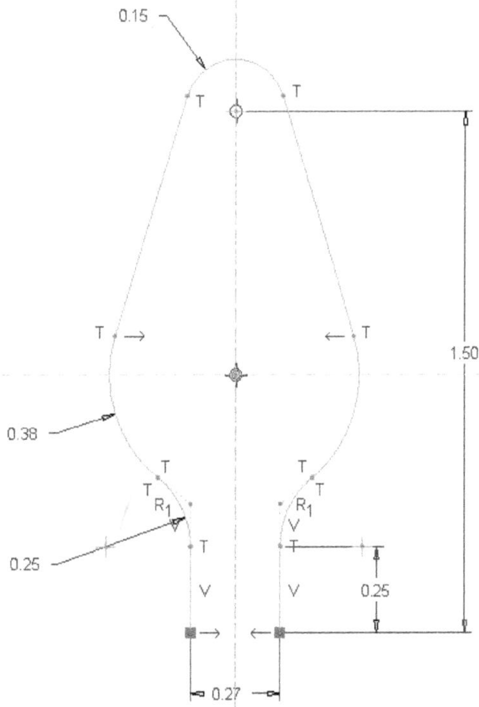

Figure 4–121

10. Complete the sketch. Press <Ctrl>+<D> to orient the model to the default orientation. It displays as shown in Figure 4–122.

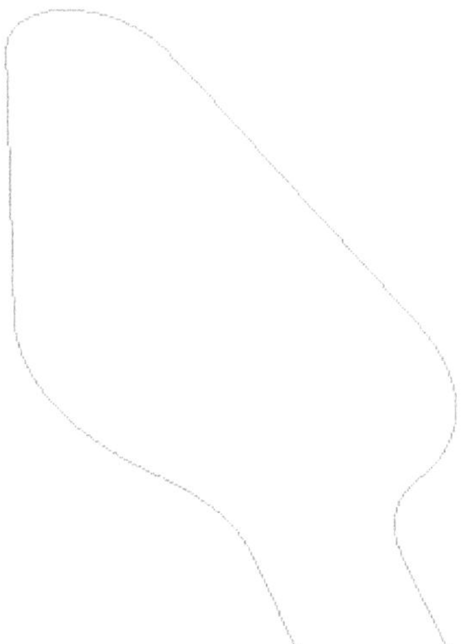

Figure 4–122

11. Save and erase the model.

Chapter Review Questions

1. Which of the following should be defined before sketching geometry? (Select all that apply.)
   a. Sketch Plane
   b. Sketch Orientation
   c. Constraints
   d. Sketcher References
2. = is used to apply the equal constraint to sketched geometry. Which of the following can be made equal with this constraint? (Select all that apply.)
   a. Angles
   b. Arc Length
   c. Lengths
   d. Radii
3. Which of the following icons enables you to create a three-point arc?
   a.
   b.
   c.
   d.
4. Construction entities can be used directly to create solid geometry.
   a. True
   b. False
5. Which of the following icons enables you to trim an entity to a corner?
   a.
   b.
   c.
   d.

6. Which of the following icons enables you to divide an entity without trimming it?
   a.
   b.
   c.
   d.
7. Which of the following are true regarding the **Delete Segment** option? (Select all that apply.)
   a. To access the **Delete Segment** option, click .
   b. To access the **Delete Segment** option, click .
   c. The **Delete Segment** option enables you to delete selected entities.
   d. The **Delete Segment** option enables you to sketch a spline through the entities to be deleted.
8. All constraints must be manually assigned to the sketched geometry.
   a. True
   b. False
9. Which of the following can be used to disable a constraint along with the right mouse button while sketching?
   a. <Tab>
   b. <Shift>
   c. <Ctrl>
   d. <Alt>
10. Which of the following can be used to create a reference in sketcher on the fly?
    a. <Tab>
    b. <Shift>
    c. <Ctrl>
    d. <Alt>

11. Which of the following can be used to disable the selection filter?

    a. <Tab>

    b. <Shift>

    c. <Ctrl>

    d. <Alt>

Command Summary

Button	Command	Location
	Centerline	• **Ribbon:** *Sketch* tab in the Sketching group
	Centered Rectangle	• **Ribbon:** *Sketch* tab in the Sketching group
	Corner	• **Ribbon:** *Sketch* tab in the Editing group
	Delete Segment	• **Ribbon:** *Sketch* tab in the Editing group
	Mirror	• **Ribbon:** *Sketch* tab in the Editing group
	Rectangle	• **Ribbon:** *Sketch* tab in the Sketching group
	Sketch Display Filters	• In-graphics toolbar

Creating the Base Feature

The first solid feature that you create in Creo Parametric is called the base feature. This feature forms the foundation on which other features are added to build the model. The first solid feature of the model adds material. You will learn how to effectively use basic base feature forms and to create extruded and revolved feature by sketching cross-sections and applying a depth or revolving it around an axis, respectively.

Learning Objectives in this Chapter

- Create a new part model based on a predefined templates.
- Understand the three default datum plane features that exist in a default template and how to control their visibility.
- Learn the different types of base features available in Creo Parametric and start the creation of the base feature.
- Start the creation of a sketch for the base feature by appropriately selecting the sketch and orientation planes.
- Create, dimension, and constrain 2D entities in a sketch so that they capture the design intent for the feature.
- Define the depth or angle and direction options to complete the base feature.
- Modify dimensional values using the Edit command.

5.1 Creating a New Part

The first solid feature in a new part is commonly referred to as the *base* feature, as shown in Figure 5–1. It is initially created by locating the new geometry using references, called *datum planes*. The base feature is a solid feature with a sketched cross-section. Once you create the initial geometry, the Creo Parametric software provides a variety of methods to edit and change it.

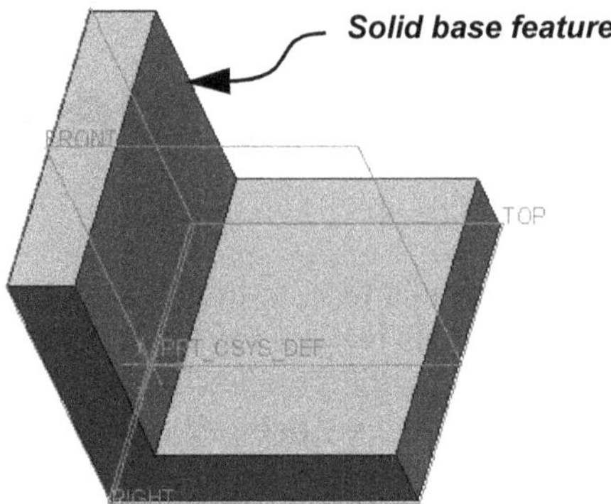

Figure 5–1

To create a new part, click (New) in the Quick Access Toolbar or the *Home* tab. The New dialog box opens, as shown in Figure 5–2. Enter the *Name* (i.e., filename) and optional *Common Name*.

Common Name is the more descriptive name of the model, e.g., 1/4-20 hex bolt. The software then creates the parameter ***PTC_COMMON_NAME*** *and puts the Common Name string into it.*

Figure 5–2

Templates

When you create a new part, Creo Parametric provides you with the option to use a template. Templates enable you to create new parts that have standardized configurations and settings. This ensures that all models start with consistent and company-specific settings (if required). Templates contain useful features and settings, such as view orientations, reference datum plane features, and unit systems.

Select the type of object that you want to create from the list in the *Type* area in the New dialog box. For most object types, the **Use default template** option displays at the bottom of the dialog box. The default template for parts uses the Inch-Pound-Second system of units, but your company may set a default template that uses a different system of units. To use a different template, clear the **Usedefault templat**e option.

You can create your own templates for creating new parts.

Once you have selected the type of model to create and have entered the filename, click **OK**. If you cleared the **Use default template** option, the New File Options dialog box opens, as shown in Figure 5–3.

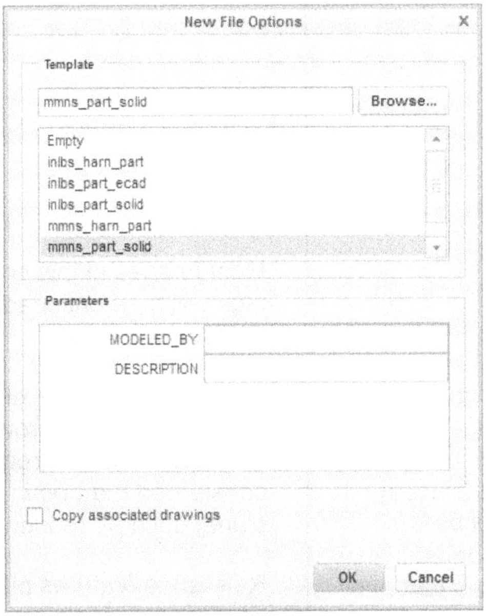

Figure 5–3

Note that you can select another template from the list in the dialog box. If you want to create a part with customized settings, select **Empty**.

Default Datum Planes

It is important to use the default datum planes when creating the base feature. Default datum planes are non-solid features that only exist in space; that is, they do not have thickness or mass. They are considered reference features because they are used as references when creating features. They also help you to orient the part. Every part template provided with Creo Parametric contains the following reference features, as shown in Figure 5–4.

- Three orthogonal datum planes named **RIGHT**, **TOP**, and **FRONT**. These are referred to as default datum planes.
- Default datum coordinate system labeled **PRT_CSYS_DEF**.

By default, the datum tags or names are toggled off. To display the tags, click (Plane Tag Display) in the Show group in the View tab.

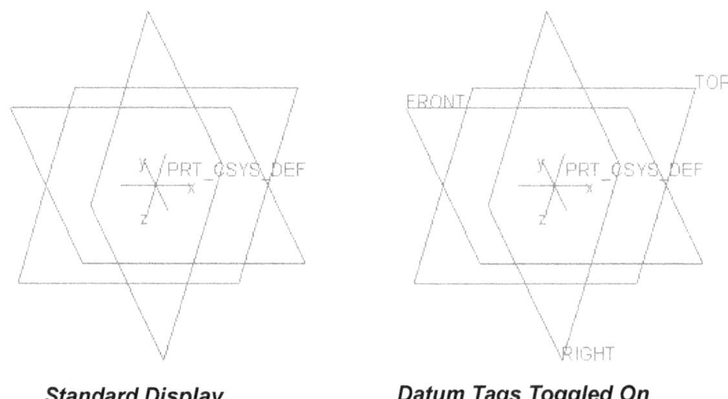

Standard Display ***Datum Tags Toggled On***

Figure 5–4

Most images in this course will not display datum tags. Datum tags will be mentioned in this chapter to help you familiarize yourself with them.

Default datum planes are very useful when your part has many non-planar surfaces. They can act as references for reorienting the part and creating features.

The datum planes extend to fit the part as its size increases. The datum planes are brown when viewed from one direction and gray when viewed from the opposite direction. The brown side is considered the *dominant* side. Actions to a selected datum plane, such as reorienting, are applied to the dominant side.

Reference features play an important role in the development of your model. While a part can be created without default datum planes, they are strongly recommended.

Model Tree

When you create a new part using a template provided with Creo Parametric, the model tree lists the three default datum planes and the default datum coordinate system, as shown in Figure 5–5.

Figure 5–5

Solid features with sketched cross-sections can add or remove material. Features that remove material are casually referred to as cuts. The first solid feature in a part must add material.

Feature Forms

You can use one of four basic feature forms to create the first solid protrusion. They are described as follows:

Feature Form	2D Cross-Section	3D Base Feature
Extrude	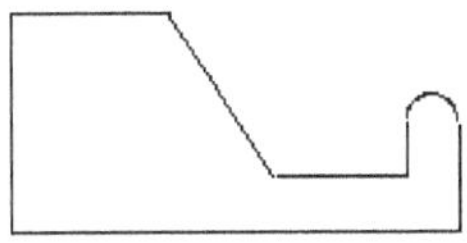	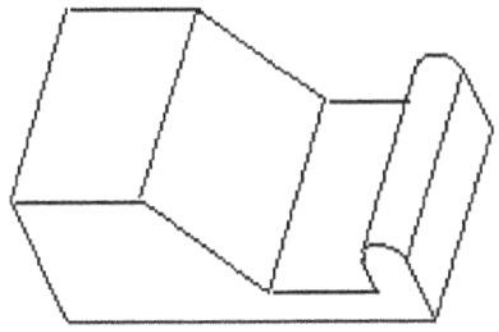
Revolve	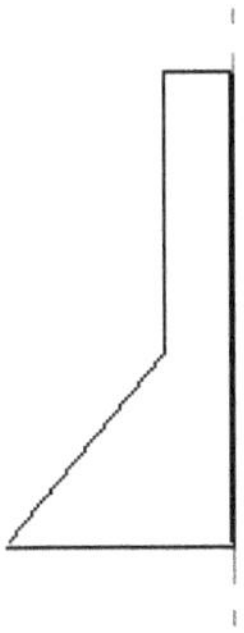	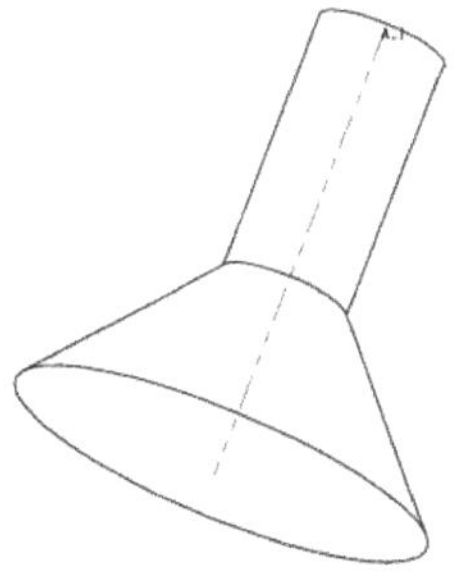
Blend	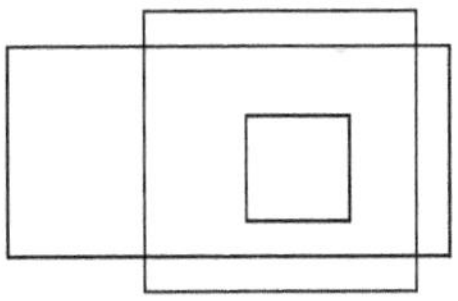	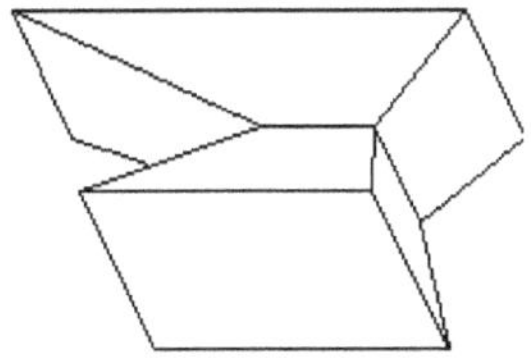

Sweep

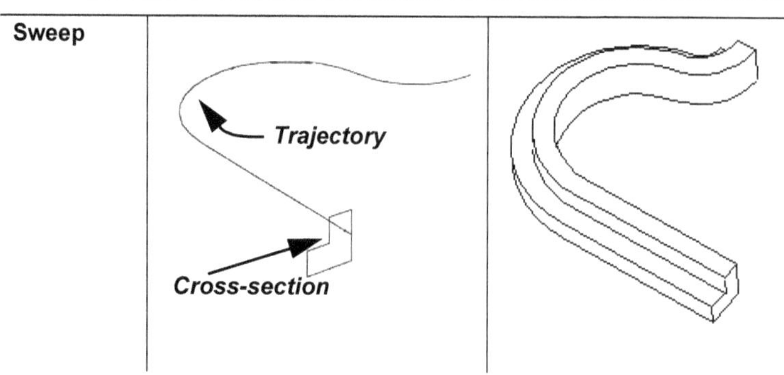

This chapter focuses on extruded and revolved solid features. Other feature forms are discussed later in this training guide.

5.2 Extruded Form

To use the extrude form, ensure that the *Model* tab is selected and click (Extrude) in the Shapes group. The *Extrude* dashboard displays as shown in Figure 5–6. You can use the message window to guide you through the creation of an extruded feature. It displays at the bottom of the main window.

Figure 5–6

The **Placement** panel heading initially displays in red, indicating that a feature section has not been fully defined. You can define the cross-section of the feature by sketching it or by selecting an existing sketch.

Selecting the Section

If you select an existing sketch to create the section, it is copied into the current sketch with an associative link. Changes made to the parent sketch update the extrusion and vice-versa. To break the associative link between the feature and the selected sketch, click **Unlink** in the Placement panel.

Sketching the Section

To sketch a section, select a plane on which to sketch and begin sketching. This method does not open the Sketch dialog box, and is the most efficient method. Note that you can also select the plane prior to clicking (Extrude), which achieves the same result.

If you require more control over the sketch orientation, use one of the following methods:

- Click **Placement** and click **Define** in the Placement panel.
- Right-click and select **Define Internal Sketch**.

With the last two options, the Sketch dialog box opens, as shown in Figure 5–7. It enables you to select the **Sketch Plane** and **Sketch Orientation** references. Generally, the orientation references are already selected based on the selection of the sketch plane. However, they can be redefined, if required. Click **Sketch** to sketch the section.

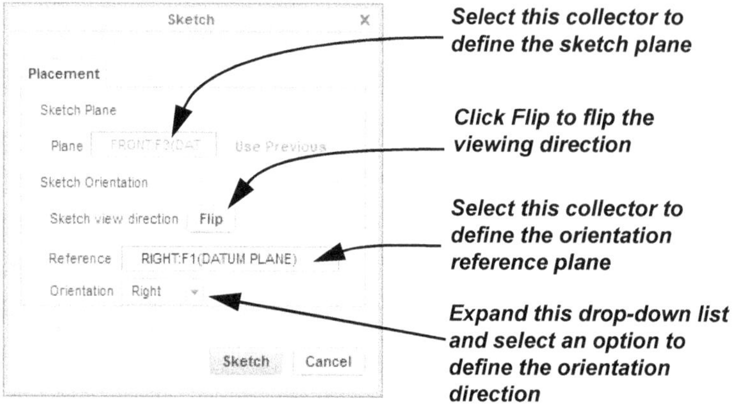

Figure 5–7

Sketch Plane

You must select a plane on which to sketch the section. The sketch plane can be any one of the three default datum planes. A 2D sketch is created on the selected datum plane and the protrusion is extruded in a direction normal to that plane. The default orientation of the model depends on the selected datum plane.

For example, consider the cylindrical extruded protrusion shown in Figure 5–8. The 2D section is sketched on datum plane **TOP** and extruded in a direction normal to the datum plane. The default orientation displays as shown in Figure 5–9.

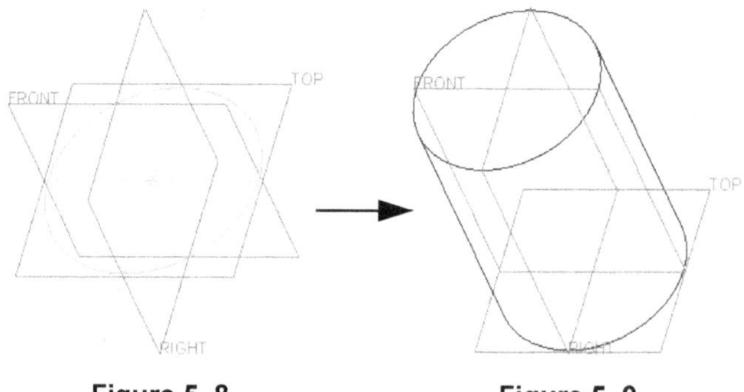

Figure 5–8 Figure 5–9

The base feature becomes a child of the datum plane you select as a sketch plane.

Similarly, the section could have been sketched on datum plane **FRONT**, as shown in Figure 5–10, or on datum plane RIGHT, as shown in Figure 5–11.

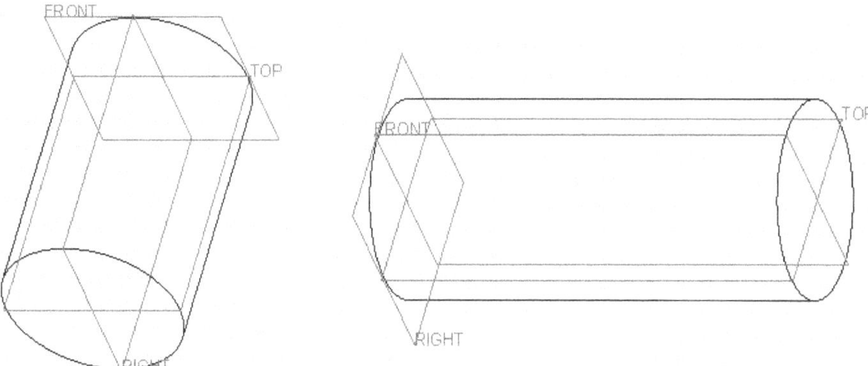

Figure 5–10 **Figure 5–11**

An arrow displays next to the datum plane when you select the sketch plane. The arrow indicates the direction in which you are viewing the sketch plane, not the direction of extrusion. When selecting a datum plane as the sketch plane, the default viewing direction is always toward its dominant side. For example, if you select datum plane **RIGHT** as a sketch plane, the brown side of the datum plane (the dominant side) displays while sketching. The protrusion is then extruded toward you, normal to the plane.

In Figure 5–12, datum plane **RIGHT** is selected as the sketch plane. The direction arrow indicates the direction in which you view the plane while sketching. The resulting protrusion is extruded in the opposite direction (i.e., toward you).

When sketching features, protrusions extrude toward you and cuts extrude away from you.

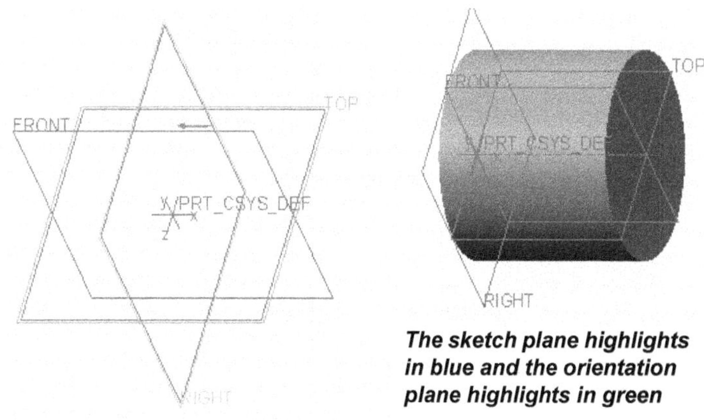

The sketch plane highlights in blue and the orientation plane highlights in green

Figure 5–12

To change the viewing direction and extrude the protrusion in the opposite direction (i.e., away from the non-dominant side), click **Flip** in the Sketch dialog box or on the head of the arrow. The protrusion extrudes in the opposite direction, as shown in Figure 5–13.

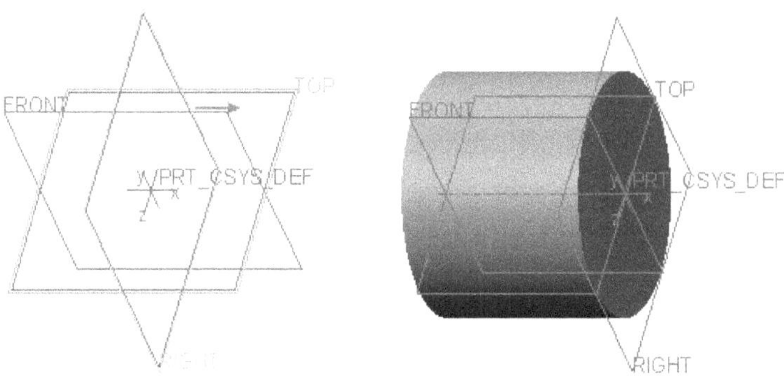

Figure 5–13

Sketch Orientation

The Creo Parametric software does not automatically reorient the part to make the sketch plane parallel to the screen when the Sketch tab becomes active.

The Creo Parametric software provides you with the option to select or change an orientation plane. The orientation plane is a horizontal or vertical reference plane that is normal to the sketch plane. It is used to orient the part while sketching. You can create your sketch entities while the model is in any orientation.

- To orient the part while sketching, click (Sketch View) in the In-graphics toolbar or in the Setup group in the *Sketch* tab.
- To make the sketching plane parallel to the screen automatically, select **File>Options>Sketcher** and select **Make the sketching plane parallel to the screen**. You can also change the **sketcher_starts_in_2d** to **yes** in the configuration editor.

Always consider your design intent before accepting default selections.

When the model does not contain a planar surface perpendicular to sketching plane, the software uses a projection of the X-axis from the default coordinate system as the horizontal orientation for the sketch. If the model contains planar surfaces perpendicular to the sketching plane, then the software provides a default sketch orientation plane. You can accept the default plane or override it by selecting your own reference. Use the **Orientation** menu to select the direction for the datum plane to face.

The base feature becomes a child of the datum plane that you select as the sketch orientation plane.

For example, if you select datum plane **FRONT** as your sketch plane, you can select either datum plane **RIGHT** or **TOP** as your sketch orientation plane. The sketch orientation plane can be selected to face top, bottom, right, or left.

In the example shown in Figure 5–14, datum plane **RIGHT** is selected as the sketch plane. Datum plane **FRONT** could be selected to face bottom or datum plane **TOP** could be selected to face left to obtain the orientation shown in Figure 5–15.

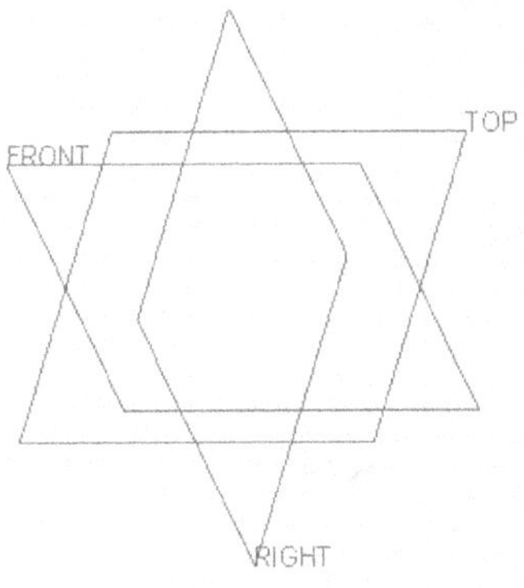

Figure 5–14

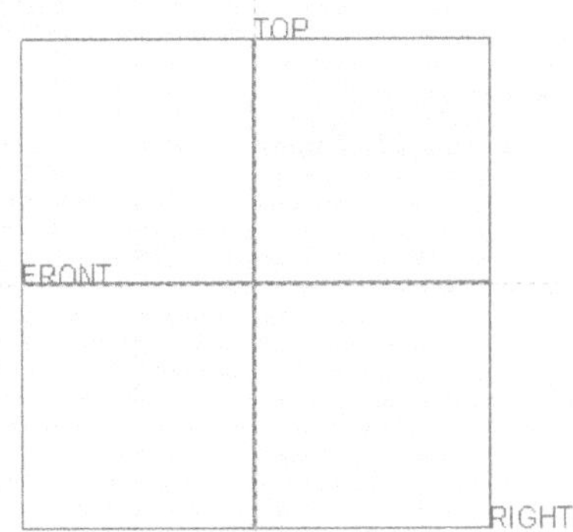

Figure 5–15

Sketching

Once the sketch references have been established, the *Sketch* tab become active, as shown in Figure 5–16. The other tabs are still available for selection, but some of the icons in the tabs are dimmed, indicating they are not currently available.

Sketch tab

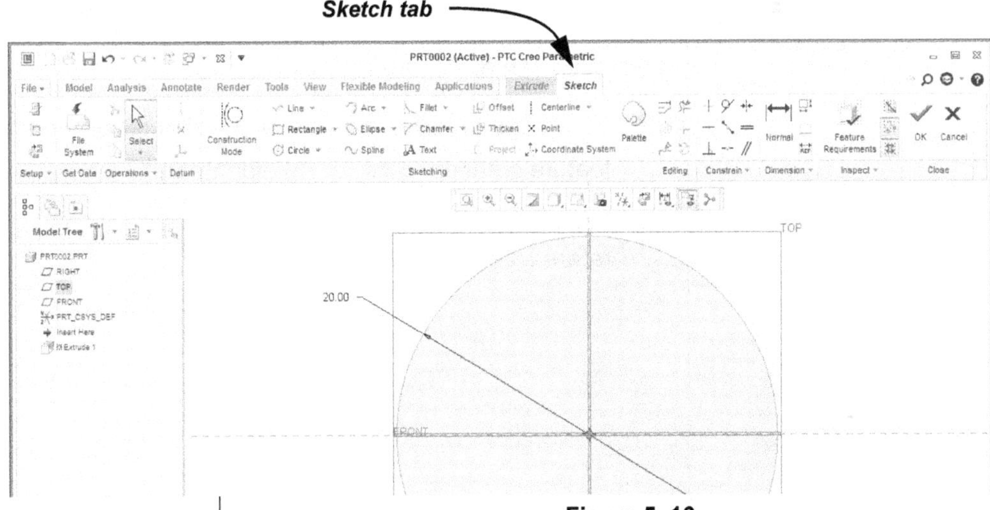

Figure 5–16

Sketched geometry must always be located with respect to existing features in the part. Before the base feature is created, the only existing features in the part are the three default datum planes and the default datum coordinate system.

In this situation, the Creo Parametric software automatically selects the two datum planes that are normal to the sketch plane. Any geometry you sketch is aligned or dimensioned with respect to these references. To change sketcher or add additional references, click (References), which opens the References dialog box, as shown in Figure 5–17.

References are represented by cyan dashed lines that are projected onto the sketch plane.

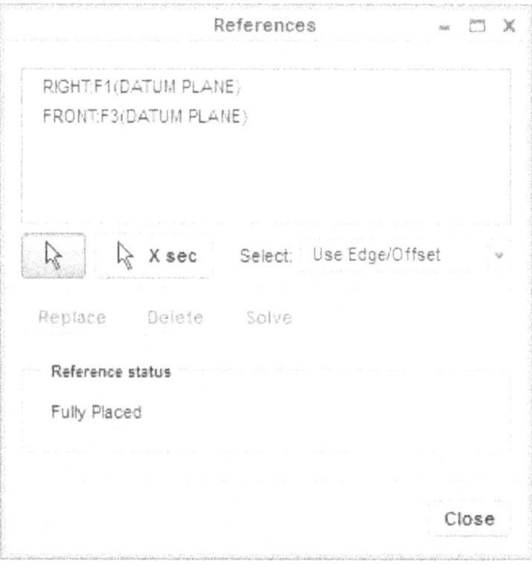

Figure 5–17

Setup

The Setup group in the sketch Ribbon enables you to specify and change your sketcher options. References, orientation, and direction can all be changed using the icons or the **Setup** menu.

- To change the sketch plane, orientation plane, or direction of feature creation, click (Sketch Setup).
- The Sketch dialog box opens and enables you to change the references.

- You can also use the **Setup** menu to override the direction reference as shown Figure 5–18.

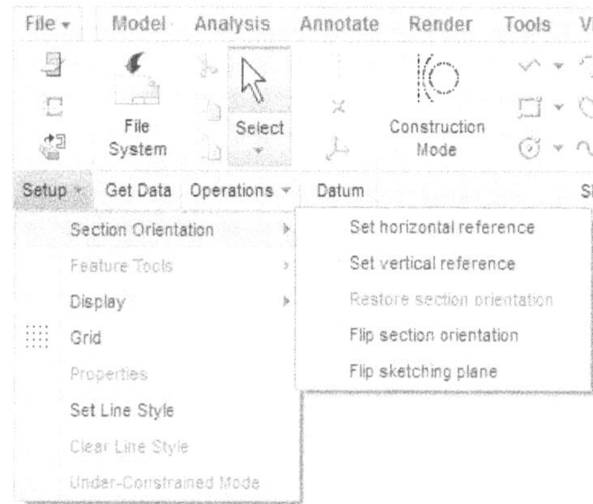

Figure 5–18

The geometry remains in the default orientation once the *Sketch* tab has been activated. To reorient so that the selected sketch plane is facing the screen, click (Sketch View) in the In-graphics toolbar or in the *Sketch* tab. This makes it easier to sketch your geometry.

*You can also right-click and select **OK** to complete the section.*

Using all the mentioned tools, you can complete the sketch.

When you have finished sketching, click (OK) to complete the section.

The Creo Parametric software provides a number of options to define the depth of extruded features. Many of these options enable you to reference other geometry to control the depth. For an extruded base feature, the depth is commonly defined with a dimension that can be easily modified. The tab for the extruded protrusion contains an entry field in which you can enter a value for the depth, as shown in Figure 5–19.

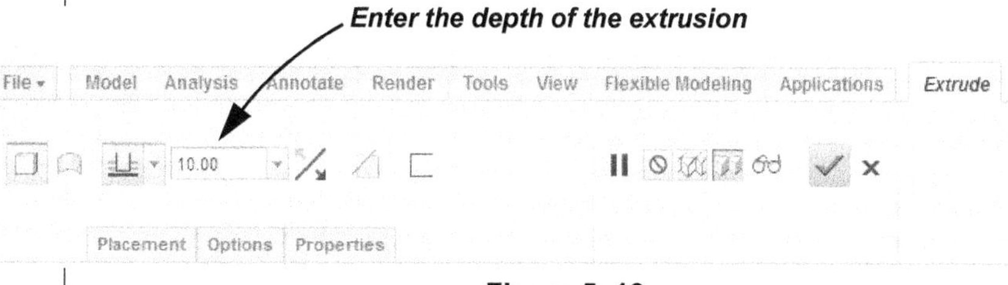

Figure 5–19

Alternatively, you can dynamically adjust the depth by dragging the handles that display on the model, as shown in Figure 5–20.

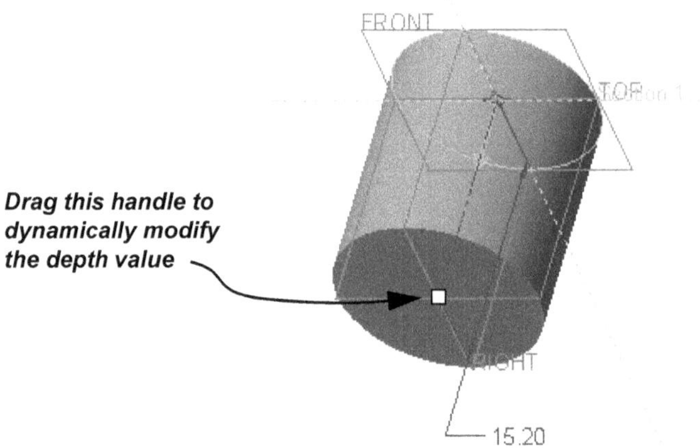

Figure 5–20

Use ✕ (Cancel Feature) *to cancel a feature.*

Once the depth of the protrusion is defined, you can complete the feature by clicking (Complete Feature). To preview the feature geometry before completing the feature, click (Verify Mode), (Attached), or (Un-Attached). The model is shaded differently depending on which icon is selected. The options are described as follows. Click (Resume), if (Verify Mode) was clicked, to resume the feature after previewing.

Options	Description
(Verify Mode)	Displays the geometry as it is going to be when the feature is completed.
(Attached)	Displays the geometry as it is going to be when the feature is completed and enables you to dynamically change the geometry.
(Un-Attached)	Displays the outline of the geometry and enables you to dynamically change the geometry.
(No Preview)	Does not display the geometry.

The model tree updates to list the base feature, as shown in Figure 5–21. The base feature displays in the model tree feature list after the default datum planes and the default datum coordinate system.

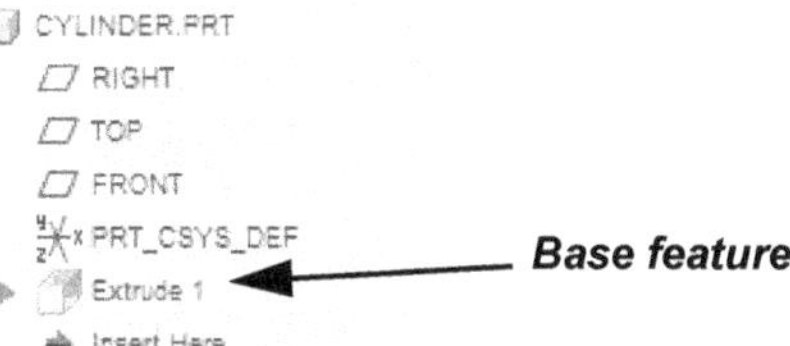

Figure 5–21

After you have created a feature, it is recommended to make changes, many of which can be initiated through the model tree. If you select the name of the feature in the model tree and right-click, a contextual menu displays with options for making changes. The (Edit) option accesses the dimensions for the feature. Any dimensions created for the sketch or depth of the feature become visible and you can modify them by double-clicking on a dimension and entering a new value in the field that displays, as shown in Figure 5–22. If the dimension has an open arrowhead, you can dynamically modify the dimension.

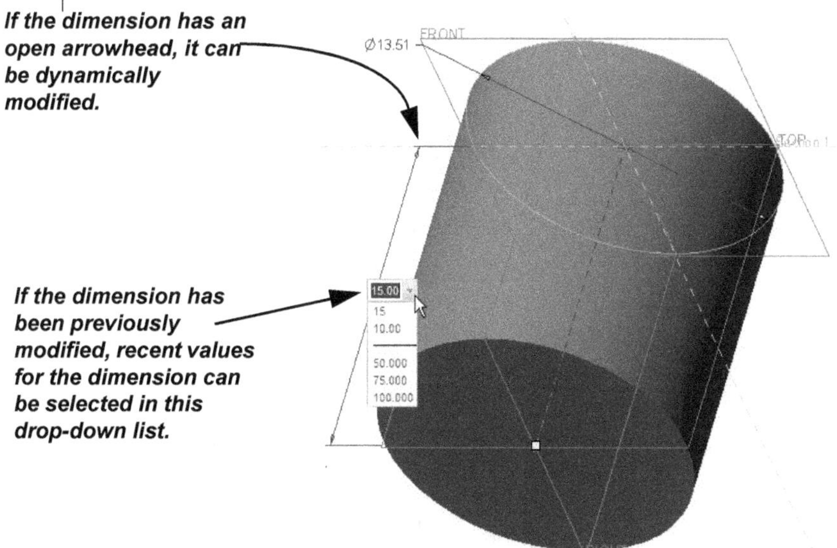

Figure 5–22

After you enter new values for dimensions, click (Regenerate) in the Quick Access Toolbar or in the *Model* tab, or press <Ctrl>+<G> to incorporate the changes. Alternatively, you can click twice in the graphics window (do not double-click) to force a regeneration.

You can change the default feature name using either of the following methods:

- Select the feature name in the model tree, right-click, and select **Rename**. Enter the new name in the model tree.
- Select the feature name twice in the model tree (do not double-click). Enter the new name in the model tree.

Assigning your own names to features can help you locate and identify features in the model tree more easily, as shown in Figure 5–23.

*Feature names cannot contain spaces and special characters, such as !, #, and *.*

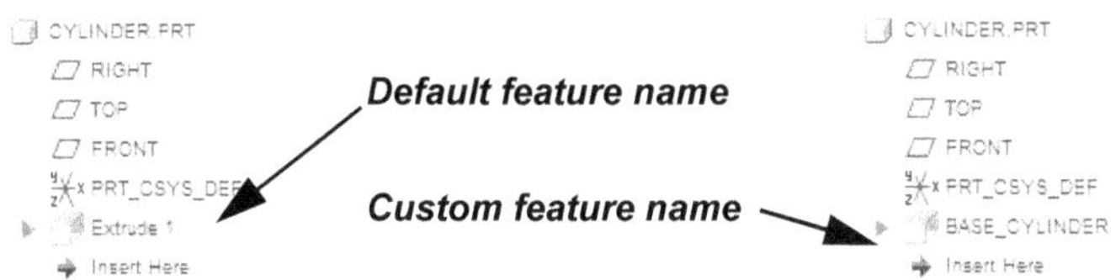

Figure 5–23

The (Edit Definition) option in the contextual menu opens the tab for the feature. From there you can make changes to the sketch for the feature (right-click and select **Edit Internal Sketch** or click **Edit** in the Placement panel) and change the direction of extrusion by clicking (Change Depth Direction).

5.3 Revolved Form

Revolved features are created in a similar manner to the extruded features. The main differences are that a revolve must contain reference an axis of revolution, which may be internal to the sketch, or an external axis, and an angle of revolution is defined instead of a depth.

To start the creation of the revolve, click (Revolve) in the Shapes group in the *Model* tab. The dashboard for revolved features displays, as shown in Figure 5–24.

Figure 5–24

As with Extruded features, you can select an existing sketch to revolve or you can create a new sketch. Sketches are initiated in the same manner as extruded features, already discussed. Sketching the geometry for the revolve feature can be done using the sketching options and editing tools which again were discussed previously.

Axis of Revolution

When you create the revolve feature, you have to specify its axis of revolution. This can be included in the sketch, or you can assign it outside the sketch.

If the axis of revolution is included in the sketch, the *Axis collector* field indicates that an internal centerline exists (**InternalCL**), as shown in Figure 5–25.

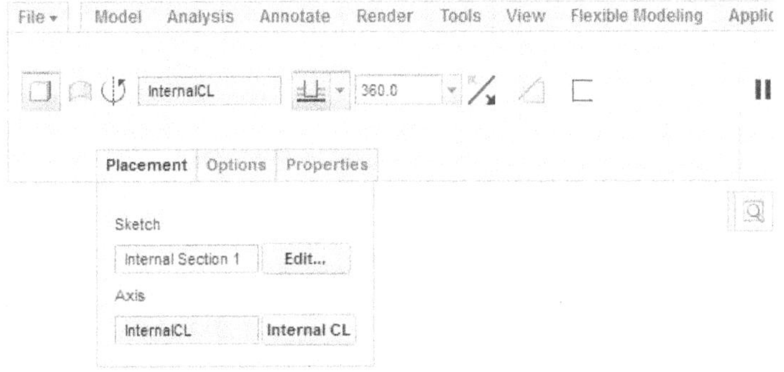

Figure 5–25

You can click (Centerline) from the Datum group to create a geometry centerline, or (Centerline) from the Sketching group to create a construction centerline.

If a sketch contains more than one centerline, the first geometry centerline created is used as the axis of revolution. If multiple centerlines exist in the sketch, select the appropriate centerline, right-click, and select **Designate Axis of Revolution**.

To clear the internal centerline, click **InternalCL** in the Placement panel, select the *Axis* collector, and select a new reference. The internal centerline in the sketch can be reused at any time by clicking **InternalCL** again.

If the axis of revolution is not included in the sketch, the *Axis collector* field indicates that you must select a reference: an existing straight curve, edge, axis, or the axis of a coordinate system that lies on the sketching plane.

The entities of the section must all lie on one side of the axis of revolution. The section cannot cross the centerline. These situations are described as follows:

Sketch	Shaft Geometry	Description
		Closed sketch with centerline aligned to one section edge.
		Closed sketch with centerline offset from section. The result is a hole in the revolve.
	Invalid	Closed sketch with centerline intersecting section. A revolve feature cannot have sketched geometry on both sides of the axis of rotation, since the geometry would overlap.

When creating a diameter dimension for a revolved section, three mouse selections are required. Two possibilities are shown in Figure 5–26.

To change the angle direction of the revolve to the other side of the sketch, click (Change Angle Direction).

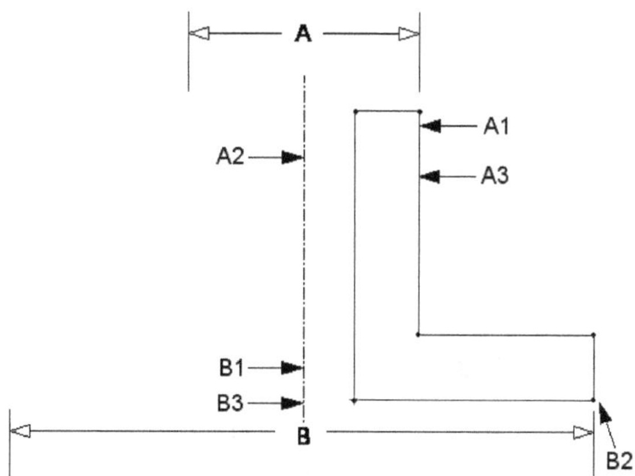

Figure 5–26

A revolve feature is automatically revolved 360° in the direction of feature creation. You can enter or select a different value in the *Revolve* tab, as shown in Figure 5–27.

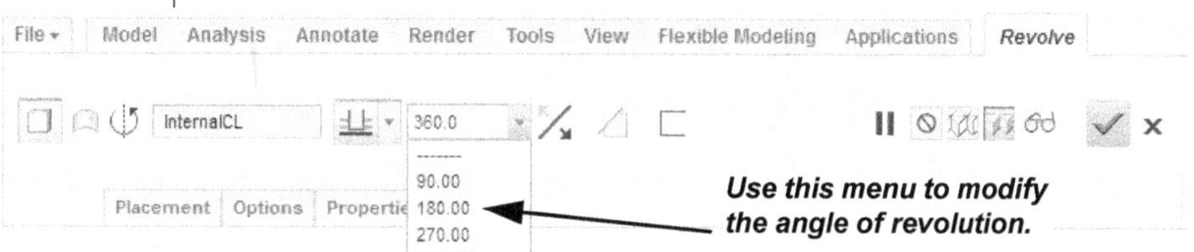

Figure 5–27

The angle value can also be defined by dragging the handles on the feature, as shown in Figure 5–28.

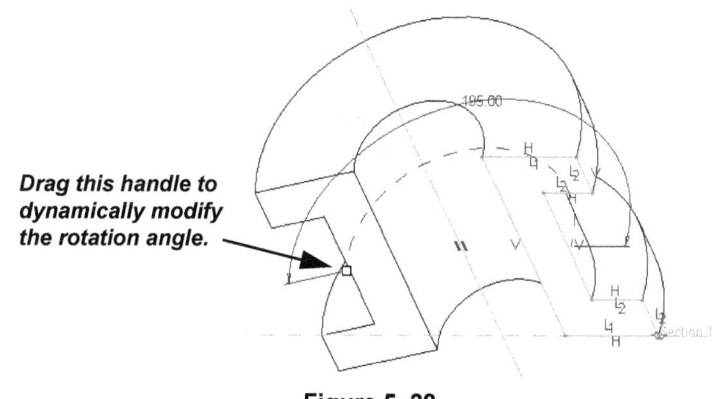

Figure 5–28

Angle Options

Additional angle options can be assigned to a revolve to capture the required design intent. describes the angle options available for revolutions.

Icon	Description
(Variable)	Revolve from sketch plane by specified angle value.
(Symmetric)	Revolve on both sides of sketch plane by half the specified angle value in each direction.
(To Selected)	Revolve to selected point, curve, plane, or surface.

Side Options

By default, a revolved feature is created in one direction from the sketching plane. If you expand the Options panel in the *Revolve* tab, you can define an angle for the second direction. This enables you to assign different angle options in each direction, as shown in Figure 5–29.

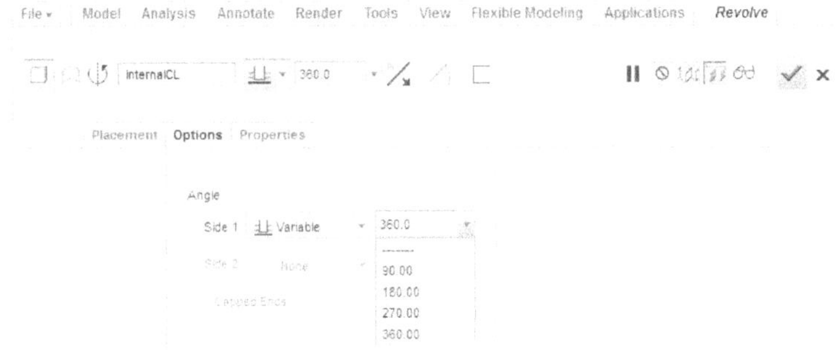

Figure 5–29

The angle options for Side 2 are the same as those for Side 1, except that the **Symmetric** side option is not available. If you have selected the **Symmetric depth** option for Side 1, the feature is revolved in both directions and the variable angle value you define is divided equally between the two directions.

When the feature is fully defined, click (Complete Feature) to complete the revolve.

Practice 5a Extruded Base Features

Practice Objectives

- Create two new part models using a predefined template.
- Create two extruded base features using default datum planes, dimensions, and constraints.

In this practice, you will create a new model using the default template provided in the Creo Parametric software. The first feature in any new model is called the base feature. The references selected when creating the base feature determine the model's default orientation. You will create extruded solids as the base features, as shown in Figure 5–30 and Figure 5–31. Sketch the extrusions using the rectangle and circle entities.

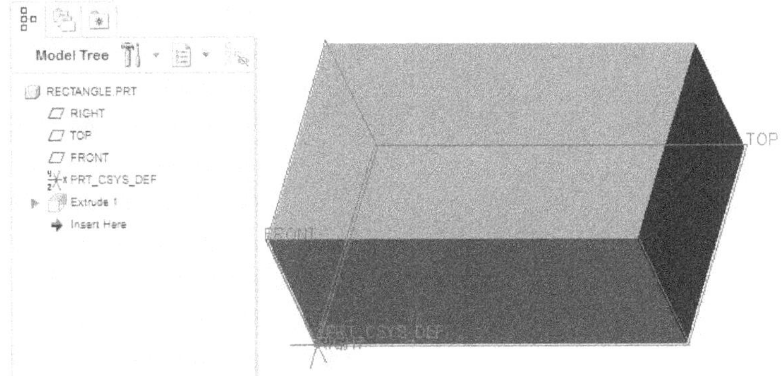

Figure 5–30

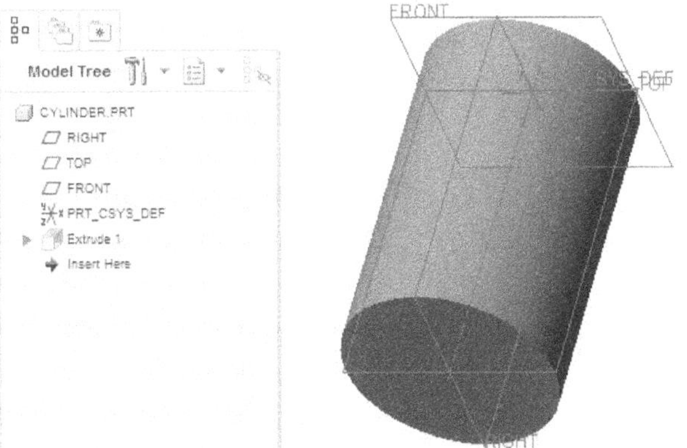

Figure 5–31

Task 1 - Create a new part using the default part template.

1. Set your working directory to the *Chapter 05/practice 5a* folder.

2. Click (New).

3. In the New dialog box, select the **Part** option, if required.

4. Set the *Name* to **rectangle** and verify that the **Use default template** option is selected. The New dialog box opens as shown in Figure 5–32.

When you create a new file or open an existing file in any mode, the software automatically knows the correct extension. You do not need to enter the extension with the filename.

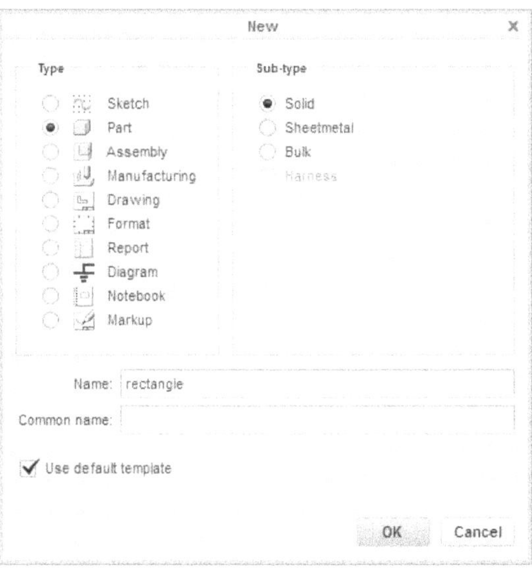

Figure 5–32

5. Click **OK**. The Creo Parametric window displays the rectangle model as the active model. The model only contains the default datum planes and coordinate system from the default template, as displayed in the model tree and main window.

Task 2 - Select the feature type of the first feature.

1. Set the model display as follows:

   - *(Datum Display Filters)*: All On
   - *(Spin Center)*: Off
   - *(Display Style)*: (Shading)

2. Select the *View* tab and click (Plane Tag Display) in the Show group to toggle on the datum plane tags. This displays the names of the datum planes as shown in Figure 5–33.

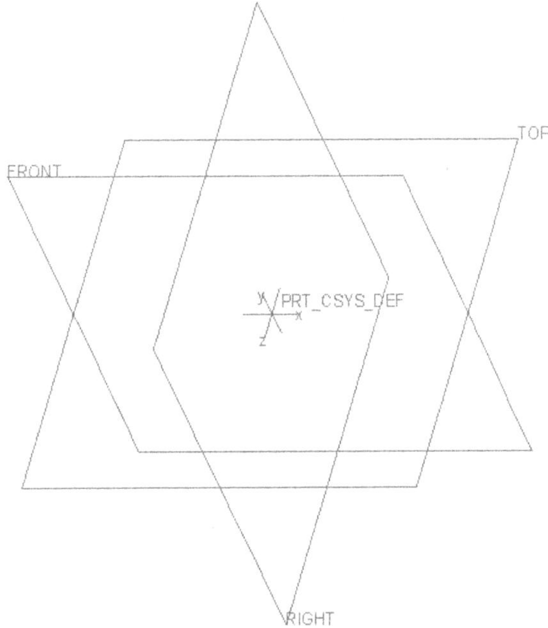

Figure 5–33

3. Select the *Model* tab, and in the Shapes group, click (Extrude) to create an extruded base feature. The *Extrude* dashboard displays as shown in Figure 5–34.

Figure 5–34

Task 3 - Sketch the section for the extruded base feature.

The system-defined reference or orientation can be changed if different references are required.

1. Select datum plane **TOP** as the sketch plane. Creo Parametric automatically chooses datum plane **RIGHT** as the orientation reference, and opens the *Sketch* tab in the ribbon.

2. The software automatically selects the two datum planes that are normal to the sketch plane as sketcher references. These references are light blue.

3. In the In-graphics toolbar, click (Sketch View) to reorient the model into 2D for sketching, as shown in Figure 5–35.

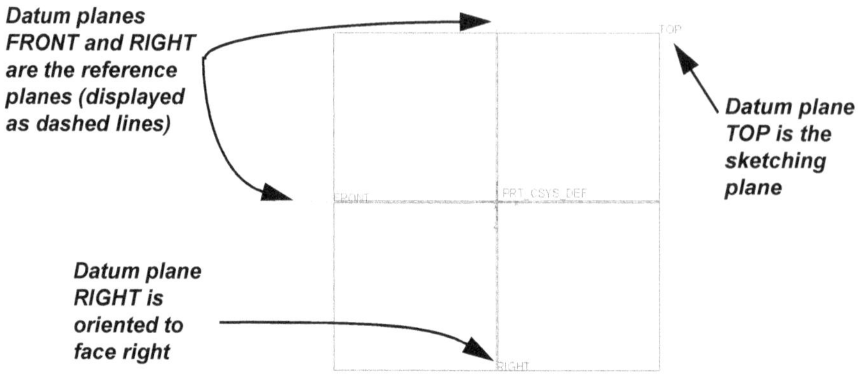

Figure 5–35

Task 4 - Sketch the rectangular section.

1. In the Sketch group, click (Rectangle) to sketch the base feature as a rectangular section.
2. Start the sketch by selecting the intersection of datum planes **FRONT** and **RIGHT**, as shown in Figure 5–36.
3. Drag the cursor upwards and to the right. Select the location shown in , to define the rectangular shape.

*To delete a sketcher entity, click (Select), select the entity, and press <Delete> or right-click and select **Delete**.*

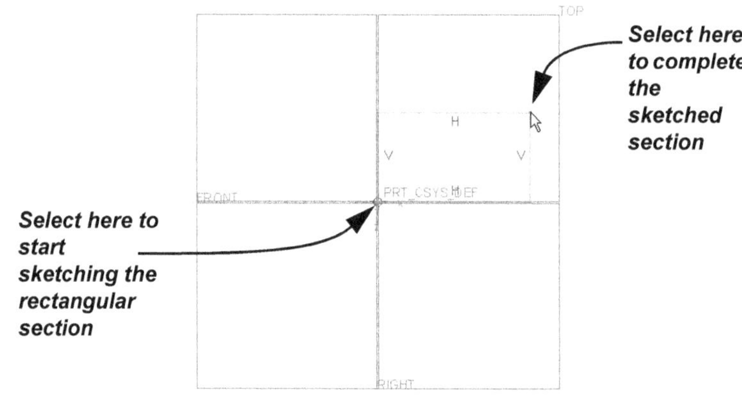

Figure 5–36

4. Click the middle mouse button to complete the rectangle. The software automatically dimensions and constrains the sketch.

You can also click <Esc> to clear the command.

5. Double-click on the *Vertical Dimension* of the rectangle and set it to **15**. Press <Enter> to accept the new value.

6. Double-click on the *Horizontal Dimension* of the rectangle and set it to **25**. Press <Enter> to accept the new value. The sketch displays as shown in Figure 5–37.

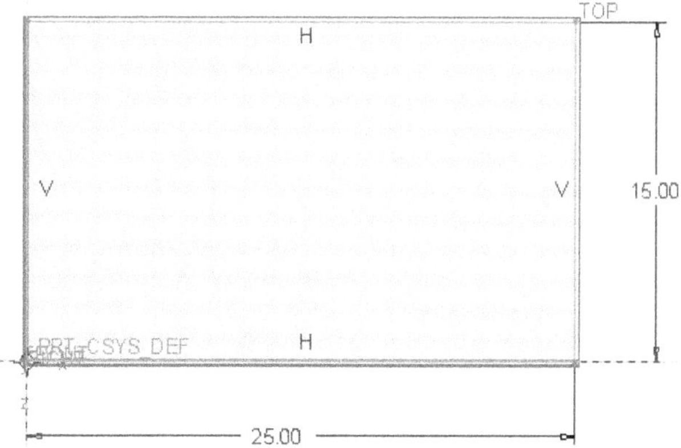

Figure 5–37

7. Click ✓ (OK) to complete the sketch and exit the *Sketcher* tab.

Task 5 - Define the depth of the extrusion.

1. The Creo Parametric software automatically applies a default depth value for the extrusion. This default value can be accepted or changed. Press <Ctrl>+<D> to orient the model to its default orientation.

*You might have to pan (<Shift> + middle mouse button) and/or zoom out (<Ctrl> + middle mouse button) to display the entire model. Select and drag the depth handle on the model to change the depth dimension to approximately **7**, as shown in Figure 5–38.*

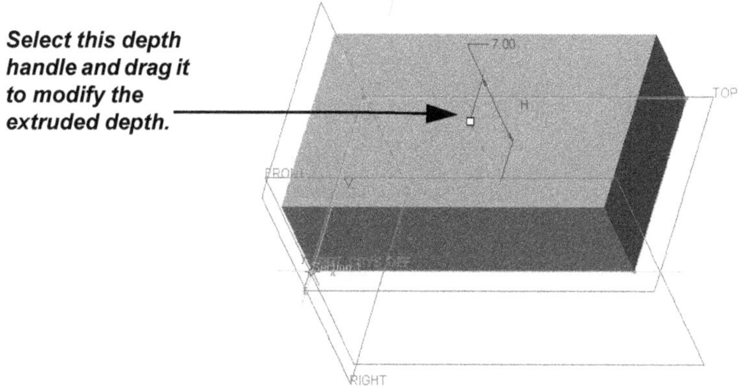

Figure 5–38

2. You can also modify the depth value in the *Extrude* dashboard to achieve an exact value. Set the *Depth* to **10**, as shown in Figure 5–39.

Figure 5–39

3. Complete the rectangular feature by clicking (Complete Feature) in the *Extrude* dashboard.

4. Orient the model to the default view by pressing <Ctrl>+<D>. The model and model tree display as shown in Figure 5–40. The model tree identifies the first solid feature in the model as **Extrude 1**.

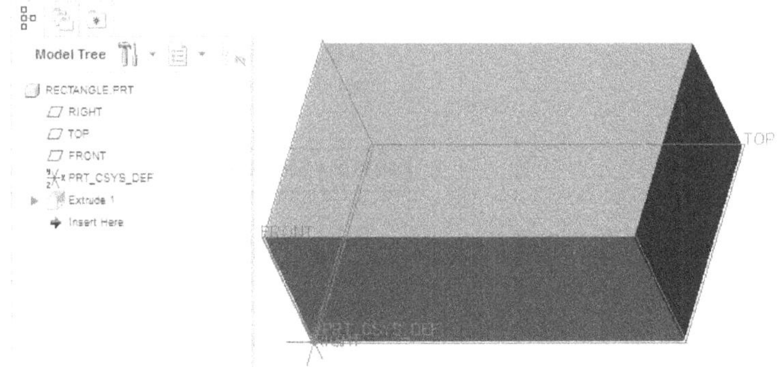

Figure 5–40

Task 6 - Save the model and erase it from the session.

1. In the Quick Access Toolbar, click (Save) to save the model.

2. Press <Enter> or click **OK** in the Save Object dialog box to save **rectangle.prt**.

3. Select **File>Manage Session>Erase Current** to erase **rectangle.prt** from the current session.

4. Click **Yes** in the Erase Confirm dialog box.

Task 7 - Create a new part using the default part template.

1. Click (New) to create a new file.
2. In the New dialog box, select the **Part** option. Set the *Name* to **cylinder**.
3. Verify that the **Use default template** option is selected.
4. Click **OK**. The Creo Parametric window now displays the cylinder model as the active model.

Task 8 - Select the feature type and define all of the sketching references.

1. Click (Extrude) from the Shapes group in the *Model* tab to create an extruded base feature.
2. Select datum plane **FRONT**. The datum plane will automatically be added as the sketch plane and maintain the default values for *Reference* and *Orientation*.

*You can also click **Define** in the Placement panel or right-click and select **Define Internal Sketch**. Use these options to control the orientation reference.*

3. Click (Sketch View) to orient the view.

Task 9 - Sketch a circular section.

1. In Sketching group in the ribbon, click (Center and Point).
2. Start the sketch by clicking the left mouse button at the intersection of datum planes **TOP** and **RIGHT**, as shown in Figure 5–41.
3. Drag the mouse outward. Click the mouse button to define the size.
4. Click the middle mouse button or press <Esc> to complete the sketch. Creo Parametric automatically dimensions and constrains the sketch, as shown in Figure 5–41.

To undo or redo sketching actions, you can click (Undo) and (Redo) in the Quick Access Toolbar, respectively.

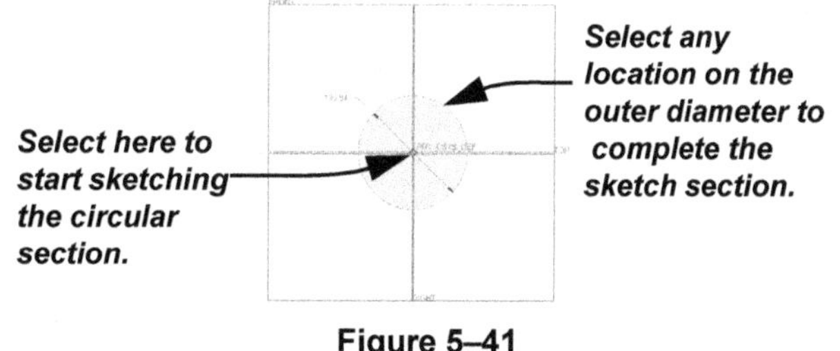

Figure 5–41

5. Double-click on the diameter dimension of the circle and set the new value to **10**. Press <Enter> to accept the new value.

6. Click ✓ (OK) to complete the sketch and exit the *Sketcher* tab.

Task 10 - Define the depth of the protrusion.

1. Press <Ctrl>+<D> to orient the model to its default orientation.

2. Double-click the *Length* dimension and set it to **15**.

3. Complete the cylindrical feature by clicking ✓ (Complete Feature) in the *Extrude* tab. The model and model tree display as shown in Figure 5–42. The model tree identifies the first solid feature in the model as **Extrude 1**.

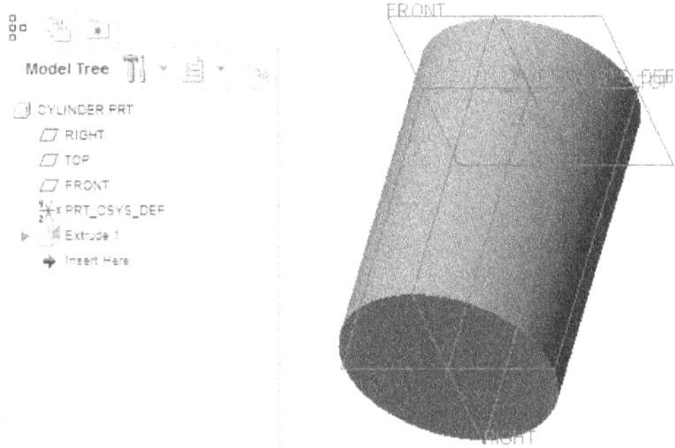

Figure 5–42

Task 11 - Save the model and erase it from the session.

1. Click (Save).

2. Press <Enter> or click **OK** in the Save Object dialog box to save **cylinder.prt**.

3. Select **File>Manage Session>Erase Current** to erase **cylinder.prt** from the current session.

4. In the Erase Confirm dialog box, click **Yes**.

Practice 5b Extruded Base Features II

Practice Objectives

- Create a new part model using a predefined template.
- Create and rename an extruded base feature.

In this practice, you will create a new model using the default template provided in Creo Parametric. You will create an extruded solid as the base feature, as shown in Figure 5–43. Sketch the feature using line entities.

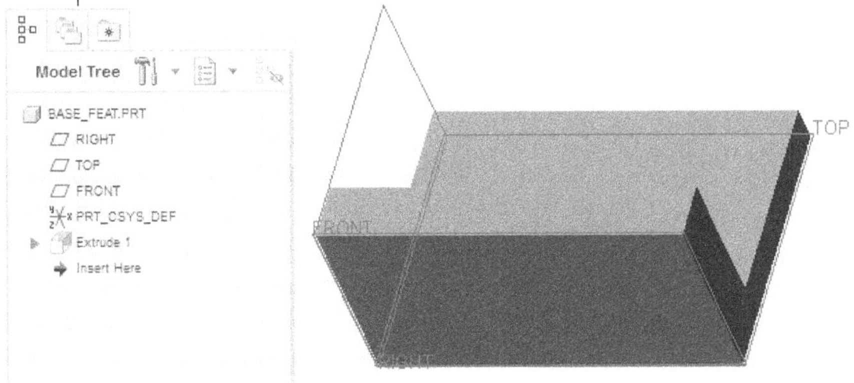

Figure 5–43

Task 1 - Create a new part using the default part template.

1. Set your working directory to the *Chapter 05\practice 5b* folder.
2. Click (New) to create a new file.
3. In the New dialog box, select the **Part** option. Set the *Name* to **base_feat**.
4. Click **OK** to create the new part model.
5. Set the model display as follows:
    - *(Datum Display Filters)*: Only (Plane Display)
    - *(Spin Center)*: Off
    - *(Display Style)*: (Shading)

6. Select the *View* tab in the ribbon and click (Plane Tag Display) if required, to toggle on the datum plane labels.
7. Select the *Model* tab.

Task 2 - Select the feature type and define all of the sketching references.

1. In the *Model* tab, click (Extrude) to create an extruded base feature.
2. Press and hold the right mouse button, and select **Define Internal Sketch**.
3. Select datum plane **RIGHT** as the sketch plane.

In this practice, the default orientation references are not the required ones, so you will need to define the orientation manually.

4. In the Sketch dialog box, select the *Reference* field and select datum plane **FRONT**. In the *Orientation* field, expand the drop-down list and select **Bottom**. The Sketch dialog box should display as shown in Figure 5–44.

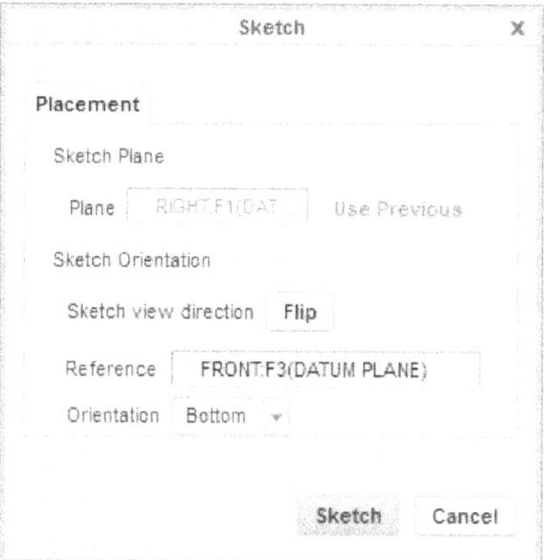

Figure 5–44

5. Click **Sketch** to begin sketching the section.
6. Click (Sketch View).

Task 3 - Sketch the section.

1. Click (Line) to use the **Line** sketching tool.
2. Sketch the six line entities as shown in Figure 5–45. Use the left mouse button to start and end each line segment.

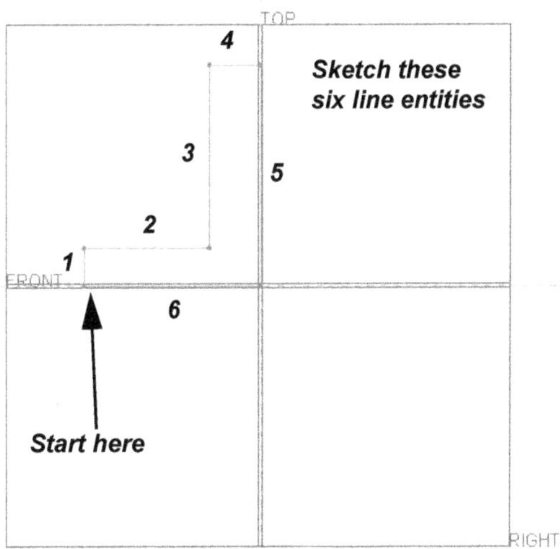

Figure 5–45

3. Click the middle mouse button to complete the line creation.
4. Click the middle mouse button a second time and the software automatically dimensions the sketch and applies constraints.

These dimensions and constraints might not represent your required design intent.

5. Click (Normal) to create new dimensions on the sketch.
6. Zoom in on the sketch to make it easier to select the entities.
7. Using the left mouse button, select entity number **1**, as shown in Figure 5–45.
8. Move the cursor to the location shown in Figure 5–46 and click the middle mouse button to locate the dimension.
9. Set the *Dimension* to **15.00**.

10. Continue to create the four linear dimensions and modify their values, as shown in Figure 5–46.

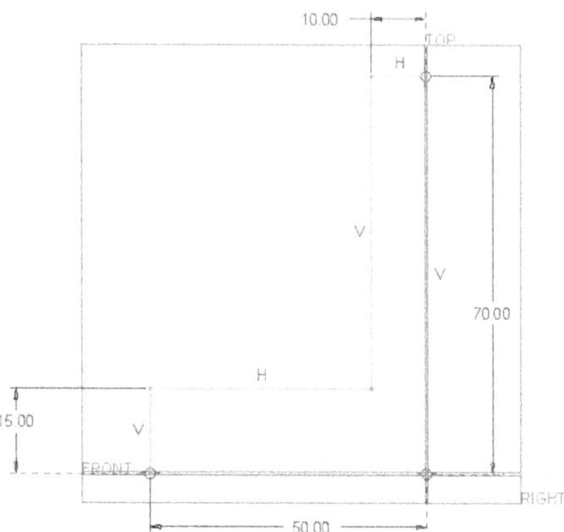

Figure 5–46

11. Click ✓ (OK) to complete the section.

Task 4 - Define the depth of the protrusion.

You can also drag the depth handle on the model.

1. Set the *Depth* field to **100**, as shown in Figure 5–47.

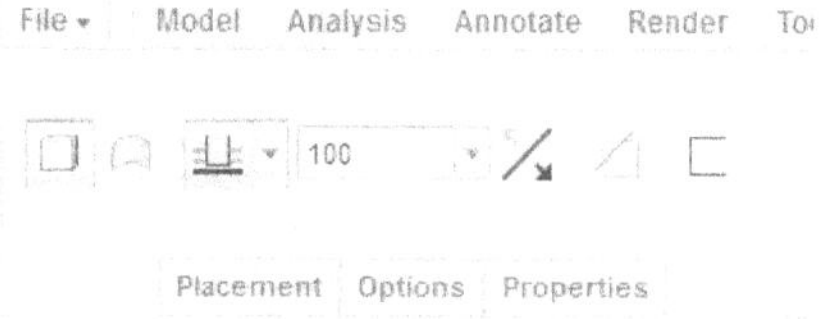

Figure 5–47

2. Click ✓ (Complete Feature) to complete the protrusion.
3. Press <Ctrl>+<D> to orient the model to the default view. The model and model tree display as shown in Figure 5–48.

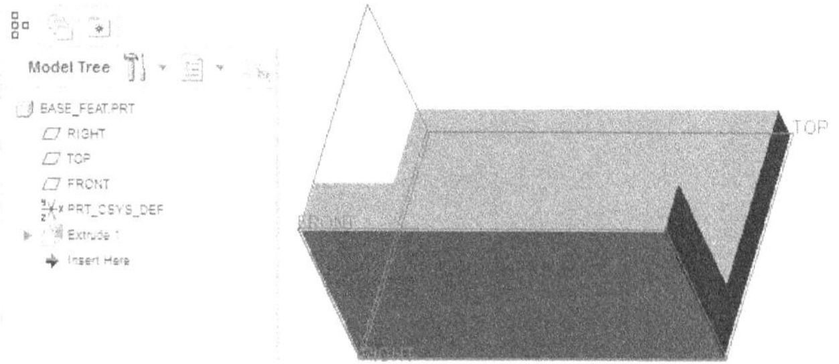

Figure 5–48

Task 5 - Modify dimension values associated with protrusion.

1. In the model tree, select the extrude that you just created.

2. Right-click and select (Edit). All of the dimensions associated with the extrusion display on the model, as shown in Figure 5–49.

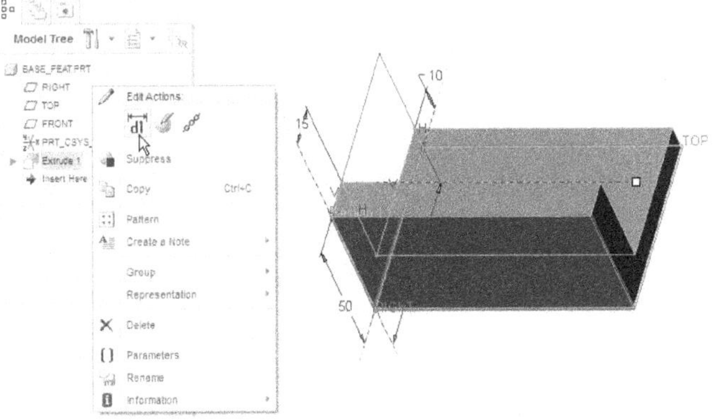

Figure 5–49

3. Double-click on the **10** dimension value.

4. Set the new dimension value to **15** and press <Enter>. The dimension displays in green when it has not been regenerated. The dimension will display in blue once it has been regenerated.

5. In the Quick Access Toolbar, click (Regenerate) to regenerate the model.

6. Alternatively, to edit the model you can double-click directly on the feature. Double-click anywhere on the extrude that you just created.

7. Double-click on the **100** *Depth* dimension.

8. Set the new *Depth* to **75** and press <Enter>.

9. Regenerate the model.

Task 6 - Redefine the extrusion direction for the protrusion.

1. Select the **Extrude 1** protrusion that you just created. You can select it in the model tree or directly on the model.

2. Right-click and select (Edit Definition). The *Extrude* dashboard displays again.

3. Click (Change Depth Direction) to switch the extrusion direction from one side of the sketch plane to the other as shown in Figure 5–50.

Figure 5–50

4. Click (Complete Feature) to complete the redefinition.

Task 7 - Rename a feature.

*You can also select **Extrude 1** in the model tree and click on the feature again to edit its name.*

1. In the model tree, right-click on **Extrude 1** and select **Rename**.

2. For the new name, enter **Lbracket**. The model and model tree display as shown in Figure 5–51.

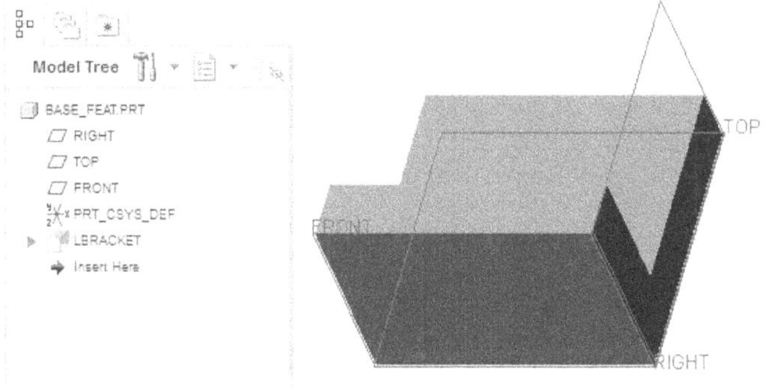

Figure 5–51

Task 8 - Save the model and erase it from the session.

1. Click (Save) to save the model.

2. Press <Enter> or click **OK**.

3. Select **File>Manage Session>Erase Current** to erase **base_feat.prt** from the current session of Creo Parametric.

4. Click **Yes** in the Erase Confirm dialog box.

Practice 5c Revolved Based Feature

Practice Objective

- Create a revolve base feature.

In this practice, you will create a revolve feature as the base feature for a part. The completed part displays as shown in Figure 5–52.

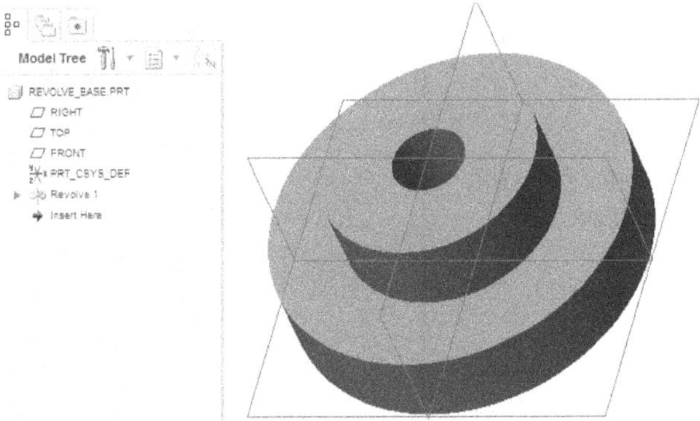

Figure 5–52

Task 1 - Create a new part file.

1. Set the working directory to the *Chapter 05\practice 5c* folder.
2. Click (New) to create a new file.
3. In the New dialog box, select the **Part** option.
4. Set the part *Name* to **drive_flange**.
5. Click **OK** to create the new part model.
6. Set the model display as follows:
   - *(Datum Display Filters)*: Only (Plane Display)
   - *(Spin Center)*: Off
   - *(Display Style)*: (Shading)
7. Select the *View* tab in the ribbon and click (Plane Tag Display) if required, to toggle off the datum plane labels.
8. Select the *Model* tab.

Task 2 - Create a revolved feature.

1. In the Shapes group in the *Model* tab, click (Revolve).
2. Select the datum plane **FRONT** from the model tree as the sketch plane.
3. Click (Sketch View).
4. In the Sketching group, create an axis by clicking (Centerline), as shown in Figure 5–53). Then, click two points on the vertical reference.

You could use (Centerline) from the Datum group as well.

Figure 5–53

To create the diameter dimension, select the vertical line, the centerline, then the vertical line a second time, and place the dimension with the middle mouse button.

5. Create and dimension the sketch, as shown in Figure 5–54. Ensure that the section is driven with a *Diameter* dimension of **2**.

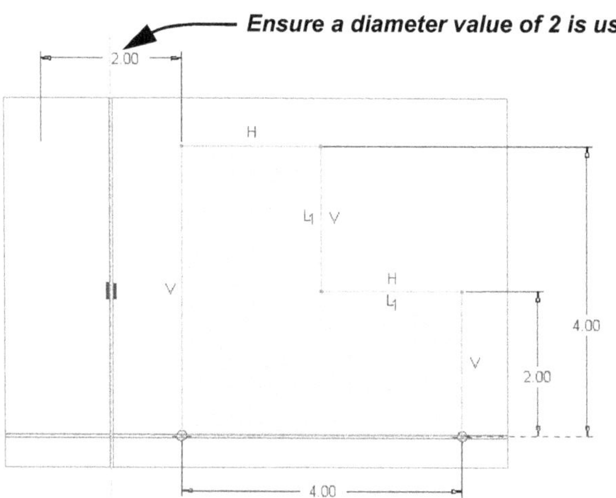

Figure 5–54

6. Click (OK) to complete the sketch.
7. In the dashboard, set the *Angle of revolution* to **270** degrees, as shown in Figure 5–55.

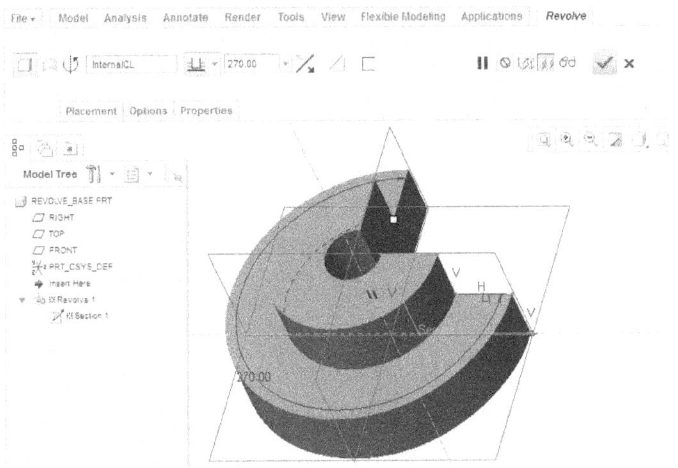

Figure 5–55

8. Set the *Angle of revolution* back to **360** degrees.
9. Click (Complete Feature).
10. Press <Ctrl>+<D>, if required, to return to default orientation.
11. The model displays as shown in Figure 5–56.

Figure 5–56

12. Click (Save) to save the part.
13. Click (Close).
14. Click (Erase Not Displayed) and **OK**.

Practice 5d Creating Additional Parts

Practice Objectives

- Create new part models using a predefined template.
- Create base features in each part model using the correct default datums that represents the geometry provided.

In this practice, you will practice creating base features as the first solid feature in a new part. Datum tags display to help you decide on sketcher orientation.

Task 1 - Create a new part.

1. Set the working directory to the *Chapter 05\practice 5d* folder.
2. Create a new part and set the *Name* to **channel**.
3. Use the extrude feature to create the base geometry shown in Figure 5–57.
4. Select a sketch plane that will result in the default view shown in Figure 5–57.

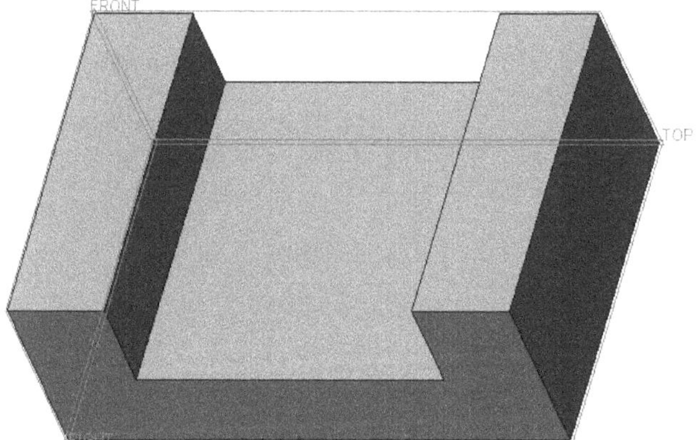

Figure 5–57

Task 2 - Create an L-shaped part.

1. Create a new part and set the *Name* to **L_part**.
2. Use the extrude feature to create the base geometry shown in Figure 5–58.

3. Select a sketch plane that will result in the default view shown in Figure 5–58.

Figure 5–58

Task 3 - Create a pipe part using an extrude.

1. Create a new part and set the *Name* to **pipe**.
2. Use the extrude feature to create the base geometry shown in Figure 5–59. Select a sketch plane that will result in the default view shown.

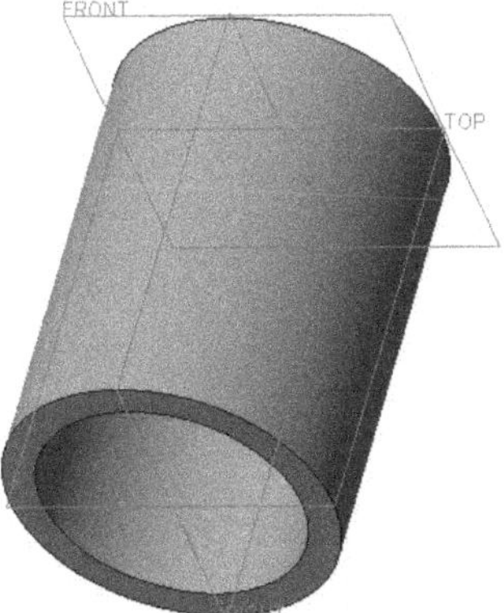

Figure 5–59

Task 4 - Undo the previous feature and create the pipe as a revolve.

1. In the Quick Access Toolbar, click (Undo).
2. Create the base feature shown in Figure 5–59 using a **Revolve**.

Task 5 - Create a wedge part.

1. Create a new part and set the *Name* to **wedge**.

2. Use the extrude feature to create the base geometry shown in Figure 5–60.

3. Select a sketch plane that will result in the default view shown in Figure 5–60.

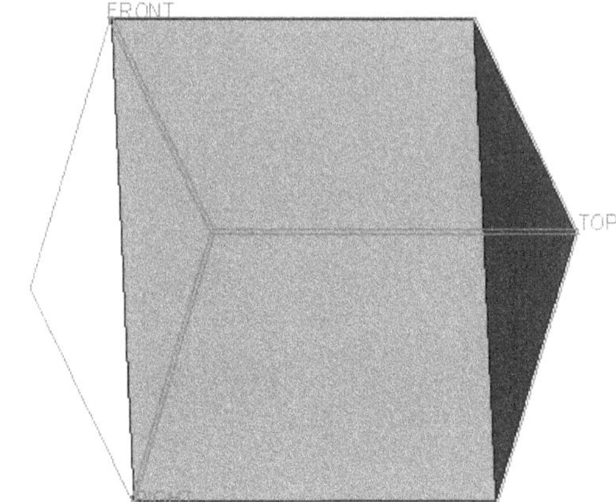

Figure 5–60

Chapter Review Questions

1. Identify the base feature form shown in Figure 5–61.

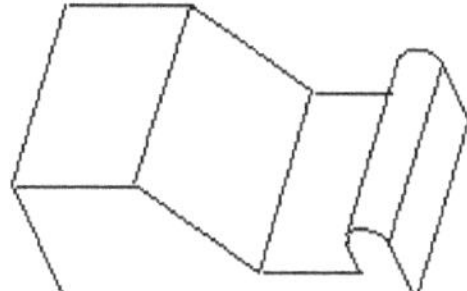

Figure 5–61

   a. Extrude
   b. Revolve
   c. Sweep
   d. Blend

2. Identify the base feature form shown in Figure 5–62.

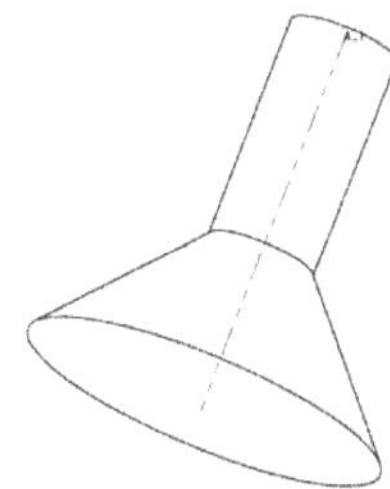

Figure 5–62

   a. Extrude
   b. Revolve
   c. Sweep
   d. Blend

3. Which of the following statements describes default datum planes? (Select all that apply.)
   a. First solid features
   b. Reference features
   c. Have mass
   d. Foundation for part

4. Which of the following can be selected as the sketching plane for the first solid feature? (Select all that apply.)
    a. Datum plane **RIGHT**
    b. Datum plane **FRONT**
    c. Datum plane **TOP**
5. What was the sketching plane for the extruded protrusion shown in Figure 5–63?

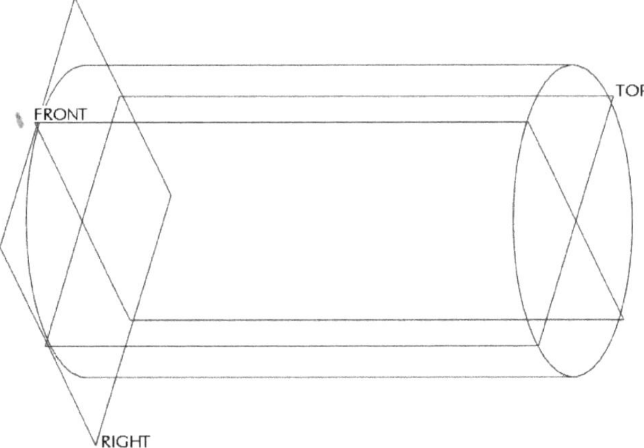

Figure 5–63

    a. Datum plane **RIGHT**
    b. Datum plane **FRONT**
    c. Datum plane **TOP**
6. The sketch orientation plane that is automatically selected by Creo Parametric must be used to orient the model while sketching the section for the base feature.
    a. True
    b. False
7. What must be selected when sketching to locate sketched geometry with respect to existing features in the part?
    a. References
    b. Sketch plane
    c. Rectangle command
    d. Circle command

8. Dimensions that you create are referred to as strong dimensions and can be automatically deleted by the system.
   a. True
   b. False

9. Which option is used to access the dashboard for an existing feature to make changes to it, such as flipping the extrusion direction?
   a. Edit
   b. Dynamic Edit
   c. Modify
   d. Edit Definition

10. Where would you click and drag to change the depth of the extrusion shown in Figure 5–64?

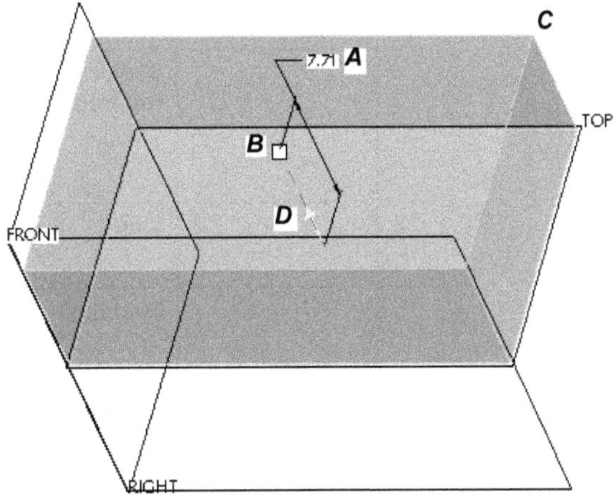

Figure 5–64

   a. A
   b. B
   c. C
   d. D

11. You can use the **Edit Definition** option to rename a feature in the model tree.
   a. True
   b. False

Command Summary

Button	Command	Location
	New File	• Ribbon: Home tab • Quick Access Toolbar • File>New • **Hot Key:** <Ctrl>+N or <Alt>+1
	Extrude	• **Ribbon:** *Model* tab in the Shapes group
	Revolve	• **Ribbon:** *Model* tab in the Shapes group
	Sketch View	• **Ribbon:** *Sketch* tab in the Setup group • Graphics Toolbar • **Hot Key:** <Alt>+Z+I
	Sketch Setup	• **Ribbon:** *Sketch* tab in the Setup group
	Sketch References	• **Ribbon:** *Sketch* tab in the Setup group • **Hot Key:** Select a sketch command, hold <Alt>, select the reference, release <Alt>.
	Line	• **Ribbon:** *Sketch* tab in the Sketching group
	Rectangle	• **Ribbon:** *Sketch* tab in the Sketching group
	Circle	• **Ribbon:** *Sketch* tab in the Sketching group
	Normal	• **Ribbon:** *Sketch* tab in the Dimension group
	Select	• **Ribbon:** *Sketch* tab in the Operations group • **Hot Key:** <Esc>

Advanced Sketching Tools

Creo Parametric provides a large variety of sketcher functions. In this chapter, you will learn about some of the sketcher functions that have not already been discussed. You will gain further knowledge about various functions to help you produce more advanced sketches.

Learning Objectives in this Chapter

- Scale, rotate, and translate the entities in a sketch.
- Import a sketch using the Palette command.
- Create multiple copies of entities in the same or a different sketch using the Copy and Paste commands.
- Create 2D sketch geometry using the Offset and Project commands.
- Fix an over-dimensioned or over-constrained sketch using the Resolve Sketch dialog box.
- Modify or drag one or multiple dimensions using the Modify Dimension dialog box.
- Move, lock, and unlock dimensions in the Sketch mode.
- Inspect 2D geometry using the diagnostic tools in the Sketch tab.
- Change and customize sketch options using the Creo Parametric Options dialog box.

6.1 Advanced Editing Tools

As your model becomes more complex, sketching tools can be used, which are accessed in the *Sketch* tab.

In addition to the editing tools introduced in the previous chapters, the following tools can also be used:

- **Scale**, **Rotate**, and **Translate**
- Import from File
- Import from Palette
- **Cut**, **Copy**, and **Paste**

Scale, Rotate, and Translate

How To: Scale, Rotate, and Translate Sketched Entities

1. Select the geometric entities to edit.
2. In the Editing group in the *Sketch* tab, click (Rotate Resize). The *Rotate Resize* dashboard opens as shown in Figure 6–1.

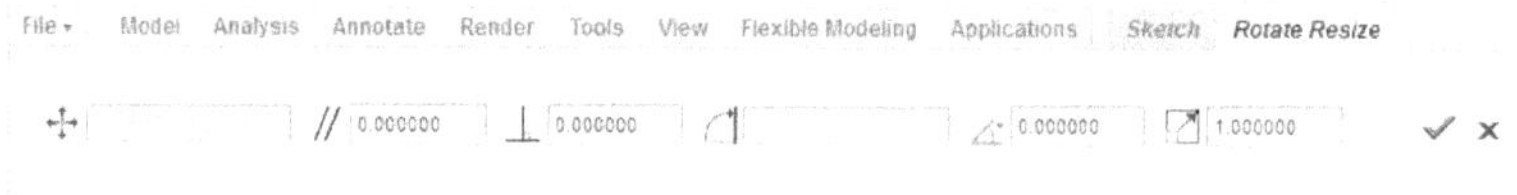

Figure 6–1

3. Use the *Rotate Resize* dashboard to enter scale and rotate values. Additionally, the (Scale), (Rotate), and (Translate) handles display on your sketch, as shown in Figure 6–2. These handles enable you to dynamically modify the geometry by dragging the appropriate handles.

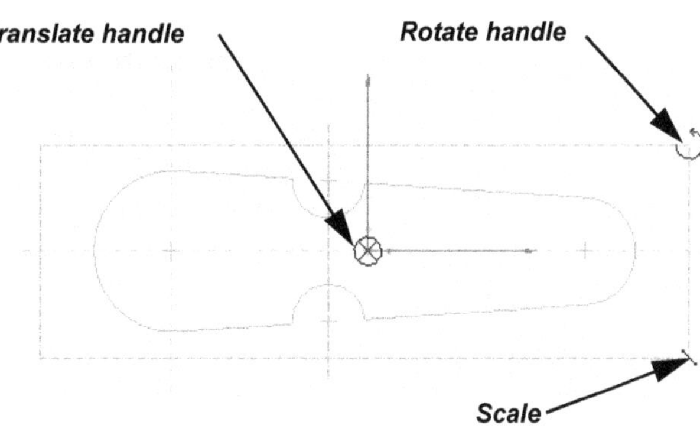

Figure 6–2

4. In the *Rotate and Resize* tab, click ✓ (OK) to apply the changes.

Import from File

A previously saved section can be retrieved into a current sketch. Complete the following steps to add a section from a file in Sketcher mode:

1. In the Get Data group in the *Sketch* tab, click (File System).
2. Enter the name of the sketch or select it from the Open dialog box and click **Open**.
3. The cursor shape changes to . Move the cursor to the appropriate location and click the left mouse button to place the section. The imported section displays in green with additional handles. The *Import Section* dashboard also opens.
4. Use the (Scale), (Rotate), and (Translate) handles to dynamically modify the imported sketch. You can also enter a scale, rotation, and translation values in the dashboard.
5. Click ✓ (OK) to close the dashboard. The section is automatically located with respect to the references.

A sketch is independent of the feature type. Any sketch can be saved while in Sketcher mode. Sketches are saved with .SEC file extensions.

Import from Palette

Similar to **Import from File**, **Import from Palette** enables you to retrieve a previously saved section into the current sketch.

How To: Add a Section from the Palette in the Sketch Tab

1. In the Sketching group in the *Sketch* tab, click (Palette). The Sketcher Palette dialog box opens, as shown in Figure 6–3.

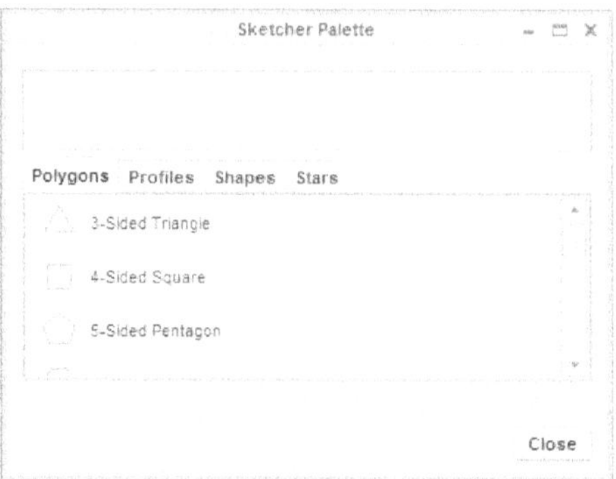

Figure 6–3

The configuration option sketcher_palette_path enables you to specify the directory in which your custom sketch library is located.

The Sketcher Palette dialog box contains a set of tabs. Each tab holds a set of section thumbnails and names. There are four predefined tabs: *Polygons*, *Profiles*, *Shapes*, and *Stars*. These can be modified and correspond to four directories located in the *PROE_LOADPOINT\text\sketcher_palette* directory. You can create any number of custom tabs (directories) and place any number of section files in them.

An additional tab will display with the name of the current working directory if the current working directory contains more than one section file.

2. Select the required tab and the section that you want to import into the active sketch. A preview of the selected section displays in the top area of the Sketcher Palette dialog box, as shown in Figure 6–4.

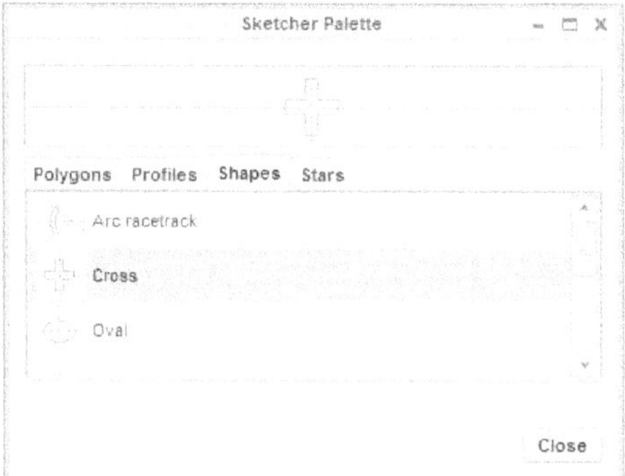

Figure 6–4

3. Drag the required section thumbnail and move the cursor to the Sketcher window. The cursor shape changes to . Move the cursor to the appropriate location and click the left mouse button to place the section. The imported section displays in green with additional handles. The *Rotate Resize* tab also opens.
4. Use the (Scale), (Rotate), and (Translate) handles to dynamically modify the imported sketch. You can also enter a scale and/or rotation value in the *Import Section* dashboard.
5. Click (OK) to close the *Import Section* dashboard. The section is automatically located with respect to the references.
6. Import another section from the palette or click **Close** to close the Sketcher Palette dialog box.

Cut, Copy, and Paste

These options enable you to cut, copy, and paste existing sketch entities.

You can also press <Ctrl>+<X>.

- **Cut:** Removes selected entities from the sketch and simultaneously puts them into the sketcher clipboard. To cut selected entities from the sketch, select the required entities and in the Operations group in the *Sketch* tab, click (Cut).

You can also press <Ctrl>+<C>.

- **Copy:** Leaves the selected entities in the sketch intact and simultaneously puts a copy of them into the sketcher clipboard. To copy selected entities from the sketch, select the required entities and in the Operations group, click (Copy).

You can also press <Ctrl>+<V>.

- **Paste:** Enables you to place entities saved in the sketcher clipboard into the current sketch as many times as required. The content of the clipboard remains unchanged until the next **Cut** or **Copy** action.

How To: Add a Section from the Sketcher Clipboard into the Sketch

1. In the Operations group, click (Paste).
2. The cursor shape changes to . Move the cursor to the appropriate location and click the left mouse button to place the section. The imported section displays in green with additional handles. The *Rotate Resize* tab also opens.
3. Use the (Scale), (Rotate), and (Translate) handles to dynamically modify the pasted sketch. You can also enter a scale and/or rotation value in the *Rotate Resize* tab.
4. Click (OK) to close the *Paste* dashboard. The pasted sketch is automatically located with respect to the references.

In the example shown in Figure 6–5, the sketch on the left is copied and pasted (scaled, rotated, and translated), as shown on the right.

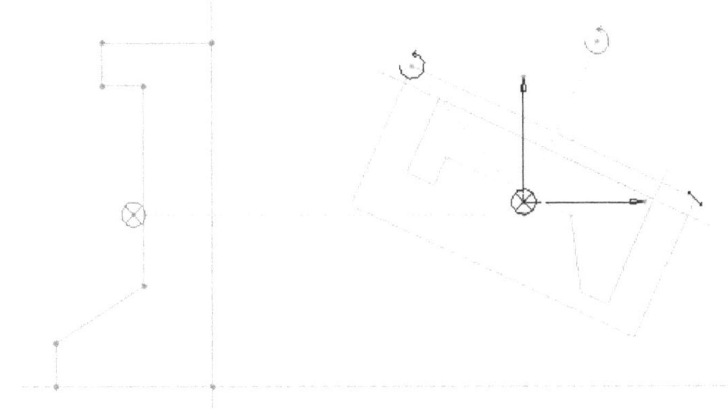

Figure 6–5

6.2 Using Existing Geometry

To sketch geometry, you must select references to dimension and constrain the new entities. As an alternative, you can use three additional sketching tools, found in the Sketching group, that enable you to create new entities based on existing geometry. These tools enable you to:

- Create an entity by offsetting it from an existing edge - Use (Offset).
- Create an entity by using an existing edge - Use (Project).
- Create entities on two sides by using an existing edge - Use (Thicken).

When using (Offset) or (Project), the Type dialog box opens, as shown in Figure 6–6. This enables you to define the method by which the entities are selected. You can select **Single** entities, a **Chain** (all adjacent entities between two selected entities) or a **Loop** (all adjacent entities).

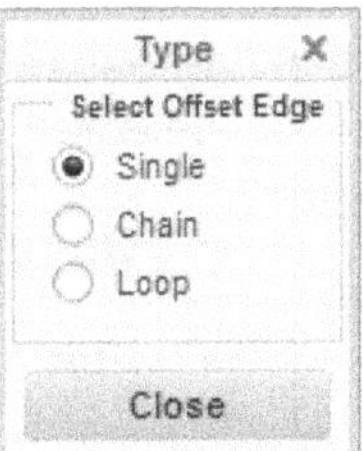

Figure 6–6

When using (Thicken), the system displays a modified Type dialog box, with several additional options, as shown in Figure 6–7.

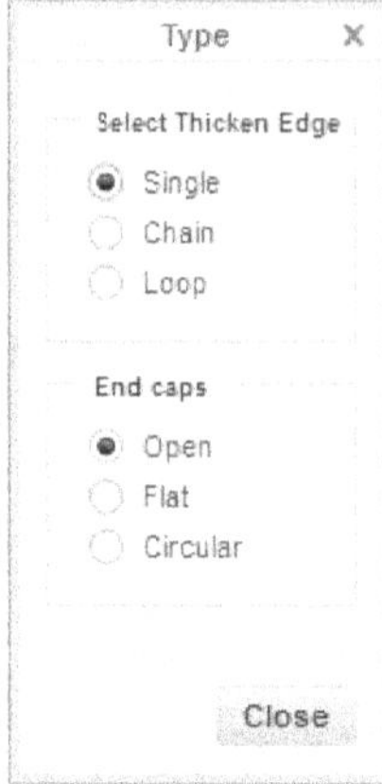

Figure 6–7

When selecting one or more edges, you are prompted for a thickness, which is the distance between the two entities the system creates. You are then prompted for an offset value, which is the distance the first entity is created from the original edge.

Because the system will create two entities for every one selected, you must tell it how to handle the ends of the entities.

- **Open** - No end cap created
- **Flat** - Straight line cap connecting the endpoints
- **Circular** - half-circle cap connecting the endpoints.

Entities that are offset are associated to a dimension. Once the entities have been selected, identifies that the new entity is based on existing geometry. Remember the parent-child relationships that you create when using existing geometry to create new entities. If you do not want these relationships, delete . The system automatically adds weak dimensions, as required.

Using Offset and Project

Figure 6–8 shows a part and the state of the model before the sketch is created. The sketched geometry shown in Figure 6–9 was created by offsetting the edge of the solid geometry by a value of **20.00**.

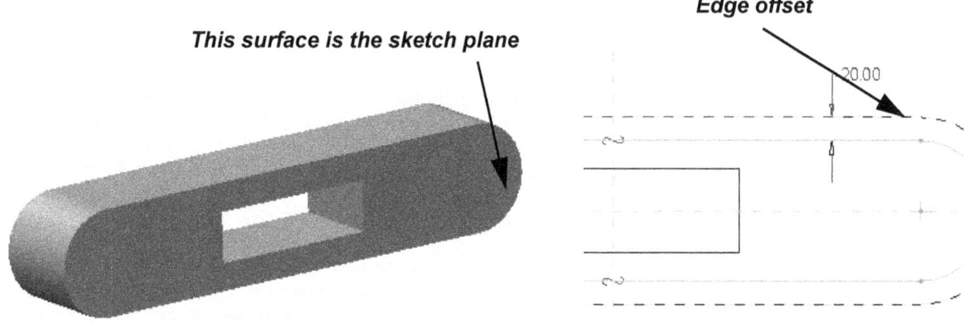

Figure 6–8

Figure 6–9

The straight edge of the solid geometry was projected, as shown in Figure 6–10. The sketched geometry has been corner-trimmed to complete a closed section, as shown in Figure 6–11.

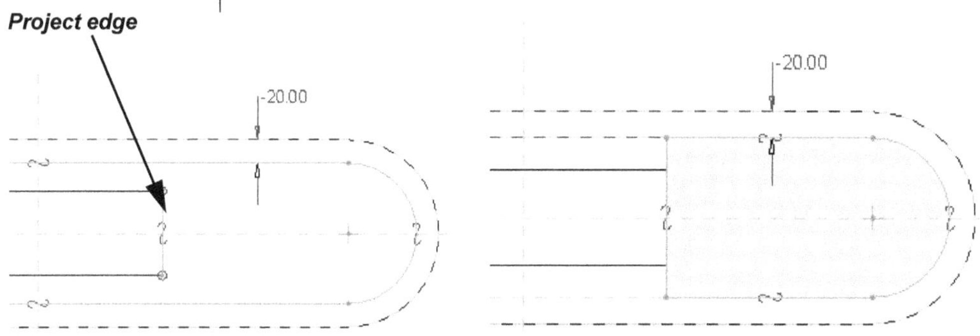

Figure 6–10

Figure 6–11

Figure 6–12 shows the resulting extrude from the sketch created with **Offset** and **Project**.

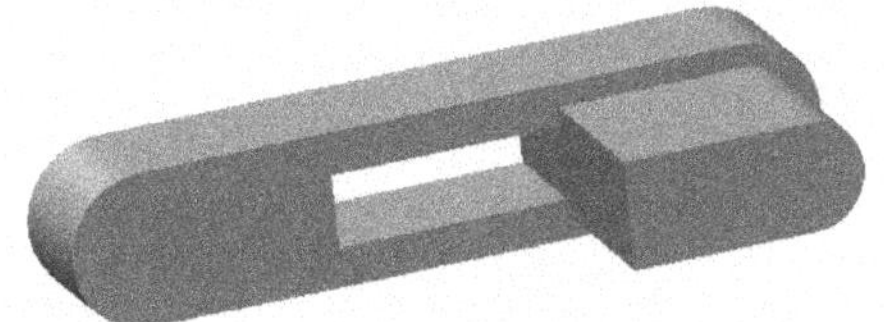

Figure 6–12

Using Thicken

Continuing with the previous example, the part shown in Figure 6–13 indicates the state of the model before the sketch is created.

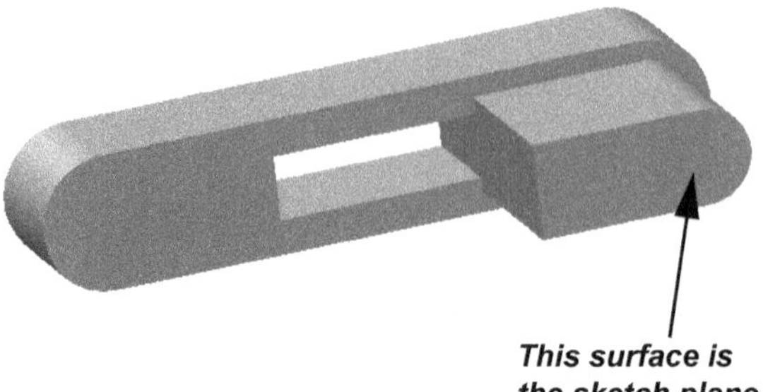

Figure 6–13

The sketched geometry shown in Figure 6–14 was created by setting a *Thickness* value of **20**, and *Offset* value of **10**, which offsets equally on both sides. The **Open** option was used for the end caps.

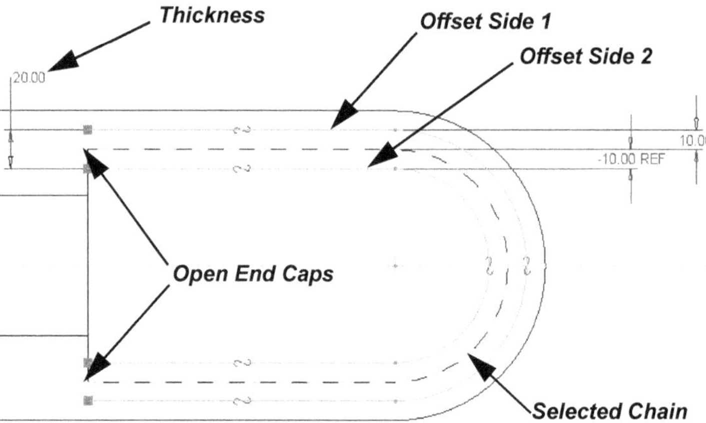

Figure 6–14

Figure 6–15 shows the same thicken, but with **Flat** selected for the end caps.

The sketched geometry has been corner-trimmed to complete a closed section, as shown in Figure 6–16.

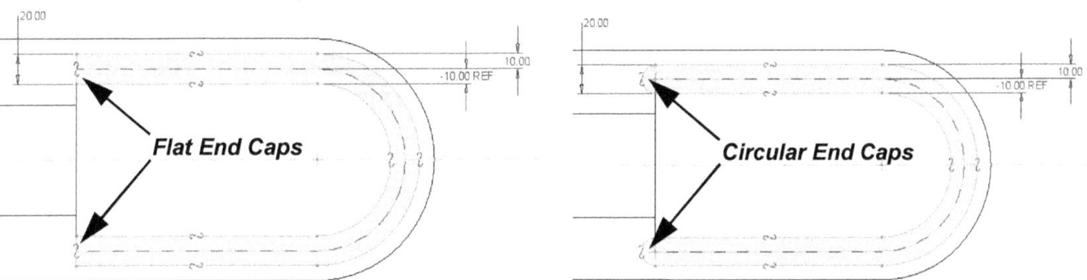

Figure 6–15

Figure 6–16

Figure 6–17 shows the resulting extrude from the sketch created with **Thicken**.

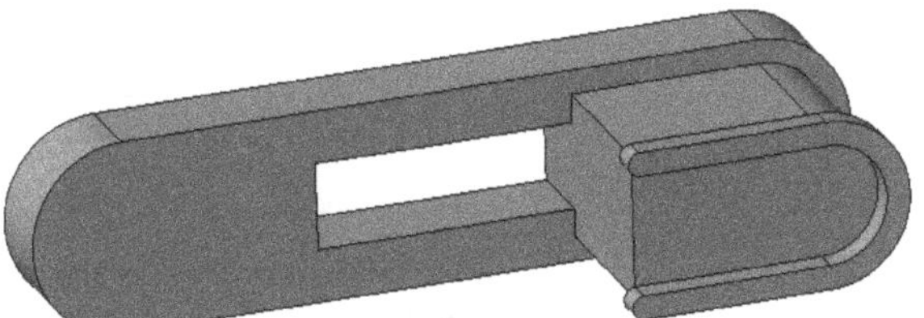

Figure 6–17

6.3 Resolving Dimension and Constraint Conflicts

If you over-dimension or over-constrain a sketch, the Resolve Sketch dialog box opens, as shown in Figure 6–18. This dialog box enables you to resolve the conflict so that you can continue working on the sketch. To resolve the conflict, you must either undo the new dimension or constraint, or delete an existing one in the sketch.

Figure 6–18

The Resolve Sketch dialog box contains a list of conflicting items. The conflicting items are also highlighted in the Sketcher window. You can select the required item in the Resolve Sketch dialog box or in the Sketcher window. In the Sketcher window, the selected item is bounded by a blue rectangle. The options for resolving conflicts are described as follows:

Icon	Description
Undo	Undoes the previous action.
Delete	Deletes the selected dimension or constraint.
Dim>Ref	Changes the selected dimension to a reference dimension.
Explain	Provides a description in the message window explaining the selected dimension or constraint.

6.4 Modify and Move Dimensions

Modify Dimensions

You can modify a dimension in the sketch by double-clicking on the dimension and entering a new value in the field that displays. You can also use the Modify Dimensions dialog box. This dialog box is useful for modifying several dimensions on a sketch at the same time. You can open the Modify Dimension dialog box by selecting the dimensions using <Ctrl> and clicking (Modify).

*You can also right-click and select **Modify** to open the Modify Dimensions dialog box.*

The Modify Dimension dialog box opens, displaying the values for the selected dimensions. You can add additional dimensions for modification by selecting them while the Modify Dimensions dialog box is open. Every selected dimension value displays in a separate text field, as shown in Figure 6–19.

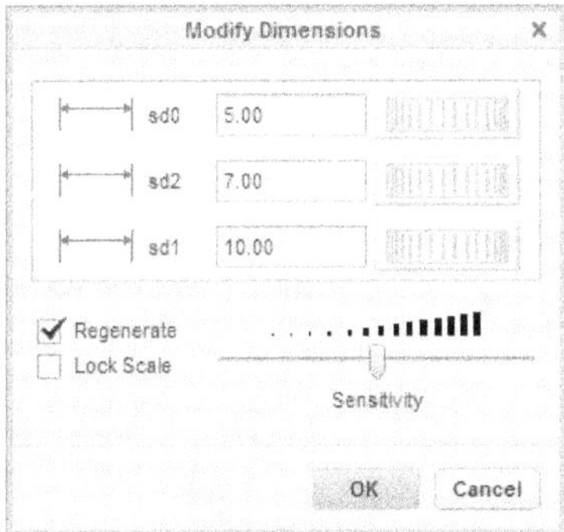

Figure 6–19

To increase the dimension by a decimal point, set a higher sensitivity.

You can modify dimensions by entering new values in the value fields or by using the thumbwheel, located next to the value field. Use the Sensitivity scale to adjust the thumbwheel's rate of change. Higher sensitivity results in a slower rate of change in values, while lower sensitivity results in a faster rate of change.

- The **Regenerate** option enables you to specify whether geometry regenerates immediately with each change of a dimension value or if it regenerates once the dialog box is closed. Consider enabling this option when you are modifying a small number of dimensions or are only making relatively small changes to the dimension values. If you are making relatively large changes to multiple dimensions, you might want to delay regeneration until you close the Modify Dimensions dialog box. To delay regeneration, clear the **Regenerate** option.

- The **Lock Scale** option enables you to scale all of the selected dimensions based on the proportion of one dimension modification. This option is useful when you want to increase or decrease the overall size of the model.

Move Dimensions

Dimensions can be moved by selecting and dragging them. To move sketcher entities, click (Select), select the entity, and drag and drop it to the required location. When moving dimensions, the dimension value does not change; only its position relative to the sketch changes.

Moving Entities

While in Sketcher mode, you can dynamically move existing sketched entities. Hover the cursor over the entity, its end point, or centerpoint, click the left mouse button and drag the entity to a new position. When moving entities, their associated dimensions update dynamically with their new placement.

Locking Dimensions

You can prevent dimensions from automatically updating when entities are moved by locking them. Locking is useful, when you want to use the **Move** functionality and keep a specific dimension unchanged.

- The **Lock** option enables you to lock a dimension. Locked dimensions display in red. Entities driven by locked dimensions do not change their sizes when they are moved.
- The **Unlock** option enables you to unlock a dimension. The locked status of dimensions is saved with the section. Therefore, if you reenter the section, the software retains the locked status for all of the previously locked dimensions.

The locked status still enables you to modify a dimension value in Sketcher mode by double-clicking on it. You can also modify the dimension value in Part mode.

6.5 Inspect Tools

When working with a sketch, you can use diagnostic tools that enable you to verify whether a sketch is valid and meets the requirements for the feature in which it is embedded. This tool is only available when creating a 3D sketch.

Shade Closed Loops

The **Shade Closed Loops** tool enables you to quickly verify whether a section is closed. This tool only shades the interior section if the entities in the sketch are closed. To access it, click (Shade Closed Loops) in the Inspect group in the *Sketch* tab. A preview of the closed sections displays, similar to that shown in Figure 6–20.

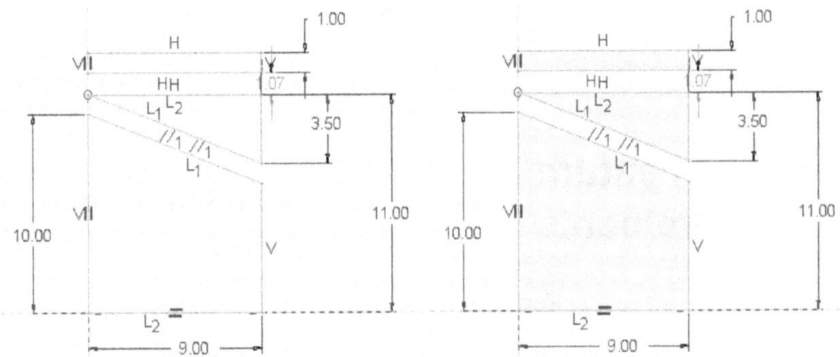

Figure 6–20

Highlight Open Ends

The **Highlight Open Ends** tool enables you to identify where open segments of sketches are located. To access it, click (Highlight Open Ends) in the Inspect group. A red square displays at the open ends of a section, as shown in Figure 6–21.

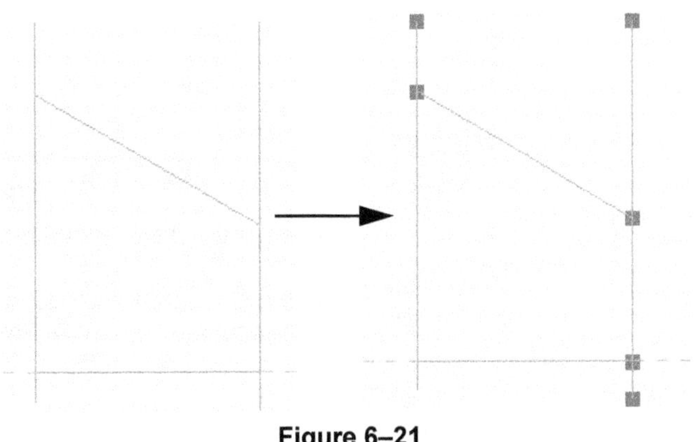

Figure 6–21

Overlapping Geometry

The **Overlapping Geometry** tool enables you to verify whether any entities are overlapping in a sketch. To access it, click (Overlapping Geometry) in the Inspect group. A preview of the overlapping geometry displays as shown in the example in Figure 6–22.

Overlapping entities are highlighted

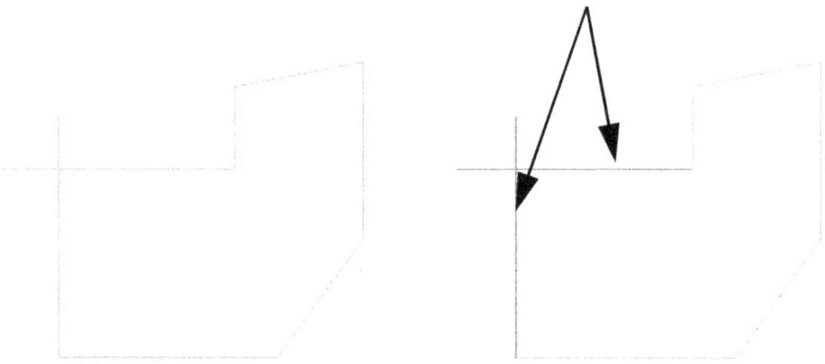

Figure 6–22

Feature Requirements

All sketched features have specific requirements to be used in a sketch. The **Feature Requirements** tool enables you to quickly determine whether your sketch meets the requirements for the feature you are creating. To access it, click (Feature Requirements) in the Inspect group. A list of the feature's requirements and their status on the current section displays, as shown in Figure 6–23.

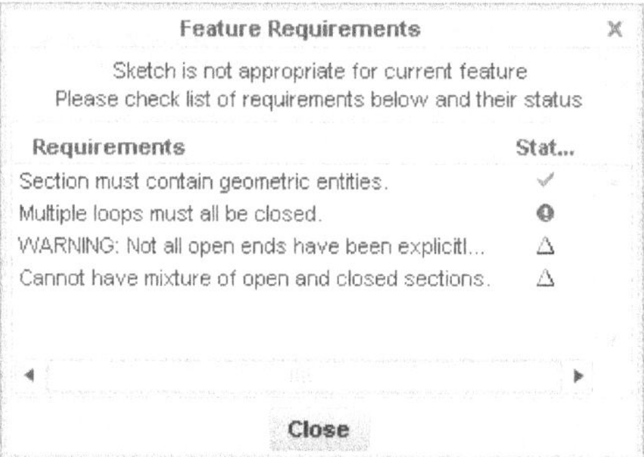

Figure 6–23

- The green check indicates that the requirement is achieved.
- The red exclamation point indicates the requirement is not achieved and must be fixed.

- The yellow triangle indicates the requirement is achieved but the sketch is unstable.

Additional inspection options are located in the **Inspect** flyout menu. They are described as follows:

Icon	Description
(Intersection Point)	Opens a separate widow with information on the intersection points between two entities.
(Tangency Point)	Opens a separate window displaying information on the point of tangency between two selected entities.
(Entity)	Opens a separate window displaying information on a selected entity.

6.6 Setting Sketcher Options

Sketch Options

To change the sketcher settings, select **File>Options> Sketcher**. This opens the Creo Parametric Options dialog box, as shown in Figure 6–24.

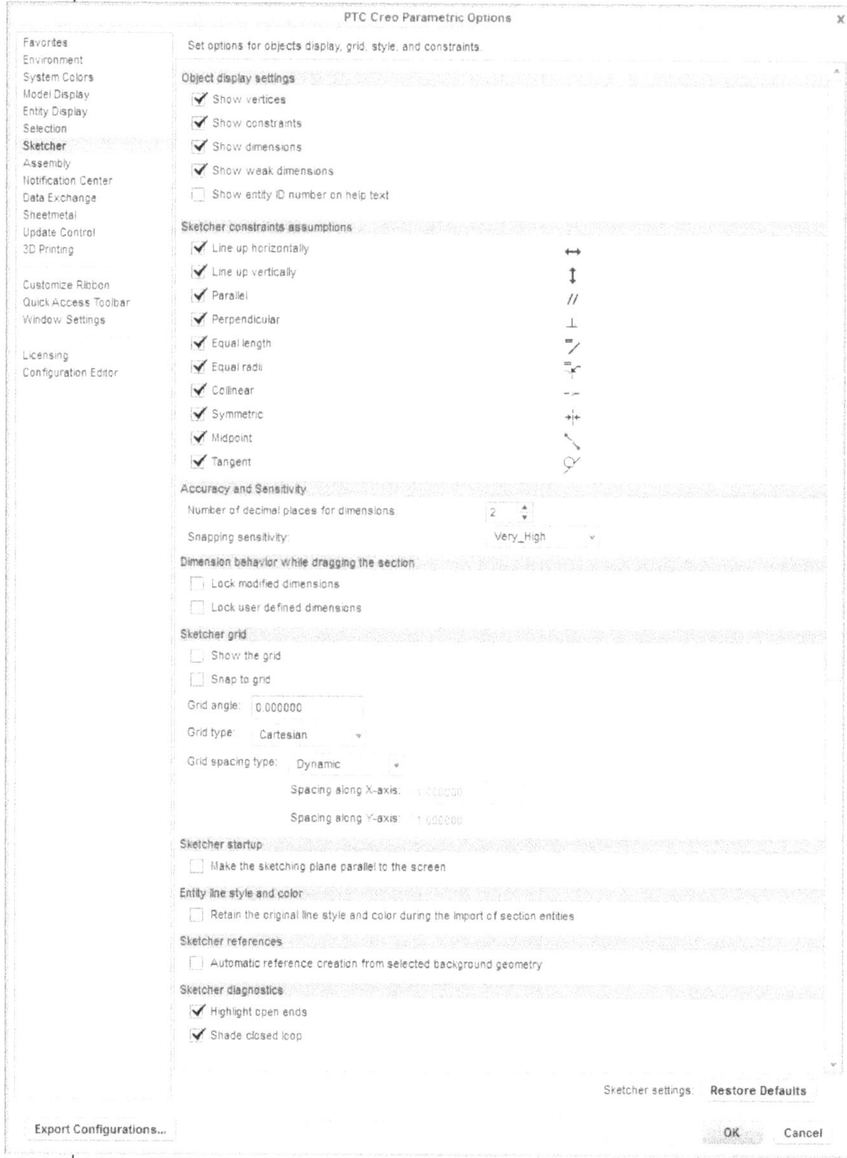

Figure 6–24

- The options in the *Object display settings* area enable you to specify preferences for the sketcher display environment. You can clean up the display on your screen by toggling on or off the display of specific entities.
- The **Make the sketching plane parallel to the screen** option is useful to orient the sketch. Some of the options available to customize the settings in the sketcher environment are described as follows:

Remember to turn weak dimensions strong when you need to dimension the sketch.

Option	Description
Show Vertices	Toggles display of endpoints of sketcher entities.
Show Constraints	Toggles display of sketcher constraint symbols (e.g., **H**, **V**, **T**, and **M**).
Show Dimensions	Toggles display of all sketcher dimensions.
Show Weak Dimensions	Toggles display of weak sketcher dimensions.
Show Entity ID on Help Text	Enriches help text displayed when cursor is hovered over sketch entity (i.e., geometry, construction geometry, sketcher reference, or constraint) with entity ID. Use the configuration option show_selected_item_id to automatically display the entity ID.
Lock Modified Dimensions	Restricts modified sketcher dimensions from changing in value when dragging sketcher entities.
Lock User Defined Dimensions	Restricts user defined sketcher dimensions from changing in value when dragging sketcher entities. Use the configuration option sketcher_dimension_ autolock to automatically lock user defined dimensions.
Show the Grid	Toggles display of sketcher grid lines.
Snap to Grid	Enables sketcher entities to snap to sketcher grid.
Highlight Open Ends	Identifies where open segments of sketches are located.
Shade Closed Loop	Enables you to quickly verify whether a section is closed. This tool only shades the interior section if the entities in the sketch are closed.

Sketcher Constraints Assumptions

The options in the *Sketcher constraints assumptions* area of the dialog box enable or disable the sketcher constraints that can be automatically assigned to a sketch (e.g., if the **Tangent** option is disabled, entities are not assumed to be tangent while sketching), as shown in Figure 6–25.

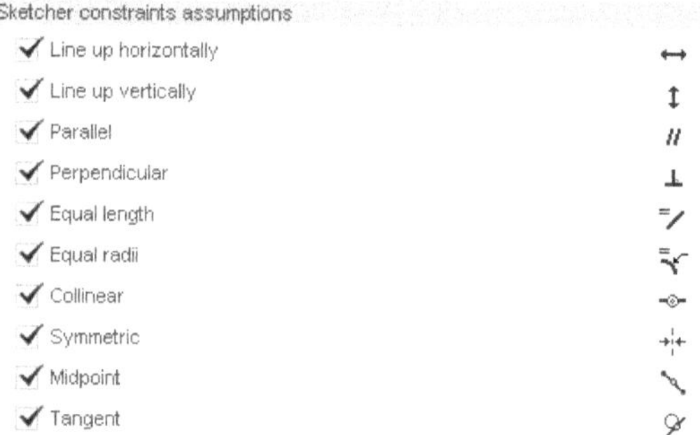

Figure 6–25

Sketcher Grid Options

The options in the *Sketcher grid* area in the dialog box enable you to set preferences for the sketcher grid and accuracy, as shown in Figure 6–26. They are described as follows.

Figure 6–26

Option		Description
Grid		Modifies sketcher grid attributes.
	Grid Angle	Modifies orientation angle of grid.
	Grid Type	Sets grid type to **Cartesian** or **Polar**.
Grid Spacing Type		Modifies spacing of grid.
	X	Sets spacing between vertical grid lines of **Cartesian** grid.
	Y	Sets spacing between horizontal grid lines of **Cartesian** grid.

The options in the *Accuracy and Sensitivity* area are shown in Figure 6–27.

Figure 6–27

Use these options to set the number of decimal places displayed in sketcher (14 maximum), and to change how sensitive the system is to snapping to references. Changes made to the sketcher options can be reset by clicking **Restore Defaults**.

Practice 6a Sketch Diagnostics

Practice Objectives

- Use the diagnostic tools in the Sketch tab to create an extruded feature.
- Fix the sketch using the Editing tools in the Sketch tab.

In this practice, you will create an extrude from an existing sketch. However, there is a problem with the sketch that will prevent you from creating an extrude feature. You will then use the inspect sketch tools to investigate the sketch to determine the problem.

Task 1 - Open a part file.

1. Set the working directory to the *Chapter 06/practice 6a* folder.
2. Open **repair_sketch.prt**.
3. Set the model display as follows:
   - *(Datum Display Filters)*: All Off
   - *(Spin Center)*: Off
   - *(Display Style)*: (Shading With Edges)

   The part displays as shown in Figure 6–28.

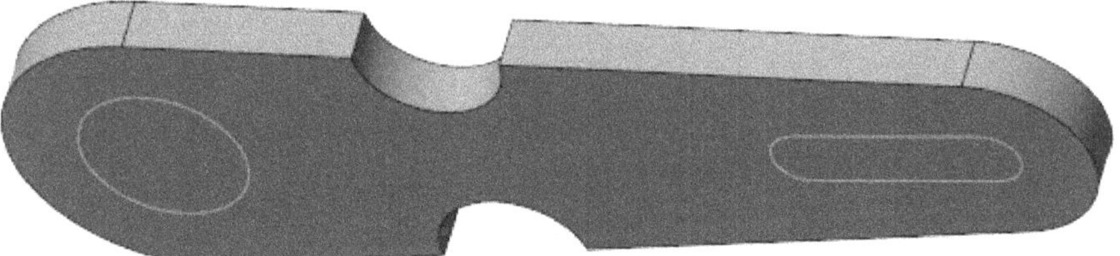

Figure 6–28

4. Note that the model contains two sketches named **PIN** and **SLOT**, as shown in Figure 6–29.

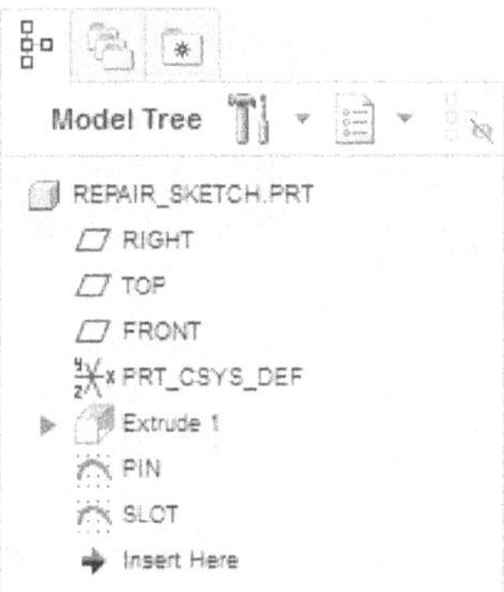

Figure 6–29

Task 2 - Create an extrude.

1. Select the **PIN** sketch.

2. Click (Extrude).

Design Considerations

The *Extrude* tab for the feature displays as shown in Figure 6–30 but the extrude is not created. The *Message* area states that the selected geometry cannot be used and that it has encountered intersecting entities in the section. The selected sketch cannot be used because it is not a single closed section.

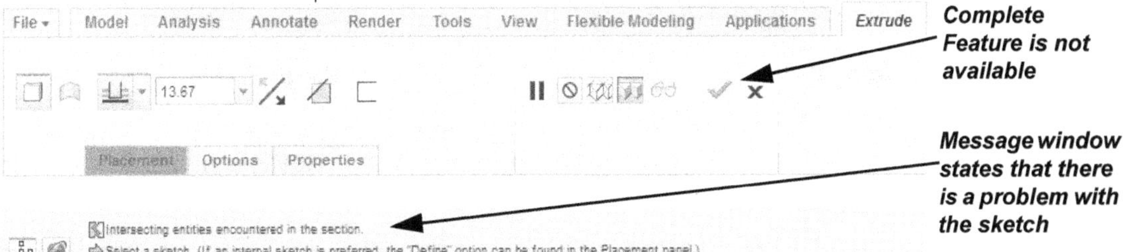

Figure 6–30

3. Click **×** (Cancel Feature) to cancel the creation of the extrude feature.

Task 3 - Edit the sketch.

1. In the model tree, select the **PIN** sketch, right-click, and select (Edit Definition).

2. The *Sketch* tab becomes active. Click (Sketch View).

Task 4 - Use sketch diagnostic tools to repair the sketch.

Design Considerations

In this task, you will use the Inspect tools in the *Sketch* tab to investigate the geometry of the **PIN** sketch.

1. Ensure that (Shade Closed Loops) is toggled on. Note that the sketch is not closed so the section does not display as shaded.

2. Ensure that (Highlight Open Ends) is toggled on. This indicates where an open section is located in the sketch. Red dots display on the end points of the open sketch geometry, as shown in Figure 6–31.

3. Hover the cursor over the right side of the sketch. A tool tip displays, indicating that this geometry is an Arc, as shown in Figure 6–32.

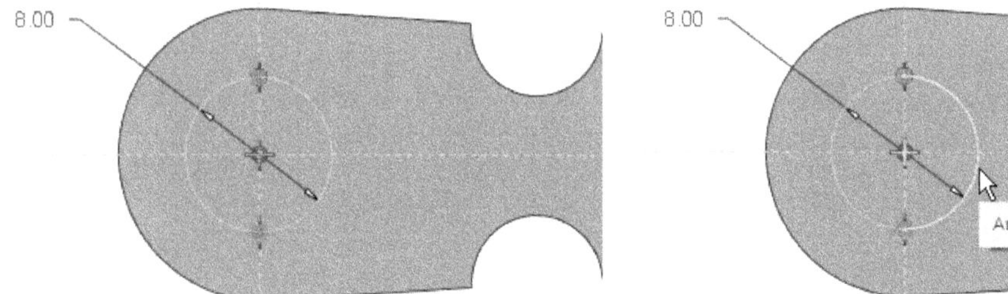

Figure 6–31

Figure 6–32

4. Hover the cursor over the left side of the sketch. A tool tip displays, indicating that this geometry is a Circle, as shown in Figure 6–33.

5. The Arc geometry is overlapping the Circle geometry. Select the arc, right-click and select **Delete**. The section displays shaded because it is now closed, as shown in Figure 6–34.

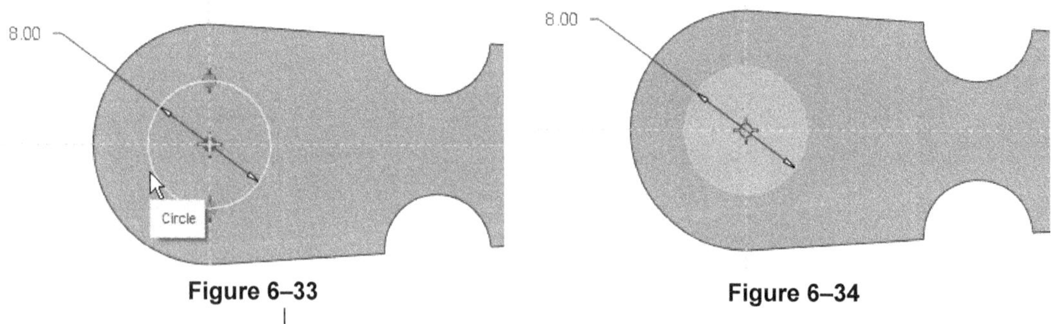

Figure 6–33

Figure 6–34

6. Click ✓ (OK) to complete the sketch.

7. Select the **PIN** sketch and click (Extrude). Set the *Depth* field to **10,** as shown on Figure 6–35.

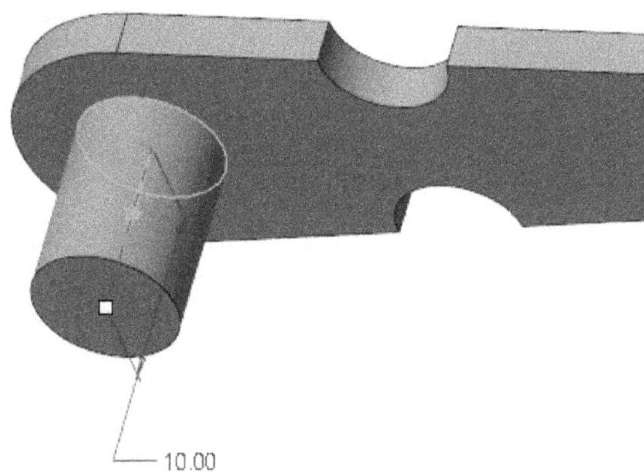

Figure 6–35

Task 5 - Edit an existing sketch.

Click (Sketch View) to orient the model into the sketched view.

The end of the arc and line, although not readily apparent, do not connect.

1. Right-click on the **SLOT** sketch and select (Edit Definition). Use the sketch diagnostic tools to identify the problem, as shown in Figure 6–36.

2. In the Editing group, click (Corner) to force the two end points to be coincident. The sketch displays as shaded, indicating that the section is now closed as shown in Figure 6–37.

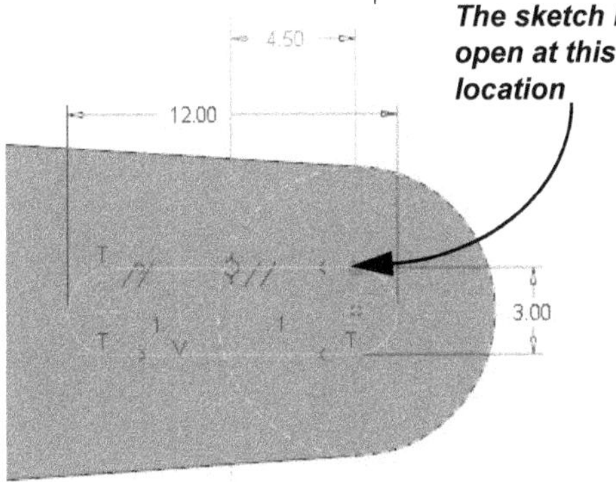

Figure 6–36

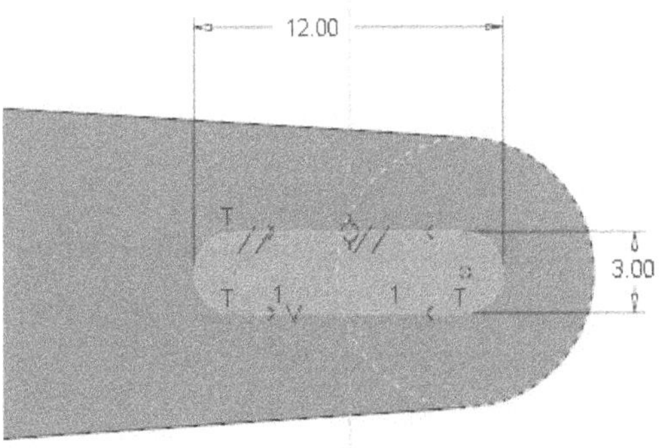

Figure 6–37

3. Click ✓ (OK).

4. Select the **SLOT** sketch and click (Extrude). In the *Depth* Field, enter **10**, as shown in Figure 6–38.

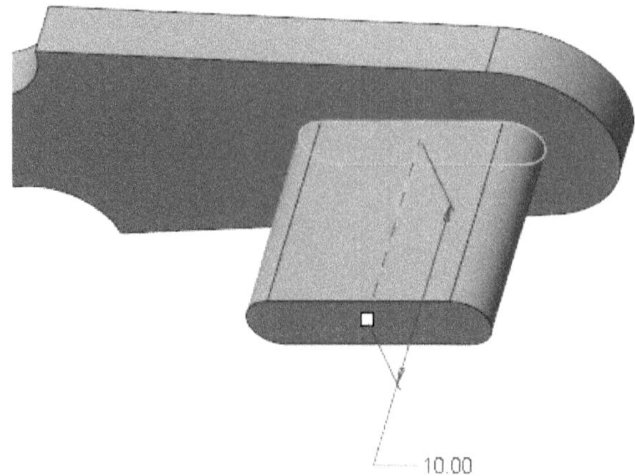

Figure 6–38

The completed model displays as shown in Figure 6–39.

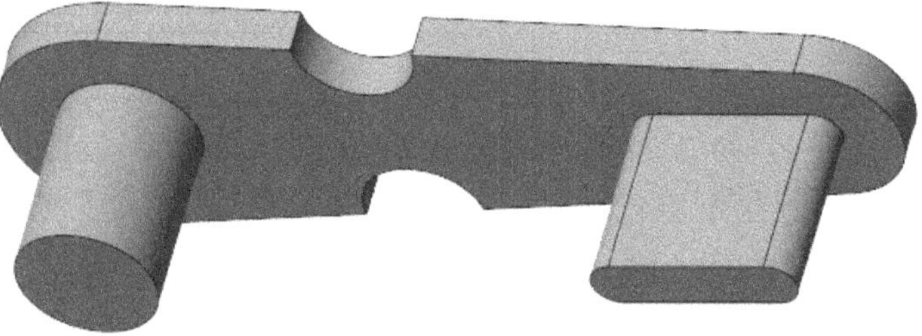

Figure 6–39

5. Save the model and erase it from memory.

Practice 6b

Import a Sketch

Practice Objectives

- Open and investigate the 2D sketch using the diagnostic tools in the *Sketch* tab.
- Fix the sketch using the Editing tools in the *Sketch* tab.
- Mirror the geometry to complete the sketch.
- Import the 2D sketch into a new part to create a base feature.

In this practice, you will open a saved sketch, and then modify, save, and import it into a part file. By importing an existing file, you are able to reuse sections in multiple models or in multiple features in one model.

Task 1 - Open a saved sketch file.

1. Set the working directory to the *Chapter 06\practice 6b* folder.
2. Open **beam.sec**. The sketch displays as shown in Figure 6–40.

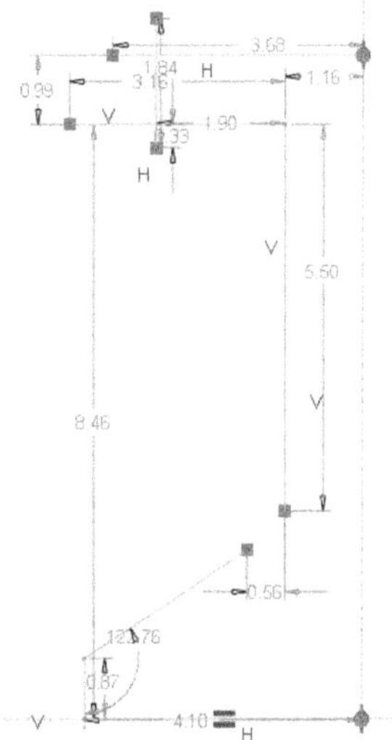

Figure 6–40

3. Set the model display as follows:

- (*Datum Display Filters*): All Off
- (*Spin Center*): Off
- (*Display Style*): (Shading With Edges)

4. In the In-graphics toolbar, click (Sketcher Display Filters) and disable (Disp Dims), to hide the display of dimensions. The sketch displays as shown in Figure 6–41.

Figure 6–41

5. In the Editing group, click (Corner) and trim the entities shown in Figure 6–42. Select the side of the entities you want to keep on both the upper and lower corner.

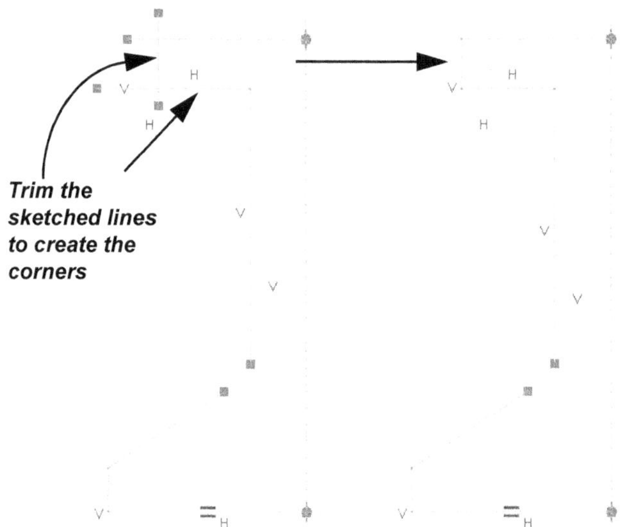

Figure 6–42

6. Trim two lines to create the corner shown in Figure 6–43.

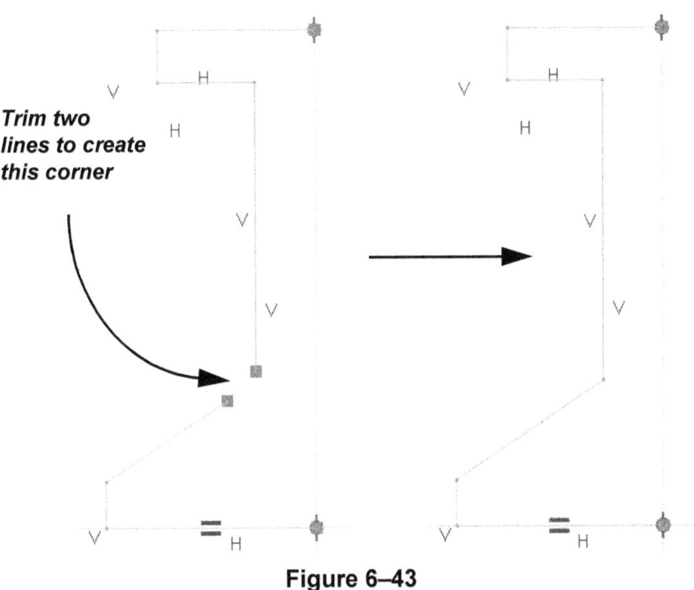

Figure 6–43

Your sketches will be more robust and stable it you strengthen all weak dimensions before conducting any operations on them.

7. In the In-graphics toolbar, click (Sketcher Display Filters), enable (Disp Dims) and dimension the sketch, as shown in Figure 6–44.

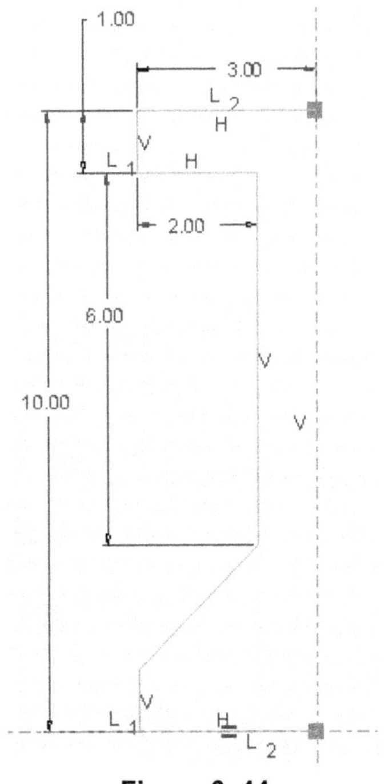

Figure 6–44

Task 2 - Mirror the sketched geometry.

1. Click (Select) and drag a box around all of the sketched geometry.
2. Click (Mirror) to mirror the sketch.
3. Select the vertical centerline as the reference to mirror about. The sketch displays as shown in Figure 6–45.

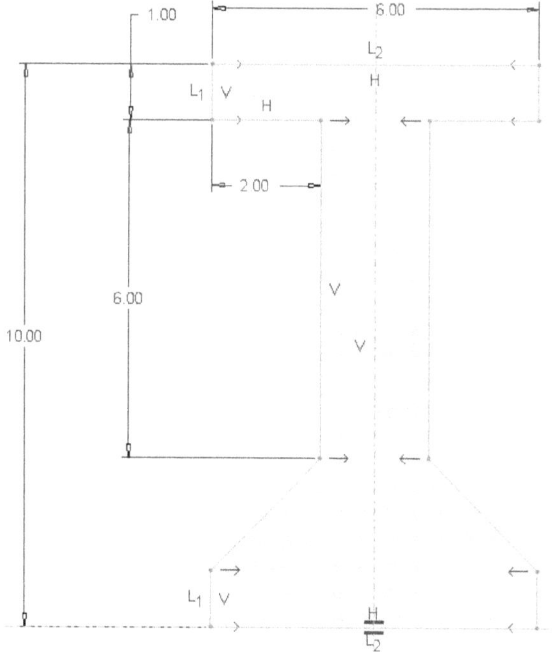

Figure 6–45

4. Save the sketch and click (Close) in the Quick Access Toolbar. Do not erase the file.

Task 3 - Create a part file and import a sketch.

1. Create a part file and name it **beam**.
2. In the Shapes group, click (Extrude) and select datum plane **FRONT** as the sketch plane.
3. Click (Sketch View).

4. In the Get Data group, click (File System) to import a sketch.

5. In the Open dialog box, double-click on **beam.sec**.

6. The cursor shape changes to . Move the cursor to the upper right quadrant, as shown in Figure 6–46. Then, click the left mouse button to place the section.

Figure 6–46

7. The *Import Section* dashboard becomes active. Set the *Scale* to **2**, as shown in Figure 6–47.

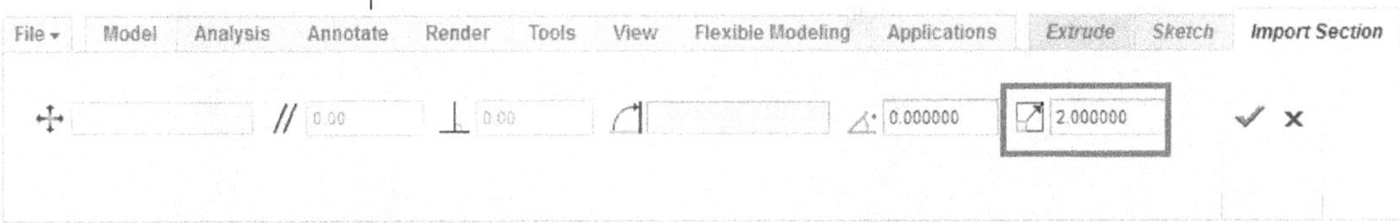

Figure 6–47

8. Click (OK) to close the *Import Section* dashboard.

9. Apply coincident constraints between the vertical centerline and the vertical sketcher reference, and between the horizontal centerline and the horizontal sketcher reference. The sketch displays as shown in Figure 6–48.

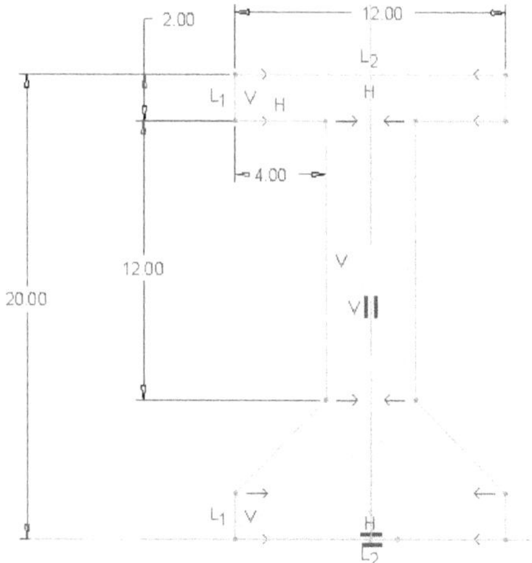

Figure 6–48

10. Click ✓ (OK) to exit the *Sketch* tab.

11. Set the *Depth* to **10**, as shown in Figure 6–49. The part displays as shown in Figure 6–50.

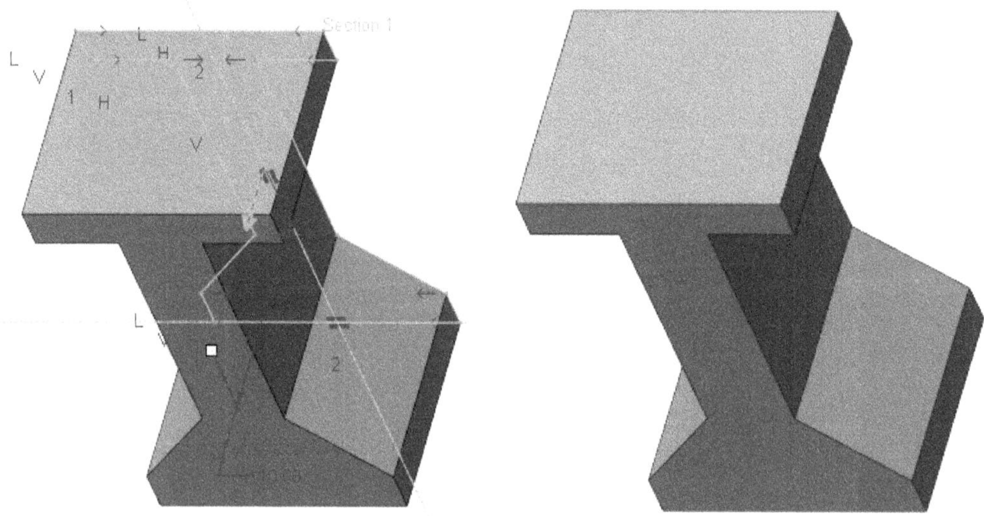

Figure 6–49

Figure 6–50

12. Save the part and erase it from memory.

Practice 6c Import Sketch From Palette

Practice Objectives

- Open and investigate the 2D sketch using the diagnostic tools in the *Sketch* tab.
- Fix the sketch using the Editing tools in the *Sketch* tab.
- Mirror the geometry to complete the sketch.
- Import the 2D sketch into a new part to create a base feature.

In this practice, you will create the sketch shown in Figure 6–51 by importing predefined sections from the palette. The sketcher palette enables you to quickly access the custom section library. When you organize commonly used sections into a library (creating a directory structure), you are able to reuse sections in multiple models or in multiple features in one model. This sketch can be used to create the cuts shown in Figure 6–51.

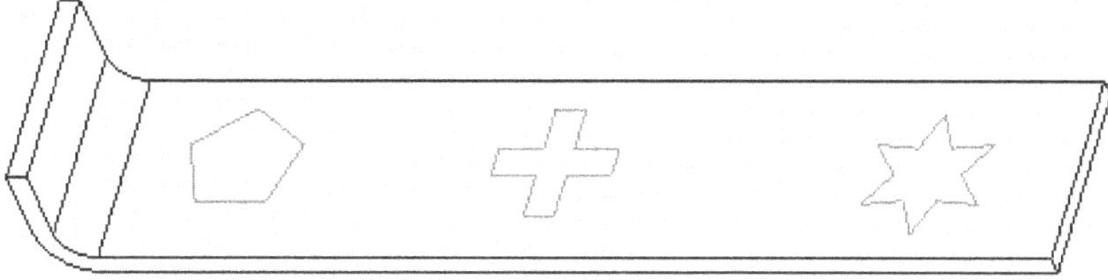

Figure 6–51

Task 1 - Open an existing Creo Parametric model.

1. Set the working directory to the *Chapter 06\practice 6c* folder.
2. Open **former.prt**.
3. Set the model display as follows:
    - *(Datum Display Filters)*: All Off
    - *(Spin Center)*: Off
    - *(Display Style)*: (Shading With Edges)

Task 2 - Create a sketch.

1. Click (Sketch).
2. Select the top surface of the part as the sketching plane and set datum plane **FRONT** to face bottom.
3. Click **Sketch** to activate the *Sketch* tab.
4. Click (Sketch View).

Task 3 - Import a predefined section from the palette.

1. Click (Palette). The Sketcher Palette dialog box opens.
2. In the *Polygons* tab, locate and select the **5-Sided Pentagon** thumbnail. The upper area of the Sketcher Palette dialog box displays a preview of the section, as shown on Figure 6–52.

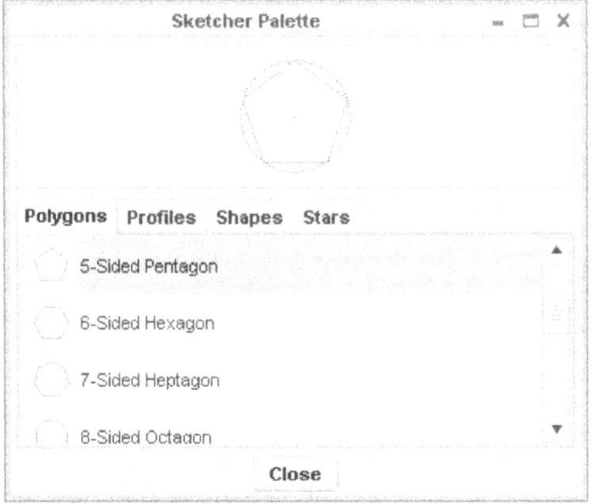

Figure 6–52

3. Select **5-Sided Pentagon** and drag it into the Sketcher window. The cursor shape changes to .
4. Release the left mouse button to place the section. The section displays as shown in Figure 6–53.

*In the Import Section tab, set the Scale to **13**.*

5. The section can be scaled, translated, or rotated using the handles on the section or by entering values in the *Import Section* dashboard. Click the (Translate) handle and snap the section to the horizontal sketcher reference. Then, click the (Scale) handle and scale the section to fit into the base feature, as shown in Figure 6–54.

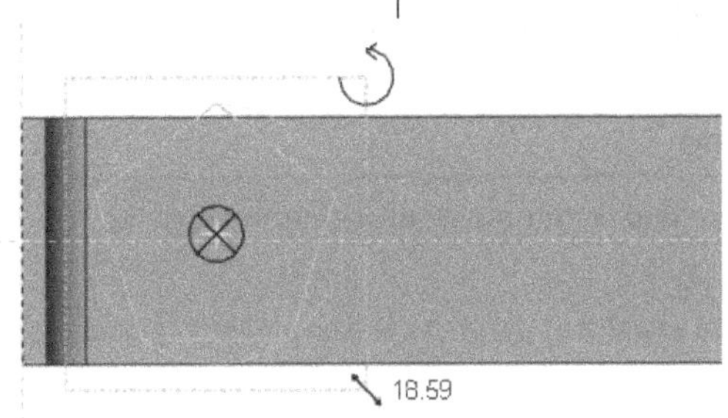

Figure 6–53

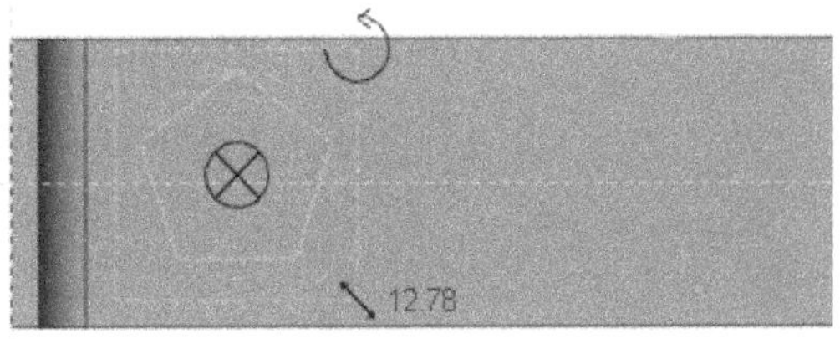

Figure 6–54

6. Click (OK) to close the *Import Section* dashboard.

Task 4 - Import two other predefined sections from the palette.

1. Use the procedure from Task 3 to import the **Cross** section from the *Shapes* tab. Set the *Scale* to **5**.
2. Use the procedure from Task 3 to import the **6-tip star** section from the *Stars* tab. Set the *Scale* to **3**.

   The resulting section displays as shown on Figure 6–55. Dimension and constraint display is toggled off for clarity.

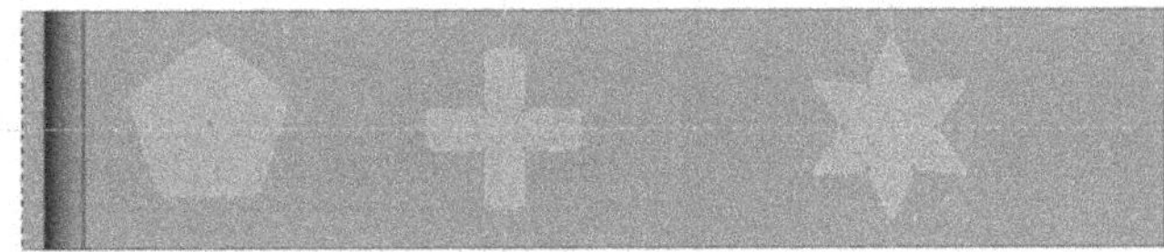

Figure 6–55

3. Close the Sketcher Palette dialog box.
4. Click (OK) to complete the sketch.
5. Reorient the model into the Default orientation. The sketch displays as shown in Figure 6–56.

Figure 6–56

6. Save the part and erase it from memory.

Practice 6d

Create and Dimension Sketches

Practice Objectives

- Open an existing part and create sketched geometry using the (Offset) command.
- Remove a coincident constraint using the Resolve Sketch dialog box.

In this practice, you will create a sketch using the (Offset) tool in the *Sketch* tab, as well as other tools and constraints. The completed sketch displays as shown in Figure 6–57.

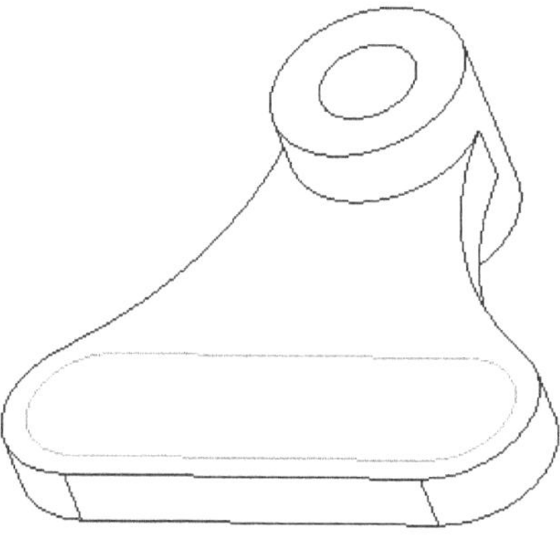

Figure 6–57

Task 1 - Open an existing Creo Parametric model.

1. Set the working directory to the *Chapter 06*\practice *6d* folder.
2. Open **bracket.prt.**
3. Set the model display as follows:
   - *(Datum Display Filters)*: All Off
   - *(Spin Center)*: Off
   - *(Display Style)*: (Shading With Edges)
4. Click (Extrude).
5. For the sketch plane, select the top surface of the part.

Task 2 - Create the sketch.

1. Click (Sketch View).

2. In the Sketching group, in the *Sketch* tab, click (Offset). The Type dialog box opens, as shown in Figure 6–58.

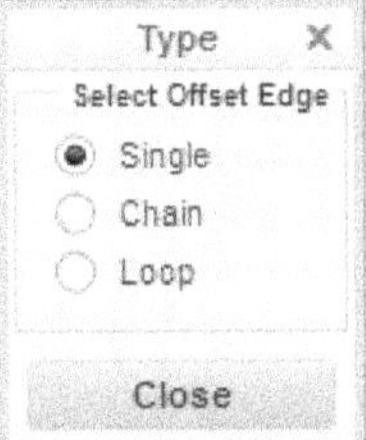

Figure 6–58

3. Select the **Chain** option.

4. Select the two arcs shown in Figure 6–59. The two arcs plus the line connecting them will be selected because you are using the **Chain** option.

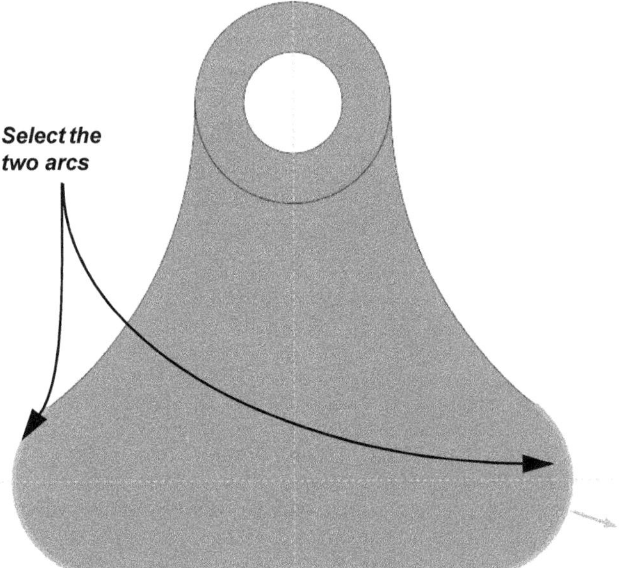

Figure 6–59

5. If the chain is created using the top loop, select **Next** until the two arcs and the bottom line are selected.

6. In the **CHOOSE** menu, select **Accept**.

The negative value is used to specify an offset value that is opposite from the displayed direction arrow.

7. Set the *Offset* to **-0.2** and press <Enter>.

8. Click **Close** to close the Type dialog box.

9. Sketch a line to join the two open ends of the arcs, as shown in Figure 6–60.

10. Click | (Vertical), and select the two endpoints shown in Figure 6–61.

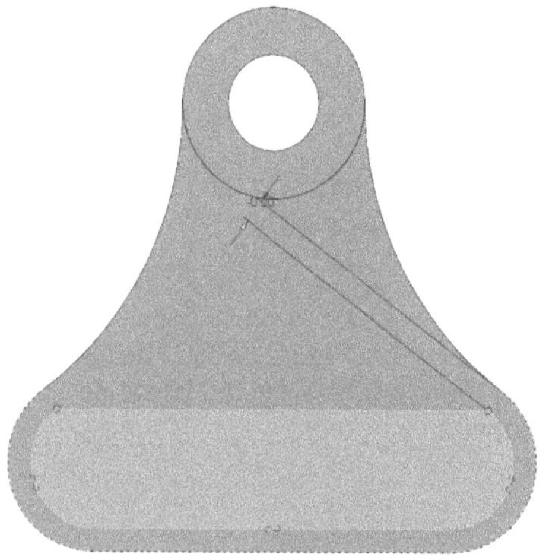

Figure 6–60

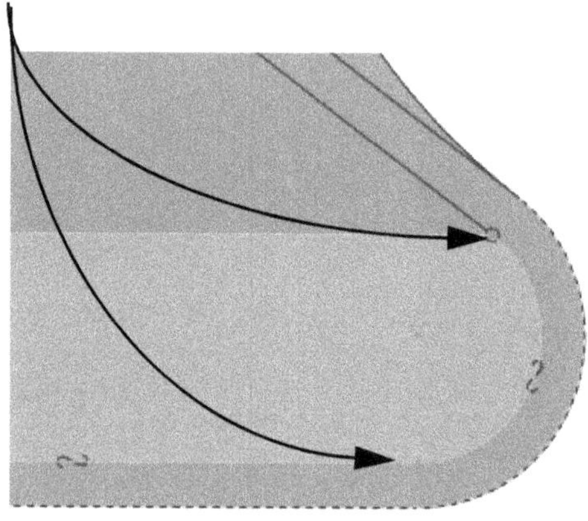

Figure 6–61

*You can select the coincident constraint and click **Explain** for a brief explanation.*

11. The Resolve Sketch dialog box opens as shown in Figure 6–62, because the end vertices of each arc are coincident with the end vertices of the line. Delete the coincident constraint.

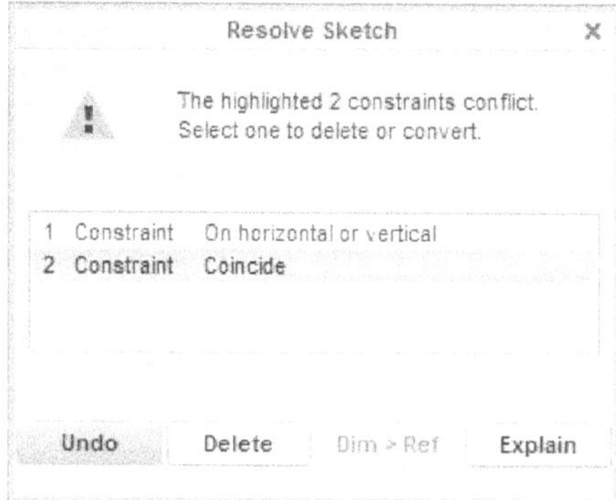

Figure 6–62

12. Assign the Vertical constraint to the other end of the line where it intersects the arc. Delete the coincident constraint.

Task 3 - Complete the extrude.

1. Click ✓ (OK).
2. Set the *Depth* to **1.0**, as shown in Figure 6–63.
3. Edit the base feature (**Protrusion id 39**), and change the *Radius R.75* value to **1.0**, as shown in Figure 6–64.

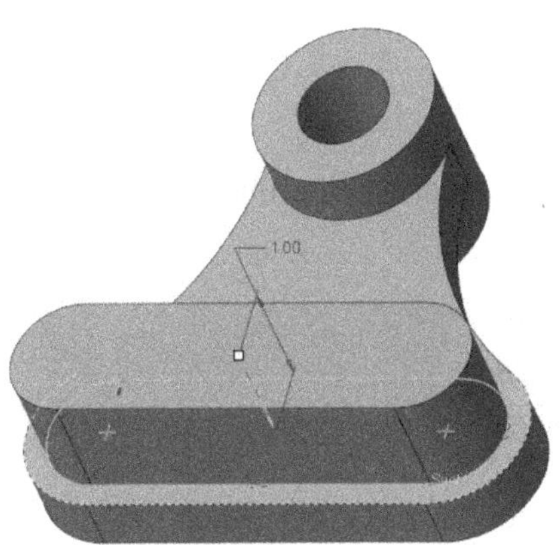

Figure 6–63

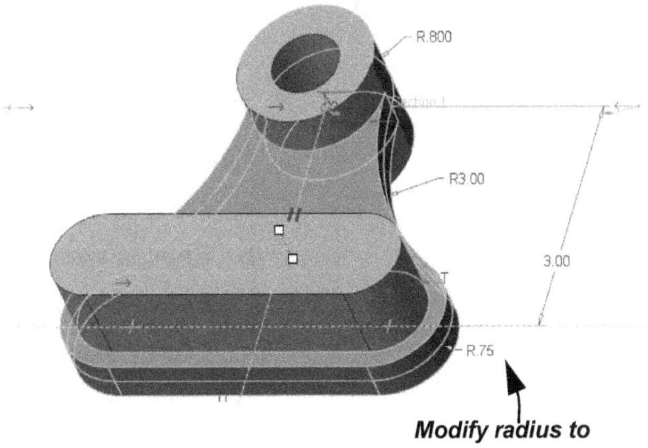

R.800
R3.00
3.00
R.75
Modify radius to

Figure 6–64

4. Regenerate the model. The offset geometry updates, as shown in Figure 6–65.

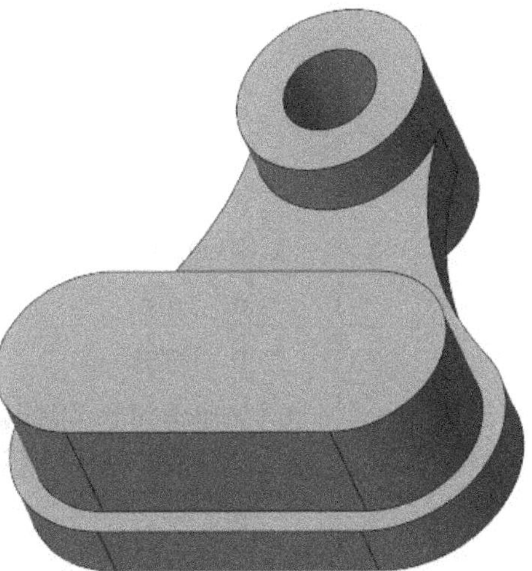

Figure 6–65

5. Save the part and erase it from memory.

Chapter Review Question

1. Which of the following icons enables you to access the **Rotate Resize** option?

    a.

    b.

    c.

    d.

2. Which of the following best describes the use of ?
    a. Translates sketched entities
    b. Rotates sketched entities
    c. Scales sketched entities
    d. Copies sketched entities

3. Which of the following best describes the use of ?
    a. Translates sketched entities
    b. Rotates sketched entities
    c. Scales sketched entities
    d. Copies sketched entities

4. When importing a sketch, the imported data can be scaled, rotated, and translated.
    a. True
    b. False

5. Pasted entities can be scaled, rotated, and translated.
    a. True
    b. False

6. Which of the following symbols identifies that existing geometry was used for offsetting sketched geometry?

    a.

    b.

    c.

    d.

7. Once automatic constraints have been assigned to the sketch, you cannot manually assign any additional constraints.

   a. True

   b. False

8. Which of the following icons enables you to manually assign the point on entity constraint?

   a.

   b.

   c.

   d.

9. Each time a constraint or dimension is manually added to the sketch, the Resolve Sketch dialog box opens requiring you to resolve the conflict.

   a. True

   b. False

10. Select the constraints that were used to sketch the geometry shown in Figure 6–66. (Select all that apply.)

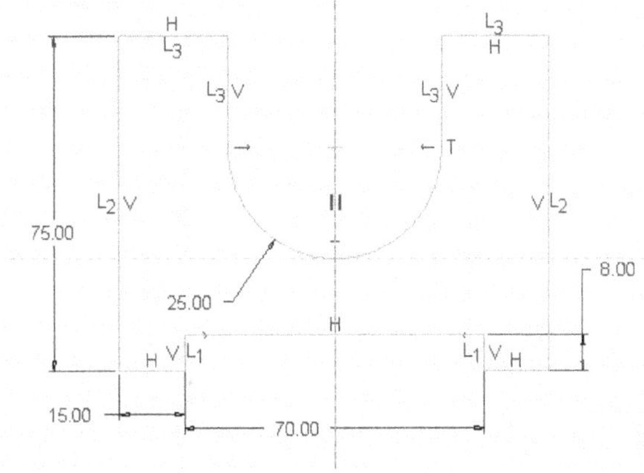

Figure 6–66

   a. Tangent

   b. Point on Entity

   c. Parallel

   d. Symmetry

   e. Equal

   f. Perpendicular

Command Summary

Button	Command	Location
	Rotate Resize	• **Ribbon:** *Sketch* tab in the Editing group
	File System	• **Ribbon:** *Sketch* tab in the Get Data group
	Palette	• **Ribbon:** *Sketch* tab in the Sketching group
	Offset	• **Ribbon:** *Sketch* tab in the Sketching group
	Project	• **Ribbon:** *Sketch* tab in the Sketching group
	Modify	• **Ribbon:** *Sketch* tab in the Editing group
	Shade Closed Loops	• **Ribbon:** *Sketch* tab in the Editing group
	Highlight Open Ends	• **Ribbon:** *Sketch* tab in the Editing group
	Overlapping Geometry	• **Ribbon:** *Sketch* tab in the Editing group

Sketched Secondary Features

Sketched features add or remove material from a model. A protrusion is a sketched feature that adds material and a cut is a sketched feature that removes material. As features and design intent become more complex, additional options are available to help you create more advanced features.

Learning Objectives in this Chapter

- Create an extruded and a revolved secondary feature and define their material removal option, extent, and direction.
- Create a Trajectory Rib feature and define its options.
- Create a Profile Rib feature and define its direction and thickness.

7.1 Sketched Secondary Features

The selection of an orientation reference is recommended, but not mandatory. The Creo Parametric software will select an orientation reference for you. The downside is the lack of control over the orientation.

The process for creating secondary features is similar to the process of creating base features. Once you select the sketching and orientation reference planes, the Creo Parametric software automatically activates the *Sketch* tab. All of the tools discussed for base features are available to create a profile. Figure 7–1 shows and example of a sketched geometry.

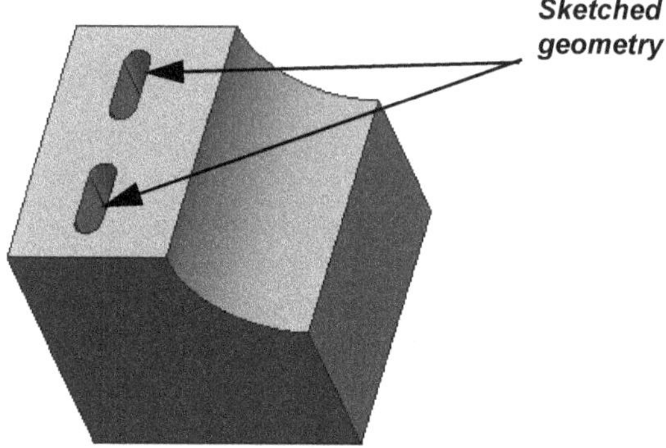

Figure 7–1

Select a feature form, either (Extrude) or (Revolve), and select the sketch plane. If the default orientation plane is unsatisfactory, select an appropriate one. In addition to orienting the sketch, you must determine where the sketch will be located relative to any existing geometry, by adding dimensions and constraints. You need various sketching references to locate the sketch both vertically and horizontally, as viewed from the 2D Sketch orientation.

Sketching references are entities to which the section is dimensioned and constrained. You can select datum planes, surfaces, edges, or vertices as references. You can add additional sketch references as required, by opening the References dialog box at any time by clicking (References) and changing the selected references. You can also open the references dialog box by right-clicking and selecting **References**.

As you add references, they are added to the References dialog box, as shown in Figure 7–2. In the example shown in Figure 7–3, the dashed lines represent the selected references.

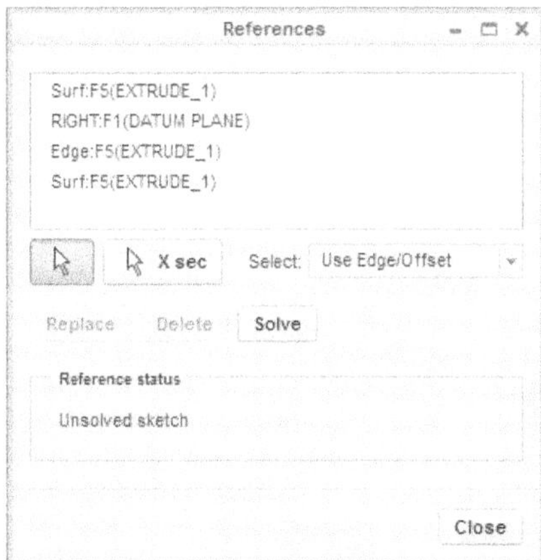

Figure 7–2

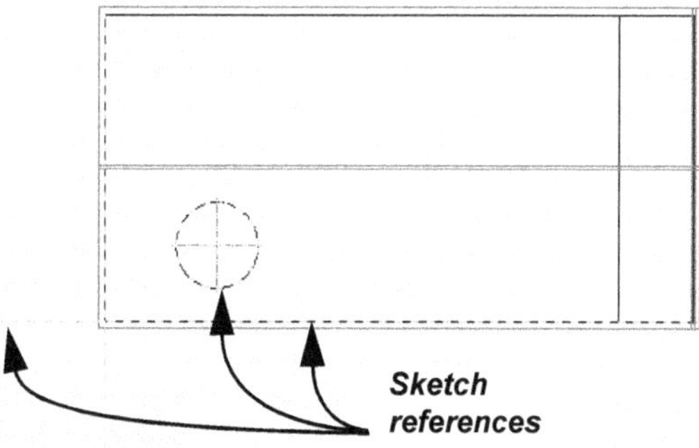

Figure 7–3

Always examine the default selections made by Creo Parametric to verify that they meet your design intent.

- To create a reference, select existing features or entities (e.g., datum planes, datum curves, sketches, surfaces, edges, etc.) on the model. The reference status in the References dialog box should be set to **Fully Placed** before you start the sketch.
- If the model is not fully placed, the Reference Status is set to **Not Placed** or **Partially Placed**. Although you can complete a sketch without fully placed references, it is recommended that it be fully placed before exiting. This prevents problems later when adding or modifying features.
- To delete a reference, highlight it in the References dialog box and click **Delete**. References that are not used in the sketch are automatically removed from the list once it has been completed.

Click **Close** to accept the references and begin sketching.A single extrude or revolve feature cannot both add and remove material.

After the first feature is created, extruded or revolved features can be defined to add or remove material.

Thicken Sketch

Base protrusions can also be created as thin extrusions.

When you select or sketch a section for an extrusion or revolve, the material to be added or removed is defined to be entirely inside or outside the section by default, as shown in the examples in Figure 7–4.

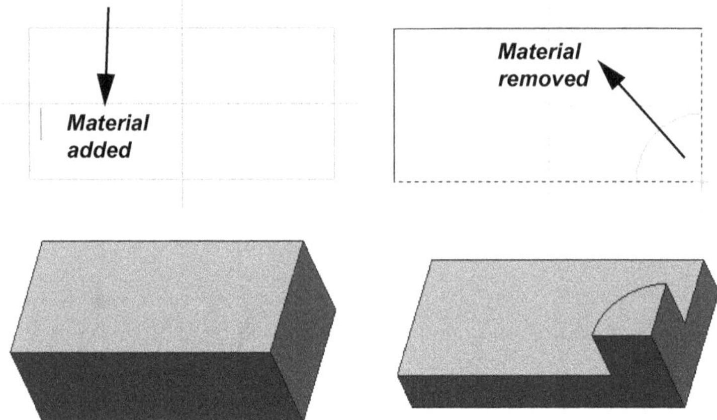

Figure 7–4

*You can also right-click and select **Thicken Sketch**.*

Using (Thicken Sketch) in the *Extrude* dashboard, you can specify a thickness for the section. Thickness can be applied on either side of the section or divided evenly on both sides using (Change Material Direction), as shown in Figure 7–5.

Select this icon to change the direction of thickening between one side, the other side, or both sides

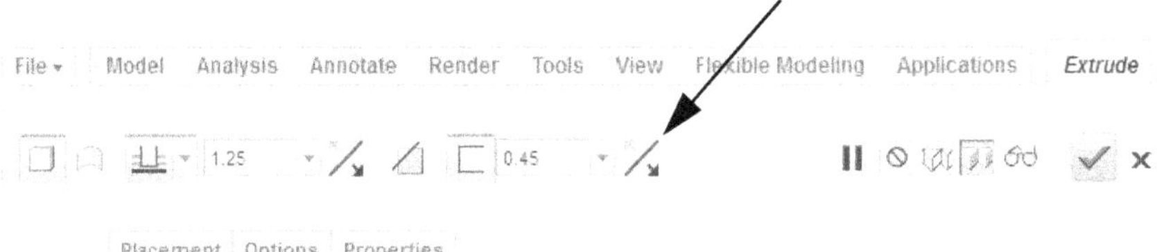

Figure 7–5

Thickness can be applied to the sections of the previous examples to obtain the geometry shown in Figure 7–6.

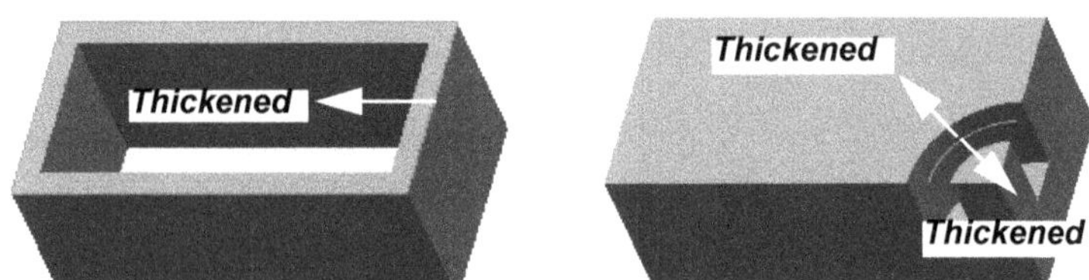

Figure 7–6

Figure 7–7 shows the section and solid geometry resulting from creating a thickened revolve.

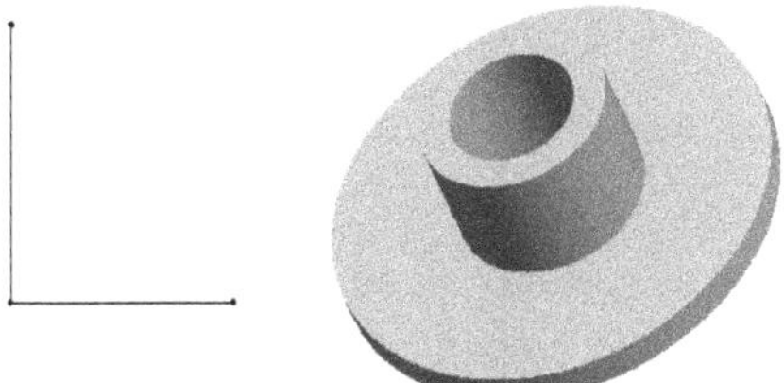

Figure 7–7

The following restrictions apply to sections that are thickened:

- The section can only contain one open chain. In Figure 7–8, the section on the left can be thickened while the section on the right cannot.

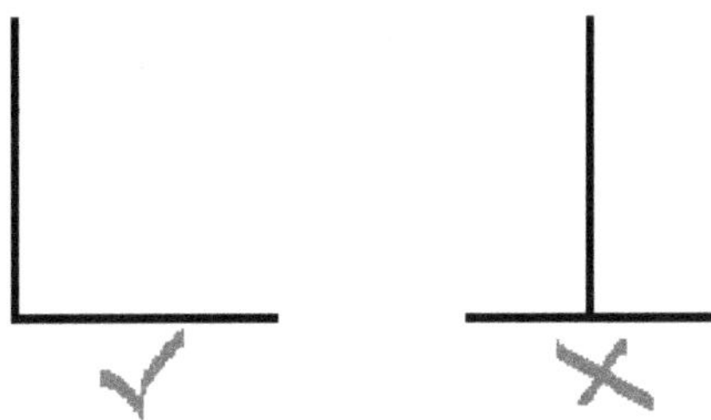

Figure 7–8

- Sections for revolves can also be open, but must only contain one open chain, as shown in Figure 7–9.

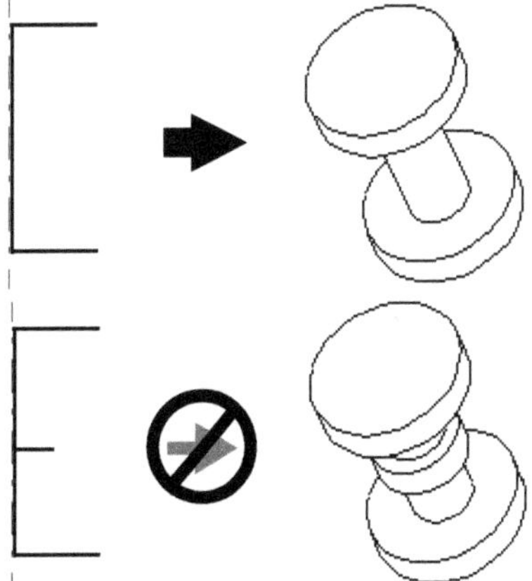

Figure 7–9

- If the section contains curvature, such as fillet arcs, the thickness added to the inside of the curvature cannot exceed the radius at any point. In Figure 7–10, the radius of the fillet arc is 5.0, therefore the thickness applied to the section cannot exceed 5.0.

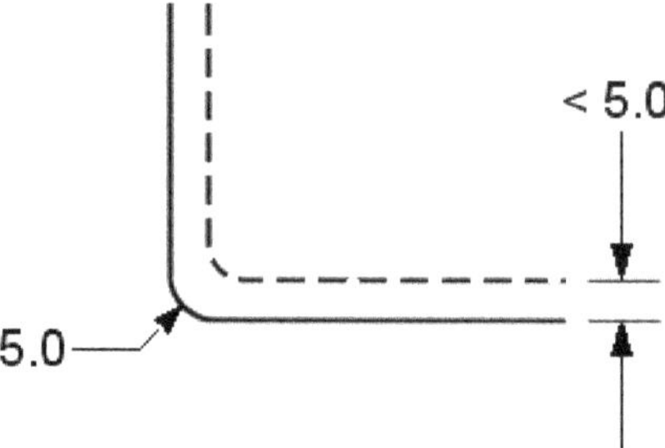

Figure 7–10

7.2 Removing Material

*You can also right-click and select **Remove Material**.*

When you create an extrusion or revolve, it is typically created to add material by default. It can be created as a cut by clicking (Remove Material) in the dashboard. If you change the feature direction such that it runs into existing solid geometry, it will automatically convert to a cut.

When you create a cut, you can define the side of the sketch from which to remove material. To change the material removal side, right-click and select **Flip Material Side** or click (Change Material Direction) in the dashboard, as shown in Figure 7–11. This icon only becomes available when a cut is being created.

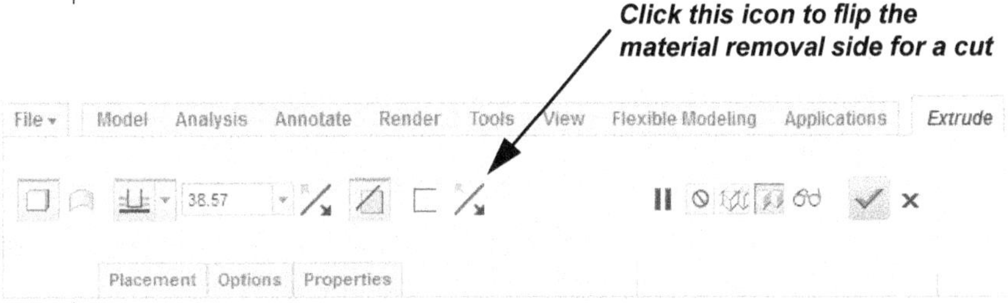

Figure 7–11

In Figure 7–12, the extrusion is shown as a protrusion on the left and a cut on the right. (Remove Material) was selected to convert the default protrusion into a cut.

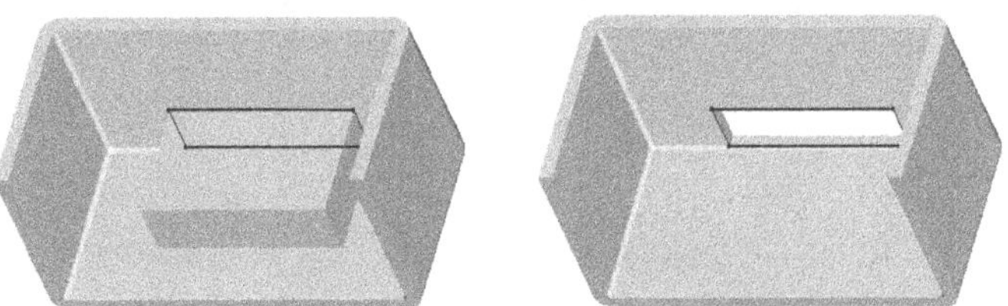

Figure 7–12

7.3 Depth Controls

You can also right-click and select ***Flip Depth Direction*** *or* ***Flip Angle Direction****.*

You can change the depth direction in which the feature is extruded from the sketching plane by clicking (Change Depth Direction) in the *Extrude* dashboard or (Change Angle Direction) in the *Revolve* dashboard, as shown in Figure 7–13.

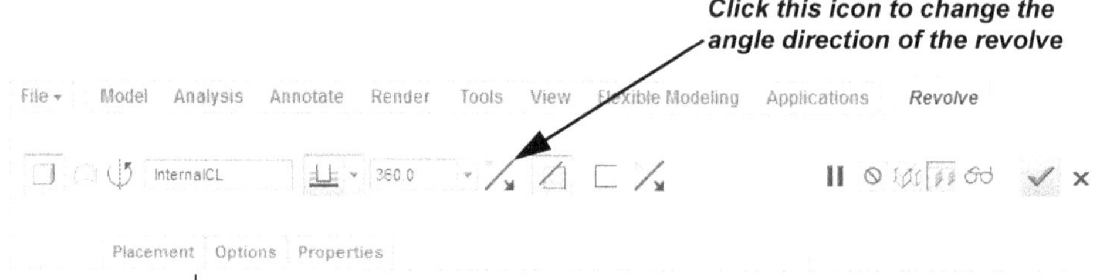

Figure 7–13

In Figure 7–14, the model on the left shows the section that is going to be used to create an extruded cut. The model in the middle shows the cut extruded below the sketching plane and the model on the right shows the cut extruded above the sketching plane. The depth direction is flipped by clicking (Change Depth Direction).

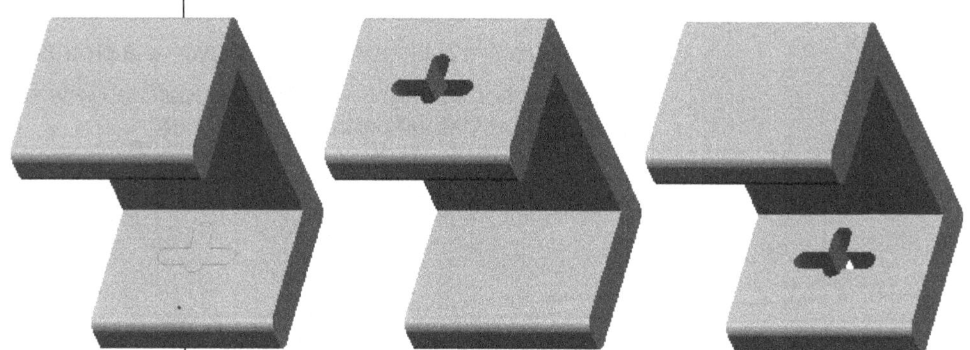

Figure 7–14

By default, Creo Parametric creates an extrusion with a blind depth that is applied to one side. The depth value can be modified in the dashboard, or by dragging the depth handle of the extrusion, as shown in Figure 7–15.

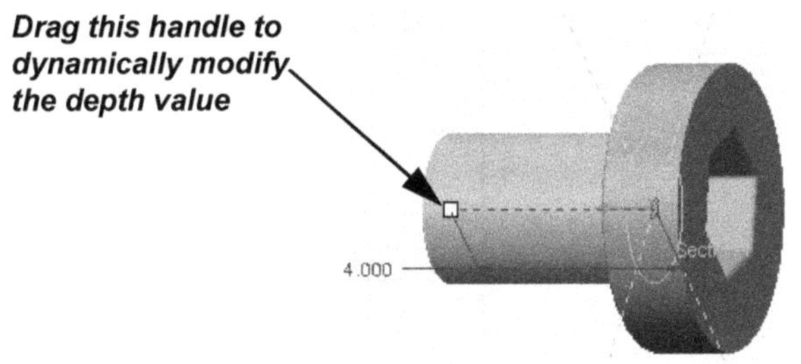

Figure 7–15

Depth and Angle Options

The depth options that can be assigned to an extrusion are described as follows:

Icon	Description
(Blind)	Extrude from sketch plane by specified depth value.
(Symmetric)	Extrude on both sides of sketch plane by half the specified value in each direction.
(To Next)	Extrude to next surface.
(Through All)	Extrude to intersect with all surfaces.
(Through Until)	Extrude to intersect with selected surface.
(To Selected)	Extrude to selected point, curve, plane, or surface.

The model in Figure 7–16 shows the resulting extruded cuts that are created by each depth option.

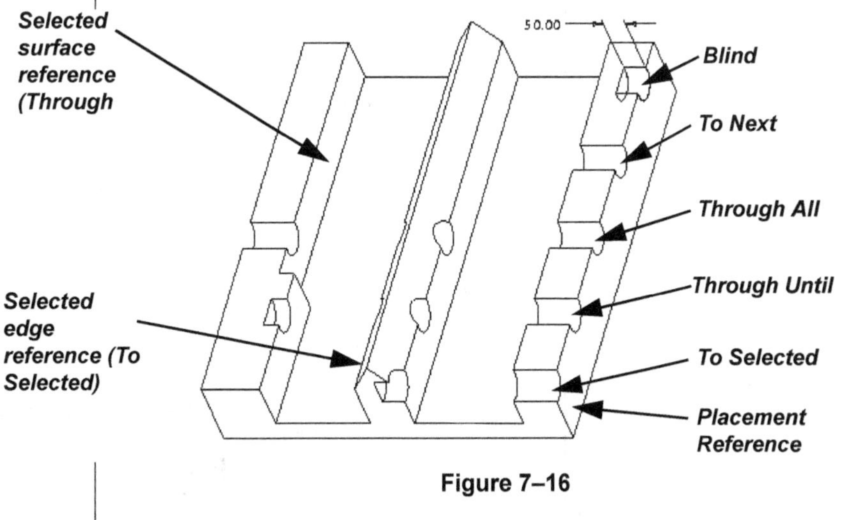

Figure 7–16

The angle options that can be assigned to a revolve are described as follows:

Icon	Description
(Variable)	Revolve from sketch plane by specified angle value.
(Symmetric)	Revolve on both sides of sketch plane by half the specified angle value in each direction.
(To Selected)	Revolve to selected point, plane, or surface.

Side Options

An extruded feature is created in one direction from the sketching plane by default. If you expand the Options panel in the *Extrude* or *Revolve* dashboard, you can define a depth (or angle for revolves) for the second direction, as shown in Figure 6-12. This enables you to define a different extent for each direction.

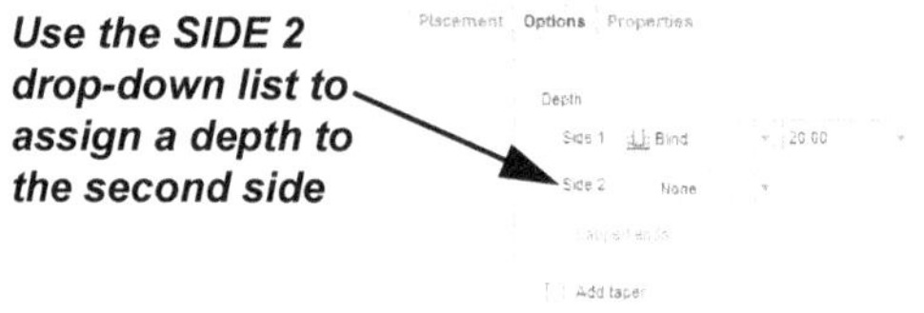

Figure 7–17

All depth options, except for the **Symmetric** depth option, are the same as those used for the primary direction. If the **Symmetric** depth option is used for the primary direction, the value is divided equally between both sides. Figure 7–18 shows cuts extruded in both directions.

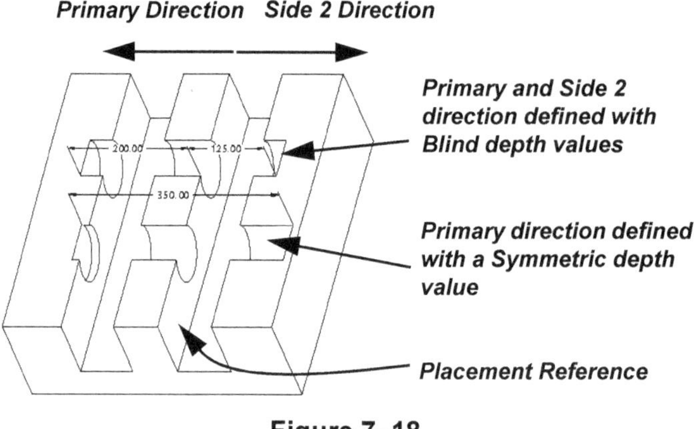

Figure 7–18

Add Taper is also in the Options panel for Extrudes. You can add a taper to an extrude if the sketch is a closed loop. This adds an angle normal to the sketching plane. You can add an angle between 30 and -30 degrees as shown in Figure 7–19.

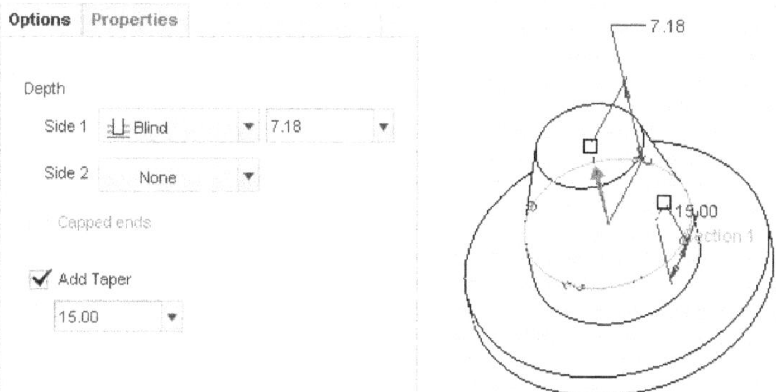

Figure 7–19

7.4 Creating Trajectory Ribs

A trajectory rib can create multiple extrusions from a selected sketching plane. In general, a rib is a feature that supports adjoining geometry, as shown in Figure 7–20.

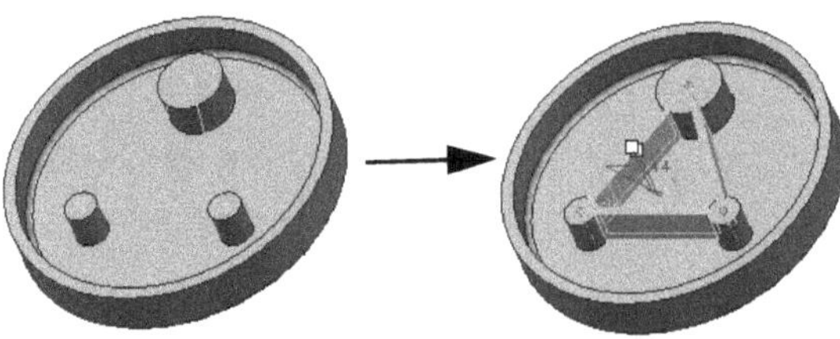

Figure 7–20

To create a trajectory rib, click (Rib) in the Engineering *group* in the *Model* tab. If you have previously created a Profile Rib, expand the flyout, select and click (Trajectory Rib). The *Trajectory Rib* dashboard displays as shown in Figure 7–21.

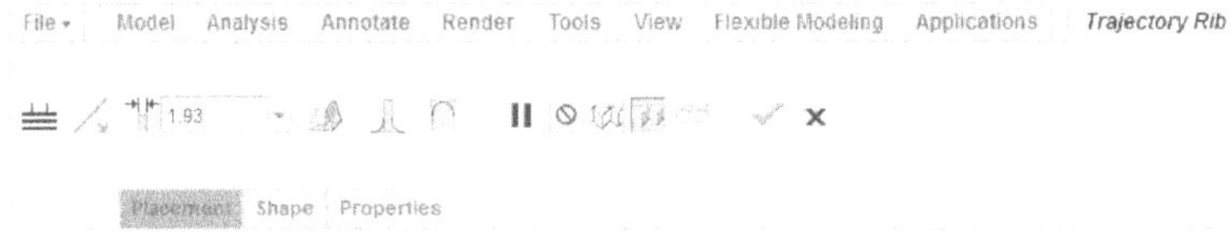

Figure 7–21

The section for the trajectory rib feature can be sketched or you can select a sketch to be copied to create the section. The section of the trajectory rib can be sketched as an open or closed section that defines the shape of the rib, as shown in Figure 7–22.

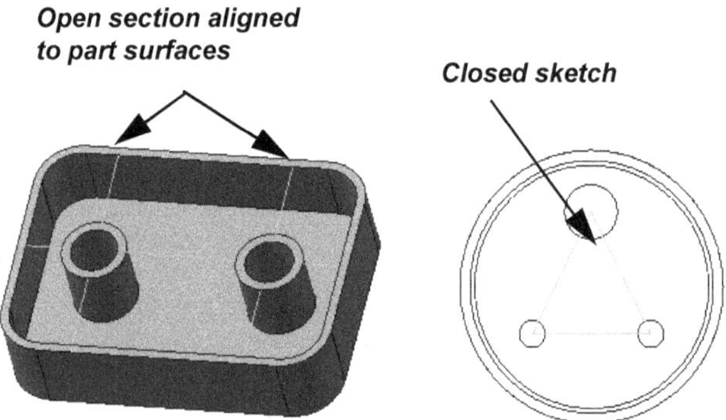

Figure 7–22

Clicking (Change Thickness Option) in the *Trajectory Rib* tab enables you to flip the direction of the rib feature. The thickness options for trajectory ribs are restricted to numeric values. You can enter the numeric value for the rib or select from the drop-down list in the *Trajectory Rib* dashboard, as shown in Figure 7–23.

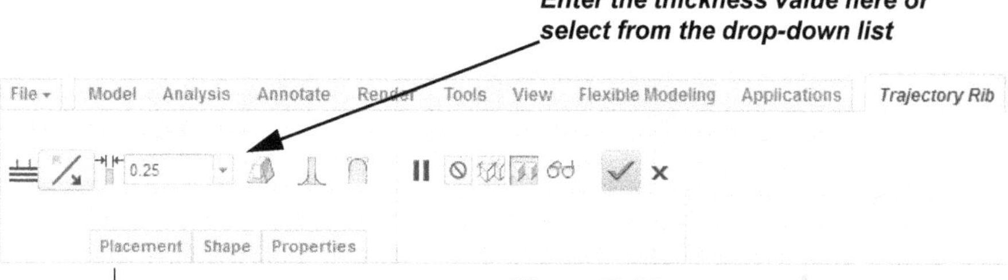

Figure 7–23

By default, the rib is extruded symmetrically on both sides of the sketching elements. Additional options can be selected as shown in Figure 7–24.

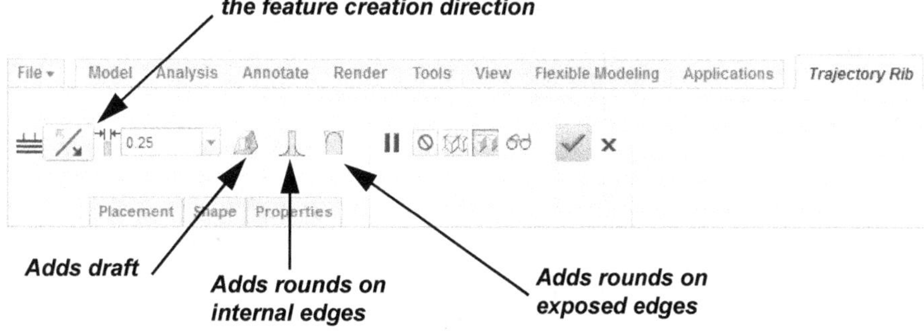

Figure 7–24

Once satisfied with the rib, click (Complete Feature) to complete the rib.

7.5 Creating Profile Ribs

A profile rib is a protrusion extruded from a selected sketching plane. In general, a rib is a feature that supports adjoining geometry, as shown in Figure 7–25.

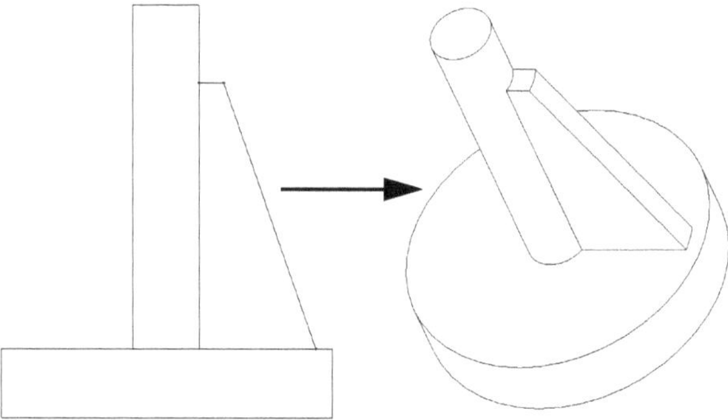

Figure 7–25

To start the creation of a profile rib, expand the (Rib) flyout in the Engineering group in the *Model* tab and click (Profile Rib). The *Profile Rib* dashboard displays as shown in Figure 7–26.

Figure 7–26

The section for the profile rib feature can be sketched or you can select a sketch to be copied to create the section.

The section of the profile rib should be sketched as an open section that defines the shape of the profile rib. In Figure 7–27, the two open end points of the sketch have been aligned to the part surfaces. By aligning to the part surfaces, the rib follows the contour of these surfaces when it is extruded.

The sketcher tools are the same as those used for creating other sketched features.

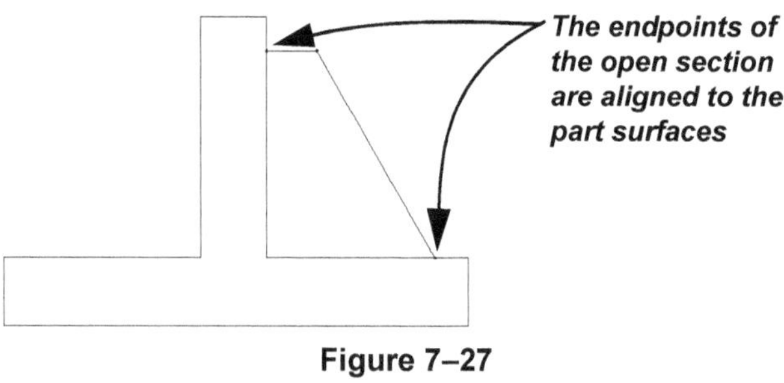

Figure 7–27

Clicking **Flip** in the References panel enables you to flip the side of the sketch on which the feature is created as shown in Figure 7–28.

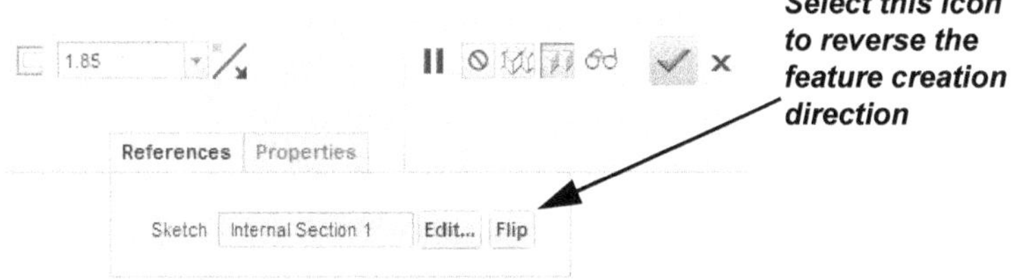

Figure 7–28

The thickness options for profile ribs are restricted to numeric values. You can enter the numeric value for the rib or select from the drop-down list in the *Profile Rib* dashboard, as shown in Figure 7–29.

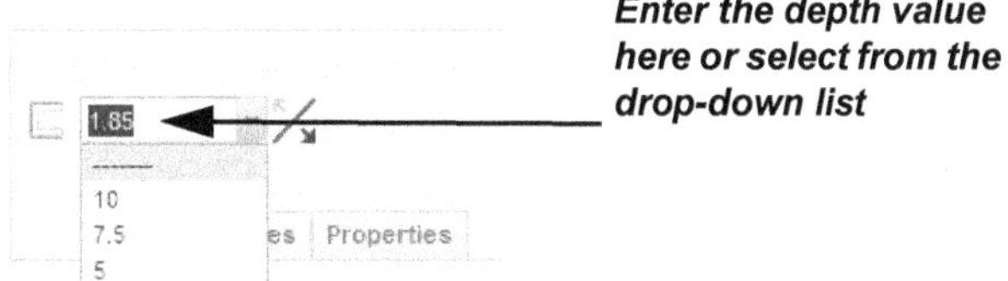

Figure 7–29

By default, the rib is extruded symmetrically on both sides of the sketching plane, as shown in Figure 7–30. To switch the feature creation from both to one side of the sketching plane, click (Change Thickness Option) in the *Profile Rib* dashboard. Each time you click this option, you toggle between extruding on once side or the other, and symmetrically.

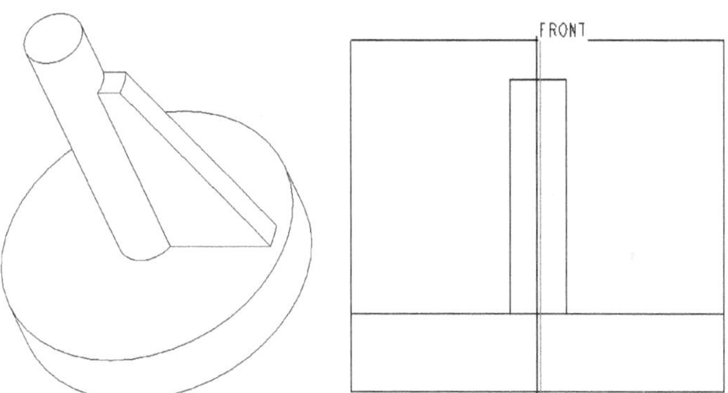

Figure 7–30

Once satisfied with the geometry, click (Complete Feature) to complete the rib.

7.6 Editing Sketched Secondary Features

Making Changes

Any of the dimensions and feature elements that were defined when the feature was created can be changed. This can be done by selecting the feature, right-clicking and selecting either the dl (Edit) or (Edit Definition). You can select the feature to be edited directly on the model or in the model tree.

If you are only making changes to the values of dimensions, right-click and select dl (Edit). This displays the dimensions for the selected feature and enables you to change the values without accessing the feature's tab. Click (Regenerate) after you have entered the modified values to regenerate the model and incorporate the changes.

You can also right-click and select (Edit Definition), as shown in Figure 7–31. This option automatically suppresses all of the features that were created after the feature you are redefining, and displays the dashboard for that feature.

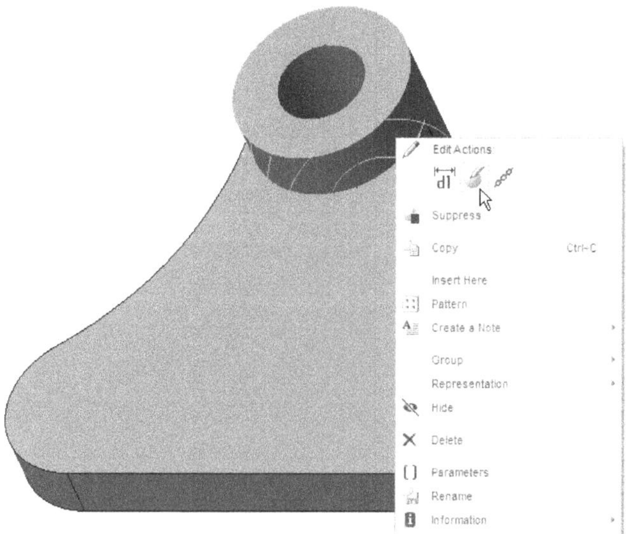

Figure 7–31

The dashboard provides access to the same options and elements that were available when the feature was created originally, as shown in Figure 7–32.

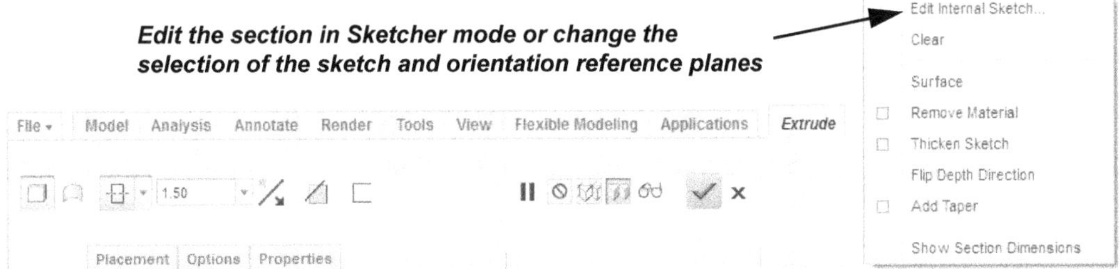

Figure 7–32

Regardless of the type of change made to a feature, be aware of any child features and how the changes are going to affect them. Sometimes a change can cause a feature creation failure because the system is no longer able to create the geometry. For example, failures occur when references are no longer present (i.e., an edge selected for a chamfer feature no longer exists) or if the geometry becomes impossible to build (i.e., the thickness of a thickened section becomes greater than the inside radius of a filleted corner).

Feature Creation Failures

When you click (Verify Mode) to preview a feature or click (Complete Feature) to complete a feature, the system might not be able to create the geometry you have defined. If a surface is removed after the depth of an extrusion has been defined using, (To Selected), the system will not be able to create the geometry. When this happens, the regeneration failure menu opens, as shown in Figure 7–33.

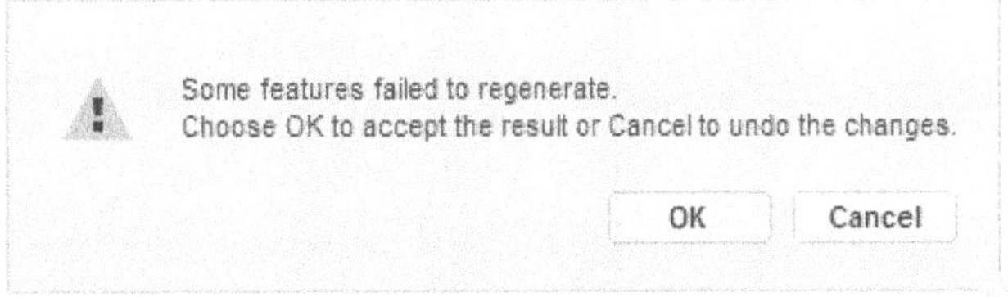

Figure 7–33

Clicking **Cancel** cancels the changes that you made to cause the failure. Clicking **OK** creates the failed feature. It displays in red in the tree as shown in Figure 7–34.

Figure 7–34

Selecting (Edit Definition) on the failed feature activates the *Feature* dashboard. Missing references display with a red dot. You can open the Troubleshooter dialog box by right-clicking and selecting **What's Wrong**, as shown in Figure 7–35.

The Troubleshooter dialog box opens as shown in Figure 7–36. The area under the feature contains notes indicating why the feature could not be created. Select each item to review its information. Items with yellow dots indicate warnings and items with red dots indicate errors. In general, warnings provide solutions and errors explain why the current combination of references and values has failed.

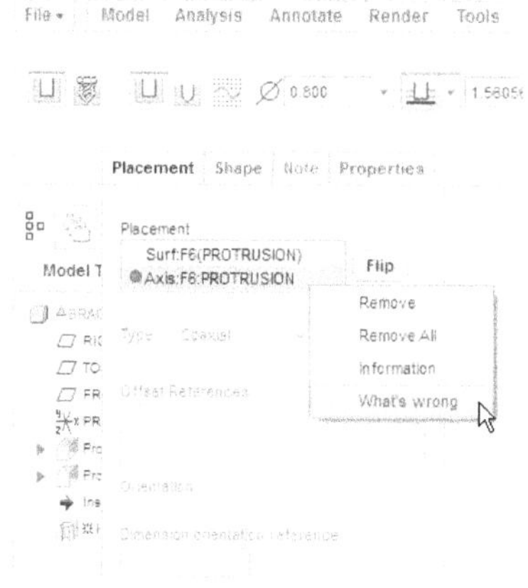

Figure 7–35

Figure 7–36

Failure to create the hole can be resolved by selecting new references. When a failure occurs while you are creating or editing a feature, review the steps used to create the feature:

1. Did you create the correct type of feature? (For example, should it have been an extrusion instead of a revolve?)
2. Was the sketch you selected or sketched correct for this type of feature? (For example, did the section contain a centerline if you are creating a revolve?)
3. If the section was thickened, could the geometry be created on the side of the section to which you applied the thickness?
4. Was the depth or angle of the feature defined correctly? (For example, did you use the correct direction and/or were the required references present?)

Practice 7a

Thicken Extrude

Practice Objectives

- Create an extrude feature using the Thicken option.
- Create a secondary extrude feature that references a face and entities in the base feature to fully constrain it.

In this practice, you will create the metal part of a USB connector. You use an extrude with the **Thicken** option as the base feature. You will also create an extrude that removes material as the secondary feature. The completed part displays as shown in Figure 7–37.

Figure 7–37

Task 1 - Create a new part.

1. Set the working directory to the *Chapter 07/practice 7a* folder.
2. Create a new part and set the *Name* to **usb_insert**.
3. Set the model display as follows:
   - *(Datum Display Filters)*: Only (Plane Display)
   - *(Spin Center)*: Off
   - *(Display Style)*: (Shading)

Task 2 - Create an extrude with the Thicken option.

1. Select the sketch and click (Extrude).
2. For the sketch plane, select **FRONT** from the model tree.

If you want to sketch in 2D, click (Sketch View) from the In-graphics toolbar.

3. In the *Sketch* tab, expand the (Rectangle) flyout and click (Center Rectangle). Sketch a rectangle that is centered about the origin, as shown in Figure 7–38.

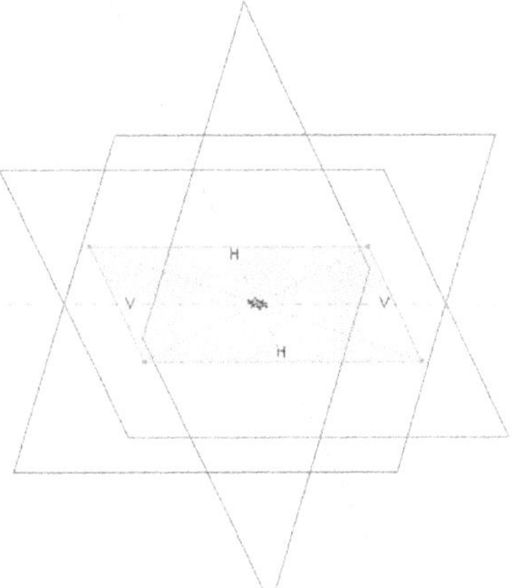

Figure 7–38

4. In the Editing group, click (Modify) and select both dimensions. Set the following, as shown in Figure 7–39:
   - *Width:* **5.0**
   - *Height:* **2.5**

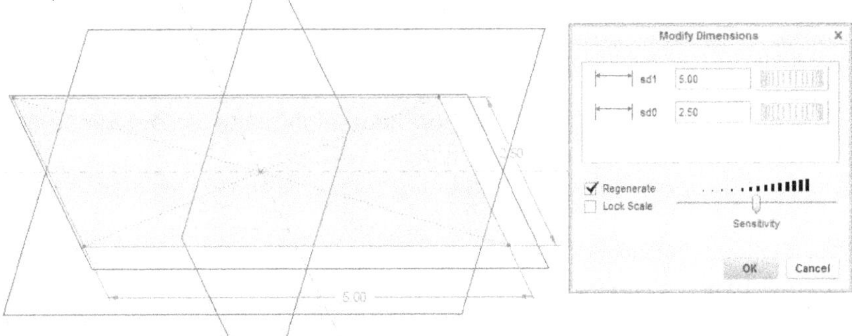

Figure 7–39

5. Click **OK** to complete the dimension modification.
6. Click (OK) to complete the sketch.
7. In the *Extrude* tab, set the *Depth* to **12.5**.
8. In the *Extrude* dashboard, click (Thicken Sketch).
9. Set the *Thickness* to **0.15**, as shown in Figure 7–40.

Figure 7–40

10. Click (Complete Feature). The completed extrude displays as shown Figure 7–41

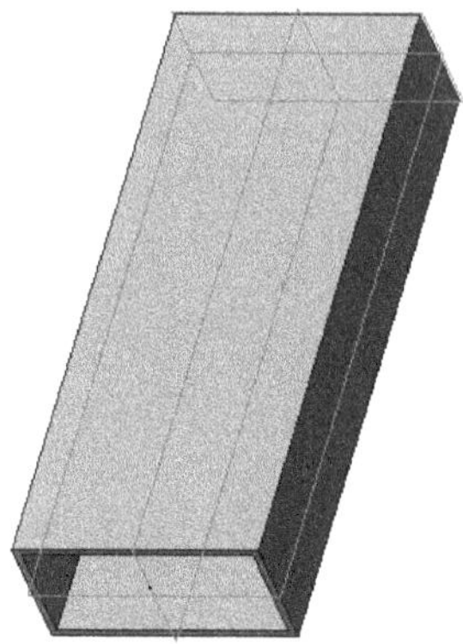

Figure 7–41

Task 3 - Create an extrude that removes material.

1. Click (Extrude).
2. For the sketch plane, select the surface shown in Figure 7–42.

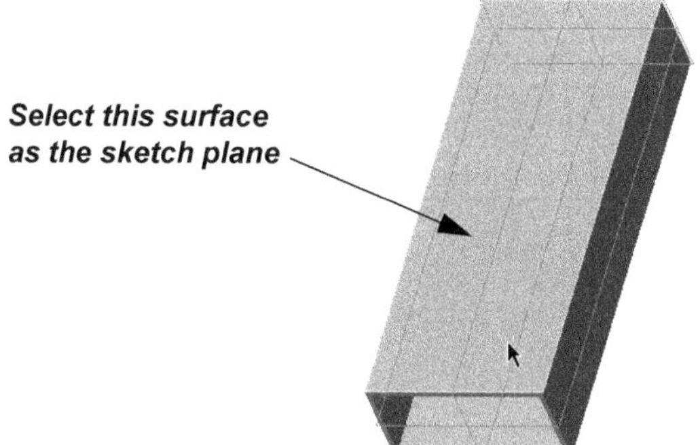

Figure 7–42

3. In the In-graphics toolbar, click (Sketch View).

4. In the Setup group, click (References).

5. Select the surface at the bottom of the screen to be a sketcher reference, as shown in Figure 7–43.

It is recommended that you select surfaces rather than edges when selecting references. As such, even when you select a reference entity in 2D orientation and it appears you are selecting the edge, the system actually selects the surface.

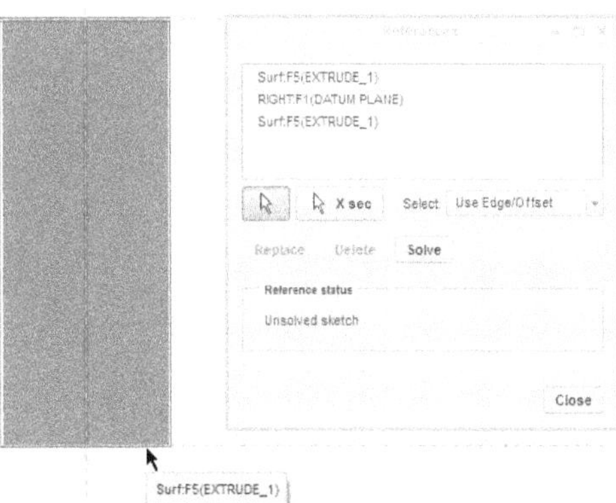

Figure 7–43

6. In the References dialog box, click **Close**.

7. In the Sketching group, click (Centerline) and sketch a centerline on the vertical reference.

To apply the symmetry constraint, click (Symmetric) in the Constrain group, then select the centerline and the two vertices of the rectangles.

8. Select the (Rectangle) flyout and click (Corner Rectangle). Sketch two rectangles and apply constraints and dimensions, as shown in Figure 7–44.

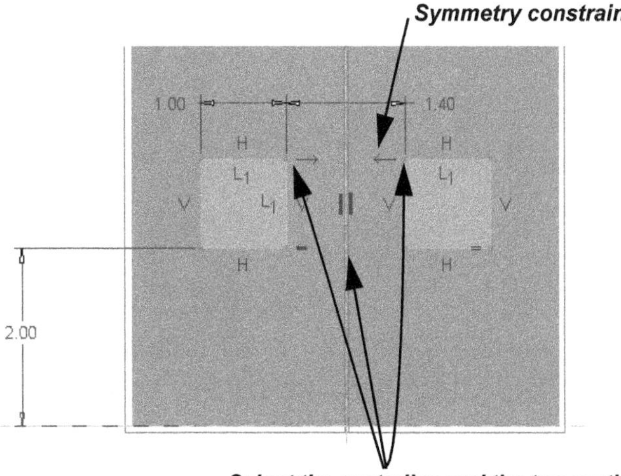

Figure 7–44

9. Click (OK) to complete the Sketch.

10. Press <Ctrl>+<D> to return to default orientation. The model displays as shown in Figure 7–45.

The default action is to create an extruded solid that adds material. To change this remove material, click (Remove Material) in the dashboard or simply change the feature direction to extrude into the existing geometry.

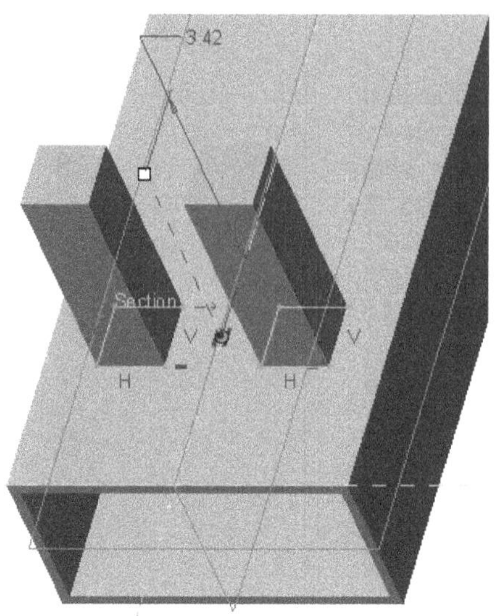

Figure 7–45

11. Click the head of the direction arrow to have the feature remove the material. Rotate the model slightly to see that the feature cuts through the entire model, but is driven by a dimension, as shown in Figure 7–46.

The (Remove Material) option is automatically enabled in the dashboard.

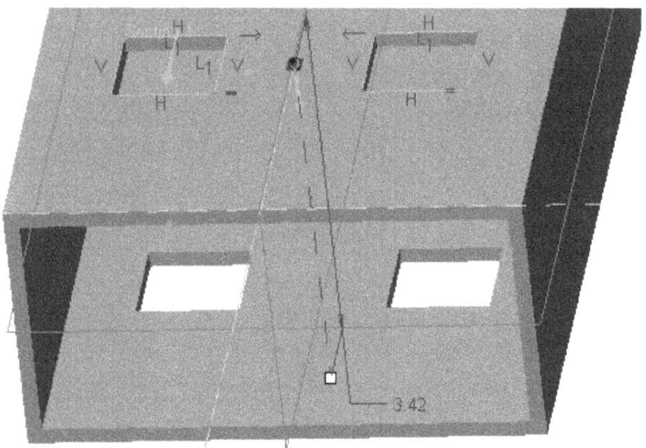

Figure 7–46

Changing the depth to ⫤ ⊨ (Through All) ensures that the cuts always go through the entire model, regardless of changes to the thickness.

12. Set the depth option to extrude ⫤ ⊨ (Through All). The dashboard should display as shown in Figure 7–47.

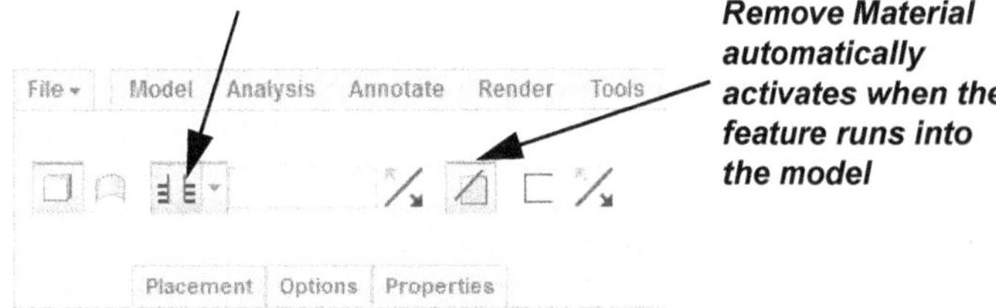

Figure 7–47

13. Click ✓ (Complete Feature) to finish the extrude feature.

14. In the In-graphics toolbar, click (Datum Display Filters) and click (Plane Display) to toggle off the display of datum planes. The model displays as shown in Figure 7–48.

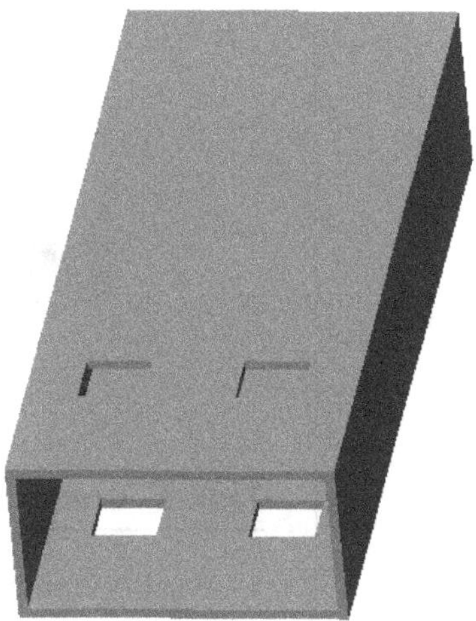

Figure 7–48

15. Save the part and erase it from memory.

Practice 7b

Secondary Features on a Revolved Base Feature

Practice Objectives

- Create two secondary features using extrude.
- Add a revolved secondary feature.
- Edit the base feature using the editing tools.
- Create a Profile Rib by sketching an open section.

In this practice, you will add two secondary extrude features that remove material from a revolved base feature. You will then create a profile rib that adds strength to the part. The completed part displays as shown in Figure 7–49.

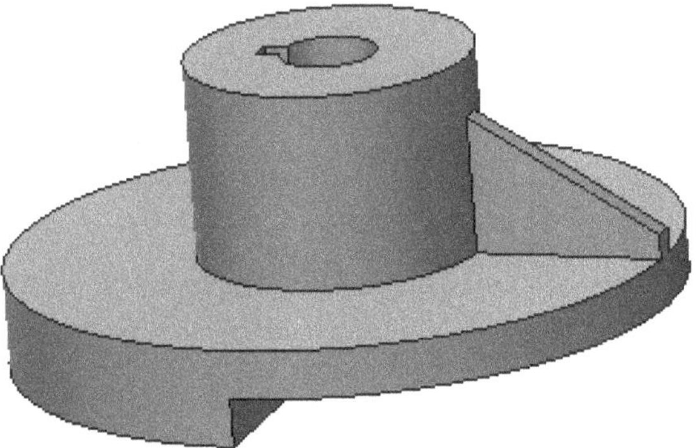

Figure 7–49

Task 1 - Create a new part file.

1. Set the working directory to the *Chapter 07\practice 7b* folder.
2. In the quick access toolbar, click (Open) and double-click **drive_flange2.prt** to open it.
3. Set the model display as follows:
   - *(Datum Display Filters)*: All Off
   - *(Spin Center)*: Off
   - *(Display Style)*: (Shading With Edges)

Task 2 - Create an extruded feature.

1. Click (Extrude).
2. Right-click and select **Define Internal Sketch**.
3. For the sketch plane, select **FRONT** from the model tree and select the bottom surface of the part as the Orientation Reference.
4. In the Orientation drop-down list, select **Bottom**. The model and Sketch dialog box display as shown in Figure 7–50.

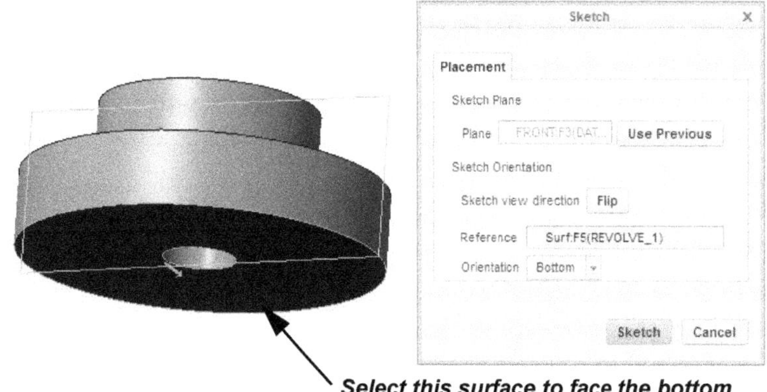

Figure 7–50

5. Click **Sketch**.
6. In the In-graphics toolbar, click (Sketch View).
7. In the Sketching group, click (Rectangle). Press and hold <Alt> and select the silhouette edge, as shown in Figure 7–51. Release <Alt>. This adds the silhouette edge as a sketcher reference.

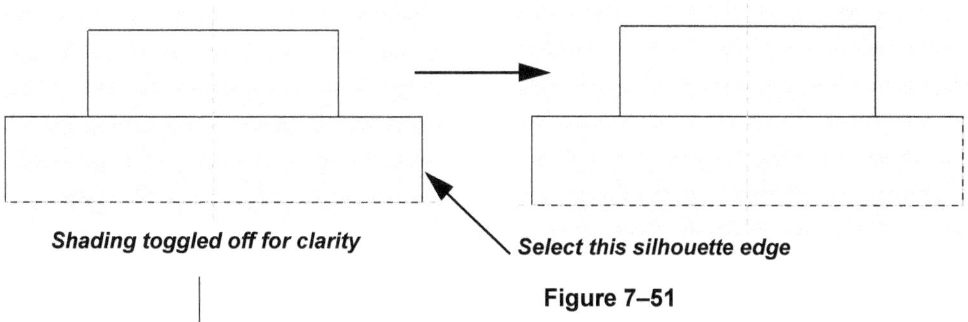

Figure 7–51

8. Move the cursor over the right sketcher reference until the **M** indicating the midpoint displays, as shown in Figure 7–52. Select this as the first point for the rectangle.

Figure 7–52

9. Move the cursor to the position shown in Figure 7–53. The sketch will snap to the sketcher references and will be complete without any dimensions.

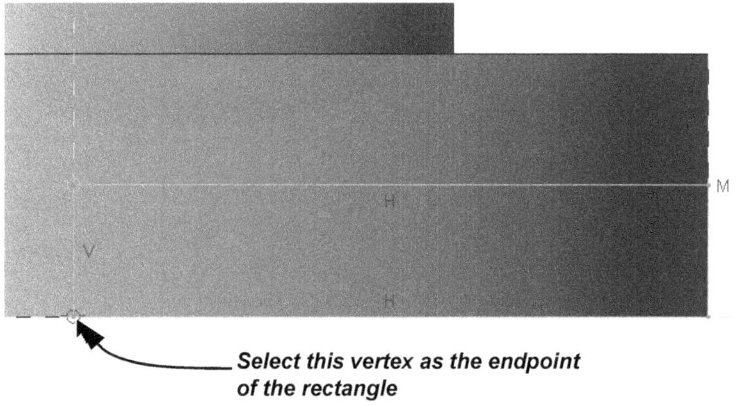

Figure 7–53

10. Click ✓ (OK) to complete the sketch.

11. In the dashboard, click ◿ (Remove Material).

12. In the *Depth* area, set the options shown in Figure 7–54.

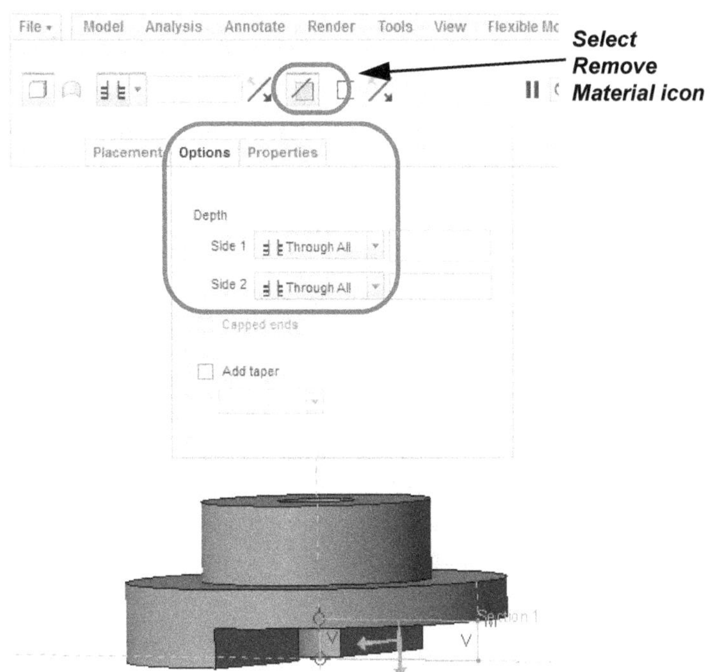

Figure 7–54

13. Click (Complete Feature) to complete the extrude. The model displays as shown in Figure 7–55.

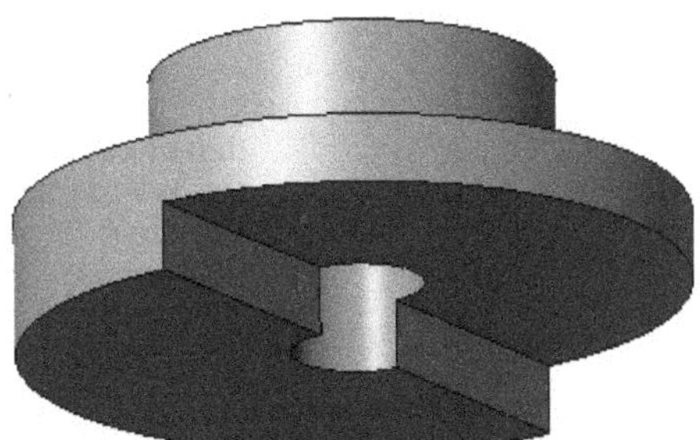

Figure 7–55

Task 3 - Create an extrude to create a key way.

1. Click (Extrude).
2. Right-click and select **Define Internal Sketch**.

3. For the Sketch plane, select the surface shown in Figure 7–56.
4. Select the datum plane **FRONT** from the model tree as the orientation Reference.
5. In the Orientation drop-down list, select **Bottom**.

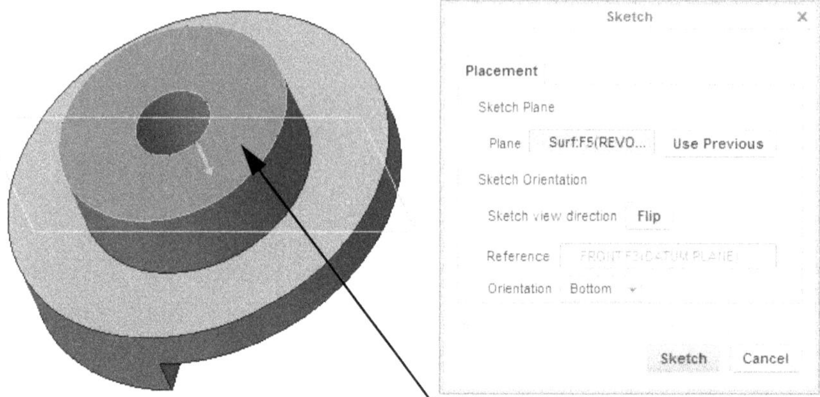

Figure 7–56

6. Click **Sketch**.
7. Click (Sketch View) and then click (References).
8. Select the appropriate sketcher references, as shown in Figure 7–57. Close the References dialog box.

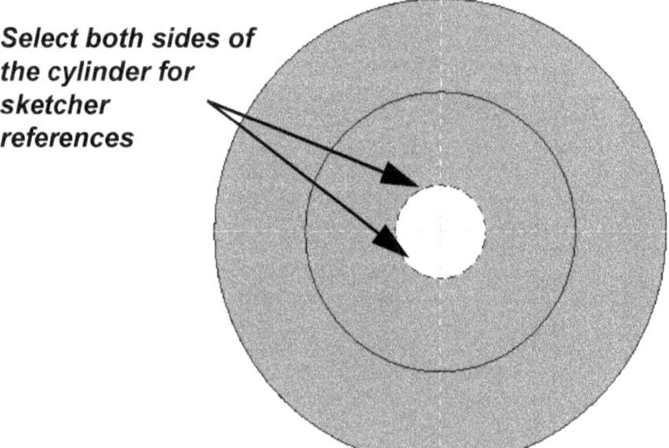

Figure 7–57

9. Create the sketch shown in Figure 7–58. The sketch consists of only three lines and a centerline to use for the symmetry constraint.

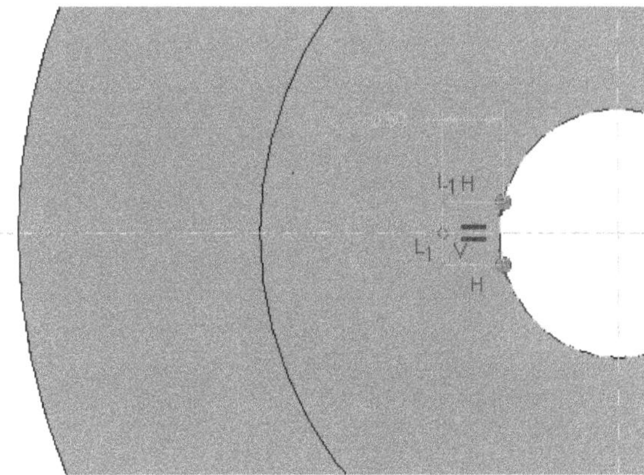

Figure 7–58

10. Click (OK) to complete the sketch.

11. Press <Ctrl>+<D> to return to default orientation.

12. Select the end of the arrow head to change the direction to extrude into the model.

Because the sketch is an open sketch, changing the direction into the model does not automatically change it to remove material.

13. In the dashboard, click (Remove Material).

14. In the *Depth* area, click (Through All).

15. Click (Complete Feature). The completed feature displays as shown in Figure 7–59.

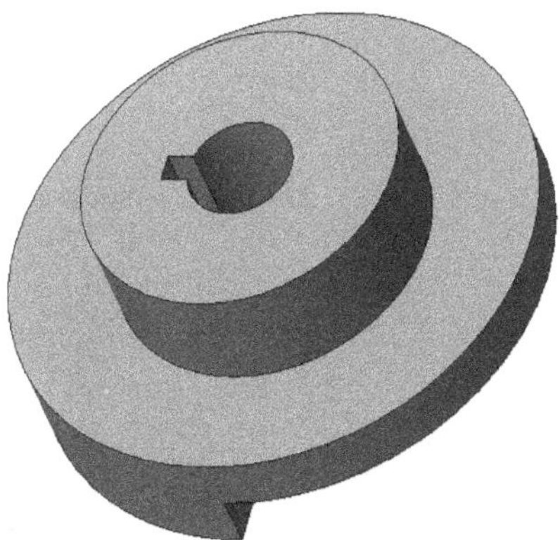

Figure 7–59

Task 4 - Create a groove in the side of the model.

1. In the Shapes group, click (Revolve).
2. For the Sketch plane, select the surface shown in Figure 7–60.
3. Right-click and select **References**.
4. Place the cursor over the edge shown in Figure 7–61 and right-click to query-select the silhouette surface.

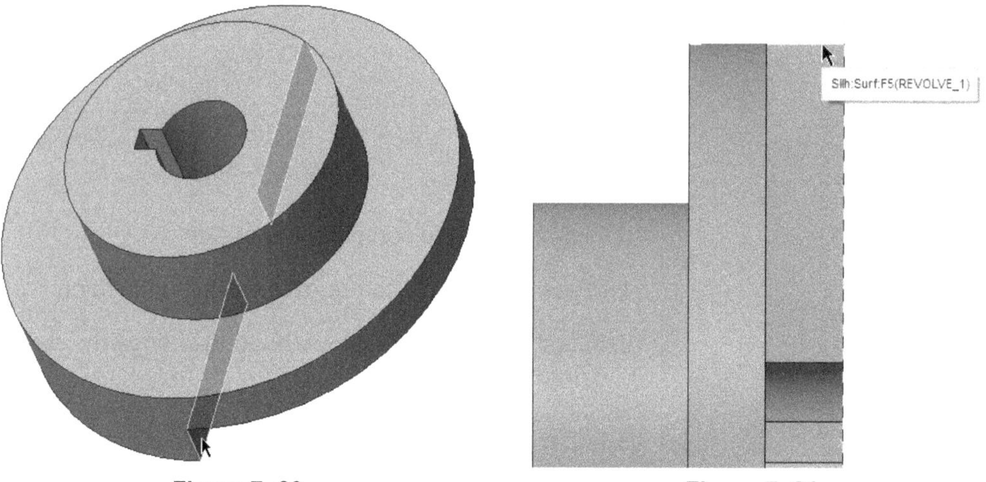

Figure 7–60

Figure 7–61

5. Close the References dialog box.
6. In the sketching group, click (Arc).
7. Click the two endpoint, then drag the center point until the center snaps to the reference, as shown in Figure 7–62.

Figure 7–62

8. In the Sketching group, click (Line) and sketch a line between the two endpoints of the arc.

The centerline should snap to the reference point.

9. Click (Centerline) and sketch a horizontal centerline through the center of the model, as shown in Figure 7–63.

10. Dimension the arc as shown in Figure 7–64.

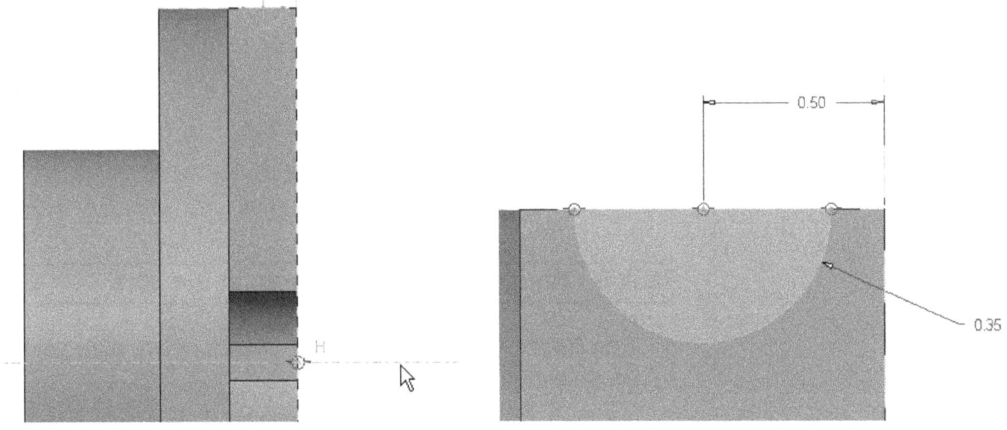

Figure 7–63 **Figure 7–64**

11. Click (OK) to complete the sketch. Note that the feature is created 360 degrees and that it is adding material, as shown in Figure 7–65.

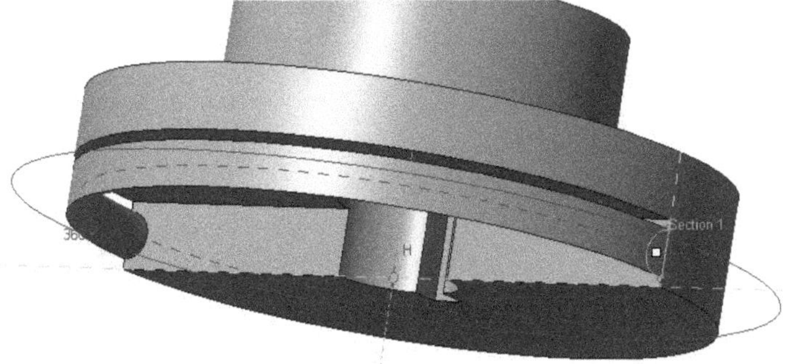

Figure 7–65

12. Set the *Angle* to **180**.

13. In the dashboard, click (Change Angle Direction).

14. Click (Remove Material).

15. Click (Complete Feature). The model displays as shown in Figure 7–66.

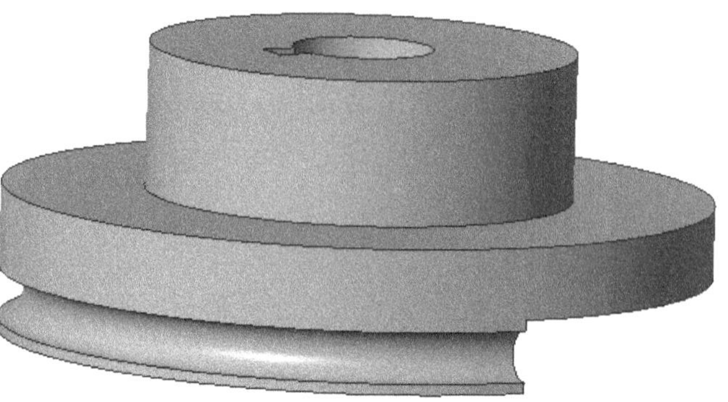

Figure 7–66

Task 5 - Modify the base geometry of the part.

1. Edit **Revolve1** and change the values of two dimensions to **6**, as shown in Figure 7–67.

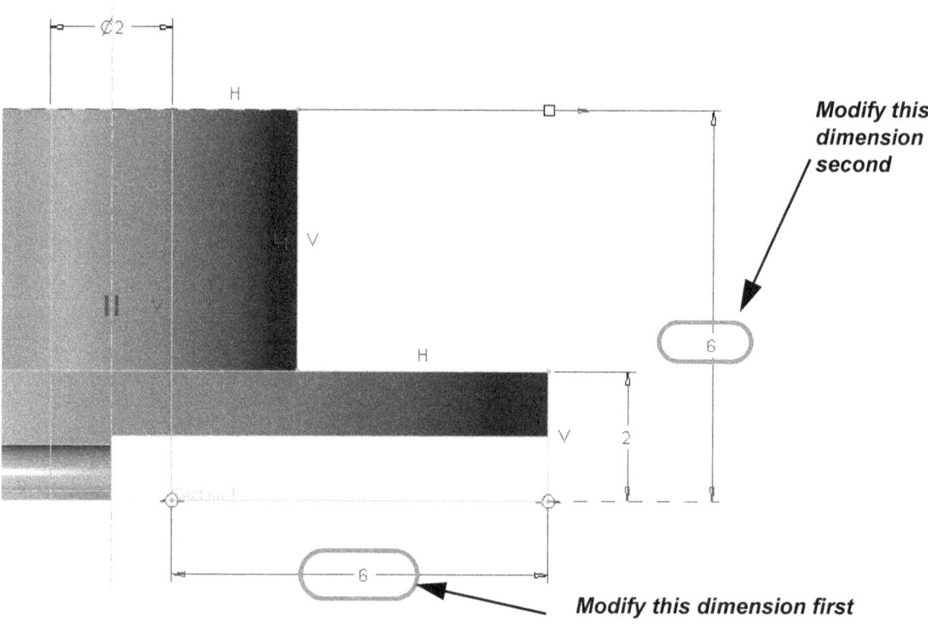

Figure 7–67

2. In the Operations group, click (Regenerate).

Task 6 - Create a rib feature.

Design Considerations

In this task, you will create a profile rib feature. Due to the thin wall section of the flange and the new dimensions, the part requires a stiffener to increase the structural integrity of the part. A rib will be used to achieve this.

1. In the Engineering group, in the *Model* tab, expand the (Rib) flyout and click (Profile Rib).
2. Right-click and select **Define Internal Sketch**.
3. For the sketch plane, select **FRONT** from the model tree.
4. Select the surface shown in Figure 7–68 as the orientation Reference
5. In the Orientation drop-down list, select **Top**.

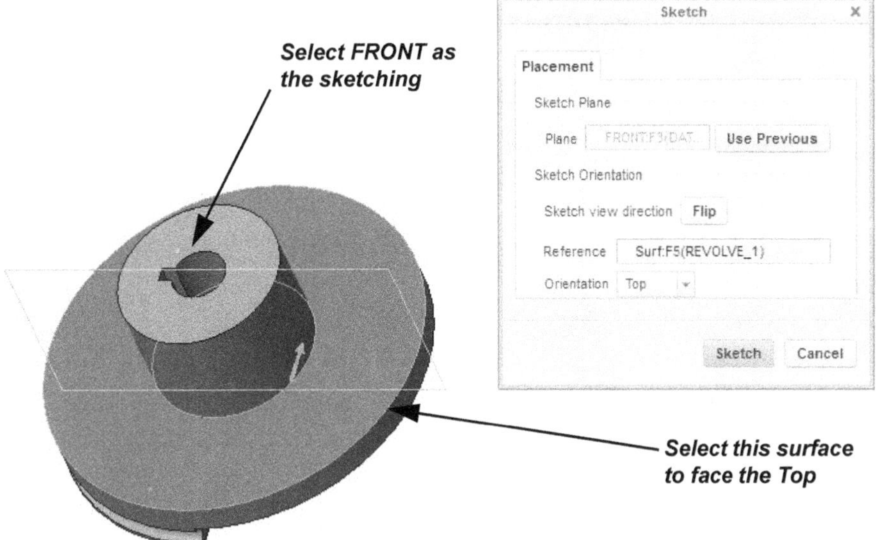

Figure 7–68

6. In the Sketch dialog box, click **Sketch**.
7. Click (Sketch View).
8. Right-click and select **References**.

9. Select the two sketcher references as shown in Figure 7–69. Note that the horizontal reference was automatically established when the surface was selected as the Top reference.

10. Create the sketch using two lines and dimension the sketch shown in Figure 7–70.

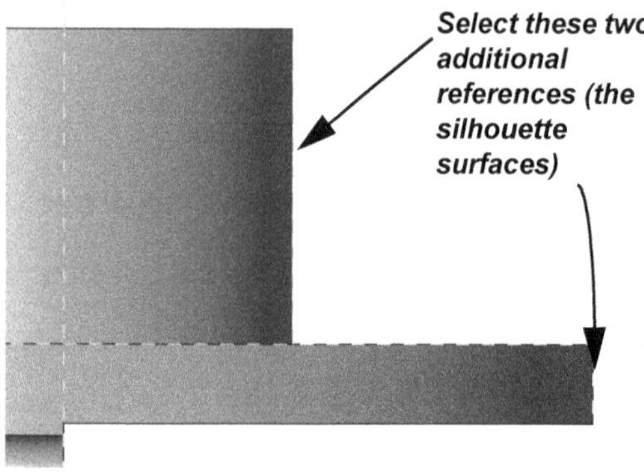

Figure 7–69

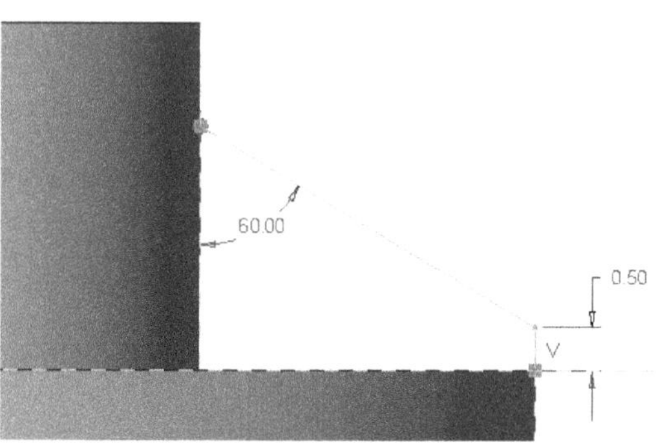

Figure 7–70

11. Click ✓ (OK) to complete the sketch.

12. Set the *Thickness* to **0.5**.

13. Click ✓ (Complete Feature). The completed profile rib displays as shown in Figure 7–71.

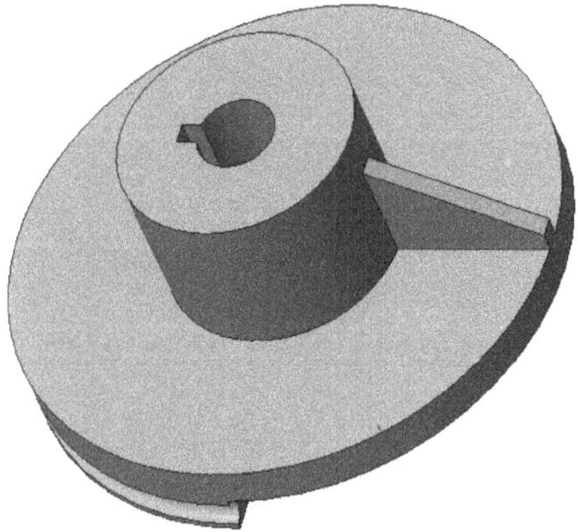

Figure 7–71

Practice 7c

Trajectory Rib

Practice Objectives

- Create a secondary Trajectory Rib feature using the appropriate references.
- Add a taper to the base feature.

In this practice, you will create a secondary Trajectory Rib feature using appropriate references and then you will add a taper to the feature using various editing tools. The complete the part shown in Figure 7–72.

Figure 7–72

Task 1 - Open the part and create the trajectory rib.

1. Set the working directory to the *Chapter 07\practice 7c* folder.
2. Open **trajectory_rib.prt**.
3. Set the model display as follows:
    - *(Datum Display Filters)*: All Off
    - *(Spin Center)*: Off
    - *(Display Style)*: (Shading With Edges)
4. To create a trajectory rib, in the Engineering group, expand the (Rib) flyout and select (Trajectory Rib).
5. Right-click and select **Define Internal Sketch**.

6. For the Sketch plane, select the surface shown in Figure 7–73.

7. Datum plane **RIGHT** should be automatically selected as the orientation Reference.

8. In the Orientation drop-down list, select **Bottom**.

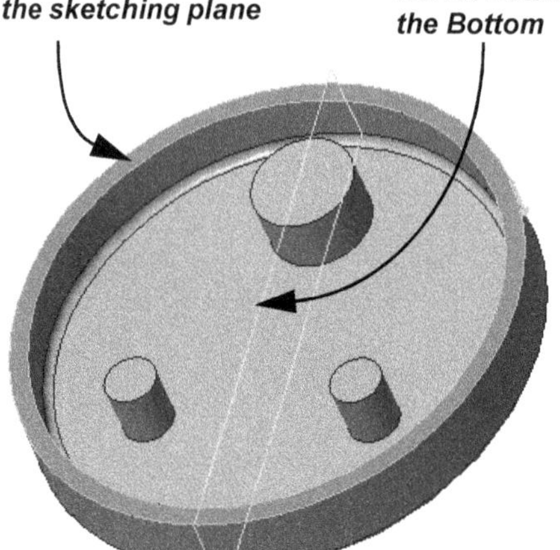

Figure 7–73

9. In the Sketch dialog box, select **Sketch**.

10. Click (Sketch View).

11. In the In-graphics toolbar, select (Datum Display Filters) and select (Axis Display) to display axes.

12. Right-click and select **References**.

13. Select the three axes shown in Figure 7–74 as references.

Mouse over the center of the axis, and click when the axis tool-tip displays.

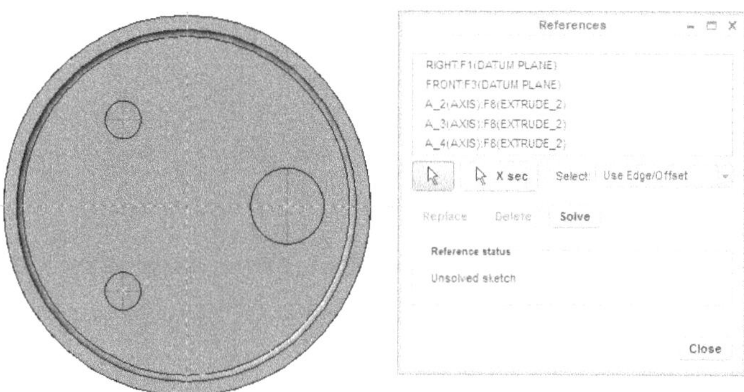

Figure 7–74

14. Click **Close** to close the References dialog box.

15. Sketch the three lines shown in Figure 7–75.

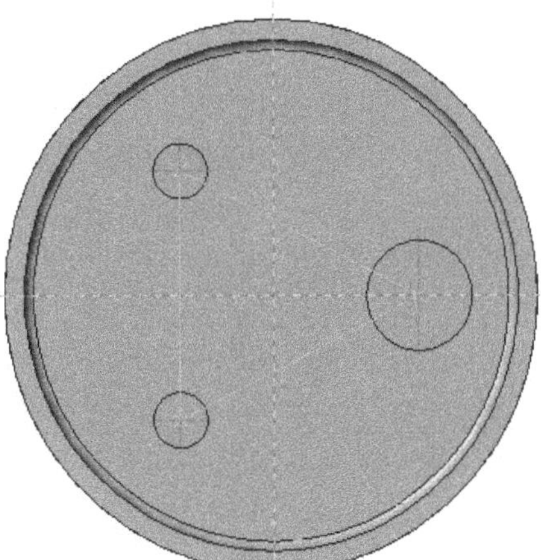

Figure 7–75

16. Click ✓ (OK) to complete the sketch.

17. Press <Ctrl>+<D>.

18. Set the *Thickness* to **0.36**.

19. In the dashboard, click (Add Internal Rounds) to add rounds on the internal edges.

20. Click ✓ (Complete Feature) to complete the trajectory rib feature. The completed model displays as shown in Figure 7–76.

Figure 7–76

Task 2 - Edit Extrude 2 and add a taper.

1. Select **Extrude 2**, right-click, and select (Edit Definition). This activates the *Extrude* tab.

2. Select the Options panel.

3. Select the **Add taper** option and then enter **10.0**, as shown in Figure 7–77.

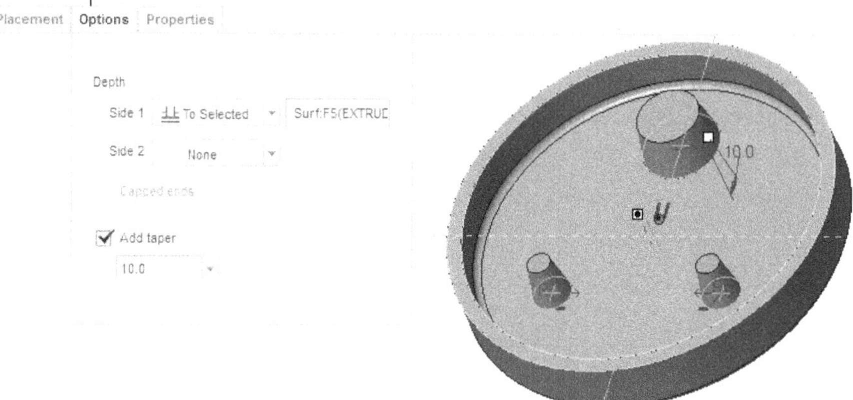

Figure 7–77

4. Click (Complete Feature) to complete the extrude feature. The completed model displays as shown in Figure 7–78.

The rib automatically updates to intersect the changed geometry.

Figure 7–78

5. Save and erase the file from memory.

Practice 7d

Extrude Depth Options

Practice Objectives

- Create entities that reference other features so that the design intent is built into the model.
- Modify features in the model to ensure that the new features update based on the references that were established.

In this practice, you will use the Offset command to create entities that reference other features so that the design intent is built into the model. You will then change the depth option of the model using various editing tools. The completed part displays as shown in Figure 7–79.

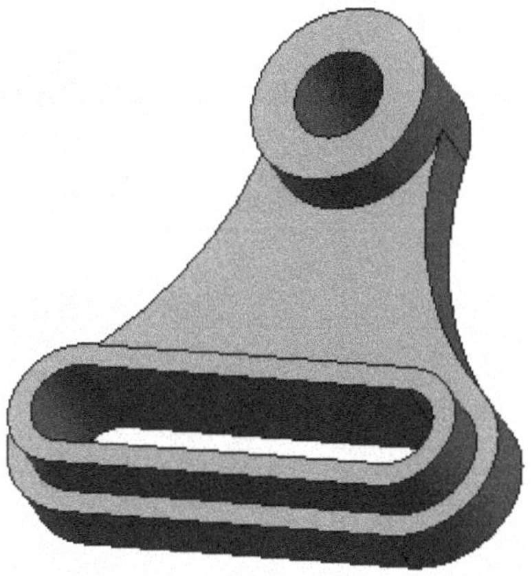

Figure 7–79

Task 1 - Open the part.

1. Set the working directory to the *Chapter 07\practice 7d* folder.
2. Open **slot_bracket.prt**. Set the model display as follows:
   - *(Datum Display Filters)*: All Off
   - *(Spin Center)*: Off
   - *(Display Style)*: (Shading With Edges)
3. Right-click on **Extrude 1** in the model tree and select (Edit Definition).

4. Change the *Depth* to extrude to a selected surface, as shown in Figure 7–80. Then, select the surface shown in Figure 7–81.

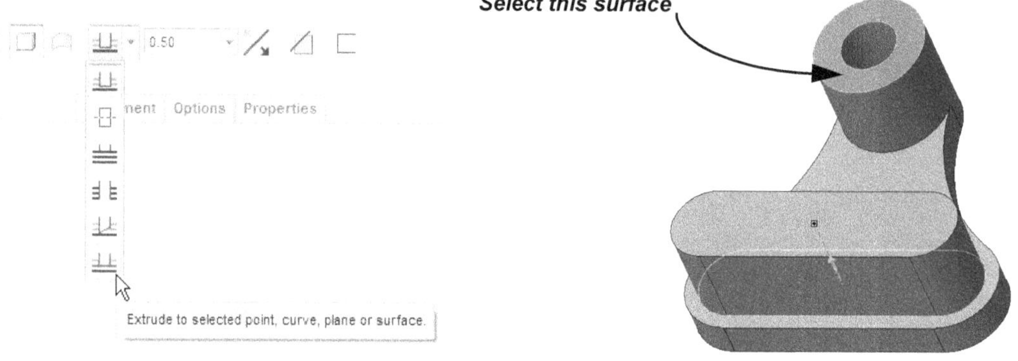

Figure 7–80

Figure 7–81

5. Click (Complete Feature).

Task 2 - Create an extrude that removes material.

1. Click (Extrude).
2. For the Sketch plane, select the surface shown in Figure 7–82.

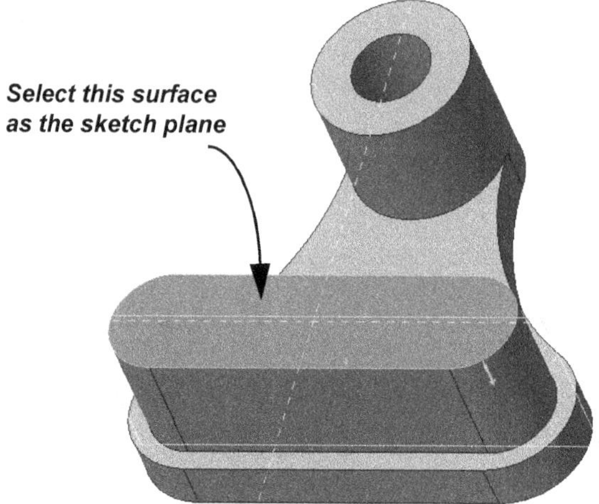

Figure 7–82

3. In the Sketching group, in the *Sketch* tab, click (Offset) to create the sketch.

4. In the Type dialog box, select **Loop**. Then, select the surface shown in Figure 7–83.

5. If the arrow is pointing to the outside as shown in Figure 7–84, enter an *Offset distance* of **-0.2**. This creates the sketch on the inside.

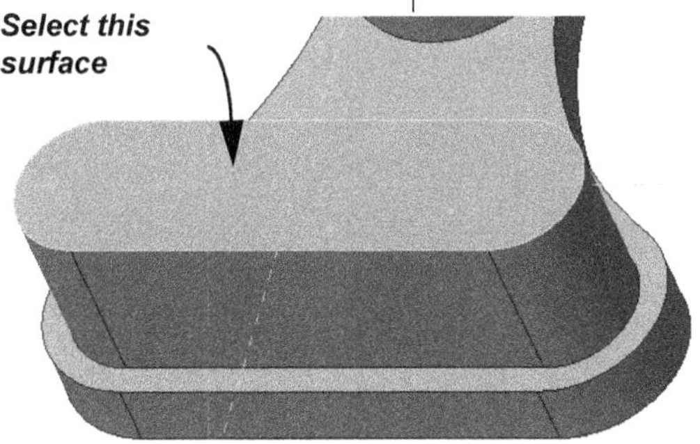

Figure 7–83

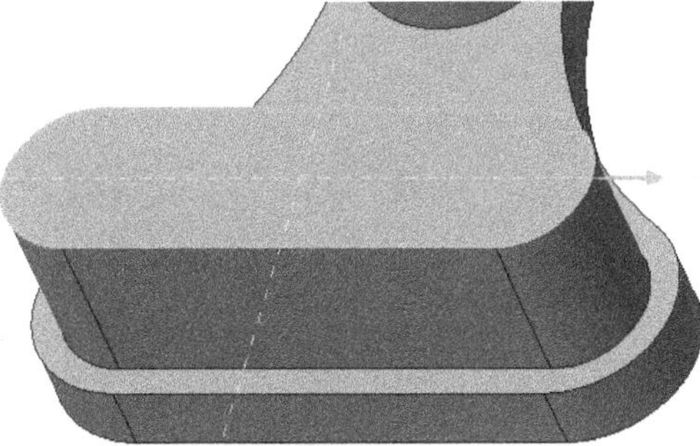

Figure 7–84

When you select the surface all of the edges surrounding the surface will be offset

6. Click **Close** to close the Type dialog box.

7. Click ✓ (OK) to complete the sketch.

8. Click the direction arrow so the extrusion runs into the model.

9. Use a *Depth* value that will extrude to the selected surface, as shown in Figure 7–85.

10. Click ✓ (Complete Feature). The completed feature displays as shown in Figure 7–86.

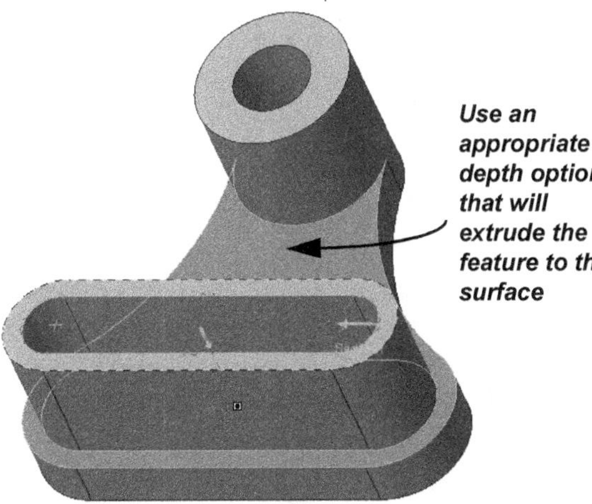

Figure 7–85

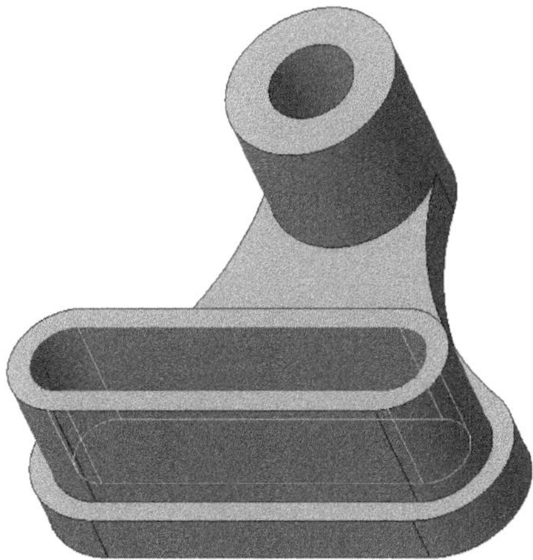

Figure 7–86

Task 3 - Edit the parent geometry.

1. Select the cylinder in the back of the model, right click and select d1 (Edit).
2. Change the *1.5* value to **0.75**, as shown in Figure 7–87.
3. Click twice on the screen to regenerate the model. It displays as shown in Figure 7–88.

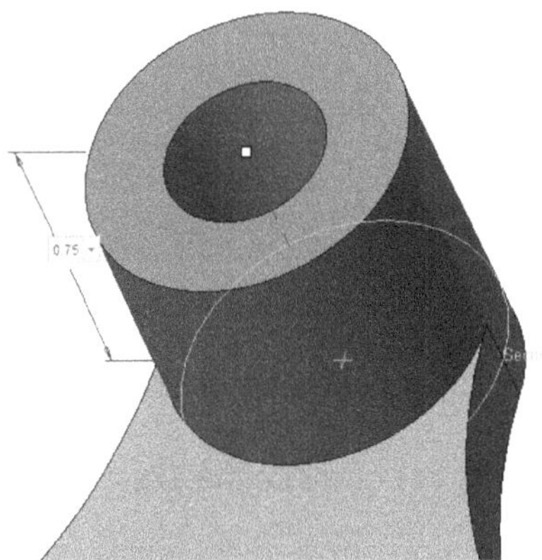

Figure 7–87

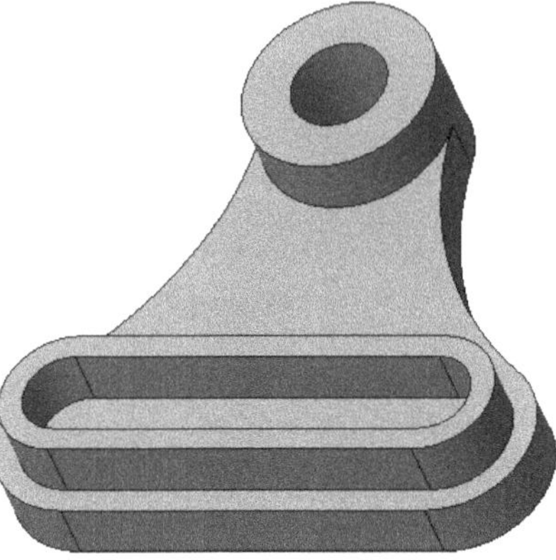

Figure 7–88

Task 4 - Edit the definition of a feature and change the depth option.

1. Right-click on **Extrude 2** and select (Edit Definition).
2. Change the depth option so that the extrude feature extrudes through all of the geometry, as shown in Figure 7–89.

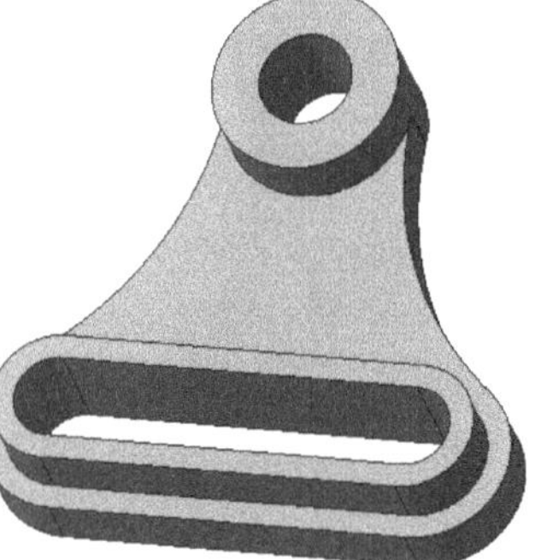

Figure 7–89

3. Save the part and erase it from memory.

Practice 7e

Create a Part with Limited Instructions

Practice Objectives

- Create a base feature using the appropriate references.
- Create secondary features using references and depth options.

In this practice, you will create the part shown in Figure 7–90. You can create the part on your own using the dimensional drawing shown in Figure 7–91.

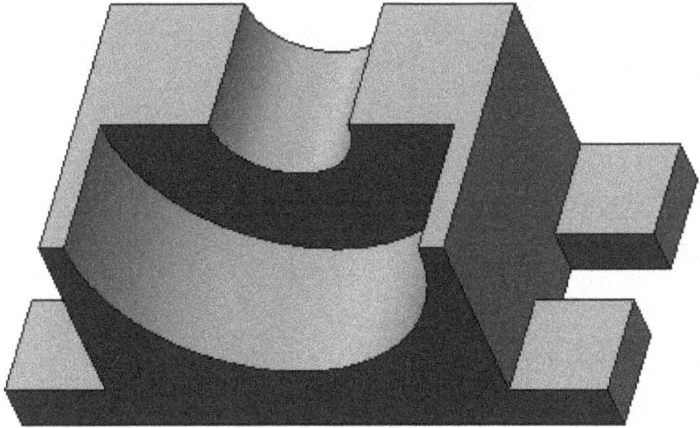

Figure 7–90

1. Set the working directory to the *Chapter 07\practice 7e* folder.
2. Create a new part file and set the *Name* to **bearing_mount**.
3. Set the model display as follows:
   - *(Datum Display Filters)*: All On
   - *(Spin Center)*: Off
   - *(Display Style)*: (Shading With Edges)
4. Consider the following before you begin modeling the part:
   - What will the base feature look like?
   - What feature will you create as the second feature?
   - Which feature forms will you use (extrude, revolve, etc.)?
   - You should be able to create this part with no more then three features.

The dimensions for the part are shown in Figure 7–91.When finished, save thee part then erase it from memory.

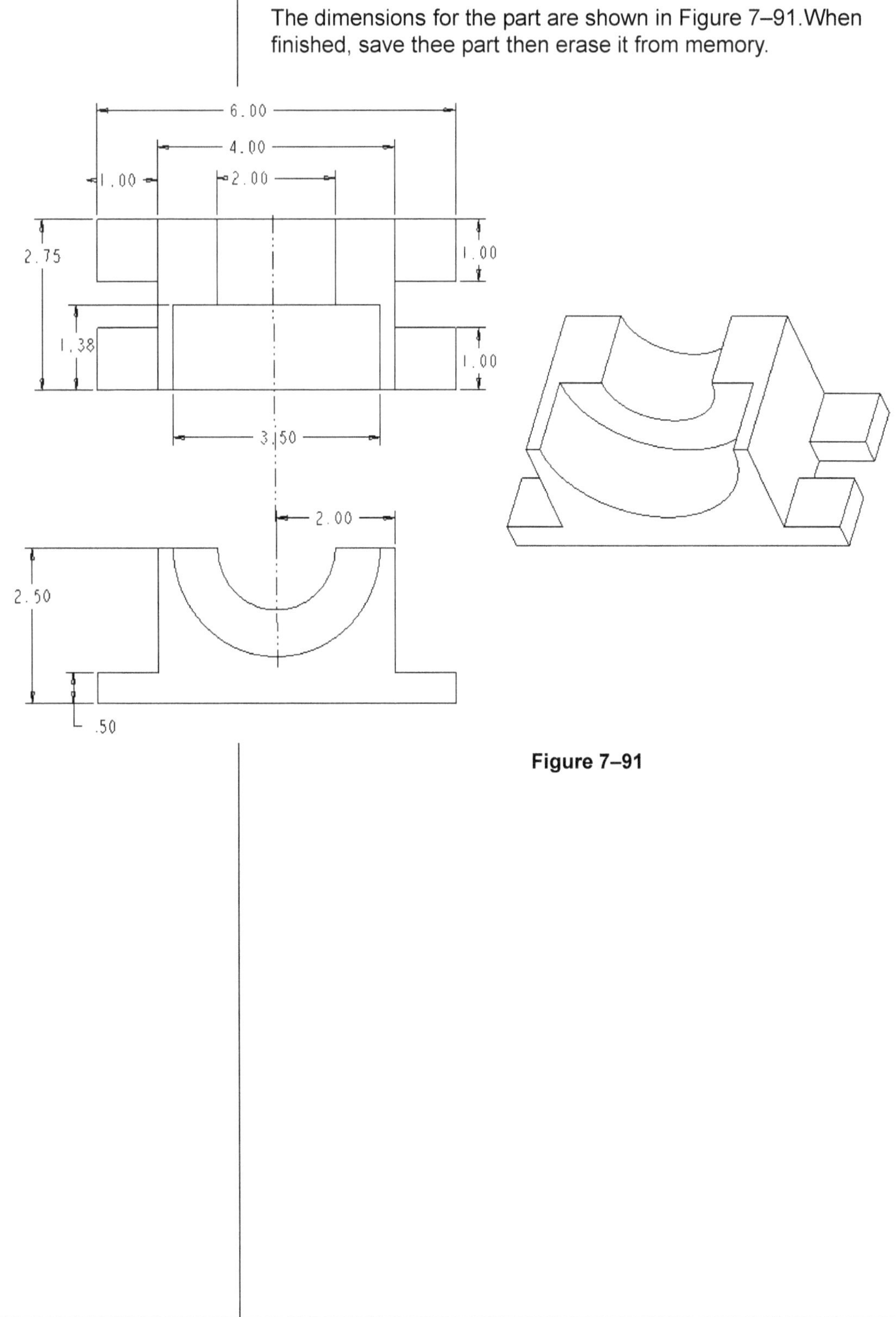

Figure 7–91

Chapter Review Questions

1. A single extrusion can add and remove material.
   a. True
   b. False
2. Which of the following happens when you select an existing sketch to create an extrusion or a revolve? (Select all that apply.)
   a. The selected sketch is copied into the new feature without an associative link.
   b. The existing sketch is removed from the model and copied to the new feature.
   c. The associative link is maintained between the existing sketch and the new feature.
   d. Subsequent modifications to the existing sketch are reflected in the new feature.
3. Which of the following are true statements regarding creating a thin extrusion or revolve? (Select all that apply.)
   a. To specify a thickness to the sketched section, click in the tab and enter a thickness value.
   b. Multiple open entities can be sketched to create a thin.
   c. The thickness applied to the inside of a radius on the sketch cannot exceed the radius at any point along the sketched section.
   d. A revolve cannot be created using a thin.
4. Which of the following icons is used to remove material instead of adding it?
   a.
   b.
   c.
   d.
5. A feature can be converted to a cut by dragging the depth handle into existing solid geometry.
   a. True
   b. False

6. Which of the following toolbar icons is used to add sketcher references?
    a.
    b.
    c.
    d.
7. Which of the following statements are true regarding a revolved feature?
    a. The section for a revolved feature can be selected or sketched.
    b. The section for a revolved feature must contain a geometry or construction centerline.
    c. The section for a revolved feature must be closed.
    d. The feature can be revolved to intersect with a selected surface.
8. All of the section entities for a revolved section must lie on one side of the centerline.
    a. True
    b. False
9. The sketched section shown on the left in Figure 7–92 generates the solid geometry shown on the right.

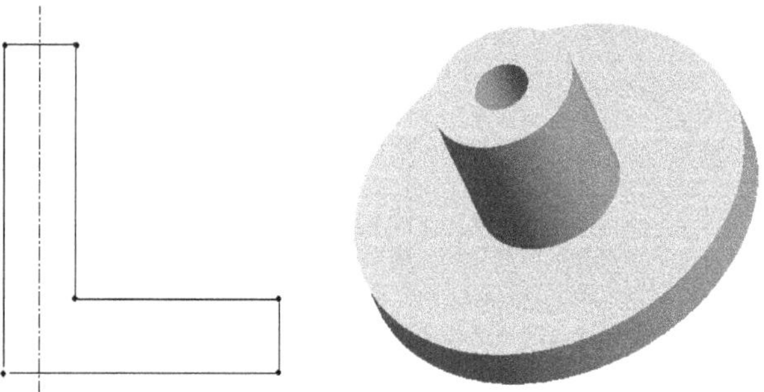

Figure 7–92

    a. True
    b. False

Command Summary

Button	Command	Location
	Thicken	• **Ribbon:** *Extrude* tab or Revolve tab
	Change Depth Direction	• **Ribbon:** *Extrude* tab or Revolve tab
	Remove Material	• **Ribbon:** *Extrude* tab or Revolve tab
	Revolve	• **Ribbon:** *Model* tab in the Shapes group
	Centerline	• **Ribbon:** *Sketch* tab in the Datum group
	Trajectory Rib	• **Ribbon:** *Model* tab in the Engineering group
	Profile Rib	• **Ribbon:** *Model* tab in the Engineering group
	Blind	• **Ribbon:** *Extrude* tab or Revolve tab
	Symmetric	• **Ribbon:** *Extrude* tab or Revolve tab
	To Next	• **Ribbon:** *Extrude* tab
	Through All	• **Ribbon:** *Extrude* tab
	Through Until	• **Ribbon:** *Extrude* tab
	To Selected	• **Ribbon:** *Extrude* tab or Revolve tab

Chamfers and Rounds

Chamfers, rounds, and holes are known as Engineering features. This means that the shape of the feature is implied and therefore, you are not required to sketch the section. Engineering features can be added once the model's base feature has been created to add detail to your model design.

Learning Objectives in this Chapter

- Create an edge chamfer that adds or removes material along an edge between two adjacent surfaces.
- Define the dimensioning scheme and placement references to create a chamfer that captures the model's design intent.
- Create a corner chamfer that removes material from a corner feature using dimensions along three adjacent edges.
- Define a dimensioning scheme to create a chamfer that captures the model's design intent.
- Create a constant round that adds or removes material along an edge.
- Create a variable fillet that adds or removes material with different values along an edge.
- Create a full round fillet when using edge fillets does not create the required geometry.
- Define the placement reference, dimension, and options, to create a fillet that captures the model's design intent.
- Create rounds on all the edges in a model automatically using the Auto Round command.

8.1 Creating an Edge Chamfer

A chamfer adds a beveled edge between two adjacent surfaces, as shown in Figure 8–1. An edge chamfer can add or remove material to/from an edge.

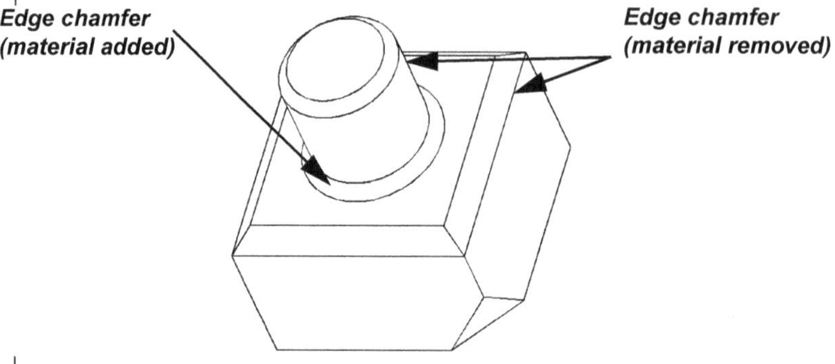

Figure 8–1

General Steps

Use the following general steps to create an edge chamfer:

1. Start the creation of the feature.
2. Select the placement references.
3. Define the dimensioning scheme.
4. Complete the feature.

Step 1 - Start the creation of the feature.

To start the creation of an edge chamfer, click (Chamfer) in the Engineering group in the *Model* tab. The *Edge Chamfer* dashboard displays with all of the options available for creating edge chamfers, as shown in Figure 8–2.

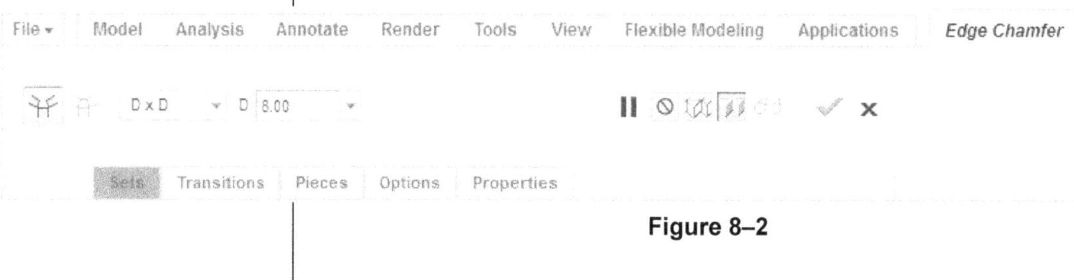

Figure 8–2

Step 2 - Select the placement references.

As an alternative, you can select the reference before clicking (Chamfer).

To create an edge chamfer you must select the edges on which the edge chamfer is going to be placed. Multiple edges can be selected individually or at the same time using <Ctrl>. If you select multiple edges individually, an independent dimension is applied to each edge. However, if you select multiple edges while holding <Ctrl>, a single dimension is applied to all of the edges. This method enables you to control changes to all of the edges with a single dimension. By default, once an edge has been selected, the software automatically creates a **DxD** chamfer on this edge.

Step 3 - Define the dimensioning scheme.

The default **DxD** chamfer that is automatically assigned to elected edges can be modified to the required dimension type using the options in the *Edge Chamfer* dashboard.

Dimension Types

Edge chamfers have six different dimension types. To change the dimension type, expand the drop-down list in the *Edge Chamfer* dashboard and select one of the six dimension types, as shown in Figure 8–3.

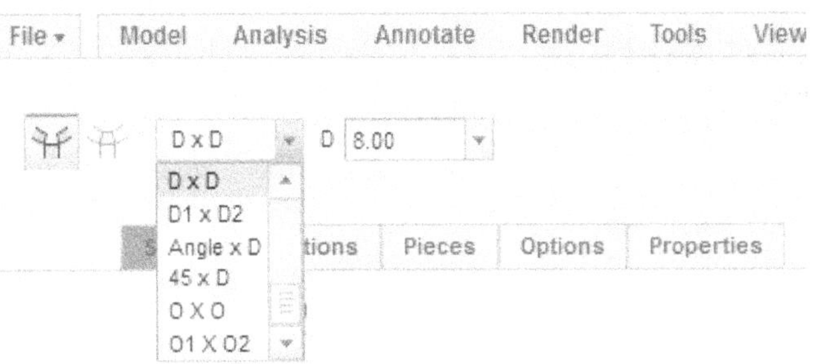

Figure 8–3

The dimension types and how they are applied to a model are shown in Figure 8–4 and Figure 8–5.

*The resulting dimensioning scheme for the **OxO** and **O1xO2** dimension types display in the same way as **DxD** and **D1xD2** on the model. However, the resulting geometry is different.*

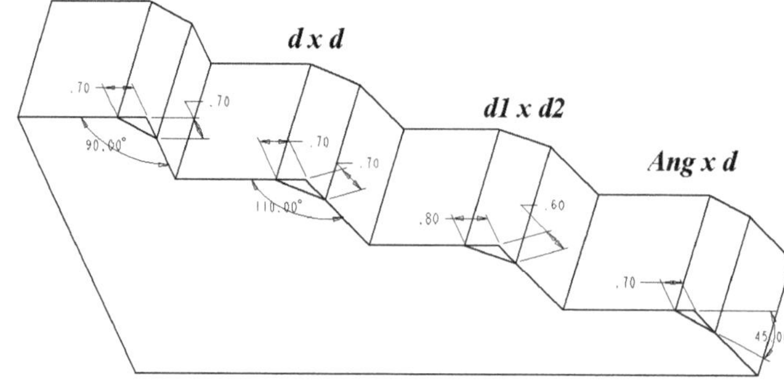

Figure 8–4

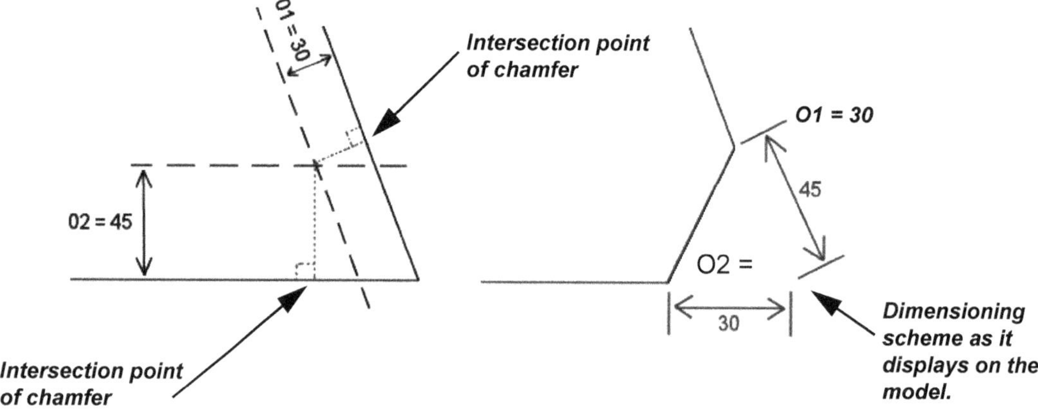

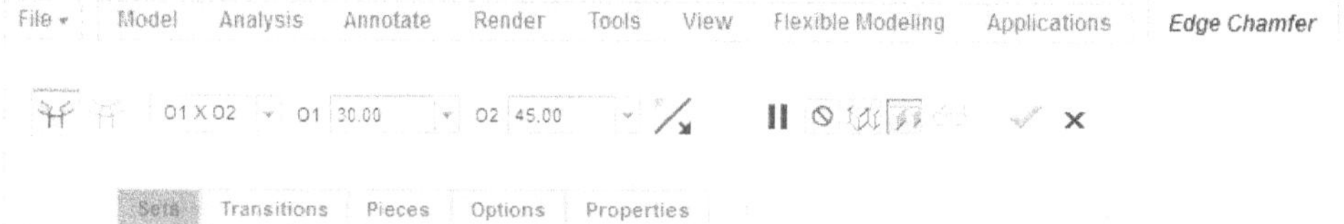

Figure 8–5

If **D1xD2**, **AnglexD**, or **O1xO2** is selected, the *Edge Chamfer* dashboard updates to display (Interchange Distance Dimensions). This icon enables you to switch the distance dimensions of the chamfer.

Dimension Values

When the dimension type has been selected, the exact dimension values can be defined. The required dimensions depend on the dimension type that has been selected. To specify the exact dimension values for an edge chamfer, you can either select and drag the handles that display on the Creo Parametric model or you can enter a value in the *Edge Chamfer* tab, as shown in Figure 8–6.

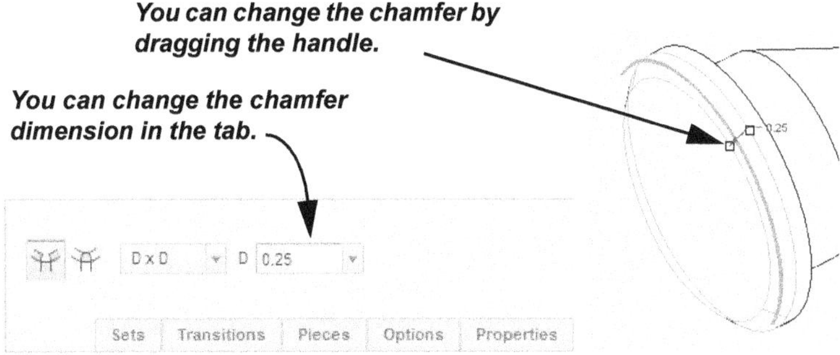

Figure 8–6

Step 4 - Complete the feature.

Once the correct dimensions have been defined, click (Complete Feature) in the *Edge Chamfer* tab to complete the edge chamfer.

8.2 Creating a Corner Chamfer

A corner chamfer removes material from the corner of a feature, as shown in Figure 8–7.

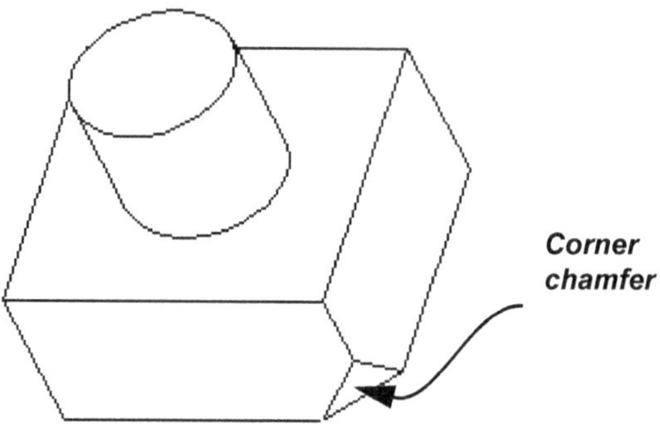

Figure 8–7

How To: To Create an Corner Chamfer

1. Start the creation of a corner chamfer by expanding the (Chamfer) fly-out in the Engineering group in the *Model* tab, and clicking (Corner Chamfer). The *Corner Chamfer* tab displays as shown in Figure 8–8, with all of the options available for creating corner chamfers.

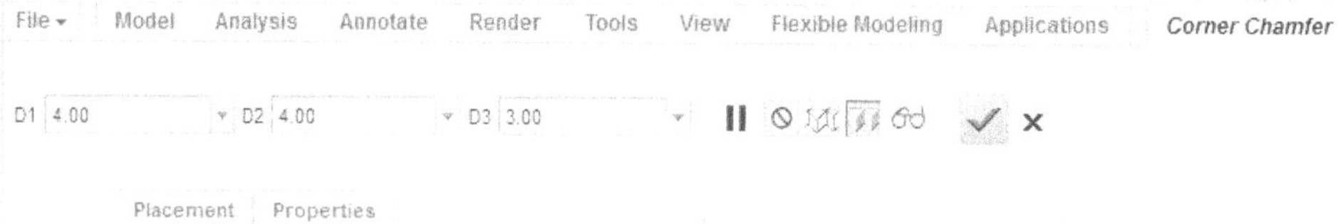

Figure 8–8

2. Select the corner to be chamfered. A corner chamfer is created at the intersection of three edges. To select this reference, select on or near the corner of the model.
3. Once the corner has been selected, define the dimensions. Each edge that intersects the corner has a drag handle that displays on the model. You can either select and drag the handles that display on the model or you can enter a value in the *Corner Chamfer* dashboard, as shown in Figure 8–9.

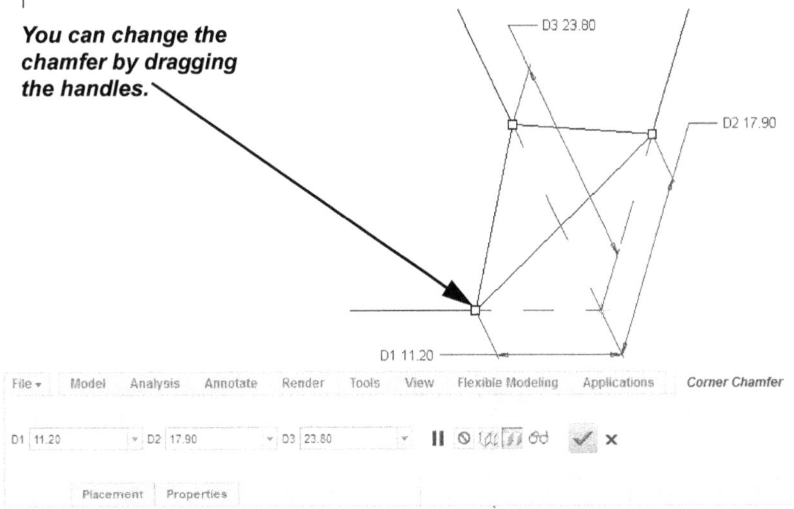

Figure 8–9

4. Once the correct dimensions have been defined, click (Complete Feature) in the *Corner Chamfer* dashboard to complete the corner chamfer.

8.3 Creating Rounds

Alternatively, you can select the reference before clicking (Round).

Rounds can add or remove material, as shown in Figure 8–10. You can create constant edge rounds (default), variable edge rounds, and full rounds.

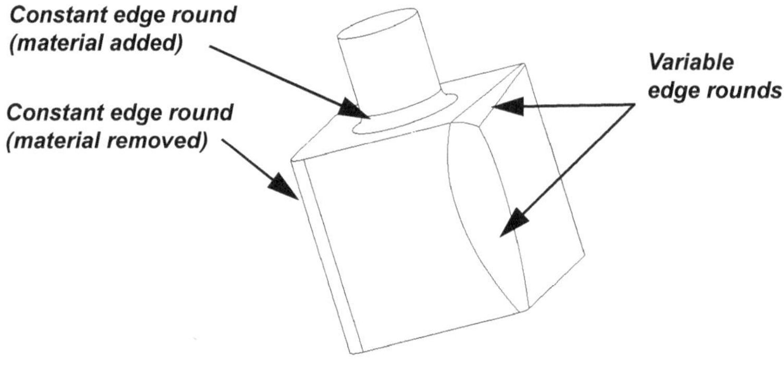

Figure 8–10

General Steps

Use the following general steps to create a round:

1. Start the creation of the feature.
2. Select the placement references.
3. Define the dimensions of the feature.
4. Complete the feature.

Step 1 - Start the creation of the feature.

To start the creation of a round, click (Round) in the Engineering group in the *Model* tab. The *Round* dashboard displays with all of the options for creating rounds, as shown in Figure 8–11.

Figure 8–11

Step 2 - Select the placement references.

You can create many different types of rounds. The surface or edge references that are required to place a round vary depending on the type of round that is required. This section covers constant edge chain rounds, variable edge chain rounds, and full rounds.

Constant Edge Chain Round

A constant edge chain round has a constant radius along its entire reference edge. To create a constant edge chain round you must select the edge(s) on which the round is to be placed. You can also select the adjacent surfaces that intersect at the edge that is to be rounded.

Multiple edges or surfaces can be selected by holding <Ctrl> while selecting the references. Alternatively, holding <Shift> while selecting an edge enables you to select a chain of edges.

By default, once references have been selected, the software automatically creates a constant edge chain round. Figure 8–12 shows an example of the default constant edge chain round.

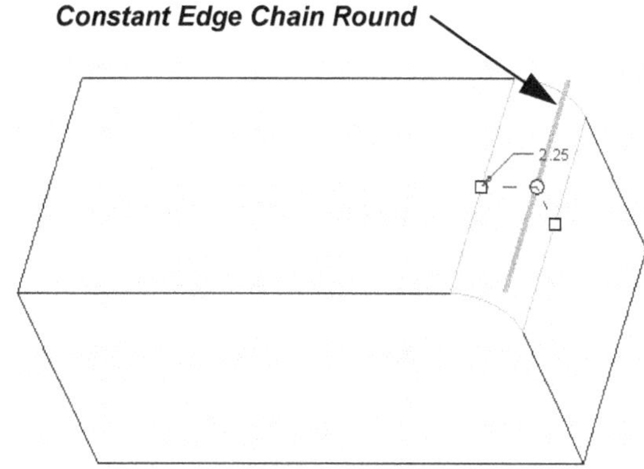

Figure 8–12

Variable Edge Chain

A variable edge chain round enables you to define at least two radii along its reference edge. Selecting the references for a variable edge chain round is the same as selecting a constant edge chain round. When the default constant edge chain round displays on the model, it can be changed into a variable edge chain round. To make the change, right-click and select **Make variable**. The round is now a variable edge chain round with two sets of handles that define the radii at each end.

It is also possible to have intermediate points between the endpoints of a variable edge chain round with different radius values. To create an intermediate point, place the cursor on one of the endpoint radii values, right-click, and select **Add radius**. An additional radius value displays that can be selected and dragged to a new location along the edge.

Figure 8–13 and Figure 8–14 describes how to create a variable edge chain round.

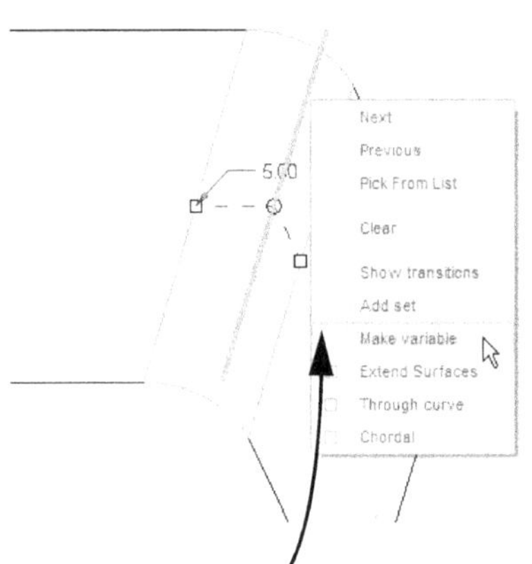

To change a constant edge chain round to a variable round, right-click and select Make variable.

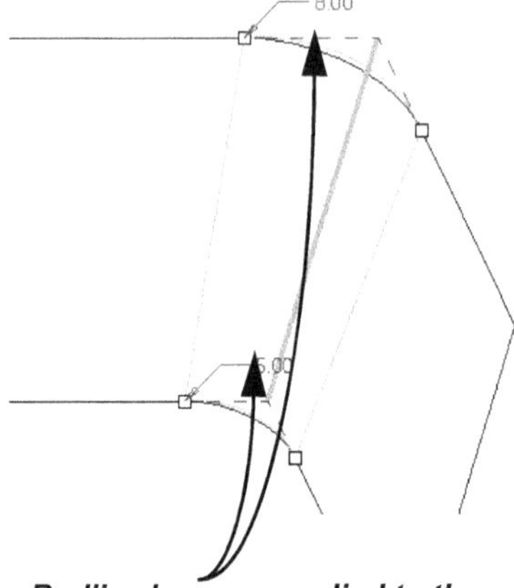

Radii values are applied to the endpoints of the reference edge. Each can be modified independently.

Figure 8–13

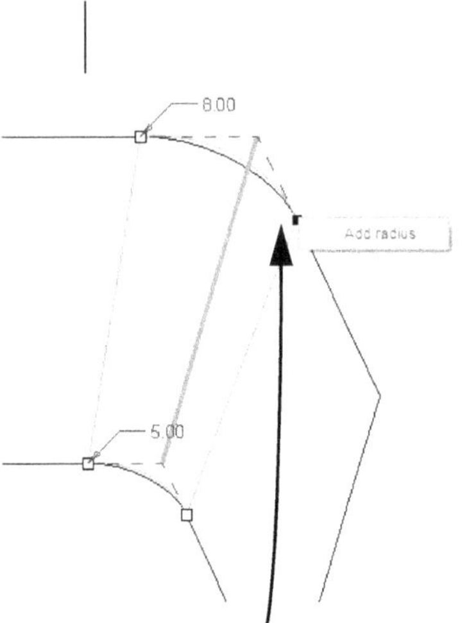

To add an intermediate radius, select an endpoint handle, right-click and select Add radius.

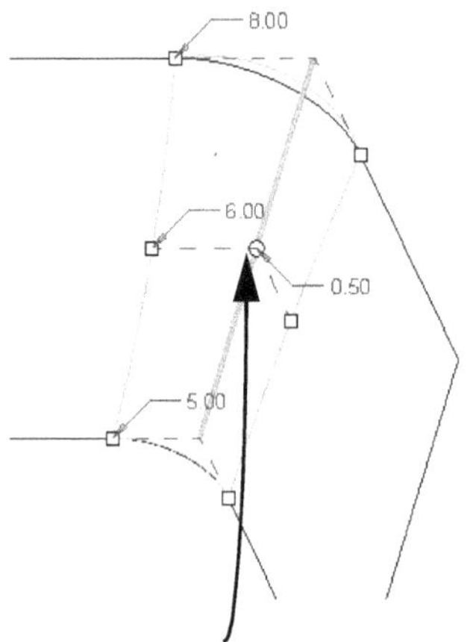

To move the intermediate radius, select the handle and drag.

Figure 8–14

Chordal Round

A chordal round is a variable round where you specify a chord length to define the round. The round radius is determined at each location along the reference edge, so that the chord length is maintained.

To create a Chordal round, right-click and select **Chordal**. The default radius is converted to a linear dimension measured between the tangency points, as shown in Figure 8–16.

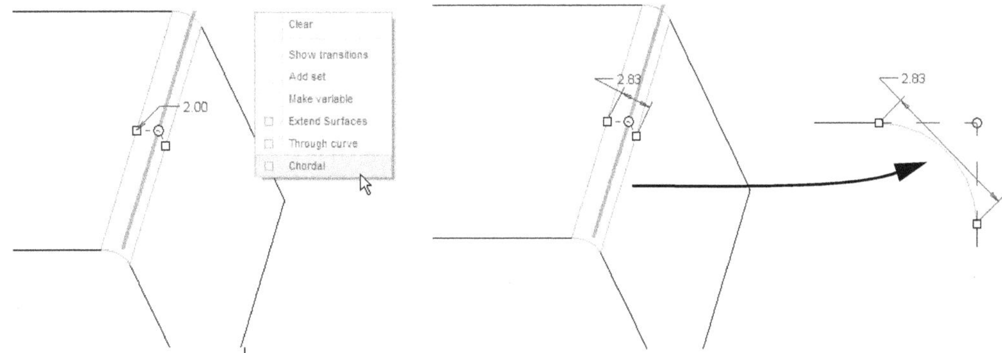

Figure 8–15

Chordal rounds are typically used when aesthetics are important. Figure 8–16 shows the difference between a chordal round, where the edges of the round appear parallel at all points on the round, and a constant radius round, where they do not.

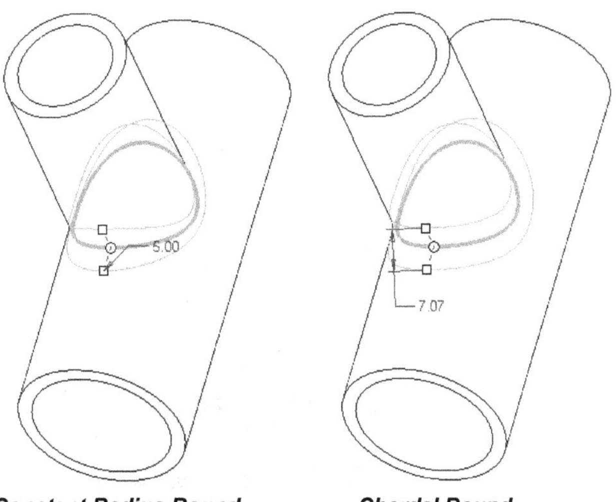

Constant Radius Round ***Chordal Round***

Figure 8–16

Full Round

A full round enables you to replace a whole surface with a rounded one. The round radius is automatically calculated to replace the bounded surface while maintaining tangency to the adjacent surfaces. A full round is placed by selecting two edges or two surfaces that are not adjacent to each other. To select multiple references at the same time, press and hold <Ctrl>. By default, once you select two edge references, the software automatically creates a constant, edge chain round. To change this to a full round, hover the cursor over one of the rounds, right-click, and select **Full round**. Figure 8–17 shows an example of a full round. Two edges are used to create the full round, as shown in Figure 8–18.

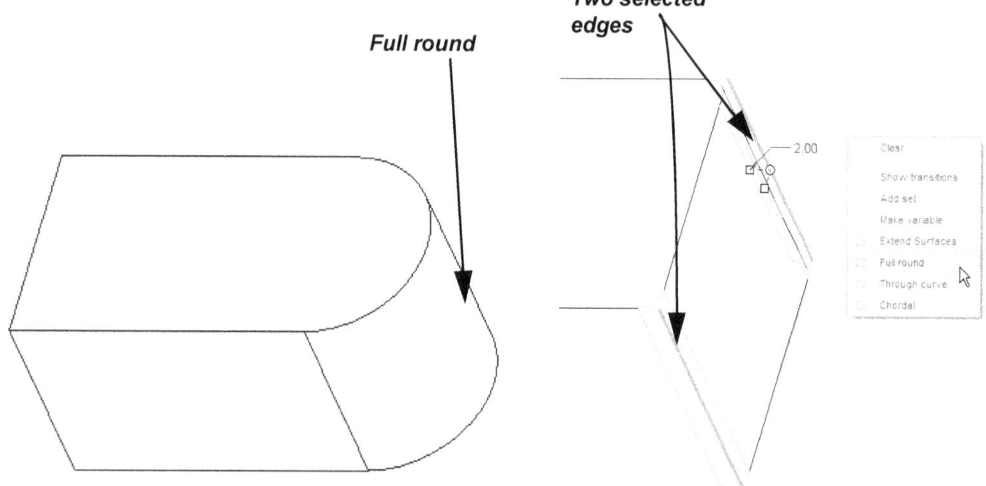

Figure 8–17

Figure 8–18

Two surfaces are used to create the full round, as shown in Figure 8–19. Once you have selected the two surfaces, select which surface is to be replaced by the full round.

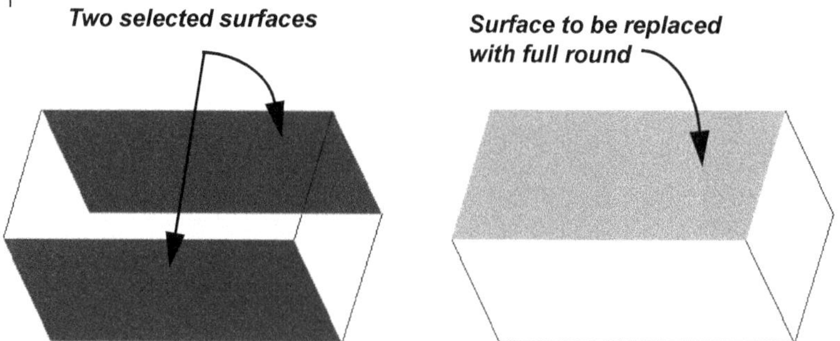

Figure 8–19

Step 3 - Define the dimensions of the feature.

Once the rounds have been placed, the radii dimensions can be changed by dragging the handles on the model, as shown in Figure 8–20. You can also change the round radii in the *Round* tab.

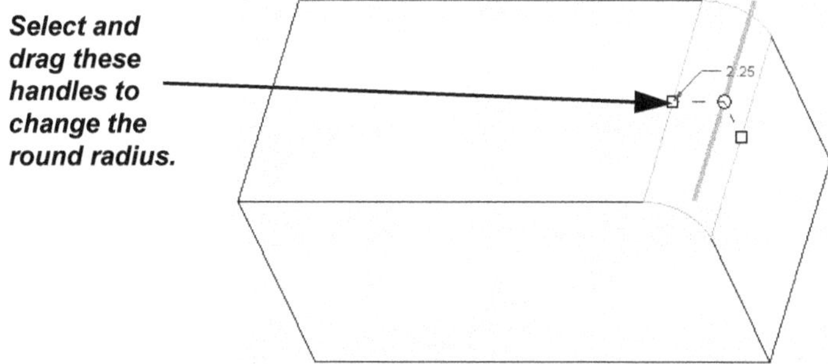

Figure 8–20

The radius of a full round is determined by the surfaces or edges that define it. Therefore, it cannot be changed.

Step 4 - Complete the feature.

Once the correct dimensions have been defined, click ✓ (Complete Feature) to complete the round.

8.4 Auto Round

The **Auto Round** option enables you to quickly create round features in your model. This feature can create rounds in Part mode on both solid or surface geometry. In Assembly mode, it is available for assembly-level surfaces. The resulting rounds created using this feature are referred to as *Auto-Round Members*. Figure 8–21 shows a model to which an auto round feature was added.

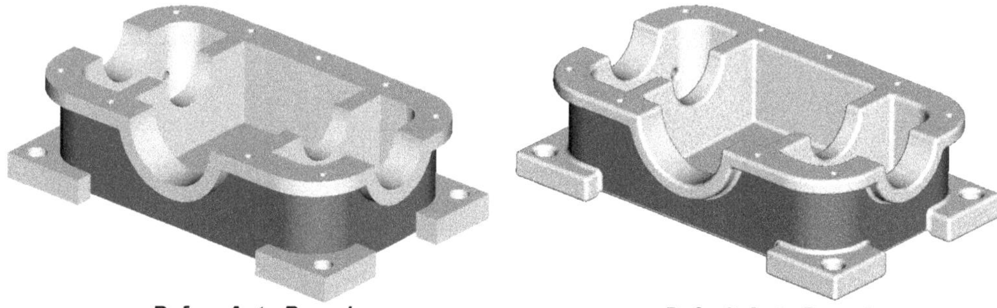

Before Auto Round ***Default Auto Round***

Figure 8–21

How To: Create an Auto Round Feature

The configuration option ***autoround_max_n_chains_per_feat*** *enables you to set the maximum number of edges in each auto round feature.*

1. To create an Auto Round, expand the (Round) Fly-out in the Engineering group in the *Model* tab, and click (Auto Round).
2. The system automatically selects the edges. The sequence and edge sets are defined to maximize the rounded chains. Enter a radius value for the (Convex) and (Concave) edges.
3. (Optional) To remove all concave or convex edges from the auto round feature, clear the checkmark to the left of the respective icon in the *Auto Round* dashboard, as shown in Figure 8–22.

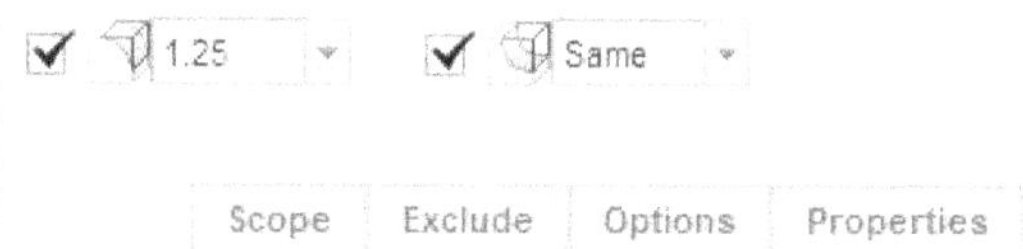

Figure 8–22

4. (Optional) To exclude edges from an auto round feature, open the Exclude panel in the *Auto Round* dashboard and select the edges on the model, as shown in Figure 8–23. Any tangent edges are automatically selected.

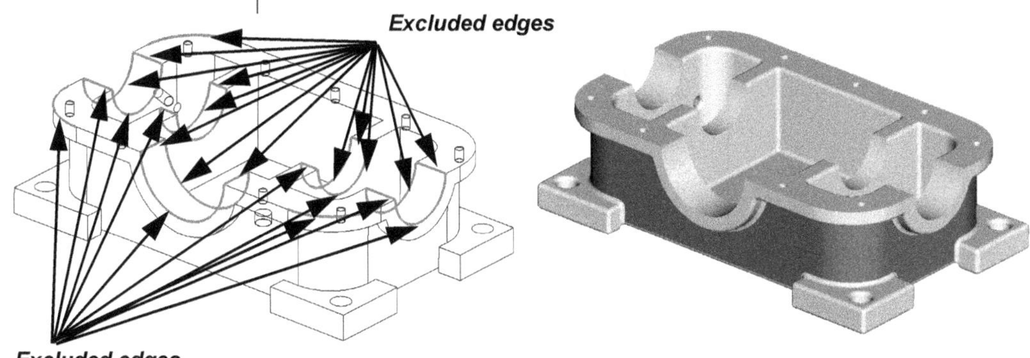

Figure 8–23

Once the edges have been excluded, they are listed in the *Excluded Edges* area. To include them again, select the edge in the list, right-click, and select **Remove**, as shown in Figure 8–24.

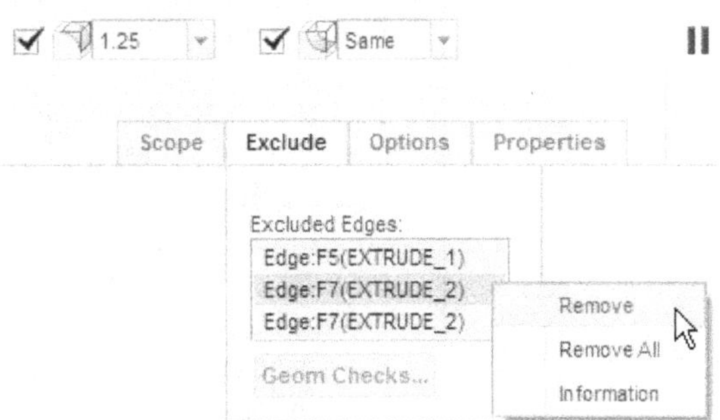

Figure 8–24

5. To complete the feature on all of the system-defined edges, click (Complete Feature).

   By default, an auto round feature displays as a single node in the model tree, as shown in Figure 8–25.

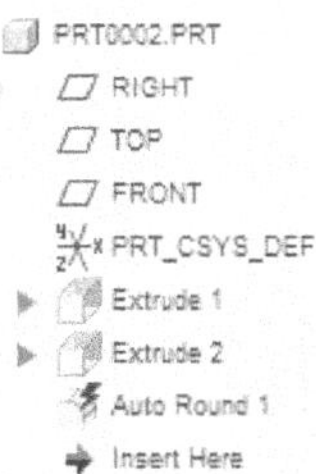

Figure 8–25

To display the list of edges in the feature, click (Settings)> **Tree Filters** in the model tree and select **Auto Round Member** in the *General* tab. Once enabled, sub-nodes of the auto round feature display, as shown in Figure 8–26.

Figure 8–26

Sub-nodes of an auto round feature are not considered standard group features. Operations such as **Suppress**, **Resume**, and **Pattern**, cannot be used.

To convert an auto round feature to a set of round features, open the Options panel and select the **Create Group of Regular Round Features** option, as shown in Figure 8–27. When you convert an auto round feature to a round group, the auto round feature is regenerated and a regular group of round features is created, as shown in Figure 8–27. Once converted, you can use the standard options available for groups and edit the definition of individual rounds in it.

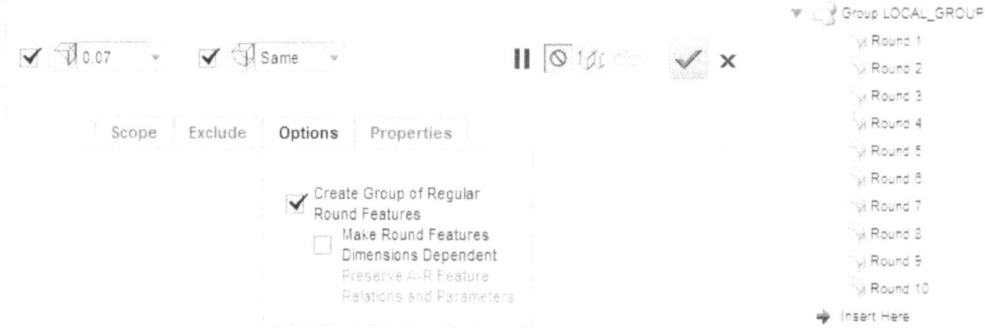

Figure 8–27

Practice 8a

Rounds

Practice Objective

- Open an existing part model and create constant and full round features along specific edges in the model.

In this practice, you will add rounds to a part. You will then add constant edge rounds and a full round. The completed part displays as shown in Figure 8–28.

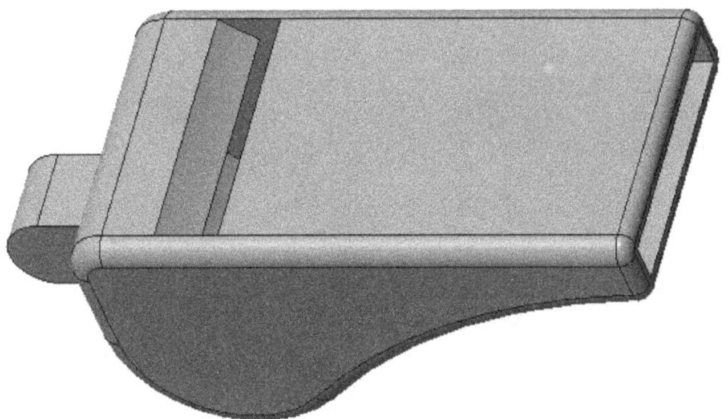

Figure 8–28

Task 1 - Open a part file.

1. Set the working directory to the *Chapter 08\practice 8a* folder.
2. Open **whistle.prt**.
3. Set the model display as follows:
   - *(Datum Display Filters)*: All Off
   - *(Spin Center)*: Off
   - *(Display Style)*: (Shading With Edges)

Task 2 - Create an edge round.

1. Select the edge shown in Figure 8–29. Then, right-click and select **Round**.
2. In the *Round* dashboard, set the *Radius* to **0.25**, as shown in Figure 8–30.

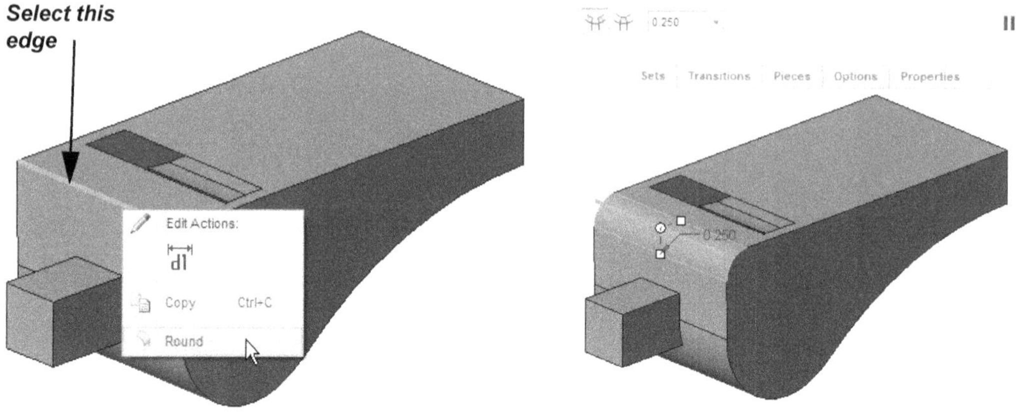

Figure 8–29

Figure 8–30

3. Click (Complete Feature) to complete the round.
4. Hold <Ctrl> and select the edges shown in Figure 8–31.
5. Right-click and select **Round**.
6. Set the *Radius* to **0.125**, as shown in Figure 8–32.

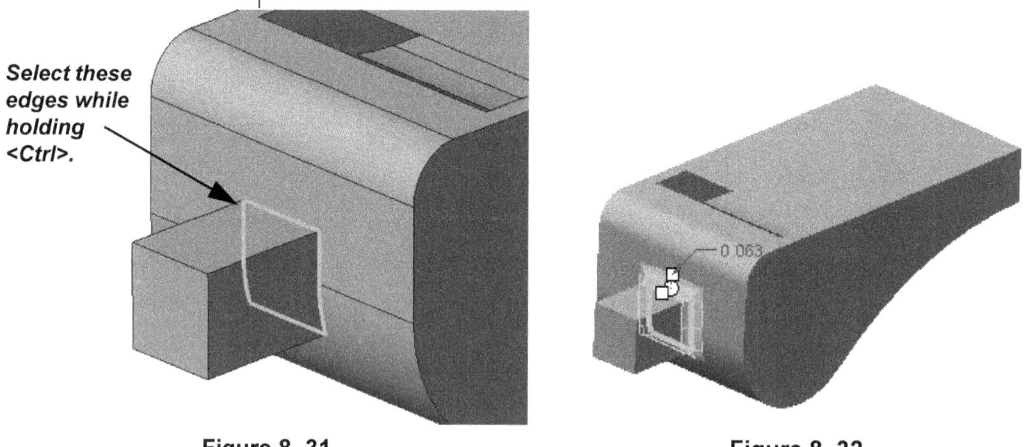

Figure 8–31

Figure 8–32

7. Click (Complete Feature) to complete the round.

Task 3 - Create a full round.

1. In the Engineering group in the ribbon, click (Round).
2. Hold <Ctrl> and select the two edges shown in Figure 8–33.
3. Right-click on one of the selected edges and select **Full Round**, as shown in Figure 8–34.

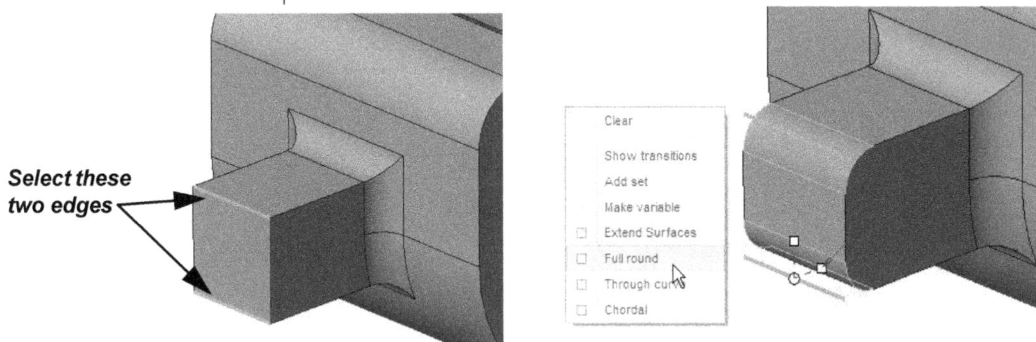

Figure 8–33

Figure 8–34

4. Click (Complete Feature) to complete the round. The full round displays as shown in Figure 8–35.

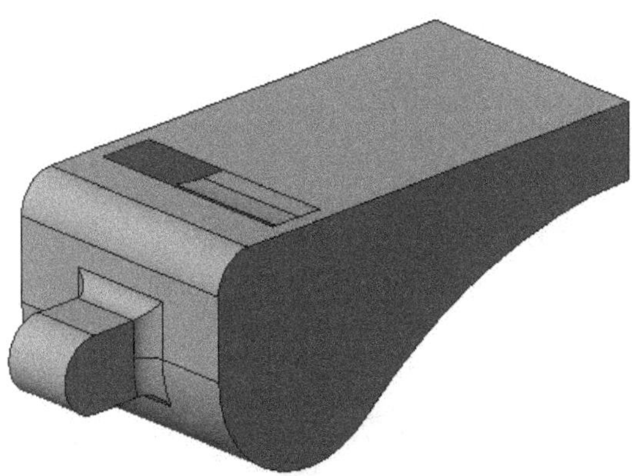

Figure 8–35

Task 4 - Create a round.

Design Considerations

In this task, you will select two edges for the round references. Note that when you select an edge, all edges that are tangent to it are also selected.

1. Click (Round).
2. Create another round and select the two edges shown in Figure 8–36.
3. Set the *Radius* to **0.125** and complete the round, as shown in Figure 8–37.

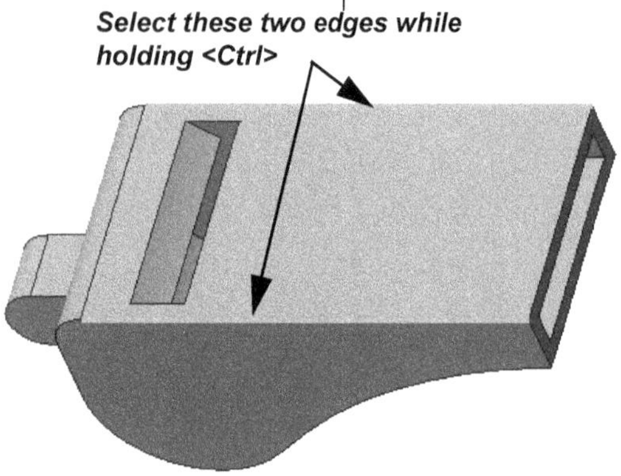

Select these two edges while holding <Ctrl>

0.125

Figure 8–36

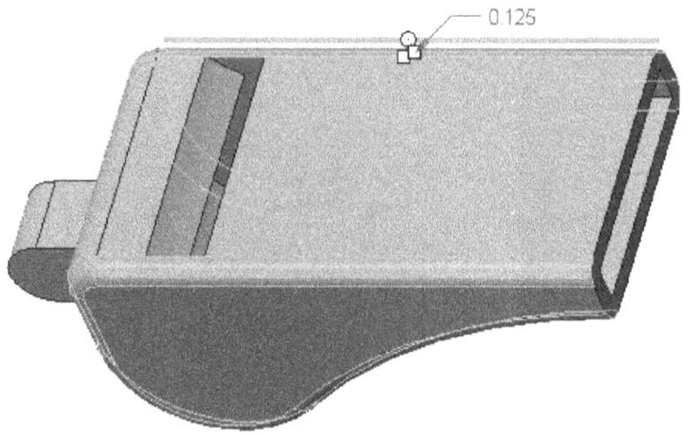

Figure 8–37

4. Create a round on the edge with a *Radius* of **0.075**, as shown in Figure 8–38.
5. Once the round has been completed, orient the model to the default view and save it. The model displays as shown in Figure 8–39.

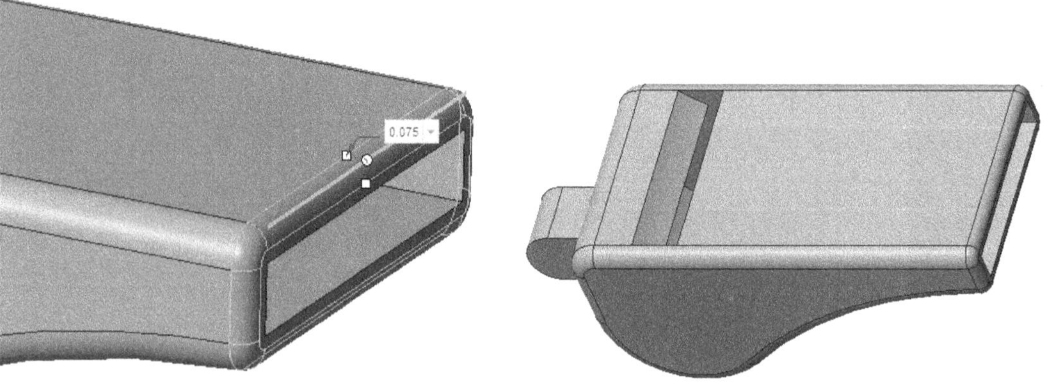

Figure 8–38

Figure 8–39

6. Save the part and erase it from memory.

Practice 8b Rounds and Chamfers

Practice Objectives

- Create constant, variable, and full round features along specific edges in the model.
- Create an edge chamfer along specific edges in the model.

In this practice, you will complete the modeling of a toy tractor by adding a full round and a chamfer to form the front of the toy, constant edge rounds to complete the cab, and a variable edge round to form the front hood area as shown in Figure 8–40.

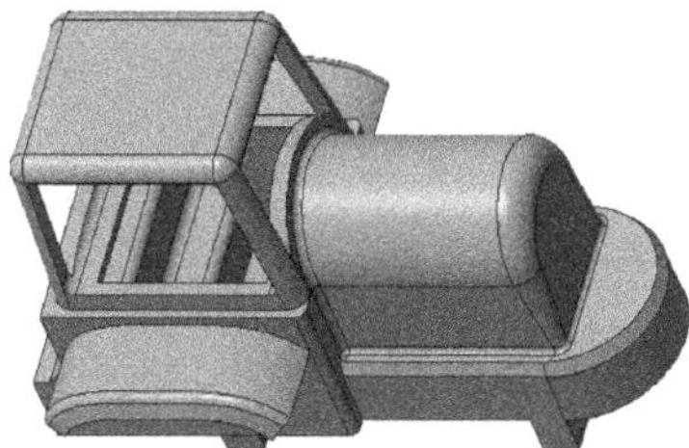

Figure 8–40

Task 1 - Open a part file.

1. Set the working directory to the *Chapter 08\practice 8b* folder.
2. Open **toy_tractor.prt**.
3. Set the model display as follows:
    - *(Datum Display Filters)*: All Off
    - *(Spin Center)*: Off
    - *(Display Style)*: (Shading With Edges)

    The model displays as shown in Figure 8–41.

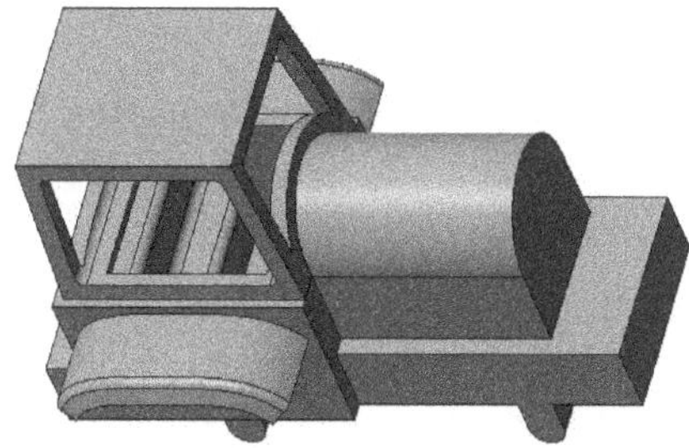

Figure 8–41

Task 2 - Create a full round.

1. In the Engineering group, click (Round).
2. Select the two edges shown in Figure 8–42, right-click and select **Full round**.

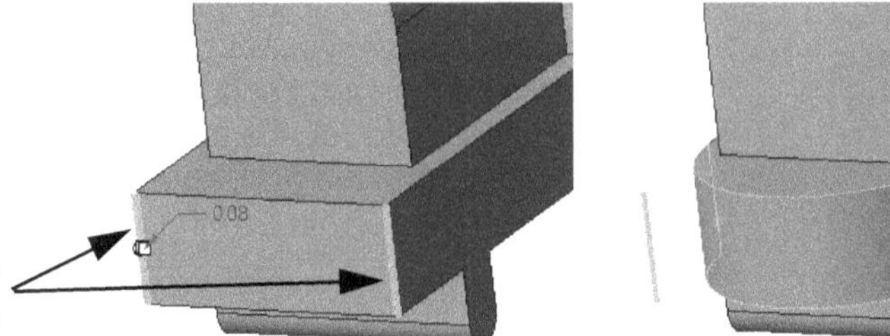

Figure 8–42

3. Press <Ctrl>+<D>. The completed round displays as shown in Figure 8–43.

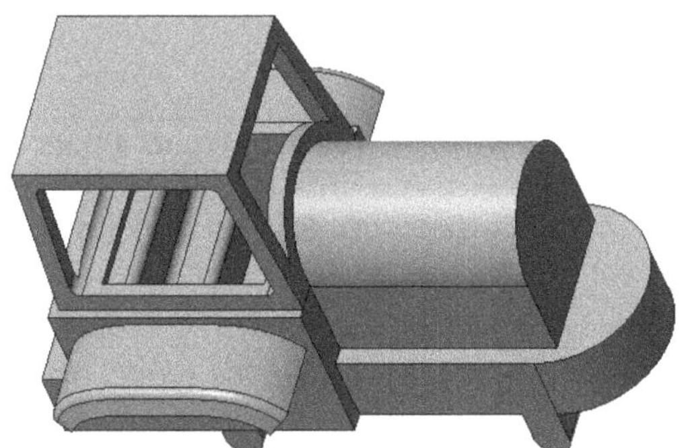

Figure 8–43

Task 3 - Create a chamfer.

1. In the Engineering group, click (Chamfer) to create an edge chamfer,
2. Select the edge shown in Figure 8–44. Leave the default **DxD** dimensioning scheme. Set the *Dimension* to **0.57**.

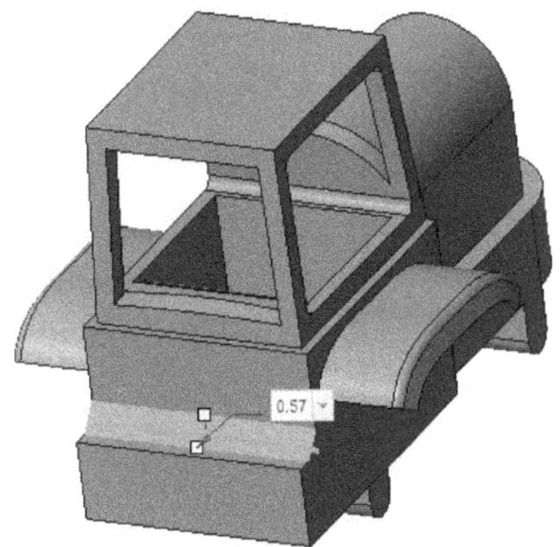

Figure 8–44

3. Click (Complete Feature) to complete the chamfer.

Task 4 - Create a D1xD2 chamfer.

1. Create a chamfer and select the edge shown in Figure 8–45. Expand the drop-down list and select **D1xD2**. Set the following values:

   - *D1:* **0.18**
   - *D2:* **0.375**

2. Complete the chamfer. The model displays as shown in Figure 8–46.

Figure 8–45

Figure 8–46

Task 5 - Create constant rounds.

1. Press <Ctrl>+<D>.
2. Create a round n all four outer edges of the cab with a *Radius* of **0.50**, as shown in Figure 8–47.
3. Create another radius round with a **0.50** value on the top edge of the cab, as shown in Figure 8–48.

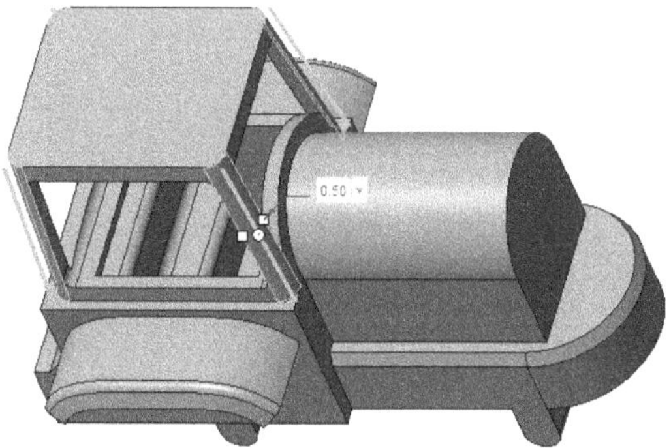

Figure 8–47

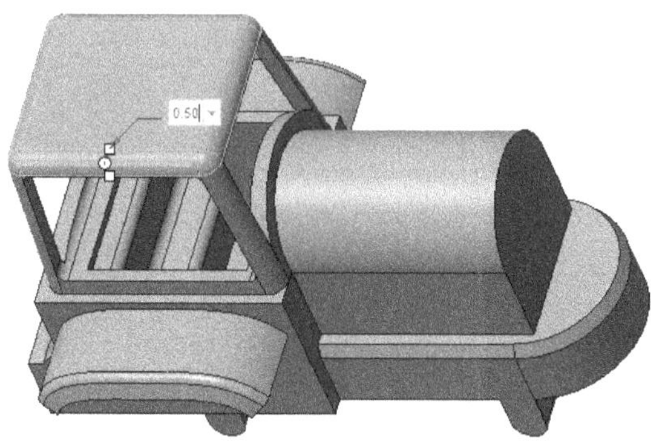

Figure 8–48

4. Create a round on the edges where the cab and the hood meet with a *Radius* of **0.18**, as shown in Figure 8–49.

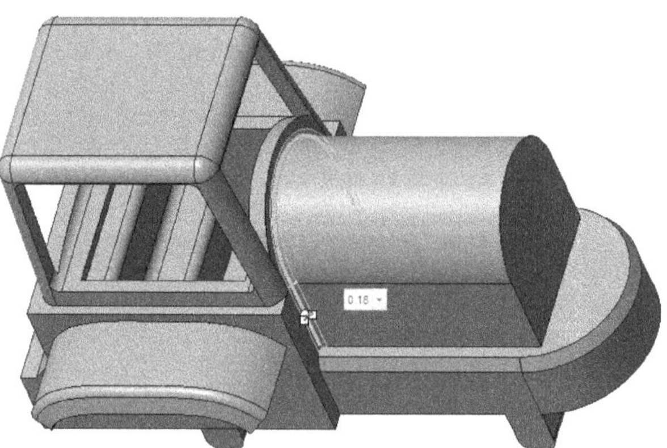

Figure 8–49

Task 6 - Create a variable radius round.

1. Create a round and select the edge shown in Figure 8–50.

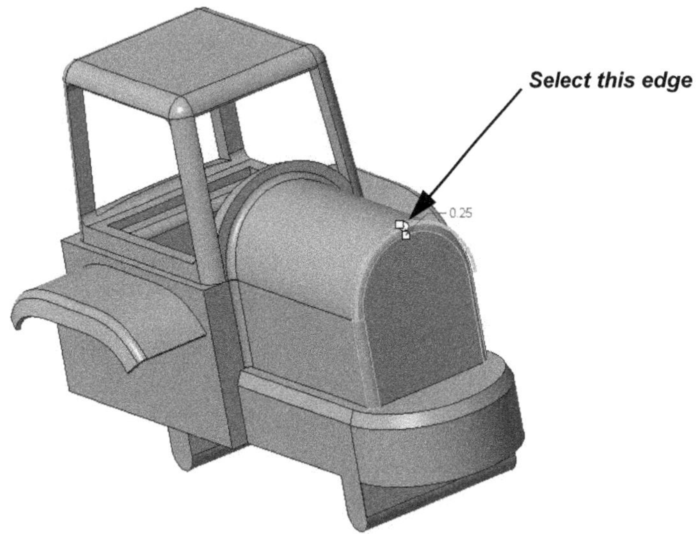

Figure 8–50

2. Hover the cursor over the selected edge, right-click, and select **Make variable**, as shown in Figure 8–51.

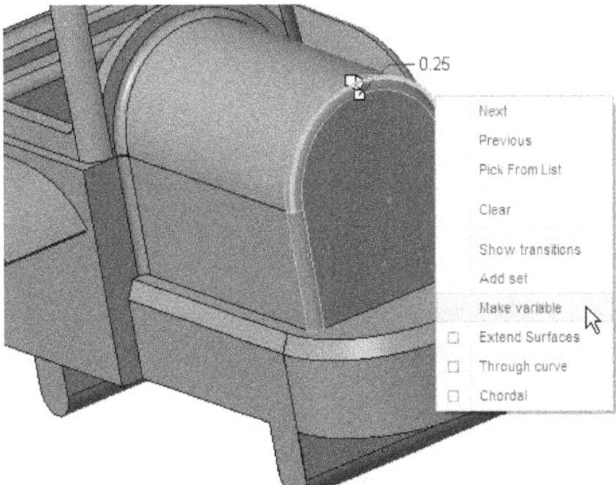

Figure 8–51

3. A radius value will display at each end of the selected edge, as shown in Figure 8–52. Ensure that both end point radii are set to **0.25**.

4. Place the cursor over one of the handles, press and hold the right mouse button, and select **Add Radius**, as shown in Figure 8–53.

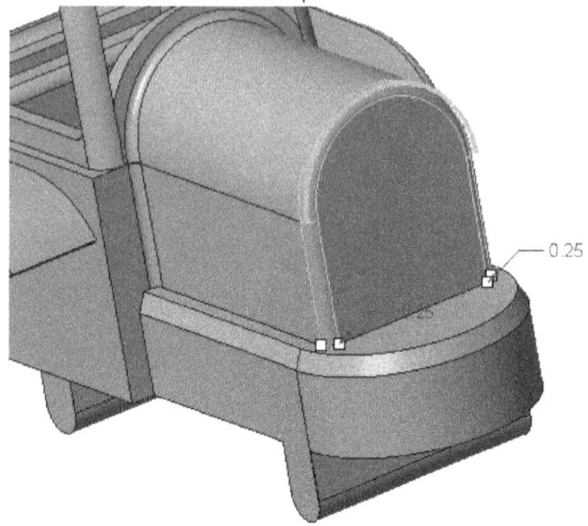

Figure 8–52

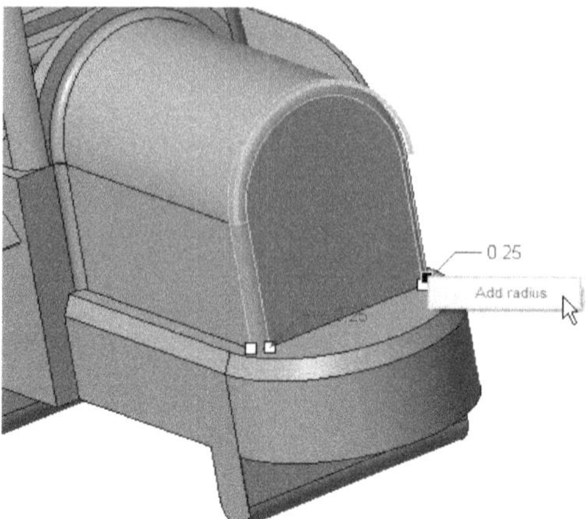

Figure 8–53

5. Drag the circular handle to the middle of the arc-shaped edge, as shown in Figure 8–54. Ensure that the *Placement* is set to a **0.5** length ratio.

6. Set the new radius value to **0.75**, as shown in Figure 8–55.

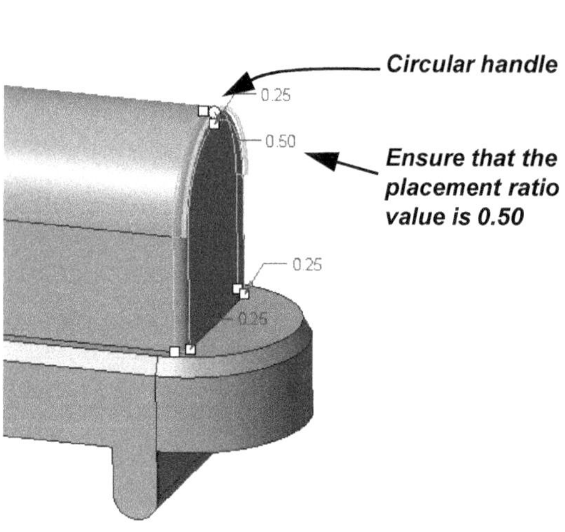

Figure 8–54

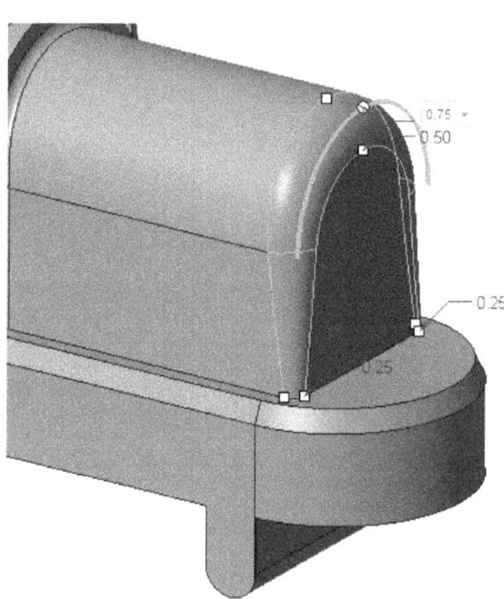

Figure 8–55

7. Complete the variable edge round. The model displays as shown in Figure 8–56.

8. Create a round with a *Radius* of **0.125**, on the edge shown in Figure 8–57.

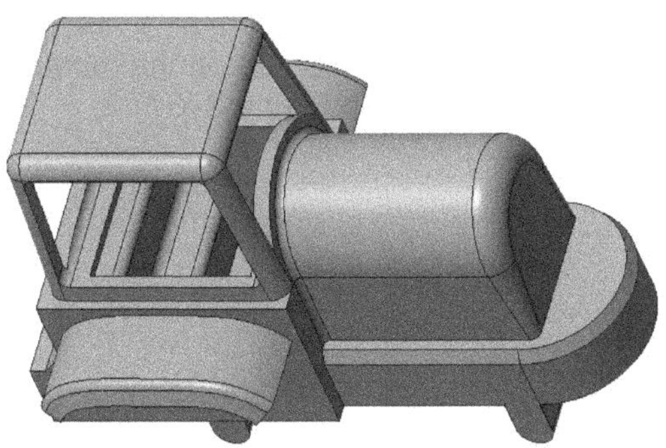

Figure 8–56

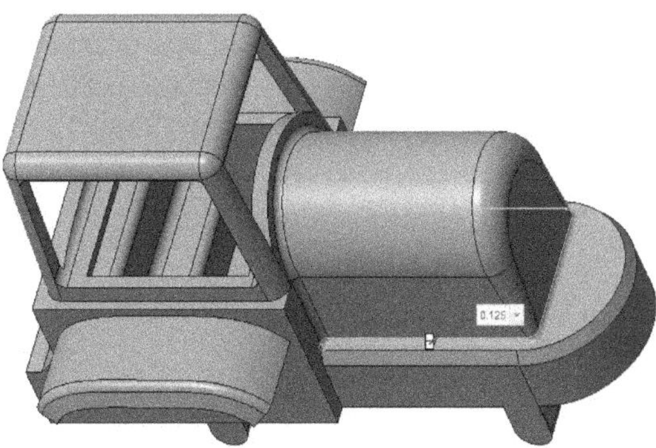

Figure 8–57

9. Create a round with a *Radius* of **0.25**, on the two edges shown in Figure 8–58. The completed model displays as shown in Figure 8–59.

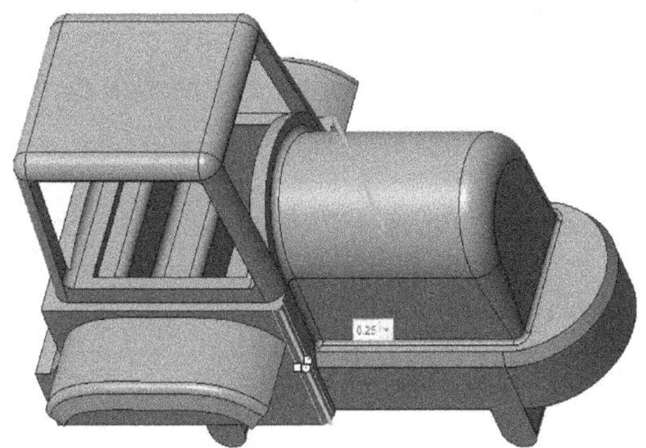

Figure 8–58

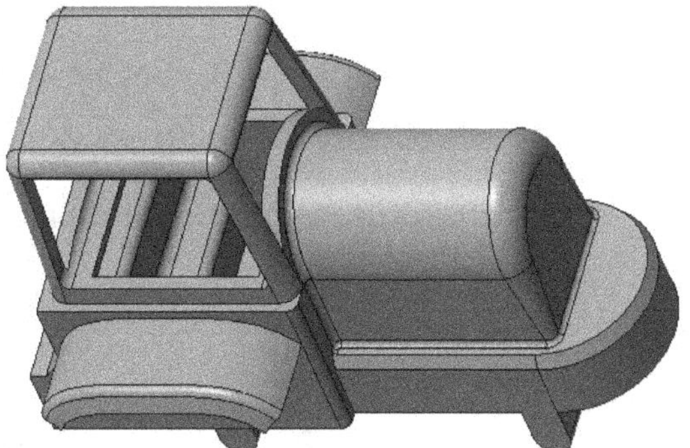

Figure 8–59

10. Save the part and erase it from memory.

Practice 8c (Optional) Additional Rounds

Practice Objective

- Create constant rounds in the model.

In this practice, you will open the **rounds.prt** part, as shown in Figure 8–60. You will create a number of rounds on the model. The resulting model displays as shown in Figure 8–61.

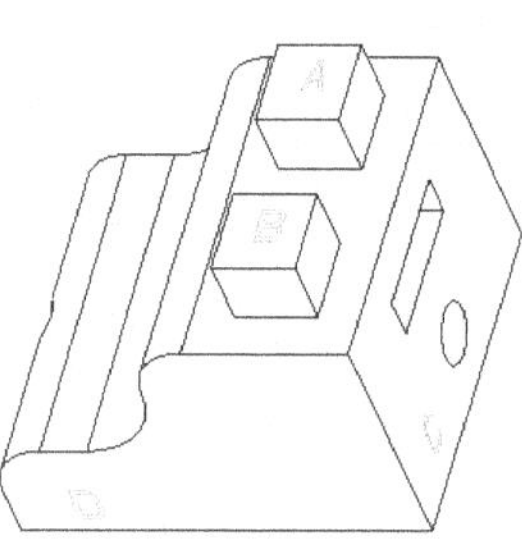

Figure 8–60

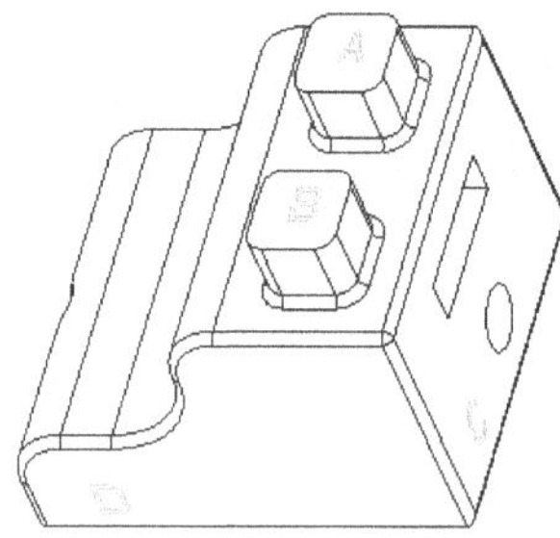

Figure 8–61

Task 1 - Open the rounds.prt part.

1. Set the working directory to the *Chapter 08\practice 8c* folder.
2. Open **rounds.prt**.
3. Set the model display as follows:
   - *(Datum Display Filters)*: All Off
   - *(Spin Center)*: Off
   - *(Display Style)*: (No Hidden)

Task 2 - Create rounds on surface C.

Alternatively, you can select a chain of edges using <Shift> while selecting two adjacent edges. All adjacent edges are automatically selected.

1. Click (Round) to create a simple round.
2. Select all four bounding edges of surface **C**. To select multiple edges at the same time, press and hold <Ctrl>. The rounds automatically display on the model.

3. Select and drag the handles for the round *Radius* to approximately **0.3**. You can also change the radius value on the tab or by double-clicking on the dimension value on the model.

4. Click (Complete Feature) to complete the feature. The part displays as shown in Figure 8–62.

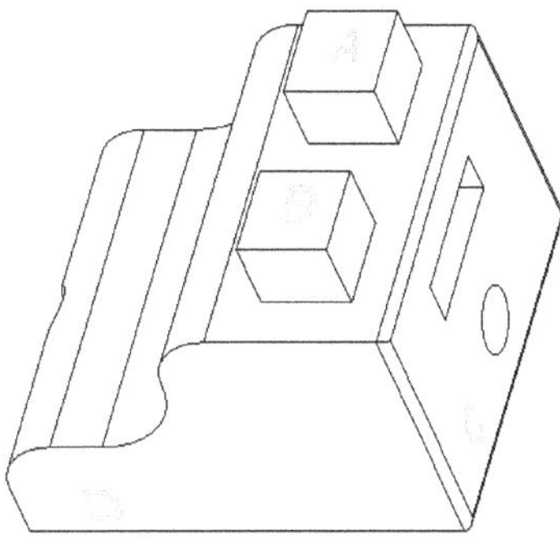

Figure 8–62

Task 3 - Create rounds on surface D.

1. Click (Round) to create a simple round.

2. Select one of the top edges of surface **D** to be rounded. All edges up to but not including the bottom edge are automatically selected because they are tangent to one another. The round displays along all of the edges.

__0.3__ remains the default value because it was the last value entered.

3. Accept the **0.3** value for the *Radius*.

4. Click (Complete Feature) to complete the round. The model displays as shown in Figure 8–63.

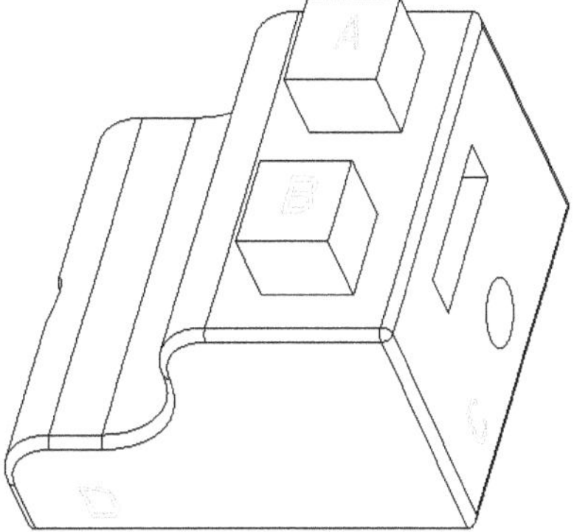

Figure 8–63

Task 4 - Create the rounds on protrusion A.

1. Create rounds with a **0.3** value for the four edges where protrusion A meets the base feature. Use <Ctrl> when selecting the edges so that they are all included as one feature and are driven by one dimension. The part displays as shown in Figure 8–64.

2. Create rounds with a *Radius* of **0.6** for the four corner edges on protrusion A. Use <Ctrl> to select the edges. The part displays as shown in Figure 8–65.

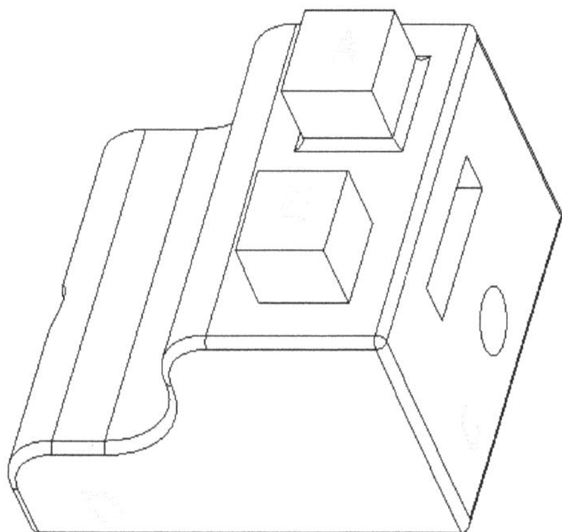

Figure 8–64

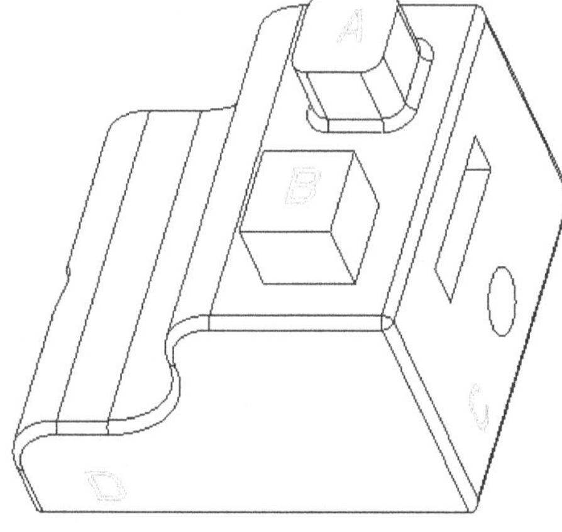

Figure 8–65

Task 5 - Create the rounds on protrusion B in the opposite order to those created on protrusion A.

1. Create rounds with a *Radius* of **0.6** for the four vertical corner edges of protrusion **B**.

2. Create rounds with a *Radius* of **0.3** for the tangent edges where the protrusion meets the base feature. It will only be necessary to select one edge, because the existing rounds create an edge chain. The part displays as shown in Figure 8–66.

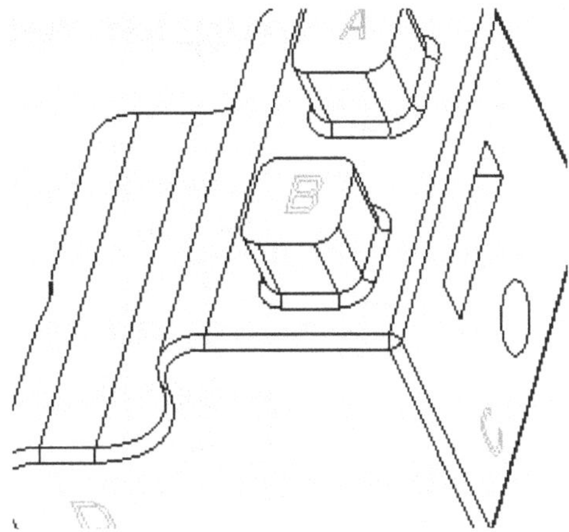

Figure 8–66

3. Save the part and erase it from memory.

Chapter Review Questions

1. Which of the following chamfer types enable you to interchange distance dimensions of the chamfer? (Select all that apply.)
   a. D x D
   b. D1 x D2
   c. Angle x D
   d. 45 x D
   e. O x O
   f. O1 x O2
2. Only ________ edges can meet at a vertex selected for a corner chamfer.
   a. One
   b. Two
   c. Three
   d. Four
3. Chamfer features always remove material.
   a. True
   b. False
4. Round features can add or remove material.
   a. True
   b. False
5. Which keyboard keys can be used to select multiple individual edges for a round or chamfer feature?
   a. <Tab>
   b. <Shift>
   c. <Ctrl>
   d. <Alt>
6. Rounds on multiple edges can be controlled by one dimension.
   a. True
   b. False

7. What is the minimum number of radius dimensions that can be attached to a variable round applied to a single linear edge?
    a. 1
    b. 2
    c. 3
    d. 4

Command Summary

Button	Command	Location
	Chamfer	• **Ribbon:** *Model* tab in the Engineering group
	Corner Chamfer	• **Ribbon:** *Model* tab in the Engineering group
	Round	• **Ribbon:** *Model* tab in the Engineering group
	Auto Round	• **Ribbon:** *Model* tab in the Engineering group

Holes

Holes are a tool for creating circular openings in a model, without having to sketch the circular section. Holes can be created on planar or cylindrical surfaces, and can have simple cylindrical sections, counterbore and countersink entry and exits. Standard holes use a predefined sketched section to generate the geometry for the hole. Creating a sketched hole gives you greater control over the hole shape, and it enables you to sketch its section as a revolved form.

Learning Objectives in this Chapter

- Create a straight hole that removes material from a model using the linear, radial, or coaxial placement options.
- Define the placement reference, dimensions, and depth options, as required, to create a hole that captures the design intent of the model.
- Create standard and sketched holes using options in the Hole dashboard.

9.1 Creating Simple, Straight Holes

Holes are Engineering features because their cross-sections are circular. Holes remove material from the model. Two types of holes are available: Straight and Standard.

Straight holes are further subdivided into Simple and Sketched holes. Examples of Simple and Sketched holes are shown in Figure 9–1.

Standard holes enable you to enter predefined parameter values to generate the hole.

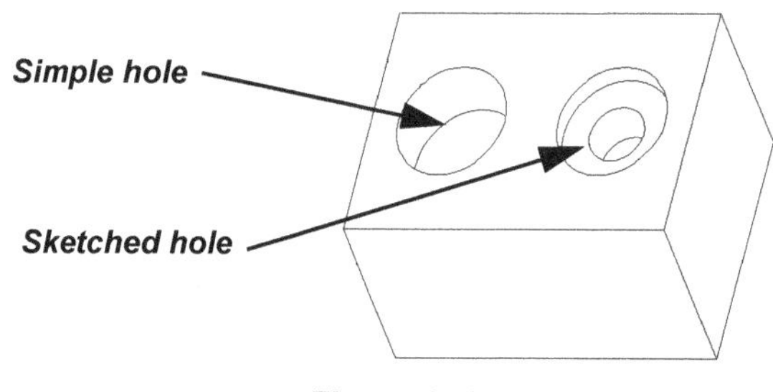

Figure 9–1

General Steps

Use the following general steps to create a simple hole:

1. Start the creation of the feature.
2. Select the placement references.
3. Define the dimensions of the feature.
4. Define the depth of the feature.
5. Complete the feature.

Step 1 - Start the creation of the feature.

To start the creation of a hole, click (Hole) in the Engineering group in the *Model* tab. The *Hole* dashboard displays with all of the options available for creating holes, as shown in Figure 9–2. Simple straight holes are the default hole types.

Figure 9–2

Step 2 - Select the placement references.

Alternatively, you can select the reference before clicking (Hole).

Holes are placed on the model by referencing existing features using one of four placement schemes:

- Linear
- Radial
- Diameter
- Coaxial

These schemes can be defined in the *Hole* dashboard under the Placement panel. It is not necessary to select a scheme because the software uses the references that you select to identify the scheme for you. Figure 9–3 shows examples of a coaxial and linear hole.

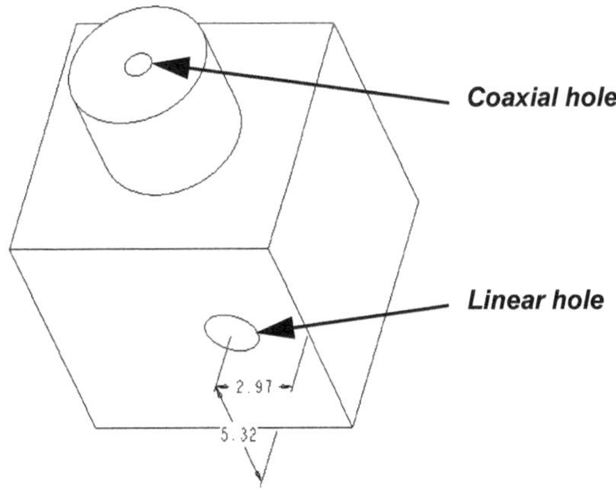

Figure 9–3

Linear Placement

To place a linear hole, you must first select a surface as the primary reference. This defines the placement surface for the hole. Once selected, the Creo Parametric software automatically places the hole, which displays with four handles. The two handles that are at 90° to each other are used to assign the secondary references.

The secondary references place the hole relative to the existing geometry. Drag and drop the handles on the required references to locate the hole. If datum references cannot be used, it is recommended to use surfaces as references planes because they are more stable than points or edges, for example. Figure 9–4 shows how references for placing the hole are assigned.

A cylindrical extrusion always includes a datum axis.

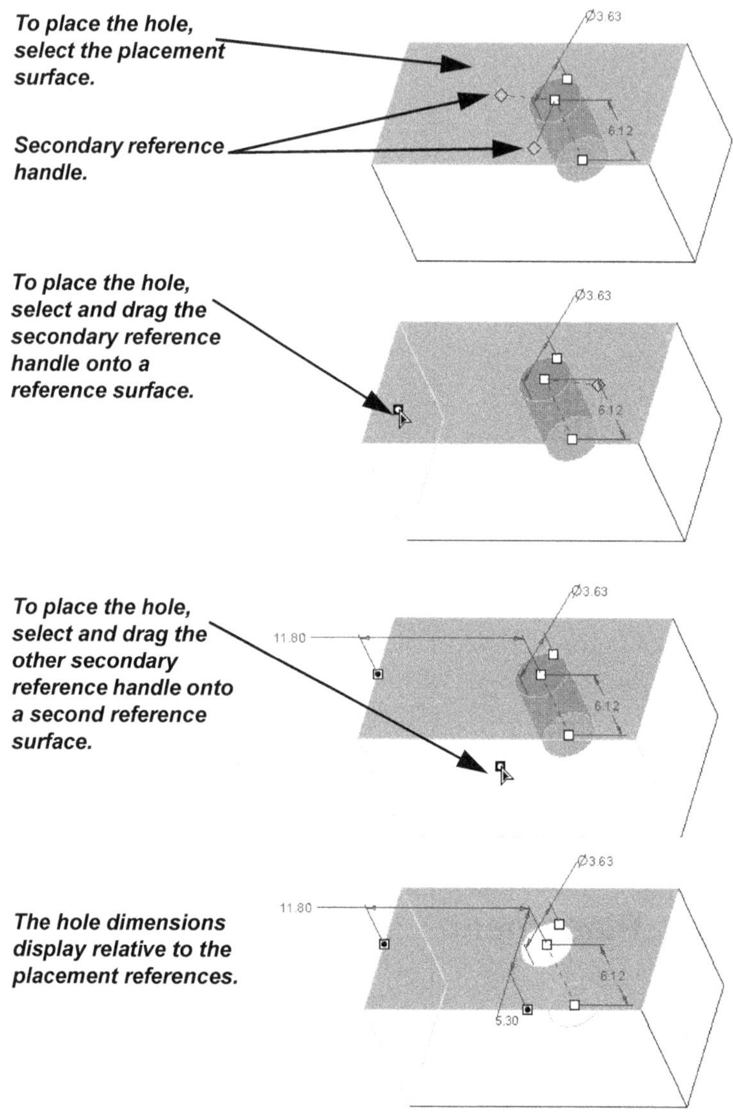

Figure 9–4

All placement references (placement and secondary) can also be assigned using the *Hole* dashboard. To display the Placement options, click **Placement** in the *Hole* dashboard. The panel displays as shown in Figure 9–5. To assign the reference, select the field and then select the reference on the model.

Figure 9–5

Once the references have been selected for a linear hole, you can assign an *Offset* value or specify to align the hole to the selected reference, as shown in Figure 9–6.

The hole is aligned to the RIGHT and FRONT datum planes.

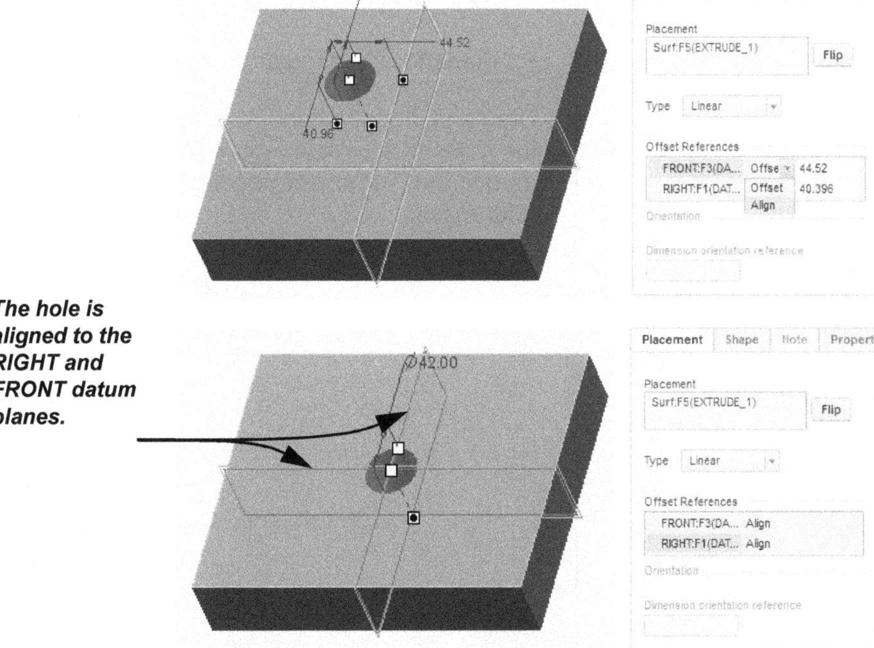

Figure 9–6

Radial Hole on a Planar Surface

To place a straight radial hole on a plane, you must first select a planar surface as the primary reference. Once selected, the software automatically places the hole. By default, it selects a linear placement because you selected a planar surface. To change the placement to radial, open the Placement panel in the *Hole* dashboard, and select **Radial** as the placement type, as shown in Figure 9–7.

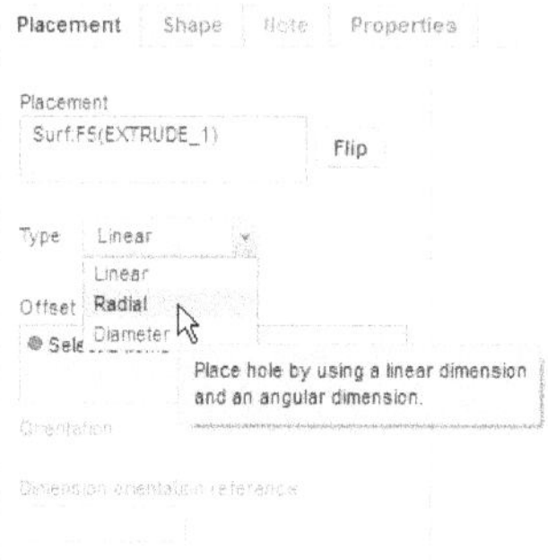

Figure 9–7

The hole displays with multiple handles to define the *Placement*, *Size*, and *Depth*. The two placement handles are 90° to each other and are used to assign the secondary references. You can assign the following secondary references:

- Axis for radial distance.
- Plane for the angular distance.

Drag and drop the handles onto the required references to locate the hole, as shown in Figure 9–8. The *Secondary References* area in the Placement panel can also be used to assign the references.

The Diameter option is the same as the Radial option, but uses a diameter dimension instead of a radius.

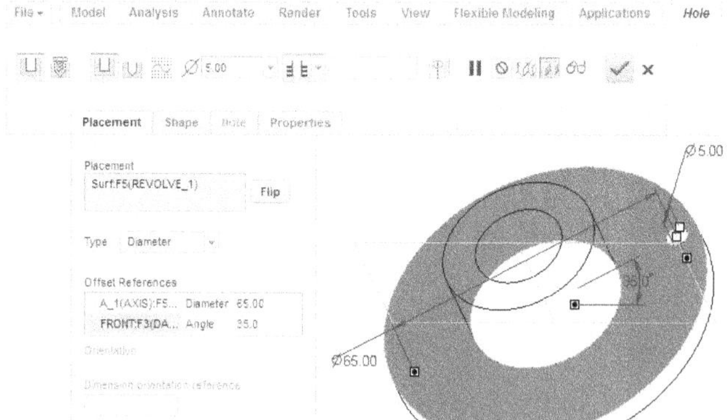

Figure 9–8

Coaxial Placement

To place a coaxial hole, an axis must be selected as the first placement reference. This defines the placement axis for the hole. Once selected, the software automatically places the hole. To finalize the hole placement, you must select a second placement reference to define the placement plane for the hole. Figure 9–9 shows how the references for placing a coaxial hole are assigned.

To place the coaxial hole, select the placement axis.

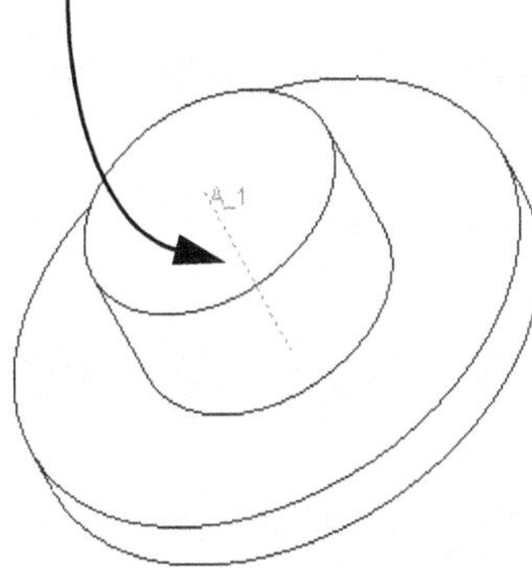

The hole now references the axis and the placement plane.

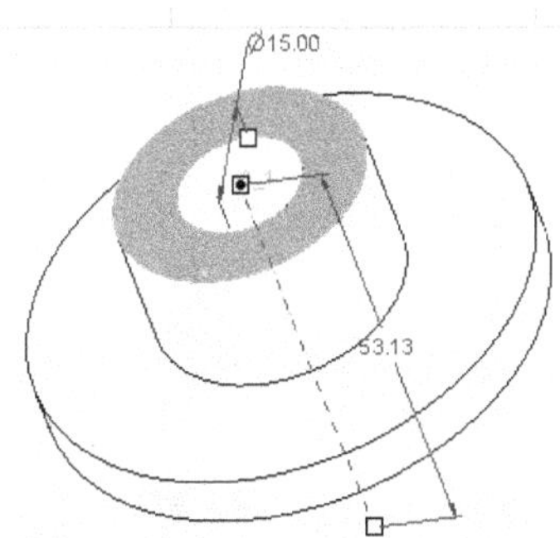

To set the placement plane, hold <Ctrl> and select the placement surface.

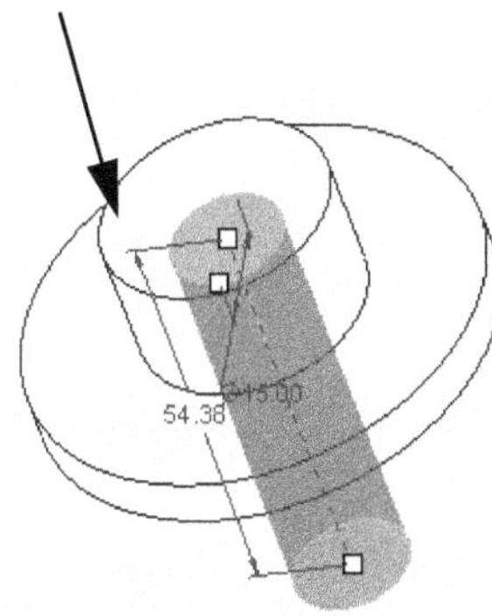

Figure 9–9

Both placement references (axis and placement plane) can also be assigned using the *Hole* dashboard. To access the **Placement** options, click **Placement** in the *Hole* dashboard. The panel displays as shown in Figure 9–10. To assign the reference, select the field and the reference on the model.

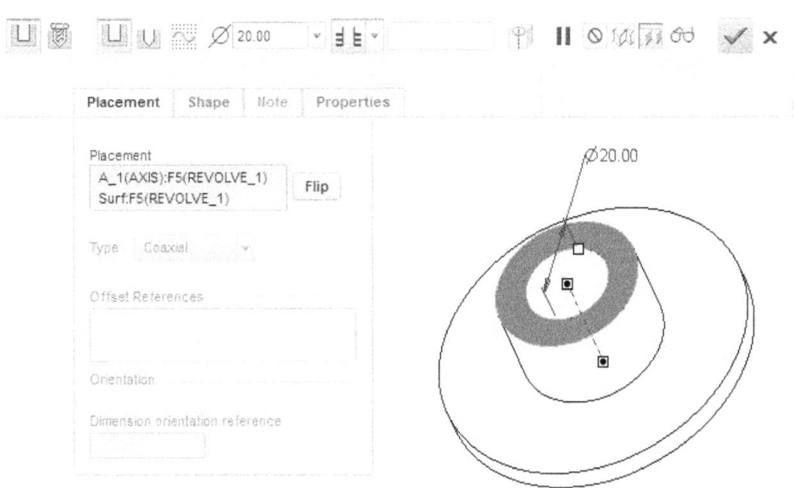

Figure 9–10

Step 3 - Define the dimensions of the feature.

Context Menu

Once you are comfortable with the required references for the various hole types, you may find it quicker to use the shortcut menu to switch between placement and reference selections.

In the example shown in Figure 9–11, the flat surface was selected as the placement reference. Instead of opening the Placement panel to select the offset references, you can simply right-click, select **Offset Reference Collector**, and select the appropriate offset references.

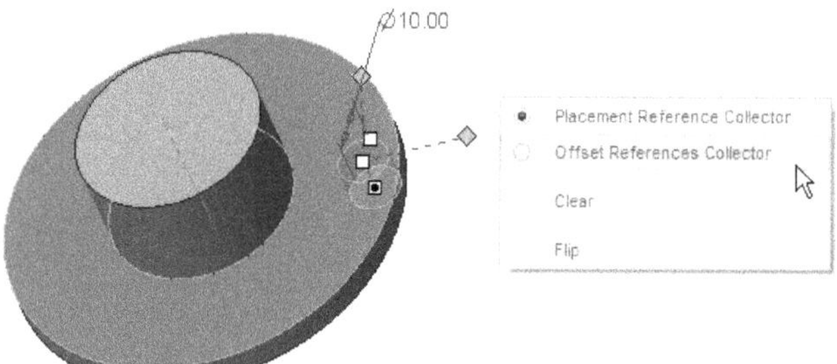

Figure 9–11

In addition to the secondary reference placement handles that display on the feature, additional drag handles display enabling you to change the diameter and depth of the hole. These dimensions can be changed by dragging the handles to the required value or by double-clicking on them and entering a value, as shown in Figure 9–12.

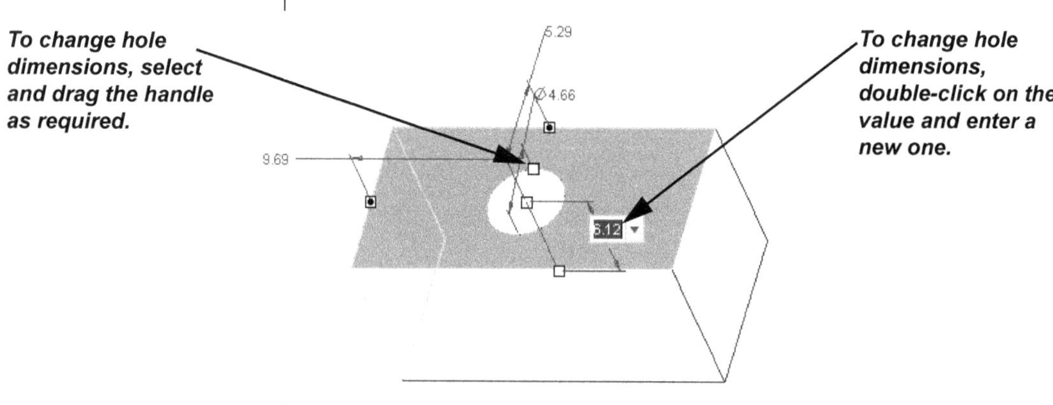

Figure 9–12

Step 4 - Define the depth of the feature.

By default, all of the holes are created in one direction from the placement reference. The Creo Parametric software determines this direction for you. Use either of the following methods to reverse the direction:

- Drag the depth handle through the placement plane so that it extrudes in the opposite direction.
- Click **Placement** in the *Hole* dashboard and click **Flip** in the panel.
- Right-click and select **Flip**.

***Flip** is also available in the Placement panel for flipping the direction of a coaxial hole.*

The hole that is automatically created when you select the placement reference has a specified value (blind depth) assigned to it and is created in one direction from the placement reference. These options do not always capture your design intent. To change these options, click **Shape** in the *Hole* dashboard. The panel displays as shown in Figure 9–13.

You can also set the depth option by pressing <Shift> while dragging the depth handle. This enables you to snap the depth to a surface.

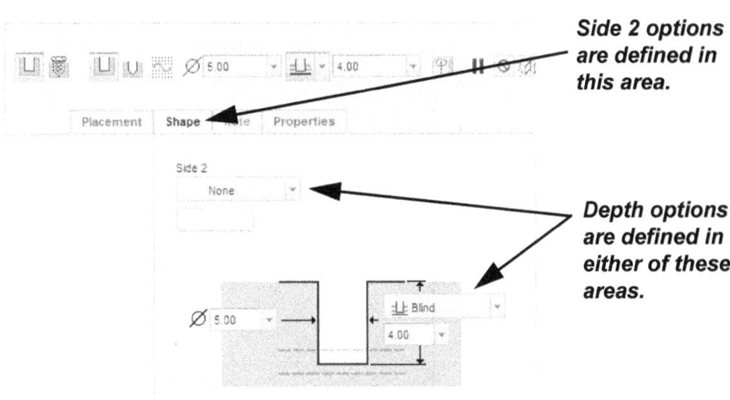

Figure 9–13

Depth Options

Six depth options are available when creating a hole, and are the same as those used to create extruded cuts. The options are described as follows:

Icon	Description
(Blind)	Extrude from sketch plane by specified depth value.
(Symmetric)	Extrude on both sides of sketch plane by half the specified value in each direction.
(To Next)	Extrude to next surface.
(Through All)	Extrude to intersect with all surfaces.
(Through Until)	Extrude to intersect with selected surface.
(To Selected)	Extrude to selected point, curve, plane, or surface.

Side Options

For many features, the design intent might require that they extrude in two directions from the placement plane or sketching plane. For holes, a second side, **Side 2**, is defined by selecting a depth option in the Shape panel on the *Hole* dashboard, as shown in Figure 9–14.

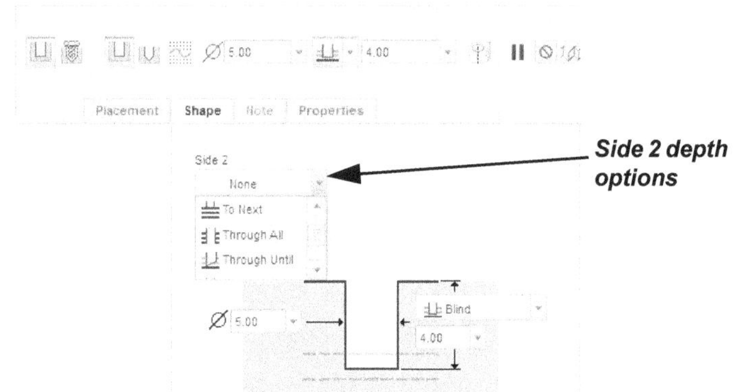

Figure 9–14

Step 5 - Complete the feature.

Once the depth has been defined, click (Complete Feature) to complete the hole.

9.2 Radial Holes

Holes are placed on a surface using one of four placement schemes: Linear, Radial, Diameter, and Coaxial. These schemes can be defined in the Placement panel in the *Hole* dashboard.

A radial hole is placed in one of the following two ways:

- On a planar surface at an angle from a planar reference, and at a distance from an axis, as shown in Figure 9–15.
- On a cylinder or cone at an angle from a planar reference, and at a distance from a dimensional reference, as shown in Figure 9–16.

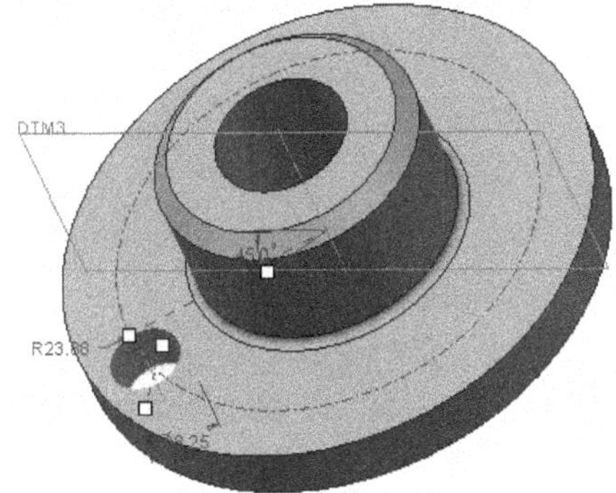

Figure 9–15

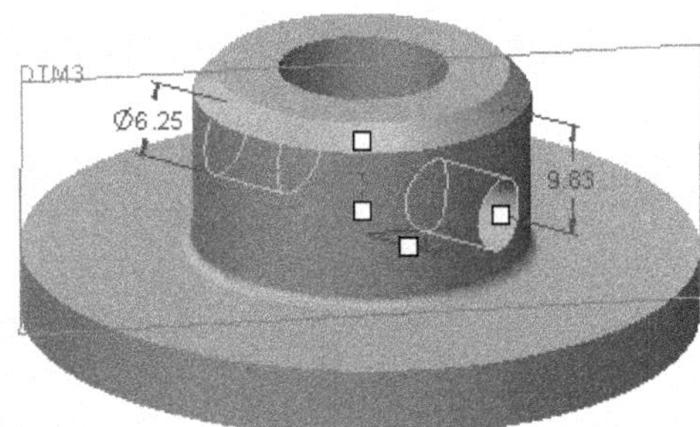

Figure 9–16

Radial Hole on a Cylinder

To place a straight radial hole on a cylinder, click (Hole) in the Engineering group in the Model tab, and select the cylindrical surface as the primary reference. The software automatically places the hole as a radial hole, which displays with multiple handles to define its *Placement*, *Size*, and *Depth*. The two placement handles are 90° to each other and are used to assign the following secondary references:

- Planar surface to provide angular distance.
- Standard linear reference to provide linear distance.

To locate the hole, drag and drop the handles onto the required references, as shown in Figure 9–17. You can also assign references in the *Secondary References* area in the Placement panel.

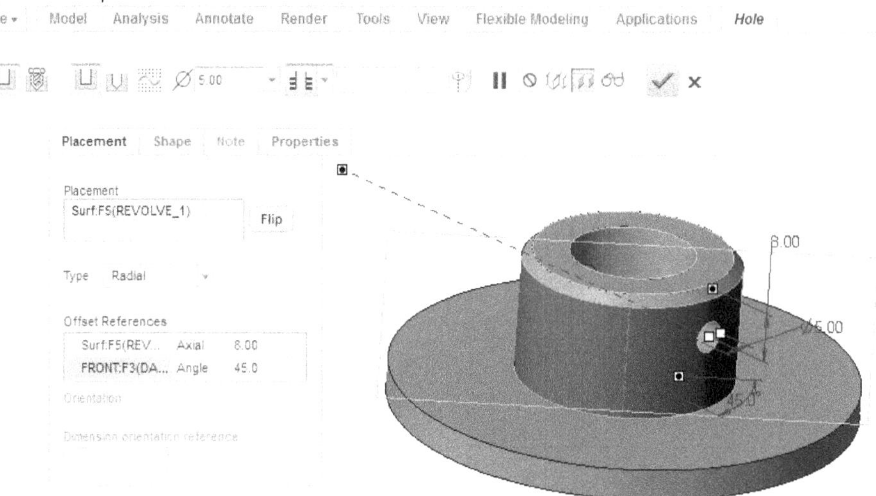

Figure 9–17

Once secondary references have been selected, specify the dimensions for the feature. The feature dimensions include the diameter and depth of the hole. Use any of the following methods to define these dimensions:

- Select and drag the handles associated with the diameter and depth of the hole.
- Double-click on the default dimension values and enter new values.
- Enter new values for the secondary references in the Placement panel.
- Enter values for the diameter and depth in the *Hole* dashboard.

By default, all holes are created in one direction from the placement reference and are extruded to a blind depth. The depth options can be changed by selecting options in the Shape panel or by selecting a depth option from the dashboard, as shown in Figure 9–18.

Figure 9–18

The Creo Parametric software determines the extrude direction for you. To reverse this direction, use one of the following methods:

- Drag the depth handle through the placement plane so that it extrudes in the opposite direction.
- Click **Flip** in the Placement panel in the *Hole* dashboard.
- Right-click and select **Flip**.

Click (Complete Feature) to complete the hole feature.

9.3 Standard Holes

Standard holes use a predefined sketched section to generate the geometry for the hole. You can enter values for the predefined dimensions to create a hole on your model. The standard hole set is based on industry-standard fastener tables.

General Steps

To create the hole, click (Hole) in the Engineering group in the *Model* tab. To create a standard hole, click (Create Standard Hole) in the *Hole* dashboard, which displays as shown in Figure 9–19.

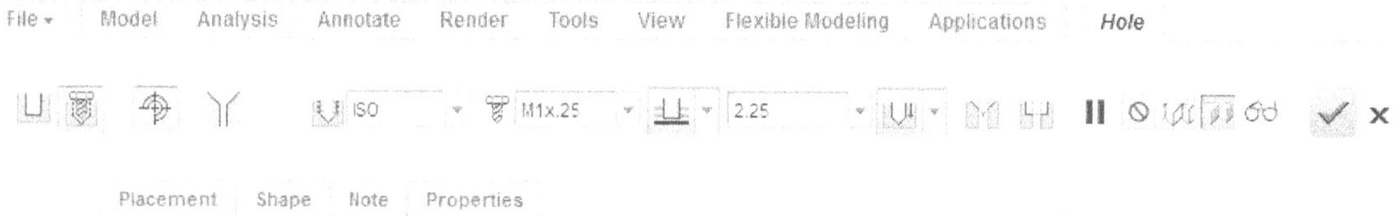

Figure 9–19

A standard hole can be placed using any hole Placement Type (Linear, Coaxial, Radial, or Diameter).

The properties and dimensions of the standard hole can be modified using any of the following methods:

- Click (Add Countersink) in the dashboard to add a countersink.
- Click (Add Counterbore) in the dashboard to add a counter bore.
- Click (Create Tapered Hole) in the dashboard to add a tapered hole.
- Select from **ISO**, **UNC** and **UNF** hole standards.
- Select or enter a screw size in the drop-down list, as shown in Figure 9–20.

Figure 9–20

- Select and edit dimensions for the hole in the Shape panel, as shown in Figure 9–21.
- Select the thread type for the standard hole using the drop-down lists.
- Select a depth option and enter a value if required, as shown in Figure 9–21.

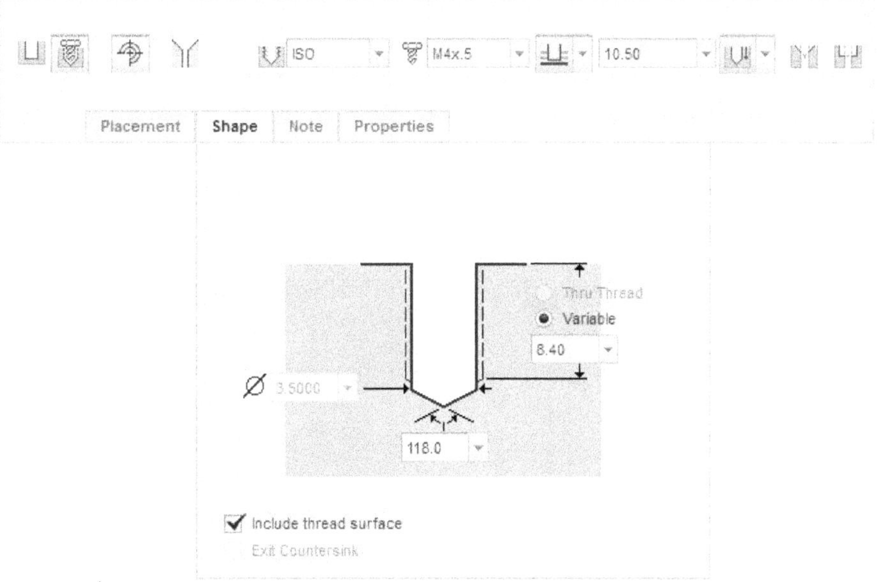

Figure 9–21

Additionally, the Creo Parametric software automatically adds a Note to all of the standard holes. To see the default note, open the Note panel in the tab, as shown in Figure 9–22.

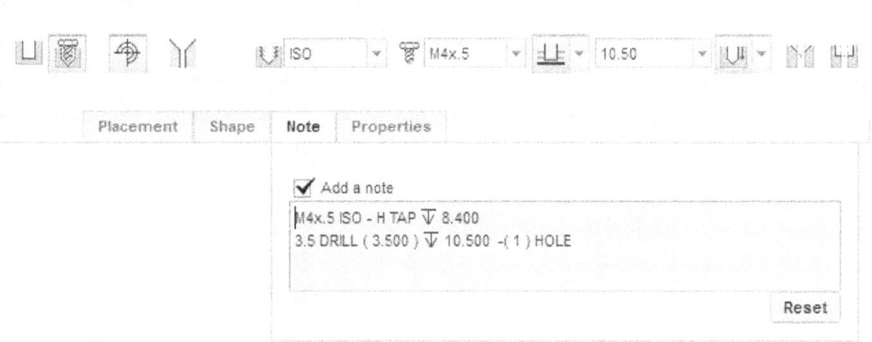

Figure 9–22

The Properties panel enables you to enter a new name for the hole. Parameter values associated with the standard hole are shown in Figure 9–23.

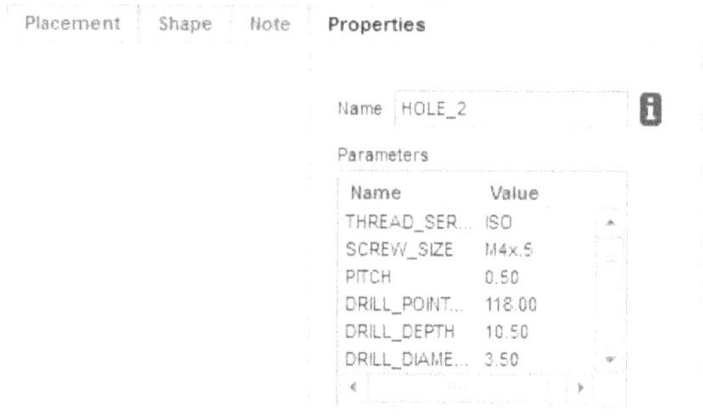

Figure 9–23

Complete the standard hole by selecting the appropriate placement references and click ✓ (Complete Feature).

9.4 Sketched Holes

A sketched hole gives you greater control for hole creation by enabling you to sketch its section as a revolved form.

How To: Create a Radial Hole

1. Create a hole by clicking (Hole) in the Engineering group in the *Model* tab. In the *Hole* dashboard, ensure the (Create Simple Hole) option is selected, then click (Use Sketch). The *Hole* dashboard updates with sketching options, as shown in Figure 9–24.

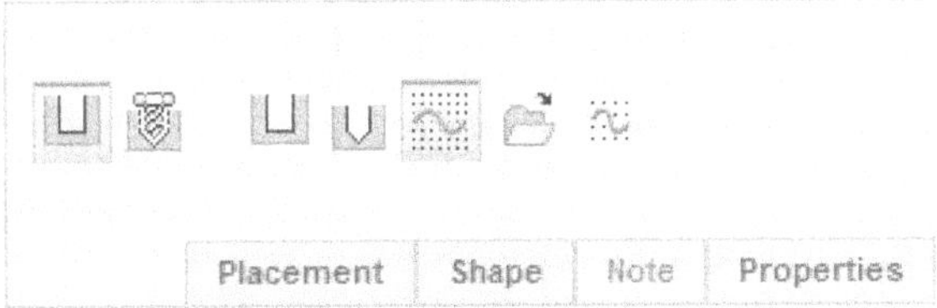

Figure 9–24

A sketched hole can be placed using any hole Placement Type (Linear, Coaxial, Radial, or Diameter).

As an alternative to sketching, you can retrieve a section using (Open Sketch Profile) in the Hole tab.

2. Once the primary reference has been selected, sketch the cross-section for the hole. Click (Activates Sketcher) to open a new window with the *Sketch* tab active. Sketch the cross-section using the standard sketching tools.

The following rules apply to the cross-sections of sketched holes:

- A vertical centerline must be sketched to represent the axis to revolve around.
- The sketched section must be closed.

- There must be a sketched horizontal line. This line is automatically aligned with the primary reference or placement surface. If more than one horizontal line exists, the top-most line is aligned with the placement surface (or primary reference, as shown in Figure 9–25).

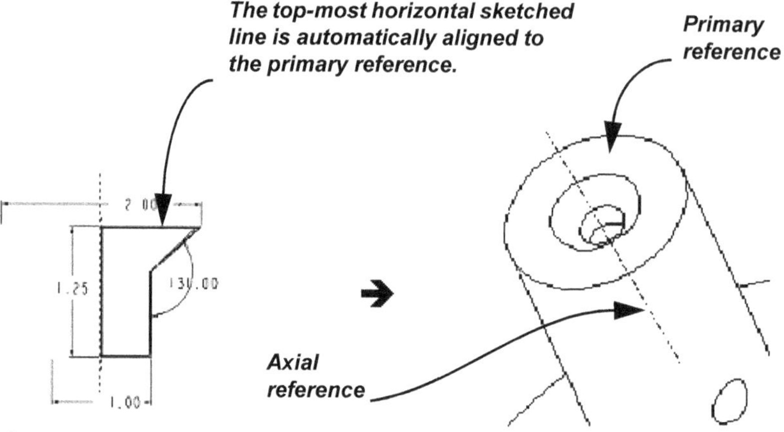

Figure 9–25

Click ✓ (OK) to complete the sketched section.

Once all of the references and options have been verified, click ✓ (Complete Feature) to complete the hole feature.

Practice 9a Holes

Practice Objectives

- Create straight holes with a linear and radial placement option in the model.
- Modify and redefine the hole to achieve a required result.
- Add a counterbore and exit countersink to one hole.

In this practice, you will create simple holes using both linear and radial placement types. You will complete the part by adding an edge chamfer and constant rounds. The completed part displays as shown in Figure 9–26.

Figure 9–26

Task 1 - Open a part file.

1. Set the working directory to the *Chapter 09\practice 9a* folder.
2. Open **hanger.prt**.
3. Set the model display as follows:
   - *(Datum Display Filters)*: Enable (Axis Display)
   - *(Spin Center)*: Off
   - *(Display Style)*: (Shading With Edges)

Task 2 - Create a hole with linear dimensions.

1. In the Engineering group, click (Hole) to start the creation of a hole.
2. Specify a location for the hole by selecting the location shown in Figure 9–27.

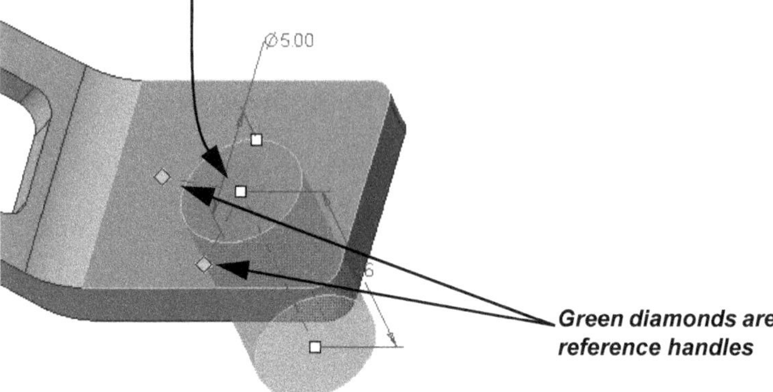

Figure 9–27

3. Drag one of the green diamond reference handles to each of the surfaces shown in Figure 9–28.
4. Set the following, as shown in Figure 9–29:
   - *Diameter*: **2.0**
   - *Offset* value: **2.5**
   - *Offset* value: **3.0**

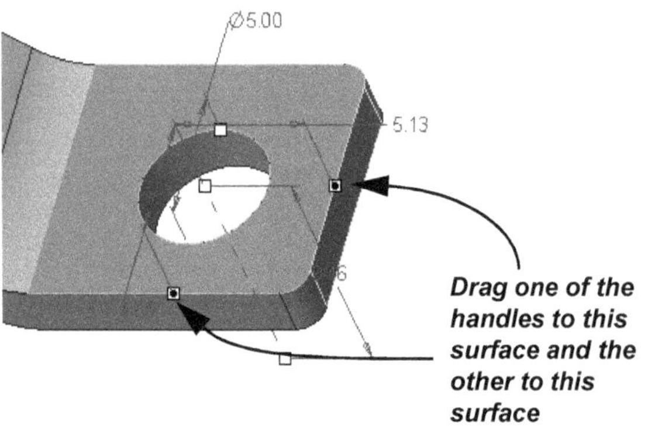

Figure 9–28

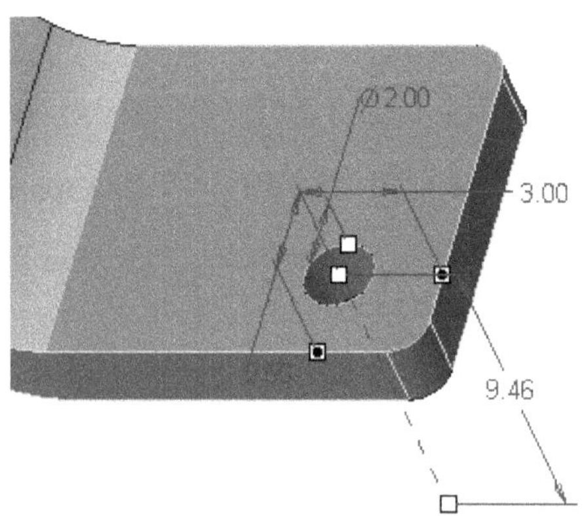

Figure 9–29

5. Click (Through All) to set the *Depth*.

6. Complete the hole. The model displays as shown in Figure 9–30.

Figure 9–30

Task 3 - Create another hole using the linear placement type.

1. Create another hole using the references shown in Figure 9–31.
2. Set the following:
   - *Diameter:* **2.0**
   - *Offset* value: **9.0**
   - *Offset* value: **2.5**
   - *Depth*: **(Through All)**

   The completed hole displays as shown in Figure 9–32.

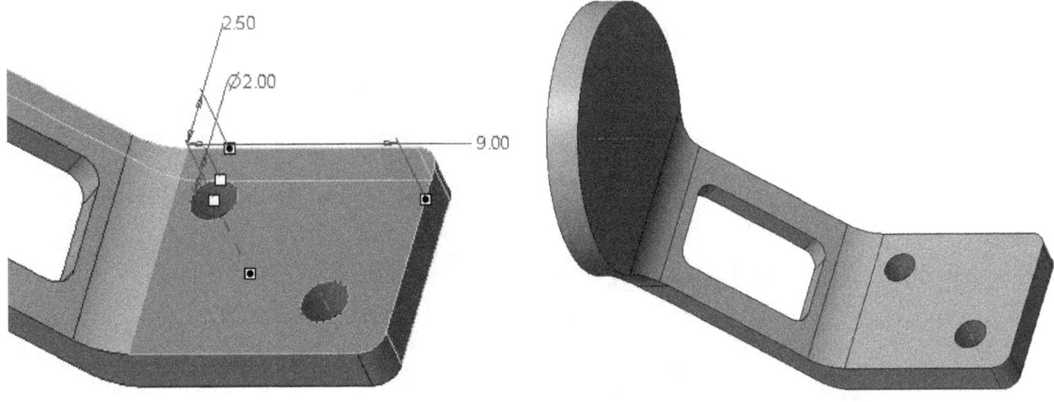

Figure 9–31

Figure 9–32

Task 4 - Create a radially placed hole.

1. In the In-graphics toolbar, click (Datum Display Filters) and select (Plane Display) to enable datum plane display. Orient the model as shown in Figure 9–33.

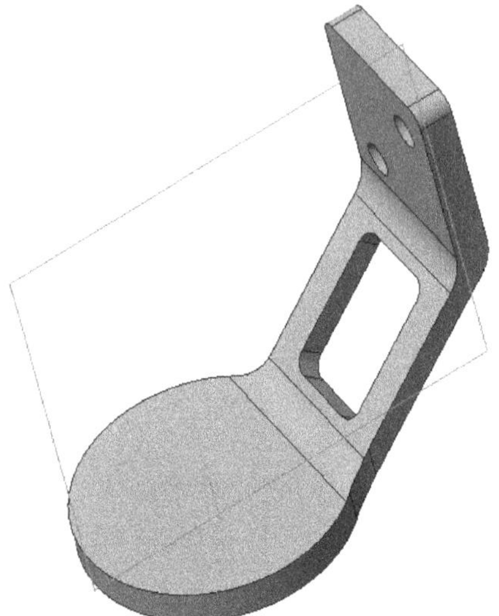

Figure 9–33

2. In the Engineering group, click (Hole).
3. For the placement reference for the hole, select the location shown in Figure 9–34.
4. In the *Hole* dashboard, select **Placement** and change the *Type* to **Radial**, as shown in Figure 9–35.

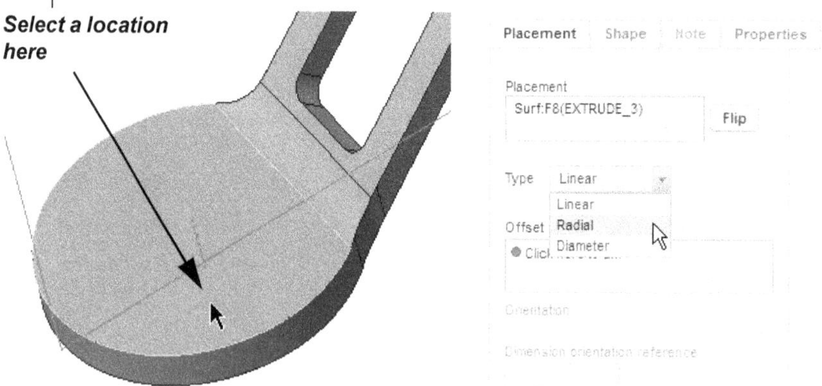

Figure 9–34

Figure 9–35

5. Drag one of the placement handles to the axis and the other to the datum plane, as shown in Figure 9–36.

Drag the handle to one of the visible "edges" of the datum plane to most select it.

Drag one handle to the axis and the other to datum plane.

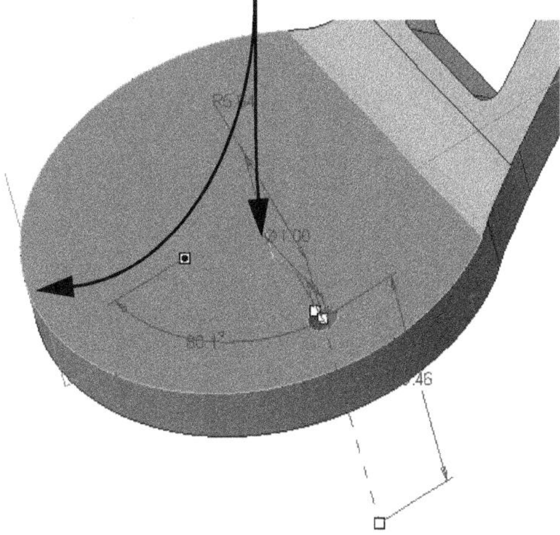

Figure 9–36

6. Set the following, as shown in Figure 9–37:

   - *Radius*: **5.0**
   - *Angle*: **45**

Angular and radius values

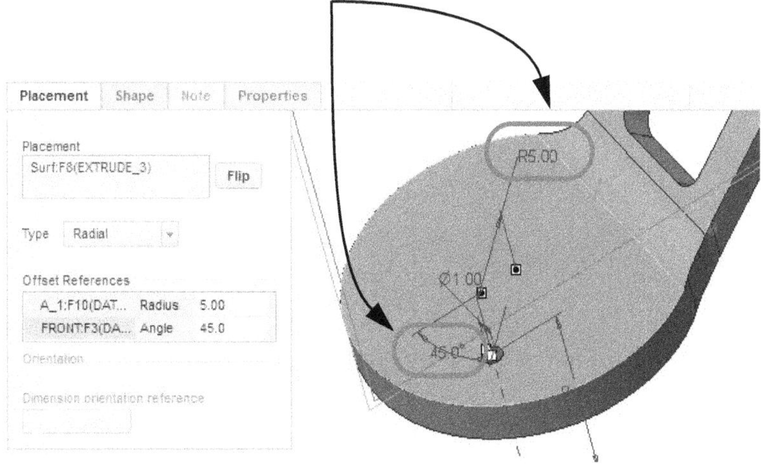

Figure 9–37

7. Set the *Diameter* to **2.0**.

8. Set the *Depth* to **(Through All)**.

Task 5 - Create another hole with a radial placement type.

1. Create another hole using the location shown in Figure 9–38.
2. Use the same axis and datum as references.
3. Set the following, as shown in Figure 9–38:
   - *Diameter:* **2.0**
   - *Radius:* **5.0**
   - *Angle:* **45**
   - *Depth:* **(Through All)**
4. Complete the hole.
5. In the In-graphics toolbar, click (Datum Display Filters) and select (Plane Display) and (Axis Display) to toggle off their display.
6. Press <Ctrl>+<D>. The completed hole and model display as shown in Figure 9–39.

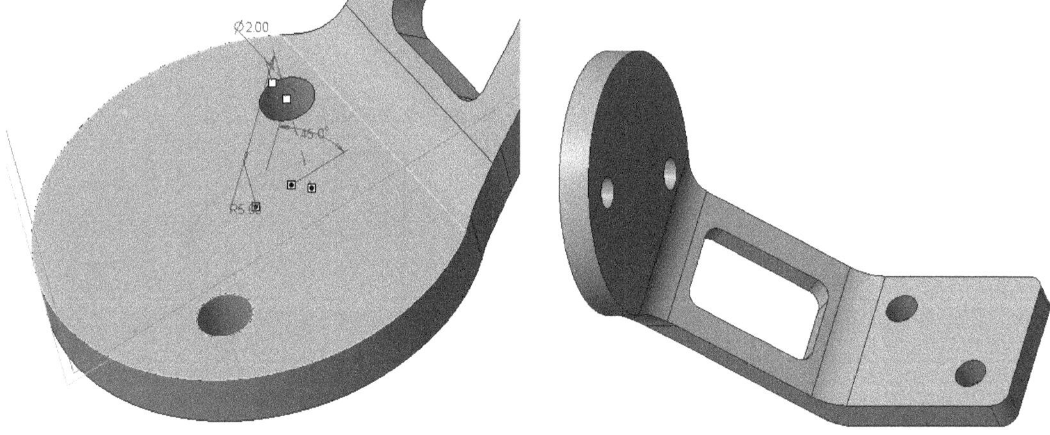

Figure 9–38

Figure 9–39

Task 6 - Edit the model.

1. Select **Hole 1** in the model tree, right-click, and select (Edit Definition).
2. Select the Placement panel. Remove the **Offset Reference**, as shown in Figure 9–40.

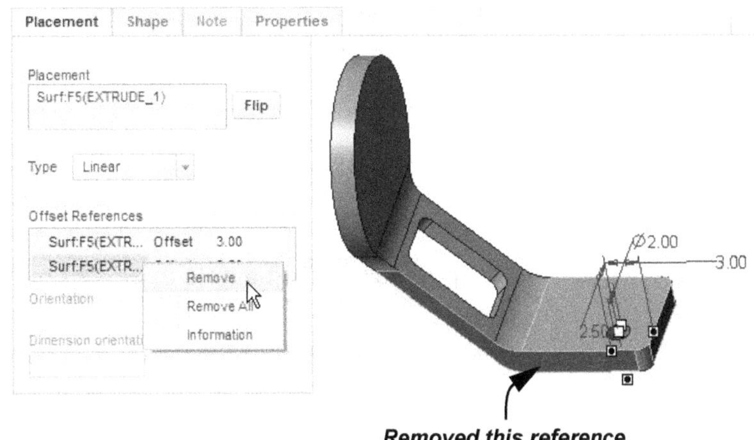

Figure 9–40

3. Hold <Ctrl> and select the **FRONT** datum plane from the model tree as the new *Offset Reference*.
4. Change the *Offset* to **Align**, as shown in Figure 9–41. This aligns the hole to the **FRONT** datum plane.

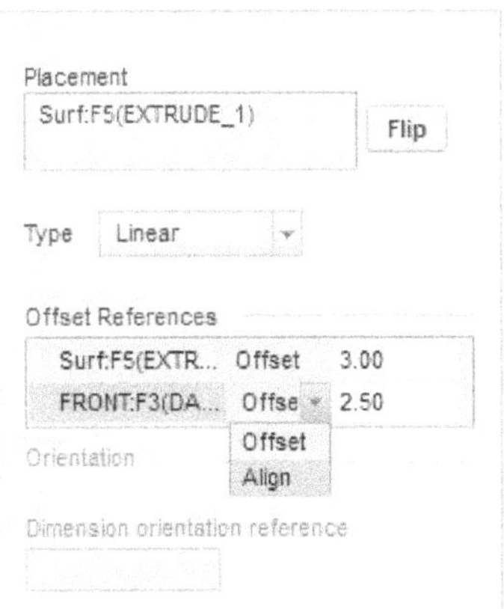

Figure 9–41

5. Complete the feature. The model displays as shown in Figure 9–42.

Figure 9–42

Task 7 - Edit a hole to add a counterbore.

1. Select **Hole 1** in the model tree, right-click and select (Edit Definition).
2. In the *Hole* dashboard, click (Use Standard Profile).
3. Click (Add Counterbore).
4. Select the *Shape* tab and enable **Exit Countersink**.
5. Edit the *Counterbore* values to match those shown in Figure 9–43.

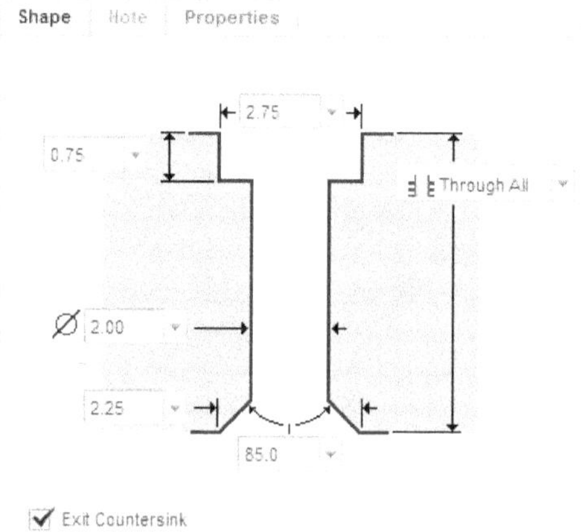

Figure 9–43

6. Click (Complete Feature).
7. In the In-graphics toolbar, click (Saved Orientations) and click (View Normal).
8. Select the surface shown in Figure 9–44.

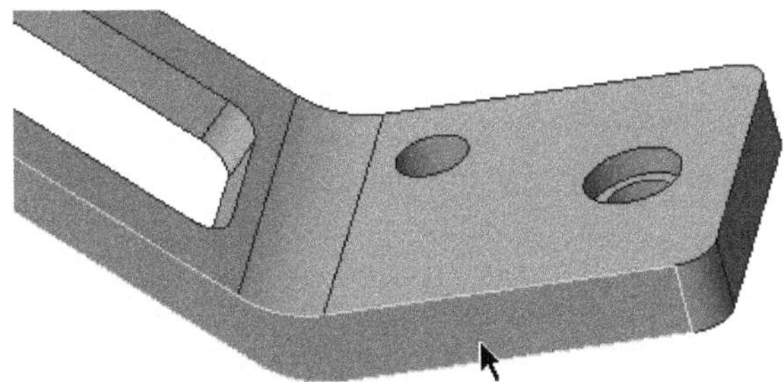

Figure 9–44

9. In the In-Graphics toolbar, click (Display Style) and select (Hidden Line) to view the profile of the hole, as shown in Figure 9–45.

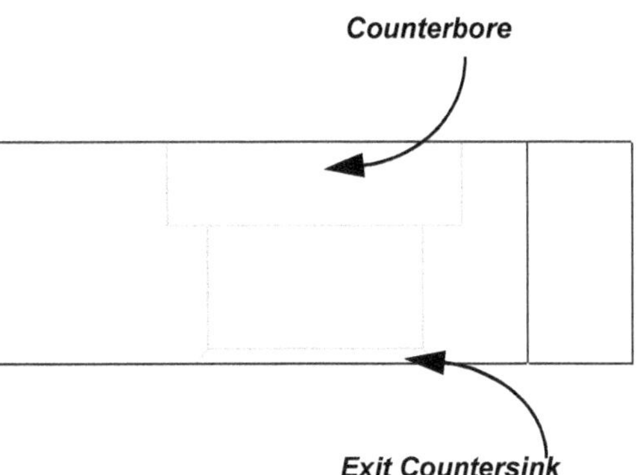

Figure 9–45

10. Save the part and erase it from memory.

Practice 9b Skid Shoe

Practice Objective

- Create a standard hole feature using the radial placement option and specified dimensions.

In this practice, you will open an existing part that requires a NTP threaded hole to accommodate a grease nipple. You will create a standard tapered hole with a radial placement to achieve this. You will then add a sketched hole in the side of the model.The completed model is shown in Figure 9–46.

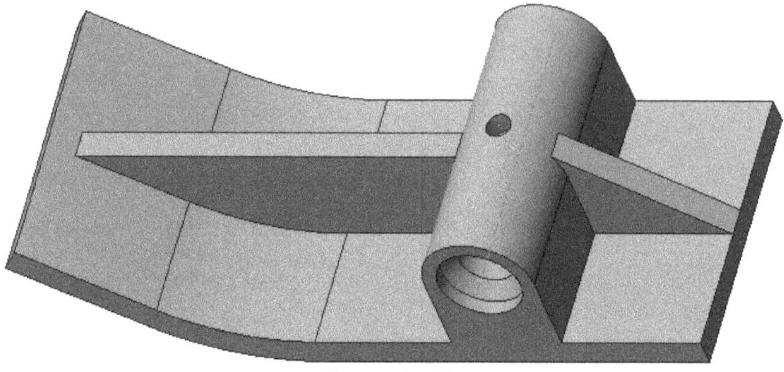

Figure 9–46

Task 1 - Open a part file.

1. Set the working directory to the *Chapter 09\practice 9b* folder.
2. Open **skid_shoe.prt.**
3. Set the model display as follows:
   - *(Datum Display Filters)*: Enable (Plane Display)
   - *(Spin Center)*: Off
   - *(Display Style)*: (Shading With Edges)
4. Create a hole and select the surface shown in Figure 9–47.

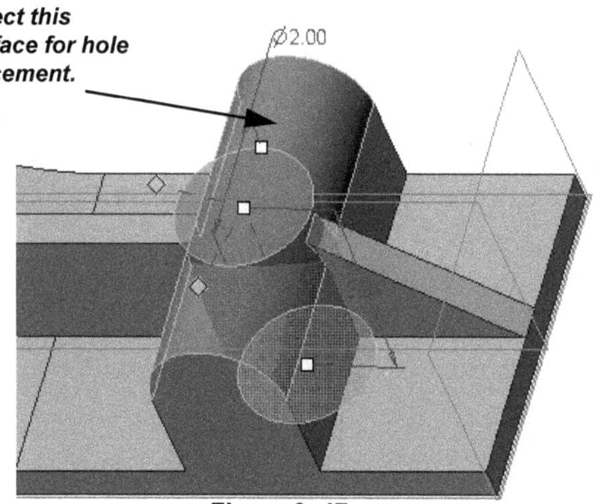

Figure 9–47

5. Drag each of the green placement handles to the two datum planes shown in Figure 9–47.

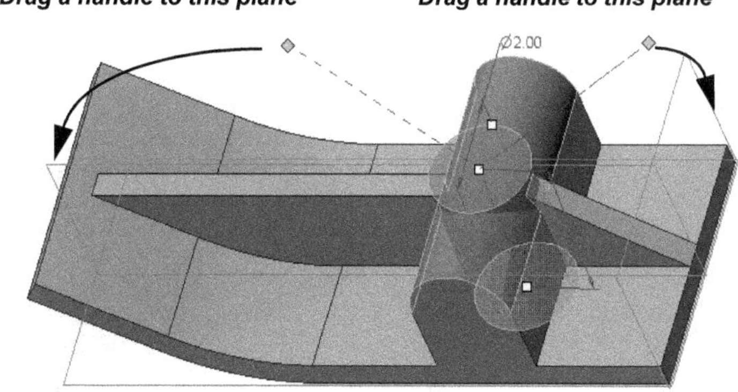

Figure 9–48

6. Change the value of both offsets to **0**.

7. In the *Hole* dashboard, click (Create Standard Hole) to change the hole type to **Standard**. The dashboard updates as shown in Figure 9–49.

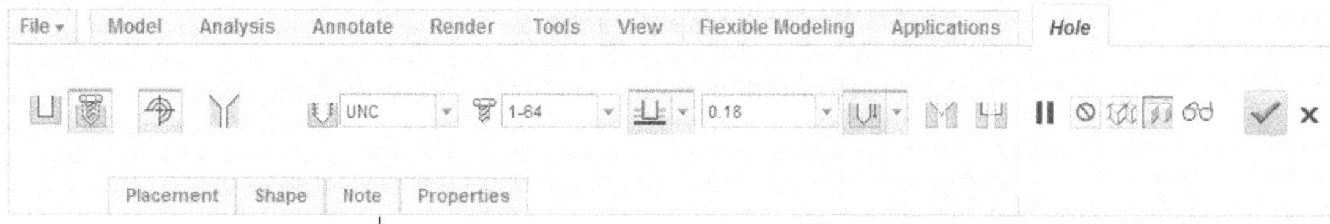

Figure 9–49

8. Click (Create Tapered Hole) to create a tapered hole with the following parameters and as shown in Figure 9–50:
   - *Thread Type:* **NPT**
   - *Thread:* **1/4 - 18**
   - *Depth:* **0.4**

Figure 9–50

9. In the In-graphics toolbar, click (Datum Display Filters), disable (Plane Display), and enable (Axis Display).

10. Click (Complete Feature) to complete the hole, as shown in Figure 9–51.

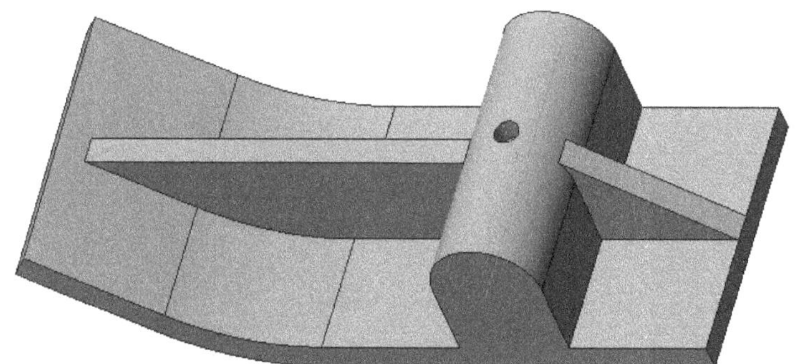

Figure 9–51

Task 2 - Create a Sketched hole.

1. In the Engineering group, click (Hole).

2. In the dashboard, click (Use Sketch) then click (Activates Sketcher).

3. Create the sketch shown in Figure 9–52.

The top-most line will be aligned with the placement plane.

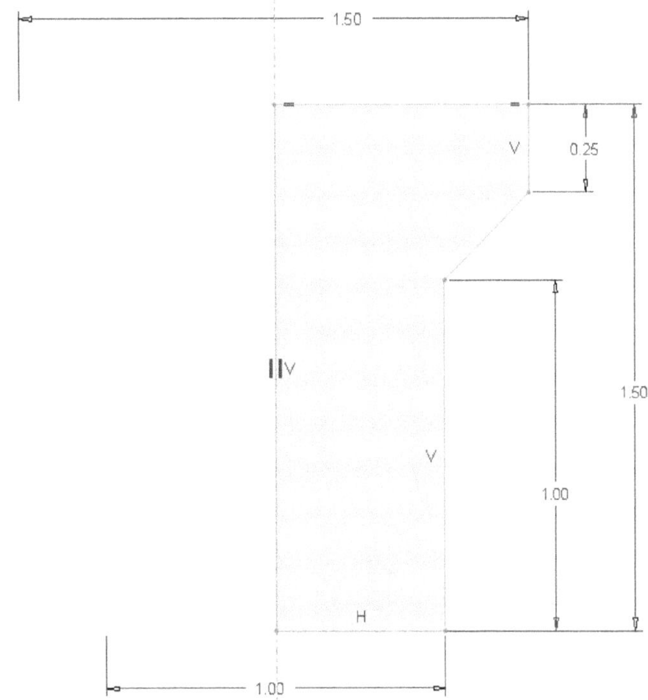

Figure 9–52

4. Click ✓ (OK).
5. For the placement reference, select the surface shown in Figure 9–53.

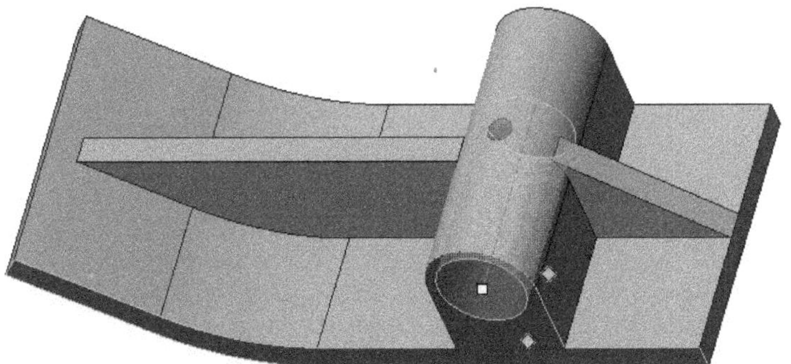

Figure 9–53

6. Press <Ctrl> and select the axis.

7. Click ✓ (Complete Feature) to complete the hole, as shown in Figure 9–54.

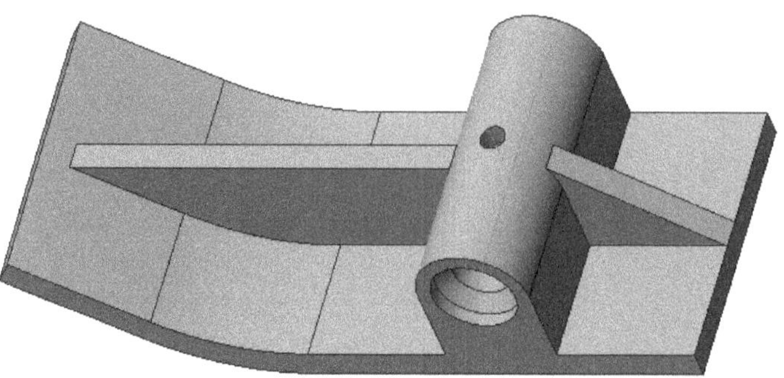

Figure 9–54

8. Save the part and erase it from memory.

Chapter Review Questions

1. On which of the following primary references can you place a radial hole? (Select all that apply.)
   a. Planar surface or datum plane
   b. Axis
   c. Cylindrical surface
   d. Point
2. Which of the following references define the two required secondary references to place a radial hole on a planar surface? (Select all that apply.)
   a. Planar surface or datum plane
   b. Axis
   c. Cylindrical surface
   d. Point
3. Standard holes enable you to sketch the cross-section for the hole.
   a. True
   b. False
4. Which of the following statements is true regarding sketching the cross-section for a hole? (Select all that apply.)
   a. A vertical centerline must be sketched to represent the axis to revolve around.
   b. The sketched section must be an open section.
   c. The top sketched horizontal line is aligned with the primary reference for the sketched hole.
   d. A horizontal centerline must be sketched that aligns the sketch with the primary reference for the sketched hole.

Command Summary

Button	Command	Location
	Hole	• **Ribbon:** *Model* tab in the Engineering group
	Standard Hole	• **Ribbon:** *Hole* dashboard
	Use Sketch	• **Ribbon:** *Hole* dashboard

Datum Features

Datum features are non-solid features that are used when creating or sketching geometry. In cast models, datum features are used to define location points to aid in assembly. They can also be added to define areas of interface between casting components. Additionally, these features are useful in effectively creating a simplified design since they regenerate quickly and their display is easily controlled. Models can exist entirely of datum features and still convey the required design intent.

Learning Objectives in this Chapter

- Understand how the use of datum planes in a model enables you to create geometry that cannot be created using existing planes or faces in the model.
- Learn the difference between internal versus external datum plane creation methods.
- Understand how the use of datum axis, points and coordinate systems in a model enables you to create geometry and other datum features that cannot be created using existing references in the model.
- Select references and constraint options using various methods.

10.1 Datum Features

Additional datum features, such as planes, axes, points and coordinate systems, are often required to complete a model. For example, a datum plane might be required if a feature's sketching plane or orientation plane are not satisfied by any of the three default datum planes or by selecting existing geometry. In these situations, datum planes can be created in a model.

- For example, to create the cut shown in Figure 10–1, the cylindrical surface does not fulfill the planar requirement for a sketching plane. Therefore, an additional sketching plane is required.
- To create the protrusion shown in Figure 10–2, an additional sketching plane is required.

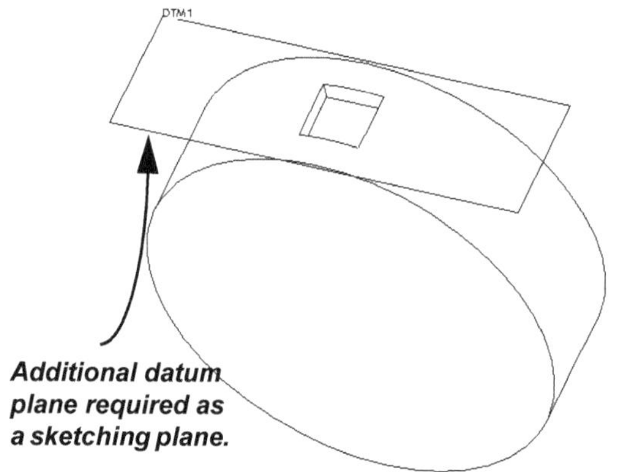

Figure 10–1

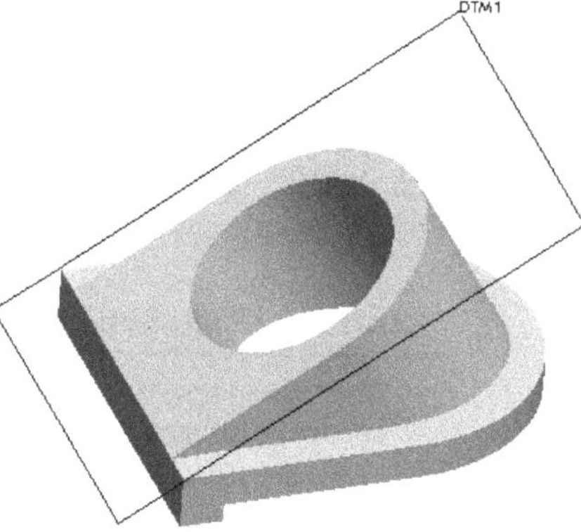

Figure 10–2

Datums that are referenced by more than one feature should be created as separate features in the model.

Datums that are only referenced by one feature should be created during that feature's creation, to simplify the appearance of the model.

A datum feature can be created as a stand-alone feature, and can then be used as a reference for other features. For example, when a datum plane is created as a separate feature, the model tree displays, as shown in Figure 10–3.

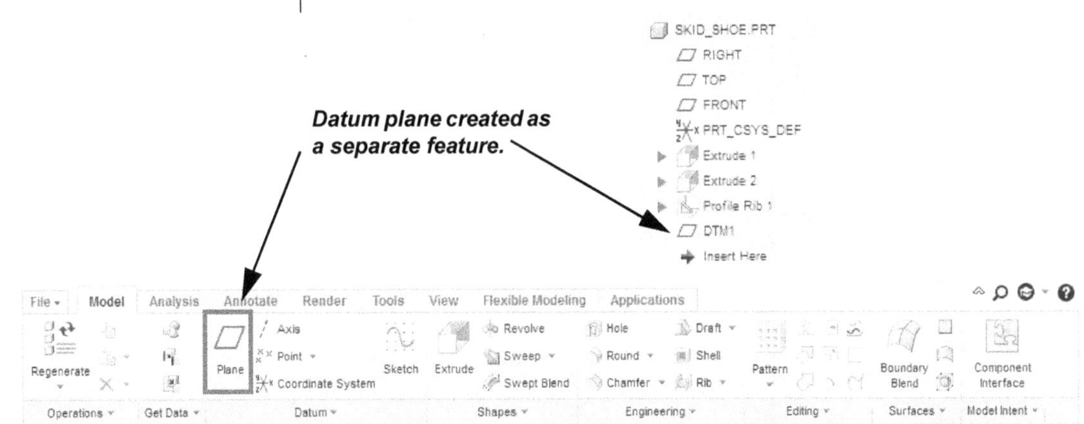

Figure 10–3

To create a datum during feature creation, expand (Datum) in the feature dashboard and click the appropriate icon to create the required datum feature. The main feature is paused, as indicated by (Pause) in its dashboard. Once you have completed the datum feature creation, you can resume the main feature by clicking (Resume). The created datum feature can be referenced as a sketch, orientation, dimension or depth reference.

When you finish the main feature creation, the datum feature is embedded inside the main feature in the model tree, such as the datum plane shown in Figure 10–4. By default, a datum feature created in another feature is hidden. To show it, select it in the model tree, right-click, and select **Unhide**.

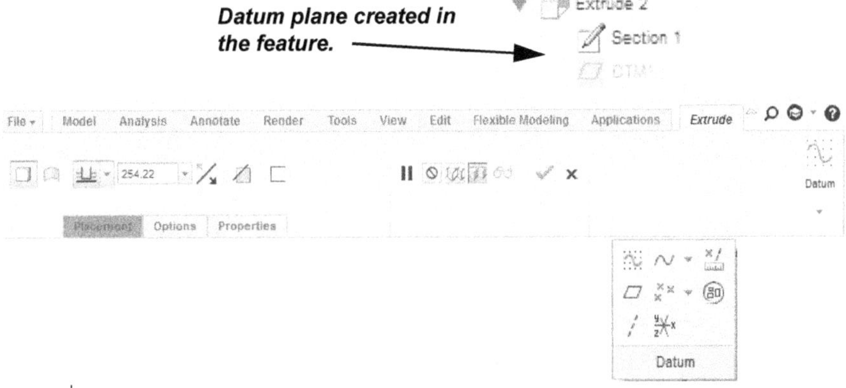

Figure 10–4

10.2 Creating Datum Planes

To start the creation of a datum plane, expand (Datum) in the dashboard of the current feature, and click (Plane). You can also click (Plane) in the *Model* tab. The Datum Plane dialog box opens, as shown in Figure 10–5.

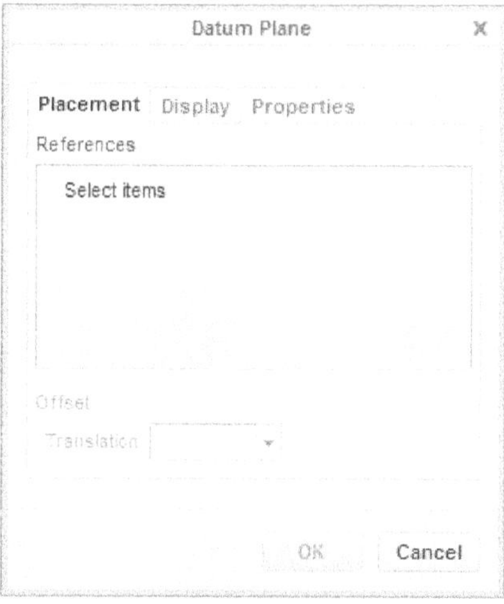

Figure 10–5

Alternatively, you can select the reference before clicking (Plane).

Once you have started the creation of a datum plane, you must select constraints and references to locate it. When creating a datum plane, its location is defined by constraining it to existing features. Constraints are required to fully locate the datum plane. To constrain a datum plane, select references from existing features in the model. You can select any of the following types of features as references:

To select multiple references at the same time, press and hold <Ctrl>.

- Axis
- Edge
- Curve
- Point/Vertex
- Plane
- Cylinder
- Coordinate System

After selecting the appropriate placement references, select a constraint type for each of them. By selecting the column to the right of the reference, you can select the required constraint in the drop-down list. Only constraints that work in combination with the previously selected references display. Figure 10–6 shows an example of a datum Tangent to the smaller cylinder and Parallel to the flat surface.

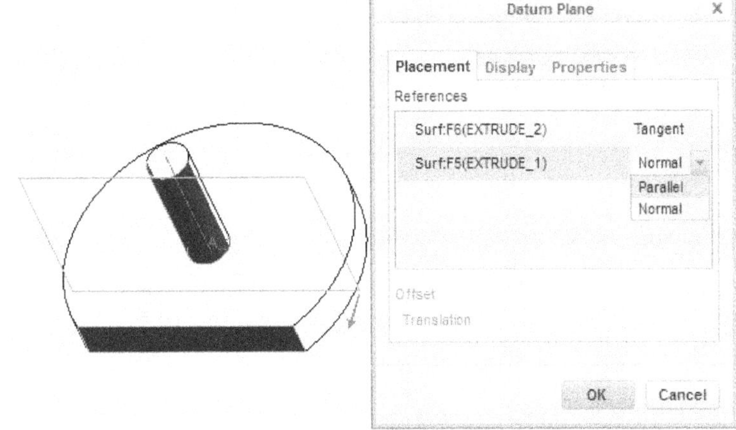

Figure 10–6

The following constraints can be used to create a datum plane:

- Through
- Normal
- Parallel
- Offset
- Tangent
- Blend Section

Only constraints that work in combination with the previously selected references display.

For example, if you select a Normal constraint for a planar reference and a Tangent constraint for a cylindrical surface, a datum plane would be successfully created. The Normal and Tangent combination of constraints is valid, indicated in the table by an **X**. All of the valid combinations of constraints used to create datum planes are described as follows:

		Through			**Normal**	**Parallel**	**Offset (rotational)**	**Tangent**	
DATUM PLANE CONSTRAINT COMBINATION		**AxisEdgeCurv**	**Point\Vertex**	**Cylinder**	**Plane**	**Plane**	**Plane**	**Cylinder**	**Stand Alone Constraints**
Through	Axis, Edge, Curve	X	X	X	X	X	X	X	
	Point/Vertex	X	X	X	X	X			
	Plane								X
	Cylinder	X	X	X	X	X	X	X	
Normal	Axis, Edge, Curve	X	X	X					
	Plane	X	X	X	X	X		X	
Parallel	Plane	X	X	X				X	
Offset	Plane								X
	Coord Sys								X
Tangent	Cylinder	X			X	X			
Blend Section									X

Figure 10–7 and Figure 10–8 shows examples of datum planes that pass through the axial reference but have different secondary constraints. In Figure 10–7, the datum plane has a parallel constraint with the vertical planar surface, whereas in Figure 10–8, the datum plane has a rotational offset constraint with the vertical planar surface.

*References can be removed from the Datum Plane dialog box. Select the reference, right-click, and select **Remove**.*

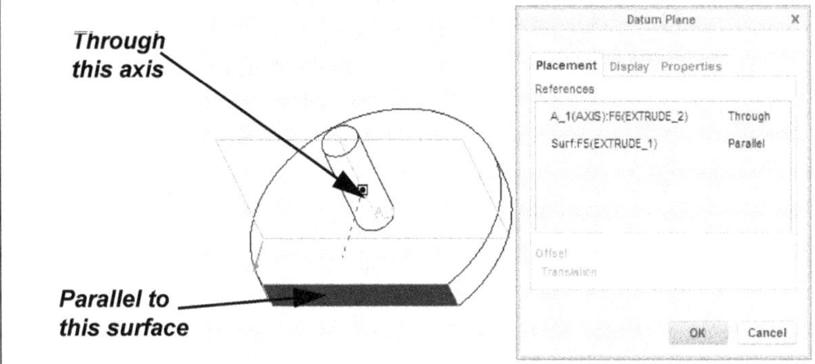

Figure 10–7

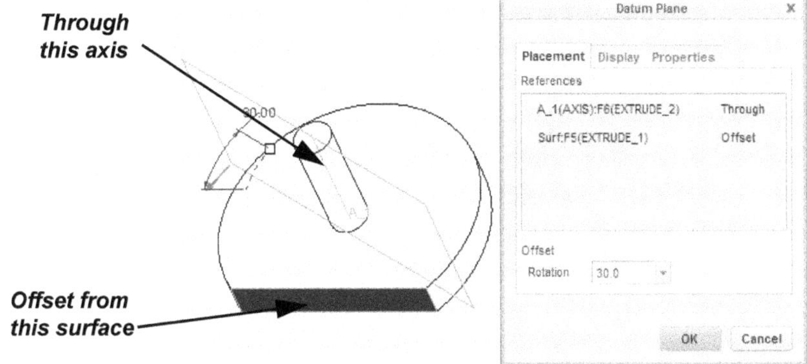

Figure 10–8

As an alternative to starting the creation of a datum plane and then selecting references, you can preselect the references required to place the datum plane before clicking (Plane).

For example, the top surface shown in Figure 10–9 was preselected. The dialog box that opens when you click (Plane) contains the preselected reference as one of the current references.

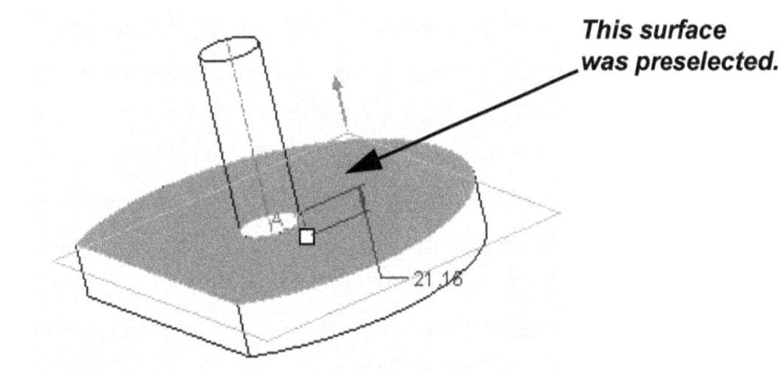

Figure 10–9

You can change the appearance, direction or name of the datum plane using the *Display* and *Properties* tabs in the Datum Plane dialog box.By default, datum planes are sized to fit the overall geometry; when working on small features, the default datum plane size might be too large.

- The *Display* tab enables you to modify the size of the datum plane to fit the feature and flip the normal direction of the datum plane, as shown in Figure 10–10.
- The *Properties* tab shown in Figure 10–11, enables you to change the name of the datum plane.

Figure 10–10

Figure 10–11

Once the datum plane has been constrained, click **OK** to place it. If the datum plane was created in another feature, proceed with its feature creation by clicking ▶ (Resume) in the dashboard.

10.3 Creating Datum Axes

Cylindrical, rotational features, and holes are the only features that automatically generate their own datum axes on creation. Because datum axes can be used as placement references for coaxial holes and rotational features, additional datum axes might be required. In the case of rotational features, a centerline can be sketched to serve as the axis of rotation. However, if this axial location is referenced by subsequent features, it is more efficient to create a permanent datum axis in the model. For example, to create the coaxial hole shown in Figure 10–12, an axial reference is required.

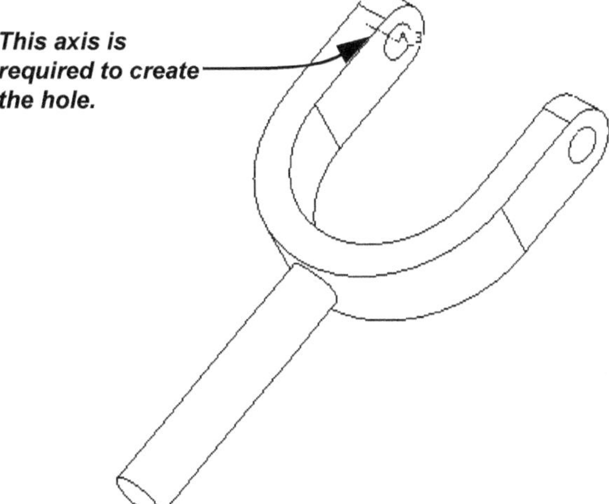

Figure 10–12

Datum axes can be created before or during feature creation. The process during feature creation is the same as with datum planes.

To create a datum axis, click (Axis) in the *Model* tab if stand-alone, or expand (Datum) in the dashboard of the current feature, and click (Axis). The Datum Axis dialog box opens as shown in Figure 10–13. Similar to datum planes, placement references and constraints must be selected to fully locate the datum axis.

Figure 10–13

- The *Display* tab enables you to modify the size of the datum axis, as shown in Figure 10–14.
- The name of the axis can also be changed from the default name to a custom name in the *Properties* tab, as shown in Figure 10–15.

Figure 10–14

Figure 10–15

Alternatively, you can select the reference before clicking (Axis).

Once you have started the creation of a datum axis, you must select constraints and references. Some constraints only require one reference, while others must be used in combination with other references to fully locate the datum axis.

To constrain a datum axis, select references from existing features in the model. References can be any of the following types:

- Edge/Curve
- Planar surfaces
- Cylindrical surfaces
- Coordinate systems
- Points/Vertices

After selecting the appropriate placement references, a default constraint type displays next to the reference in the dialog box. If multiple constraints are available, you can access a drop-down list by selecting the constraint column. Only constraints that work in combination with the previously selected references display.

This axis can also be created without having to use the dialog box, by preselecting the cylindrical surface formed by the round and then clicking (Axis).

Figure 10–16 shows an example where the created datum axis references the existing cylindrical surface that was generated by the rounds. This is the only reference required to fully constrain the datum axis.

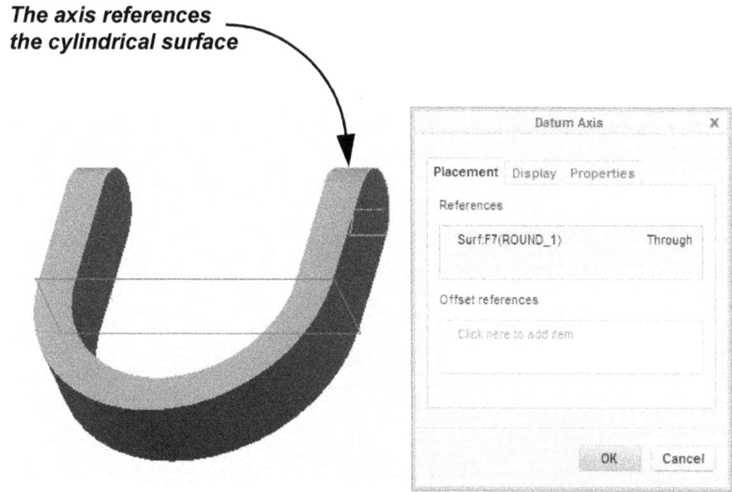

Figure 10–16

In the example shown in Figure 10–17, the top planar surface is selected as a placement reference with a Normal constraint. When a planar surface is selected as a reference, two linear placement handles display. They can be dynamically dragged to fully locate the datum axis. By dragging the handle to adjacent edges or surfaces, offset references are added to the dialog box that can be modified to locate the datum axis as required.

*References can be removed using the Datum Plane dialog box. Select the reference, right-click, and select **Remove**.*

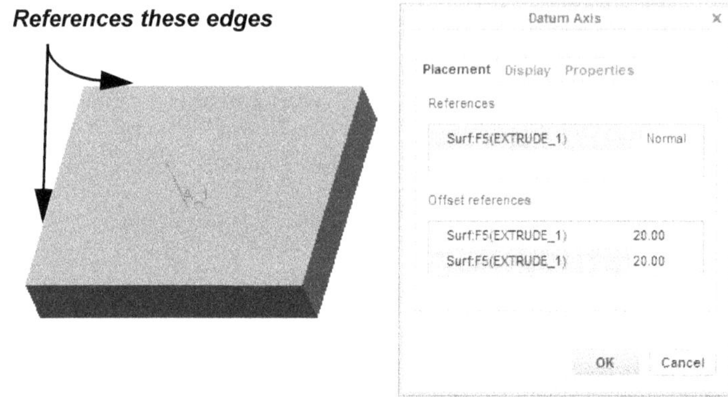

Figure 10–17

10.4 Creating Datum Points

Datum Points can be used as construction elements for modeling or as known points for analyses. Similar to Planes and Axes, you can add points at any time, including during the creation of other features.

A single datum point feature can contain multiple individual points. When multiple points are created in a single point feature, the following apply:

- All datum points display under one Datum Point feature in the Model Tree.
- All points in the Datum Point feature act as a group, so deleting will apply to all points in the feature.
- To delete an individual point in the Point Feature, you must edit the definition of the Datum Feature.

There are three types of datum points:

- (Point) - A datum point created on or offset from an entity, or at the intersection of entities.
- (Offset Coordinate System) - A datum point created by offsetting from a selected datum coordinate system.
- (Field) - A field point identifies a geometric domain, and is used in Behavioral Modeling analyses. Field points will not be covered in this guide.

Offset Coordinate System points are covered in the Creo Parametric 3.0: Advanced Modeling course.

To create a datum point, expand the (Point) fly-out in the *Model* tab if stand-alone, or expand (Datum) in the dashboard of the current feature, and expand the (Point) fly-out. Select either (Point) or (Offset Coordinate System), as required.

To create a general point, click (Point). The Datum Point dialog box opens as shown in Figure 10–18. Placement references and constraints need to be selected to fully locate the datum points.

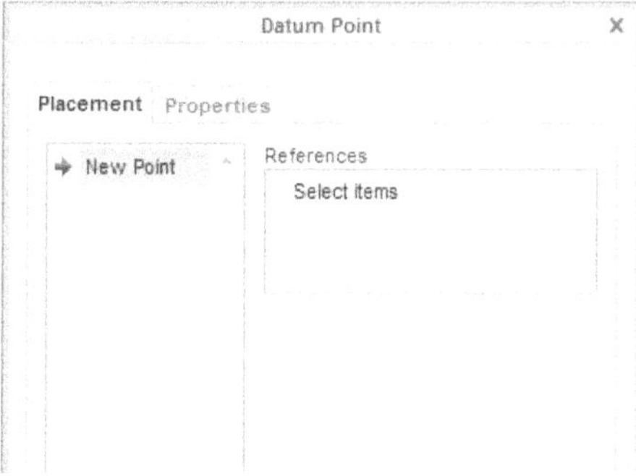

Figure 10–18

Datum points can be created in the following locations:

- On a curve, edge, or axis.
- At the center of a circular or elliptical entity.
- On a surface or quilt, or offset from a surface or quilt.
- On a vertex or offset from a vertex.
- Offset from an existing datum point.
- Offset from a coordinate system.
- At the intersection of entities.

Figure 10–19 shows a point labeled **PNT0** created at the edge formed between the cylinder and the block.

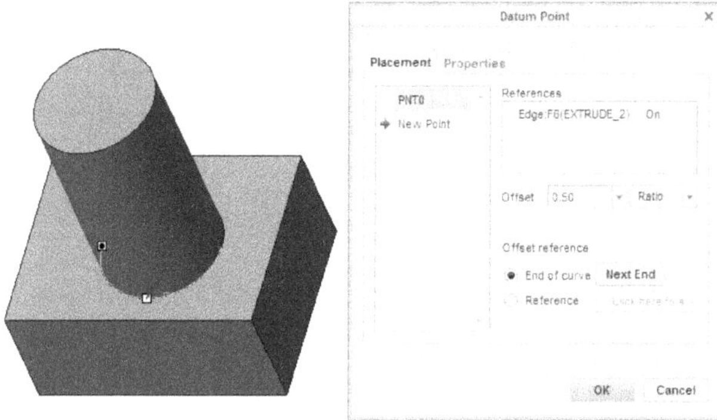

Figure 10–19

When you create a point on an edge, you must locate the point. The most common option is to Offset the point a ratio between 0 (the start) and 1 (the end). In this example, the point was created half way around the curve, or a ratio of 0.50.

In a single datum point feature, you can create multiple individual points by creating a point, clicking **New Point**, and adding an additional point with new references, as shown in Figure 10–20. This can be repeated as many times as required. In Figure 10–20, the surface and axis were selected as references to create **PNT1**.

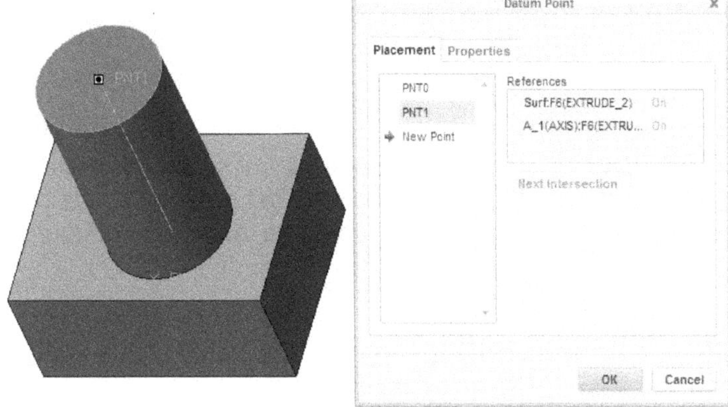

Figure 10–20

In Figure 10–21, the point **PNT2** is created on the surface shown, and offset from the two perpendicular surfaces, in a similar fashion to how a linear hole is located.

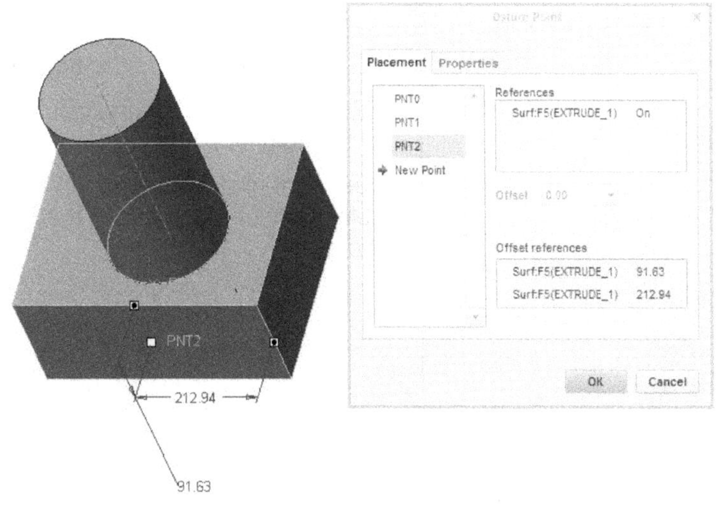

Figure 10–21

In the final example, the point **PNT3** is created at the selected vertex shown in Figure 10–22.

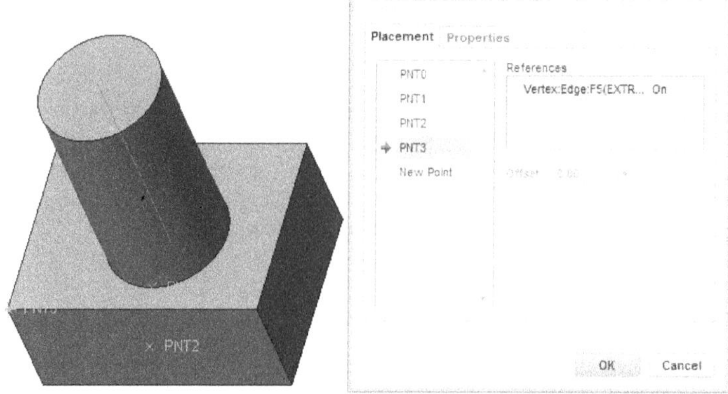

Figure 10–22

Once the points are complete, click **OK** to create the datum point feature. The grouped points display as a single feature in the model tree, as shown in Figure 10–23,

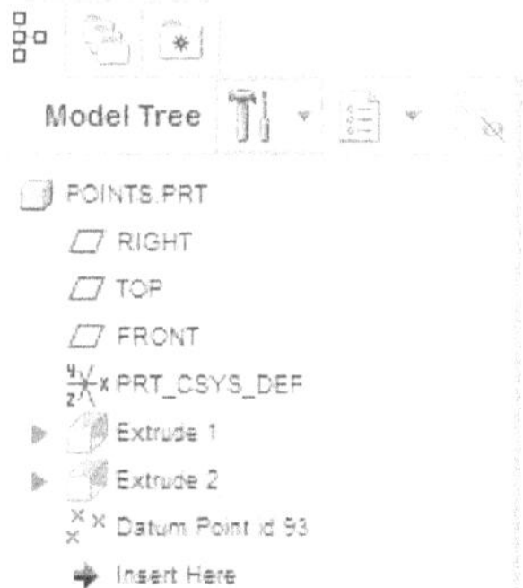

Figure 10–23

To change any of the individual points in the feature, select any of the points on screen, or the Datum Point feature in the model tree, right-click and select (Edit Definition). You can then select any of the points in the Datum Point dialog box to change them.

10.5 Creating Datum Coordinate Systems

Coordinate systems are used as reference features in parts and assemblies for the following scenarios:

- Serving as a reference for positioning other features.
- Direction references for most modeling tasks.
- Conducting mass property calculations.
- Assembling components.
- Placing constraints for Finite Element Analysis (FEA).
- Providing manufacturing operation references for tool paths.

Coordinate systems can be created by:

- Clicking (Coordinate System) in the *Model* tab.
- Clicking (Datum) and then (Coordinate System) while in a feature's dashboard
- Sketching a coordinate system while in sketcher.

In ether case, the Coordinate System dialog box opens as shown in Figure 10–24.

Figure 10–24

You can select placement references, such as surfaces, edges, vertices, or other coordinate systems, and then define the orientation of the coordinate system axes. Figure 10–25 shows a coordinate system created in a surface, using a Linear dimensioning scheme. The two perpendicular surfaces are used as dimensioning references.

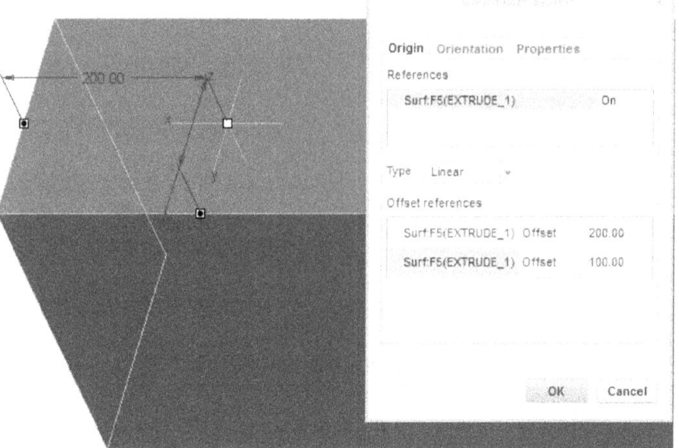

Figure 10–25

The system automatically determine the orientation for the X, Y, and Z-axis. You can control the orientation using the *Orientation* tab, as shown in Figure 10–26. You can use references to determine the direction in which any two of the coordinate system axes face. The third is then automatically set.

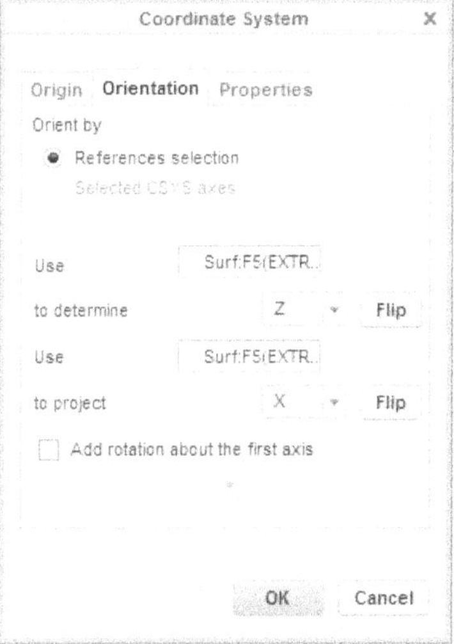

Figure 10–26

10.6 Datum Display

The display of datum features can be toggled on and off by selecting or clearing the appropriate option in the In-graphics toolbar, as shown in Figure 10–27.

Figure 10–27

By default, the datum names are not displayed for datum entities other than Coordinate Systems. To display datum tags, select the *View* tab, and select the appropriate option from the Show group, as shown in Figure 10–28.

Figure 10–28

The datum display can be controlled from the Show group as well.

Hiding Datum Features

The options in the In-graphics toolbar enable you to control the display of all the features of the same type.

The **Hide** option enables you to control the display of individual datum features. For example, you can select the datum plane **FRONT** and hide it, which only removes that datum from the display.

To hide a datum feature, select it in the model or from the model tree, right-click and select **Hide**. To show it again, select it in the model tree, right-click and select **Unhide**.

Practice 10a Reference Elements

Practice Objectives

- Create reference elements.
- Create solid features using reference elements.

In this practice, you will create the part shown in Figure 10–29. You will create reference elements to use as sketch planes. From these you will create the features.

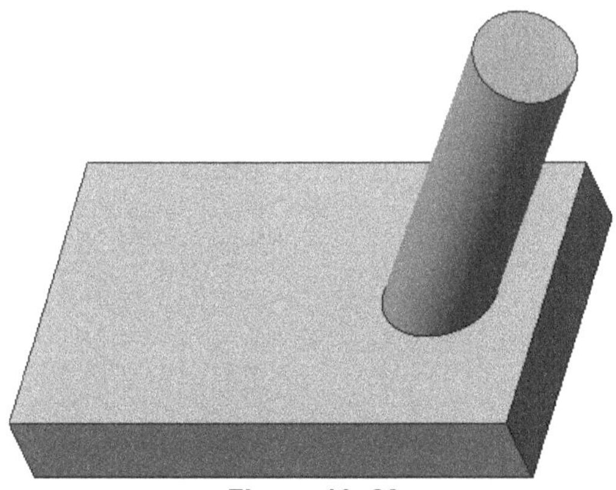

Figure 10–29

Task 1 - Open a model with an initial Pad feature.

1. Set your working directory to the *Chapter 10/practice 10a* folder.
2. Open the **Datum Refs.prt**.
3. Set the model display as follows:
   - *(Datum Display Filters)*: All On
   - *(Spin Center)*: Off
   - *(Display Style)*: (Shading With Edges)

Task 2 - Create a point at the center of the part.

Design Considerations

The point you create here is used later to constrain the sketch of an extrude feature. It is also used as a starting point for an axis, which will serve as a reference for datum planes.

1. Select the top surface of the part as shown in Figure 10–30.

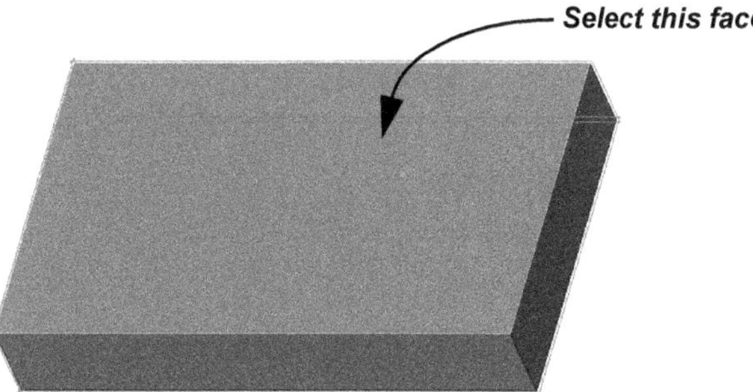

Figure 10–30

2. In the *Model* tab, click (Point) to create a point. The Point Definition dialog box opens, as shown in Figure 10–31.

Figure 10–31

3. Note the two drag handles on the model.

4. Move the drag handles to the two surfaces shown in Figure 10–32.

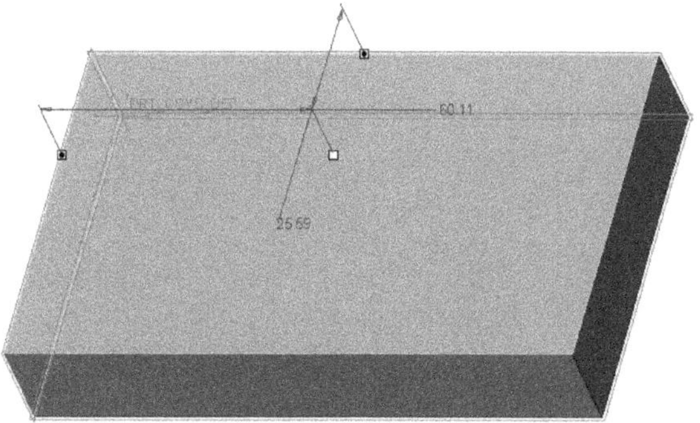

Figure 10–32

5. Set the *Vertical Dimension* to **38** and the *Horizontal Dimension* to **63.5**, as shown in Figure 10–33.

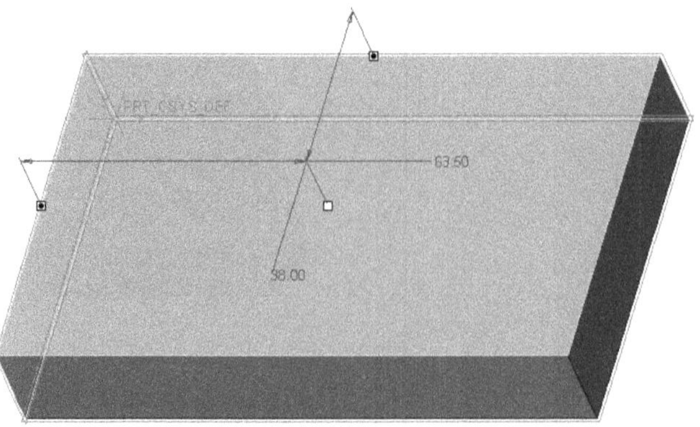

Figure 10–33

6. Click **OK** to complete the point.

Task 3 - Create an axis.

Design Considerations

This axis will reference the point you previously created. It is used as a pivot axis for an angled plane.

1. In the Datum group in the *Model* tab, click (Axis).
2. Select the datum point.
3. Press and hold <Ctrl> and select Datum **FRONT** from the model tree.
4. The Datum Axis dialog box should display, as shown in Figure 10–34.

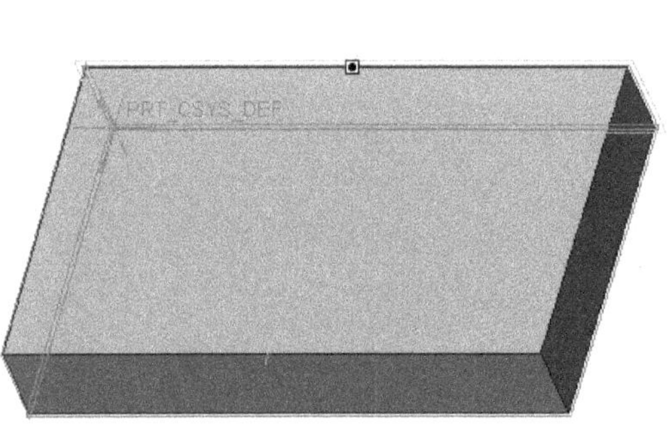

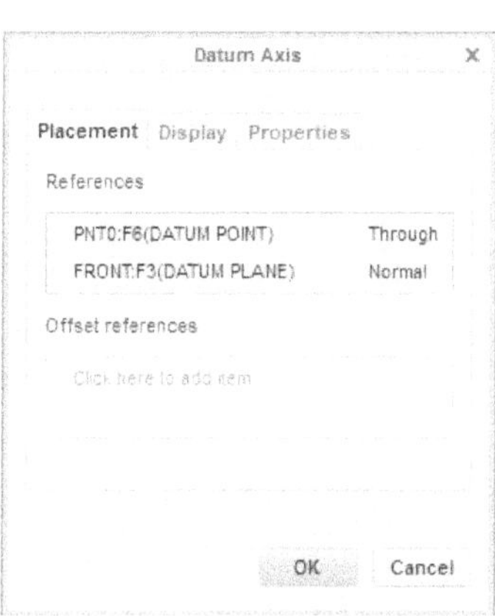

Figure 10–34

5. Click **OK** to complete the axis. The resulting part displays as shown in Figure 10–35.

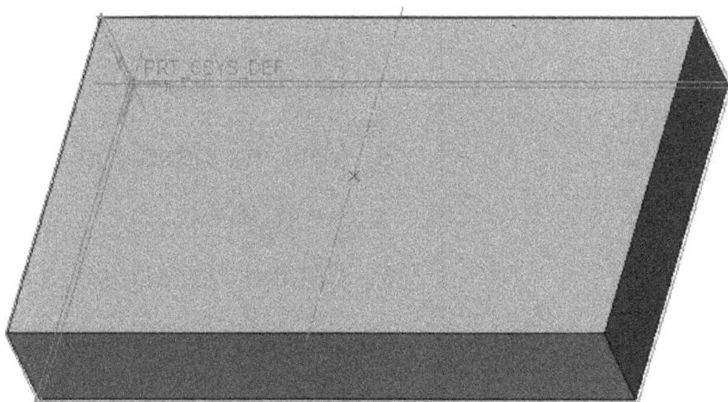

Figure 10–35

Task 4 - Create planes to locate a sketch.

Design Considerations

Using the previously created axis and one of the datum planes, you will create an angled plane. This plane will be used as a reference for the following plane that you will create.

1. In the Datum group in the *Model* tab, click (Plane).
2. Select the datum axis previously created.
3. Press and hold <Ctrl> and select datum plane **TOP** from the model tree as the plane to measure the angle from.
4. Set the *Angle* to **60**.
5. The Datum Plane dialog box displays as shown in Figure 10–36.

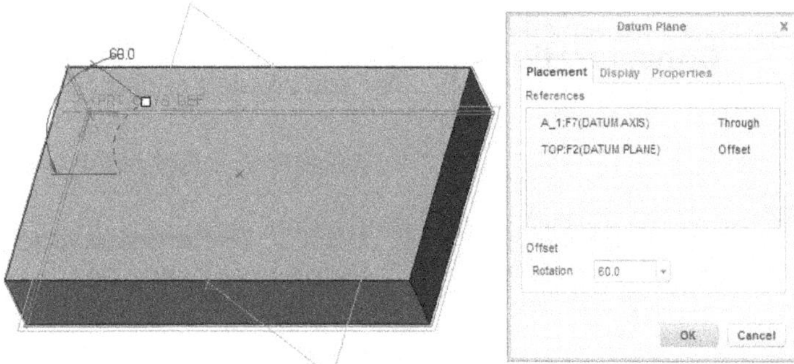

Figure 10–36

6. Click **OK** to complete the datum plane.

Design Considerations

The following plane will be used as a sketching plane for the profile sketch of a Pad feature. The plane will be offset from the angle plane.

7. Make the second plane offset from the first plane. You will use it as the sketching plane in the next task.
8. With the plane you just created still selected, click (Plane).
9. Set the *Translation* to **50.00**.
10. Click **OK** to complete the creation of this plane. The resulting part displays as shown in Figure 10–37.

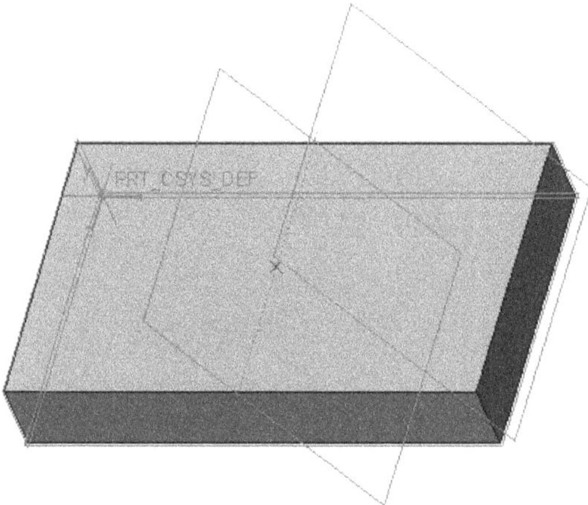

Figure 10–37

Task 5 - Create an extrusion on the offset plane.

Design Considerations

This sketch will be used as a profile for an extruded feature. It is created on the offset plane and will be constrained to the point that you created earlier.

1. Select the offset plane and click (Extrude).
2. Click (References) and select the datum point. Close the References dialog box.
3. Click (Sketch View).
4. Sketch a circle that is centered on the point, as shown in Figure 10–38.

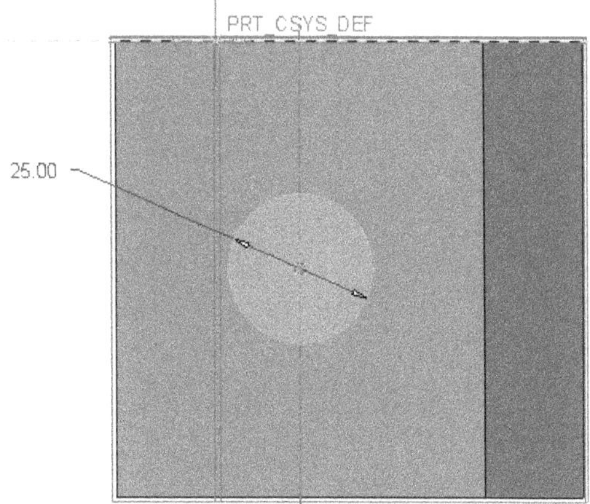

Figure 10–38

5. Click (OK) to complete the sketch.
6. Press <Ctrl>+<D> to return to default orientation.
7. Select the white square drag handle.
8. Press and hold <Shift> and drag the handle until it snaps to the top surface of the model, as shown in Figure 10–39.
9. Click (Complete Feature) to complete the extrusion.
10. The resulting part displays as shown in Figure 10–40.

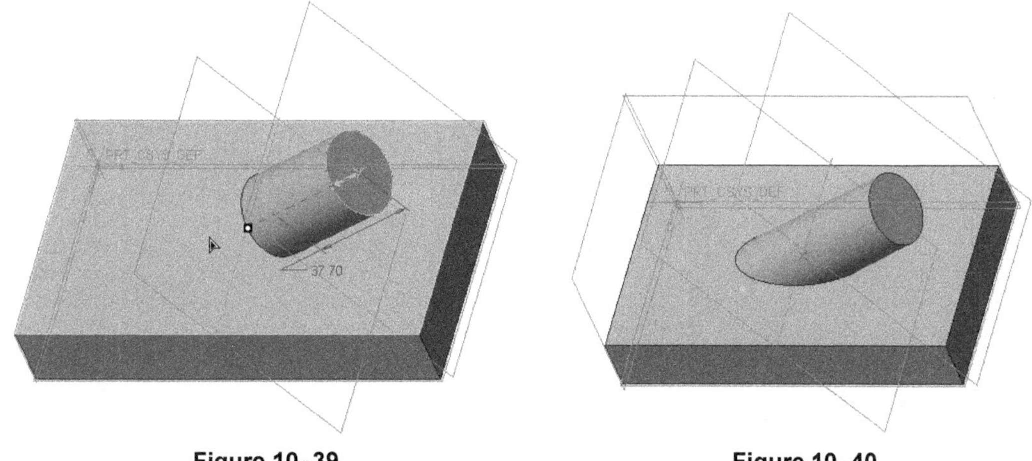

Figure 10–39

Figure 10–40

Figure 10–41

Task 6 - Modify the angle, offset distance, and location of the extrusion.

1. Double-click the offset datum (**DTM2**), and change the *50 Translation* to **100.00.**
2. Double-click on the angle datum plane (**DTM1**) and set the *Angle* to **30.00**.
3. Double-click on **PNT0** and change the *63.5* value to **100.00**.
4. Click (Regenerate).
5. Toggle off the display of all datum entities. The model displays as shown in Figure 10–42.

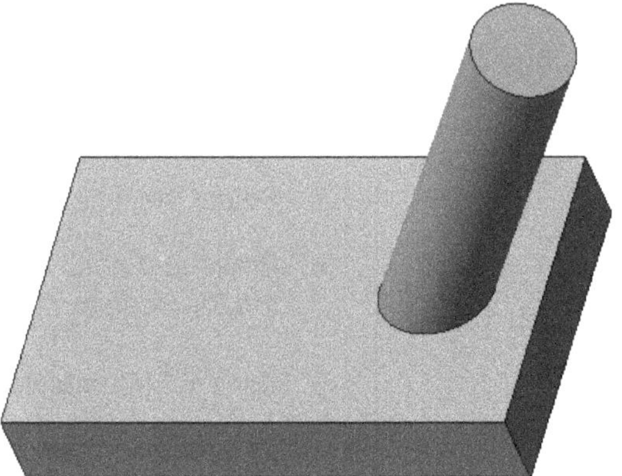

Figure 10–42

6. Save the model and erase it from memory.

Practice 10b Creating Datum Features

Practice Objective

- Create internal datum planes and datum axes that can be used as references in the creation of a solid feature.

In this practice, you will create the model shown in Figure 10–43. To create the geometry for this model, you must create an additional datum plane and axis.

Figure 10–43

Task 1 - Create a new part.

1. Set the working directory to the *Chapter 10\practice 10b* folder.
2. Create a new part using the default template and set the *Name* to **bevel_washer**.
3. Set the model display as follows:
   - *(Datum Display Filters)*: Only (Plane Display) and (Axis Display)
   - *(Spin Center)*: Off
   - *(Display Style)*: (Shading With Edges)

Task 2 - Create the base feature.

1. Click (Extrude) to create the base feature.
2. For the sketching plane, select datum plane **TOP** and sketch the section of the protrusion.
3. Click (Sketch View).

4. Sketch the section shown in Figure 10–44, using the default references.

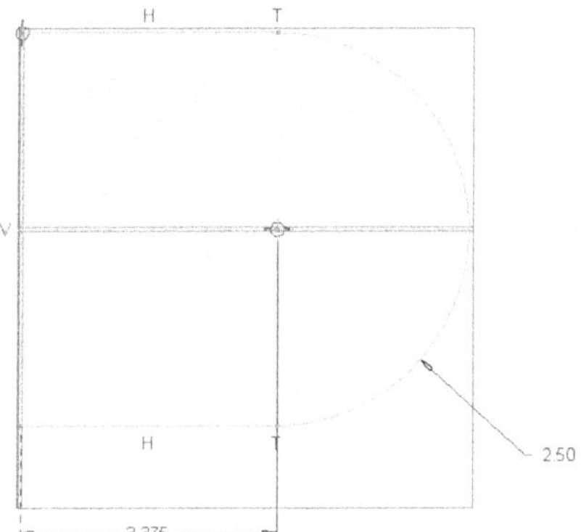

Figure 10–44

5. Click ✓ (OK) to complete the sketch.
6. Pres <Ctrl>+<D> to return to default orientation.
7. Set the *Depth* to **0.75**.
8. Click ✓ (Complete Feature) to complete the extrusion. The model displays as shown in Figure 10–45.

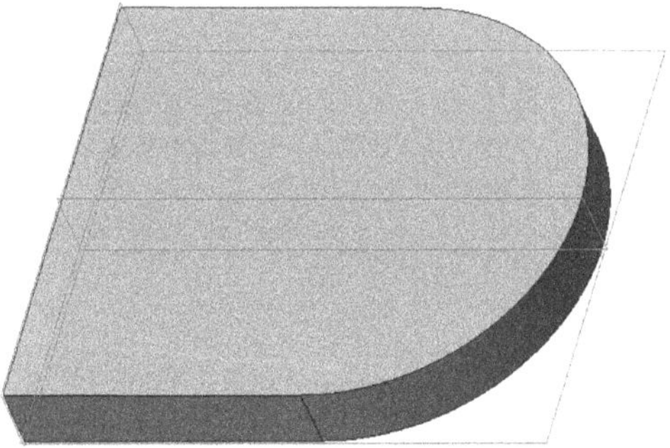

Figure 10–45

Task 3 - Create the angled protrusion.

1. Click (Extrude) to create the angled extrusion.

Creation of the extrusion is paused automatically.

2. An additional datum plane is required as a sketching plane. In the *Extrude* dashboard, expand (Datum) and click (Plane) to create an additional datum plane. The Datum Plane dialog box opens as shown in Figure 10–46.

3. Press and hold <Ctrl>, and select the edge and surface shown in Figure 10–47. The datum plane displays once the references have been selected.

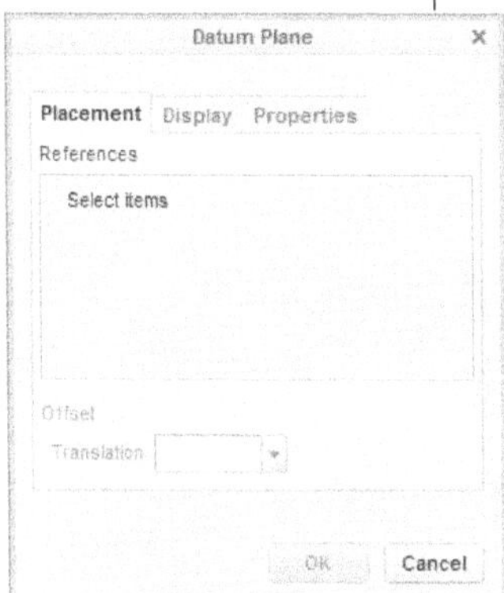

Figure 10–46

Select this edge and this surface

Datum Plane
Placement Display Properties
References
Edge:F5(EXTRUDE_1) Through
Surf:F5(EXTRUDE_1) Offset
Offset
Rotation 30.0
OK Cancel

Figure 10–47

*The constraint types (i.e., **Through** or **Offset**) are dependent on the reference type (i.e., edge or surface). A default constraint type is assigned for each reference. However, it can be changed by selecting the constraint and using the drop-down list to select from the list of available constraints.*

4. In the Datum Plane dialog box, note that the **Through** constraint is selected for the edge, and the Offset constraint is selected for the surface.

5. Set the *Rotation* to **30** if required. If you need to flip the datum plane to the opposite side of the selected surface, set the *Rotation* to **-30**. In the Datum Plane dialog box, select the *Properties* tab. Change the *Name* of the datum plane to **Angled_datum**, as shown in Figure 10–48.

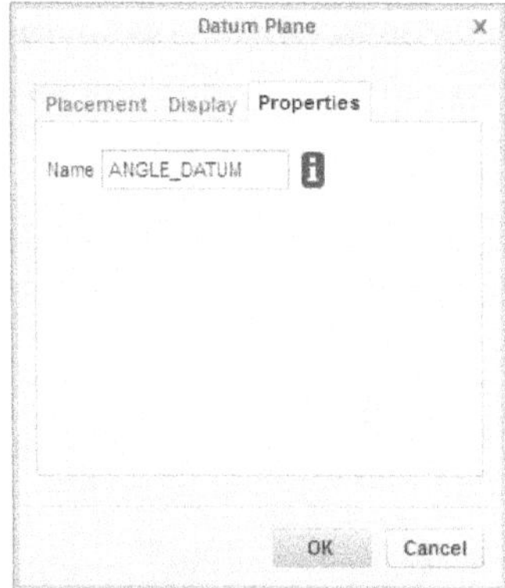

Figure 10–48

6. Click **OK** to complete the creation of the datum plane.

7. Click (Resume) to continue creating the protrusion. The *Sketch* tab is now active. The system automatically uses the new plane as the sketching plane and the **FRONT** plane to face the bottom direction.

8. Press and hold <Alt>. Move the cursor over the left edge, and right-click until the edge is highlighted as shown in Figure 10–49.

9. Select the edge, right-click and select **Add references**.

10. Sketch the section shown in Figure 10–50. Select the appropriate references to create the geometry.

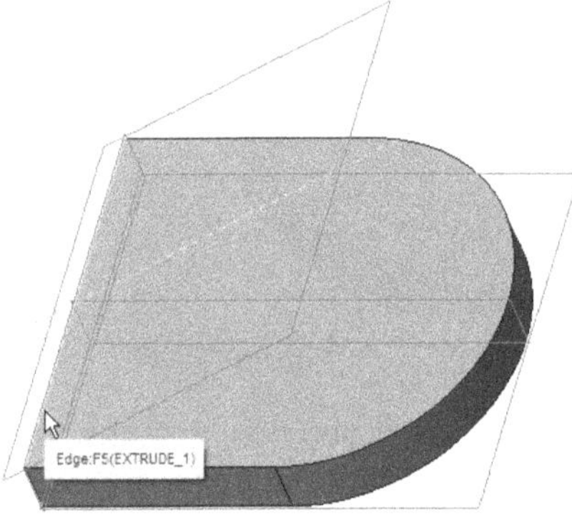

Figure 10–49

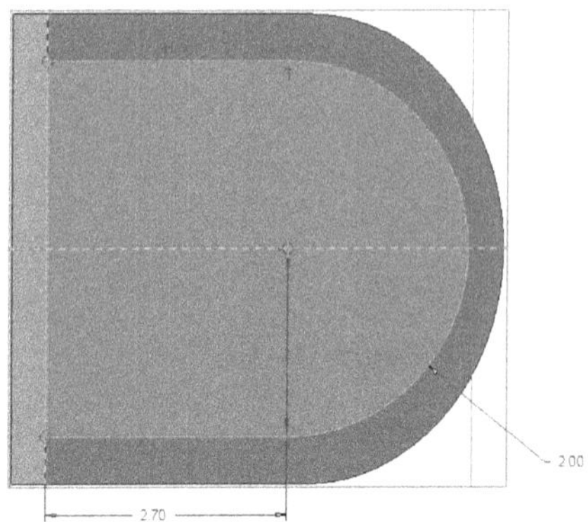

Figure 10–50

11. Click ✓ (OK) to complete the sketch.

12. If required, click the arrow head so the feature extrudes toward the existing geometry.

13. In the Depth drop-down list, click (To Next). The preview displays as shown in Figure 10–51.

14. Click ✓ (Complete Feature) to complete the feature. The model displays as shown in Figure 10–52.

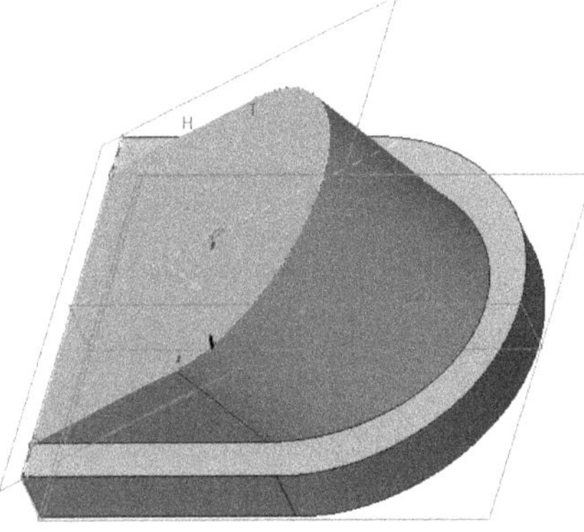

Figure 10–51

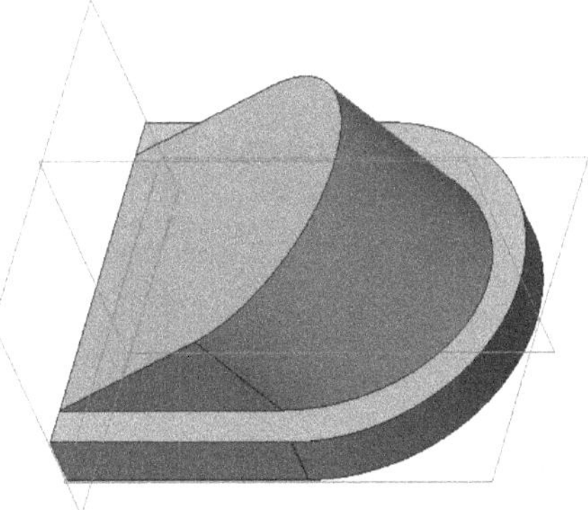

Figure 10–52

The feature that has been added to the model tree is an extrude feature. If you expand the feature it consists of the section and the datum plane, as shown in Figure 10–53.

Figure 10–53

Task 4 - Create a coaxial hole.

1. In the Shapes group, click (Hole).
2. To create the hole, an axis is required as a reference. In the *Hole* dashboard, expand (Datum) and click (Axis) to create a datum axis. The Datum Axis dialog box opens.

Creation of the hole is paused automatically.

3. Select the surface shown in Figure 10–54 as a reference. The constraint type should automatically be set to **Through**.

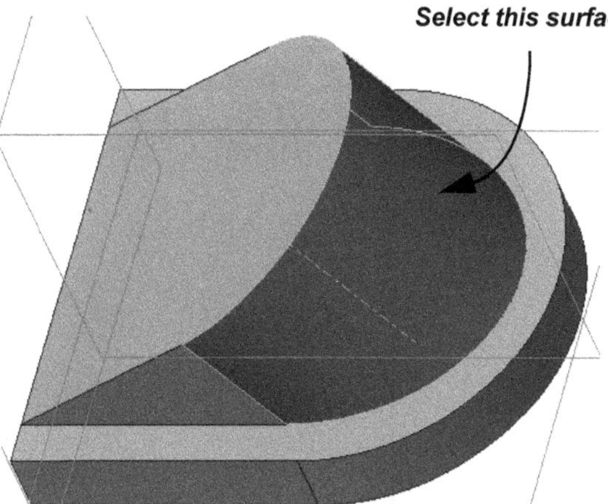

Figure 10–54

4. The Datum Axis dialog box updates, as shown in Figure 10–55. Click **OK** to complete the datum axis.

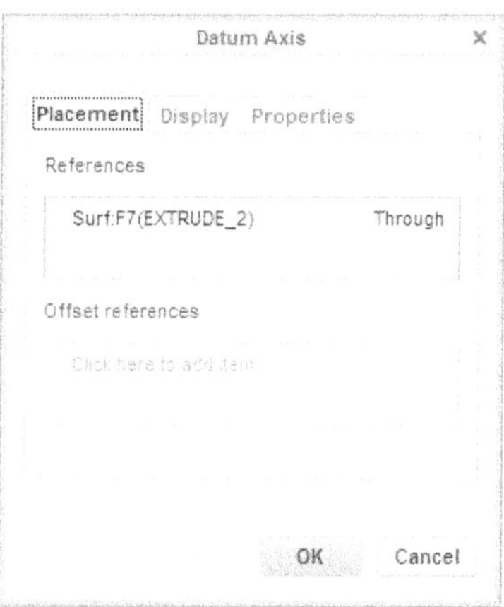

Figure 10–55

5. Click (Resume) to continue creating the hole. The *Hole* dashboard is now active.

*The **Placement** panel can be selected to review or change the references.*

6. The newly created axis is automatically selected as a primary placement reference. This establishes a coaxial constraint.
7. Move the cursor into the Creo Parametric window, hold <Ctrl>, and select the top surface of the angled protrusion, as shown in Figure 10–56.

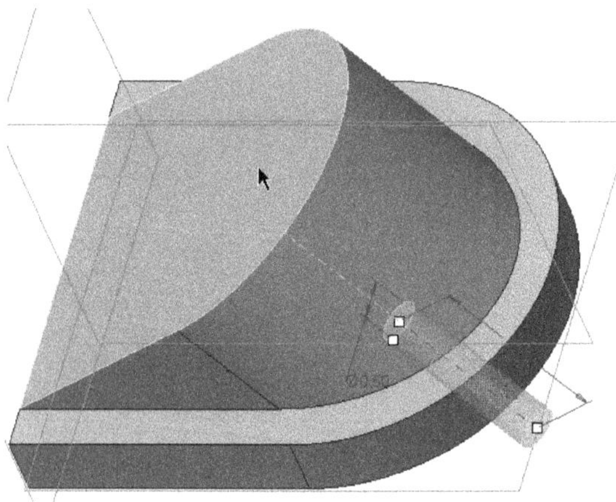

Figure 10–56

8. Click (Through All) to set the *Depth* option to intersect with the through all surfaces.
9. Double-click the *Diameter* of the hole and set it to **3.00**.

10. Click (Complete Feature) to complete the feature. The model displays as shown in Figure 10–57.

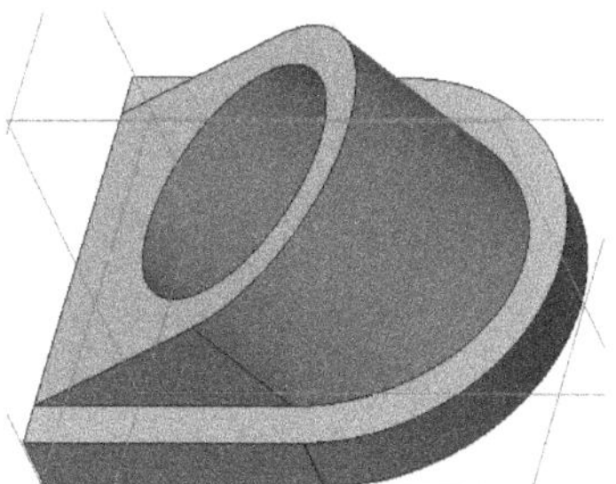

Figure 10–57

Task 5 - Create an extruded lip.

1. Create an extrusion on the underside of the model with the dimensions shown in Figure 10–58.

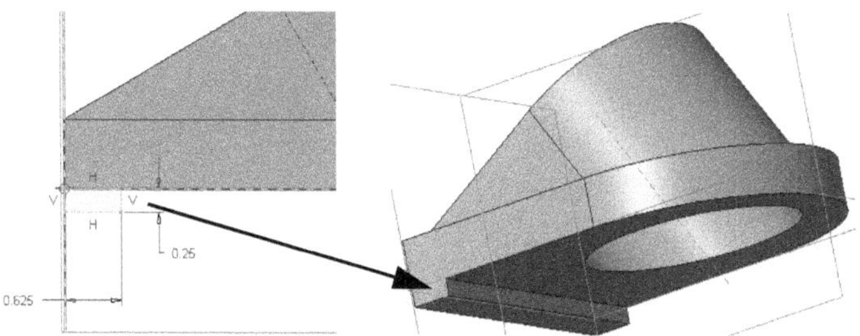

Figure 10–58

2. In the In-graphics toolbar, click (Datum Display Filters) and toggle off (Axis Display) and (Plane Display).
3. The completed model displays as shown in Figure 10–59.

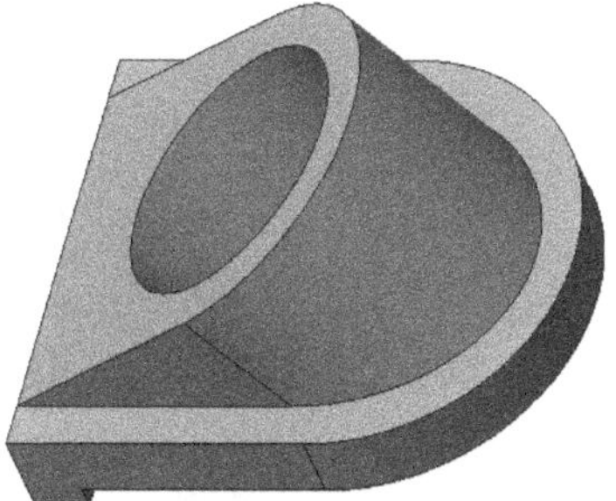

Figure 10–59

4. Save the model and erase it from memory.

Practice 10c Additional References

Practice Objective

- Create datum planes and axis that can be used as references in the creation of a solid feature.

In this practice, you will create the model shown in Figure 10–60. To create the geometry for this model, you must create an additional datum plane and axis.

Figure 10–60

Task 1 - Create a new part.

1. Ensure that the working directory is set to the *Chapter 10\ practice 10c* folder.
2. Use the default template to create a new part and set the *Name* to **fork**.
3. Set the model display as follows:
   - *(Datum Display Filters)*: Only (Plane Display) and (Axis Display)
   - *(Spin Center)*: Off
   - *(Display Style)*: (Shading With Edges)

Task 2 - Create the base feature.

1. Click (Extrude) to create the base feature.
2. Click (Thicken Sketch) to specify that the feature will be a thin extrusion.

*You can also click **Placement** in the tab and then click **Define** in the Placement panel.*

3. For the sketching plane, select datum plane **TOP** to activate the *Sketch* tab.

4. Click (Sketch View) and sketch the section shown in Figure 10–61.

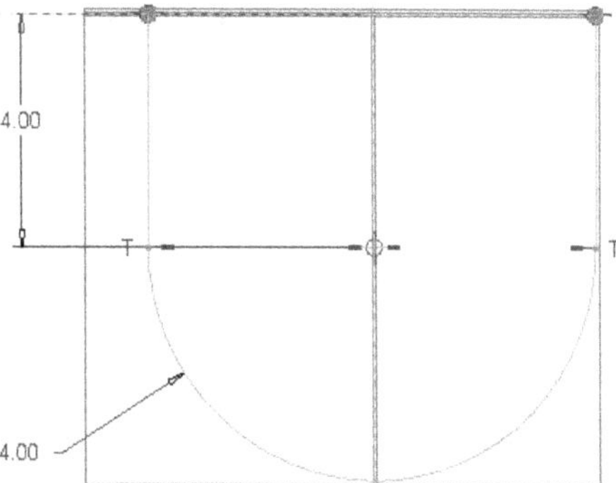

Figure 10–61

5. Click (OK).

6. Set the *Thickness* to **1.00**. Ensure that the thickness is to the inside of the sketch.

7. Click to extrude the feature on both sides of the sketching plane. Set the *Depth* to **2.00**.

8. Click (Complete Feature) to complete the feature. Return to default orientation and the model displays as shown in Figure 10–62.

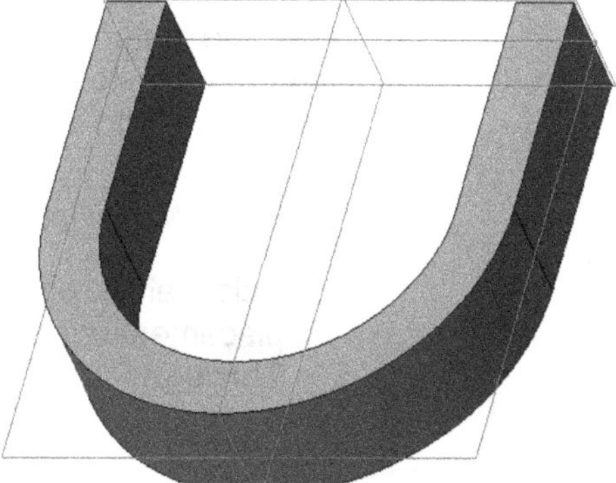

Figure 10–62

Task 3 - Create two full rounds.

1. Click (Datum Display Filters) and toggle (Plane Display) off.
2. Select one of the edges shown in Figure 10–63. Press and hold <Ctrl> and select the other edge.
3. Right-click and select **Round**. Then, right-click again and select **Full round**.
4. Click (Complete Feature) and the model displays as shown in Figure 10–64.

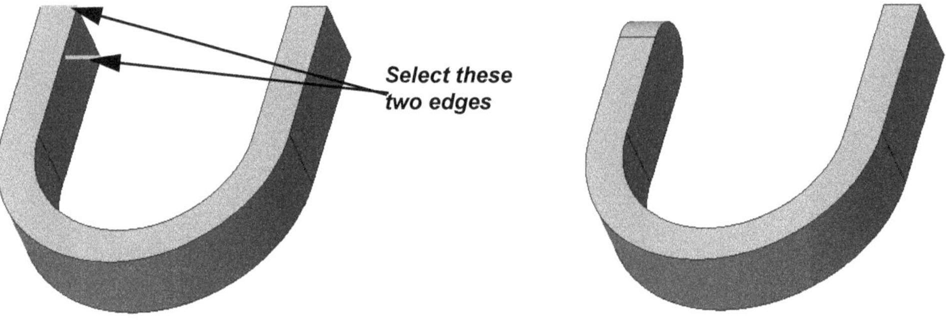

Figure 10–63 Figure 10–64

5. Repeat the previous steps to create the full round on the other side.

Task 4 - Create a coaxial hole.

An axis is required to create a coaxial hole through the ends of the base feature. Because this axis might be referenced by other features, create the axis before the hole so that it is not embedded with the hole feature.

1. In the *Model* tab, click (Axis) to create the datum axis.
2. Select either of the surfaces formed by the full rounds as the placement reference. Ensure that the constraint type is set to **Through**.

The axis should still be active after creation.

Note that if the default hole diameter, which is set from the last hole you created, is too large, it might cut off the end of the model. Simply drag the diameter handle to make it fit.

3. Click **OK** in the Datum Axis dialog box.
4. With the axis still selected, In the *Model* tab, click (Hole) to create a hole through the ends of the base feature so that it is coaxial with the full rounds.
5. Press <Ctrl> and select the surface shown in Figure 10–65.

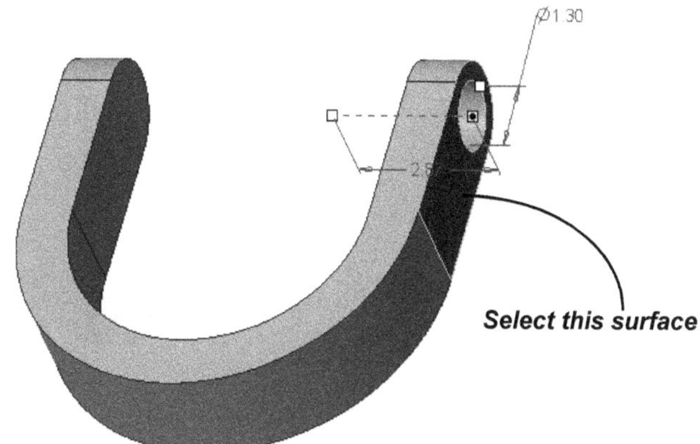

Figure 10–65

6. Set the hole *Diameter* to **1.00**.
7. Select the depth to intersect through all surfaces.
8. Click (Complete Feature) to complete the feature.

Task 5 - Create the post.

1. Click (Extrude) to create an extruded feature.
2. Click (Datum Display Filters) and toggle (Plane Display) on.

Creation of the protrusion is paused automatically.

Press and hold <Ctrl> to select more than one reference.

3. A sketching plane is required that does not currently exist in the model. In the *Extrude* dashboard, expand (Datum), and click (Plane). Press and hold <Ctrl> and multi-select the surface and datum plane **FRONT** as references, as shown in Figure 10–66. Constrain the datum plane to be **Tangent** to the cylindrical surface and **Parallel** to datum plane **FRONT**. The resulting datum plane displays as shown in Figure 10–66.

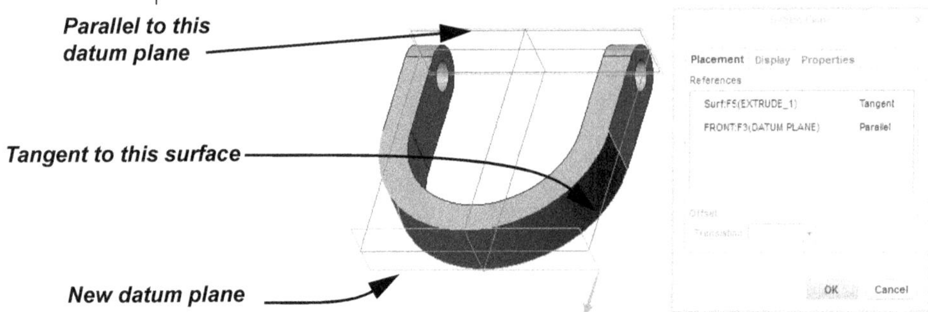

Figure 10–66

4. Click **OK** to complete the datum plane.
5. Click (Resume) to continue creating the extruded feature.
6. Click (Sketch View).
7. Sketch the section shown in Figure 10–67 on the newly created datum plane.

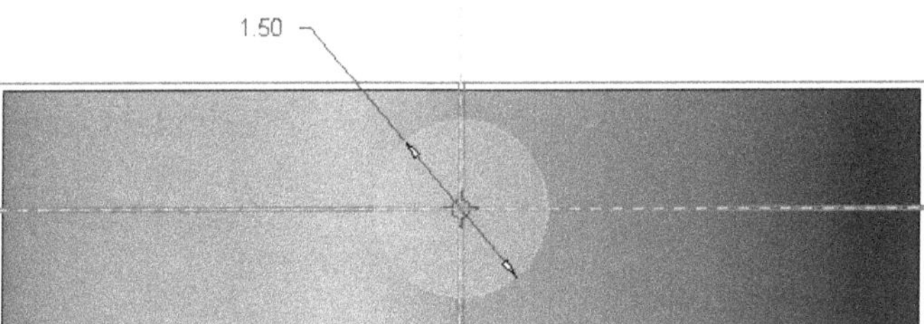

Figure 10–67

8. Click (OK) to complete the sketch.

The Options panel must be used to set options for Side 2. Alternatively, the Extrude tab can be used for Side 1.

9. In the *Options* tab, in the *Side 1* field, set the *Depth* to **Blind** and enter a value of **7.50**. In the *Side 2 field,* set the *Depth* to **To Next**. The panel is shown in Figure 10–68.

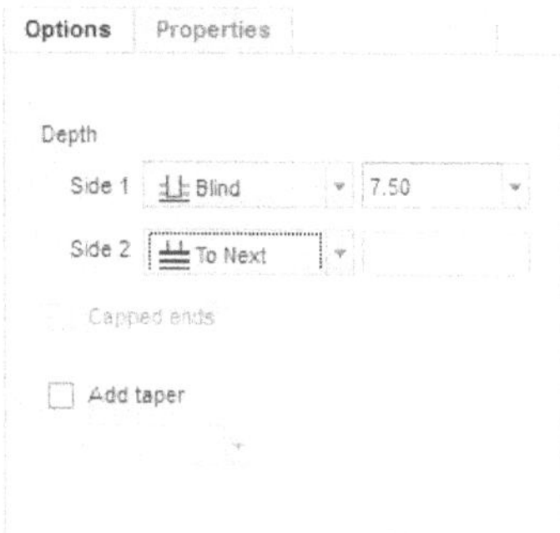

Figure 10–68

What would have happened if the Side 2 depth was not set?

10. Click (Complete Feature) to complete the cylindrical protrusion. Toggle off the display of datum features. The model displays as shown in Figure 10–69.

Figure 10–69

11. Save the model and erase it from memory.

Practice 10d (Optional) Using Datum References

Practice Objectives

- Create datum elements.
- Create solid features using datum references.

In this practice, you will complete the features of a coat stand by, creating and using datums. Limited instructions will be provided. The finished model displays as shown in Figure 10–70.

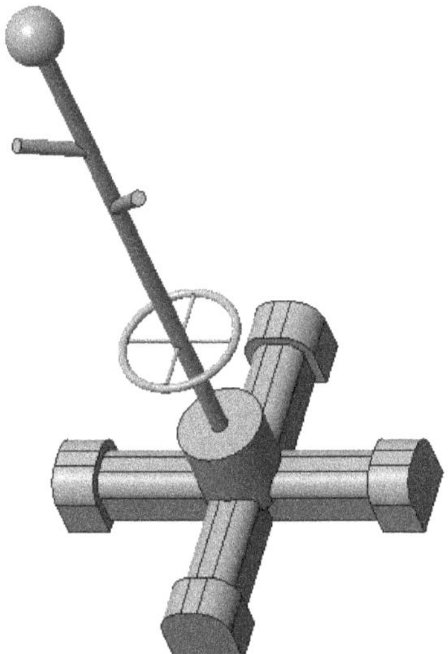

Figure 10–70

Task 1 - Create arms for the coat hanger.

1. Ensure that the working directory is set to the *Chapter 10\ practice 10d* folder
2. Open **CoatStand.prt**.
3. Set the model display as follows:
   - *(Datum Display Filters)*: Only (Plane Display) and (Axis Display)
   - *(Spin Center)*: Off
   - *(Display Style)*: (Shading With Edges)

Design Considerations

Create an arm above the **TOP** plane with the following stats:

- *Length:* **300mm**
- *Diameter:* **50mm**
- *Height*: **1500mm**
- *Angle*: **45 degrees** (pointing up)
- *Rotation:* **45 degrees** (from the **FRONT** plane)

4. Create a datum plane through the axis and **45** degrees to datum **FRONT**.

5. Create a datum point on the axis and set the *Offset* to **1500mm** from datum plane **TOP**.

6. Create a datum Sketch. Use the Datum group in the *Sketch* tab and sketch a point and two centerlines, as shown in Figure 10–71.

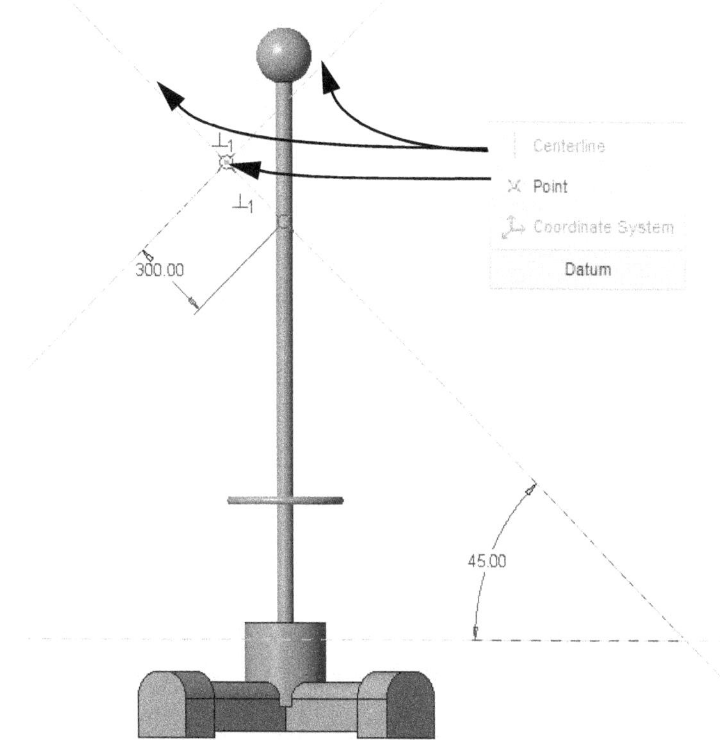

Figure 10–71

7. Complete the datum sketch.

8. Create a datum plane **Through** the axis that is offset from the point and **Normal** to the first plane you created.

9. Create an extrusion using the plane you just created as the sketch plane. The sketch is shown in Figure 10–72. Use the point from the Datum Sketch as your sketch reference. Set the depth option to through next and complete the feature.

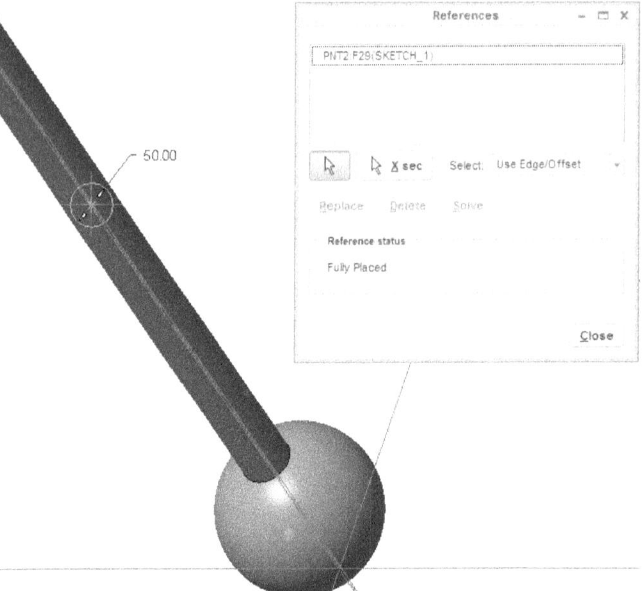

Figure 10–72

10. Toggle off the display of datum entities. The model displays as shown in Figure 10–73.

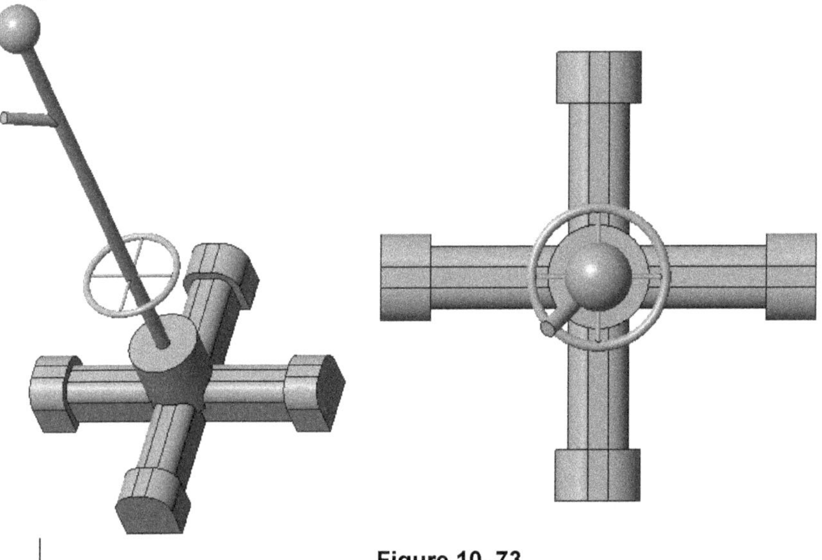

Figure 10–73

Task 2 - Create another arm.

1. Create another arm with a the following stats:

    - *Length*: **600mm**
    - *Diameter*: **50mm**
    - *Height*: **1200mm** (above the **FRONT** plane)
    - *Angle*: **45 degrees** (points upwards)
    - *Rotation:* **45 degrees** (from the **FRONT** plane, in the opposite direction as the other arm)

    The completed model displays as shown in Figure 10–74.

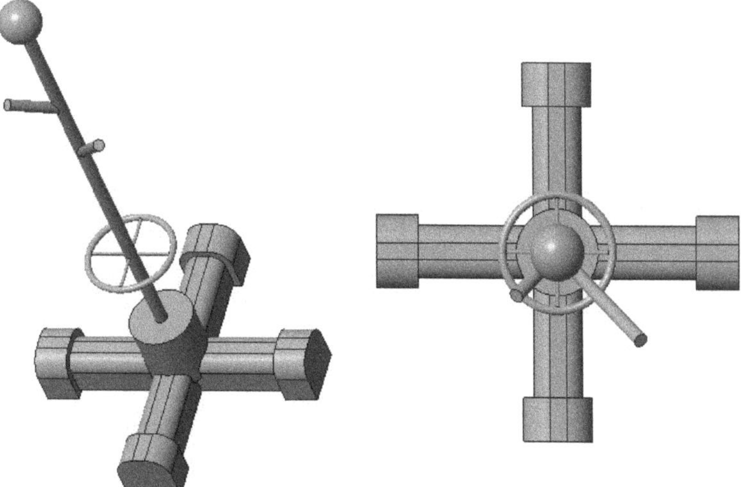

Figure 10–74

2. Save the model and erase it from memory.

Chapter Review Question

1. Default datum planes are the only datum planes that can be created in the model.
   a. True
   b. False
2. Which icon enables you to create a datum plane?
   a.
   b.
   c.
   d.
3. Which icon enables you to create a datum axis?
   a.
   b.
   c.
   d.
4. By default, datum axes are automatically generated with cylindrical features.
   a. True
   b. False
5. Both datum planes and datum axes can be renamed using the *Properties* tab in their associated dialog boxes.
   a. True
   b. False

6. Which combination of constraints enables you to create **DTM2**, as shown in Figure 10–75?

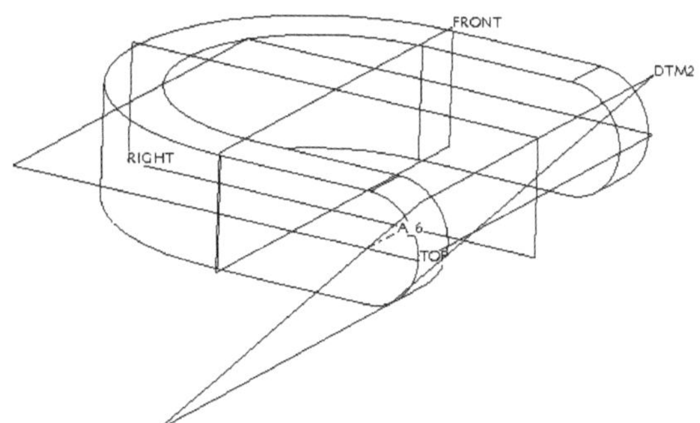

Figure 10–75

   a. Tangent to the Round at an Angle to **TOP**.
   b. Through **A_6** at an Angle to **TOP**.
   c. Through **A_6** at an Angle to **FRONT**.
   d. Through **TOP** at an Angle to **FRONT**.

7. Which of the following are valid constraint combinations to create a datum plane? (Select all that apply.)
   a. Through a plane and parallel to an axis.
   b. Through a plane and offset from a surface.
   c. Tangent to a surface and parallel to a surface.
   d. Through an axis and Normal to a surface.

8. Which of the following statements is true regarding the model tree shown in Figure 10–76?

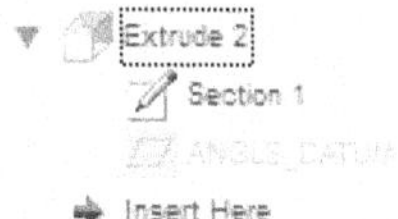

Figure 10–76

   a. The datum plane was created as a separate feature.
   b. The datum plane was created in the extrusion.
   c. The datum axis is created with the feature.
   d. **DTM1** is hidden.

9. A datum axis can be fully constrained through a round.
   a. True
   b. False

Command Summary

Button	Command	Location
	Datum Plane	• **Ribbon:** *Model* tab in the *Datum* group
	Datum Axis	• **Ribbon:** *Model* tab in the *Datum* group
	Datum Point	• **Ribbon:** *Model* tab in the *Datum* group
	Datum Coordinate System	• **Ribbon:** *Model* tab in the *Datum* group
	Plane Display	• **Ribbon:** *View* tab in the *Show* group • In-graphics toolbar
	Axis Display	• **Ribbon:** *View* tab in the *Show* group • In-graphics toolbar
	Point Display	• **Ribbon:** *View* tab in the *Show* group • In-graphics toolbar
	CSys Display	• **Ribbon:** *View* tab in the *Show* group • In-graphics toolbar

Shell and Draft

Drafts, shells, and ribs are quick methods of adding detail to your models. These features are generally added late in the design cycle.

Learning Objectives in this Chapter

- Create a closed internal shell feature that maintains uniform wall thickness in the resulting geometry.
- Create a shell feature that removes selected faces and maintains uniform wall thickness in the resulting geometry.
- Create a shell feature that removes faces and assigns unique wall thickness to the resulting faces in the model.
- Create a draft feature by selecting a draft hinge and pull direction.
- Define the direction and draft angle to create a draft that captures the design intent of the model.

11.1 Creating Shells

A shell is an Engineering feature that creates a hollowed out solid with a specified wall thickness. The geometry must be a constant thickness; shell features cannot create tapered geometry. They can also be used for castings and molded parts.

Two types of shells can be created:

- Open Shells (select surfaces to remove)
- Closed/Internal cavity shells

Open Shell

An open shell feature removes specified surfaces and leaves a hollowed out solid. Figure 11–1 shows the cross-section of a bottle before and after an open shell feature has been added to the model.

A constant wall thickness is applied to all surfaces when you add a shell feature to the model.

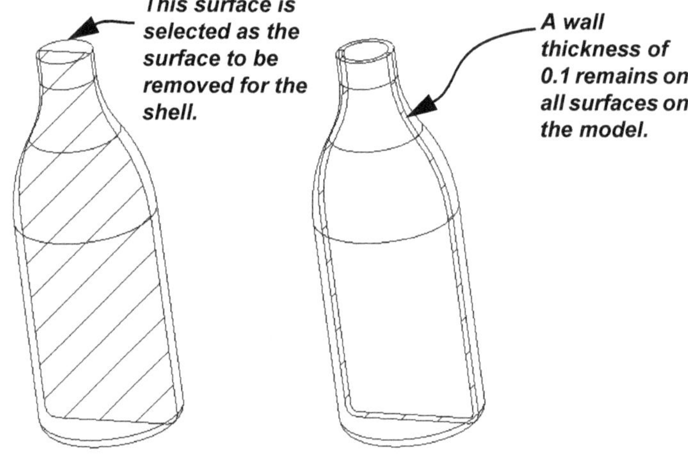

Figure 11–1

Closed/Internal Cavity Shell

A Closed/Internal cavity shell creates a model that has an internal hollow cavity, but does not remove a surface. For example, you could use a closed shell in modeling situations where a surface cannot be selected for removal (i.e., all surfaces have tangent edges).

General Steps

Use the following general steps to create a shell:

1. Start the creation of the shell.
2. Select the surfaces to remove.
3. Define the wall thickness.

4. (Optional) Select surfaces with a non-default wall thickness.
5. (Optional) Exclude surfaces to create a partial shell.

Step 1 - Start the creation of the shell.

To start the creation of a shell, click (Shell) in the Engineering group in the *Model* tab. The *Shell* dashboard displays with all of the options available for creating shells, as shown in Figure 11–2.

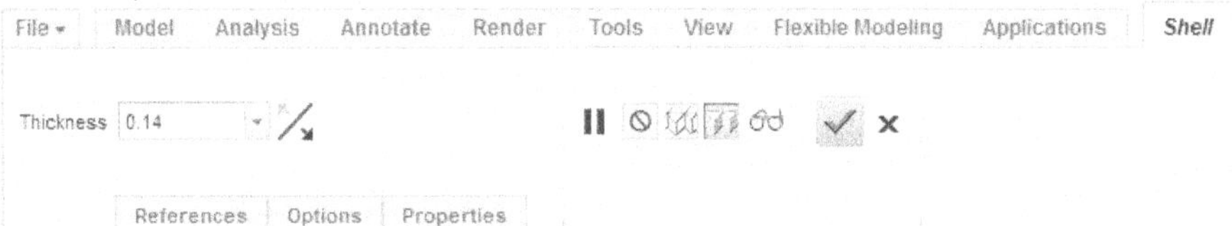

Figure 11–2

Step 2 - Select the surfaces to remove.

By default, a closed/internal shell is created. If the intent is to create a closed/internal shell, you can continue to the next step.

- To create an open shell, select the surface you want to remove. To remove multiple surfaces, press and hold <Ctrl> while selecting.
- To view or make changes to the selected references, open the References panel option in the *Shell* dashboard.
- Figure 11–3 shows the References panel with a single surface selected for removal.

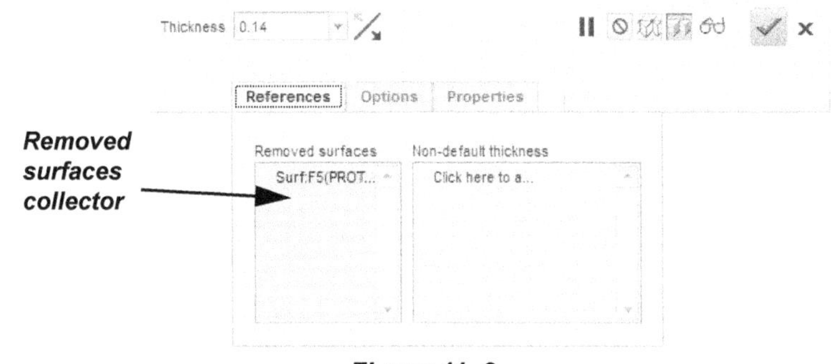

Figure 11–3

Shell Restrictions

The geometry of the model can control whether or not a shell feature can be added to the model. Some additional restrictions are:

- The surface that is being removed for a shell must be surrounded by edges (i.e., not a fully revolved feature). Alternatively, use a closed shell.
- While creating a shell, you cannot select surfaces in multiple collectors. For example, a surface cannot be selected in both the Removed surfaces and Non-default thickness collectors.

Step 3 - Define the wall thickness.

You can accept the default wall thickness value or enter a new value. To enter a new value, select the *Thickness* field in the *Shell* tab and enter a new value. You can also select a value in the drop-down list, as shown in Figure 11–4. The drop-down list displays the most recently used values.

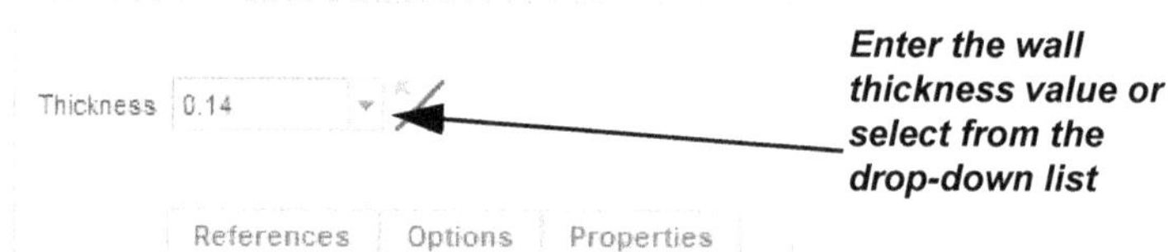

Figure 11–4

The wall thickness value for a shell feature can be positive or negative. Use a positive or negative value depending on whether the initial geometry represents the final shape of the inside or outside of the model. Figure 11–5 shows the difference between adding the shell value as a positive (left side) or negative (right side) value.

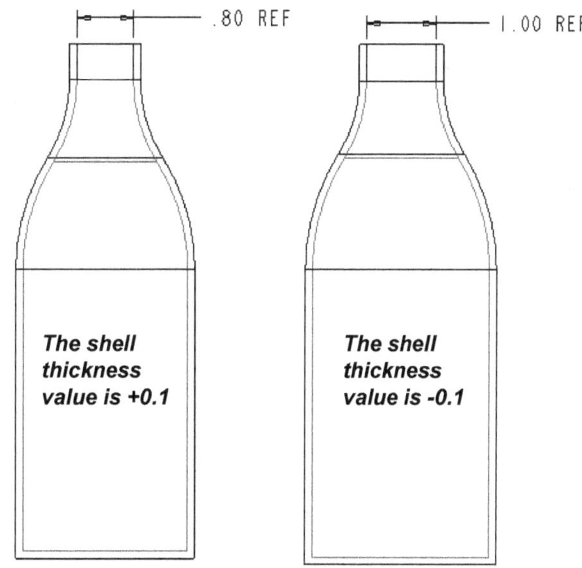

Figure 11–5

Step 4 - (Optional) Select surfaces with a non-default wall thickness.

By default, all walls in a shell feature have a constant thickness. However, you do have the option of applying a different wall thickness to selected surfaces. This enables you to have greater design flexibility when using shell features in your models.

To add a non-default wall thickness, open the References panel in the *Shell* tab and activate the *Non-default thickness* collector. Select the surface for which you are defining the non-default wall thickness and enter a dimension, as shown in Figure 11–6.

Multiple surfaces can be selected and assigned a non-default wall thickness by pressing and holding <Ctrl> while selecting references.

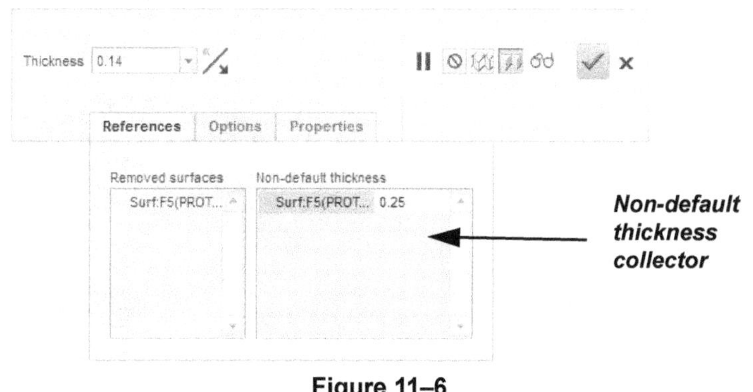

Figure 11–6

You can also activate the Non-default thickness collector using the shortcut menu.

Figure 11–7 shows an example in which the thickness at the bottom of a bottle was assigned a different thickness value than the other surfaces in the model.

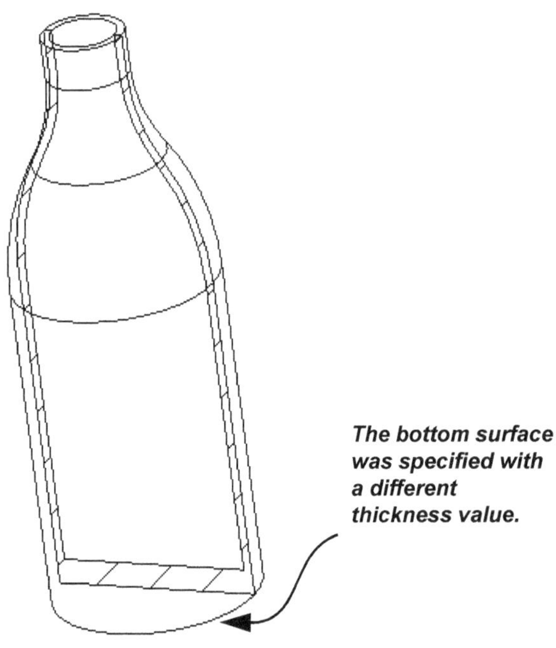

Figure 11–7

Step 5 - (Optional) Exclude surfaces to create a partial shell.

By default, the shell feature affects the whole model, as shown in Figure 11–8. However, you have the option of excluding some surfaces from the shell. The excluded surfaces remain intact after the shell feature creation.

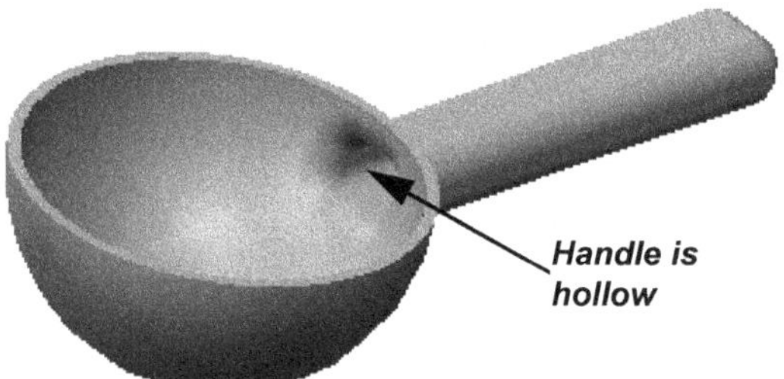

Figure 11–8

To exclude surfaces from the shell feature, open the Options panel in the *Shell* dashboard and activate the *Excluded surfaces* field. Then, select the required surfaces shown in Figure 11–9.

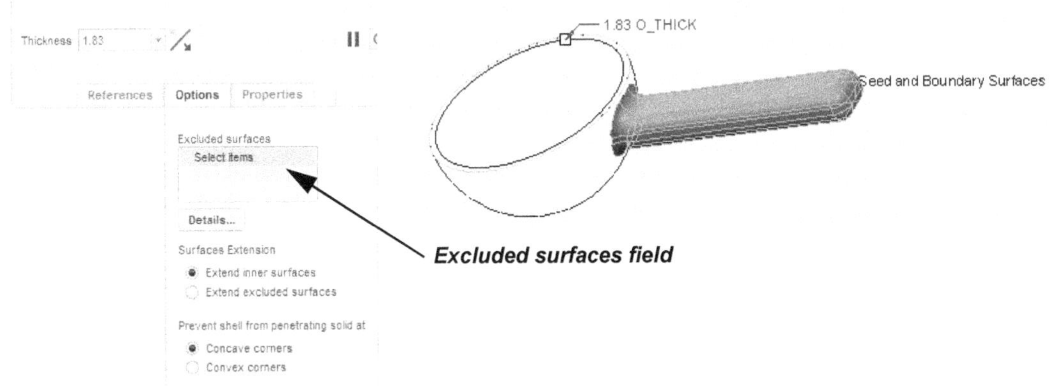

Figure 11–9

The options available in the Options panel are described as follows:

Extend inner surfaces	Create a cover over the inner surfaces of the shell feature
Extend excluded surfaces	Create a cover over the inner surfaces of the shell feature.
Concave corners	Prevent the shell from cutting through the solid at any concave corners
Convex corners	Prevent the shell from cutting through the solid at any convex corners.

Figure 11–10 shows the model with a partial shell. Note that the handle is filled with material.

Figure 11–10

To complete the shell feature, click ✓ (Complete Feature) in the *Shell* dashboard.

11.2 Creating Drafts

A draft feature creates sloped or angled surfaces at a maximum of +/- 89.9°.

General Steps

Use the following general steps to create a draft:

1. Start the creation of the draft.
2. Select the surfaces that require drafting.
3. Select the draft hinges.
4. Define the pull direction.
5. Enter the draft dimension.

Step 1 - Start the creation of the draft.

To start the creation of a draft, click (Draft) in the Engineering group in the *Model* tab. The *Draft* dashboard displays with all of the options available to create drafts, as shown in Figure 11–11.

Figure 11–11

Step 2 - Select the surfaces that require drafting.

Select the surface that you want to draft directly on the model. Single or multiple surfaces can be selected for drafting.

Once a surface has been selected, it displays an Individual Surfaces tag. The References panel updates to indicate that **Individual Surfaces** have been selected, as shown in Figure 11–12.

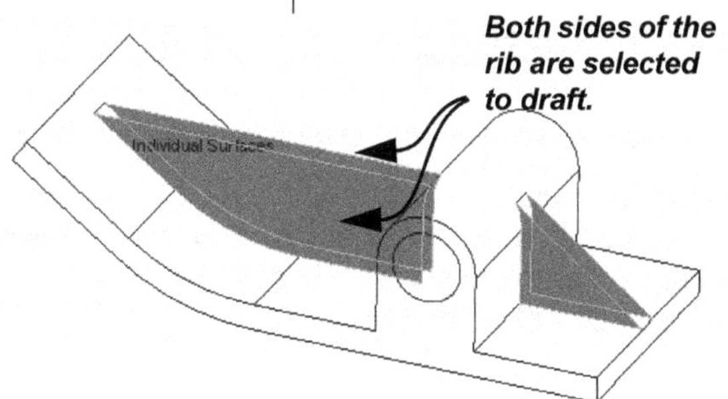

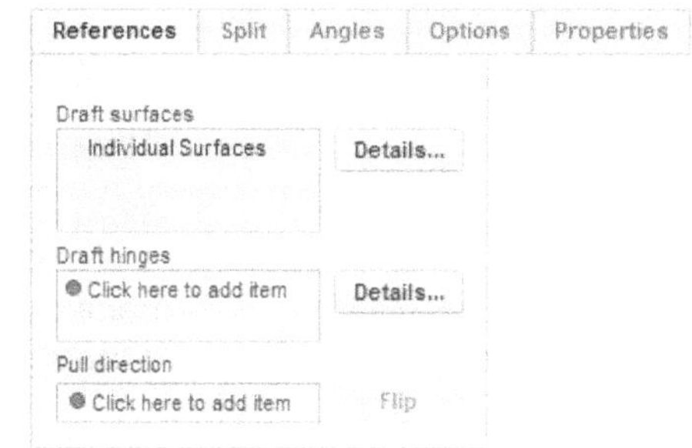

Figure 11–12

To select multiple surfaces, press and hold <Ctrl>. Even if multiple surfaces are selected, the **Individual Surfaces** tag remains, and each surface is highlighted in green.

Step 3 - Select the draft hinges.

The draft hinge is an internal axis that represents the pivot line (or *hinge*) about which the drafted surfaces rotate when the draft angle is applied. The draft hinge exists at the intersection of the draft surface and the draft hinge surface. The draft hinge surface is not required to physically intersect the draft surfaces. The angle can be measured from an implicit intersection.

Once draft surfaces have been selected, you must select the draft hinge. It can be defined directly in the *Draft* tab or using the References panel. To define the hinge using either of these locations, select the *Draft hinges* collector to activate and then select a planar surface, edge, or curve on the model. Once the draft hinge is selected, the draft angle displays on the model, as shown in Figure 11–13.

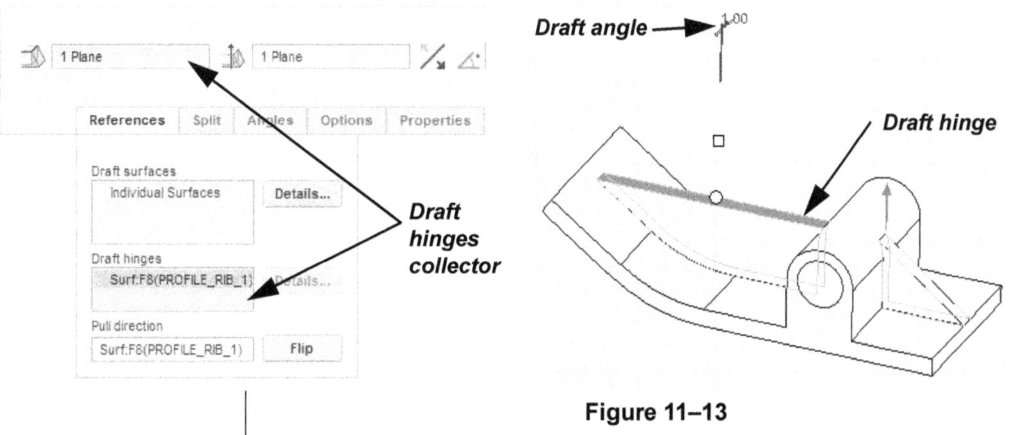

Figure 11–13

Step 4 - Define the pull direction.

The pull direction represents the direction in which the positive mold is being removed from the negative. Click (Reverse Pull Direction) in the *Draft* dashboard or click **Flip** in the References panel to reverse the pull direction. This also enables you to change the draft direction, as shown in Figure 11–14.

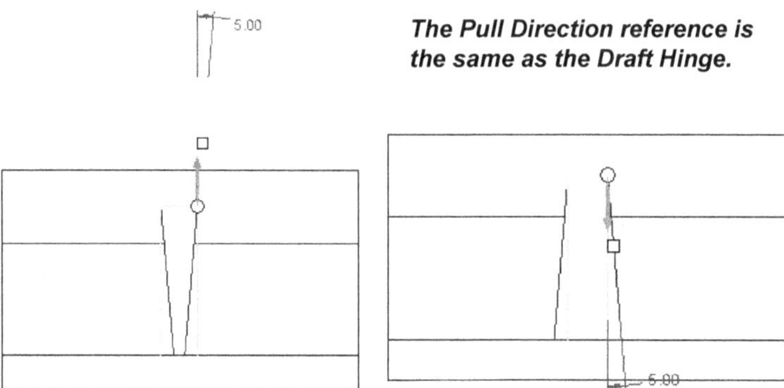

Figure 11–14

By default, the pull direction is assigned the same reference as the draft hinge (as long as it is a surface). This can be changed directly in the *Draft* tab or in the References panel. To define the pull direction reference using either of the locations shown in Figure 11–15, activate the *Pull Direction* collector and select a planar surface, axis, or two points.

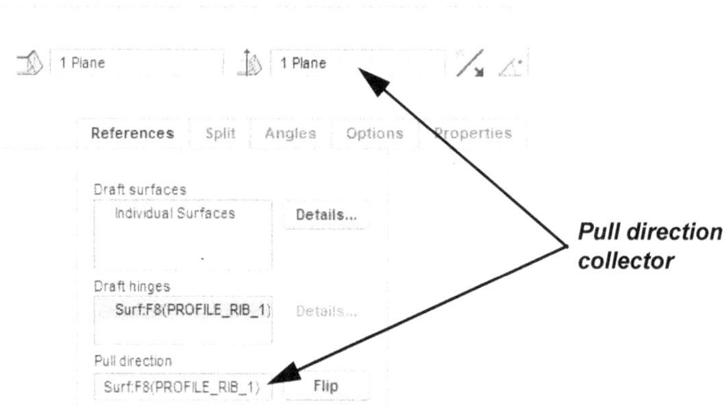

Figure 11–15

Step 5 - Enter the draft dimension.

To reverse the draft angle direction, click (Reverse Angle) or enter a negative value.

The last step is to enter the draft angle value of less than or equal to 89.9°, as shown in Figure 11–16.

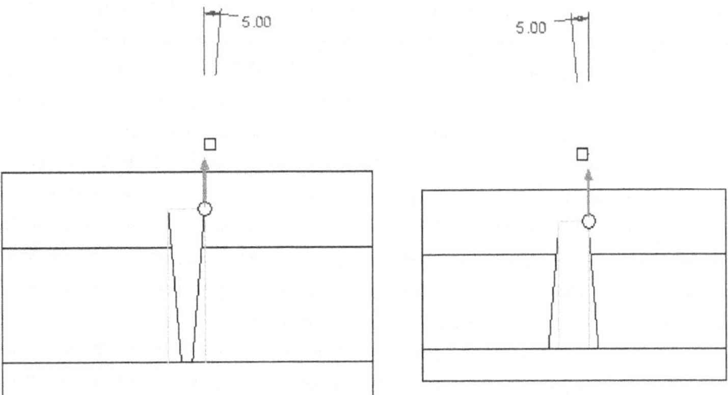

Figure 11–16

To complete the draft, click (Complete Feature) in the *Draft* dashboard.

Practice 11a Y Pipe

Practice Objectives

- Create simple round features to specified edges on the model.
- Create a Shell feature that removes required geometry from the model.

In this practice, you will open an existing part and complete it by adding rounds and then shelling the part. Consider the feature order when working with the shell. Try to create all of the rounds before creating a shell. The completed part displays as shown in Figure 11–17.

Figure 11–17

Task 1 - Open a part file.

1. Set the working directory to the *Chapter 11\practice 11a* folder.
2. Open **y_pipe.prt**.
3. Set the model display as follows:
   - *(Datum Display Filters)*: All Off
   - *(Spin Center)*: Off
   - *(Display Style)*: (No Hidden)

Task 2 - Create a round.

1. Create a round with a *Radius* of **0.38** on the edge shown in Figure 11–18.

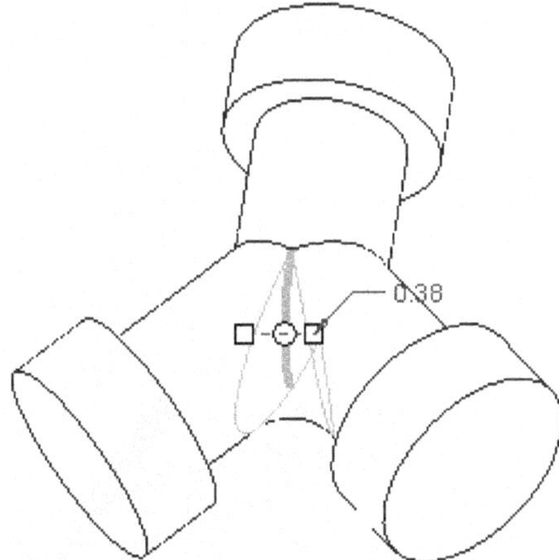

Figure 11–18

Task 3 - Create another round.

1. Create round with a *Radius* of **1.0** on the two edges shown in Figure 11–19.

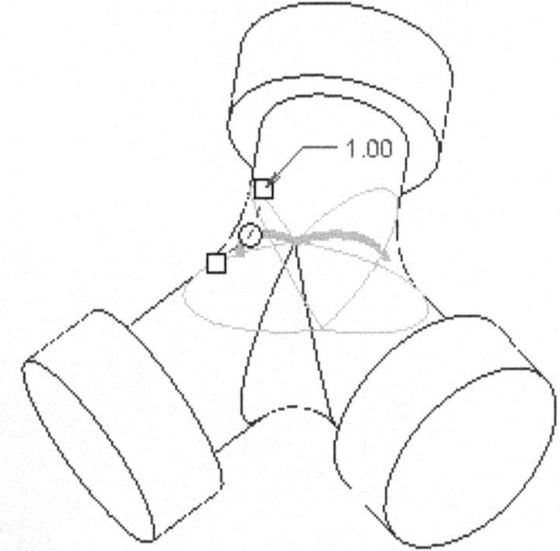

Figure 11–19

Task 4 - Shell a part.

1. In the Engineering group in the *Model* tab, click (Shell) to create a shell. Hold <Ctrl> and select the three surfaces shown in Figure 11–20.

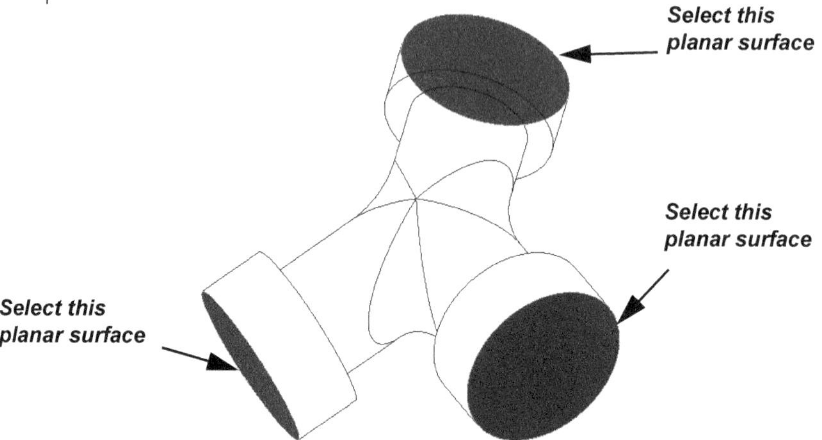

Figure 11–20

2. Set the *Thickness* to **0.125** and complete the shell.

3. Set the model display to (Shading With Edges). The completed part displays as shown in Figure 11–21.

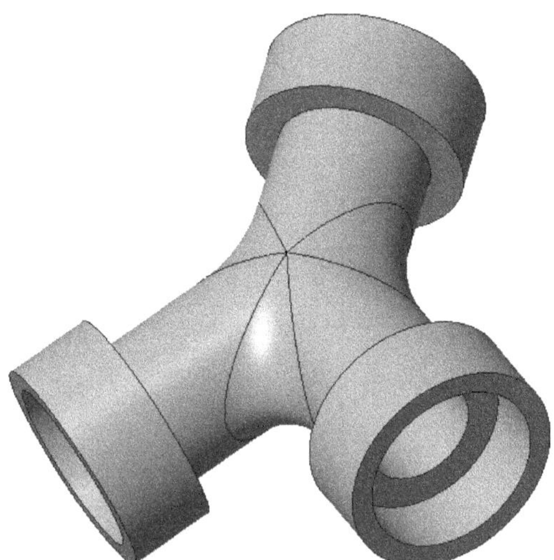

Figure 11–21

4. Save the part and erase it from memory.

Practice 11b Shell an Axle Bracket

Practice Objectives

- Change a wall to have a unique thickness.
- Investigate the order of feature creation.

In this practice, you will create a partial shell of a model. The completed part is shown in Figure 11–22.

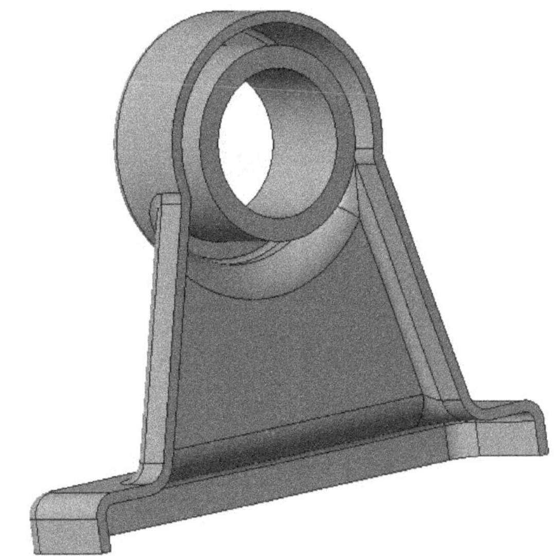

Figure 11–22

Task 1 - Open a part file.

1. Set the working directory to the *Chapter 11\practice 11b* folder.
2. Open **axle_bracket.prt**.
3. Set the model display as follows:
   - *(Datum Display Filters)*: All Off
   - *(Spin Center)*: Off
   - *(Display Style)*: (Shading With Edges)

Task 2 - Create a shell feature in the model.

1. In the Engineering group, click (Shell).
2. For the surfaces to remove, spin the model and select the two surfaces shown in Figure 11–23. The model displays as shown in Figure 11–24.

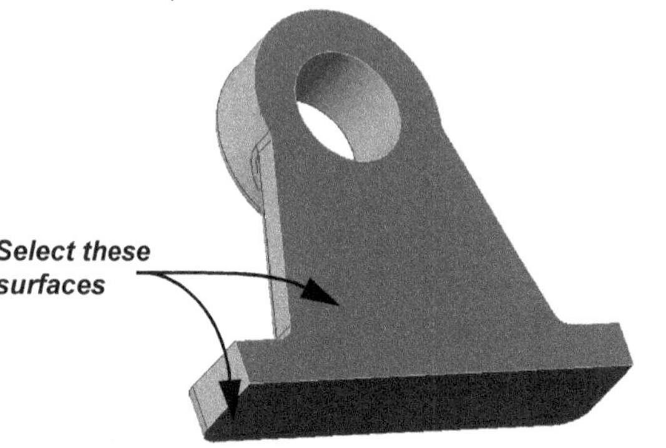

Figure 11–23

Figure 11–24

3. Set the *Thickness* to **4.00**.

Task 3 - Set one wall to have a unique thickness.

1. Right-click and select **Non-default thickness**.
2. Select the surface shown in Figure 11–25.
3. Set the additional dimension to **8.00**, as shown in Figure 11–26.

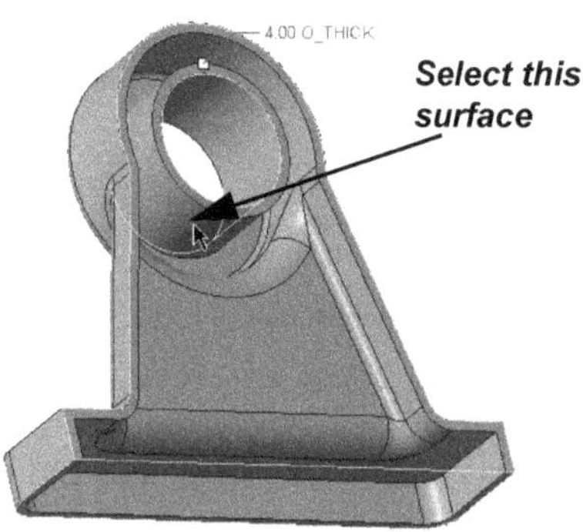

Figure 11–25

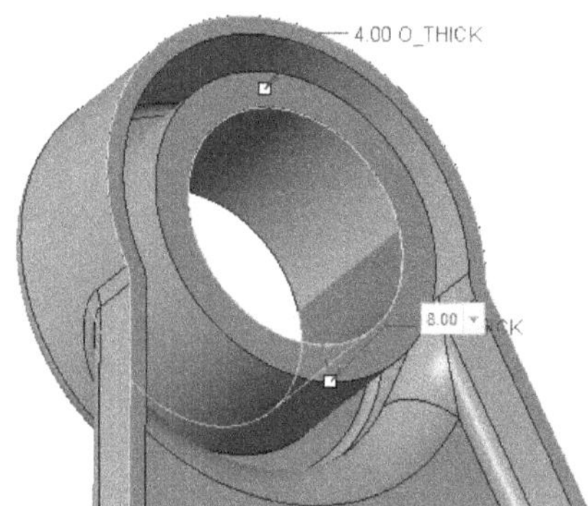

Figure 11–26

4. Click (Complete Feature).

Task 4 - Add a round to the model and investigate the shell behavior.

1. Return the model to default orientation.

2. Select the edge shown in Figure 11–27, right-click and select Round.

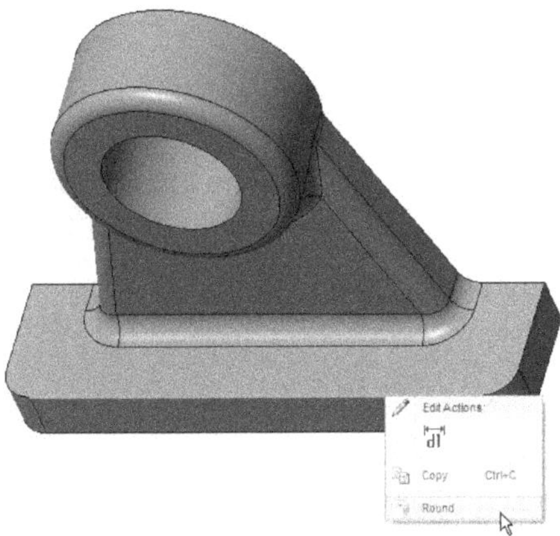

Figure 11–27

3. Set the *Radius* to **8.00**.

4. Click (Complete Feature).

5. In the In-graphics toolbar, click (Saved Orientations) and select **BACK**. Note that the surface of the shell does not take on the contour of the round, since the round was create after the shell, as shown in Figure 11–28.

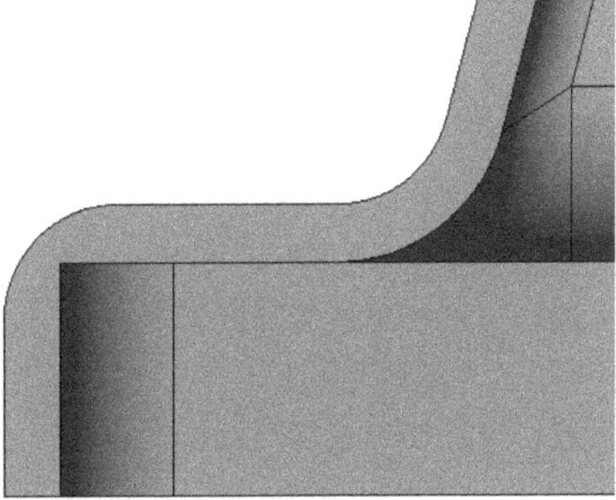

Figure 11–28

6. Select **Shell 1** in the model tree.

This procedure is referred to as reordering features. This is covered in detail in another chapter.

7. Drag the Shell to be positioned after **Round 4**, as shown in Figure 11–29.

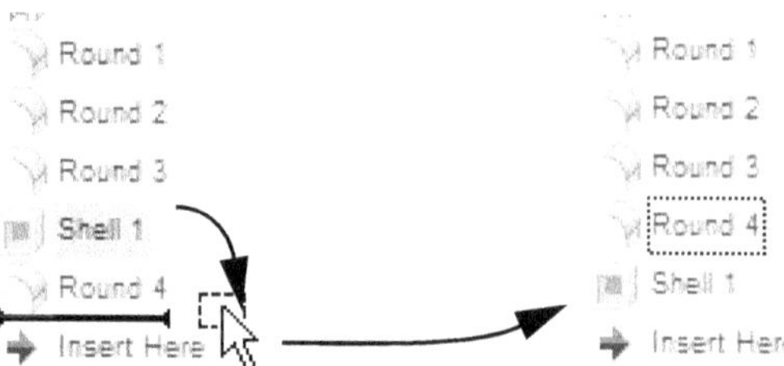

Figure 11–29

8. The model updates such that the shell now follows the contour of the round, because it now regenerates after the round. The result is shown in Figure 11–30.

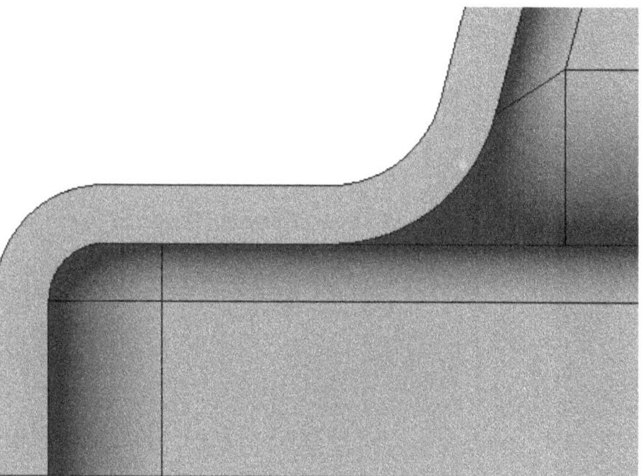

Figure 11–30

9. Save the part and erase it from memory.

Practice 11c Skid Shoe

Practice Objective

- Create a draft feature with a specified draft hinge and angle dimension.

In this practice, you will open an existing part. Since you will create a cast part, drafts must be added. The finished model is shown in Figure 11–31.

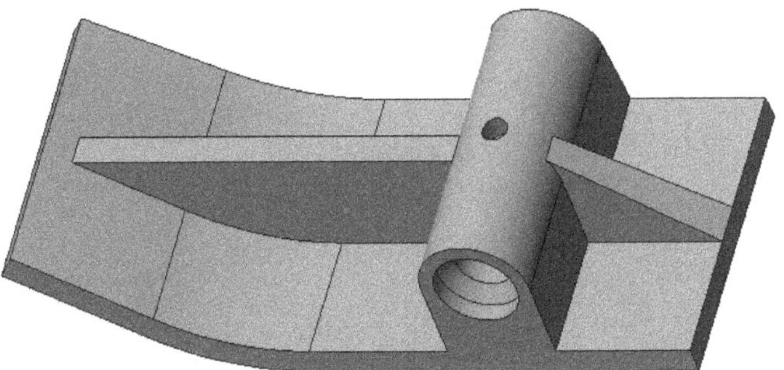

Figure 11–31

Task 1 - Open a part file.

1. Set the working directory to the *Chapter 11\practice 11c* folder.
2. Open **skid_shoe2.prt.**
3. Set the model display as follows:
    - *(Datum Display Filters)*: All Off
    - *(Spin Center)*: Off
    - *(Display Style)*: (Shading With Edges)
    - *(Annotation Display)*: Off

Task 2 - Add draft to the part.

The shading is toggled off for clarity.

1. In the Engineering group in the *Model* tab, click (Draft) to create the draft.

2. Hold <Ctrl> and select the four planar surfaces shown in Figure 11–32.

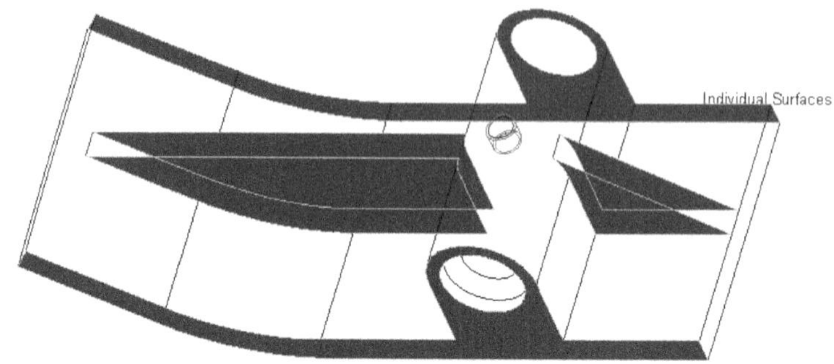

Figure 11–32

3. Right-click and select **Draft Hinges**.

4. For the draft hinge, select the surface shown in Figure 11–33. (You might need to zoom in on the part.)

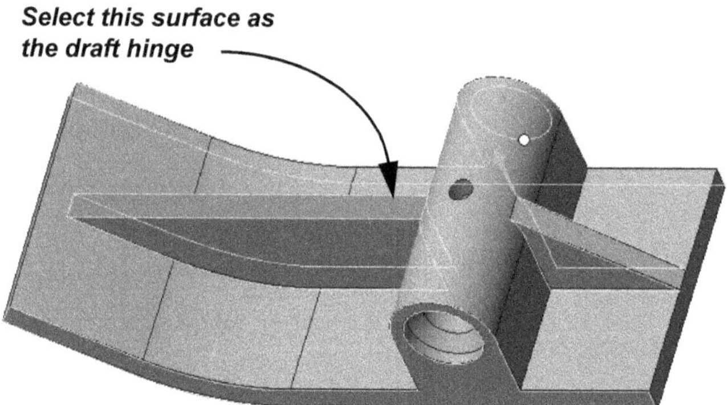

Figure 11–33

You can click (Reverse Angle) and (Reverse Pull Direction) as required, to achieve the result shown.

5. Set the draft *Angle* to **3.0**. Ensure that the draft is created in the direction as shown in Figure 11–34.

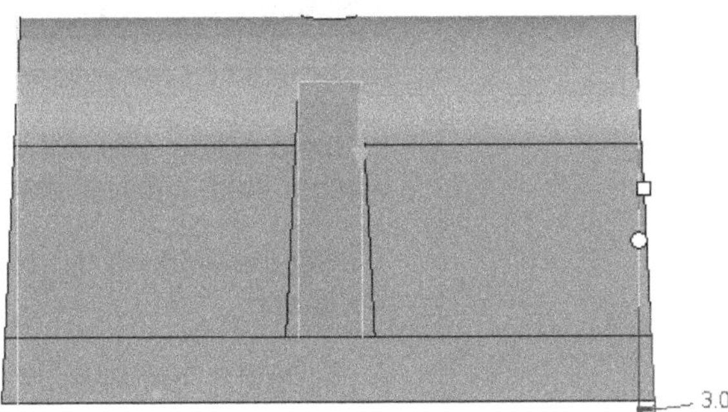

Figure 11–34

6. Click (Complete Feature) to complete the draft. The part displays as shown in Figure 11–35.

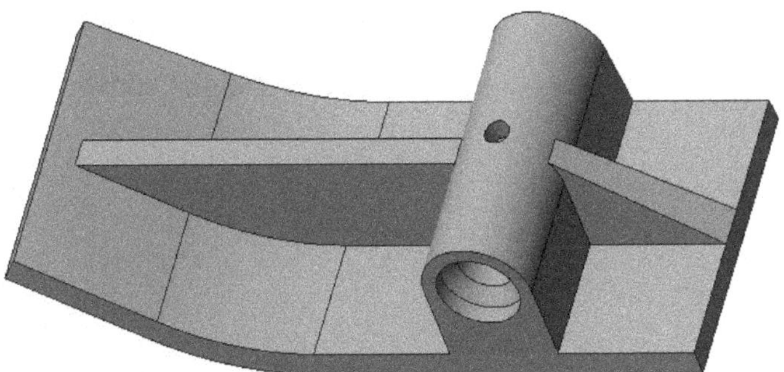

Figure 11–35

7. Save the part and erase it from memory.

Practice 11d (Optional) Tank

Practice Objective

- Create a new part using sketched and engineering features.

In this practice, you will create a tank that holds windshield washer fluid. Limited instructions are given.

1. Set the working directory to the *Chapter 11\practice 11d* folder.
2. Create a new part file and set the *Name* to **tank**.
3. Set the model display as follows:
    - (*Datum Display Filters*): All Off
    - (*Spin Center*): Off
    - (*Display Style*): (Shading With Edges)
4. Create the part shown in Figure 11–36.

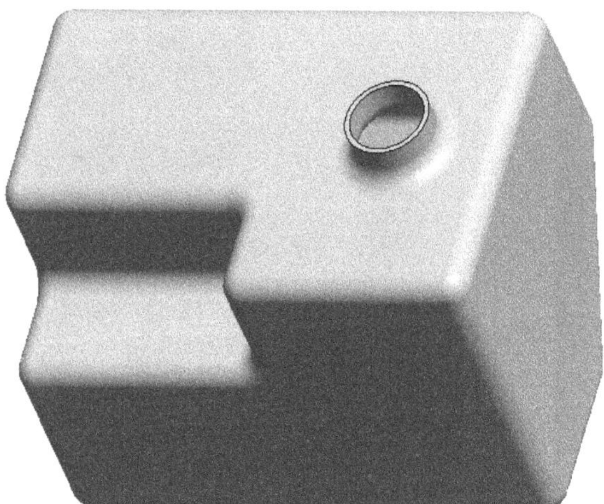

Figure 11–36

5. Consider the following:
    - Form and shape of the base feature.
    - Feature order.
    - This part can be created using no more then five features.

6. Dimensions are shown in Figure 11–37.

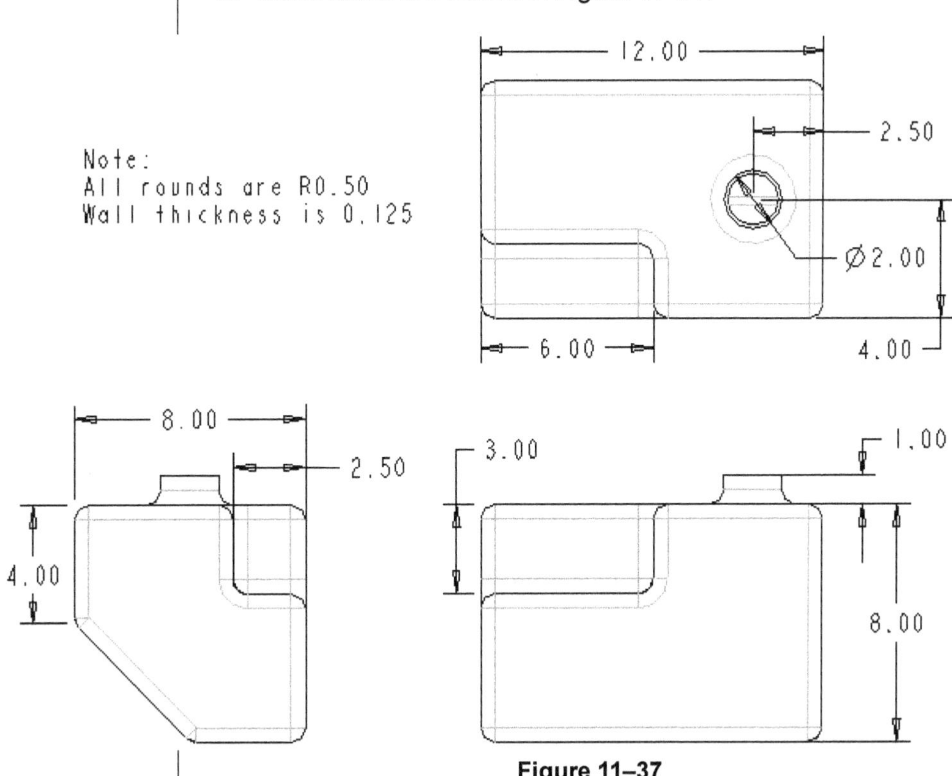

Figure 11–37

7. Save the part and erase it from memory.

Chapter Review Questions

1. Which of the following statements is true regarding the creation of a draft?
   a. Multiple surfaces can be selected for drafting by pressing and holding <Ctrl> while selecting the surfaces.
   b. Multiple surfaces can be selected as references when defining the draft hinge by pressing and holding <Ctrl> while selecting the surfaces.
   c. To define the draft hinge reference, you can only select an existing edge on the model.
   d. The pull direction reference must be a reference independent of the draft hinge reference.
2. A closed/internal shell is the default shell type.
   a. True
   b. False
3. Which of the following statements is true regarding shell features? (Select all that apply.)
   a. To create an open shell, based on the default options, you must select which surface(s) are to be removed.
   b. The thickness of a shell can be manually entered in the dashboard or you can select from the drop-down list values.
   c. A closed shell cannot have walls of varying thickness.
   d. Wall thickness can be added to the inside or outside of a model by entering a positive or negative wall thickness value.

Command Summary

Button	Command	Location
	Draft	• **Ribbon:** *Model* tab in the Engineering group
	Shell	• **Ribbon:** *Model* tab in the Engineering group

Sweeps and Blends

Sweep features can be used to create advanced geometry that standard extrusions cannot create. These features enable you to effectively sketch a cross-section and sweep it along a defined trajectory.

Learning Objectives in this Chapter

- Create a sweep feature and set the required options to create the required geometry.
- Create a blend feature and set the required options by sketching sections and ensuring they each have the same number of entities.
- Sketch or select the section for the blend feature various tools.
- Ensure that each section has the same number of entities to create the blend using tools such as Blend Vertex or Trim.

12.1 Creating a Sweep Feature

A sweep feature form enables you to create advanced geometry that cannot be created using an extrusion. Basic sweep features enable you to create geometry by sweeping a cross-section along a single trajectory, as shown in Figure 12–1.

Advance sweeps using multiple trajectories are explained in the Creo Parametric: Advanced Part class.

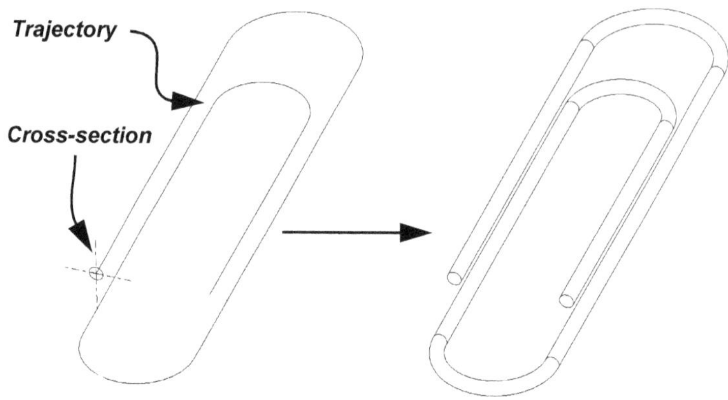

Figure 12–1

General Steps

Use the following steps as a general guideline to create a sweep:

1. Start the creation of a sweep.
2. Define the trajectory for the sweep.
3. Sketch the cross-section for the sweep.

Step 1 - Start the creation of a sweep.

To start the creation of a sweep, click (Sweep) in the Shapes group in the *Model* tab. The *Sweep* dashboard displays, as shown in Figure 12–2.

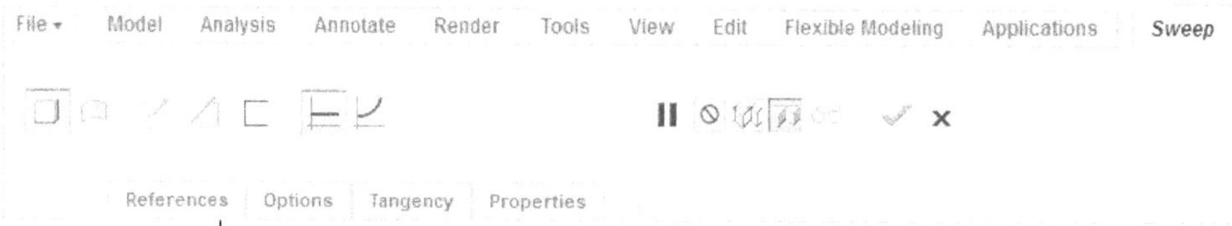

Figure 12–2

A sweep can add or remove material by clicking (Remove Material). You can also click (Thicken Sketch) and specify a *Thickness* value.

Step 2 - Define the trajectory for the sweep.

The trajectory defines how the geometry of the feature is created. The entities can be an open or closed loop. The trajectory can be a selected edge, curve, or sketch that exists in the model. Once you select a trajectory it displays in the Reference panel, as shown in Figure 12–3. The cross-section remains normal to the trajectory as it is swept.

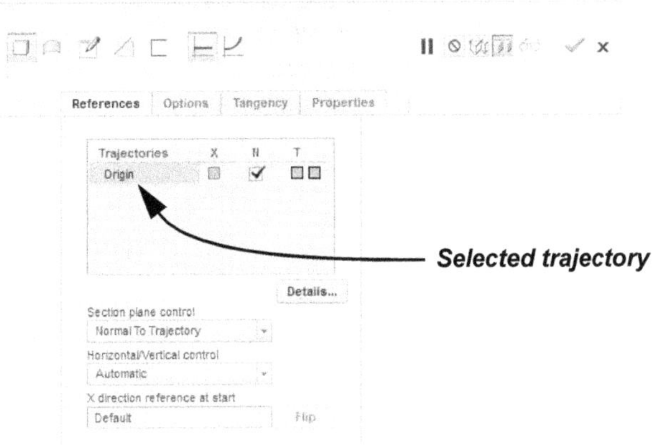

Figure 12–3

Select Trajectory

You can select existing edges or datum curves to define the trajectory for the sweep. Selecting the Reference panel and clicking **Details** can be used to select multiple curves to define the trajectory, as shown in Figure 12–4.

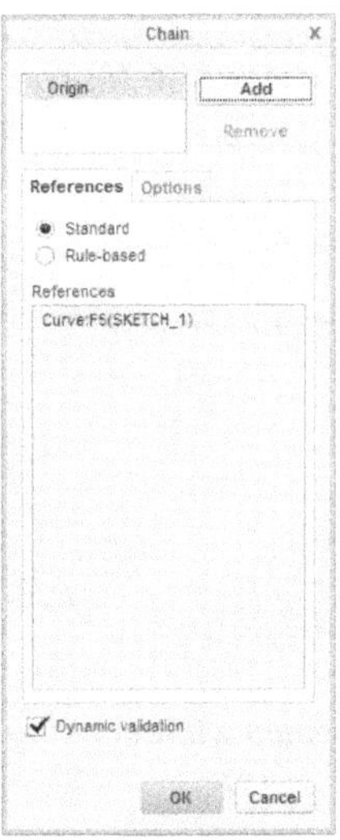

Figure 12–4

Sketched Trajectory

You can sketch the trajectory by clicking (Datum) and clicking (Sketch). This creates a sketched curve that is copied into the swept feature with an associated link. Any subsequent modification to the sketch is reflected in the swept feature.

Additionally, you can select the *Model* tab and click (Sketch).

Options Panel for Sweep

If the trajectory forms an open loop and solid geometry already exists in the model, you can define whether the cross-section merges to the existing geometry at both ends of the trajectory or remains free, as shown in Figure 12–5.

Figure 12–5

By default, the merge option is not selected. This option enables the cross-section to remain perpendicular to the trajectory at all points along it. For the **Merge Ends** option, at least one end of the swept feature must have a surface to merge into. If **Merge Ends** is selected and is not a viable option, the feature aborts. The sweep shown on the right in Figure 12–6 is created using the **Merge Ends** option, while the model shown on the left is created without it.

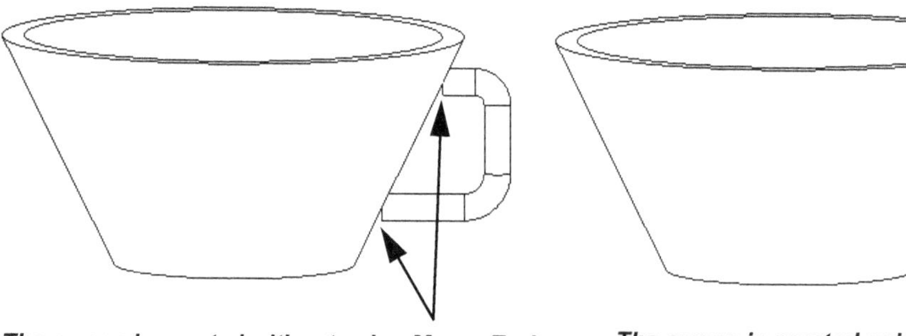

The sweep is created without using Merge Ends ***The sweep is created using Merge Ends***

Figure 12–6

Start Point

The start point of a trajectory defines the location where the cross-section is sketched. The start point, identified with an arrow, must be at one of the trajectory endpoints for an open trajectory. It can be at any internal point for a closed trajectory.

Once a trajectory has been selected from the existing geometry, you can change the start point by selecting the arrow on the trajectory, right-click, and select **Flip Chain Direction**. You can also change the start point by selecting the References panel and clicking **Details**. This opens the Chain dialog box, as shown in Figure 12–7. Select the *Options* tab and click **Flip** to move the start point to the other end of the trajectory.

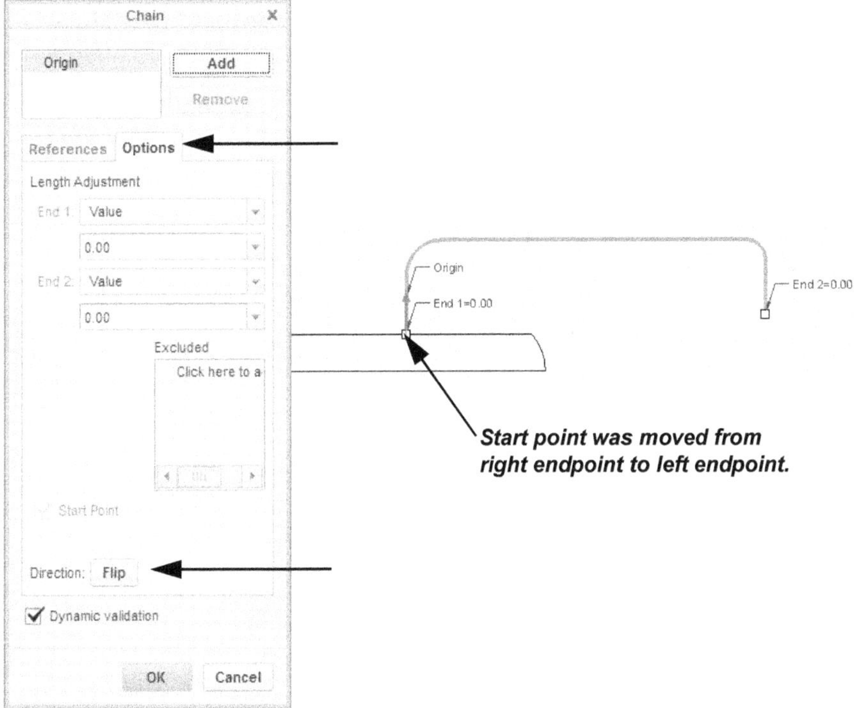

Figure 12–7

Step 3 - Sketch the cross-section for the sweep.

To make it easier to sketch and locate the cross-hairs in the sketch, consider clicking (Sketch View) to orient the model in 2D.

Once the trajectory has been defined, click (Create or Edit Section). The *Sketch* tab becomes active. Cross-hairs display identifying the start point on an open trajectory, as shown on the left in Figure 12–8. Sketch the cross-section for the sweep relative to the start point. It maintains this relationship along the entire trajectory.

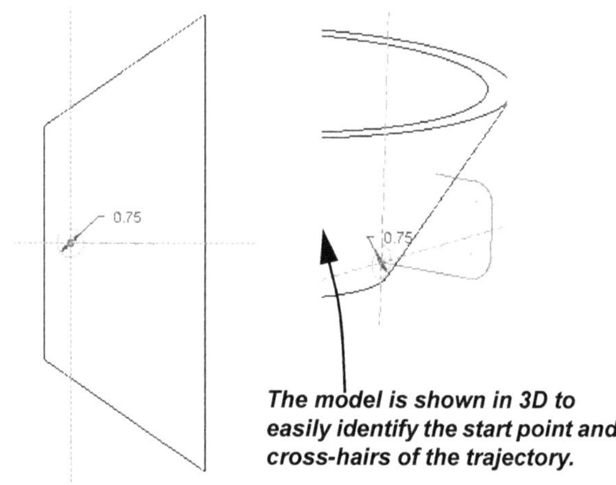

Figure 12–8

Figure 12–9 shows an example of a closed trajectory.

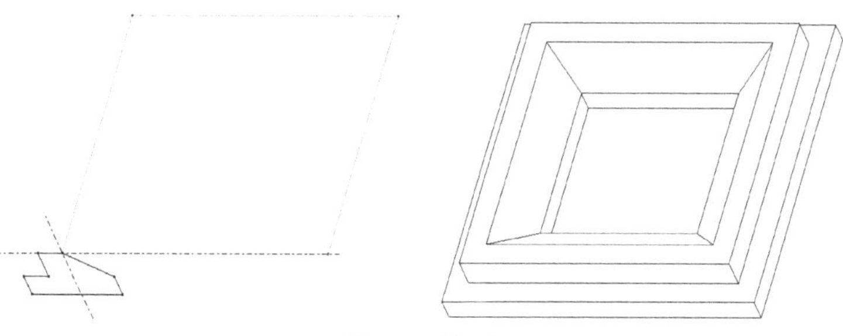

Figure 12–9

A cross-section does not have to lie directly on the cross-hairs. If the cross-section is offset, it maintains the offset as it travels along the trajectory.

If the cross-section overlaps itself as it travels along the trajectory, the feature might abort, as shown in Figure 12–10. If this occurs, edit the definition of the cross-section or trajectory to correct the failure.

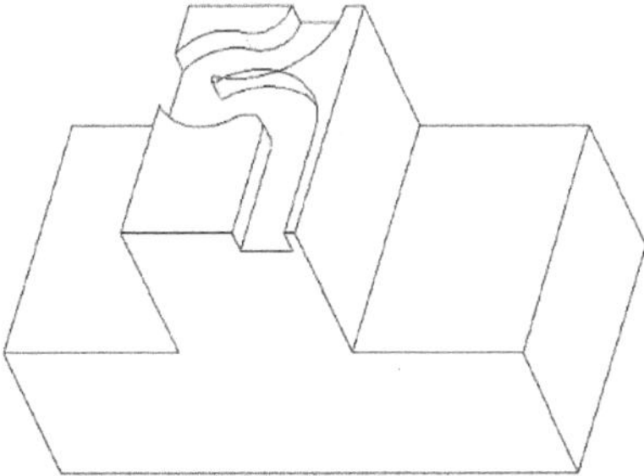

Figure 12–10

Sweeps can be made along trajectories consisting of non-tangent entities. Trajectory entities that are not tangent produce mitered corners, as shown in Figure 12–11.

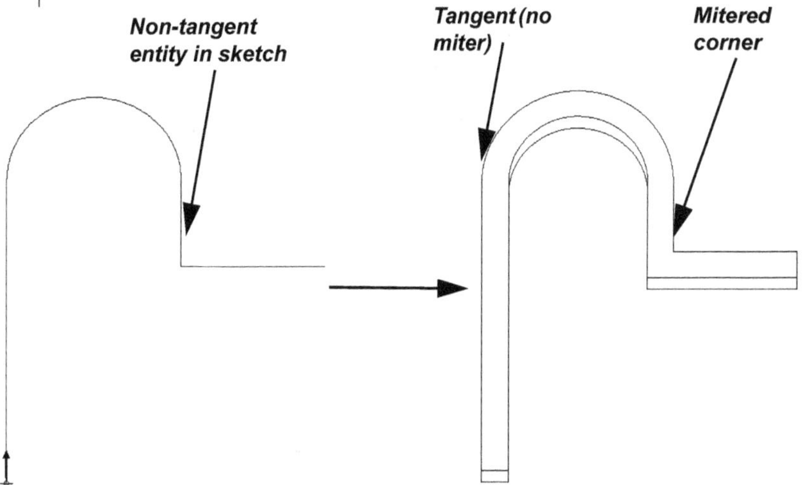

Figure 12–11

12.2 Creating a Blend Feature

A blend feature enables you to create advanced geometry that cannot be created using a single extrusion. The geometry is defined by blending between multiple sub-sections, as shown in Figure 12–12.

A blend can either remove or add material to a model.

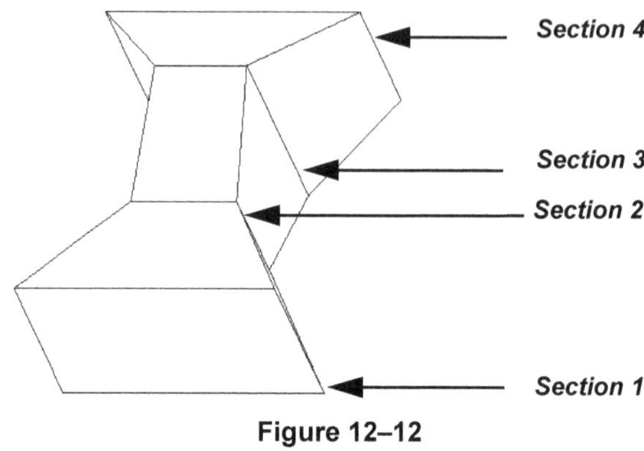

Figure 12–12

General Steps

Use the following general steps to create a parallel blend feature:

1. Start the creation of the blend feature.
2. Specify additional options for a blend.
3. Select or sketch the sections for the blend.
4. Complete the feature.

Step 1 - Start the creation of the blend feature.

To start the creation of a blend, select **Shapes>Blen** in the *Model* tab, as shown in Figure 12–13.

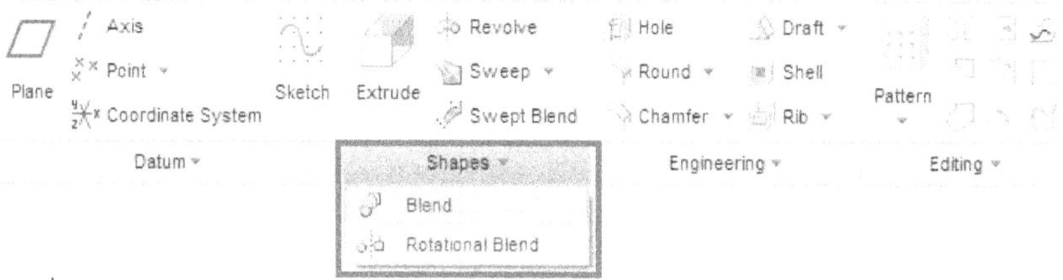

Figure 12–13

The *Blend* dashboard displays as shown in Figure 12–14.

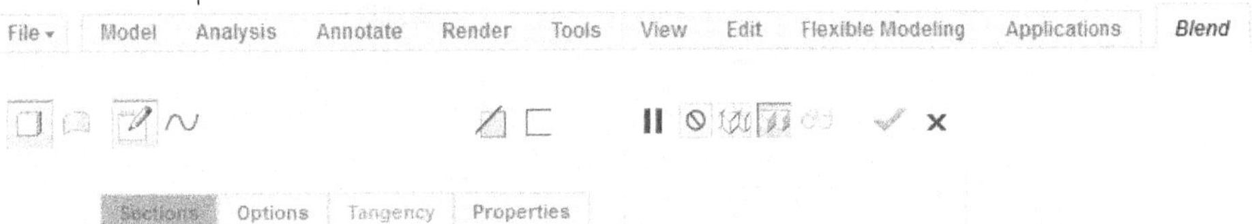

Figure 12–14

This training guide discusses simple parallel blend types. They are sections that are parallel with one another.

Step 2 - Specify additional options for a blend.

A blend can be created using the **Smooth** or **Straight** option, as shown in Figure 12–15.

- For a **Straight** Blend, the vertices of each adjacent section are connected with linear edges, as shown in Figure 12–16.
- For a **Smooth** Parallel Blend, a spline passes through the vertices of the intermediate sections, as shown in Figure 12–17.

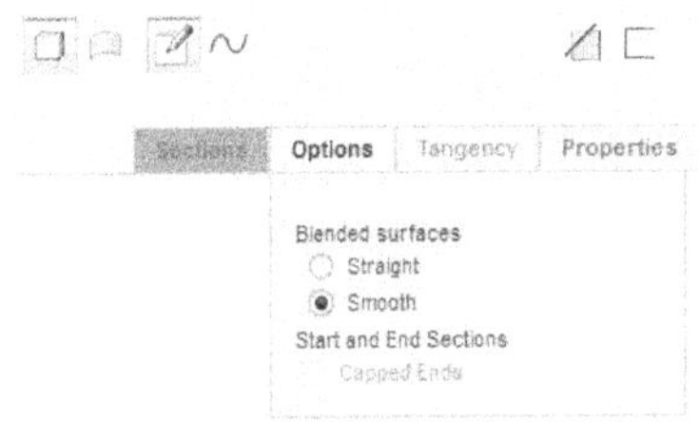

Figure 12–15

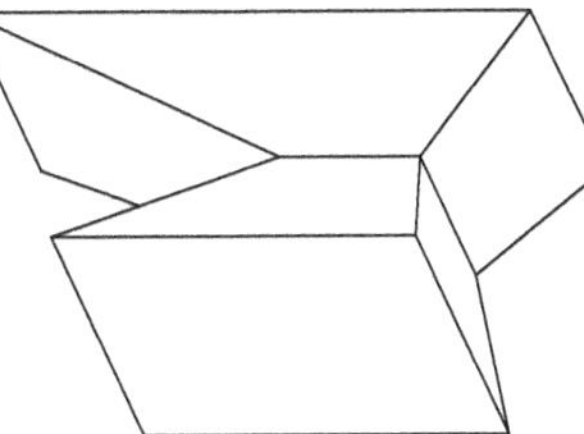

Figure 12–16

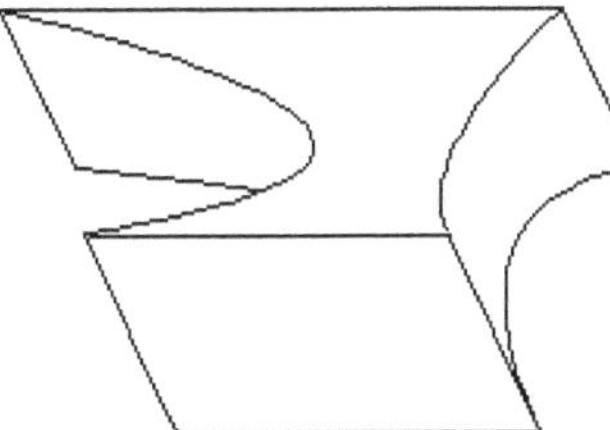

Figure 12–17

Step 3 - Select or sketch the sections for the blend.

A blend is created from multiple sections. At least two sections are required to create a blend, and they can be selected or sketched.

Selected Sections

To select the sections, click (Selected Sections) or enable **Selected sections** in the Sections panel, as shown in Figure 12–18. Click **Insert** to select additional sections.

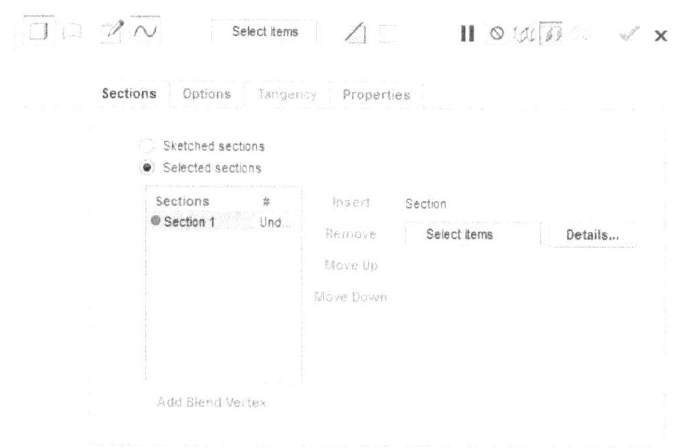

Figure 12–18

Sketched Section

As with any sketched feature, you must select a sketching plane and sketch orientation plane. You can select planes or surfaces as references. The sketch references must also be defined and can be datum planes, surfaces, edges, or vertices. To sketch the blend section, use the *Sketch* tab and the previously discussed tools.

How To: Create a Blend using Sketched Sections

You can also click (Offset Dimension) or (Reference) in the Blend dashboard to specify the Offset dimensional or Reference options.

1. Click (Sketched Sections), if required.
2. Click **Define** in the Sections panel, as shown in Figure 12–19. Additionally, right-click and select **Define Internal Sketch**. Then, select a sketching plane, orientation plane, and additional references.

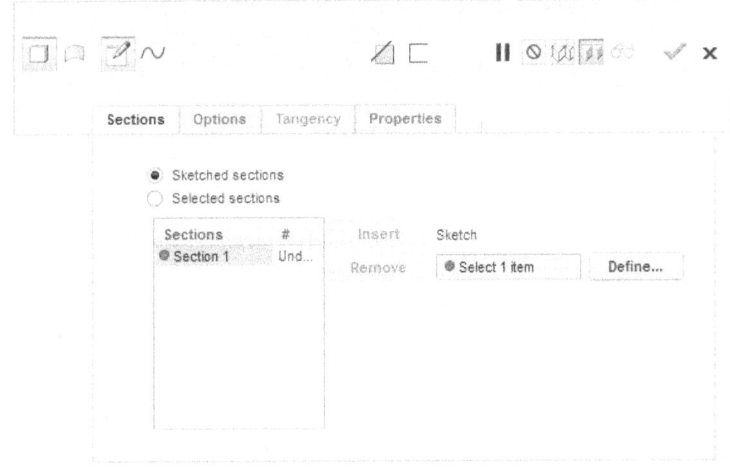

Figure 12–19

3. Sketch the first section using the *Sketch* tab and click ✓ (OK).
4. If required, click **Insert** to create a new section.
5. Specify a depth between the sections in the Sections panel.

The depth is determined by the offset option of the next section. You can use **Offset dimension** to enter a specified value, as shown in Figure 12–20. You can also select **Reference** and select an existing datum plane or surface, as shown in Figure 12–21.

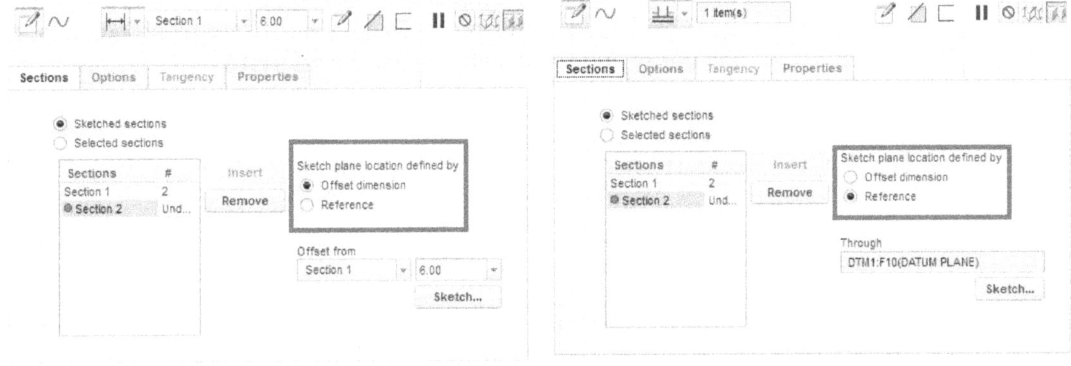

Figure 12–20

Figure 12–21

You can also right-click and select ***Sketch****.*

6. Click **Sketch** in the Sections panel or click (Sketched Sections) in the *Blend* dashboard to create an additional section. At least two sections are required to create a blend.
7. Sketch the next section and click ✓ (OK).
8. Add additional sections, as required.

Vertices

Each sub-section can contain geometry of any shape. However, each sub-section must have an equal number of vertices. Consider the following techniques for accomplishing this.

Equal Entities

(Divide) can be used in conjunction with construction entities to split the entities as required. For example, a circle must be broken into four arcs to blend a circle with a square, as shown in Figure 12–22.

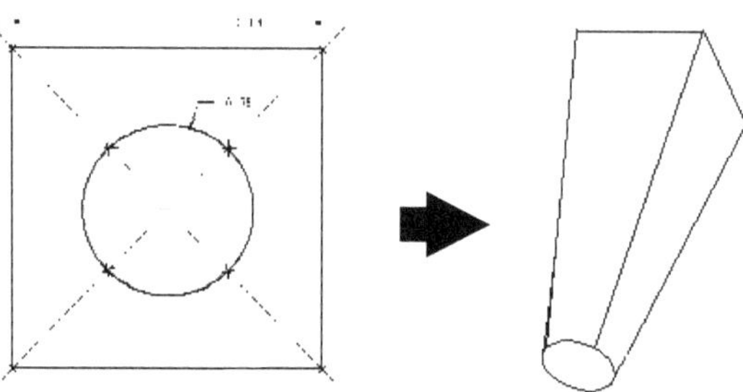

Figure 12–22

Blend Vertex

You can also click ***Setup>FeatureTools>Blend Vertex****.*

The **Blend Vertex** option can be used if the design intent calls for unequal numbers of vertices per section. Figure 12–23 shows a square section being blended with a triangular section. A Blend Vertex is placed on a triangle vertex, enabling the extra square vertex to blend to this point. To set a vertex for blending, select the vertex, right-click and select **Blend Vertex**.

A blended vertex cannot be located at the start point of a section.

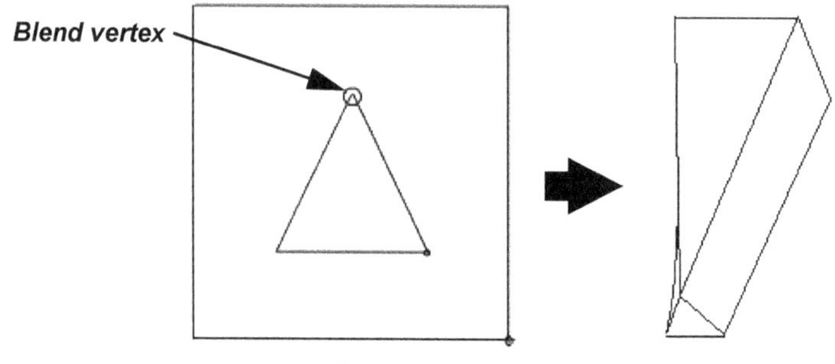

Figure 12–23

Sketcher Point

The first and last sub-sections in a parallel blend can consist of a sketcher point. This enables you to blend a sub-section with multiple entities to a single point, as shown in Figure 12–24. To add a sketcher point, click ⨯ (Point) and place the point on the sketch, as required.

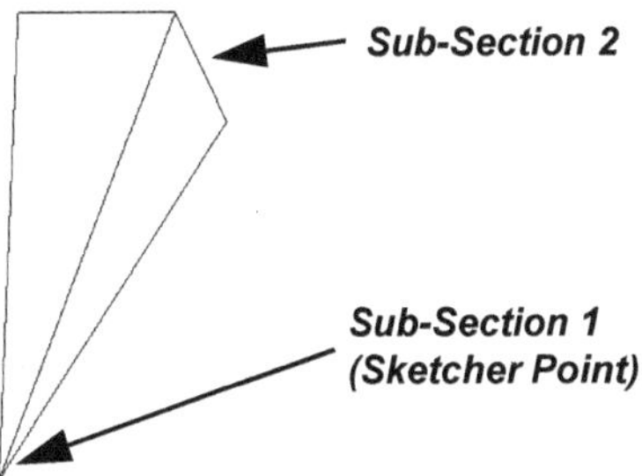

Figure 12–24

Start Point

A start point (indicated by a orange arrow) is located at the first vertex sketched in each sub-section. The Creo Parametric software creates the geometry for a blend by connecting these start points. It continues to match each subsequent vertex moving in a clockwise direction to create the feature.

*You can also select **Setup>Feature Tools> Start Point**.*

To move the start point, select the vertex that is going to be the start point, right-click and select **Start Point**. Figure 12–25 shows how the blended geometry can be affected when the start points for each section are not located in the same relative location for each sub-section.

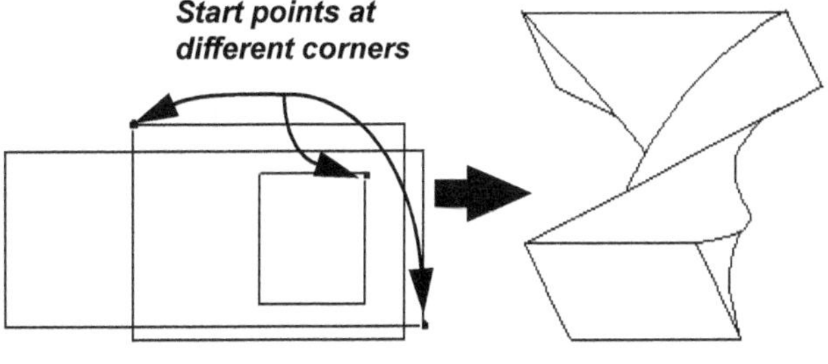

Figure 12–25

Step 4 - Complete the feature.

Once all the sections and options have been specified, click ✔ (Complete Feature) to complete the feature.

Practice 12a Paper Clip

Practice Objectives

- Create the sweep by selecting the curve for the trajectory.
- Sketch the profile for the swept feature by changing the start point.
- Sketch the profile entities to create required swept geometry.

In this practice, you will create a part using a sweep as the base feature, as shown in Figure 12–26. A sweep must have a trajectory and a section. Since trajectories can be sketched or selected, you will then select a trajectory.

Figure 12–26

Task 1 - Open a part file.

1. Set the working directory to the *Chapter 12/practice 12a* folder.

2. Open **paper_clip.prt.** The part contains a completed sketch that you will use as the trajectory for the sweep.

3. Set the model display as follows:

    - *(Datum Display Filters)*: All Off
    - *(Spin Center)*: Off
    - *(Display Style)*: (No Hidden)

4. In the Shapes group in the *Model* tab, click (Sweep).

5. Select **Sketch 1** as the trajectory. The system automatically selects a start point as shown in Figure 12–27.

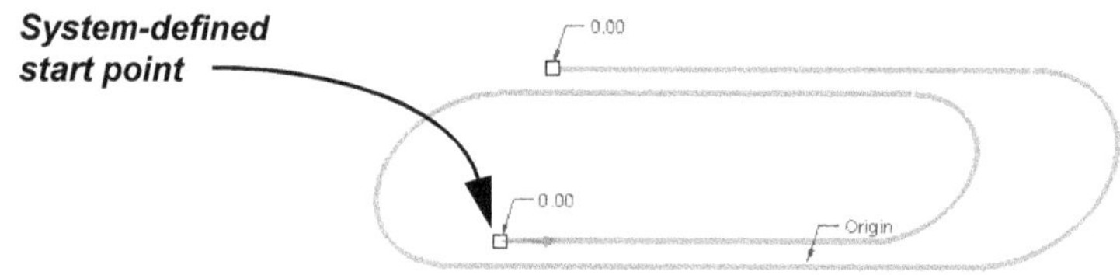

Figure 12–27

Task 2 - Change the start point for a sweep.

Design Considerations

The location of the start point is the location at which the section will be sketched. Its location is a user preference and has no real impact on feature creation.

1. To change the start point, right-click on the arrow and select **Flip Chain Direction**, as shown in Figure 12–28.

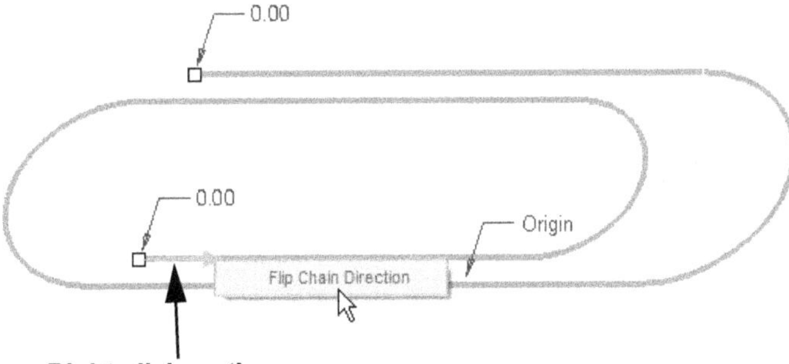

Figure 12–28

2. This changes the start point and moves it to the other end of the trajectory as shown in Figure 12–29.

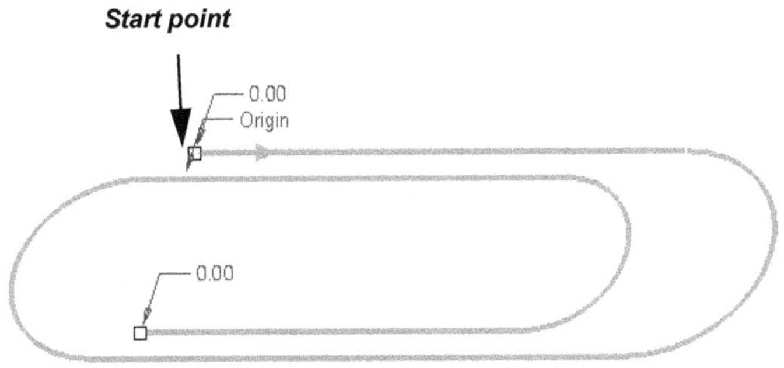

Start point

0.00
Origin
0.00

Figure 12–29

Task 3 - Sketch a section for the sweep.

1. Now that the trajectory has been defined, click (Create or Edit Section) to sketch the cross section.
2. The *Sketch* tab becomes active and displays horizontal and vertical center lines at the start point, as shown in Figure 12–30.

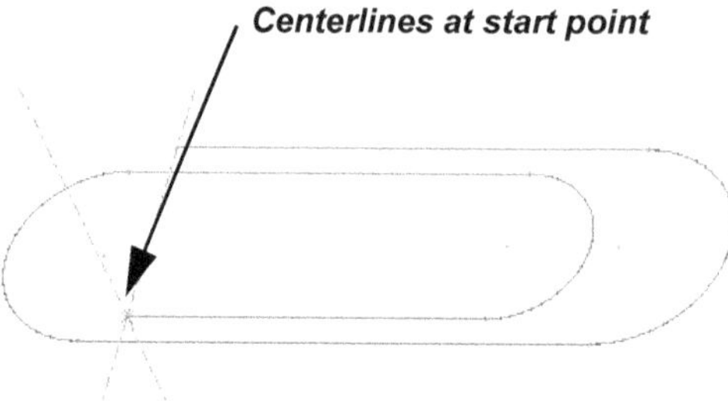

Figure 12–30

3. Sketch and dimension the cross-section for the paper clip, as shown in Figure 12–31.

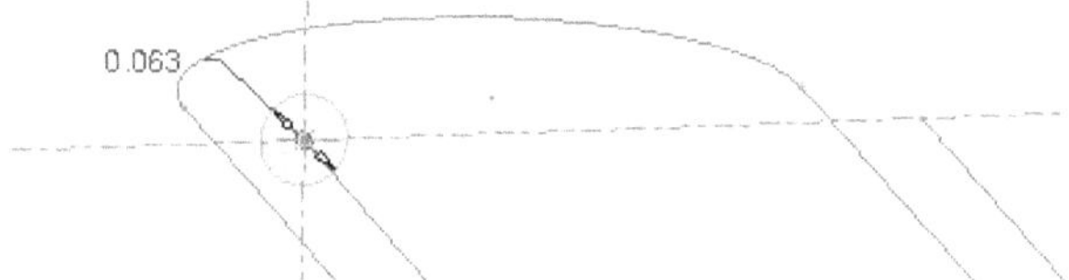

Figure 12–31

4. Click (OK) to complete the sketch.
5. Click (Complete Feature) to complete the feature.
6. Orient the model to the default orientation. The part displays as shown in Figure 12–32.

Figure 12–32

7. Save the part and erase it from memory.

Practice 12b Swept Features

Practice Objectives

- Select existing edges in the model as the path for a sweep feature.
- Set the required options in the Sweep tab and create the profile entities to create the required swept geometry.
- Edit a sweep feature and change the feature options to merge ends.

In this practice, you will create the part shown in Figure 12–33. You will sketch appropriate path and profile entities to create required swept geometry.

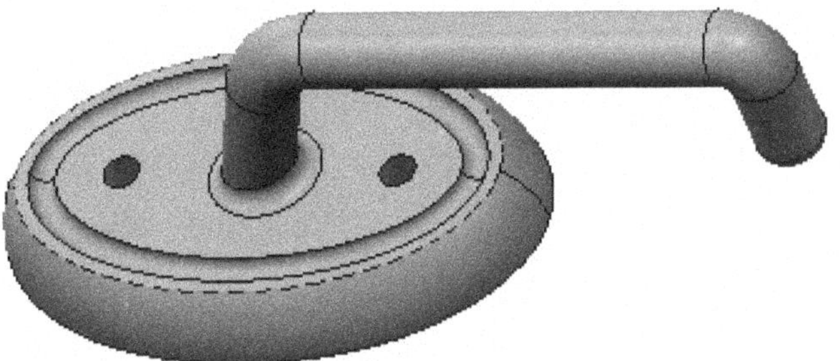

Figure 12–33

Task 1 - Open a part file.

1. Set the working directory to the *Chapter 12\practice 12b* folder.
2. Open **door_handle.prt**.
3. Set the model display as follows:
   - *(Datum Display Filters)*: All Off
   - *(Spin Center)*: Off
   - *(Display Style)*: (No Hidden)

Task 2 - Create a sketched swept protrusion.

In this task, you will create the swept protrusion for the handle, as shown in Figure 12–34.

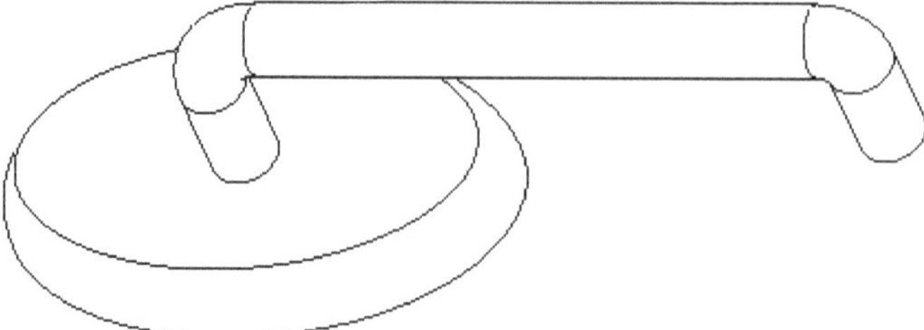

Figure 12–34

1. In the Shapes group in the *Model* tab, click (Sweep).

2. In the *Sweep* dashboard, expand (Datum) and click (Sketch) to sketch a trajectory.

3. For the sketching plane for the trajectory, select datum plane **FRONT.**

4. Click **Sketch** to activate the *Sketch* tab.

5. Sketch and dimension the trajectory, as shown in Figure 12–35.

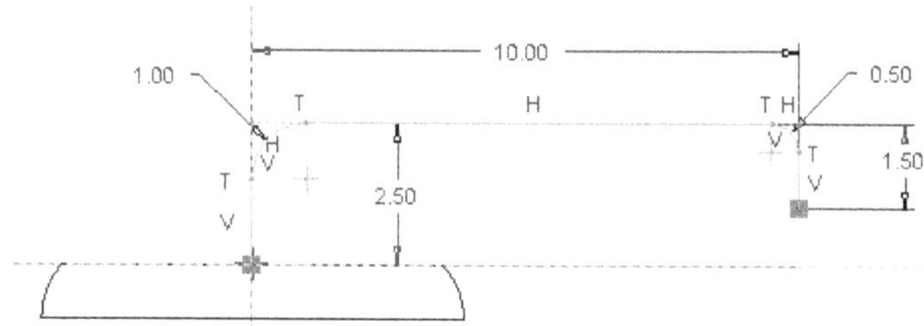

Figure 12–35

6. Click (OK) to complete the sketch for the trajectory.

7. Click (Resume) to activate the *Sweep* dashboard. Note that the new sketch is selected as the trajectory.

8. If required, change the start point by right-clicking on the arrow and selecting **Flip Chain Direction**. The model displays as shown in Figure 12–36.

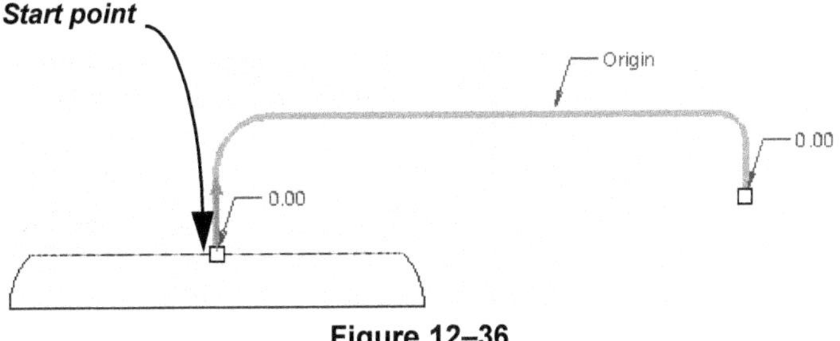

Figure 12–36

9. Click (Create or Edit Section) to sketch the cross-section.

10. Click (Sketch View) to orient the view. The crosshairs display, indicating the start point for the trajectory. Sketch and dimension the cross-section at the intersection of the crosshairs, as shown in Figure 12–37.

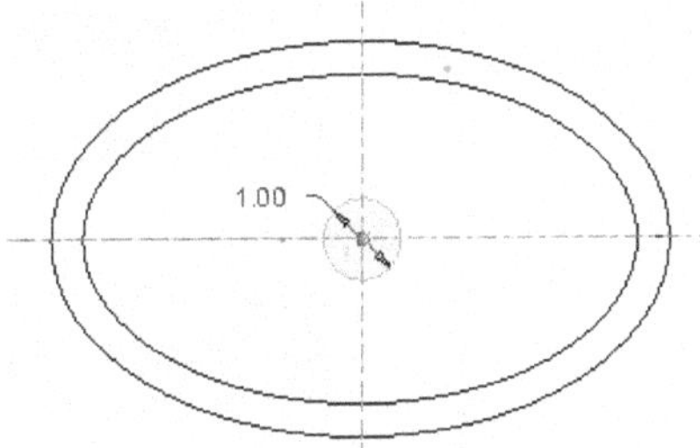

Figure 12–37

11. Click (OK) to complete the cross-section.

12. Click (Complete Feature).

13. Rename the sweep you just created to **HANDLE**, as shown in Figure 12–38.

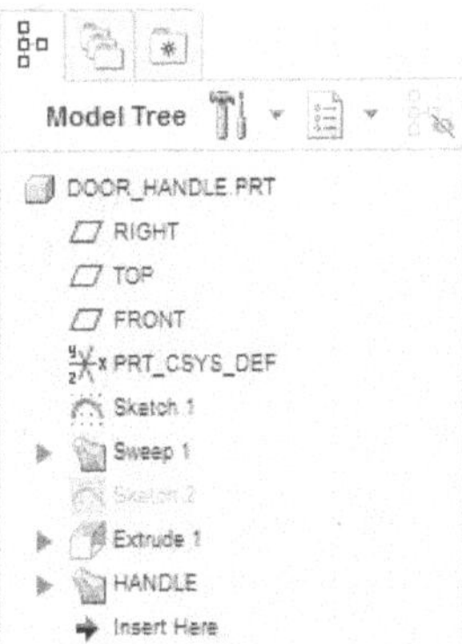

Figure 12–38

14. Set the orientation to the default orientation. Set the display to (Shading With Edges), and the model displays as shown in Figure 12–39.

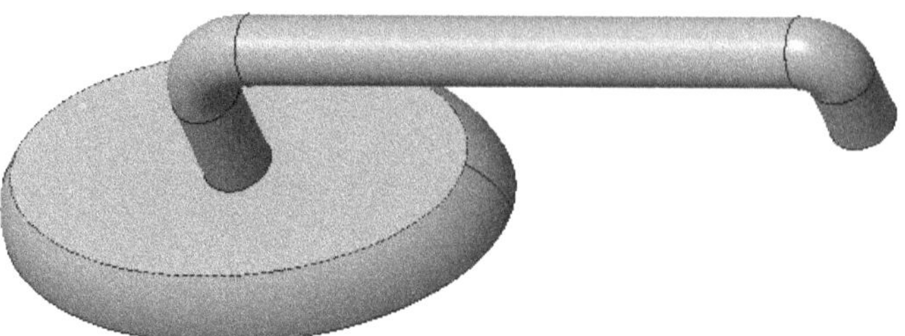

Figure 12–39

Task 3 - Create a swept cut using a selected trajectory.

1. In the *Model* tab, click (Sweep).
2. In the *Sweep* dashboard, click (Remove Material).
3. Select the top edge of the base protrusion for the trajectory as shown in Figure 12–40. If required, drag the start point to the location as shown in Figure 12–40. Click the heading of the arrow to change the direction to match the direction shown.

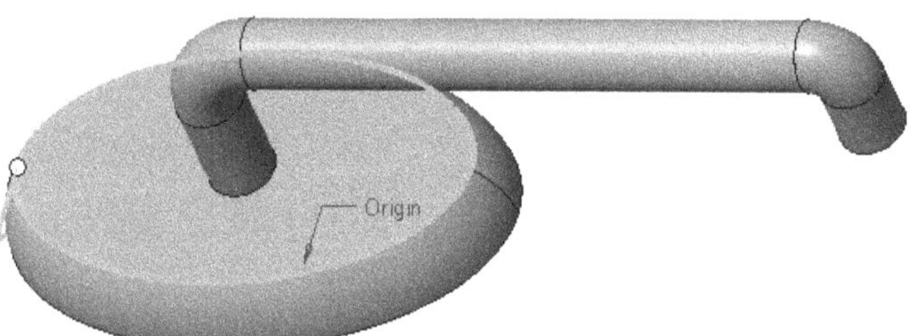

Figure 12–40

4. In the *Sweep* dashboard, click (Create or Edit Section) to sketch the cross-section.
5. Click (Sketch View) and sketch and dimension a circle section, as shown in Figure 12–41.
6. Click (OK) to complete the cross-section.

7. Click ✓ (Complete Feature) to complete the sweep. The model displays as shown in Figure 12–42.

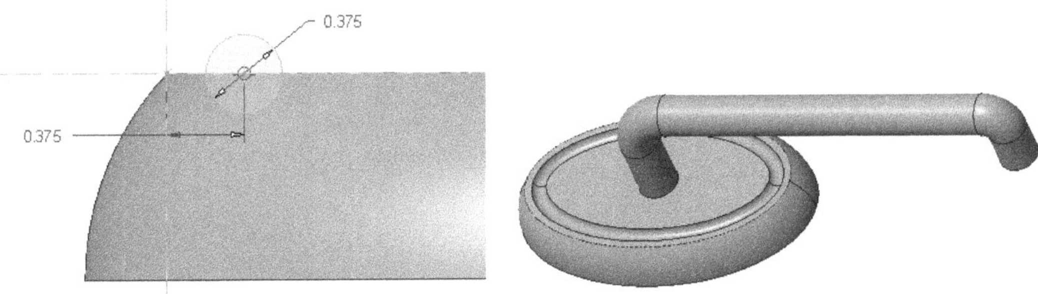

Figure 12–41

Figure 12–42

Task 4 - Edit the trajectory of the swept handle.

1. In the model tree, expand the **HANDLE** feature.

Additionally, you can drag the open arrow on the sketch.

2. Select **Sketch 3**. Then, right-click and select **Edit**.

3. The trajectory dimensions display as shown in Figure 12–43. Change the *10* dimension to **7**.

Change this dimension to 7

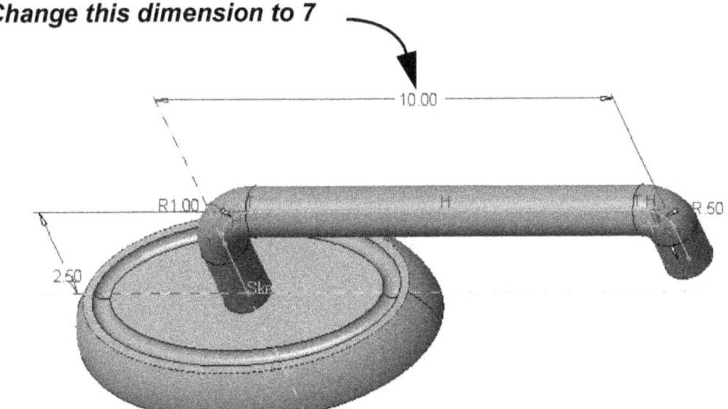

Figure 12–43

4. Regenerate the model. It displays as shown in Figure 12–44.

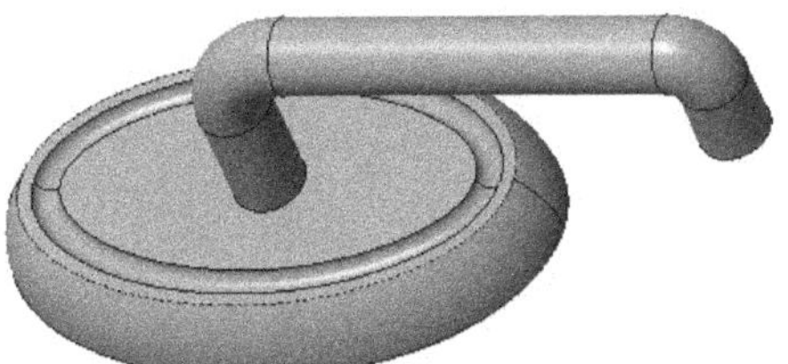

Figure 12–44

Task 5 - Edit the definition of the swept handle.

1. In the model tree, select **Sketch 3**, right-click and select **Edit Definition** to change the trajectory sketch.
2. Add the angular dimension and delete the vertical constraint, as shown in Figure 12–45.

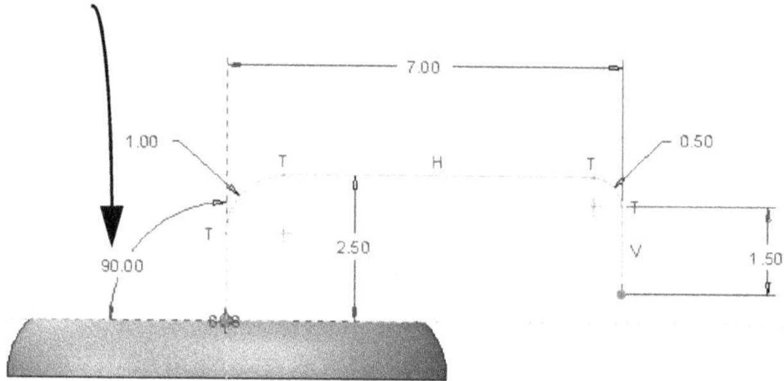

Figure 12–45

3. Set the following, as shown in Figure 12–46:
   - *Angle* value*:* **110**
   - *Horizontal* dimension: **8**

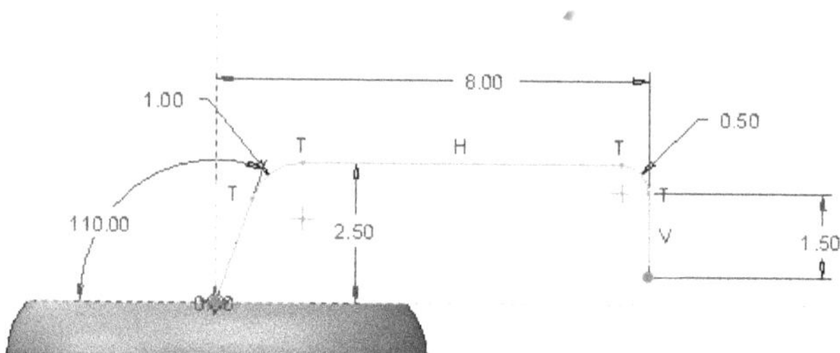

Figure 12–46

4. Click ✓ (OK).
5. Display the resulting geometry. Note that the handle does not extend up to the base due to the angle of trajectory, as shown in Figure 12–47.
6. Edit the definition of the **HANDLE**.
7. Select the Options panel and select **Merge ends**.

8. Click ✓ (Complete Feature). The model displays as shown in Figure 12–48.

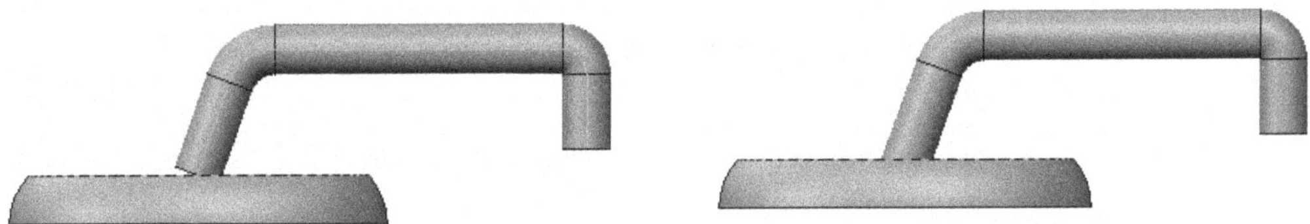

Figure 12–47 **Figure 12–48**

Task 6 - (Optional) Create additional features on the model.

1. Create two holes with a *Diameter* of **0.5**, as shown in Figure 12–49.
2. Create a round on the two edges, as shown in Figure 12–50.

Figure 12–49 **Figure 12–50**

3. Save the part and erase it from memory.

Practice 12c Swept Base Features

Practice Objective

- Create swept geometry by sketching appropriate path and profile entities.

In this practice, you will use the sweep tool to create several parts.

1. Set the working directory to the *Chapter 12\practice 12c* folder.

2. Create the parts shown in Figure 12–51 using swept protrusions.

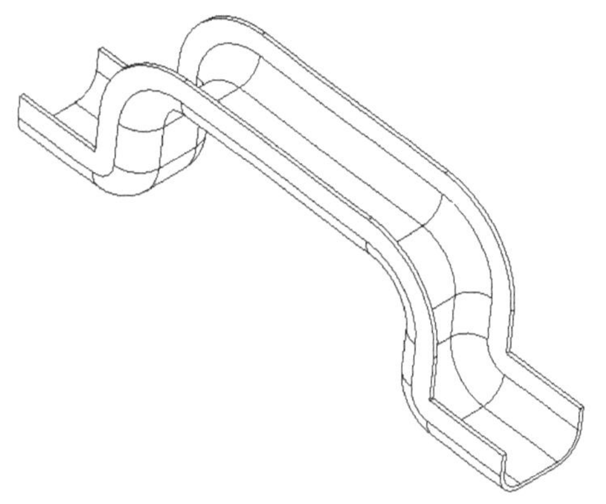

Figure 12–51

Practice 12d Keyboard Key

Practice Objective

- Create a blend feature by sketching two sections.

In this practice, you will create a key used on a keyboard. You will create the base feature using a blend with two sections, finish the part with rounds, and then shell the part. The completed part is shown in Figure 12–52.

Figure 12–52

Task 1 - Create a new part file.

1. Set the working directory to the *Chapter 12\practice 12d* folder.
2. Create a new part file and set the *Name* to **key**.
3. Set the model display as follows:
   - *(Datum Display Filters)*: All Off
   - *(Spin Center)*: Off
   - *(Display Style)*: (No Hidden)
4. In the *Model* tab, select **Shapes>Blend**. The *Blend* dashboard activates, as shown in Figure 12–53.

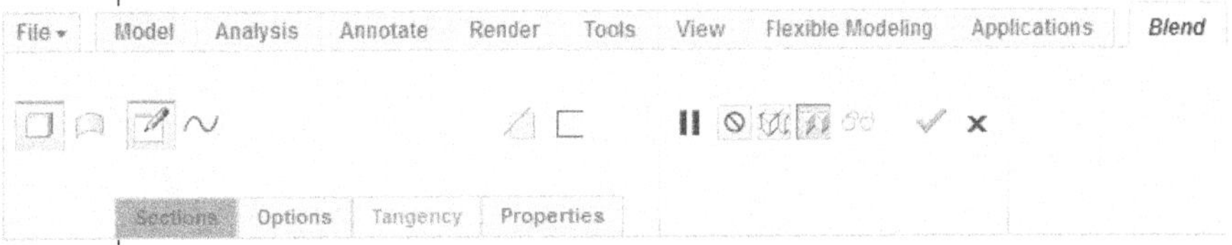

Figure 12–53

*You can also right-click and select **Define Internal Sketch**.*

5. Click **Sections** and click **Define**. The Sketch dialog box opens.

6. Select datum plane **TOP** from the model tree as the sketching plane and set datum plane **FRONT** to face bottom.

7. In the Sketch dialog box, click **Sketch**.

8. In the Sketching group, expand (Rectangle) and click (Center Rectangle). Select the center point at the intersection of the sketch references.

9. Sketch and dimension a square as shown in Figure 12–54, ensuring that the lines are equal lengths.

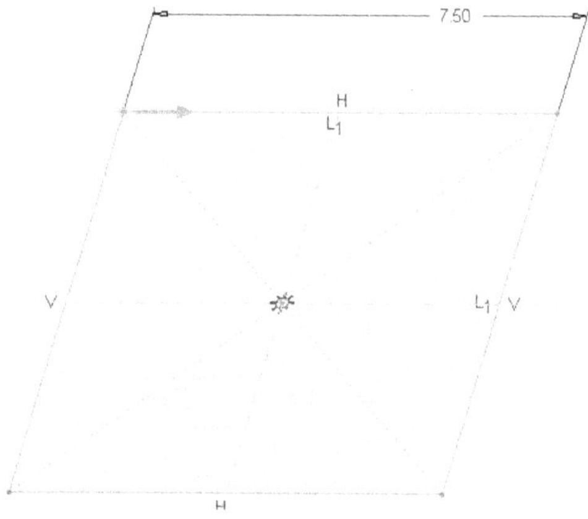

Figure 12–54

10. Click (OK) to complete the sketch.

11. Select the Sections panel and set the *Depth* value to **2.5**, as show in Figure 12–55. You can also change this value using the drag handle in the view window.

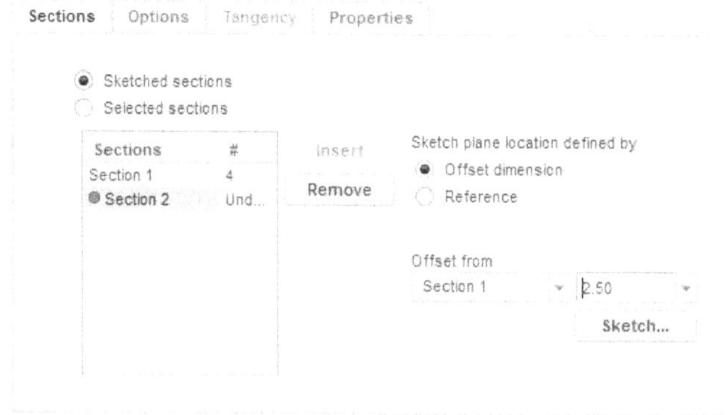

Figure 12–55

You can also click in the Blend dashboard right-click and select Define Internal ***Sketch****.*

12. Click **Sketch** to create the next section.

13. Sketch a second square, as shown in Figure 12–56. Begin the sketch in the upper left corner and permit coincidence with the horizontal line of the first sketch. Verify that the lines are of equal lengths. Ensure that the start points of both sections are in the same corner. If the start points do not line up, select the required location for the start point, right-click, and select **Start Point**.

Note that the sketches are lined up directly above one another.

14. Click (Sketch View) to view the sketches in 2D, as shown in Figure 12–57.

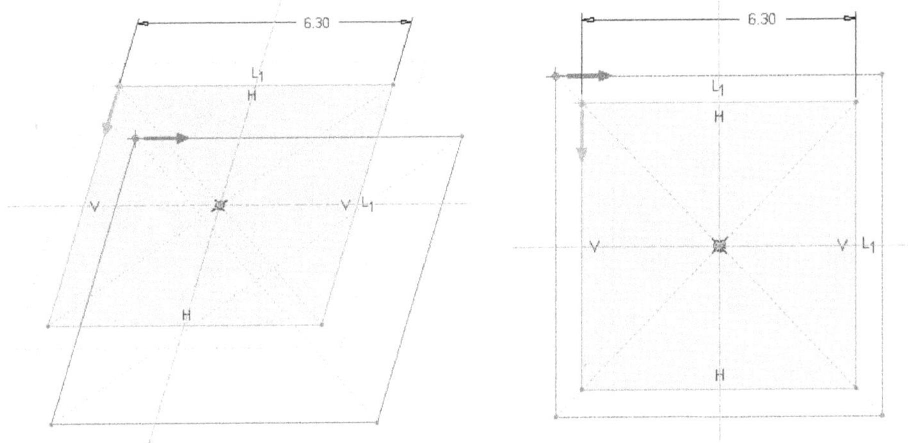

Figure 12–56 **Figure 12–57**

15. Press <Ctrl>+<D> to return to default orientation.

16. Click (OK).

17. Click (Complete Feature) to complete the blend.

18. In the In-graphics toolbar, click (Shading With Edges). The completed blend displays as shown in Figure 12–58.

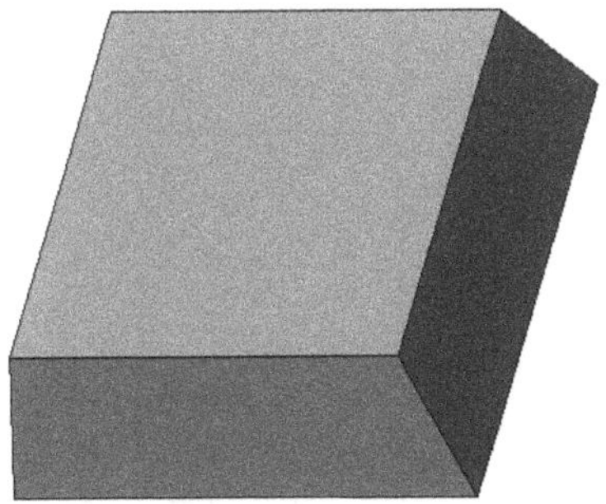

Figure 12–58

Task 2 - Create an extruded cut.

1. Click (Extrude).
2. Click (Remove Material).
3. Select **FRONT** from the model tree as the sketch plane.
4. Add the appropriate sketch references and sketch a single arc, as shown in Figure 12–59.

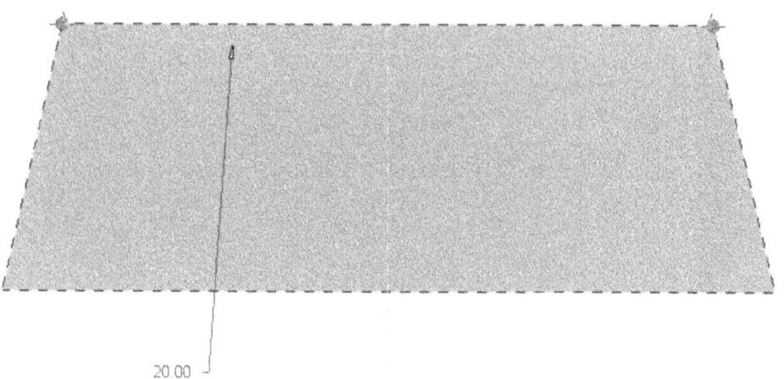

Figure 12–59

5. Click (OK).
6. Remove material on both sides of the sketch. The *Extrude* tab and model display as shown in Figure 12–60.

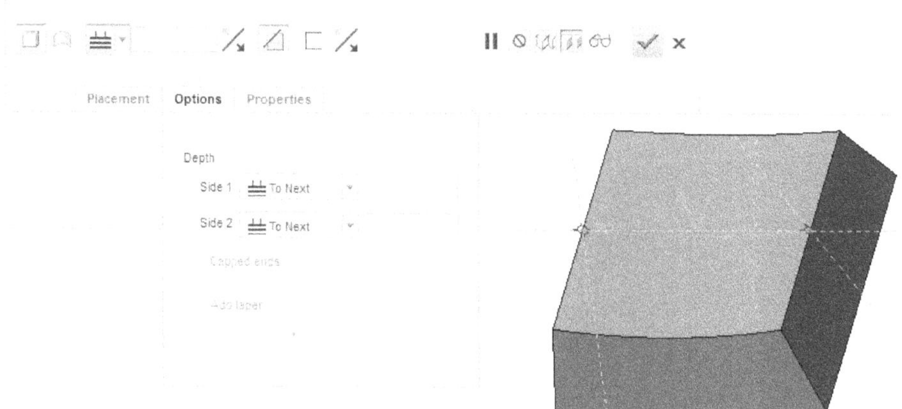

Figure 12–60

7. Click ✓ (Complete Feature). The completed extrude displays as shown in Figure 12–61.

Figure 12–61

Task 3 - Create rounds.

1. Create a round with a *Radius* of **0.63**, on the four edges shown in Figure 12–62.
2. Create a round with a *Radius* of **0.10**, on the edge shown in Figure 12–63.

Figure 12–62

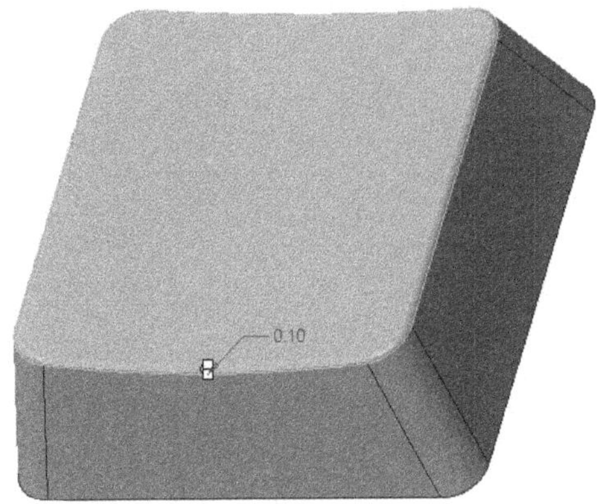

Figure 12–63

Task 4 - Shell the part.

1. Shell the part by setting the *Thickness* to **0.20**. Remove the bottom surface, as shown in Figure 12–64.

2. Set the orientation to the default one. The model displays as shown in Figure 12–65.

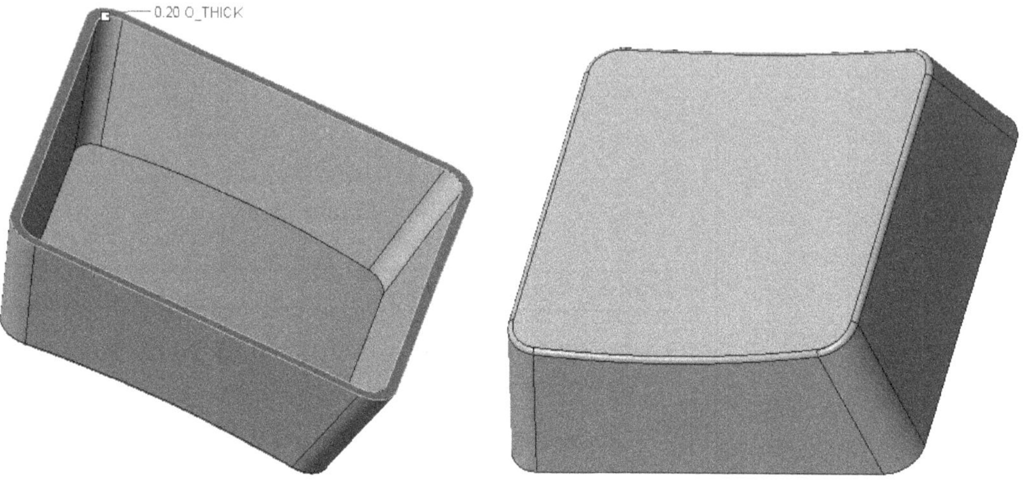

Figure 12–64

Figure 12–65

3. Save the part and erase it from memory.

Practice 12e Horn Speaker

Practice Objectives

- Create a blend feature by sketching three sections and ensuring they each have the same number of entities.
- Check each section has the same number of entities using the sketch tools.

In this practice, you will create the geometry for a horn speaker. You will use a three-section blend to create the base feature. One of the sections is a circle which will be divided into four entities, so that it can be blended with the four vertices of the rectangle sections. The completed part is shown in Figure 12–66.

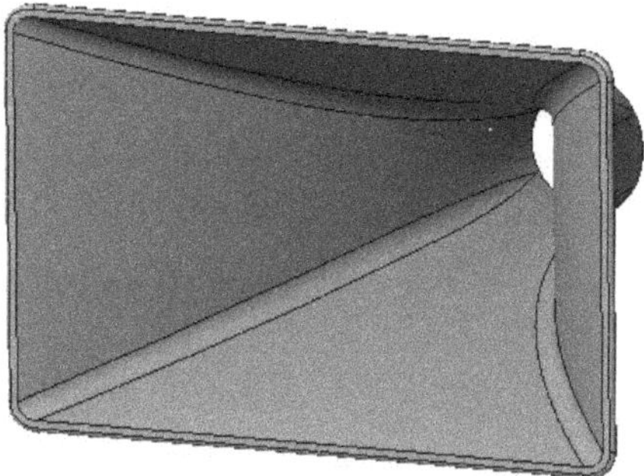

Figure 12–66

Task 1 - Create a new part file.

1. Set the working directory to the *Chapter 12\practice 12e* folder.
2. Create a new part file and set the *Name* to **horn_flare**.
3. Set the model display as follows:
   - *(Datum Display Filters)*: All Off
   - *(Spin Center)*: Off
   - *(Display Style)*: (No Hidden)
4. In the *Model* tab, select **Shapes>Blend**.
5. Select the Options panel and note that **Smooth** is selected by default.
6. Right-click and select **Define Internal Sketch**.

7. Select datum plane **FRONT** from the model tree as the sketch plane and click **Sketch**.

8. Expand (Rectangle) and click (Center Rectangle). Sketch and dimension the rectangle shown in Figure 12–67.

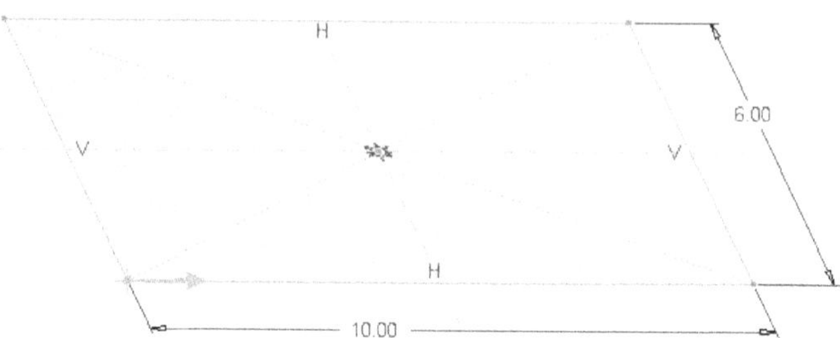

Figure 12–67

9. Click (OK).

10. Select the Sections panel and set the *Depth* between the first two sections to **4**.

11. Click **Sketch** to create the next section.

12. Click (Sketch View).

Your start point might vary depending on how the geometry was sketched

13. Click (Center Rectangle). Sketch and dimension the rectangle shown in Figure 12–68. Verify that the start points are aligned. If the start points do not line up, select the required location for the start point, right-click, and select **Start Point**.

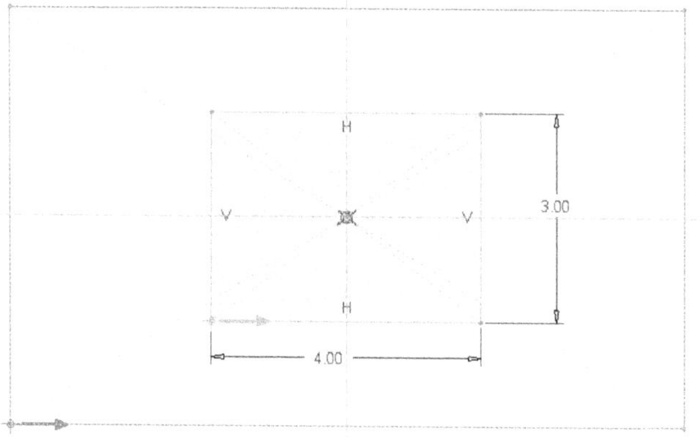

Figure 12–68

14. Click (OK).

15. Right-click and select **Insert** to insert a third section.

16. Select the Section panel and set the *Depth* between the next two sections to **4**.

17. Click **Sketch** to create the third section.

18. Click (Circle) and sketch and dimension the circle shown in Figure 12–69.

19. The first two sections contain four vertices. The circle must also be divided into four sections. Create two centerlines and constrain each one using the (Coincident) constraint to the vertex of the large rectangle, as shown in Figure 12–70.

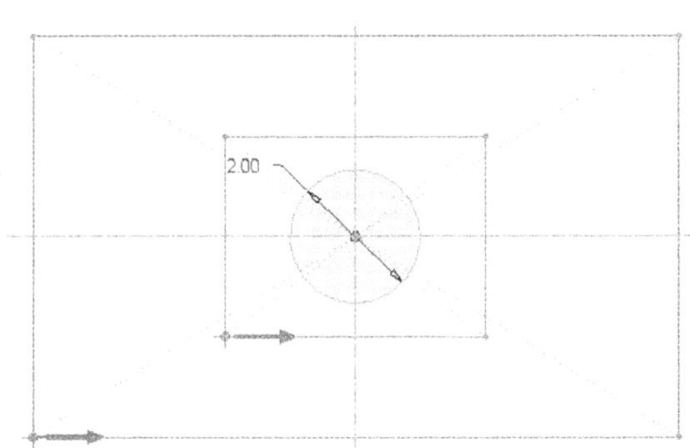

Figure 12–69

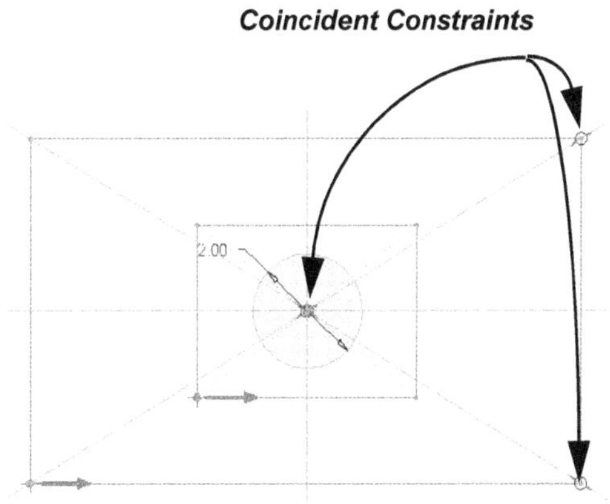

Coincident Constraints

Figure 12–70

20. Click (Divide) to divide the circle into four entities. Begin with the intersection that corresponds to the start point of the rectangles, as shown in Figure 12–71.

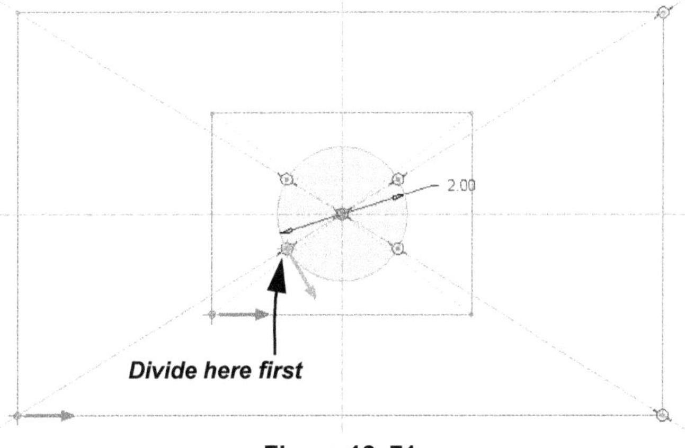

Figure 12–71

21. Click ✓ (OK) to exit the *Sketch* tab.

22. Click ✓ (Complete Feature) to complete the blend and orient the model to the Default orientation, as shown in Figure 12–72.

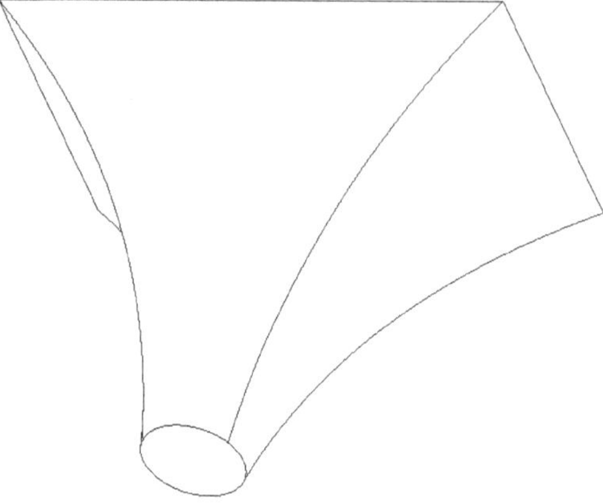

Figure 12–72

Task 2 - Create rounds.

1. Create a round with a *Radius* of **0.5**, on the four edges shown in Figure 12–73.

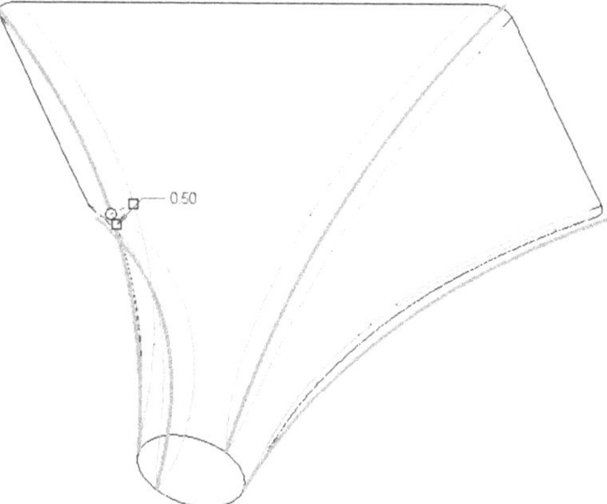

Figure 12–73

Task 3 - Shell the part.

1. In the Engineering group, click (Shell) and shell the part by setting the *Thickness* to **0.188**. Remove the two surfaces shown in Figure 12–74.

2. Create a round with a *Radius* of **0.063**, on the edge shown in Figure 12–75.

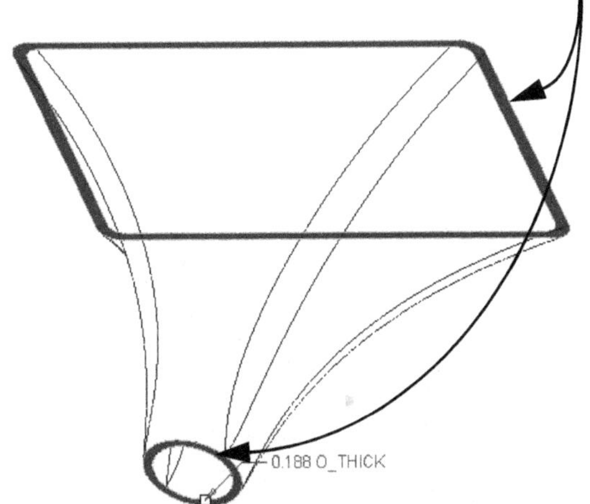

Figure 12–74

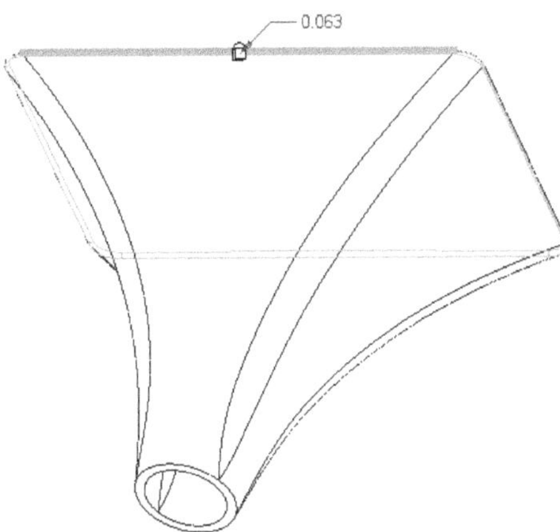

Figure 12–75

3. In the In-graphics toolbar, click (Shading With Edges) and set the display to default orientation. The completed part displays as shown in Figure 12–76.

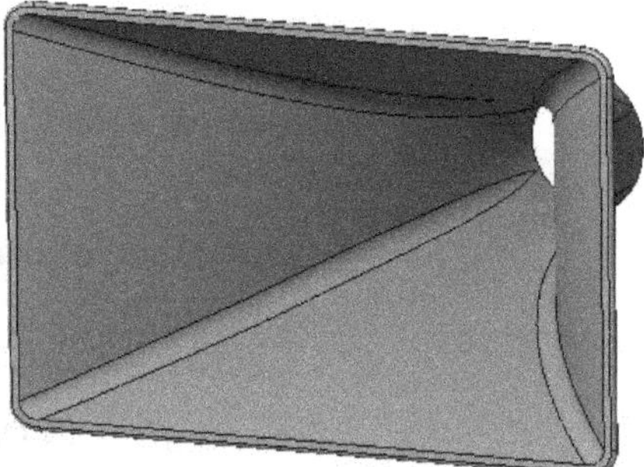

Figure 12–76

4. Save the part and erase it from memory.

Practice 12f (Optional) Bucket

Practice Objectives

- Create a blend feature by sketching sections and ensuring they each have the same number of entities.
- Create a bend feature using two sections.

In this practice, you will create the part shown in Figure 12–77. It is created using two separate blend feature forms. One feature will add material as the base feature and the second will remove material. To complete the model, you will add rounds and shell the model.

Figure 12–77

Task 1 - Open a part file.

1. Set the working directory to the *Chapter 12\practice 12f* folder.
2. Open **bucket.prt**.
3. Set the model display as follows:
   - *(Datum Display Filters)*: All Off
   - *(Spin Center)*: Off
   - *(Display Style)*: (No Hidden)

4. Edit the definition of **Sketch 1** to investigate the sketch geometry, as shown in Figure 12–78. Note the number of entities and dimensions at the bottom of the section. This is where the spout for the bucket will be created.

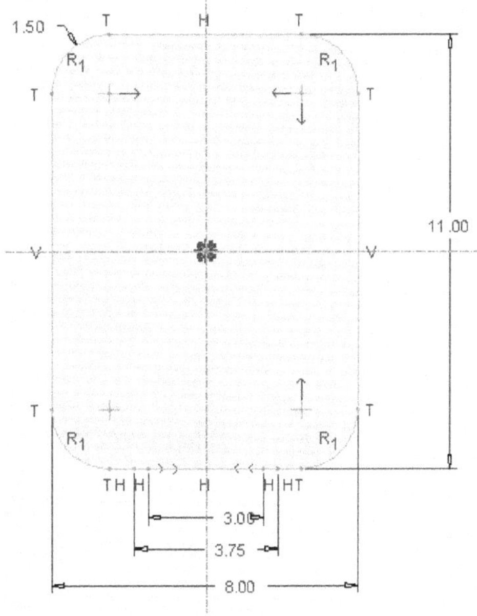

Figure 12–78

5. Click ✓ (OK) to exit Sketcher without making any changes.

Task 2 - Create a Blend feature.

1. Select **Shapes>Blend**.
2. Select the Options panel and change the blend to **Straight**.
3. Right-click and select **Define Internal Sketch**.
4. Select datum plane **Top** as the sketch plane and maintain the default orientation reference. Click **Sketch**.
5. Click (Project) to project the existing sketch as the first sub-section in the blend.
6. In the **TYPE** menu, select **Loop** as the method of selection.
7. Select any of the entities in the sketch.

8. Close the **TYPE** menu. Note that an arrow displays on the sketch, similar to that shown in Figure 12–79. This arrow is the section's start point. The start point location might vary depending on the entity selected.

Figure 12–79

9. Click ✓ (OK).
10. Set the offset between the first two sections to **6**.
11. Right-click and select **Sketch** to create the next section.

*You can also click **Sketch** in the Sections panel.*

12. Ensure that the sketch is oriented in the default position. To sketch the second section, click (Offset) in the *Sketch* tab to offset from the existing sketch.
13. Select **Loop** and select any entity on the sketch, as shown in Figure 12–80.
14. An arrow displays indicating the positive direction of the offset, as shown in Figure 12–81.

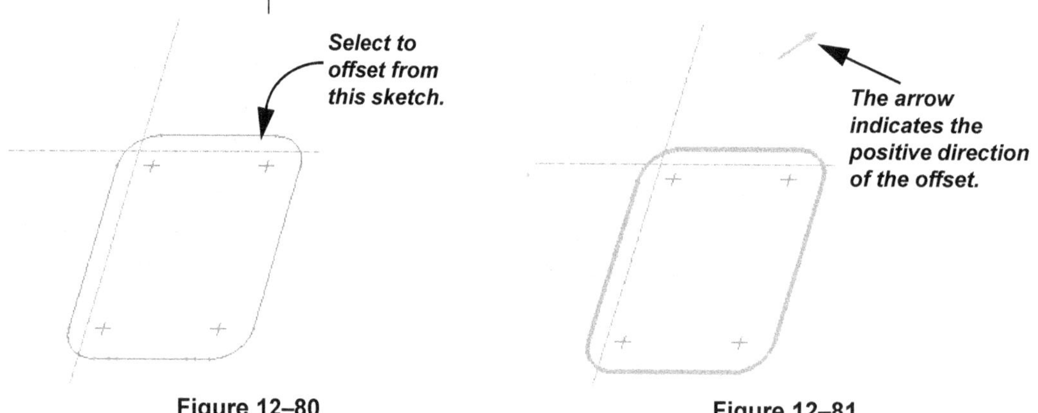

Figure 12–80

Figure 12–81

15. In the message window, enter **0.5** to create a second section that is larger than the first. If the arrow is pointing the opposite direction, enter **-0.5**. Ensure that the sketch is larger than the first section.

16. The second section's start point should be in the same position relative to the previous section's start point. If it is not, select the vertex that you want to use as the section's start point, right-click, and select **Start Point**.

17. Click ✓ (OK).

18. Select the Sections panel and click **Insert** to create a third section.

19. In the Sections panel, set the *Offset from* distance to **0.25**.

20. Click **Sketch** to create the next section.

21. Orient to the default view. Offset the datum curve again by a value of **0.85**. Ensure that the sketch entities are offset to the outside of the selected sketch. Use a negative value if required. The third section should be larger than both the first and second. If required, correct the start point position for the section.

22. Click ✓ (OK).

23. Insert a fourth section and set the *Offset from* distance to **3.00** and then offset the datum curve by **1.00**. Ensure that the sketch entities are offset to the outside of the selected sketch. Use a negative value if required. The fourth section should be larger than all of the other sections.

24. In the fourth section, you need to sketch additional geometry to create the bucket's spout. Trim away or delete the unwanted offset geometry shown in Figure 12–82.

Delete these three entities

Figure 12–82

25. Add the sketched lines and dimensions, as shown in Figure 12–83. You might also need to add a centerline and symmetry constraint to the sketch.

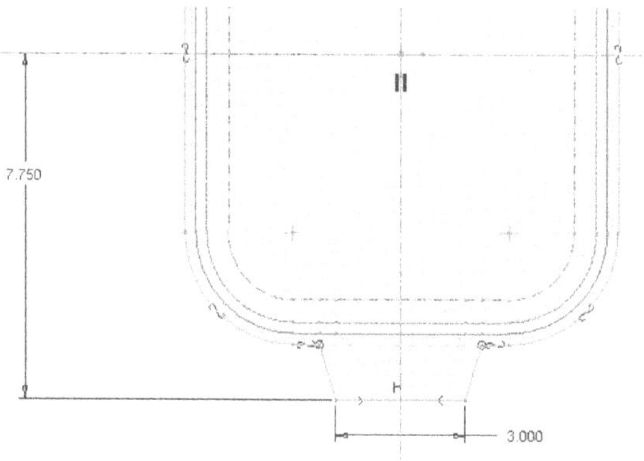

Figure 12–83

26. Click ✓ (OK).

27. Click ✓ (Complete Feature) to complete the blend as shown in Figure 12–84

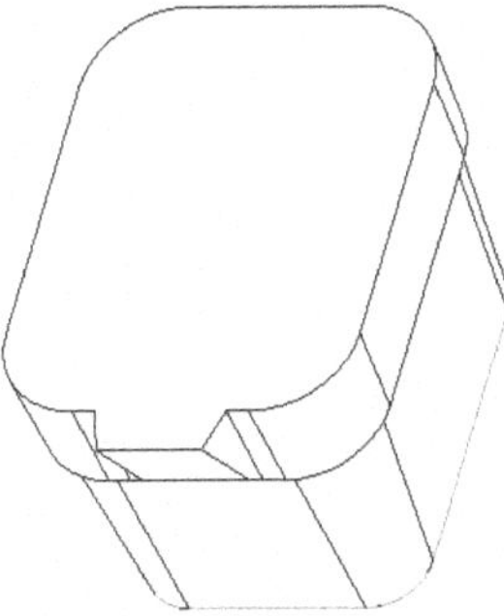

Figure 12–84

Task 3 - Create a blended cut to remove material from the model.

In this task, you will create an additional blend feature that removes material from the model, as shown in Figure 12–85.

1. Select **Shapes>Blend**.
2. In the *Blend* dashboard, click (Remove Material).
3. Select **Straight** in the Options panel.
4. Right-click and select **Define Internal Sketch**.
5. Select the bottom surface of the bucket as the sketching plane and maintain the default orientation plane, as shown in Figure 12–86.

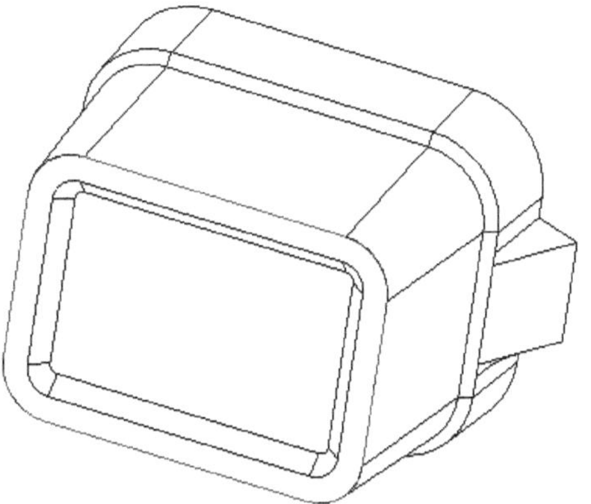

Figure 12–85

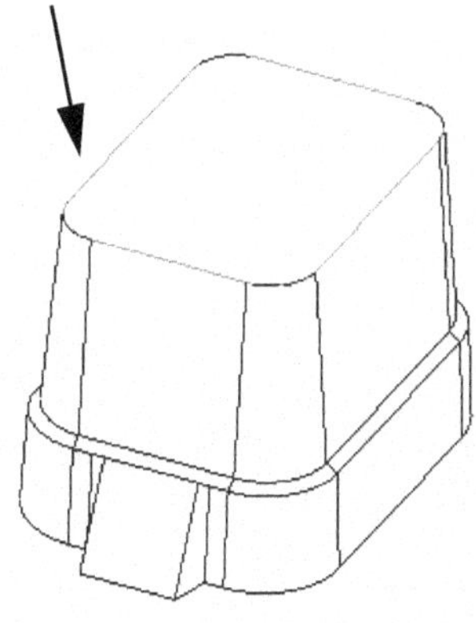

Figure 12–86

6. If required, select datum plane **FRONT** as the second sketcher reference. Close the References dialog box.

7. Create the first sub-section so that it is offset from the existing sketch by a *Distance* of **0.75** (the section is smaller than the original sketch), as shown in Figure 12–87.

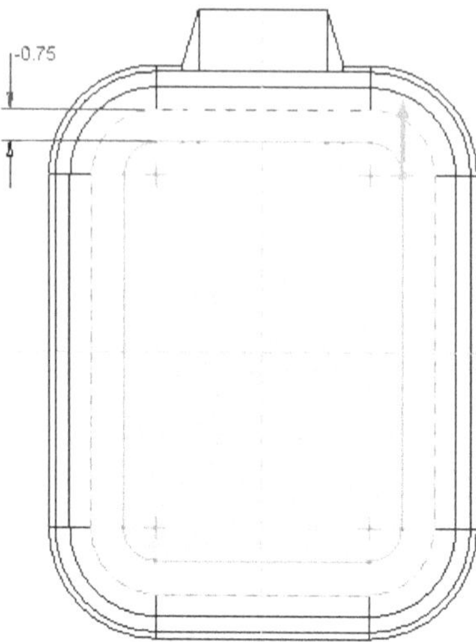

Figure 12–87

8. Click ✓ (OK).

9. Set the *Offest* from field to **0.5**.

Ensure you rotate the model and select the original edges to offset.

10. Click **Sketch** and create the entities by offsetting from the existing sketch by a *Distance* of **1.25** (the section is smaller than the original sketch).

11. Click ✓ (OK) to complete the sketch.

12. Click ✓ (Complete Feature) to complete the feature.

Task 4 - Create the round features.

Use <Ctrl> to select more than one edge at a time for the set.

1. Create round with a *Radius* of **0.50**, on the edges shown in Figure 12–88.

2. Create another round with a *Radius* of **0.40**, on the edge shown in Figure 12–89. All adjacent tangent edges are included in the round.

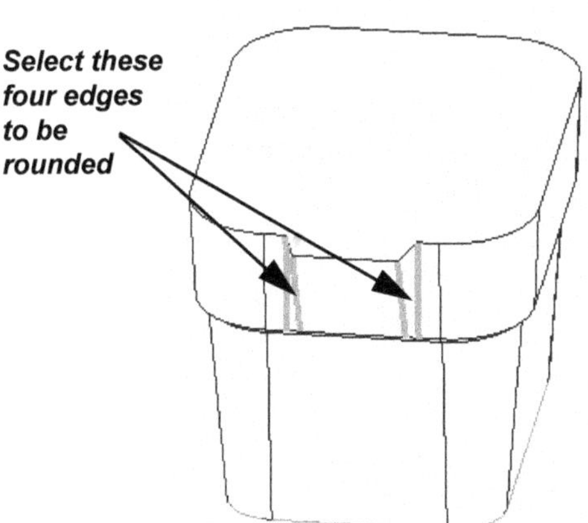

Figure 12–88

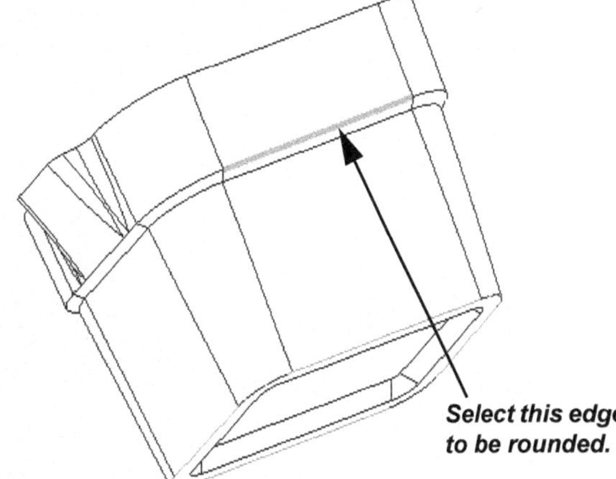

Figure 12–89

3. Create another round with a *Radius* of **0.40**, on the edge shown in Figure 12–90. All adjacent tangent edges are included in the round.

4. Create a final round with a *Radius* of **0.40**, on the edges shown in Figure 12–91.

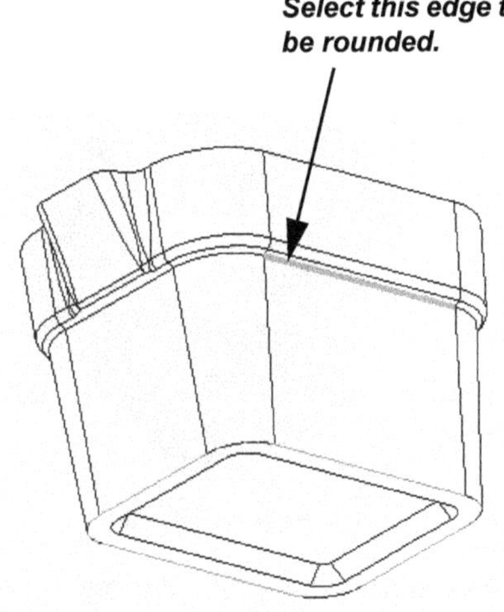

Figure 12–90

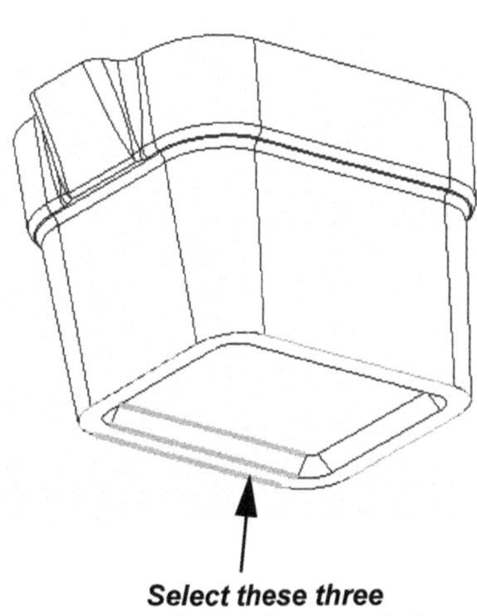

Figure 12–91

Task 5 - Create a shell feature.

1. In the Engineering group, click (Shell) to shell the part.
2. Select the top surface of the bucket as the surface to remove, as shown in Figure 12–92.

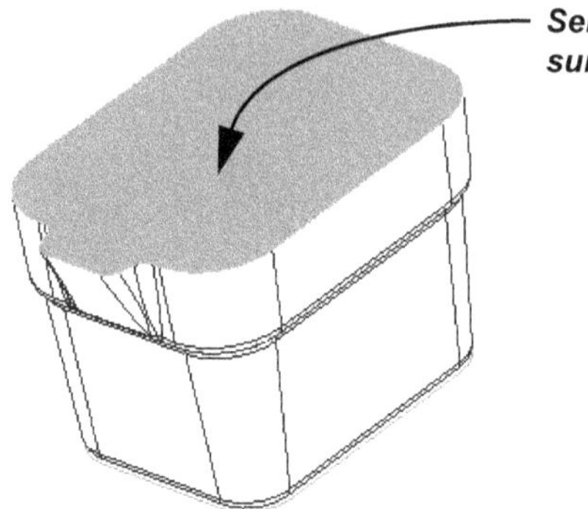

Figure 12–92

3. Set the *Thickness* to **0.125**.
4. Click (Complete Feature) to complete the feature.
5. In the In-graphics toolbar, click (Shading). The model displays as shown in Figure 12–93.

Figure 12–93

6. Save the model and close the window.

Chapter Review Questions

1. A Sweep can be used in a model to add or remove material.
    a. True
    b. False
2. Which of the following statements are true regarding Sweeps?
    a. A Sweep creates a single feature whose geometry is blended between multiple sub-sections.
    b. A Sweep creates a single feature whose geometry is swept along a defined trajectory.
    c. A Sweep can only be added to the model after the base protrusion has been created.
    d. The trajectory for a sweep must be sketched.
3. What are the two elements that must be defined to create a Sweep feature?
    a. Trajectory and section
    b. Trajectory and depth
    c. Section and depth
4. Why is it important to rename your features in the model tree?
    a. To identify the feature.
    b. To edit the feature.
    c. To organize the features in alphabetical order.
5. The start point of an open loop trajectory can be anywhere on the curve.
    a. True
    b. False
6. Which of the following criteria are required to use the **Merge Ends** or **Free Ends** options? (Select all that apply.)
    a. Solid geometry already exists in the model.
    b. The trajectory forms a closed loop.
    c. The trajectory forms an open loop.
    d. The cross-section is circular.

7. Which of the following are true statements regarding the start point of a trajectory? (Select all that apply.)
   a. The start point defines the location where the cross-section is sketched.
   b. Start points must be located at the start or end of an open trajectory.
   c. To change the start point for a trajectory, select the Reference panel and click **Details**.
   d. To change the start point for a selected trajectory, right-click on the arrow and select **Flip Chain Direction**.
8. The cross-section remains perpendicular as it follows the trajectory.
   a. True
   b. False
9. The trajectory cannot contain any sharp corners.
   a. True
   b. False
10. A Blend can be used in a model to add or remove material.
    a. True
    b. False
11. Which of the following statements are true regarding Parallel Blends?
    a. A Parallel Blend creates a single feature in which the geometry is blended between multiple sub-sections.
    b. A Parallel Blend can only be added to the model after the base protrusion has been created.
    c. All of the sections for a Parallel Blend are created in one sketch.
    d. A Blend Vertex is a feature similar to a Parallel Blend in that it enables you to blend geometry between selected vertices.
12. What is the minimum number of sub-sections that must exist in a Blend feature?
    a. 1
    b. 2
    c. 3
    d. There is not a minimum number of sections.

13. What is the maximum number of sub-sections that can exist in a Blend feature?

    a. 2

    b. 3

    c. 100

    d. There is not a maximum number of sections

14. The sub-sections for Parallel Blends can only be sketched.

    a. True

    b. False

15. Which of the following techniques enables you to change the geometry shown on the left in Figure 12–94 to that shown on the right in Figure 12–94?

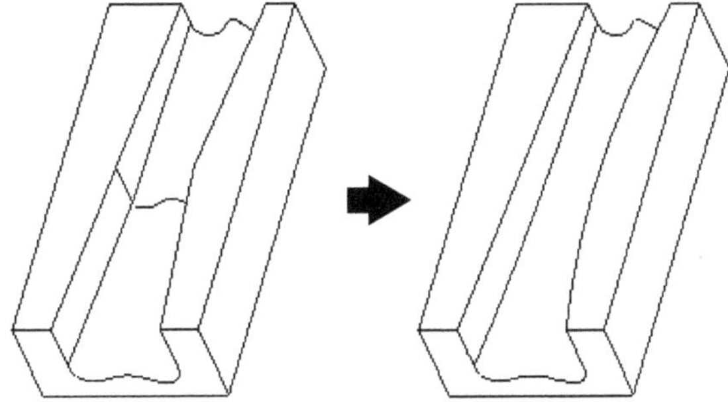

Figure 12–94

    a. Change the attributes element from *Straight* to **Smooth**.

    b. Add a **Blend Vertex** to the first sub-section in the sketch.

    c. Change the start points for each sub-section so that they start in the same relative location.

    d. Create an additional sub-section with the sketch for the blend.

16. Which of the following techniques can be used to blend a triangular sub-section that contains three entities to a circle that only contains one entity?

    a. Blend Vertex

    b. Trim tools

    c. Sketcher Point

    d. Toggle Section

17. Sections in a blend feature can be reordered.
    a. True
    b. False

Command Summary

Button	Command	Location
	Divide	• **Ribbon:** *Sketch* tab in the *Editing* group
	Sweep	• **Ribbon:** *Model* tab in the *Shapes* group